D1710552

A GUIDE TO ──────────

AMERICAN
TRADE
CATALOGS 1744-1900

by Lawrence B. Romaine

DOVER PUBLICATIONS, INC. · *New York*

Published in Canada by General Publishing Company, Ltd., 30 Lesmill Road, Don Mills, Toronto, Ontario.

Published in the United Kingdom by Constable and Company, Ltd., 3 The Lanchesters, 162-164 Fulham Palace Road, London W6 9ER.

This Dover edition, first published in 1990, is an unabridged and unaltered republication of the work first published by the R.R. Bowker Company, New York, in 1960.

Manufactured in the United States of America
Dover Publications, Inc., 31 East 2nd Street, Mineola, N.Y. 11501

Library of Congress Cataloging-in-Publication Data

Romaine, Lawrence B.
   A guide to American trade catalogs, 1744-1900 / Lawrence B. Romaine.
      p.   cm.
   Reprint. Originally published: New York : R.R. Bowker, 1960.
   Includes bibliographical references and index.
   ISBN 0-486-26475-0 (pbk.)
   1. Catalogs, Commercial—United States—Bibliography. I. Title.
Z7161.C8R6   1990
[HF5861]
016.381′029′473—dc20   90-3914
                                                                CIP

CONTENTS

FOREWORD

by A. Hyatt Mayor, Curator of Prints, Metropolitan Museum of Art

For several centuries historians have been moving steadily away from the ancient bare chronicles of battles and reigns in order to explore fresh approaches to man's past. Ever since the 1540's when Vasari discovered the history of art - or at least the history of artists - ever since Voltaire found that ideas have a parentage like people, historians have roamed around for new viewpoints from which to look toward the central subject of man. Thus the history of science has taken shape in the last couple of decades, and now the history of business is beginning to emerge.

The new historians of business will find a basic tool in Mr. Romaine's bibliography of American catalogues, for it is the first general listing of these scarce ephemera in any country. Like any pioneer survey, its structure will always endure under the additions that the years must inevitably bring. Henceforth no American trade catalogue can be listed respectably without a Romaine reference, or boasting (while perhaps adding a penny to the price) "Not in Romaine."

The United States has probably issued more business catalogues than any other country. We were by no means the first to do so, for by the 1780's the metal manufactures of Birmingham and Sheffield were already sending out elaborately illustrated brochures to their agents in France, Italy, Spain, the Americas, and very probably India and Russia. These early British catalogues usually omit the name of the manufacturer lest the customer circumvent the agent by ordering direct from England. American catalogues much more often state the manufacturer's address so as to solicit direct orders from the customer, because in the United States money and goods could travel over great distances to vast markets without needing agents to negotiate barriers of exchange and customs' duties. The American opportunity for direct sales produced a fascinating profusion of small, inexpensive catalogues that vividly picture the epic of muscle, thought and enterprise which built up our commerce, and dominated our history.

The lavish illustrations in catalogues of every country constitute the main historical source for the development of nineteenth century ornamental design. For previous centuries the record of design lies in the sets of prints published in great artistic centers in order to supply ideas when gentlemen were conferring with local craftsmen to create elegant and individual household furnishings. But when craftsmen's shops gave way to big factories in the world's progression toward larger and larger unities, the old design books gave way to commercial catalogues. So the history of nineteenth century design cannot really be written until foreign scholars imitate Mr. Romaine by compiling the bibliographies of the commercial catalogues of other countries.

Some time ago a number of far-sighted collectors became aware that such catalogues, while mere curiosities when gathering dust by twos and threes, become history - history with the fascination of anecdote and image - when they are arranged by thousands. This present Guide would have been impossible without the pioneer enthusiasm of a few librarians, collectors and dealers who preserved what everybody else was clearing out and throwing away.

INTRODUCTION

Have you lived for days, weeks, months and years with one small idea pricking your conscience? Have you slept with it, wakened with it, shaved with it, breakfasted with it, allowed it to drive you to work, sit with you through business conferences and struggles, and, after a long and tedious day jump right back into bed with you again? Your little gremlin may be an 1847 stamp, a copy of Tamerlane or the first pamphlet printed in Texas, but mine is Benjamin Franklin's 1744 catalog of books; its real meaning to the history of the American mail order business, and its influence on the industrial development of the United States.

One of the considerations that strengthened my determination is the generally held impression that the first mail order catalogs were offered to the American public about 1872. Nothing could be farther from the truth. Most people still seem to think that the huge miscellaneous catalogs issued by Montgomery Ward & Co., Sears Roebuck & Co., Butler Brothers, The House Wrecker, Charles Williams and dozens of others from about 1880 on are representative of this facet of Business Americana. As industrial records they are well over a hundred years late, and as examples of paper, printing and illustration they are surely very poor specimens.

Compare Dr. Franklin's 1744 catalogs with Montgomery Ward & Co.'s 1872 circular. Compare William A. Carr's Hardware Catalog for 1838 with any Gay Ninety mammoth printed by Sears Roebuck & Co., allowing, of course, in all fairness, for what was available in each case. Compare A. B. Allen's New York Agricultural Warehouse catalog for 1852 with any of our mail order giants at the turn of the 20th century.

It is high time that someone compiled and printed a record proving that Americans recognized the value of advertising catalogs and the mail order business even before they recognized the real value of freedom. There are ten thousand volumes that tell and retell the story of the American Revolution. I offer one that will, without bloodshed, convince you of the creative ability, imagination and Yankee ingenuity of the builders of this Republic throughout the 18th and 19th centuries.

As you use this guide and study this colorful panorama you will begin to share my enthusiasm. The American trade catalogs to which I call your attention are drawn from our earliest beginnings. They were printed by the best printers and are fitting bedfellows for the best Evans and Sabin listings. As our methods of illustration and printing developed, so they grew in size and quality. During the last half of the nineteenth century their copy was often written by outstanding authors and historians, and embellished with woodcuts and lithographs executed by the best artists and engravers.

Permission from the California Historical Society to announce in this guide its plan to include in the forthcoming edition of "California Local History: A Centennial Bibliography," all located California trade catalogs is the recognition I hope may eventually sweep the country. This means that at long last these lowly give-aways have been acknowledged as historical records from coast to coast. Run through the list of library symbols and you will visualize exactly what this announcement means.

I have read anything and everything that I thought might throw some light on the history of trade catalogs and the mail order business in the United States. A great many chronicles and commentaries have been written about advertising by advertising executives, yet very few of them even mention catalogs. Those that do, mention only the Montgomery Ward, Sears Roebuck era, and scarcely do justice to these huge mass production contributions to the American way of life. Even Larsen's "Guide to Business History," (Harvard University Press, 1950) merely says: "Trade cards, catalogs and other similar materials have generally been considered too ephemeral in value to warrant the cost of saving them." This otherwise outstanding work notes only five collections in the entire country. I have found there are hundreds from Maine to Texas and from Florida to Washington. Unfortunately, these institutional collections are not properly cataloged and consequently not available at the moment for research.

During this search for dates, details and other data I have collected thousands of examples, which in the course of my business have been placed in institutional as well as private collections. For this very reason I am probably in the fortunate position of being able to locate accurately a greater number of American Trade Catalogs than any other dealer, collector or librarian. It is my responsibility to see that this guide is made available in printed form to those who will understand that it provides one of the best and clearest pictures of our development during the 19th century.

That these listings must be inconsistent is evident. They are supplied from sales records, correspondence and file cards. The descriptive details vary with the interest of the collector and the librarian, just as they do in Evans or Sabin, or in any current out of print bookseller's catalog. I have letters from American librarians boasting collections of over 100,000 trade catalogs. In some cases these collections date from 1920 to 1940, are still stored in cases and trunks, and have never been checked and cataloged. In others, fine collections dating from 1800 to 1900 are stored in shoe boxes labeled Drugs, Glass, Pottery, etc. Several of our outstanding repositories have large collections set aside ready to catalog as soon as funds and staff can handle them. After all this is only a guide. Where possible I have given obtainable description, but with the firm's name indexed, and his goods and products classified in sixty two chapters, it is up to you to check the locations and ferret out the specific information you need.

I have checked with over two hundred of our largest libraries, historical societies and museums before attempting to compile this preliminary survey. Much as I would like to give credit where credit is due I have explained my position under acknowledgments. The thousands of locations should speak for themselves.

It is both amusing and confusing to find that in many cases my own records of sales for nearly thirty years must stand as the locations because of this dearth of funds for staffs to classify, file and cataalog. On the other hand, if these same institutions had not listened to my detailed descriptions of these catalogs, accepted my claims to their importance as a very real force in the development of America, and purchased them for future research, I would not have been financially able to exploit their preservation or even consider this Guide. It may sound as though I criticize those very libraries that have backed my convictions. If there is any fair criticism, it is of the boards and "angels" who provide funds for Gutenburg Bibles and Tamerlanes but NOT for the greatest panorama of industrial development ever printed.

A good many experienced librarians and collectors have thought checking Charles Evans' American Bibliography for trade catalogs sheer folly. However, though I claim only a very selective list for this preliminary examination, I do want it to be as thorough as I can possibly make it. Since our oldest libraries do not have their trade catalogs segregated, or filed under this term, there is no other way of checking what might have been issued from 1639 to 1800.

Samuel Willard's "Heavenly Merchandise: or the Purchasing of Truth Recommended, and the Selling of it Dissuaded," printed by Samuel Green in Boston in 1686 (Evans Vol. #424), might possibly be suggested as the first American mercantile brochure . . . if, of course, you are willing to smile and shed that dusty cloak of bibliography for a second. Following this perhaps rather questionable attempt at humor come the booksellers' auction lists that continue right through the 19th century.

The first real trade catalog is Benjamin Franklin's 1744 catalog of books, in which he offers those who live remote the same justice as though present . . . provided they send him the necessary cash purchase prices as listed. To me, as a 20th century out of print bookseller, his warning that after three weeks the remaining books will be sold at advanced prices, is a challenge to all of us. I wish I had his confidence in my own appraisals and evaluations. Can any of us today honestly state that the lowest price is marked in each book, and stick to it? No. We are asked to allow 10% for this one, 20% for that one, and 33-1/3% for another to begin with; then if business is poor we have to take what we can get . . . but not Dr. Franklin. What has become of that world of individuals?

I might, I suppose, select amusing and educational bits from many of these booksellers' offerings listed in Brigham, Evans, McKay, Sabin and Silver, but, like the White Rabbit, I'm late now and I dassent daudle . . . the Red Queen is waiting. Those located on the following pages in the Books, Booksellers & Publishers' Chapter are only to supplement the exhaustive bibliographies already printed and waiting for you in your local or nearby library.

Dr. Franklin's brochure offering his then miraculous fireplaces or stoves is the first in the manufacturing field, and was printed in the same year. I doubt very much that this was the only one before 1750. I think it better to say the only one that has been rescued and preserved. I am convinced that there were others. Dr. Franklin's have survived because of his prominence and popularity. Those issued by Mr. Smith, Mr. Jones and perhaps Mr. White were probably "considered too ephemeral in value to warrant the cost of saving them." Becoming one of the greatest Americans of all time, Dr. Franklin's catalogs and pamphlets were at least saved, and have surely proved themselves worth the cost of preservation.

This "Essay", which I claim as a catalog - "An Account of the New Invented Pennsylvania Fire-Places . . . etc." . . . will bring criticism. "Believing that inventions were for the benefit of mankind, Franklin refused to profit by the manufacture and sale of the 'Pennsylvanian Fire-Place' . . ." (The Colonial Scene. 1602-1800). On the other hand it is my contention that the "Advertisement" on the verso of the title page designates it as a trade catalog. This small pamphlet presents a thorough description of these new modern "stoves", it also names three sales agents from whom they may be purchased, with their places of business, and to boot explains that there are three different sizes. Wherein does this differ from the color pictorial automobile catalogs of today? True, he doesn't give prices, but I still think this 1744 pamphlet is a trade catalog way before its time, printed by a man whose common sense genius might well have split the atom had he lived long enough.

In 1756 (Evans #7631) a catalog was printed by James Chattin of Philadelphia. Since the compiler added a question mark, we cannot be certain whether this was a broadside or a pamphlet. There is apparently no copy located. However, it is a trade catalog in wording, and adds variety to our meager knowledge of what the colonists were offered to make life more colorful. "A Catalogue of a very curious collection of Prints, consisting of several hundred representations of trees, shrubs, plants, herbs, fruits, flowers, etc. To be sold cheap, the lowest price being mark'd in the Catalogue. Printed by James Chattin ? Philadelphia: 1756."

Years roll by under the competent hand of Charles Evans, and the American bookseller continues to be the outstanding cataloguer. Other manufacturers didn't issue as many catalogs because they couldn't produce the goods. Business records in manuscript ledgers and family papers tell and retell the struggles of the craftsmen to supply the demands of their own small communities. There seems to have been little need for catalogs of goods for sale. The blacksmith in New Haven had more trade than he could attend to and quite naturally didn't ask for trouble by printing lists of skillets and spiders he couldn't possibly make to sell in Boston or New York. If any smith or artisan had any surplus manufactures, there were local outlets begging for more goods. Books were apparently imported in far greater quantity than anything else, or, the American booksellers were better merchants than their contemporary craftsmen and jobbers.

Not counting "A Short Treatise of the Virtues of Dr. Bateman's Pectoral Drops etc." reprinted for James Wallace by John Peter Zenger in New York in 1731, since such nostrums are considered patent medicines, the first American drug catalog appeared in 1760. This catalog was issued by one John Tweedy of Newport, Rhode Island, and is well worth looking up and reading. Located by Alden 228, Evans 8753, Hammett page 34 and Winship page 16 at the Rhode Island Historical Society and the National Library of Medicine only, the title page reads: "A Catalogue of Druggs, and of Chymical and Galenical Medicines; sold by John Tweedy at his shop in Newport, Rhode-Island. And For Him In New-York, At The Sign Of The Unicorn and Mortar. (Newport ? Printed by James Franklin? 1760 ?)" Evans notes (32) pages. Alden accuses him of supplying the Newport imprint. DNLM's copy is apparently complete with 28 pages, and Alden comments that Evans may have counted the additional pages in manuscript in the RHi copy, listing it as 32 pages. The fact remains, in spite of the bibliographical squabbling, that John Tweedy issued the first real American drug catalog, and that we can locate it for use. I feel quite confident that a gentleman in Boston might order a bottle of ipecac by post as easily as he might step into the Tweedy shop in Newport or at the Sign of the Unicorn & Mortar in New York.

It seems possible that by 1744 a few craftsmen and merchants were producing more than their next door neighbors could absorb. The "New Invented Pennsylvania Fire-Places" were apparently being made in more numbers than Philadelphia could install, and Dr. Franklin also felt that the rest of the countryside ought to have the benefit of their warmth and comfort. Whether or not any but the British soldiers used books as fuel in them, I can't say. The number of booksellers' catalogs might suggest that there were more books and pamphlets than folks could read. If you will check Mr. McKay's bibliography of the auction catalogs issued from about 1713 to 1800, I think this might occur to you as a possibility. Yet the burning of most of Thomas Prince's library in Old South Church by the British troops makes one wonder how or why we should expect to find a complete check list of everything printed in New England in Evans, or anywhere else. In 1771 John Dunlap printed for John Day and Company the second drug catalog of which we have a record. This catalog, Evans 12024, shows the growth of the drug business even since 1744. The title page in full follows:-

Day, John & Co. "A Catalogue of Drugs, Chymical and Galenical Preparations, Shop Furniture, Patent Medicines, and Surgeons' Instruments, sold by John Day & Co., Druggists and Chymists, in Second-Street, Philadelphia." Printed by John Dunlap, in Market-Street, Philadelphia: M, DCC, LXXI. 8vo., 33pp.

Shop Furniture and Patent Medicines! Shades of Sears Roebuck of the Gay Nineties! What have we here? In 1765 a medical school was formed in the College of Philadelphia which is now the University of Pennsylvania. These patent medicines were undoubtedly different from those of our Gay Nineties, and there was no American Medical Association to sift out the good ones, and ban the junk. Probably they were harmless pink pills such as our own doctors use today, whose value lies in their psychological curing powers.

In the same year William Prince issued "A List of Fruit Trees . . . on Sale at Flushing, Long-Island, August, 1771. New York: 1771." (Evans #12206). Today, with our billions of circulars and stuffers, this might not be considered a catalog. However, since almost all advertising in our 18th century seems to have been placed in the newspapers, I think it worth while to make a record of those who first recognized the value of printing all forms of catalogs both for their own clientele, and unwittingly, for the annals of trade history.

Although Rita Susswein Gottesman in her compilation "The Arts and Crafts in New York 1726-1776," published by the New-York Historical Society, notes newspaper advertising of gardeners, seedsmen and fruit trees, there is no listing for William Prince. In a circular dated October 1, 1823, Mr. Prince states that "This establishment commenced about the middle of the last century . . . well known for the great extent of its Botanic acquisitions, as well in Exotic and Native Fruits, as for its large collection of Trees, Flowers and Plants . . . etc." This circular is headed "Linnaean Botanic Garden and Nurseries, New-York."

There is an interesting sidelight on Mr. Prince's enthusiasm in General Washington's Diary during the period 1789 to 1791: "Saturday, 10th (1789). Pursuant to an engagement formed on Thursday last, I set off about 9 o'clock in my barge to visit Mr. Prince's fruit gardens and shrubberies at Flushing, on Long-Island . . . These gardens, except in the number of young fruit trees, did not answer my expectations. The shrubs were trifling, and the flowers not numerous." It is a known fact that Washington bought his seeds, plants, shrubs and trees directly through British agents, because he felt that the run of the mill exported to American agents were of inferior quality. At the turn of the century, I gather that he did patronize the famous Bernard M'Mahon of Philadelphia whose catalogs I will consider later.

As I skim along through Volume 4 of Mr. Evans' monumental compilation, I must remind you of grand old General Henry Knox's "Catalogue of Books Imported and to be sold by . . . 1772," as well as many hundred examples of the printed records of the colonial booksellers. If you are especially interested in this field, Mr. McKay offers a complete bibliography, and Mr. Brigham a carefully condensed analysis. That these booksellers' catalogs are without doubt the best exponents of American cataloging in the 18th and 19th century is undeniable. They belong in this volume, but if I include them, this volume will become ten!

In 1774, Evans #13201, Matthew Clarkson issued an "Advertisement," apparently listing millstones for sale. This was printed by Robert Aitken of Philadelphia, and is probably a broadside list. However, since there is no copy located, I can't be sure that it should be included.

In the same year, we find a catalog comparable to the much touted first by A. Montgomery Ward in 1872, almost a hundred years earlier. I shall not copy the entire list, which may be consulted in the Boston Public Library.

Evans #13233. Cranch, Robert G. "Robert G. Cranch, Saddlers' Ironmonger and Bridle-Cutter, on the Exchange, Boston, has imported on the last Ship from Bristol, Bought of the Manufacturers, and sells wholesale and retail, on the lowest terms, viz: (three columns of goods). Printed by I. Thomas, near the Mill Bridge, Boston. (1774)." This is a broadside catalog, copy located in BPL.

Reading Evans page for page, title for title, and word for word, instead of using the index has been an experience I wouldn't trade for anything. The only trouble with it is that I hate to leave out some of the choice bits like "Heavenly Merchandise," "Jewels and Diamonds for Sentimentalists at Bell's Bookstore" and the small significant fact that, as far as I can determine, Robert Bell was the first bookseller to charge "one quarter of a dollar" for his book catalog in 1783.

Printing began in what is now the United States in 1639, but catalogs of type or of printers' equipment or services seem to have lagged. As already noted, there was good reason. Presses and type were virtually unobtainable. Evans #19272 is a specimen of Isaiah Thomas' printing types. (See The Colonial Scene, page 62) "Isaiah Thomas. A Specimen of Isaiah Thomas's Printing Types. Being as large and complete an Assortment as is to be met with in any one Printing-Office in America. --- Worcester, 1785." However, as Lawrence Wroth points out, this is not a type-founder's catalog of types for sale addressed to printers, but a brochure of printer's specimens addressed to customers, displaying the sizes and styles of type available in his cases for use in printing he hopes to do for them. On the other hand, I believe it is as much a trade catalog as those issued by R. R. Donnelley of Chicago today. The 20th century has yet to produce anything to equal them. Mr. Wroth also notes a broadside of specimens issued by Mein & Fleeming of Boston in 1766. Dr. Sachse in his "German Sectarians of Pennsylvania," reproduced a printer's specimen of types and a price list which he attributes to Christopher Sauer of Germantown, and says further that this broadside is supposed to have been issued as early as 1740. All of which makes it evident that we know little of the trade catalogs issued during the 18th century. One will wonder what difference it makes WHICH was the first trade catalog issued by an American printer, and another will be indignant if I make the slightest error. However, I have so much to report in the 19th century that I cannot stay in the 18th much longer.

In 1788 we find the first catalog reference to silverware and jewelry. Evans 21153. Hubley, A. & Co. "A Catalogue of Prints, Plate, Plated-Ware, Jewelry &c. to be sold Wednesday, September 3, 1788 at the Southward Vendue-Store. Phil.: 1788." No copy is located. It seems reasonable that the "Prints" were calicos or other colorful textiles, but they might have been engravings. At any rate, THIS is not a catalog of just one line, and it IS a catalog.

"The New invented friction roller, made and sold by John Martin at his manufactory, No. 207, Queen street, near the corner of Golden Hill," is another of those border line cases. This folio broadside (Evans #21219) was printed by W. Morton in New-York, in 1788. It is embellished with a cut, but since there is no copy located, I can't check to see whether or not there is a list of types and sizes offered for sale. Like Dr. Franklin's fireplaces, there will be those who agree that it might have been a catalog, and many who won't.

In the same year, Evans #21568, George Wall, Junior, issued a very complete descriptive pamphlet of 32 pages concerning the invention and sale of his "newly-invented surveying instrument, called the trigonometer." He obtained an exclusive right for its manufacture and sale from the Pennsylvania Legislature. This pamphlet is most certainly a piece of printed matter for the sole purpose of selling the instruments. The plate and recommendations remind one of recent automobile brochures, most of which are considered catalogs in every sense of the word. In building up this short list of American trade catalogs in the 18th century, other than books, I shall most certainly include it.

Since the dictionary states that a catalog should be a list, I am again bucking accepted terms when I list "Joyce and Snowdon's American ink powder for records, equal to any imported, or offered for sale in the Thirteen United States" (Evans 22594). This was offered in a 4to. broadside as "Sold by most stationers, booksellers, ironmongers, &c. in New York, and in other principal cities and towns in America." This enterprising cataloger uses the U. S. Arms, engraved by Rollinson in New-York in 1790. There are directions in Dutch and English, and this "catalogue" (?) that was used as a wrapper for the powder, may be inspected at the New-York Historical Society.

In 1791, our friend William Prince issued another folio broadside with a fine list of his "large collection of fruit trees, shrubs, &c.", and in spite of George Washington's scathing remarks, for 1791, it looks pretty tasty.

Whether the booksellers of 1791, like the drug stores of today, the mighty First National Stores and their competitors, felt the pinch of high rents with the high cost of marketing it is hard to tell, but Carey, Stewart and Co. of Philadelphia did add "stationery and cutlery" to their twelve page catalog in this year. I don't mean to be critical, but it does seem as though book stores ought to be able to live on books, and food stores on food. I have often mourned this departure from old times, and am surprised to find the same thing happened in 1791.

By using the John Carter Brown set of Evans, as well as their kindly, cooperative, comfortable hospitality, I stumbled over a very unusual, "not in Evans", broadside. It is apparently the only known broadside catalog of shipbuilding materials in the 18th century. The addition of fish at the bottom of the list adds a salty flavor. This broadside catalog was offered by Jonathan Davis & Son, and printed in Bath, Maine, in 1792. I wonder if they also carved figure-heads, and if so why they didn't mention them. Probably this was a separate occupation whose craftsmen didn't need catalogs. For a complete listing see the Chapter on Boats & Ships, Marine Hardware and Supplies.

"Price Current" lists were published here and there from about 1750 on to 1850. These are not exactly catalogs, and yet they are lists of merchandise with a slant on values. Evans #28315 is a good example:- "The Boston Price-current and Marine-Intellingencer. Commercial and Mercantile No. 1, Monday, Sept. 7 - (No. XVII, December 28, 1795)." Established by John and Joseph N. Russell as a weekly it was enlarged to crown folio in March 1796. Whereas I think it originally might have been called a catalog of prices, it was really a periodical. It continued until about 1840.

The booksellers continued their furious pace through 1792, 1793 and 1794. At last in 1795 we find another industry that calls for attention. I offer you Evans 28428, "Boston Paper Staining Manufactory. Ebenr. Clough, Paper Stainer, Charles River Bridge, Boston, Manufactures & Keeps Constantly for Sale, a Great Variety of Paper Hangings, etc." No location is given, but John Carter Brown Library has since acquired a copy of this small but significant record.

Although this is listed as a 1795 broadside, there is note stating that it is a billhead engraved by Samuel Hill. This checks exactly with the copy at RPJCB. There is unfortunately no list of designs of wall and other paper hangings because the lower half bearing the items on the bill has been lost. Perhaps there is another copy still buried in an attic that may one day give us a list of fantastic Yankee peacocks and harbor views -- who knows? If you feel that this listing is a gross stretch of the imagination please consider that it is perhaps the first reference in printed form of American wall papers and paper hangings. The engraving by Samuel Hill is a complete panorama of paper making and deserves a place in this Guide.

As we near the end of Charles Evans' bibliography, it would seem that the druggists and "chymists" are to take second place to the booksellers, with the seedsmen and horticulturalists coming in third, upheld almost entirely by William Prince of Long Island. From the catalog standpoint it is not an imposing list. On the other hand many a librarian, collector and dealer has told me there were none, so I'm far from "skunked" -- in fact I feel that the work so far is definitely a contribution. If I have lifted Benjamin Franklin's stoves into the trade catalog classification, I'm proud of it.

Evans #29537 offers another combination catalog which, though essentially drugs, again emphasizes the fact that many manufacturers and merchants issued catalogs offering a great variety of goods for the American public of the 18th century. This catalog by Messrs. Smith and Bartlett of Boston offered the following in 1795:- "Catalogue of Drugs and Medicines, instruments and utensils, dyestuffs, groceries and painters' colours, imported, prepared and sold, by Smith & Bartlett, at their druggists store and apothecaries shop, No. 61, Cornhill, Boston." This catalog of 22 pages, 12mo. in size, (copy in LC) offers the customer everything from a head of lettuce to a surgeon's saw and I think will compare favorably with Montgomery Ward's first, second and even No. 11 for May, 1874 in which they announce that they will add a complete line of Groceries, Teas and Wooden Ware on June 1st. It would not be reasonable to compare the bag of 1795 flour with one offered in 1874, but it seems to be a fair statement that Smith & Bartlett offered a comparatively varied stock.

1796 and 1797 passed catalog-wise with the usual number of booksellers' lists and offerings, broadsides and pamphlets, good and bad, with no other trades represented. In 1798 John Langdon of New York offered the following (Evans #33978): "A Catalogue of English Kitchen-garden and fancy flower seeds, imported in the snow (?) (possibly ship), Hazard, from London, and for sale at the store of John Langdon, No. 6 Fletcher-street, near the Fly-Market, wholesale and retail." This broadside was printed by J. Buel, New-York, 1798. Whether President Washington would have found this array more to his liking is doubtful. This catalog makes it a close race between the seedsmen and the druggists as we close this section on the 18th century. 1799 passed like so many others, with the irrepressible booksellers' rampant, and these you can examine and study as previously recommended.

The small scraps recorded by Mr. Evans do not make an imposing exhibition even when added to the discoveries of recent years. They do stand as proof that trade catalogs were issued during the 18th century, and as such they are important to this preliminary survey. Much as I would like to supply it, a continuation of this same sort of short-short story of trade catalogs during the 19th century is out of the question. With the invention of the rotary press, followed by almost annual improvements in every field of American industrial development, a complete roster, even of those preserved and located in collections today, would mean fifty volumes.

For a better understanding of what this pictorial panorama meant to the people of the U. S. A. as it grew from 1800 to 1900 the reader might do well to select a few of the Bibliographical Suggestions provided for further study. The compilers tell you little about trade catalogs or where to find the examples they use, but they do give you a solid background. They will point out better than I can the truth of Robert Cantwell's "America's Unknown History," an excellent article that appeared in The Nation, April 25th, 1959. Mr. Cantwell states in no uncertain terms that since James Leander Bishop's "History of American Manufactures 1608-1860," the story of our industrial development has been completely forgotten and entirely neglected.

If a complete history of American manufactures is ever to be compiled, American trade catalogs will unquestionably be one of the most valuable sources of material available. As I recently explained in a short tirade in Vol. 4, No. 1 of Library Resources and Technical Services, one good sixty four page catalog with lithographed illustrations of a full line of products in any given field will, for such an undertaking, be worth seven tons of manuscript ledgers, day books, copy books and correspondence. If this volume encourages our library boards and "angels" to recognize these invaluable records, and to provide funds and staffs to take care of them, not stored in boxes and cartons and trunks, unchecked, but rather properly cataloged and shelved where historians can find them, I shall feel amply paid for the time and effort that has gone into it.

Lawrence B. Romaine

ACKNOWLEDGMENTS

There is no page in the history of literature less interesting than a page of names, titles and addresses, unless it be a page of goods and manufactures. Since we offer a complete library symbol roster, why should we burden you further with pages of names with the customary clutter of "I want to thank," "I am deeply indebted," "Without so and so we could not have gone to press," and "I especially want to . . ." Sweet nothings, though they are colorful at a cocktail party, are not necessarily sincere thanks at all.

I include this page only to sincerely thank those librarians . . . and in this instance librarians stands for collectors, curators, custodians, directors and all assistants . . . whose enthusiasm and interest has not only preserved the catalogs, but has extended to listing and classifying, sorting and carding, corresponding and mailing the material, both at work and after hours, to the humble compiler of this volume. I would like to include the dealers who have conscientiously collected and rescued these basic records of American industry that have found their way to the repositories and built these collections.

Those of you who have lent a hand know that I know and appreciate the time and effort you have made. I thank you, one and all . . . and I thank you again. Is this better than three pages of names and addresses? I think so, and, I'm in the driver's seat.

ABBREVIATIONS

bds.	boards
bkrm.	buckram
book sizes (approx.)	
4to	9 x 12
8vo	6 x 9
12mo	5 x 7-1/2
16mo	4-1/4 x 6-3/4
18mo	4 x 6-1/4
24mo	3-1/2 x 6
32mo	3-1/4 x 5
c.	circa
cl.	cloth
cm.	2.4 to the inch
co.	company
col.	color
col(s)	column(s)
cvs.	covers
dec.	decals, decorated
desc.	description, descriptive
diag(s)	diagram(s)
ed.	edition
ellipsis	indicated by . . .
enc.	enclosed
est.	established
fig(s)	figure(s)
fld.	folding
fol.	folio
frs.	frontispiece
glt.	gilt

ill(s)	illustrated, illustrations
lea.	leather
lg.	large
mfg.	manufacture(d) (rs)
mor.	morocco
ms(s)	manuscript(s)
nd.	no date
no.	number
n.p.	no place
orig.	original
p.	after
pat.	patent(ed)
photo(s)	photograph(s)
pict.	pictorial
pls.	plates
port(s)	portrait(s)
pp.	pages
ptd.	printed
ref.	reference
resp.	respectively
rev.	revised
sm.	small
spec(s)	specification(s)
sq.	square
test(s)	testimonials
unbd.	unbound
v.d.	various dates
vol(s)	volume(s)
wrap(s)	wrapper(s)

SYMBOLS

ADA	American Dental Association, Chicago, Ill.	CtY	Yale University Library, New Haven, Conn.
CaNBSM	New Brunswick Museum, St. John, New Brunswick, Can.	CU	University of California, Berkeley, Calif.
CBaK	Kern County Museum, Bakersfield, Calif.	CU-A	University of California, Davis, Calif.
CBevT	20th Century-Fox Film Corporation, Beverly Hills, Calif.	CU-D	Should read CU-A.
CCuMGM	Metro-Goldwyn-Mayer, Culver City, Calif.	DA	U. S. Dept. of Agriculture Library, Washington, D.C.
CHi	California Historical Society, San Francisco, Calif.	DAIA	American Institute of Architects, Washington, D. C.
CLU	University of California, Los Angeles, Calif.	DAPh	American Pharmaceutical Association, Washington, D.C.
COCAC	California College of Arts & Crafts, Oakland, Calif.	DeWE	Eleutherian Mills Hagley Foundation, Wilmington, Del.
CoD	Denver Public Library, Denver, Colo.	DeWint	Henry F. DuPont's Winterthur Museum, Winterthur, Del.
CSf	San Francisco Public Library, San Francisco, Calif.	DLC	Library of Congress, Washington, D. C.
CSmH	Henry E. Huntington Library & Art Museum, San Marino, Calif.	DLNM	National Library of Medicine, Washington, D.C. & Cleveland, O.
Ct	Connecticut State Library, Hartford, Conn.	DSi	Smithsonian Institution, Washington, D. C.
CtBrAM	American Clock & Watch Museum, Bristol, Conn.	F	Florida State Library, Tallahassee, Fla.
CtHi	Connecticut Historical Society, Hartford, Conn.	GU	University of Georgia Library, Athens, Ga.
CtMerK	Kelsey Press Library, Meriden, Conn.	IaHi	Iowa Historical Society, Iowa City, Ia.
CtMyM	Marine Historical Association, Mystic, Conn.	ICHi	Chicago Historical Society, Chicago, Ill.
CtNlC	Connecticut College Library, New London, Conn.	ICJ	John Crerar Library, Chicago, Ill.
CtWAB	The American Brass Co., Waterbury, Conn.	ICN	Newberry Library, Chicago, Ill.

ICRMc	Rand McNally & Co., Chicago, Ill.	MdBelW	H. P. White Co., Bel Air, Md.
ICRRD	R. R. Donnelley & Sons, Chicago, Ill.	MdBJ-W	Welch Medical Library, Johns Hopkins University, Baltimore, Md.
ICTPA	Telephone Pioneers of America, Ill. Division, Chicago, Ill.	MdHi	Maryland Historical Society, Baltimore, Md.
ICU	University of Chicago, Chicago, Ill.	MdTanSW	"Spinning Wheel" Magazine, Taneytown, Md.
IHi	Illinois State Historical Library, Springfield, Ill.	MdU-D	University of Maryland - Medical Library, Baltimore, Md.
In	Indiana State Library, Indianapolis, Ind.	MeBa	Bangor Public Library, Bangor, Me.
InELK	Elkhart Public Library, Elkhart, Ind.	MH	Harvard University, Cambridge, Mass.
InFw	Public Library of Fort Wayne & Allen Co., Fort Wayne, Ind.	MH-BA	Harvard - Baker Library - Graduate School of Business Administration, Cambridge, Mass.
InHi	Indiana Historical Society, Indianapolis, Ind.	MH-D	Harvard University Dental School, Boston, Mass.
IU	University of Illinois Library, Urbana, Ill.	MHi	Massachusetts Historical Society, Boston, Mass.
IU-M	University of Illinois - Medical Library, Chicago, Ill.	Mi	Michigan Historical Commission, Lansing, Mich.
KU	University of Kansas, Lawrence, Kan.	MiD	Detroit Public Library, Detroit, Mich.
KyBdnB	Barton Distilling Co. Museum, Bardstown, Ky.	MiDbF	Ford Motor Co. Archives & Greenfield Village, Dearborn, Mich.
KyU	University of Kentucky, Lexington, Ky.	MiFli	Flint Public Library, Flint, Mich.
MB	Boston Public Library, Boston, Mass.	MiK	Kalamazoo Public Library, Kalamazoo, Mich.
MBAt	Boston Athenaeum, Boston, Mass.	MiLSU	Michigan State University, Lansing, Mich.
MBH	Massachusetts Horticultural Society Library, Boston, Mass.	MiU-H	University of Michigan, Michigan Historical Collections, Ann Arbor, Mich.
MBM	Boston Medical Library, Boston, Mass.	MiU-T	University of Michigan, Transportation Library, Ann Arbor, Mich.
MBP	Massachusetts College of Pharmacy, Boston, Mass.		
MBSPNEA	Society for Preservation of New England Antiquities, Boston, Mass.	MMidHi	Middleborough Historical Association, Inc., Middleborough, Mass.
MdBE	Enoch Pratt Library, Baltimore, Md.	MnHi	Minnesota Historical Society, St. Paul, Minn.

MnU	University of Minnesota, St. Paul, Minn.	NhHi	New Hampshire Historical Society, Concord, N. H.
MnU-B	University of Minnesota - Medical, St. Paul, Minn.	NHi	New York Historical Society, New York, N. Y.
MoSHi	Missouri Historical Society, St. Louis, Mo.	NIC-B	Cornell University, Liberty H. Bailey Hortorium, Ithaca, N. Y.
MoU	University of Missouri, Columbia, Mo.	NjN	Newark Public Library, Newark, N. J.
MSaE	Essex Institute, Salem, Mass.	NjOE	Edison Laboratory National Monument, East Orange, N. J.
MSanHi	Sandwich Historical Society, Sandwich, Mass.		
MSC	Springfield College Library, Springfield, Mass.	NjR	Rutgers University, New Brunswick, N. J.
MStOSV	Old Sturbridge Village, Sturbridge, Mass.	NLIAM	Long Island Automotive Museum, Southampton, L. I., N. Y.
MSwanHi	Swansea Historical Society, Swansea, Mass.	NN	New York Public Library, New York, N. Y.
MWA	American Antiquarian Society, Worcester, Mass.	NNC	Columbia University, New York, N. Y.
N	New York State Library, Albany, N. Y.	NNC-A	Columbia University, Avery Library, New York, N. Y.
NBmlAM	Adirondack Museum, Blue Mountain Lake, N. Y.	NNCoo	Cooper Union Library, Cooper Union, New York, N. Y.
NBuHi	Buffalo Historical Society, Buffalo, N. Y.	NNGr	Grolier Club Library, New York, N. Y.
NCaS	St. Lawrence University, Canton, N. Y.	NNHome	Home Insurance Co., H. V. Smith Museum, New York, N. Y.
NcGW	Women's College of North Carolina, Greensboro, N. C.		
NCooHi	New York State Historical Association, Cooperstown, N. Y.	NNMM	Metropolitan Museum of Art, New York, N. Y.
NCorniC	Corning Glass Museum, Corning, N. Y.	NNNAM	New York Academy of Medicine Library, New York, N. Y.
NcU	University of North Carolina, Chapel Hill, N. C.	NNQ	Queensborough Public Library, New York, N. Y.
NcUPh	University of North Carolina - Medical, Chapel Hill, N. C.	NNU	New York University Libraries, New York, N. Y.
NhD	Dartmouth College, Hanover, N. H.	NOCSM	Shaker Museum, Old Chatham, N. Y.
NhDY	Yankee Magazine Library, Dublin, N. H.	NR	Rochester Public Library, Rochester, N. Y.
NHerkHi	Herkimer County Historical Society, Herkimer, N. Y.	NRGE	George Eastman House, Rochester, N. Y.
		NSbSM	Suffolk Museum, Stony Brook, N. Y.

NStIHi	Staten Island Historical Society, Richmond, Staten Island, N. Y.	PPL	The Library Company of Philadelphia, Philadelphia, Pa.
NSyHi	Onondaga Historical Association, Syracuse, N. Y.	PPPCPh	Philadelphia College of Pharmacy & Science, Philadelphia, Pa.
NTRHi	Rensselaer County Historical Society, Troy, N. Y.	PPPMilk	Pennbrook Milk Co., Gwinn Museum, Philadelphia, Pa.
OAkF	Firestone Tire & Rubber Co. Archives, Akron, O.	PShipL	The Lincoln Library, Shippensburg, Pa.
OC	Public Library of Cincinnati, Cincinnati, O.	PU	University of Pennsylvania, Philadelphia, Pa.
OCl	Cleveland Public Library, Cleveland, O.	PWcHi	Chester County Historical Society, West Chester, Pa.
OCLloyd	Lloyd Library, Cincinnati, O.	RHi	Rhode Island Historical Society, Providence, R. I.
OCP&G	The Proctor & Gamble Co., Cincinnati, O.	RP	Providence Public Library, Providence, R. I.
OHi	Ohio Historical Society, Columbus, O.	RPB	Brown University Library, Providence, R. I.
OrHi	Oregon Historical Society, Portland, Ore.	RPJCB	John Carter Brown Library, Providence, R. I.
OrU	University of Oregon, Eugene, Ore.	RU	University of Rhode Island, Kingston, R. I.
OT	Toledo Public Library, Toledo, O.	TxDa	Dallas Public Library, Dallas, Tex.
PBS	Bethlehem Steel Co., Bethlehem, Pa.	TxDaDeG	DeGolyer Foundation, Dallas, Tex.
PC	Private Collections. This symbol is used for outstanding libraries like Thomas W. Streeter's, not at the moment available to the general public.	TxLT	Texas Technological College Library, Lubbock, Tex.
		TxU	University of Texas, Austin, Tex.
PHi	Historical Society of Pennsylvania, Philadelphia, Pa.	Vi	Virginia State Library, Richmond, Va.
PKsL	Longwood Library, Kennett Square, Pa.	ViNewM	Mariners' Museum, Newport News, Va.
PLACC	Armstrong Cork Co., Lancaster, Pa.	ViRm	Medical College of Virginia, Richmond, Va.
PP	Free Library of Philadelphia, Philadelphia, Pa.	ViU	University of Virginia - Alderman Library, Charlottesville, Va.
PPAmP	American Philosophical Society, Philadelphia, Pa.	ViWc	Colonial Williamsburg Library, Williamsburg, Va.
PPF	Franklin Institute Library, Philadelphia, Pa.	VtHi	Vermont Historical Society, Montpelier, Vt.
PPiU	University of Pittsburgh, Pittsburgh, Pa.	VtSM	Shelburne Museum, Shelburne, Vt.

WaMaG	Gannon Museum, Mabton, Wash.	WUPh	University of Wisconsin - Medicine, Madison, Wis.
WHi	Wisconsin Historical Society, Madison, Wis.	Wv-Ar	West Virginia Department of Archives & Library, Charleston, W. Va.
WM	Milwaukee Public Library, Milwaukee, Wis.	WvWO	Oglebay Institute, Wheeling, W. Va.
WU	University of Wisconsin, Madison, Wis.		

Chapter 1

Agricultural Implements, Tools & Machinery

The American seedsman was among the first to recognize the value of circulating lists of his products for sale. It happens that he was also the first to manufacture and sell the implements, tools and machinery to produce the seeds, plants, trees, shrubs and vegetables he sold to make his living. Consequently, many of the finest examples of illustrated catalogs of American agricultural implements will be found in the chapter on seed catalogs, where some of the earliest woodcuts of plows, fanning mills, cider presses, pruning knives, etc. appear. Since windmills served factories, railroads and even whole communities during the 19th century, they will be found in a separate chapter. Although one might expect to find beekeeping equipment, millers' supplies, mills and livestock and poultry under agriculture, these too have been listed by themselves.

This chapter, therefore, is confined to farm implements and machinery as nearly as possible, even though seeds, fences, garden and fire engines, mills, ornamental iron castings, and dozens of other artifacts appear, because the manufacturers and jobbers slipped them in many of the listings to swell their sales.

1886 Peoria   MnHi
ACME HAY HARVESTER CO. Catalog of hay rickers, loaders and rakes. 16mo., 16pp., ill., pict. wrap.

c.1886 Poughkeepsie
ADRIANCE, PLATT & CO. Buckeye mower and reapers. Buy the best. 8vo., 16pp., ill., pict. wrap. of plant.

1890 Poughkeepsie   DSi
------ Catalog of mowers, reapers and binders. 20pp., litho. of plant, ill.

1894 Poughkeepsie   PKsL
------ Catalog of harvesting machinery. Ill. (Issued by agent at Wilmington, Del.)

ALBANY AGRICULTURAL WORKS. See Emery Brothers and Luther Tucker.

1848 New York   NCooHi
ALLEN, A.B. & CO. New York Agricultural Warehouse. Desc. catalog of agricultural and horticultural implements. np., ill., pict. wrap. Fine early woodcuts.

1852 New York   NCooHi
------ Desc. catalog. Woodcuts of implements, churns, mills, garden furniture, fire engines and coaches. 8vo., 110pp., pict. wrap.

1854 New York   NCooHi
------ Ill. catalog.

1853 New York   MStOSV
ALLEN, R.L. (Late A. D. Allen & Co.) Catalog of agricultural implements, etc. 12mo., 32pp., ill., wrap.

1873 New York   PKsL
------ Catalog of agricultural implements, machinery, hardware, garden fire engines, apple parers, bull rings, mills and weather-vanes. 8vo., 264pp., ill., pict. wrap. 16th ed.

1880 Philadelphia   PKsL
ALLEN, S.L. & CO. Desc. catalog and price list of Planet Jr. drill, wheel hoe, Firefly plow, etc. 8vo., 16pp., pict. wrap.

1884 Philadelphia   CtHi
------ Ill. catalog and price list of Planet Jr. and Firefly farm and garden instruments. 4to., 32pp. (Agent R.D. Hawley, Hartford.)

1885 Philadelphia   NNQ
------ Ill. catalog of Planet Jr. and Firefly farm and garden implements. (Agent D.T. Bayles, Stony Brook, N.Y.)

1885 Philadelphia   PKsL
------ Ill. catalog. Ptd. Morrell Bros., Philadelphia. Pict. wrap of 22 implements.

c.1885 Philadelphia   NCooHi
------ Ill. catalog of farm implements. 32pp. Ptd. Albany.

1888 Philadelphia   CtHi
------ Ill. catalog and price list of Planet Jr. and Firefly farm and garden tools. 8vo.,

32pp., wrap. (Agents Parker & Barber, Rockville, Conn.)

1891 Philadelphia   NCooHi
------ Greetings for 1891. First season in new works. Implement catalog. 32pp., ill.

1892 Philadelphia   PHi
------ The Planet Jr. implement catalog. 8vo., 32pp., ill.

1893 Philadelphia   CSmH
------ Catalog of Planet Jr. garden seed drills. 32pp., ill.

1894 Philadelphia   PKsL
------ The Planet Jr. A memorable year. 8vo., 32pp., pict. wrap. World's Fair Exhibition.

1895 Philadelphia   PKsL
------ Catalog of Planet Jr. implements. 8vo., 32pp., col. pict. wrap.

1897 Philadelphia   PKsL
------ Catalog similar to 1895. 8vo., 32pp. N.B. Later catalogs to 1912 may be found at PKsL.

1881 Chicago   MnHi
AMERICAN GRINDING MILL CO. Desc. catalog and price list of fodder grain mills, farm mills, grinders, etc. 8vo., 25pp., ill., wrap.

c.1900 Richmond, Ind.   In
AMERICAN SEEDING MACHINE CO. 8vo., 32pp., ill., col. pict. wrap. by Detroit Litho.

nd. Richmond, Ind.   OHi
------ Ill. folder. Ptd. Springfield, Ohio.

1885 Oswego   MnHi
AMES IRON WORKS. Agricultural catalog of straw burner traction engines and threshers. 8vo., 29pp., ill.

1876 Worcester & Ayer   MH-BA
AMES PLOW CO. Successors to Nourse, Mason & Co. Catalog of plows, agricultural implements and machines. 7-1/2x11, c.300pp., ill., hard cover.

1893 Boston & New York   NCooHi
AMES PLOW CO. Catalog and price list of agricultural implements and machines, farm wagons, carts, vehicles, etc. 8 lvs., and 112pp., ill.

1887 Boston & New York   CtY
------ Ill. catalog.

1887 Ashland, O.   OHi
ASHLAND PUMP & HAYING TOOL WORKS. Ill. catalog of haying tools and carriers. 8vo., 11pp.

c.1890 Indianapolis   In
ATLAS ENGINE WORKS. Catalog #110. Engines for agricultural purposes. 8vo., 56pp., ill., wrap.

1871 Canton, O.   ICHi
AULTMAN, C. & CO. Catalog of threshers, mowers and separators. Ill.

1878 Canton, O.   ICHi
------ Ill. catalog of mowers, engines, etc.

1886 Canton, O.   MnHi
------ Ill. catalog of steam threshers. 4to., 24pp., pict. wrap.

c.1889 Akron, O.   NCooHi
AULTMAN, MILLER & CO. Catalog of harvesting machines. 12mo., 32pp., ill., wrap. Buckeye written in symbols.

1887 Mansfield, O.   OHi
AULTMAN & TAYLOR MACHINERY   KU
CO. Compliments of 1868-1887. Catalog of traction engines, straw burners, separators for farmers and threshermen. 4to., 16pp., col. ills.

1897 Mansfield, O.   MH-BA
------ Catalog of water tube steam boilers, 4th ed. 6x9, 98pp., ill.

1899 Mansfield, O.   OHi
------ Catalog of Dixie, Matchless, Eureka tractors and threshers. 4to., 32pp., ill.

1899 Louisville, Ky.   CU-A
AVERY, B.F. & SONS. 74th annual catalog of plows and cultivators. 8vo., 176pp., ill., pict. wrap.

1876 San Francisco   CHi
BAKER & HAMILTON'S BENICIA AGRICULTURAL WORKS. Est. c.1859. Catalog of hardware, agricultural implements and engines. 8vo., ill., wrap.

1883 San Francisco   CHi
------ Ill. catalog of agricultural implements.

1888 San Francisco   CHi
------ Catalog of agricultural implements including wagons, etc. 4to., bds.

c.1857 Cleveland   ICHi
BALDWIN, DEWITT & CO. Catalog of plows, reaping and mowing machinery. Ill.

1879 Canton, O.   MH-BA
BALL, E. & CO. Manufacturers   ICRMc
of Tornado thresher and separator, Carey horse power, world mower and reaper. 5-1/2x8-1/2, 18pp., ill.

1873 Chicago   ICHi
BANKS, W.H. & CO. Catalog of shellers,
windmills, etc. Ill.

BARBED WIRE FENCES. See Fences.

c.1885 Freeport, Ill.   MnHi
BARNES MFG. CO. A choice line of cultivators. 16mo., 16pp., ill.

1833 Boston
BARRETT, GEORGE C. See Seedsmen.
Fine woodcut ills. of farm mills, tools,
churns, etc.

1876 Chicago   ICHi
BATCHELLER & SONS. Catalog of implements and sulky rakes. Ill.

c.1886 Chicago   ICHi
BATES, J.C. Catalog of grain dryers.

c.1865 New York   NCooHi
BEACH WHEEL HORSE RAKE MFG. CO.
4p. circular, ill., won 1st prize at Am. Inst.
Fair 1865.

BEEKEEPING SUPPLIES. See Beekeeping.

1871 Springfield, O.   MH-BA
BELCHER & TAYLOR AGRICULTURAL
TOOL CO. Manufacturers of Bullard's
improved patent hay tedder and agricultural
tools. 6x9, 12pp., ill.

1871 Springfield, O.   WHi
------ Price list of planters, plows, etc.
8vo., 8pp., ill.

1871 Springfield, O.   WHi
------ Circular for Feb. 1872. 8vo., 4pp.,
ill.

1894 Springfield, O.   WHi
------ Ill. catalog. 8vo., 81pp., cl.

c.1883 Macedon, N. Y.   NCooHi
BICKFORD & HUFFMAN. Mfg. of farmers'
favorite grain drills. 12pp., ill., wrap.

1875 Chicago   ICHi
BLAIR, WILLIAM & CO. Catalog of agricultural tools, lawn mowers, wire and farm
implements. Ill.

1876 Chicago   ICHi
------ Ill. catalog.

1877 Chicago   ICHi
------ Ill. catalog of agricultural machinery, hardware, etc.

1871 Concord, N. H.   NhHi
BLANCHARD'S, PORTER SONS. What
people say of the Blanchard churn. 24mo.,
48pp., ill., wrap.

nd. Cincinnati   OHi
BLYMER MFG. CO. Desc. circular of corn
and cob crushers, shawing machines and
agricultural implements. 8vo., ill. folder.

nd. Cincinnati   MnHi
------ Catalog of agricultural implements.
Ill.

1857 Reading, Pa.   PKsL
BOAS & SPANGLER MFG. Catalog of
Ketchem's celebrated mowing machine and
combined mower and reaper. One ill., 24pp.,
wrap.

1881 Syracuse, N. Y.   ICHi
BOOMER & BOSCHERT PRESS CO. Catalog
of presses, cider mills, machinery, wine
presses, hand and power. 8vo., 36pp., ill.,
pict. wrap.

1882 Syracuse, N. Y.   MH-BA
------ Ill. catalog. 8vo., 34pp.

1890 Syracuse, N. Y.   NSyHi
------ Ill. catalog. 8vo., 92pp.

1895 Syracuse, N. Y.   DSi
------ 23rd annual catalog. 8vo., 82pp.,
ill., wrap.

1882 New York   MH-BA
BOOMER, GEORGE B. Catalog of the
Boomer evaporator for cider jelly, sorghum
and maple sugar. 8vo., 20pp., ill.

1890 Boston & New York   MH-BA
BOWKER FERTILIZER CO. Catalog of
Stockbridge manures and fertilizers. Test.,
8vo., 32pp., ill.

1869 Syracuse, N. Y.   NCooHi
BRADLEY, C.C. & SON. Est. 1832. Catalog
of Hubbard's pat. two horse rear bar single
mowers. 12pp., ill., wrap.

1888 Syracuse, N. Y.   KU
------ Catalog of mowers, rakes and reapers. 24pp., ill., col. pict. wrap.

c.1885 Minneapolis & Chicago
BRADLEY, DAVID MFG. CO. Catalog of
agricultural implements, wagons, wire, buggies, etc. Catalog #6. 4to., 131pp., ill.

1895 Minneapolis & Chicago   MnHi
------ Pocket annual of plows,   IHi
etc. 16mo., 64pp., ill., pict. wrap.

nd. Minneapolis & Chicago   MnHi
------ Catalog of caster colters, seeders,
etc. 16mo., 8pp., ill., wrap.

1871 Chicago   ICHi
BRAYLEY & PATTERSON MFG. Catalog
of farm machinery, belting, etc. Ill.

3

1838 Boston   MStOSV
BRECK, JOSEPH & SONS. Catalog of herb,
flower and grass seeds, bulbs, trees, tools
and implements, mills, churns, etc. 7th ed.
16mo., 66pp., ill.

1880 Boston   DSi
------ Spring catalog of agricultural implements, machines, etc. 8vo., 64pp., ill.

1897 Boston   CBKCoM
------ Ill. cata- GEU ICHi   MMNN
log of agricultural implements, machines,
cow bells to rat traps, hardware and woodenware. Hundreds of cuts. 4to., 288pp., cl.

1900 Boston   GEU
------ Catalog.

c.1876 Chicago   ICHi
BRISTOL, E.S. & CO. Catalog of hay
machinery. Ill.

1881 Chicago   MnHi
------ Catalog of corn shellers, etc.
12mo., 27pp., ill., pict. wrap.

1881 Chicago   MnHi
BRISTOL & GALE CO. Catalog of agricultural machinery, corn shellers, etc. 12mo.,
27pp., ill., wrap.

1883 Chicago   MnHi
------ Catalog of horse hay forks, etc.
12mo., 19pp., ill., wrap.

1883 Chicago   MnHi
------ Catalog of farm machinery. 12mo.,
35pp., ill., wrap.

1884 Chicago   MnHi
------ Catalog of hay machinery. 12mo.,
19pp., ill., wrap.

1884 Chicago   MnHi
------ Catalog of agricultural implements.
12mo., 39pp., ill., wrap.

1885-89 Chicago   MnHi
------ Miscellaneous catalogs.

c.1861 Worcester   MWA
BROWN, ALZIRUS. Est. 1858. Manny's
pat. combined mower and reaper. Whit-
comb's spring-tooth horse hay rake. Lyon's
pat. stone extractor. 8vo., ill., pict. wrap.

1866 Worcester   MH-BA
------ Catalog of union mowing machines,
first built in 1861. 8vo., 24pp., ill.

c.1885 Baltimore   PKsL
BROWN CHEMICAL CO. Catalog of Powell's
fertilizers. 12mo., 48pp., ill., col. wrap.

nd. Canton, O.   MnHi
BUCHER & GIBBS PLOW CO. Catalog of
imperial plows, etc. 79pp., ill.

1890 Sidney, O.   OHi
BUCKEYE CHURN CO. Special catalog of
items of profit to butter makers. Delightful
pict. wrap. of small boy working the churn.
8vo., 16pp.

c.1859 Buffalo, N. Y.   CU-D
BUFFALO AGRICULTURAL MACHINE
WORKS. Catalog of Kirby's American
Harvester and Little Buffalo. Woodcuts.
8vo., pict. wrap.

c.1880 Minneapolis   MnHi
BUSHNELL, J.B. Catalog of farm machinery. 4to., 40pp., ill.

1888 Chicago   ICHi
CALDWELL, H.W. Catalog of mill and
grain elevator supplies and conveying machinery. Ill.

nd. San Francisco   OrU
CALIFORNIA POWDER WORKS. Stump
blasting. Champion powder mfg. 8pp.,
29x14cm.

1861 Richmond, Va.   ViU
CARDWELL, JOHN W. & CO. Catalog of
buckeye mower and reaper and Geiser's
threshing machines. Ill.

c.1882 Carlisle, Pa.   PKsL
CARLISLE CARBONITE OF LIME WORKS.
Mfg. of oyster shell preparations for poultry,
etc. 16mo., 16pp.

c.1880 Newburgh, N. Y.
CHADBORN & COLDWELL MFG. CO.
Excelsior lawn mowers for hand and horse,
rollers, etc. $11. to $23. for two horses.
8vo., 4pp., col. ill.

1876 Springfield, O.   MoSHi
CHAMPION MACHINE CO. Champion handbook and price list.

1859 London   MH-BA
CLUBB & SMITH. Catalog of agricultural
implements, steam engines and machinery.
8vo., 136pp., ill.

1871 Hartford, Conn.   ICHi
COLLINS & CO. Catalog of plows, scales,
etc. Ill.

1895 Atkinson, Wis.   PPPMilk
CORNISH, CURTIS & GREEN MFG. CO.
Ill. catalog of butter and cheese apparatus.

1898 Chicago   PPPMilk
CREAMERY PACKAGE MFG. CO. Ill. catalog of supplies and apparatus for creamery,
cheese factory and dairy farms.

1883 Milwaukee   MnHi
CRIBB, GEORGE C. Catalog #14 of agricultural implements. 8vo.,176pp.ill., wrap.

c.1883 Carlisle, Pa.   PKsL
CUMBERLAND COUNTY FERTILIZER CO.
Compliments of . . . a book worth reading.
8vo., 16pp., pict. wrap.

c.1888 Carlisle, Pa.   PKsL
------ 16mo., 44pp., wrap.

nd. Higganum, Conn.   CtHi
CUTAWAY HARROW CO. Catalog of farm
implements. 8vo., 39pp., ill., map, wrap.

c.1888 Ottumwa, Ia.   IaHi
DAIN MFG. CO. Catalog of baling presses,
horse, motor and belt power hay presses.
8vo., 28pp., some col. pls., wrap.

1872 Littleton, N. H.   MH-BA
DAVIS, THAYER & CO. The Grafton
mineral fertilizer and destroyer of insects.
Tests. 8vo., 32pp., not ill.

nd. Dayton, O.   OHi
DAYTON MACHINE CO. The Dayton sulky
rake. 18mo., ill. folder.

1873 Albany, N. Y.   N
DEDERICK, P.K. Albany Agricultural and
Machine Works. Catalog of lever hay presses,
etc. Price list. Ill.

1884 Moline, Ill.   ICHi
DEERE & CO. John Deere. Est. 1847.
Farmer's pocket companion, 18th ed. Details
of plant and medals won, wallet format, fld.
litho., 16mo., 48pp., ill.

1885 Moline, Ill.   MiDbF
------ 19th ed. Ill., pict. wrap.

1886 Moline, Ill.   ICHi
------ Ill. catalog of farm machinery.

1879 Moline, Ill.   ICHi
DEERE & MANSUR CO. Ill. catalog of
planters, cultivators, etc.

1881 Moline, Ill.   MoSHi
------ Ill. catalog of farm machinery.

1895 Minneapolis   MnHi
DEERE & WEBBER MFG. General catalog
A - farm machinery, vehicles, harness, etc.
4to., 481pp., ill., index, cl.

1880 Chicago   ICHi
DEERING, WILLIAM & CO. Catalog of
harvesting machinery. Ill., pict. wrap.

1882 Chicago   ICHi
------ Ill. catalog of harvesting machinery.

c.1887 Chicago   NNMM
------ Ill. and desc. catalog of harvesting
machinery. 10 unbd. lvs., wrap.

1890 Chicago   OHi
------ Catalog of grass cutting machinery.
12mo., 24pp., ill., wrap.

1893 Chicago   OHi
------ Around the world on a harvester.
4to., 40pp., ill.

c.1897 Chicago   ICHi
------ Catalog of harvesting machinery.

1900 Chicago   OHi
------ Deering harvesting machinery. Ill.

nd. Chicago   TxU
------ Official retrospective exhibition of
development of Deering harvesting machinery for Paris Exposition. Not a catalog, but
important for a complete picture of American
harvesting creations.

c.1884 New York   PPL
DeLAVAL SEPARATOR CO. Ill. catalog of
milk separators, etc.

1893 New York   ICHi
------ Ill. price list of separating machines.

c.1869 Auburn, N. Y.   ICHi
DODGE & STEVENSON MFG. CO. Catalog
of reapers, rakers, etc. Ill.

1889 Dowagiac, Mich.   MnHi
DOWAGIAC MFG. CO. Ill. catalog of
agricultural machinery. 16mo.,16pp., pict.
wrap.

c.1900 Philadelphia   PKsL
DREER, HENRY A. Est. 1838. See Seedsmen for complete list of locations of earlier
catalogs. Desc. catalog of tools, implements,
supplies for nurserymen and farmers. 4to.,
48pp., ill., pict. wrap.

c.1880 Chicago   ICHi
EATON & PRINCE. First catalog so noted.
Ill. catalog of hoisting machinery, ice
elevators, etc.

1847 Albany, N. Y.   DeWe
EMERY, HORACE L. Successor to Luther
Tucker. Albany Agricultural Works. Annual
desc. catalog of agricultural implements,
tools, seeds, mills and horse powers.
12mo., 32pp., woodcuts, pict. wrap.

1848 Albany, N. Y.
------ Annual catalog. 12mo., 32pp., ill.,
pict. wrap.

1849 Albany, N.Y.
------ Annual catalog. 16pp., ill., wrap.

1850 Albany, N.Y.
------ Annual catalog. 16pp., ill., wrap.

1851 Albany, N.Y.
------ Annual catalog. 40pp., ill.

1853 Albany, N.Y.   NNMM
------ Annual circular of Albany Agricultural Works. 9 lvs., unbd., ill.

1854 Albany, N.Y.   NNMM
------ Annual circular. 18 lvs., unbd., ill.

1855 Albany, N.Y.   PPPMilk
------ Annual ill. and desc. catalog of
churns, yokes, presses, windmills, tubs and
firkins. 8vo., 36pp., woodcuts.

1856 Albany, N.Y.   PPPMilk
------ Catalog of horse powered   PPL
machinery, dairy and farm equipment, saws,
threshers and plows. Ill., wrap.

c.1890 Richmond, Ind.   In
EMPIRE MFG. CO. Catalog of Empire
grain drills, disc, hoe and shoe harrows,
sowers, etc. 8vo., 30pp., ill., wrap.

c.1890 Quincy, Ill.   IHi
ERTEL, GEORGE CO. Ertel's improved
Victor double-acting perpetual hay and
straw presses, wire tying machines, etc.
8vo., 4pp., ill.

c.1876 Whitewater, Wis.   NCooHi
ESTERLY, GEORGE & SON MFG. Ill. cir-
cular of agricultural machinery. 12pp.

1882 Whitewater, Wis.   MH-BA
------ Light draft twine-binding harvester.
Tests. 8vo., 16pp., ill.

1883 Boston   MH-BA
EVERETT & SMALL. Catalog of agricul-
tural implements. 8vo., 40pp., ill.

1885 Boston   MH-BA
------ now T. B. Everett & Co. 8vo.,
64pp., ill.

c.1882 Chicago   ICHi
FAIRBANKS MORSE & CO. Ill. catalog of
shellers, windmills, etc. See also Hardware,
Machinery and Windmills.

FENCES. See Fences.

1885 Springfield, O.   MnHi
FOOS MFG. CO. Ill. catalog of mills,
gears, corn shellers, etc.

1889 Springfield, O.   MnHi
------ Ill. catalog of farm machinery.

1893 Springfield, O.   OHi
------ 10th annual. Fair ed. Scientific
catalog of harvesters, windmills, shellers,
horse powers, etc. 12mo., 71pp., ill. Litho.
by Winters Art Co.

1895 Rochester, N.Y.   NR
FOSTER, JOHN. Ill. catalog of churns,
mills, butter moulds, windmills, cutters,
grinders and machines. 8vo., 60pp., pict.
wrap.

1861 Philadelphia   MH-BA
FOWLER, JOHN. Patent steam ploughing
and cultivating machinery. 8vo., 32pp., ill.

1862 Rutland, Vt.   MH-BA
FRENCH & KINGSLEY. Coe's super phos-
phate of lime. Tests. 8vo., 24pp., not ill.

nd. Gasport, N.Y.   MdTanSW
FRIEND MFG. CO. Formerly Hull Bros.
Est. 1891. Catalog of spraying outfits for
garden and orchard with history of company.
12mo., 40pp., ill., wrap.

c.1885 Philadelphia   PKsL
FRONEFIELD CATTLE POWDER CO.
Breinig, Fronefield & Co., successors to
F. A. Miller. Important knowledge. 16mo.,
28pp., ill., wrap.

1875 Chicago   ICHi
FURST & BRADLEY MFG. CO. Ill. catalog
of cultivators, plows, etc.

c.1877 Chicago   IHi
------ Desc. circular of gang and sulky
plows and harrows. Ill.

1877 Chicago   MiU-H
------ (Agents Bloss & McNaughton,
Galesburgh, Mich.) Collection of valuable
information, tables and recipes. 24mo.,
62pp., ill. of farm machinery, pict. wrap.

1859 St. Louis   MoSHi
GARNETT, JOHN & CO. Catalog of agricultural and horticultural implements and
machines. Ill.

c.1894 Waynesboro, Pa.   PKsL
GEISER MFG. CO. Ill. catalog and   PHi
letters - Peerless threshing machinery.
16mo., 8pp.

1885 Quincy, Ill.   MoSHi
GEM CITY MOWER CO. Catalog of the
Quincy mower.

1884 Geneva, O.   MnHi
GENEVA TOOL CO. Ill. catalog of hand
farming tools. 12mo., 24pp., wrap.

1886 Geneva, O.   MnHi
------ Ill. catalog. 12mo., 28pp., wrap.

1887 Geneva, O.   MnHi
------ Ill. catalog of farm tools and implements. 12mo., 28pp., wrap.

nd. Canton, O.   MnHi
GIBBS LAWN RAKE CO. Catalog of lawn
rakes, post hole diggers, etc. 24mo., 16pp.,
ill., wrap.

1887 Chicago   MnHi
GOULDS & AUSTIN MFG. CO. Ill. catalog
of hay tools, etc. 4p. ill. circular.

c.1885 Middletown Springs, Vt.   VtHi
GRAY, A.W. SONS. Gray's horse powers,
latest pat. threshing and cleaning machines.
8vo., 50pp., fine woodcuts, pict. wrap.

1887 Middletown Springs, Vt.   VtSM
------ Gray's latest improved pat. horse
powers. Ill. circular with 12 engravings of
machines in action.

c.1870 Middletown, Vt.   NCooHi
GREGG PLYER & CO. Meadow King
Mower. Fourth annual circular. 12mo.,
14pp., ill., pict. wrap.

c.1895 Rutland, Vt.   MdTanSW
GRIMM, G.H. & CO., MFG. Catalog of
Champion evaporator, regulators and
siphons for maple sorghum, etc. 24mo.,
28pp., priced, ill., wrap.

c.1870 Hagerstown   PKsL
HAGERSTOWN IMPLEMENT MFG. CO.
Catalog of the BEST spring tooth rake.
32mo., 8pp., ill., pict. wrap.

1876 Hagerstown   PKsL
------ Catalog. 8vo., 32pp., ill., pict.
wrap.

1881 Hagerstown   PKsL
------ Catalog. 8vo., 32pp., ill., wrap.

1870 Hamilton, O.   OC
HAMILTON PLOW CO. Ill. catalog and
price list of plows, wagons, cultivators,
rakes and straw cutters. 16mo., 24pp.

1876 Chicago   ICHi
HANNA, W.J. & CO. Catalog of shellers
and hay presses. Ill.

c.1878 Chicago   ICHi
------ Catalog of seeds and cultivators, in
English and German. Pict. wrap.

1900 Alton, Ill.   IHi
HAPGOOD PLOW CO. General catalog of
wholesale prices direct to farmer. Hand
tools to windmills. 4to., 144pp., fine ills.,
pict. wrap.

1860 New Haven   CtHi
HARRISON, EDWARD. Illuminated catalog

of Harrison's grinding mills. 8vo., 48pp.,
frs. and wrap. 8th ed.

c.1875 New Haven   CtHi
------ Catalog of Harrison's grinding and
flouring mills. 8vo., 16pp., ill., wrap.

nd. Massillon, O.   OHi
HARRISON, W.R. & CO. Catalog of
Tornado feed and ensilage cutters, carriers
and blowers. 16mo., ill. folder.

1893 Decatur, Ill.   IHi
HAWORTH & SONS. Haworth's planting
machinery. 7 lithos. in detail with a calendar To Our Patrons. 12mo., 8pp., lithos.
by Gies of Buffalo, N. Y.

1856 Sandusky, O.   IHi
HENDERSON, D.C. A challenge to the
world! The best grain and grass harvester
in use! Sole manufacturer. 15pp., ill.

1889 Philadelphia   MoSHi
HENDERSON, PETER & CO. Catalog of
everything for the garden. 4to., ill., some
in col. Col. pict. wrap. See Seedsmen for
complete list of dates and locations in both
implements and seeds.

nd. Lancaster, Pa.   PPPMilk
HERR & CO. Ill. catalog of milk cans, pans,
strainers, skimmers, kettles, dairy pails,
etc. Pict. wrap.

nd. Racine, Wis.   MnHi
HERRICK, C.B. & CO. Catalog of agricultural machinery. Ill.

c.1866 Valley Falls, N. Y.   NCooHi
HERRINGTON, H.J. & CO. Eagle mower
and Eagle combined mower and reapers.
Ill. price list of 4pp.

nd. Ashland, O.   OHi
HESS & CLARK CO. Catalog of farming
equipment. Ill. with col. pict. wrap.

1886 Chicago   MnHi
HIBBARD, SPENCER, BARTLETT & CO.
Catalog of agricultural implements. 4to.,
36pp., ill., pict. wrap.

1888 Chicago   MnHi
------ Catalog of agricultural implements.

1876 Higganum, Conn.   CtHi
HIGGANUM MFG. CORP. Ill. catalog of
cider mills, wine presses, jacks, lard
presses, hay cutters, etc. 8vo., 20pp.,
wrap.

nd. Higganum, Conn.   CtHi
------ Higganum specialties - Clark's
harrows, seeders, corn shellers, etc.
8vo., 40pp., ill., wrap.

1880 Higganum, Conn.   MnHi
------ Ill. price list of harrows. 16mo.,
40pp., wrap.

1886 Higganum, Conn.   MnHi
------ Ill. price list of drills, cultivators,
horse shoes, presses, cutters and jacks.
8vo., 36pp., wrap.

1889 Higganum, Conn.   MnHi
----- Ill. catalog as in 1886.

1900 Avery, O.   OHi
HOOVER PROUT CO. Catalog of Hoover
potato digger and sorter. 4to., 20pp., ill.,
wrap.

nd.   CtHi
HORTON-GALLO-CREAMER CO. Ill.
catalog of dairy equipment.

1888 Chicago   MnHi
HORTON, GILMORE, McWILLIAMS & CO.
Catalog of wholesale hardware, farming
tools, etc. 4to., 12pp., ill., wrap.

1889 Chicago   MnHi
------ Catalog of farming tools. 4to.,
48pp., ill., pict. wrap.

1861 Sharon Valley, Conn.   PKsL
HOTCHKISS & SONS. Salesrooms - New
York. Price list of malleable iron castings,
bull rings, steel yards, ox bow pins, etc.
12mo., 26pp., ill., glt. pict. wrap.

1859 Buffalo, N. Y.   NCooHi
HOWARD, R.L. Ketchum's improved
mower and reaper. 12mo., 57pp., ill., wrap.

1886 Minneapolis   MnHi
HOWELL, R.R. & CO. 7th annual catalog
of grain registers, baggers, weighers,
threshing machines and steam engines.
8vo., ill., wrap.

1888 Minneapolis   MnHi
------ 9th annual catalog. Ill., wrap.

1889 Marion, O.   OHi
HUBER MFG. CO. To threshermen of the
U. S. - catalog of traction engines, threshers, straw burners, etc. 8vo., 32pp., ill. of
plant, tinted ills. of details. Gies lithos.

1893 Marion, O.   OHi
------ Fair catalog of threshers, engines,
etc. 24mo., 8pp., col. ill., wrap. Gies
lithos.

1904 Marion, O.   OHi
------ Fine example of photo. catalog work.

1891 Gilead, O.   ICHi
HYDRAULIC PRESS MFG. CO. Catalog and
price list of cider and wine presses,graters,
evaporators, etc. 8vo., 80pp., ill.,pict.wrap.

1900 Gilead, O.   OHi
------ To cider makers of the world.
8vo., 96pp., ill., pict. wrap.

1900 Richmond, Va.   V
IMPLEMENT CO. Wholesale price list of
agricultural implements, plows, harrows,
buggies, harness, threshers, mills, presses,
horse powers, etc. 16mo., 18pp., ill., wrap.

c.1900 Chicago   MdTanSW
INTERNATIONAL HARVESTER CO. Cata-
log of Cloverleaf manure spreaders. 8vo.,
28pp., ill., col. pict. wrap.

1884 Fort Madison, Ia.   MnHi
IOWA FARMING TOOL CO. Catalog of
scythes, grain cradles, stable forks, etc.
12mo., 48pp., ill., wrap.

c.1884 Janesville, Wis.   MnHi
JANESVILLE HAY TOOL CO. Ill. catalog
of haying tools and machinery. 12mo.,
16pp., wrap.

c.1895 Janesville, Wis.   NCooHi
------ Catalog of haying tools. 36pp., ill.,
wrap.

c.1880 Racine, Wis.   WiHi
JOHNSON & FIELD MFG. CO. Catalog of
Racine dustless separators, mills, grinders,
etc. Pict. folder with col. ills., prices, etc.

1881 Oswego, N. Y.   NCooHi
JOHNSON, GERE & TRUMAN. The
Champion grain drill. 20pp., ill., wrap.

1882 Oswego, N. Y.   MH-BA
------ Whipple's spring harrows and cultivators. 16mo., 8pp., ill., wrap.

c.1878 Moline, Ill.   ICHi
JOHNSON, J.S. Post hole diggers. 4pp.,
with pict. wrap.

c.1873 Brockport, N. Y.   ICHi
JOHNSTON HARVESTER CO. Catalog of
harvesters. Ill.

1899 Batavia, N. Y.   ICHi
JOHNSTON HARVESTER CO. Greetings -
annals of 1898 will be outdone by 1899, etc.
8vo., 32pp. of fine ills., double spread of
plant, col. pict. wrap.

1877 Joliet, Ill.   ICHi
JOLIET MFG. CO. Catalog of power corn
shellers. Ill.

1859 Middletown, Conn.   CtHi
KETCHUM MOWING MACHINE CO. Prospectus of Ketchum's improved reaper and
mower - endorsements. 8vo., 24pp., woodcuts, wrap.

c.1879   IHi
KING & HAMILTON, Mfg. Catalog of
Gilman's sheller, Ball's Ohio reaper and
mower, Northwestern planter, Champion
corn plow, etc. 4to., 6pp., ill.

1895 Peoria   DSi
KINGMAN & CO., Mfg. Catalog #29 - The
Wild Irishman Plow, Russell compound
steam farm engines, etc. 4to., 308pp., ptd.
cl., fine ills.

1882 Minneapolis   MnHi
KIRKWOOD, H. Ill. catalog of agricultural
implements and farm machinery. 4to.,
77pp., wrap.

1880 Rockford, Ill.   CBKcoM
KNOWLTON MFG. CO. Catalog of mowers,
reapers, cultivators, rakes, etc. 8vo.,
16pp., ill., wrap.

1869 St. Louis   MoSHi
KOENIG, WILLIAM & CO. Ill. catalog of
Buckeye reapers and mowers.

1871 St. Louis   MoSHi
------ Ill. catalog of agricultural machinery.

c.1886 Milwaukee   MuIIi
LINDSAY BROTHERS, Mfg. & Jobbers.
Catalog of agricultural machinery and farming tools. 12mo., 94pp., fine ills., index,
wrap.

1884 Mansfield, O.   MoSHi
LITTLE GIANT PLOW CO.   OHi
Catalog of the Little Giant riding plow.

1877 Hamilton, O.   CU-D
LONG & ALLSTATTER CO. Ill. catalog of
mower and reaper knives, sulky plows, etc.
8vo., 24pp., wrap.

c.1900 Lynchburg   V
LYNCHBURG PLOW CO. Catalog of
chilled and hillside plows, etc. Ill.

1878 Chicago   ICHi
McCORMICK, C.H. & L.J. Ill. catalog of
threshing machines.

1871 Chicago   MoSHi
McCORMICK HARVESTING MACHINE CO.
Ill. catalog.

1880 Chicago   ICHi
------ Ill. catalog.

1881 Chicago   ICHi
------ Ill. catalog.

1882 Chicago   ICHi
------ Ill. catalog.

1883 Chicago   MoSHi
------ Annual fair circular. Ill. catalog.

1888 Chicago   MnHi
------ Ill. catalog. 12mo., 51pp., ill.
pict. wrap.

1893 Chicago   ICHi
------ Ill. catalog.

1900 Chicago   ICRMc
------ First in the field. Catalog and
history. 4to., 40pp.

nd. Manitowac, Wis.   MnHi
MANITOWAC MFG. CO. Catalog of farm
implements. 16mo., 4pp. of ills.

c.1889 Rockford, Ill.   MnHi
MANNY, JOHN P. MOWER CO. Catalog of
chain power mowers. 16mo., 16pp., ill.,
wrap.

1861 New York   ICU
MAPES, CHARLES V. Ill. catalog of plows,
implements, machines, harrows, washing
machines, windmills and weathervanes.
8vo., 250pp., ills. of great value, pict. wrap.

1889 Chicago   MnHi
MARKLEY, ALLING & CO. Catalog of
farming tools and seasonable goods. 8vo.,
32pp., fine ills., pict. wrap.

1875 Springfield, O.   MoSHi
MAST, P.P. Buckeye Agricultural Works.
Est. 1856. Ill. catalog of Buckeye grain
drills.

1876 Springfield, O.   MoSHi
------ 1856-1876 catalog of drills, seeders, cultivators, cider mills, presses, etc.
Ill., pict. wrap.

c.1885 Springfield, O.   NCooHi
------ Catalog. 18pp., ill., wrap. OHi

1886 Springfield, O.   NCooHi
------ Ill. catalog. New walking cultivators, presses and improved machinery.
16pp., wrap.

1870 New York
METROPOLITAN AGRICULTURAL WORKS.
(agent H.B. Griffing.) Ill. catalog of drills,
mowers, reapers, presses, bells, churns,
fire engines, wagons, weathervanes and
hitching posts. 4to., 62pp.

c.1900 Brooklyn   NNQ
METROPOLITAN MATERIAL CO. Catalog
of hot bed sash and greenhouse material.

1892 St. Louis   MoSHi
MILLARD IMPLEMENT CO. Ill. directory.

1888 Richfield, Pa.   PKsL
MILLS, S.V., Inv. & Pat. Mills' farmyard
ammoniator. 12mo., 16pp., ill., pict. wrap.

1890 Scotch Grove, Ia.   IaHi
MILNE, JAMES & SON. Annual catalog of
Hawkeye grub and stump machines, pat.
wire rope couplers, etc. 8vo., 48pp., ill.,
glt. pict. wrap.

1892 Monticello, Ia.   IaHi
------ Annual catalog I.X.L. Grubber, etc.
8vo., 60pp., ill., pict. wrap., pls.

1886 Milwaukee   MnHi
MILWAUKEE HARVESTER CO. Catalog of
agricultural machinery, two horse binder,
light mowers, etc. 12mo., 32pp., col.
lithos., wrap.

1888 Milwaukee   MnHi
------ Catalog of junior harvester and
binder. 12mo., 32pp., ill., pict. wrap.

1880 Moline, Ill.   ICHi
MOLINE PLOW CO. Est. 1865. Branches
in Kansas City and St. Louis. Ill. catalog
of Moline plows, harrows, planters, cultivators, etc. Pub. Kansas City branch.

nd. Moline, Ill.   IHi
------ Ill. catalog #48. 4to., 262pp.,
col. pls.

1885 Moline, Ill.   MnHi
------ Ill. catalog. 16mo., 92pp., pict.
wrap.

1886 Moline, Ill.   IHi
------ Ill. catalog - issued Deere, Mansur
& Co.

1888 Moline, Ill.   MnHi
------ Ill. catalog of parts, etc. 12mo.,
120pp., wrap.

1897 Chicago   ICHi
MONTGOMERY WARD & CO. Special ill.
catalog B of agricultural implements and
general farm machinery. 4to., 200pp., wrap.

1887 Bryan, O.   MnHi
MORRISON & FAY MFG. CO. Catalog of
Bryan Plows. 12mo., 24pp., ill., wrap.

c.1879 Rutland, Vt.   ICHi
MOSELEY & STODDARD MFG. CO. Oldest
in New England. Ill. catalog of pyramidal
milk strainers.

c.1890 Rutland, Vt.   VtHi
------ Moseley's Cabinet Creamery.
8 page ill. brochure in good detail.

1897 Rutland, Vt.   VtHi
------ Superior butter making appliances

DeLaval separators, Moseley's cabinet,
Stoddard's churns. 4to., 8pp., ill., wrap.

nd. Rutland, Vt.   VtHi
------ Catalog #275. 20th century
machinery. 16pp., ill.

1894 Ashland, O.   OHi
MYERS, F.E. & BRO. Est. 1870. Catalog
#25. Pumps, haying tools, carriers, forks,
track, grapples, etc. 8vo., 192pp., ill., glt.
pict. wrap. Gies & Co., litho.

1883 Millington, N.J.   PKsL
NASH & BROTHER. Acme pulverizing
harrows, crushers and levelers. Ill. catalog. 12mo., 26pp., pict. wrap.

1875 Pittsburgh   PKsL
NELLIS, A.J. & CO. Formerly in Bath,
N.Y.* Nellis' original harpoon horse hay
fork. 8vo., 16pp., ill., pict. wrap.

1884 Pittsburgh   MnHi
------ Catalog of hay forks, agricultural
machinery, etc. 12mo., 16pp., ill., wrap.

*1858 Bath, N.Y.
------ In 1858 A.J. Nellis sold Manny's
reaping and mowing machines for Walter A.
Wood. A large heavy stamp on one of
Wood's catalogs for this date makes this
entry possible.

nd. Washington, Ill.   MnHi
NESMITH, C.L. Catalog of Nesmith's pat.
grain registers.

1884 Columbus, O.   OHi
NEWARK MACHINE CO. Ill. price list of
imperial straw stacker and agricultural
machinery. 8vo., 16pp., col. pict. wrap.

1886 Columbus, O.   OHi
------ Ill. catalog of Victor double huller
clover machines, etc. 4to., 40pp., list of
clients. Col. pict. wrap.

1887 Columbus, O.   MnHi
------ Ill. catalog of straw stackers, etc.
12mo., 15pp., test., pict. wrap.

1829 Boston
NEWELL, J.R. & RUSSELL, JOHN B. See
Seedsmen.

1867 Hinsdale, N.H.   MH-BA
NEWHALL & STEBBINS. Granite state
mowing machine. Ref. 8vo., 22pp., ill.

1882 New York   MH-BA
NEW YORK PLOW CO. Successor to
Peekskill Plow Works. Est. 1826. Adamant
Plows and agricultural implements. 8vo.,
16pp., ill.

1866 Albany, N. Y.   TxU
NEW YORK STATE AGRICULTURAL
SOCIETY. 2nd national trials of mowers,
reapers, horse powers, etc. Includes ill.
catalogs of various manufacturers.

1874 Albany, N. Y.   DSi
NEW YORK STATE AGRICULTURAL
WORKS. Catalog of railway and horse
power threshers, cleaners, etc. 8vo.,
16pp., ill., pict. wrap.

1867 Battle Creek   ICHi
NICHOLS & SHEPARD. Ill. catalog of
threshing machinery. Ptd. in Chicago. In
the comfortable 1880's, Battle Creek had
some seven thousand democratic residents
and not a single millionaire. Those were
halcyon days. Sometimes the entire force
at Nichols & Shepard thresher works, with
wives and shoe-box lunches, would pile into
a Grand Trunk Special, drawn by the pony
engine, to spend a bright August day in the
blackberry patch near Olivet. See Gerald
Carson's Cornflake Crusade. Rinehart:
1957, p. 10.

1873 Battle Creek   ICHi
------ Ill. catalog of threshing machinery.

1881 Battle Creek   MnHi
------ Improved clover hulling   MiU-H
attachment, parts, etc. 16mo., 32pp., ill.,
wrap.

1884 Battle Creek   MnHi
------ Factory price list of repair parts.
16mo., 32pp., ill., wrap.

1885 Battle Creek   MnHi
------ Telegraphic cipher price   MiU-H
list, engines, etc. 16mo., 24pp., ill., wrap.
Also general catalog. 12mo., 52pp., ill.,
pict. wrap.

1886 Battle Creek   MnHi
------ Ill. price list of engines. MiU-H

c.1890 Battle Creek   MoSHi
------ Catalog of vibrator threshers.
72pp., ill., wrap.

1886 Stillwater, Minn.   MnHi
NORTH WESTERN MFG. AND CAR CO.
Minnesota Chief threshing machinery. 8vo.,
60pp., ill., col. litho. cvs.

1847 Rochester, N. Y.   N
NOTT & ELLIOTT. Rochester Agricultural
warehouse, at the sign of the plow, implements of husbandry. Adze and axe to fire
engines, mills and presses. 8vo., 32pp.,
woodcuts, pict. wrap.

1857 NOURSE & CO., Mfg. & Dealer. Eagle
Agricultural Warehouse. Ill. catalog of

agricultural and horticultural implements
and machines, fertilizers, seeds and trees.
In English and Spanish. 8vo., 100pp., woodcuts throughout plus two pls., pict. wrap.

1857 Worcester   MStOSV
NOURSE, MASON & CO., Mfg. Plants in
Worcester and Groton. Desc. and ill. catalog of agricultural and horticultural implements and machines, apple parers, bull
rings, ox yokes, mills and weathervanes.
8vo., 160pp.

1861 Worcester   NCooHi
------ Catalog of Davis' improved mowing
machines, Ketchum's pat. 8vo., 12pp., ill.

1868 Chicago   MH-BA
NOVELTY MACHINE WORKS. Est. 1868.
Catalog of agricultural equipment. 8vo.,
20pp., ill.

nd. South Bend   OHi
OLIVER CHILLED PLOW WORKS. Ill.
catalog - including a practical farmer's
instructions to his son. 12mo., 16pp.

c.1898 South Bend   ICHi
------ Ill. catalog of plows, etc.

c.1900 East Rochester, N. Y.   MdTanSW
ONTARIO DRILL CO. Catalog of grain and
fertilizer drills. 8vo., 24pp., ill.

1871 Auburn, N. Y.   ICHi
OSBORNE, D.M. & Co. Est. 1856. Annual
catalog of mowers, reapers, etc. Ill., pict.
wrap.

1872 Auburn, N. Y.
------ 16th annual pamphlet - the Kirby
mower and reaper. 8vo., 24pp., ill., wrap.

1875 Auburn, N. Y.   NCooHi
------ Osborne sulky plow. 8 page ill. folder.

1876 Auburn, N. Y.
------ Kirby & Wheeler's reapers and
mowers. 8vo., 24pp., ill.

1887 Auburn, N. Y.
------ 31st annual catalog. 4to., 36pp.,
ill., col. pict. wrap.

1888 Auburn, N. Y.   NSyHi
------ 32nd annual catalog. 4to., 48pp.,
ill., col. pict. wrap.

c.1890 Auburn, N. Y.   MdTanSW
------ Handy book #2 for house and farm.
Harvesters, binders, reels, elevators, hay
rakes and tedders. 8vo., 64pp., ill., col.
pict. wrap.

1895 Auburn, N. Y.   NCooHi
------ 39th annual catalog of farm imple-

ments, with a history of new binders for farmers of the world. 56pp., ill., pict. wrap.

1884 St. Louis   MoSHi
OYLER, GEORGE K. Repair catalog of parts for Eureka, Modern, Rural and Oyler's Pearl hand and power corn shellers and Pitt's horse powers and wagon jacks. Ill.

1885 St. Louis   MnHi
------ Catalog of farm equipment. Ill., test.

1886 St. Louis   MnHi
------ Catalog of rolling colters, colter blades and hubs.

1887 St. Louis   MnHi
------ Catalog of above, power, etc. 56pp., ill.

1888 St. Louis   MnHi
------ Fall catalog of corn shellers, feed mills, cutters, etc. 12mo., 32pp., ill.

1876 Boston   MH-BA
PACIFIC GUANO CO. Est. 1865. Works at Woods Hole, Mass. Soluble pacific guano, fertilizer. Tests. 8vo., 30pp., not ill.

1881 Boston   MH-BA
------ Catalog. 8vo., 60pp., not ill.

1886 Boston   NBuHi
PARKER & WOOD. Ill. price list of agricultural implements, woodenware, mills, butter moulds, plant stands, farm tools, fancy iron garden furniture, 48 weathervane designs, etc. 8vo., 208pp., woodcuts throughout, pict. wrap.

1891 Boston   ICJ
------ Ill. catalog of agricultural tools, machines, woodenware, adze to yoke, fancy ironware. 8vo., 216pp.

1878 Newark & Baltimore   PKsL
PASSAIC AGRICULTURAL CHEMICAL WORKS. Lister Bros. Catalog of standard fertilizers. 8vo., 64pp., ill., wrap.

1887 Utica, N.Y.   MnHi
PECKHAM, J.S. & M. Ill. catalog of cultivator teeth and parts. 12mo., 48pp., pict. wrap.

1871 Peekskill   DeWe
PEEKSKILL PLOW WORKS. Ill. catalog of Hutchinson's cider and wine presses and agricultural implements. 8vo., 8pp., wrap.

c.1895 Quincy, Ill.   ICHi
PEERLESS INCUBATOR & BROODER CO. Successors to Sheer, Berrian & Co. Est. 1892. Improved Peerless hatchers and

brooders. 12mo., 58pp., ills. and pls., pict. wrap.

nd. Pekin, Ill.   MnHi
PEKIN PLOW CO. Catalog of Pekin plows and plow goods. 16mo., 32pp., ill., pict. wrap.

1883 York, Pa.   CU-D
PENNSYLVANIA AGRICULTURAL WORKS Ill. catalog and price list of agricultural implements, tools and machines. 8vo., 24pp., wrap.

nd. Peru, Ill.   MnHi
PERU CITY PLOW CO. Ill. catalog of plows, etc. 16mo., 22pp., wrap.

c.1895 Philadelphia   MnHi
PHILADELPHIA LAWN MOWER CO. PHi Ill. catalog. 24mo., 16pp., col. pict. wrap.

1871 New London, Conn.   MH-BA
PHOENIX GUANO CO. (agents Williams, Haven & Co.) Guano for fertilizer. 8vo., 21pp., not ill.

1889 Pike Station, N.H.   NhD
PIKE MFG. CO. Headquarters for Pike's scythe stones. 8vo., 32pp., ill., limp lea. cvs.

1880 St. Paul, Minn.   MnHi
PILKINGTON, BUSCH & CO. Annual catalog of agricultural machinery, buggies, wagons and seeds. 4to., 59pp., ill., wrap.

1886 Buffalo, N.Y.   MnHi
PITTS AGRICULTURAL WORKS. Also Buffalo Pitts Co. Est. 1837 in Winthrop, Maine by brothers Hiram A. and John A. Pitts. Moved business to Albany, Rochester, N.Y., Springfield, Ohio, and finally to Buffalo, N.Y. and Chicago. John was known as Buffalo Pitts and Hiram as Chicago Pitts. 36th annual catalog of wood and straw burning engines, threshers, tractors and horse powers. 8vo., 32pp., ill., wrap.

1888 Buffalo, N.Y.   MnHi
------ 38th annual catalog. 12mo., 32pp., ill., pict. wrap. See also Road Building Machinery.

1873 Marseilles, Ill.   ICHi
PITTS, H.A. MFG. CO. Ill. catalog of threshing machines.

c.1870 Burlington, Vt.   VtHi
POST, C.C. Sugar Maker's Friend - a catalog of Eureka sap buckets, hangers and evaporators with A Poem to a Maple Tree. 16mo., 12pp., ill.

1869 Philadelphia   PKsL
Barrows, Savory & Co. for

PRINDLE, D.R. of East Bethany, N. Y.
Prindle's agricultural steamer and cauldron.
Prize essays on cooked and cooking food for
domestic animals of the farm. 8vo., 64pp.,
woodcuts with prices, wrap.

1883 New London, Conn.   MH-BA
QUINNIPIAC FERTILIZER CO. Est. 1852.
High grade phosphate. Tests. 12mo., 34pp.,
not ill.

1884 Des Moines   OrU
RACINE SEEDER CO. Catalog of Strow-
bridge broad-cast seeders, mfg. for Knapp,
Burrel & Co. of Portland, Ore. 32pp., line
drawings of sower and factory.

1871 Utica, N. Y.   MH-BA
RALPH, WILLIAM & CO. Cheese factory,
dairy apparatus and furnishing goods. 8vo.,
30pp., ill.

1850 Rochester, N. Y.   NHi
RAPELJE & BRIGGS. Catalog of   N
agricultural implements, machines, seeds,
tools, mills, cutters, etc. 8vo., 48pp.,
woodcuts, wrap.

c.1885 Kalamazoo   MiU-H
REED, D.C. & H.C. CO. Catalog of original
spring tooth harrows, cultivators, seeders,
etc. Litho. ills. and wrap.

1883 Philadelphia   PKsL
REID, A.H. Ill. catalog of dairy fixtures,
butter workers, printer, little giant animal
powers and Reid's lightning braces. 8vo.,
12pp., pict. wrap.

1879 St. Louis   MoSHi
REINSTEDLER, H. Ill. wholesale catalog
of farm machinery.

1868 Ilion & Utica, N. Y.   NCooHi
REMINGTON AGRICULTURAL WORKS.
Catalog and price list of Wood's self-rake
reaper and world prize mower. 40pp., ill.,
wrap.

1882 Ilion & Utica, N. Y.   NCooHi
------ Ill. catalog of agricultural implements, pat. clipper steel plows, etc. 32pp.,
wrap.

c.1869 North Bridgewater, Mass. MH-BA
REYNOLDS, E.D. & O.B. Catalog of Eagle
seed sower and clipper wheel hoe.
3-1/2x5-1/2, 20pp., ill.

1884 Providence   MoSHi
RHODE ISLAND HORSE SHOE CO. Ill.
catalog of Perkin's pat. machine hammered
horse and mule shoes.

1878 Worcester   MWA
RICHARDSON MFG. CO. Est. 1857. Cata-

log of new Buckeye mower, standard
harvester of the age. 8vo., 12pp., ill.,wrap.

1880 Worcester   MWA
------ Ill. catalog, 80pp., view of plant.

1881 Worcester   MWA
------ Ill. catalog of agricultural implements.

1881 Worcester   MH-BA
------ Catalog of the Buckeye mower.
8vo., 28pp., ill.

1872 Rochester, N. Y.   NCooHi
ROCHESTER AGRICULTURAL WORKS.
Meadow Lark - cheapest mower in the
market. 4to., 3 page ill. folder.

1876 Rochester, N. Y.   DSi
------ Catalog of Hubbard changeable
motion and the Meadow Lark. 8vo., 32pp.,
ill., pict. wrap.

1876 Madison, O.   MH-BA
ROE, H.H. & CO. Catalog of cheese and
butter making apparatus and separators for
factory, farm, dairy and creamery. 4x7,
32pp., ill.

1868 Somerset, nr. Liberty Mills, Va. V
ROUTT, A.P. & CO. Catalog of agricultural machinery and implements, threshing
machines, plows, etc. 8vo., 10pp., ills.,
pict. wrap. Ptd. Baltimore.

1886 Beaver Dam, Wis.   MnHi
ROWELL, J.S. SONS & CO. Catalog of
Tiger seeder, drills, etc. 24mo., 18pp., ill.

1846 Boston   VtSM
RUGGLES, NOURSE & MASON. Desc. catalog of agricultural implements, tools,
machines, mills, cutters, shellers, churns,
cranberry rakes, etc. 8vo., 84pp., woodcuts throughout, wrap.

1849 Boston   MH-BA
------ Mfg. of agricultural implements
and machinery. Wholesale and retail
dealers in implements, seeds, fertilizers,
agricultural and horticultural products and
nursery stock. Quincy Hall agricultural
warehouse and seed store.

1853 Boston   MH-BA
------ Catalog of plows. 8vo., 72pp., ill.

1053 Boston   MH-BA
------ Catalog of agricultural implements.
8vo., 143pp., ill.

nd. St. Louis   MnHi
RUMSEY& SIKEMEIER. Special ill. catalog #7 of cider and cane mills, butchers'
machines, belting, hose and agricultural
machines. 12mo., 96pp., index, wrap.

1882 St. Louis MoSHi
RUMSEY, L.M. MFG. CO. Ill. catalog and
price list of agricultural implements, wire
fences, pipe, belting, machinery, cider
mills, mowers, hay presses and road
scrapers. 12mo., 40pp.

1884-5 St. Louis MoSHi
------ Ill. catalog. 4to., 512pp.

1887 St. Louis MnHi
------ Special catalog #43. Feed cutters,
corn shellers, mills, etc. 12mo., 80pp.,
ill., pict. wrap.

1893 St. Louis MoSHi
------ Catalog #70. Agricultural machinery. 4to., 604pp., ill., cl.

1896 St. Louis MoSHi
------ Catalog #96. Pumps, railroad and
contractors' supplies and agricultural
implements. 4to., 575pp., ill., cl.

1897 St. Louis MoSHi
------ Catalog #100. 4to., 62pp., ill.,
wrap.

1897 St. Louis MoSHi
------ General catalog. 50th ed. Pumps,
etc. 8vo., 192pp., ill., cl.

1898 St. Louis MoSHi
------ Discount sheet #4. Pumps and
agricultural implements. 4to., ill.

c.1900 St. Louis ICJ
------ Catalog #96. Pumps, agricultural
machines, railroad supplies, tools - anvils
to yokes, village fire engines, wagons, bells,
fences, etc. 4to., 575pp., ill., dec. cl.

1882 Massillon, O. MnHi
RUSSELL & CO. Price list of threshing
machines, etc. 12mo., 8pp., ill., wrap.

1882 Massillon, O. MnHi
------ Ill. catalog.

1884 Massillon, O. MnHi
------ Factory price list of OHi
threshers, improved engines, etc. 12mo.,
24pp., ill., wrap.

1885 Massillon, O. MnHi
------ List of improved threshers, etc.
12mo., 26pp., ill., wrap.

1886 Massillon, O. MnHi
------ Ill. catalog. 12mo., 32pp.,
pict. wrap. See Road Machinery for other
listings and locations.

1874 Chicago & Canton, O. IHi
RUSSELL, C. & CO. Catalog of the
Peerless machine, Russell's mower and
reaper. 8vo., 8pp., ill., tests.

1870 St. Albans, Vt. VtHi
ST. ALBANS FOUNDRY. Buckeye mower,
the premium machine of America. 12mo.,
10pp., ill., wrap.

1879 St. Albans, Vt. VtHi
------ Catalog of new improvement in
horse powers with Old's pat. combination
link. 12mo,, 32pp., ill., wrap.

1888 St. Albans, Vt. VtHi
------ Catalog of threshing MnHi
machines, churns, saws, castings, wagon
jacks, tools, agricultural machinery and
fodder stoves. 8vo., 36pp., ill., pict. wrap.

c.1876 Sandwich, Ill. NCooHi
SANDWICH MFG. CO. Ill. catalog of
Adam's pat. self feeding power corn shell-
ers. 6 page folder.

1879 Sandwich, Ill. ICHi
------ Ill. catalog of corn shellers,
harvesters, etc.

nd. Sandwich, Ill. IHi
------ Ill. catalog of Sandwich excess
power gas and kerosene engines, for grinding, sawing, hay and wood machines. 69th
year in business. 8vo., 32pp., photo. ills.,
col. pict. wrap.

1892 San Francisco CSmH
SAN FRANCISCO TOOL CO. Ill. catalog of
irrigation machinery, etc. 72pp.

1894 San Francisco CHi
------ Ill. catalog, 7th ed. 8vo., 72pp.,
wrap.

nd. Chicago ICHi
SEEBERGER & BREAKLEY. Ill. catalog of
wheelbarrows, milk cans, ox yokes, etc.

1872 Akron ICHi
SEIBERLING, J.F. & CO. Ill. catalog of
self-raking reaper and mowers.

1886 Akron DSi
------ Ill. catalog. 12mo., 32pp., MnHi
pict. wrap.

1887 Akron MnHi
------ Ill. catalog. 12mo., 36pp., pict.
wrap.

1893 Akron OHi
------ New Empire mowers, reapers and
binders. 4to., 32pp., col. pict. wrap. Litho.
by Werner Co. Columbus discovers
America, Indians discover reaping
machines.

1878 New York PPPMilk
SELF-ACTING COW MILKER MFG. CO.
Geo. E. & T.W. King, pat. Desc. catalog -
Time is Money - 12mo., test. letters.

Delightful reading, pict. wrap. of cow in operation!

c.1898 Albany, N. Y.   NCooHi
SELF SHARPENING PLOW CO. Catalog of plows, plow shares and castings. 24pp., ill.

1876 St. Louis   MoSHi
SEMPLE, BIRGE & CO. Ill. catalog of farm implements and hardware.

1869 Brockport, N. Y.   NCooHi
SEYMOUR, MORGAN & ALLEN MFG. CO. Est. 1845. Catalog of New Yorker self-raking reaper and mowers. 36pp., ill.

c.1900 West Chester, Pa.   PKsL
SHARPLES SEPARATOR CO.   PWcHi
Ill. price list of Tubular A cream separators. 16mo., 24pp., col. pict. wrap.

c.1900 West Chester, Pa.   PKsL
------ Science of making cows pay - convincing tale from cow to can. 8vo., col. pict. wrap. Later catalogs available at PPPMilk.

c.1890 Philadelphia   PHi
SHEPPARD, ISAAC & CO. Catalog of Chasewood mowers - simple, strong and durable! 8vo., 8pp., ill., wrap.

1879 Philadelphia   PHi
SHOEMAKER, M.L. & CO. What of Fertilizers? 4to., 32pp., ill.

c.1849-50 Rockland, N. Y.
SIPPLE, LOUIS. The Rockland Cooperage. Price list of butter churns, well buckets, firkins, pails, tubs - white oak and iron hoops. 48mo., 4pp. An early record of manufacture in this field with amazing prices. Pride the Printer, Sandburgh, N.Y.

1883 LaCrosse, Wis.   MnHi
SMITH & MERRELL. Catalog of threshing machines. 12mo., 20pp., ill., wrap.

1868 Richmond, Va.   ViU
SMITH, H.M. & CO. General ill. catalog of churns, mills, harvesting machines, saw mills and steam engines.

1876 Richmond, Va.   ViU
------ Retail price list of Malta plows, Studebaker wagons, Keller drills, Blanchard churns, Gieser threshers, Smith horse powers, etc. Ill.

1882 Richmond, Va.   ViU
------ General ill. catalog of harvesting machinery.

c.1890 Richmond Va.   PKsL
------ Ill. catalog of grain and guano drills, American fruit evaporator, etc. 8vo., 8pp.

1875 Pittsburgh   DSi
SPEER, ALEX & SONS. Late Hall & Speer. Ill. catalog of plows and agricultural implements. 16mo., 40pp., wrap.

1873 Providence   CBKcM
SPRAGUE MOWING MACHINE CO. Catalog of mowing machines. 8vo., 32pp., woodcuts, wrap.

1887 Springfield, O.   OHi
SPRINGFIELD ENGINE & THRESHER CO. Kelly duplex grinding mills. 16mo., 16pp., ill., wrap.

1898 Quincy, Ill.   ICHi
STAHL, GEORGE H. Pat. and sole mfg. Ill. desc. catalog of Excelsior Incubators and brooders. 12mo., 210pp., with col. pls. by Gugler Litho. Co. of Milwaukee, also ills. with col. pict. wrap.

c.1890 Quincy, Ill.   IHi
STAHL, WILLIAM CO. Excelsior fruit and vegetable evaporators. 12mo., 32pp. Gies lithos. showing the famous Drownics at work - you can almost see the flies on the dried apples in the corner store.

1884 Chicago   MnHi
STAVER, H.C. IMPLEMENT CO. Annual catalog #12 of agricultural machinery. 12mo., 26pp., ill., pict. wrap. Text in English and German.

1887 Chicago   ICHi
------ Ill. catalog of seeders and sawing machines.

1888 Chicago   MnHi
------ Annual catalog of farm machinery. 12mo., 32pp., ill., pict. wrap.

1868 Albany, N. Y.   N
STRONG & DOUW CO. Ill. catalog of agricultural implements, ironwork, engines, machinery, threshers, fountains, weathervanes, garden furniture, etc. 4to., 32pp., pict. wrap.

1882 Springfield, O.   ICHi
SUPERIOR DRILL CO. Ill. catalog of agricultural machinery and tools.

1885 Springfield, O.   ICHi
------ Ill. catalog of grain and fertilizer drills, etc.

1878 Wheeling, W. Va.   ICHi
SUPERIOR MACHINE WORKS. Catalog of Superior mowers and reapers, no cogs, noiseless machines. 8vo., 12pp., pls., pict. wrap.

1881 Baltimore   PKsL
SUSQUEHANNA FERTILIZER CO., LTD. Works at various places - Canton, O.,

Oxford, Pa., Perryville, Md. Catalog of
pure fertilizers. 12mo., 8pp.

1883 Baltimore   PKsL
------ Catalog of pure fertilizers. 12mo.,
24pp., wrap.

1883 Syracuse, N. Y.   NSyHi
SYRACUSE CHILLED PLOW CO. Ill. catalog of plows and agricultural machinery.
12mo., 48pp., with ill. almanac to boot.

1897 Syracuse, N. Y.   MdTanSW
------ Catalog #7. Barrows, trucks, carts
and tools. 8vo., 36pp., ill., wrap.

1898 Syracuse, N. Y.   NCooHi
------ Ill. catalog and price list. 8vo.,
56pp., wrap.

nd. Syracuse, N. Y.   NSyHi
------ Catalog #27. Ill., 8vo., 80pp., wrap.

c.1875 Boston
THOMPSON, C.H. & CO. Ill. catalog of
agricultural tools, implements, machines,
woodenware, pumps, hardware, etc. 8vo.,
296pp., fine ills., ref., wrap.

c.1876 Towanda, Pa.   NCooHi
TOWANDA EUREKA MOWER CO. Wilber's
direct draft Eureka mower. 8vo., 4pp., one
ill.

c.1888 Mendota, Ill.   IHi
TOWER, J.D. & BRO. Treatise and catalog,
corn cultivators, etc. 28pp., ill.

c.1883 San Francisco   CHi
TRUMAN, HOOKER & CO. Catalog #18,
agricultural machinery, engines, carriages,
etc. 4to., 144pp., ill., wrap.

1847 TUCKER, LUTHER. See Horace L.
Emery, Albany Agricultural Works.

1899 Newark, N. J.   NjR
U. S. BUTTER CO. Catalog of Empire easy
running cream separators. 8vo., ill., pict.
wrap.

c.1900 Bloomfield, N. J.   MdTanSW
U. S. BUTTER EXTRACTOR CO. Catalog
of hand power cream separators. 8vo.,
32pp., ill. in two col., wrap.

c.1876 Batavia, Ill.   ICHi
UNITED STATES WIND ENGINE & PUMP
CO. Ill. catalog of windmills, corn shellers, etc. 52pp., fine ills. with col. pict.
wrap.

c.1876 Batavia, Ill.   ICHi
------ Ill. catalog of agricultural machinery. 16pp., col. wrap.

1882 Batavia, Ill.   IHi
------ Price list for March. 20pp., ills.

c.1885 Batavia, Ill.   MnHi
------ Ill. catalog of agricultural machinery. 12mo., 24pp.

1886 Batavia, Ill.   MnHi
------ General catalog. 12mo.   IHi
28pp., ill., wrap.

1888 Batavia, Ill.
------ Catalog of windmills, gears, parts,
mills, shellers, etc. 12mo., 24pp., ill.,
pict. wrap.

c.1880 Appleton, Wis.   MnHi
VALLEY IRON WORKS MFG. CO. Ill. catalog of agricultural implements. 12mo.,
8pp., pict. wrap.

c.1882 Horicon, Wis.   MH-BA
VAN BRUNT & DAVIS CO. The Monitor
adjustable force-feed seeder and cultivator.
4x6, 20pp., ill.

1872 New York   WiHi
VANDERBILT SEED & IMPLEMENT CO.
Price list of churns, choppers, grinders,
mills, shellers, barrows, etc. 8vo., 24pp.,
ills., pict. wrap.

c.1871 Sandwich, Ill.   IHi
VAN OSDEL & CO. Ill. catalog of patent
hedge trimmers, etc.

1874 Chicago   ICHi
VANT, COOK & CO. Ill. catalog of corn
shellers, cleaners, etc.

1876 Chicago   ICHi
------ Ill. catalog of agricultural machinery.

1877 Bellows Falls, Vt.   MH-BA
VERMONT FARM MACHINE CO. Ill. catalog of dairy fixtures - How to Manufacture
gilt edged butter with Cooley's portable
creamery, Davis' oscillating churn. 12mo.,
12pp.

c.1880 Bellows Falls, Vt.   PPPMilk
------ Catalog #26. churns, butter workers and cans. Ill.

1883 Bellows Falls, Vt.
------ Ill. catalog of dairy and creamery
supplies. 8vo., 24pp., wrap.

1885 Bellows Falls, Vt.
------ Ill. catalog of dairy supplies.
Davis' swing churn, etc. 8vo., 16pp., pict.
wrap.

1885 Bellows Falls, Vt.   VtHi
------ Pat. improved evaporators for
maple sap, cider, etc. 8vo., 8pp., ill.

1886 Bellows Falls, Vt.   VtHi
------ Davis swing churn. 8vo., 16pp.,
ill., pict. wrap.

1889 Bellows Falls, Vt.   VtHi
------ Ill. price list #19, special dairy
supplies and appliances. 8vo., 96pp., pict.
wrap.

c.1890 Bellows Falls, Vt.   MdTanSW
------ Catalog #30, pat. improved evaporators for maple sap, cider jelly, etc.
8vo., 12pp., ill., wrap.

c.1890 Bellows Falls, Vt.   PPPMilk
------ Ill. brochure of Cooley Creamers.

1892 Bellows Falls, Vt.   NCooHi
------ Ill. price list #42 of U. S. Cream
separators and butter extractors. 32pp.,
wrap.

1894 Bellows Falls, Vt.   MdTanSW
------ Catalog #78 of Williams improved
pat. evaporators, cans and pails. 8vo.,
32pp., ill., wrap.

1898 Bellows Falls, Vt.   PPPMilk
------ Special catalog of Cooley Creamers. Ill.

1900 Bellows Falls, Vt.   PPPMilk
------ Catalog of Davis swing churns,
workers, moulds, printers, carriers, etc.
Ill.

1886 Chicago   MnHi
VICTOR GRINDING MILL CO. Ill. catalog
of mills for farm use. 16mo., 34pp.,
wrap.

1897 Delaware City   PKsL
VON GULIN INCUBATOR CO. Ill. catalog
of poultry equipment. 8vo., 64pp., col. pict.
wrap.

c.1883 Muncy, Pa.   PKcL
WALDRON & SPROUT. Sprout's elevator
and hay carrier. Fol. ill. folder showing
elevator in action filling barn loft. 4pp.

1880 Springfield, O.   MnHi
WARDER, BUSHNELL & GLESSNER. Ill.
catalog of threshers and farm machinery
and extra parts. 8vo., 64pp., wrap.

1882 Springfield, O.   MnHi
------ Revised catalog of extra parts.
8vo., 64pp., ill., pict. wrap.

1886 Springfield, O.   MnHi
------ Ill. catalog of harvesting machinery. 8vo., 52pp., wrap. Also copy of the
same in Dutch.

1890 Springfield, O.
------ America's Presidents. 16mo.,
ills. of machines, ports. of presidents, col.
pict. wrap.

1893 Springfield, O.   ICHi
------ Ill. catalog of Champion harvesters.

1894 Springfield, O.   NCooHi
------ New Champion binders and mowers,
etc. 32pp., ill., wrap.

1872 Chicago   ICHi
WARDER, MITCHELL & CO. Ill. catalog of
reapers and mowers.

c.1876 Chicago   IHi
------ Ill. catalog of Champion mowers
and reapers. 12pp., wrap.

1836 Worcester   MWA
WARREN, E. Warren's newly invented
wheat threshing machine, pat. May 29, 1835.
Broadside. Ill. of machine with details,
small hand power size $20. - one horse
$25., two horses $30.

1870 Little Falls, N. Y.   MH-BA
WARRIOR MOWER CO. The Young Warrior
mower, Black's hay hoisting machine.
8vo., 18pp., ill.

1893 Rochester, N. Y.
WEAVER, PALMER & RICHMOND. Ill.
catalog of tools and supplies for nurserymen. 8vo., 56pp., wrap.

1882 Chicago   ICHi
WEBSTER & COMSTOCK MFG. CO. Ill.
catalog of specialties for grain elevators,
flour mills, etc.

1884 Chicago   MnHi
------ Catalog of scoops, Fulton steel
pulleys and agricultural machinery. 16mo.,
48pp., ill., wrap.

c.1869 St. Louis   MoSHi
WESTERN AGRICULTURAL DEPOT &
SEED STORE. Ill. catalog of Buckeye
mowers and reapers, etc.

1871 Schenectady
WESTINGHOUSE MFG. CO. Ill. catalog of
horse powers, threshing machines, hullers,
etc. 8vo., 12pp., wrap.

1888 Schenectady   CU-D
------ Ill. catalog of machinery, traction
engines, threshers, etc. 8vo., 32pp., wrap.

1893 Schenectady   ICJ
------ Ill. catalog of portable agricultural
engines, saw mills, mills for farm produce,
etc. 4to., 32pp., pict. wrap.

1876 Albany, N. Y.   MH-BA
WHEELER & MELICK CO. New York State
Agricultural Works. Est. 1830. Wheeler's
patent railway horse powers agricultural
machinery. 8vo., 16pp., ill.

1887 Rutland, Vt.   VtHi
WHEELER & SHELDON. Est. by L.L.
Crocker. Rise of a mighty industry founded
by L.L. Crocker with price list. 12mo.,
32pp., ill., pict. wrap.

1889 Rutland, Vt.   VtHi
------ Results - January 1889. 12mo.,
32pp., ill., pict. wrap.

1876 Springfield, O.   PPL
WHITELY, FASSLER & KELLY. Est. 1854.
Ill. catalog of Champion harvester machinery, improvements and parts, with 5 fine
col. lithos.

1878 Springfield, O.   OHi
------ Ill. catalog of Champion reaping and
mowing machines, new improved standard
engines, etc. 8vo., 62pp., tests., col. litho.
wrap.

1879 Springfield, O.   MH-BA
------ Ill. catalog of reaping and mowing
machines. 8vo., 40pp., wrap.

1882 Springfield, O.   OHi
------ Catalog of Champion harvester
machines. 4to., 32pp., ill., col. pict. wrap.

1883 Springfield, O.   OHi
------ Ill. catalog of binders, mowers and
reapers, detailed desc., parts and repairs.
8vo., 16pp.

1895 St. Louis   MoSHi
WHITMAN AGRICULTURAL CO. Price
list of repairs, Eclipse full circle steel
presses, etc. 8vo., 8pp., ill.

1882 Boston   CBKoM
WHITMAN & BARNES MFG. CO. Complete
catalog of parts for mowing machine repairs, harvesters, etc. 8vo., 72pp., ill.,
wrap.

1893 Boston   CHi
------ San Francisco - branch office.
Catalog of agricultural machinery. 4to.,
ill., wrap.

1882 Boston   KyU
WHITTEMORE BROTHERS. Ill. catalog of
agricultural implements and machines.
8vo., 48pp., dec. wrap.

1874 East Avon, N. Y.   NCooHi
WIARD PLOW WORKS. Est. 1806. Orig.
Wiard & Hough. Ill. catalog of plows and
cultivating implements. 48pp., wrap.

1875 East Avon, N. Y.   PKsL
------ Ill. catalog of farm implements,
etc. 32pp., wrap.

1890 East Avon, N. Y.   PKsL
------ Moved to Batavia, N. Y. The great
pulverizers, a catalog of Wiard plows. Ill.

1891 East Avon, N. Y.   NR
------ Ill. catalog. 12mo., 24pp., wrap.

1873 Poughkeepsie, N. Y.   NCooHi
WILBER'S EUREKA MOWER & REAPER
MFG. CO. Wilber's direct draft Eureka
mower. Ill. 8 page circular.

1873 Poughkeepsie, N. Y.   NCooHi
------ Ill. catalog of mowers.

1882-83 St. Johnsville, N. Y.   MH-BA
WILLIAMS, M. St. Johnsville Agricultural
Works. Horse powers, threshers and
cleaners. 8vo., 20pp., ill.

1886 New York   PKsL
WILLIAMS, CLARK & CO. Plants in
Staten Island and New Jersey. Catalog of
high grade bone fertilizers, blood, bones
and meat for NYC. 16mo., amusing ills.,
wrap.

1871 Syracuse, N. Y.   ViU
WILLIAMS MOWER & REAPER CO. Ill.
brochure of Johnston's Sweepstakes self-
raking reapers.

nd. Dubuque, Ia.   MnHi
WILLIAMS, V.J. IMPLEMENT CO. Catalog
of horse hay forks, etc. 12mo., 20pp., ill.,
wrap.

nd. St. Louis   MoSHi
WILSON, H. McK. & CO. Ill. catalog of
dairy machinery and supplies.

1884 Jackson, Mich.   MnHi
WITHINGTON & COOLEY MFG. CO. Ill.
catalog of farm and garden tools. 12mo.,
41pp., pict. wrap.

1886 Jackson, Mich.   MnHi
------ Ill. catalog. 12mo., 47pp.,
wrap.

1887 Jackson, Mich.   MnHi
------ Ill. catalog. 12mo., 48pp.,
wrap.

1888 Jackson, Mich.   MnHi
------ Ill. catalog. 12mo., 48pp.,
wrap.

1858 Dublin, Ind.   In
WITT, BUTLER & CO., Mfg. (agent
Holloway & Davis, Richmond, Ind.) Ill. catalog of mowers and reapers, etc. 44pp.,
pict. wrap.

1858 Dublin, Ind.   In
------ Ill. catalog. 16mo., 16pp., wrap.
Details of trials and tests of machines.

1859 Dublin, Ind.   In
------ Ill. and desc. catalog. 14pp., pict.
wrap.

1857 Hoosick Falls, N. Y.   N
WOOD, WALTER A. Est. 1854. Catalog of
New York Reaping & Mowing Machine manu-
factory. 8vo., 68pp., ill., woodcuts, wrap.

1858 Hoosick Falls, N. Y.   N
------ Catalog of Manny's mowing
machines with Wood's improvement in reels,
frames, etc. 8vo., 66pp., ill. and fld. plate,
pict. wrap.

1867 Hoosick Falls, N. Y.
------ Catalog of mowing and reaping
machines. 8vo., 40pp., ill., wrap.

1868 Hoosick Falls, N. Y.   DSi
------ Ill. circular of Agricultural Machinery. 1st prize at Paris Exposition, etc.
8vo., 48pp., pict. wrap.

1871 Hoosick Falls, N. Y.   OHi
------ Annual circular. 8vo., 56pp., ill.,
wrap.

1873 Hoosick Falls, N. Y.   OHi
------ Ill. circular of harvesting machinery. 8vo., 28pp.

1874 Hoosick Falls, N. Y.   CBKcoM
------ 21st annual catalog. 8vo., 24pp.,
ill., wrap.

1876 Hoosick Falls, N. Y.   CBKcoM
------ 26th annual catalog. 8vo., ill.,
pict. wrap.

1877 Hoosick Falls, N. Y.   MoSHi
------ Inventory of parts for mowers,
reapers and machines for J.E. Hayner & Co.
of St. Louis, agent. Priced. 4to., 42pp.,
ill., wrap.

1877 Hoosick Falls, N. Y.
------ Fair circular. Wood's self-binding
harvester. Will it work? Answers by 600
farmers, Maine to Texas. 4to., 16pp., ill.,
wrap. (also ptd. for J.E.Hayner, agent.)

1880 Hoosick Falls, N. Y.   N
------ Price list of mowers and reapers.
8vo., 62pp., ill., pict. wrap.

1880 Hoosick Falls, N. Y.   CtHi
------ Catalog of world renowned harvesting machines, self-rake reapers, etc. 4to.,
12pp., ill., wrap. (agent Southmayd &
Gardiner, Middletown, Conn.)

1881 Hoosick Falls, N. Y.   CBKcoM
------ Catalog of harvesting   ICHi
machines, etc. Ill. Issued by Chicago
branch.

1884 Hoosick Falls, N. Y.   MoSHi
------ Special circular #1. Ill.

1889 Hoosick Falls, N. Y.   MoSHi
            Inventory of extra parts. Ill., wrap.

1891 Hoosick Falls, N. Y.   MoSHi
------ Price list of extra parts. Ill.

1895 Hoosick Falls, N. Y.   MoSHi
------ Ill. price list of extra parts for all
harvesting machines. (Ptd. in St. Paul,
Minn. for local agent.)

1880 Youngstown, O.   OC
WOODS, WILLIAM A. Ill. catalog of
mowing and reaping machines. 16mo.,
32pp., pict. wrap.

1888 Coatsville, Pa.   PKsL
YEARSLEY, ISAAC JR. Ill. catalog of
Philadelphia standard acidated phosphate,
national Chester Co. superbone chemicals.
8vo., 32pp., tests.

It may seem odd that at the end of a chapter of agricultural equipment there should be any rhyme or reason for further suggestions. However, the very nature of the American trade catalog, being merely the printed record of America's multi-industrial development, dictates that no one craftsman can produce one artifact. In the first place the craftsman, or factory, wouldn't be satisfied, and in the second, especially by 1900, the profits wouldn't pay the overhead.

Since definite classification is impossible even in the best and most exhaustive dictionary or encyclopaedia, one cannot expect to find every tool and implement in any one chapter. This may sound repetitious, but I think it only fair to remind you again that in using this volume you have got to use both your head and other chapters to find the complete pictorial panorama. Many mills are used on a farm, but windmills were once used in every walk of life. Just because the farmer's wife used a hand pump during most of the 19th century is no reason to expect to find every pump and water supply catalog listed in this chapter.

Chapter 2

Alcoholic Beverages & Tobacco

There is no catalog of the pipes in which Sir Walter Raleigh first broke smoke with the American Indians. The history of American drinking and smoking may be found in dozens of authoritative volumes; this guide is only concerned with the printed price lists and catalogs.

At this stage in the game of recognizing, appreciating and preserving these records of American social and economic life reports of holdings are necessarily incomplete. The Turner & Fisher brochure for 1841 indicates that the brewers, distillers and tobacconists were conscious of the selling powers of mail order and print at this time. Other examples right down to 1900 should prove that catalogs in this field were numerous, and that further exploitation will provide a more complete list in the future. To date, the Missouri Historical Society has the most outstanding collection of catalogs relating to American beer, and the Barton Museum of Whiskey History the greatest collection of ephemera concerning American distilling.

1885 St. Louis   MoSHi
ANHEUSER BUSCH BREWING ASSOCIATION.
Price list and trade circular.

1889 St. Louis   MoSHi
------ A symphony in malt and hops - origin and growth - autobiography of a child of which Uncle Sam is proud - account of march from humble obscurity in wild west to a glorious supremacy in all world centers. 6-3/4x10-1/2, 32pp., pls. by A. Gast Bank Note Co. Breweries in many cities. Ills. of glasses, canes, pipes, etc. A great job.

p.1900 MoSHi has a fine reference library in this field after 1900.

1897 Cincinnati   KyBardBM
BILES, THE J.W. CO. Est. 1878. Biles Odds and Ends bulk whiskies. 32mo., 40pp., wrap.

c.1890 Cleveland   MoSHi
BISHOP & BABCOCK CO. Ill. catalog of beer pumps and supplies, bars, counter accessories, iceless soda fountains and equipment, fancy drinks and toasts to go with them. 12mo., 104pp.

c.1900 Cleveland, St. Louis & New York
------ Ill. catalog of bar equipment   MoSHi and soda fountains, etc. 8vo., 56pp.

c.1895 Roanoke, Va.   NNU
CASPER CO. Latest premium   V booklet - the best .35 per quart - no scull-duggery - honest values. Ills. of premiums,

watches, clocks, guns, notions, trunks, etc. 8vo., 28pp., ills., pict. wrap.

c.1887 St. Louis   MoSHi
CLAES & LEHNBEUTER MFG. CO. Ill. catalog of bar fixtures, show cases, bars, counter ware and store fixtures.

1894 Cleveland   MoSHi
CLEVELAND FAUCET CO., Mfg. Ill. catalog of Beer preserving air pressure apparatus, Cleveland beer pumps, etc. Ills. of coolers, cabinets and bars, models Famous Landmark, Star, Schooner, Great Eastern, Manhattan, Superior Outfit #10, and novelty ice boxes. Sq. 8vo., 40pp., pict. wrap.

1891 New York   KyBardBM
COOK & BERNHEIMER CO. Ill. catalog of American specialties. Bottles of the best. 12mo., 92 col. pls. and fld. frs. with col. pict. wrap.

c.1900 New York   NNMM
DEMUTH, WILLIAM & CO. WDC catalog. Ill. catalog of smokers' articles. Pls. and col. pls., without any question the best pict. record of American Gay Ninety smoking. 4to., 95pls., many in col. - applewood, briar and rosewood, meerschaum, cherry, corn and clay - the fanciest and best - pouches, cases, racks, fancy glass stand lighters and even Turkish water pipes. Pict. wrap. N.B. Largest American mfg. and jobbers before 1900. Swallowed up by S. M. Frank, who was taken over by Frank Medico, who recently absorbed Kaywoodie. If some of Demuth's best men had stuck instead of

going to Kaywoodie c.1900, perhaps the story might have been different; however, that's American business history, and always will be.

1863 London   MH-BA
DENMAN, JAMES L. 7th annual wine report and price current. 24mo., 28pp. Probably used in the U.S.A. as in England.

1881 New York   N
DEWEY, H.T. & SONS. The American Wine House. Ill. catalog of pure American wines from the Pioneer American wine house. 12mo., 32pp. with ills. of plant, equipment and produce. Pict. wrap.

1893 Hudson, N.Y.   N
EVANS, C.H. & SONS. Est. 1786. Facts about the Worlds Fair and Evans' India pale ale, etc. 24mo., col. pict. wrap.

c.1890 Saratogs Springs   KyBardBM
GOLDSMITH, B.J. Ill. catalog of fancy groceries, wines, liquors and cigars. 12mo., 62pp., wrap.

1869 New York   NNMM
GOODWIN, WILLIAM H. & CO. Price list of tobacco, segars and snuffs. 20 lvs., wrap.

c.1860 New York   KyBardBM
HADDEN, DAVID H. Est. 1850. A catalog of liquors - at the sign of the big Demijohn - selected for family use, fine brandies and wines and cigars. Deliveries in city and adjoining towns free.

1895 Dayton, O.   KyBardBM
HAYNOR DISTILLING CO. A treatise on whiskey, its mfg. and use - history of company price list of American whiskies - photos. of plant, and tinted half tones. 16mo., 16pp., pict. wrap. One of the best located.

1891 New York   PShipL
HELL GATE BREWERY. George MoSHi
Ehret, prop. 24 Years of Brewing with an ill. History of Beer - dedicated to friends of George Ehret. A fine ill. job, swimming in American suds with a readable history - 1635 to 1866 to boot. Sm. 4to., 120pp.

1893 Louisville, Ky.   KyU
KENTUCKY DISTILLERS' BUREAU CO. Worlds Fair brochure listing Kentucky's distilling interests, history of leading makers and brands, old woodcuts, trademarks, etc. 4to., 100pp., pict. wrap.

1893 St. Louis   MoSHi
LEMP, WILLIAM J. BREWING CO. Souvenir booklet with historical sketch and 42 lithos. of plant and branches with 3 col. pls. of bottles and labels, etc. 32mo. A fine col. pict. record.

1876 Cincinnati   KyBardBM
LEVY, JAMES & BROTHER. Catalog of specialties - Kentucky whiskies, etc. Ill. circular with price lists.

1899 Denver   CoD
LOUISVILLE LIQUOR HOUSE. Ill. catalog of wines and liquors for family use, carefully selected, etc.

c.1890 Philadelphia   PKsL
MIDDLETON, JOHN. Pointers.   Or
A catalog of pipes and smokers' supplies, with a short history. Ills. of briars, meerschaums, jars, moistening boxes, stogies, etc. 16mo., 36pp., col. pict. wrap. of Cox's Brownies in action.

c.1893 Milwaukee   WHi
PABST BREWING CO. An invitation to Milwaukee. Col. lithos. of plant, etc. by Gugler Co., col. pict. wrap. 16mo., 12pp.

1855 Boston   KyBardBM
PIERCE, S.S. CO. Est. 1831. Catalog of groceries, cigars and liquors. 16mo., 15pp., wrap.

1889 Boston   KyBardBM
------ The Epicure. 4to., 36pp., ills., wrap.

1897 Boston   KyBardBM
------ Wholesale price list. 8vo., 16pp., ills., wrap.

1898 Boston   KyBardBM
------ Wholesale price list. 12mo., 16pp., ills., wrap.

c.1893 New York   NNMM
ROTHSCHILD'S, R. SONS & CO. Catalog #19. Ill. and desc. price list of saloon equipment. 34pp. with fine ills.

c.1885 Boston   MH-BA
SPIRIT PURIFYING & AGING CO. Desc. brochure on only successful apparatus for purifying and aging liquors. 12mo., 14pp.

c.1890 Boston   KyBardBM
STACK, JAMES H. Est. 1875. Liquor and wine catalog and price list. 12mo., 22pp., ills., wrap.

1892-95
STEVENS, B.A. Liquors and bar equipment. See Sporting Goods.

1895 Chicago   MdTanSW
STRICKLAND CO., INC. Our Traveler - ill. price list of brandies, gins, good old California wines, whiskies, Strickland's wine of life, rock & rye, bitters, juniperine, etc. 24pp. of ills.

nd. Albany, N. Y.   MoSHi
TAYLOR, JOHN & SONS. Account of rise
and progress of John Taylor Brewery - a
history in prose and verse - a good messenger for sales. 4to., 100pp., with fine ills.
and pls.

1841 Philadelphia   DNLM
TURNER & FISHER.   MH   PKsL
The Smokers', Chewers' and Snuff Takers'
Companion and Tobacconists' Own Book. A
defense of tobacco - history of - beneficial
effects, etc. with a selection of segars, etc.
Sold by all respectable tobacconists throughout the Union. 16mo., 49pp. Published for
the author. If this isn't a catalog in essence,
the history of American business will never
be written.

c.1900 New York   KyBardBM
WEBSTER, H. CO. Est. 1852. Catalog.
4to., 4pp., ills., wrap.

c.1900 New York   KyBardBM
------ Price list of Sunset wines and Con-
solation whiskies. 16mo., 8pp., wrap.

1852 Philadelphia   PHi
WOLBERT, C.J. & CO. Catalog of a grand
classic and unique world's fair of wines,
brandies and liquors. 8vo., 9pp. Dec.18,1852.

1884 New Orleans   KyBardBM
YARNYAN'S. A catalog of Yarnyan's vacuum distilling apparatus for producing fine
liquors, etc.

Though this is a very small chapter it covers one of the largest fields of American activity -- ask
any doctor. Under Food & Drink I have undoubtedly neglected several cases of the best bourbon
and innumerable meerschaum pipes. Don't forget that drug stores carry pipes and have for a long
time stocked bottles with familiar labels. Take a look at some of the pages of strange creations
in pipes with gold stems, silver mountings and bowls carved in the form of Mount Vesuvius illustrated in The Busiest House in America, A. C. Becken and other catalogs in the Department, Dry
Goods and Miscellaneous Stores. Better still, be sure to ask your local historical society curator
and librarian so that he or she will hunt for the thousands that should be found, cataloged and
located.

Chapter 3

Architectural Building Materials

Shelter has always been considered one of the basic requirements of human life. The original materials were stone, mud, grass and hay for thatched roofs, and later on wood. The creator who provided shelter for the human race must have a hard time today accepting the glass, plastic and steel structures in which we live and work. The once humble dwellings are no more.

Building materials have multiplied like rabbits. Stone is synthetic, mud, grass and hay are unknown quantities, and though wood is still on the shelf it is slowly but surely being pushed off by glass and plastic products.

The catalogs located should offer data and illustrations for a log cabin, colonial home, eccentric Gay Ninety mansion, farm houses and outbuildings throughout the 19th century, and even a ten acre factory.

Since Henry Russell-Hitchcock includes bridges in his Bibliography of American Architectural Books before 1895, catalogs of bridge building materials are listed herein. Ornamental ironwork is also found in this chapter when the illustrations are definitely for structural rather than ornamental use.

1892 Syracuse, N. Y.   N
ADAMANT MFG. CO. OF AMERICA.
Adamant wall plaster. Ills. of buildings
from Boston to Milwaukee with architect's
names. 16mo., 52pp., pict. wrap.

1884 Minneapolis   MnHi
ADAMS-HORR CO. Catalog of doors, sash
and blinds. 8vo., ill., wrap.

1884 Minneapolis   MnHi
------ Rural architecture. 12mo., 68pp.,
plans, ills.

nd. Allegheny   PKsL
ALBREE, CHESTER B. IRON WORKS CO.
Catalog #4. Designs of bridge railings,
portals, newels, gates, lamp posts and
cornices. 8vo., 130pp., pls. of bridges in
various cities, wrap.

nd. Allegheny   NNMM
------ Catalog #7. Ill. catalog of bridges
and ornamental and structural iron. 118pp.,
fine pls., wrap.

1895 Allegheny   PKsL
------ Ill. catalog of designs for   NNMM
bridges and ironwork. 8vo., 122pp., fine
pls., wrap.

c.1890 Grand Rapids   CCuMGM
ALDINE MFG. CO. Artistic mantels and
grates, etc. A word to the wise! 4to.,
32pp., pls., wrap.

c.1893 Grand Rapids   NNMM
------ Ill., desc. and priced catalog of
mantels and fireplaces. 32pp.

1898 Grand Rapids   CtY
------ Ill. catalog of mantels and grates.

c.1900 Zanesville   NNMM
AMERICAN ENCAUSTIC TILE CO., LTD.
Catalog A - artistic tiles and ceramic
mosaic tile floor designs. 8vo., looseleaf,
col. pls.

c.1890 Corona, L. I., N. Y.   NNQ
AMERICAN PATENT PORTABLE HOUSE
MFG. CO. Ill. catalog of portable houses.

1887 Boston   NNMM
ANDERSON & DICKEY. Ill. and desc.
catalog of architectural wood turnings and
spiral mouldings. 18pp., wrap.

1889 Boston   DeU
------ Supplementary catalogue of stock
patterns of wood turnings, spiral mouldings
and mantels. 12mo., 12pp., pict. wrap.
Ills. of newel posts, etc.

c.1910 New York   MdTanSW
ATLAS PORTLAND CEMENT CO. Concrete
Garages. 48pp., photo. ills. and specs.

1894 Concord, N. H.   NNMM
AUSTIN, FLINT & DAY CO. Ill., desc., and

priced catalog of builders' merchandise -
fireplaces, mouldings and hitching posts.
93pp., wrap.

1888 Boston   PKsL
BAILEY, J.W. & SONS. MBSPNEA TxDa
Ill. catalog of wood mantels, CU   PU
brackets, mouldings, etc. 12mo., 32pp.,
pict. wrap.

1890 Boston   NNMM
------ The mantel catalog - special on
shelves, mantels, tub rims, curtain frames,
etc. 12mo., 40pp., pls., wrap.

1887 Salem, O.   NNMM
BAKEWELL & MULLINS CO. Architectural ornaments. Ill., desc. and priced catalog
of designs in sheet zinc, brass or copper.
196pp., wrap.

1888 Mason City, Ia.   MnHi
BARNARD, W.O. & SON. Ill. catalog of
white lime cement, stucco and brick
chimney pipe. 16mo., 32pp., wrap.

1889 Swanton, Vt.   VtHi
BARNEY MARBLE CO. (Successor to Geo.
& R.L. Barney). Ill. price list of plain and
fancy floors, hearths, tiles, borders,
columns and wainscoting. 8 page circular.

c.1870 Detroit   MiD
BARNUM, E.T. IRON & WIRE WORKS. Ill.
catalog of builders' wire and iron work.
Crestings, finials, weathervanes, etc. 4to.,
32pp., pict. wrap.

1883-4 Detroit   NNMM
------ Ill., desc. and priced catalog of
railings, fire escapes, stairs, gates, vanes
and crestings. 32pp.

1891 Detroit   N
------ Ill. catalog. 4to., 36pp.

1900 Detroit   NNMM
------ Ill. catalog #1294. 40pp., wrap.

c.1900 Cincinnati   CO
BARRETT MFG. CO. Mills at Beliot, Wis.
Catalog B - roofing, paving and building
papers, cardboards tarred, etc. 8vo.,
32pp., ill., wrap.

1888 New York   NNMM
BECK, FRANK & CO. Ill. and desc.
catalog of Lincrusta-Walton designs for
decoration. 208pp., wrap.

1893 Canton, O.   NNMM
BERGER MFG. CO. Ill., desc. and priced
catalog of steel roofing, cornices and crestings. 7th annual. 120pp., wrap.

1895 Canton, O.   N
------ Architectural sheet metal work -

ornaments, crestings, vanes, steel ceilings,
etc. 12mo., 100pp., fine ills., wrap.

nd. East Berlin, Conn.   NNMM
BERLIN IRON BRIDGE CO. Catalog of
designs for iron construction of bridges,
railings, gates, etc. 70pp., fine ills., wrap.

1884 Boston   PPL
BOSTON TERRA COTTA CO. Architectural and dec. terra cotta of every desc. Pls.
of buildings, naming architects all over
eastern USA. Sq. 8vo., pict. cl., col. pls.

1885 Boston
------ Ill. catalog of tiles, panels,
moulded brick, arches, coping and friezes.
Fine pls., sq. 8vo.

1890 Boston   N
------ Ill. catalog with plates of examples
of work in well known buildings throughout.

1889 Brooklyn & Philadelphia   PKsL
BOUGHTON, JOHN W., Mfg.   NNMM
Est. Philadelphia 1871.
BOUGHTON & TERWILLIGER. Est.
Brooklyn 1868.   Largest mfg. of wood
flooring in the world. Catalog of new
styles, designs of parquet floors, wood carpets, wainscoting, walls and ceilings. 8vo.,
32pp., col. pls., col. pict. wrap.

nd. Brooklyn & Philadelphia   PPL
------ Ill. catalog of wood carpeting.

1893 Brooklyn & Philadelphia   NNQ
------ Catalog of interior decorations,
fret work, grilles, screens and floors.
12mo., 66pp., col. pls., wrap.

1869 Trenton, N. J.   NNMM
BOWMAN, O.O. & CO. Ill., desc. and
priced catalog of fire brick and terra cotta
work. 32pp., wrap.

1877 New York   NNMM
BRADLEY & CURRIER CO., LTD. Ill.
catalog of doors, mantels, mouldings and
fireplaces.

1885 New York   NNMM
------ Ill. catalog of mantels, windows,
mouldings, etc. 100pp., excellent reference. Wrap.

nd. New York   MH-BA
------ Ill. catalog of fireplaces, tiles, etc.
12mo., 36pp., wrap.

1896 New York   NNMM
------ Ill. catalog of balusters, railings,
stairs, mouldings, etc. 64pp., index, wrap.

c.1870 Chicago   ICHi
BRIDGES, LYMAN & CO. Ill. catalog of
building materials and ready-made houses.

1896 Brooklyn, N.Y.   NNMM
BROOKLYN CITY MOULDING MILL. John
S. Loomis. Est. 1846. Catalog #1 - new
ed., mouldings, architraves, trimmings,
rails, newels, frames and brackets. A fine
ill. ref.

1854 Buffalo, N.Y.
BUFFALO EAGLE IRON WORKS. Ill. catalog of architectural designs in window caps,
sills, columns for store fronts, etc. 8vo.,
26pp., pict. wrap.

1878 Portland, Me.   MoSHi
BURROWES, E.T. & CO. Est. 1873. (St.
Louis agent.) Ill. catalog of sliding wire
window screens.

1892 Portland, Me.   NNMM
------ Ill. catalog of wire window and door
screens, wood for frames, details. 18pp.

1892 Portland, Me.   MH-BA
------ Ill. catalog of frames, etc. 24mo.,
4pp.

1895 Portland, Me.   MH-BA
------ Ill. catalog. Largest screen factories in the world. P.T. Barnum's house in
Bridgeport, Thomas Edison, etc. 8vo.,
30pp., wrap.

1883 Philadelphia   MoSHi
BYAR COMBINATION CELLAR WINDOW
GUARD CO. Ill. price list.

1897 Wheeling, W. Va.   Wv-Ar
CALDWELL & PETERSON MFG. CO. Steel
ceilings, all styles and prices, steel roofings, etc. Estimates. 24mo., 16pp., ill.

1883 Calumet, O.   OHi
CALUMET FIRE CLAY CO. Ill. catalog of
stove pipes, sewer pipes, fire brick and
terra cotta faience work. 52pp., wrap.

1898 Johnstown, Pa.   PPL
CAMBRIA IRON CO. Handbook of diagrams,
shapes, etc. of structural steel. 350pp., ill.

c.1868 Cincinnati   OC
CAMERON, WESLEY M. Ill. catalog of
window frames, mantels, pilasters, columns
and flooring. Pre-fabricated stairs complete with rail and newel post for shipment
to any point. Accounts for sameness in
older farm and small town houses in mid-
west and south. Particular attention paid to
southern and western work. 4to., 30pp.,
fine pict. ref.

1889 Canton, O.   NNMM
CANTON STEEL ROOFING CO.   MnHi
Est. 1877. Ill. catalog of iron and steel
roofing, siding and ceilings. 16mo., 40pp.,
col. tinted pict. wrap.

1890 Pittsburgh   PKsL
CARNEGIE STEEL CO., LTD. Pocket
companion for architects, engineers and
builders. Tinted pls. by Bien, shapes and
forms.

1896 Pittsburgh   PKsL
------ Pocket companion. Tinted pls.
16mo., leather.

1898-99 Peoria, Ill.   NNMM
CARR & ADAMS CO. Ill., desc. and priced
catalog of sash, doors and mouldings.
343pp. in red cl., with fine pls.

1895 St. Louis   MoSHi
CENTRAL MANTEL CO. Ill. catalog #32.
Science of mantel making. 4to., 80pp., fine
pls., wrap.

1880 CHAMPION CO. See ornamental iron.

1855 CHASE BROTHERS. See ornamental
iron for fancy metallic chimney pieces and
mantels.

1867 Chicago   ICHi
CHICAGO BUILDING BLOCK CO. Desc.
catalog of artificial stone, tests. Not ill.

1883 Cincinnati   MoHi
CINCINNATI CORRUGATING CO. Ill.
catalog of superior corrugated sheet iron,
steel and zinc roofing. 16mo., 16pp., wrap.

1887 Cincinnati   CtY
------ Ill. catalog.

1888 Cincinnati   CtY
------ Ill. catalog.

1893 Cincinnati   CtY
------ Ill. catalog.

1898 Cincinnati   PPF
------ Ill catalog #33. 87pp., Ptd. Piqua.
Wrap.

1899 Cleveland   NNMM
CLEVELAND HYDRAULIC PRESS BRICK
CO. Ill., desc. and priced catalog of bricks.
121pp., glt. ptd. wrap.

c.1885 New York   NNMM
COMPOSITE IRON WORKS CO. Catalog of
iron railings, gates, stable fixtures, window
and tree guards, fences and bedsteads. Ill.
of work on Brooklyn Bridge, Central Park,
etc. 4to., 16pp. of pls., pict. wrap.

1885 Milwaukee   NNMM
CONWAY MFG. CO. Ill. catalog of
Champion sliding blinds. 32pp., wrap.

c.1876 Memphis   DAIA
COOK, JAMES B. Prisons: Construction
according to the Cook & Heath perfected

system. Fine pls., one leaf, 98pp., diags., ptd. Price, Jones & Co.

1882 St. Paul   MnHi
CORLIES, CHAPMAN & DRAKE, INC. Ill. price list of doors, blinds, sash, windows, balusters, posts and mouldings. 12mo., 32pp., wrap.

c.1864   NNMM
CRAWFORD. Crawford's Bronze Doors - Cost Book #1. 12 lvs. of pls., wrap.

1886 Clinton, Ia.   IaHi
CURTIS BROS. & CO. Est. 1866. Catalog of doors, sash, blinds, stairs, railings, posts, mouldings, balusters and lumber.

c.1878 Beloit, Wis.   NNMM
DAVIS, F.N. & CO. Ill. catalog of aluminous and ornamental building paper, oilcloth and carpeting.

c.1880 Beloit, Wis.   NNMM
------ Ill. catalog. 12mo., 12pp., wrap.

nd. Chicago   NNMM
DECORATORS' SUPPLY CO. Ill. catalog of plastic ornaments, mouldings, brackets and cornices. 176pp., cl. and bds.

1898 Seattle   WaS
DENNY CLAY CO. Ill. catalog of clay products, chimney tops, foundation blocks and sewer pipe.

1880-96 San Francisco   CHi
DOE, B. & J.S. Prices current of doors, blinds, windows, pulley cords, etc.

1895 Boston   NNMM
EMMEL, CHARLES. Specimens of relief ornamentation for interior and exterior use. Tall fol., 36 detailed pls. of mantels, ceilings, mouldings, etc. Stiff wrap.

1899 Boston   CtY
------ Ill. catalog.

c.1875 Delpsburg & Philadelphia   PKsL
EMPIRE SLATE WORKS. J.B. Kimes & Co. 4 page col. ill. folder of slate mantels, ice boxes, pulpits, pedestals, roofing, flooring tiles, etc.

c.1887 New York   MH-BA
ENDOLITHIC MARBLE CO. Endolithic marbles, their history and use, test. 8x9, 20pp., 11 pls, 1 col.

1900 Essex, Conn.   CtHi
ESSEX WOOD TURNING CO. Catalog of turned and twisted mouldings, spindles in all styles and shapes, metalized wood, machine wood turning in all branches. 4to., 65 and 2pp., 31 fine pls., view of plant.

1884 St. Louis   MnHi
EVANS & HOWARD MFG. CO. Catalog of fire clay goods, gas retorts, fire brick, pipe, terra cotta, etc. 16mo., 20pp., ill., wrap.

1886 St. Louis   CtY
------ Ill. catalog of fire bricks.

1887 St. Louis   CtY
------ Ill. catalog of clay goods.

1897 St. Louis   MoSHi
------ Ill. catalog of brick, terra cotta, culvert pipe, etc. 12mo., 20pp., wrap.

1890 Camden, N. J.   NjR
FAY, W.H. Fay's waterproof building manila for roofing. 8vo., 32pp., ill. of dwellings and buildings in many states using Fay's products. Pict. wrap.

1884 Troy, N. Y.   PKsL
FIRE BRICK WORKS. Ill. catalog of fire brick, clay, tile, ground clay, brick and kaolin.

c.1885 New York   NNMM
FISKE, J.W. Ill. catalog of iron railings, gates, window and door guards, etc. 122pp., cl.

1899-1900 Worcester   NNMM
FLEXIBLE DOOR & SHUTTER CO. Catalog of patent improved flexible specialties for schools, dwellings, railroad stations, halls, and even trolley cars. 8vo., 62pp., photo. ills., dec. wrap.

1900 Chicago   ICHi
FOSTER-MUNGER CO. Official catalog for 1900. 8vo., 626pp., doors, sash, blinds, mouldings and mantels with 32 col. pls. of stained glass windows.

1902 Chicago   NNMM
------ Official catalog for 1902. 8vo., 752pp., col. pls., ill., wrap.

1893 Camden, N. J.   MoSHi
FRAND, MARTIN J. & CO. Ill. catalog of ornamental iron work. 3rd series.

1900 Camden, N. J.   MoSHi
------ Ill. catalog of ornamental iron work. 5th series.

1883 Minneapolis   MnHi
FRASER & SHEPHERD. Ill. price list of doors, sash, blinds, balusters, posts, mouldings, etc. 12mo., 55pp., wrap.

c.1869 Chicago   NNMM
FREAR ARTIFICIAL STONE MFG. CO. Ill. and desc. catalog of mantels, mouldings, etc. 16pp. with 19 pls., wrap.

1884 Philadelphia   NNMM
FRENCH, SAMUEL H. & CO. Catalog of
builders' supplies. Ills. of mantels,
embossed and cut glass windows, fire
frames, grates, etc. 4to., 209pp., wrap.

1880 Camden, N. J.   PKsL
FRENCH, W.A. & CO. Ill. catalog of
builders' supplies: centres, cornices, cut
glass windows, mantels, newel posts, terra
cotta, etc. 12mo., 133pp., wrap.

1882 Camden, N. J.   PU
------ Ill. catalog. 12mo., 208pp., ornaments, brackets, doors, etc.

c.1890 Camden, N. J.   NNMM
------ Ill. catalog of marbelized slate
mantels. 18pp., wrap.

1889 Chicago   MoSHi
FRIEDLEY & BOSHARDT. Ill. catalog of
zinc and copper ornaments.

nd. Philadelphia   PHi
GALLOWAY TERRA-COTTA CO. 2 ill.
catalogs of products.

1872 Cleveland   DeU
GARRY IRON ROOFING CO. Ill. catalog
pat. iron roofing for all building. Largest
producers in the world. 16mo., 20pp., pict.
wrap.

1888 Cleveland   MnHi
------ Ill. catalog. 16mo., 54pp., pict.
wrap.

nd. Cleveland   MnHi
------ Ill. catalog. 16mo., 32pp., pict.
wrap.

1898 Louisville, Ky.   MoSHi
GENERT BROS. LUMBER CO. Catalog.

c.1900 Easton, Pa.   PHi
GENUINE BANGOR SLATE CO. Slate and
its uses. 2nd ed., 4to., 74pp., ill., wrap.

1881 Troy, N. Y.   MnHi
GLOBE VENTILATOR CO. Ill. catalog of
Globe ventilators, chimney caps, etc.

p.1900 Davenport, Ia.   NNMM
GORDON-VAN TINE CO. Ill., desc. and
priced catalog. Grand plans for everybody.
52pp., cl.

nd. Davenport, Ia.   NNMM
------ Ill. catalog for home builders.
General supplies. 116pp., wrap.

1884 Chicago, Ill.   MnHi
GOULDS & AUSTIN CO. Ill price list of
brick, cement, lime, pipe, etc. 16mo.,
24pp., wrap.

c.1887 Grand Rapids, Mich.   NNMM
GRAND RAPIDS PORTABLE HOUSE CO.
Ill. catalog of portable houses: cottage,
cabin, bath house, hunter's cabins, etc.
8vo., 22pp., fine ills., wrap.

1865 Boston   MH-BA
GREEN MOUNTAIN SLATE & FILE CO.
Catalog, 8vo., 24pp. See Sabin 28578.

1888 Philadelphia   PKsL
HALL & GARRISON. Ill. catalog of wood
mantels mfg. by . . . 4to., 48pp., fine pls.
of designs, wrap.

c.1890 New Haven   NNMM
HALSTED & HARMOUNT LUMBER CO. Ill.
and priced catalog of mouldings. 32pp., 31
litho. pls., wrap.

1872 Philadelphia   DSi
HANSON, WILLIAM R. Desc. pamphlet of
Vermont variegated marbles for builders,
architects, etc.

1893 Philadelphia, New York & Cincinnati
HARRISON BROTHERS & CO. Ill.   NNMM
catalog and price list of white leads, colors,
chemicals, etc. 90pp., cl.

1890 Wooster, O.   DSi
HARTMAN & DURSTINE CO. Catalog of
inside sliding window blinds. 75pp., ill.,
wrap.

1873 Albany, N. Y.   NNMM
HAWLEY, H.Q. & SONS. Ill., desc. and
priced catalog of wood mouldings, casings,
etc. 66pp., bds.

c.1890 Rochester, N. Y.
HAYDEN FURNITURE CO. Ill. catalog of
wood mantels. 4to., 70pp. of pls., pict.
wrap.

1874 New York & Cincinnati   NNMM
HAYES BROTHERS. Dunn & Witt,   OC
Cincinnati. Ill. catalog of Hayes' pat.
ventilating fireproof skylights, shutters,
conservatories, blinds, gates, partitions
and fire escapes. An unusually good reference. Weathervanes: $410. for an eagle
with 14 ft. wing spread down to $7. for a
game cock. Circular comfort stations for
parks. 7x10, 92, XVI pp., excellent ills.,
wrap.

c.1900 Brooklyn   DeU
HECLA IRON WORKS. Formerly Poulson
& Eger. Ill. catalog of ornamental iron and
bronze work for stair, elevator, gates,
grills, guards and doors, with names of
architects and buildings all over the country. 11x14, 40 pls.

1871 Chicago   NNMM
HEENEY & CAMPBELL. Catalog of mouldings. Ill., numbered and priced. 74pp.,
wrap.

c.1885 Minneapolis   MnHi
HERZOG MFG. CO. Ill. catalog of architectural ironwork, grills, gates, jail works,
etc. 8vo., 116pp., wrap.

c.1900 Newport, Ky.   DSi
HIGGINS MFG. CO. Catalog of Higgins
metal window screens. 24pp., tests., ills.

1862 Cincinnati   OC
HINKLE, GOULD & CO. Plans of buildings,
mouldings, architraves, stairs, newels,
balusters, rails, mantels, sash, columns
and doors for carpenters and builders.
Adapted to styles in U. S. Valuable information with 422 ills. 4to., 54pp., wrap. One
of the most important catalogs in this field.
House plans include architect and locations
in many states. Our factory is the largest
of its kind in the United States.

1869 Cincinnati   MoSHi
------ Plans, etc. . . 4to.,   OC
80pp., ills., wrap.

c.1895 San Francisco   CHi
HOLMES, H.T. & CO. Catalog of cements,
limes, etc. 12mo., 14pp., ill., wrap.

c.1898 San Francisco   CHi
Ill. catalog. 12mo., 19pp., ill., wrap.

c.1880 New York   NNMM
HOWARD & MORSE, MFG. Est. 1856. Ill.
catalog of steel, iron and brass screens,
guards, finials, crestings, fences, railings,
bank interiors, summer houses for architects and builders. 8vo., 96pp., pict. wrap.

c.1886 New York   DeU
------ Catalog #59. 8vo., 128pp., fine
ills., pict. wrap.

c.1890 New York
------ Catalog #104. 8vo., 58pp., ills.,
wrap.

1885 Indianapolis   In
INDIANA PAINT & ROOFING CO. Catalog
of rubber roofing, sheathing, paints, marbelized mantels, etc. 8vo., ill., pict. wrap.

1886 Indianapolis   In
------ Free booklet on rubber roofing,
slate mantels, etc. 8vo., 40pp., pict. wrap.
of mantels.

1836 Indianapolis   InHi
INDIANAPOLIS, TOWN OF. House carpenters' and joiners' book of prices for the
town of Indianapolis. Adopted June 1. 44,
one page, 1 blank leaf.

Not strictly a catalog, but like the Boston
1774, and other labor and material price
books, a guide to costs useful for research
with trade catalogs of whatever period they
concern.

c.1895 Indianapolis   NNMM
INTERIOR HARDWOOD CO.   In
Design book of parquet floors, borders, etc.
8vo., 26 lvs., col. pls., col. pict. wrap.

1889 St. Louis   MoSHi
ITTNER, ANTHONY. Successors to Ittner
Bros. Ill. catalog of pressed, moulded and
ornamental bricks.

1866 New York   NSbSM
JACKSON ARCHITECTURAL IRON WORKS.
Est. 1840. Ill. catalog of new and improved
stable fittings, plans, stalls, hitching posts,
crestings, lamps, gates, etc. 4to., 70pp.,
fine pls., stiff pict. wrap. with 4to., 16pp.
price list.

1873 New York   NNMM
JACKSON, JAMES L. & BRO. Catalog of
improvement in faulty construction of
buildings. 4 lvs., ill. and desc., wrap.

c.1900 New York   DeU
JACKSON, WILLIAM H. CO. Brass, bronze,
and iron work. Book #244 ptd. Meriden
Gravure Co. 11x14, 162 pls., view of works,
names architects and buildings.

1881 New York   CtY
JACOBSON & CO. Ill. catalog of mantels
and chimney pieces.

1882-92 New York   CtY
------ 5 ill. catalogs containing many new
original designs for this period.

1894 New York   NNMM
------ Supplement #1, chimney pieces.
40 fine pls. in original wrap.

1896-97 New York   CtY
------ 2 more ill. catalogs of designs.

1884 New York   KU
JOHNS, H.W. MFG. CO. Est. 1858. Ill.
catalog of standard asbestos materials for
roofs, walls, pipes, etc. 12mo., 48pp.,
pict. wrap.

c.1889 New York   KU
------ Ill. folder of roofing and coverings.
Pict. wrap. in original envelope.

nd. New York   PPF
------ Ill. catalog of asbestos materials
for builders. 16mo., 20pp., pict. wrap.

1882 Minneapolis   MnHi
JOHNSON & HURD. Ill. price list of sash,

doors, blinds, mouldings, window frames, stairs, newels, balusters and railings. 16mo., 27pp., wrap.

1890 Racine, Wis.   CtY
JOHNSON, S.C. & SON. Ill. catalog of parquetry and fine flooring. Col. pls. and pict. wrap.

1893 Racine, Wis.   CtY
------ Ill. catalog.

1895 Racine, Wis.   CtY
------ Ill. catalog.

nd. Racine, Wis.   PPF
------ Artistic wood finishes and designs. 8pp.

c.1900 Racine, Wis.   PBS
------ Ornamental hardwood floors, parquetry, borders and strips. 7x10, 26pp., col. pict. wrap.

1874 Pittsburgh   MH-BA
KEYSTONE BRIDGE CO. Est. 1865. Ill. catalog of wrought iron bridges, with desc. list of bridges built in many States, etc. 4to., 60pp., fine pls., bds.

1000 Pittsburgh   N
------ Examples of bridges built with details. Fol., 16 fine pls., dec. buckram.

1884 Cleveland   OHi
KING IRON AND BRIDGE MFG. CO. Est. 1858. Catalog of wrought iron bridges. 4to., 16pp., fine litho. pls. by Johns & Co.

1898 New York   DeU
KING, J.B. & CO. King's windsor cement for architects. 12mo., wrap., good sales talk.

1891 Toulon, Ill.   MoSHi
KNOX & STONIER. Ill. catalog of architectural ornaments: spun urns, balls in zinc and copper.

1891 Toulon, Ill.   MoSHi
------ Further designs in zinc and copper.

1895 St. Louis   MoSHi
KOKEN IRON WORKS. Ill. catalog of designs of work in iron, steel and brass for office, public buildings, dwellings and bridges. 4to., 90pp.

1886 New York
KUMP, ALBERT. Ill. catalog of natural wood ornaments, corner blocks, mouldings, etc. 8vo., 16pp., pict. wrap.

1884 St. Louis   MoSHi
LACLEDE FIRE BRICK MFG. CO. Ill. catalog of fire brick, gas retorts, sewer pipe, culverts, etc. 16mo., 16pp., pict.wrap.

1882 New York   NNMM
LANSING & CO. Ill. and desc. booklet of theater interiors, ornamental and decorative materials. 32pp., wrap.

1854 New York   MH-BA
LEFFERTS, MARSHALL & BROTHER. Patented galvanized iron for roofs, etc. Tests. 4x7, 49pp., ill.

1883 Lima, O.
LIMA IRON FENCE CO. See fences.

c.1885 Chicago   MnHi
LLOYD IRON ROOFING & PAINT CO. Ill. catalog of corrugated iron and sheet metal roofing in all its branches. 12mo., 32pp., pict. wrap.

1896 New York   NNMM
LOOMIS, JOHN S. Brooklyn City Moulding Mill. Ill. catalog of mouldings and woodwork for builders. 132pp., fine pls., wrap.

nd. Worcester   NNMM
LUGRIN FLEXIBLE DOOR CO. Ill. and desc. catalog of doors, etc. 4 lvs., wrap.

nd. Philadelphia   PHi
LUPTON, DAVID'S SONS CO. Catalog of architectural sheet metal work and Lupton's fireproof windows. 4to., 163pp., pls.

1850 New York & Liege, Belguim   MH-BA
McCALL & STRONG. (Late Mosselman, agent.) Ill. catalog of zinc roofing materials. 8vo., 40pp., wrap.

1851 New York   MH-BA
------ Ill. catalog. 4to., 48pp., wrap.

1886 Cleveland & Berea, O.   OHi
McDERMOTT & BEREA STONE CO. CtY Catalog of block and fine sawed stone for churches, court houses and public buildings. 8vo., 28pp., pls. of buildings, wrap.

1884 Philadelphia   N
MANLY & COOPER. Catalog of ornamental iron work. 8vo., 64pp., pls., pict. wrap.

1886 Philadelphia   NNMM
------ Ill. catalog of bridge railings, crestings, gates, fences and railings. 13 lvs., pict. wrap.

1893 Chicago   NNMM
MARITZEN, AUGUST. Ill. catalog of architectural and engineering work for brewers. 44pls., glt. ptd. cl.

1885 New York   TxDa
MAURER, HENRY. Ill. catalog of fireproof building materials, arches, beams, columns, etc. 8vo., 32pp., wrap.

1897 New York   CtY
------ Ill. catalog

1898 New York   CtY
------ Ill. catalog.

1890 Philadelphia   MoSHi
MERCHANT & CO. Ill. catalog of roofing
plates and tin roofs.

1901 Philadelphia   PHi
------ 20th century catalog of tin plates,
mixed metals, ventilators, shingles and
tiles. 8vo., 135pp., ill.

        Evansville, Ind. & St. Louis
MESKER, JOHN B., MESKER, GEORGE L.
& CO., MESKER & BROTHER. John B.
Mesker born in Holland, came to USA. at
8 yrs. old. Grew up in Cincinnati and went
into hardware business. Moved to Evansville, Ind. and was leading merchant until
his death Dec. 21, 1899. Son Frank born
Jan. 8, 1861 went to St. Louis in 1877. He
learned architectural and mechanical draft-
ing in office of Arch't. J.B.Legg & Co.
Associated with brother Bernard T. Mesker
1879 in structural and sheet metal, Mesker
Brothers Iron Co. Brother George ran
George L. Mesker & Co. in Evansville, Ind.
Frank died at 93 in 1952, and George at 84
in 1936.

c.1875 Evansville, Ind. & St. Louis   In
------ Ill. catalog of modern store fronts,
roofs, grills, railings, columns, blocks,
crestings, weathervanes, etc. 8vo., 32pp.,
fine pls., pict. wrap.

1888 Evansville, Ind. & St. Louis   MoSHi
------ Ill. catalog with details of   In
named buildings all over the USA. 4to.,
20pp., pict. wrap.

1897 Evansville, Ind. & St. Louis   NNMM
------ Ill. catalog. 4to., 32pp.,   In
pict. wrap.

1899 Evansville, Ind. & St. Louis   In
------ Ill. catalog.

1901 Evansville, Ind. & St. Louis   MoSHi
------ Ill. catalog. 20th ed., 4to., 40pp.,
pict. wrap.

c.1901 Evansville, Ind. & St. Louis   MoSHi
------ Ill. catalog of store fronts, street
scenes and public buildings. 4to., 48pp.,
pict. wrap.

c.190? Evansville, Ind. & St. Louis   MoSHi
------ Ill. catalog. 4to., 32pp., pict. wrap.

1894-5 Grand Rapids   NNMM
METAL STAMPING & SPINNING CO. Ill.,
desc. and priced catalog of architectural

sheet metal, ornaments and steel ceilings.
80pp., wrap.

1891 Boston   NNMM
MILLEN, CHARLES A. & CO.   CtY
Ill. catalog of mouldings, builders' trimmings, stair rails, posts, balusters and
mantels. 12mo., 96pp., pict. wrap.

1887 Milwaukee   MoSHi
MILLER, WILLIAM. Ill. catalog of
Miller's pat. inside sliding blinds.

c.1875 Cincinnati   OC
MILLS & SPELMIRE MFG. CO. Ill. catalog
of mouldings, doors, sash, blinds, frames,
etc. 4to., 74pp., wrap. N.B. The beginning of mass production. This one catalog
offers nearly 500 patterns.

c.1880 Minneapolis   MnHi
MINNEAPOLIS FENCE & IRON   MnM
WORKS. H.L. Woodburn, Prop. Ill. catalog of wood and iron fences, roof crestings,
finials, balustrades, window guards, stairs
and wire railings, hitching posts, etc.
12mo., 48pp., fine ills., dec. wrap.

1880 Minneapolis   MnHi
MINNEAPOLIS GALVANIZED IRON
CORNICE WORKS. Catalog of designs of
architectural sheet metal ornaments, cornices, window caps, ventilators, iron, slate
and gravel roofing. 4to., fine ills.

1884 Minneapolis   MnHi
------ Ill. catalog.

c.1885 St. Louis   MoSHi
MIRAGOLI, E.S. & CO. Ill. catalog of
plastic relief ornaments.

1867 St. Louis   MoSHi
MISSOURI CONCRETE STONE CO. Mfg. of
Ransome's pat. apparatus for building
bridges, gateways, mantels, vases, tiles,
grave stones and ornaments.

1898 St. Louis   MoSHi
MISSOURI SHEET METAL ORNAMENT CO.
Ill. catalog.

c.1890 Chicago   NNMM
MOORE, E.B. & CO. Ill. catalog of parquet
floors. Sq. 8vo., 44pp., col. pls., throughout, pict. wrap.

1893 Chicago   NHi
------ Catalog. 8vo., 48pp., col. pls.,
col. pict. wrap.

1869 Philadelphia   DSi
MOORHEAD CLAY WORKS. Ill. catalog of
clay and terra cotta architectural products,
etc. 48pp., wrap.

1853 New York   NNMM
MOREWOOD, GEORGE B. & CO. Ill., desc.
and priced catalog of galvanized tinned iron
and plumbic zinc goods. 32pp., wrap.

1885 Louisville, Ky.   KyU
MORTIN, D. Ill. catalog of architectural
plans for churches, parsonages and dwellings. 8vo., 90pp., elevations and plans,
wrap.

1867 Boston   MH-BA
MOSELEY IRON BUILDING WORKS. DLC
Ill. catalog of buildings, iron bridges, iron
roofs, etc. 8vo., 22pp., fine pls., wrap.

1887 New York   MoSHi
MOSEMAN, GEORGE H. & CO. Ill. price
list of Globe ventilators.

1887 New York   NNMM
MOTT, J.L. IRON WORKS. Ill. catalog F -
stable fittings, plans, stalls and accessories. 4to., 224pp. of pls., pict. wrap.

1889 New York   ICHi
------ Ill. catalog F with supplement.
Stables complete, hitching posts, weathervanes, crestings and ornaments. 4to.,
240pp., pict. wrap. See also ornamental
ironwork, fences, weathervanes and horse
goods for other ill. catalogs.

1896 Salem, O.   OHi
MULLINS, W.H. CO. Ill. catalog   DeU
of architectural sheet metal work, art
metal roofing, cornices, crestings and
statuary. Plates of statuary for Cotton
States and International Exposition, factory
interiors, etc. Tall 4to., 172pp., dec. cl.

1909 Salem, O.   DLC
------ Ill. catalog of architectural sheet
iron work. Tall 4to., 86pp. of pls., wrap.

1913 Salem, O.   NNMM
----- Ill. catalog. 80pp., wrap.

1899 New York   NNMM
MURALO CO. Catalog of Muralo relief
decorations for the home. 12mo., 38pp.,
22 pls., samples in col., col. pict. wrap.

1881-97
NATIONAL MOULDING BOOK. See Rand,
McNally & Co.

1888 New York   PU
NATIONAL SHEET METAL ROOFING CO.
Practical hints to builders. 12mo., 80pp.,
plans and designs from attic to cellar.
Pict. wrap.

1890 New York   DAIA
------ Ill. catalog of plans and elevations.
12mo., 100pp., a few comic ills., pict. wrap.

c.1875 New York   DeU
NATIONAL WOOD MFG. CO. Catalog, ill.
by litho. pls. of wood carpeting, parquet
floors and wainscoting. Price list. 16mo.,
24pp. of designs, pict. wrap.

c.1882 Boston
NEW ENGLAND PRESS BRICK MFG. CO.
Front or Face Bricks, ornamental, shaped
and moulded bricks, history and tests.
16pp. fld. col. pls., wrap. Fine bit of
merchandising though not priced.

1870 Trenton, N. J.   CtY
NEW JERSEY STEEL & IRON CO. Ill.
catalog of rolled beams and channels for
builders.

1874 Trenton, N. J.   PKsL
------ Ill. catalog of beams and channels.
16mo., 50pp., fld. pls., pict. cl.

1887 New York   MoSHi
NEW YORK ARCHITECTURAL TERRA-
COTTA CO. Ill. catalog of building
materials.

1903 New York   NNMM
NEW YORK BELTING & PACKING CO.,
LTD. Ill. catalog of interlocking rubber
tiling. 18 col. pls. with wrap. Fine reference.

1893 New York   PKsL
NEW YORK IRON ROOFING & CORRUGA-
TING CO. Ill. catalog of roofing. 16mo.,
10pp., tests. from Pa., Ind., etc.

1874 New York   MH-BA
NEW YORK SLATE ROOFING CO. George
E. Glines patent slate roofing paint, cement,
roofs, tests. and list of users. 8vo., 80pp.,
ill.

c.1876 New York   NNMM
------ Ill., desc. and priced catalog of
roofs, mantels, grates, etc. 28 lvs.

1882 New York   PPL
NEW YORK TERRA COTTA LUMBER CO.
Ill. catalog showing types of flooring,
sheathing, insulation, etc.

1857 New York   NNMM
NEW YORK WIRE RAILING CO. Ill., desc.
and priced catalog of iron wire railings,
gates, fences, etc. 84pp., cl.

c.1880 New York   NNMM
NEW YORK WOOD TURNING CO. Ill.
catalog of moulded cornices, curtain poles,
ornamental wood work, etc. 8vo., 15pp.,
wrap.

nd. New York   NNMM
------ Ill. catalog of balusters, mouldings
and furniture turnings. 22pp., wrap.

nd. New York   NNMM
------ Ill. catalog of newel posts, railings,
etc. 8vo., 32pp., pict. wrap.

c.1890 Berkeley, Calif.   CHi
NIEHAUS BROS. & CO. West Berkeley
Planing Mills. Ill. catalog of stairs, hardwood interiors, windmills, water tanks,
etc. 12mo., pict. wrap.

1900 New York   NNMM
NORTHROP, COBURN & DODGE CO. Ill.
catalog of stamped steel for ceilings, side-
walls, etc. 48pp. of designs, etc. Price
list at back, wrap.

1889 New York   CtY
NORTHROP, HENRY S. Ill. catalog of
metal ceilings.

1886 Milwaukee   MnHi
ORMSBY LIME CO. Ill. catalog of limes,
cements and supplies. 16mo., 10pp., wrap.

1895 Boston   NNMM
PAINE FURNITURE CO.   CtY   TxDa
A Mantel Book. Sm. 4to., 40 pls. with text
and details, tinted pict. wrap. Offers list
of Paine's catalogs free for the postage.

1893 Oshkosh, Wis.   NNMM
PAINE LUMBER CO. Ill. catalog of sash,
doors, blinds, mouldings, stairs and
mantels. 332pp., cl. cover.

1900 Chicago   MdTanSW
PALMER, FULLER & CO. Wholesale
catalog of building supplies, doors, sash,
etc. with 16 col. pls. of leaded art glass
windows, grilles, parquet floors, borders,
etc. 8vo., 380pp., cl., fine reference.

1893 Syracuse, N. Y.   NSyHi
PARAGON PLASTER CO. Paragon -
perfection in wall plasters. Photos. of
sample work. 16mo., 54pp., ill., wrap.

1892 Paterson, N. J.   NjR
PASSAIC ROLLING MILL CO. Ill. catalog
of steel and iron beams, angles, channels,
bars, nuts for builders and contractors.
8vo., 42pp., cl.

1879 Philadelphia   PPL
PEERLESS BRICK CO. Ill. catalog of
moulded ornamental bricks, detailed desc.
of 289 designs.

1892 Pencoyd, Pa.   PKsL
PENCOYD IRON WORKS. A. & P. Roberts
Co. Near Philadelphia. Wrought iron and
steel construction: rules, formulae, beams,
shapes, channels for buildings and bridges.
16mo., 257 and IXpp., 43 tinted pls., cl.

1892 Pencoyd, Pa.   PKsL
------ 8th ed.

1899 PHILADELPHIA & BOSTON   PKsL
FACE BRICK CO.   Sketch Book.

1872 Philadelphia   PHi
PHILADELPHIA ARCHITECTURAL DSi
IRON CO. Catalog of structural and
decorative architectural iron. 27pp. with
18 fine pls., wrap.

1888 Philadelphia   TxDaDeG
PHOENIX BRIDGE CO.   DSi   PWcHi
Successors to Clark Reeves & Co. Album
of designs. 4to., 32pp. of pls. of the plant,
designs A to S, bridges built in Pa., N.J.,
N.Y., O., etc.

c.1900 Detroit   MiD
PHOENIX WIRE WORKS. Catalog of
architectural and ornamental wire and iron
railings, fences, crestings, finials, weathervanes and cornices. 4to., 24pp., fine ills.,
dec. wrap.

1855 Boston   NNMM
POND & DUNKLEE. Warming and ventilating warehouse. Ill. catalog of ventilating
heaters, 5 sizes of Boynton's pat., Pond &
Dunklee's portable furnace The Coronet,
railroad car stoves, etc., plus a section of
mantels, mirror mantels, stone, slate,
marbelized, metallic grates and fire frames,
etc. 8vo., 64pp.

c.1870 Charlestown, Mass.   TxDa
POND, MOSES & CO. Ill. catalog of
marbelized (sic) slate for hospitals, railroad stations, hotels; also ornamental
mantels, shelves and brackets. 12mo.,
58pp., pict. wrap.

1883 Cincinnati   MH-BA
PORTER IRON ROOFING CO. Mfg. of
sheet iron roofing. Tests. 8vo., 20pp., ill.

1855 New York   N
PORTER'S STONE DRESSING MACHINE.
Pat. August 8, 1854. 8vo., 20pp., 2 pls.,
wrap.

1890 Wilmington, Del.   PKsL
PUSEY & JONES. Ill. catalog of Gould
screens.

1873 Philadelphia   DSi
QUIGG, J. TRAVIS & CO. Desc. catalog of
Marezzo marbles. 46pp.

1881 Chicago   MnHi
RAND, McNALLY & CO., Publishers. Compiled by W.L. Churchill. Universal Moulding Book, full size designs in great variety,
architraves, stair and pew railings, pickets,
lattice, balusters, newels, pew ends, wood
mantels with working plans, etc. 4to., 84
and 2pp., pls. throughout, stiff wrap.

1892 Chicago   NNMM
------ Universal Moulding Book; combined
book of sash, doors, blinds, mouldings,
stairs, mantels, embossed, ground and cut
glass windows, etc. 8vo., 312pp., fine pls.
and ills., cl.

1897 Chicago   ICHi
------ National Moulding Book - adopted
by the wholesale sash, door and blind mfg.
of Northwest and East. 8vo., 140pp., fine
ills. throughout, pict. wrap.

1896 St. Louis   MoSHi
READY ROOFING ROCK ASPHALT CO.
Ill. catalog of roofing materials.

c.1882 New York, Philadelphia & Chicago
RENDLE, ARTHUR E. Ill. catalog   NNMM
of pat. systems of glazing without putty -
skylights, greenhouses, etc. 40pp., wrap.

1893 New York, Philadelphia & Chicago
------ Ill. catalog. 8vo., 16pp.,   PKsL
wrap.

1899 New York, Philadelphia & Chicago
------ Desc. catalog of Paradigm   DSi
skylights.

c.1886 San Francisco   CHi
RANSOME, ERNEST L. Catalog of concrete
apparatus for moulding walls. See also
Missouri Concrete Stone Co. 8vo., ill.,
fld. col. plate, wrap.

1883 Detroit   NNMM
RAYL, T.B. & CO. Ill. catalog and price
list of artificial and natural wood ornaments.
34 lvs., wrap.

1889 Kansas City. Mo.   MoSHi
RITZLER, J.A. Ill. catalog of architectural
ornaments.

1900 Chicago   ICHi
ROBERTS, F.L. & CO. Official catalog of
blinds, doors, sash, stairs, parquetry floors,
etc. Startling col. ill. circular of OOM-
BULL and JOHN-PAUL doors tipped in.
7x10, 350pp., ills., pls., col. pls., cl.

c.1900 Chicago   NNMM
------ General catalog #500. Blinds, sash,
mantels, interior woodwork, grilles, etc.
443pp., ill. throughout, cl.

1898 Rock Island, Ill.
ROCK ISLAND SASH & DOOR WORKS
Design book for stairs, store fronts, mouldings, parquetry floors, hardware, stained
glass windows, etc. 8vo., 392pp., ills., col.
pls., cl.

1900 Milwaukee   CCuMGM
ROCKWELL MFG. CO. Ill. catalog of mill-
work, original pat. doweled doors, panels,
mouldings, plans, etc. 12mo., 282pp., pict.
wrap.

1877 Trenton, N. J.   MnHi
ROEBLING, JOHN A. & SONS CO. See also
machinery. Ill. catalog of cables and wire
for tramways, bridges and power transmission.

1886 Trenton, N. J.   MnHi
------ Ill. catalog.

1896 Trenton, N. J.   NjR
------ Ill. catalog - new method   CHi
of transmitting power, etc., cables, wire
bridges, etc. 8vo., 40pp., pict. wrap.

1882 Rochester, N. Y.   NNMM
RUNYON, W.C. & CO. Ill. catalog of wood-
mosaic floors and borders. 50 patterns in
16pp., wrap.

1886 Cincinnati   MnHi
SAGENDORPH IRON ROOFING, CORRUGAT-
ING & PAINT CO. Ill. catalog of roofing
materials. 12mo., 32pp., pict. wrap.

1888 Cincinnati   OC
------ Tinted ills., 16mo. 10 page folder
of bricks, clapboards, cleat roofing and
shingles.

1891 St. Louis   OrU
ST. LOUIS CORRUGATING CO. Ill. catalog
of sheet iron building materials, interior
and exterior - designs furnished in all
gauges. 4to., 7pp.

1893 Baltimore   N
SCHERER, JOHN & SON. Ill. catalog of
sash, doors, mouldings, pews, balusters,
newels, bay windows and store fronts. 4to.,
155pp., fine ills., pict. wrap.

c.1898 St. Louis   MoSHi
SEIFERT, FRANK A. PLASTIC RELIEF CO.
Ill. catalog of ornaments.

1873 Rome, N. Y.   N
SELDEN, G.V. Price list of mouldings,
ornaments, brackets, doors, gables, newels,
cornices, stairs, etc. 8vo., 52pp., pls.
throughout, wrap.

1862 New York & Boston   DAIA
            MBAt DoU   KU   DLC
            NN   PU   MH   MB
SKILLINGS, D.N. & FLINT, D.B. Ill. catalog of Portable Sectional Houses. Pat. Nov.
19, 1861. 4to., 54pp. with 49 pls. covering
24 designs, with separate price list from
$125. to $650. First house catalog issued
in U. S.

1862   New York & Boston
------ No. 1 - $125. is a railroad station,
but suggested also for a lodge or summer
house. No. 23 was shipped to Port Royal
to Adams & Co. to be used as an express
office. No. 22 is a seaside villa with a de-
tached kitchen, but also recommended as a
plantation or country residence. The P.T.
Barnum of the firm goes on to explain that
with a chapel and school house, a village
can be built in an incredibly short time.
No. 18 is a hospital for $550. Officers'
Quarters building is also suggested for
bathing houses.

These buildings, the manufacturers point
out, can be set up in less than three hours
by two or three men with no knowledge of
construction! They can also be taken down
and moved to another location, and set up
again in the same time.

Patent rights are for sale on reasonable
terms. These buildings, ready for use, will
be sent per order, neatly packed, to any
part of the United States, or to any foreign
country. There is no mention as to who
pays the postage.

1882   Minneapolis   MnHi
SMITH & WYMAN. Successors to Smith,
Parker & Co. Ill. price list of balusters,
blinds, doors, mouldings, newels, stair railings, etc. 12mo., discount sheet, wrap.

1885   Minneapolis   MnHi
------ Ill. catalog.

1886   Minneapolis   MnHi
------ Ill. catalog.

1884   Canton, O.   MnHi
SNYDER, T.C. & CO. Ill. catalog   DeU
of improved sheet iron roofings and iron
ore paints for roofs. 16mo., 16pp., pict.
wrap.

1899   Chicago   MoSHi
SOUTH CHICAGO & CALUMET LUMBER
CO. Ill. catalog and price list of mouldings,
shingles, etc.

1901   Chicago   ICHi
SOUTH SIDE LUMBER CO. Ill. catalog of
lumber, lath, mill work, shingles, mantels,
mouldings, newels and rails. 8vo., 48pp.,
wrap.

1895   St. Louis   MoSHi
SOUTHER, E.E. IRON CO. Ill. catalog -
roofing department - roofing, siding, ceilings, etc. 7x10, 40pp., wrap.

c.1900   St. Louis   MoSHi
------ Catalog #18. Store fronts,   NNMM
roofs, ceilings, crestings, finials, weathervanes, tools, etc. 8vo., 210pp., fine ills.,
red ptd. wrap.

1874   Boston   NNMM
SPURR, CHARLES W. Ill. catalog of wood
hangings. 10 lvs., wrap.

c.1880   Boston   NNMM
------ Ill. catalog of papered wood hangings. 16mo., 20pp., pls. of decorated rooms,
wrap.

c.1890   Boston   NNMM
------ Designs of Spurr's pat. wood
carvings, veneers, etc. for panelling, parquetry floors and ceilings. 4to., 48pp. of
ills., pict. wrap.

1881   Jersey City   NjR
STANDARD WOOD TURNING CO. Catalog
of machine turned balusters, posts, newels,
roof ornaments, mantels and porch brackets. 12mo., 32pp., fine ills., pict. wrap.

1884   Jersey City   PKsL
------ Ill. catalog. Revised prices. 8pp.,
wrap.

1896   Jersey City   OHi
------ Ill. catalog. 12mo., 40pp., wrap.

1900   Jersey City   MoSHi
------ Ill. catalog of wood turnings,
mantels, etc.

1879   Washington, D. C.   DSi
STOCKSTILL, D.W. & CO. Ill. catalog of
architectural sheet metal work. 60pp.,
wrap.

1893   Philadelphia   PKsL
SWEENY, GEORGE. See Stoves and Heating Appliances, fire bricks, etc.

1892   Niles, O.   OHi
SYKES IRON & STEEL ROOFING CO. 15th
annual catalog of architectural building
materials. 8vo., 40pp., fine ills., wrap.

1891-2   Hartford, Conn.   NNMM
TAFT CO. Ill., desc. and priced catalog of
natural and artificial wood ornaments and
turnings. 20pp., wrap.

1886   Columbus, O.   OHi
TEACHOUT, A. & CO. Ill. catalog of sash,
doors, blinds, mouldings, balusters, newel
posts, window glass and hardware for
builders.

1886 Chicago   NNMM
THOMPSON, C.C. & WALKUP CO. Ill.
catalog of finish, mouldings, doors, frames,
brackets, stair work, etc. 98pp., fine ills.

1890 Trenton, N. J.   NjR
TRENTON IRON CO. Bleichert pat.
system of wire rope tramways showing
spans for river, factory and mine. Sq.
8vo., 36pp., fld. pls.. maps and plans.

1887 Mason City, Ia.   MnHi
TURNER, I. & CO. Ill. catalog of   IaHi
coal, lime, stucco, cement, plastering hair,
brick, tile, chimney pipe, etc. 16mo., 24pp.,
pict. wrap. of freight car ill. all products.

1885 Chicago   ICHi
UNION FOUNDRY & PULLMAN CAR
WHEEL WORKS. N.S. Bouton, Pres.
Manual of ills. for architectural iron work
patterns; information for architects and
builders. Tall 16mo., 144pp., fine pls. of
architectural columns, caps, pilasters and
ornamental iron in use in Chicago buildings.

1899 St. Louis   MoSHi
UNION PRESS BRICK WORKS. Ill. catalog
and price list of bricks.

1892 Chicago   NNMM
UNIVERSAL MOULDING BOOK. See Rand,
McNally & Co.

1898 Cleveland   ICHi
VAN DORN IRON WORKS CO. Jail Archi-
tects and Builders. Catalog #53. 4to.,
24pp., fine ills. of Maryland State Pen,
Hartford Co. Jail and others in New York,
Pennsylvania, Michigan, etc.

1882 Rutland & Proctor, Vt.   VtHi
VERMONT MARBLE CO. Partners:
Vermont Marble Co., Sheldon & Sons, Gilson
& Woodfin, Ripley Sons and Sherman,
Gleason & Proctor. Price list for finished
monuments in Rutland and Sutherland Falls
marble for season, subject to change.
Separate titles for each partner. 12mo.,
ills. throughout.

1891 Rutland & Proctor, Vt.   VtHi
------ Ill. catalog of marble work from
quarries. 7x10, 34pp., photo. engraved pls.,
wrap.

c.1900 Rutland & Proctor, Vt.   VtHi
--- Miracles in marble applied to one
of America's oldest industries. 12mo.,
22pp., fine ills. VtHi also has a collection
of Vermont Marble Co. catalogs, col. pls.,
memorial issues showing national and state
buildings and monuments right up to 1943.

1857 New York   NNMM
VIEILLE MONTAGNE ZINC MINING CO.
Ill. and priced circular on zinc roofing.

c.1858 Lancaster, Pa.   NNMM
WATER STREET IRON WORKS. Ill., desc.
and priced catalog of cast iron railings.
34pp. with 17 col. pls. of designs, wrap.

c.1850 Boston   NNMM
WEBSTER & KINGMAN. Broadside catalog
of the Papier Mache Depot - carved ornaments for house and ship. 16x24 offering
1200 designs, 40 woodcuts of ornaments.

1890 Cortland, N. Y.   MiDbF
WICKWIRE BROTHERS. Ill. catalog of
scenic and pictorial wire cloth for screens,
etc. 8vo., 24pp., pict. wrap.

1895 San Francisco   CHi
WILSON & BROTHER. Prices current of
balusters, blinds, doors, sash, stairs, newel
posts, railings, etc. 12mo., 80pp., fine ills.,
wrap.

1885 Philadelphia   PHi
WILSON BROTHERS & CO. Architects.
Catalog of work executed. 4to., 70pp.,
fine pls.

1888 New York   N
WILSON, JAMES G. Catalog of Wilson's
pat. rolling blinds and shutters. Gold Medal
awards, etc. 8vo., 65pp., ills. of designs -
Eastlake, Queen Ann carved partitions, etc.
Pict. wrap.

1889 New York   DSi
WILSON, J. GODFREY. Ill. catalog of
blinds and shutters. 66pp., wrap.

c.1886 St. Louis   MoSHi
WINKLE, JOSEPH TERRA COTTA CO. Ill.
catalog of stock designs in terra cotta work
and architectural materials.

1894 Chicago   DeU
WINSLOW BROTHERS CO. Ornamental
Iron Works. Catalog of architectural ornamental iron. Photo. edition. 4to., 168 pls.
of buildings from Maine to Florida and
Texas, naming architects using Winslow
products.

1877 New York   MH-BA
WOOD CARPET CO. Parquet and inlaid
floors, wood carpets. 3x4, 16pp., ill.

1893 Boston   NNMM
WOOD MOSAIC CO. Branches in New York
& Chicago. Ill. and desc. catalog of parquetry. 4to., 16pp., 16 tinted litho. pls. of
designs, wood carpets, borders, strips,
corners, etc.

1897 Boston   CtY
  ------ Ill. catalog.

1874 Canton, O.   OHi
  WROUGHT IRON BRIDGE CO. Catalog of
  designs for wrought iron bridges. 8vo.,
  56pp., fine ills., wrap.

1871 Chicago   MoSHi
  ZINC ROOFING & ORNAMENTAL WORKS.
  Ill. catalog #1.

1873 Chicago   MoSHi
  ------ Ill. catalog #2.

If when you have checked this section you find that your dictionary definition of architectural building materials differs from mine, let me make a few suggestions. Experience with library interest and classification has been my guide to selections. Because of definite interest in weather-vanes, bathrooms, ornamental ironwork, decorative fences and other embellishments, such goods have been segregated and given chapters of their own.

Chapter 4

Artists' Materials & Supplies

This group of catalogs offers a small but well selected library for research in the field of the brushes whose delicate strokes modern experts study, the carefully cabinet-made wooden paint boxes of the last century with their assortment of available colors, canvasses and stencils for amateurs and professionals, boards, papers, wax, inks and other supplies, that, like the accumulations at a country auction, are too numerous to mention. Frames and framing tools are also included in these pictorial records.

For those who like first dates and earliest known catalogs, I call attention to the Devoe and Raynolds listings which will in themselves explain why I do not feel justified in making definite statements. Even if Mr. Bishop's History of American Manufactures is ever brought up to date - or even to 1900 - the question as to when a firm established in 1825 actually compiled and issued its first catalog will not necessarily be solved. Very few catalogs definitely identify themselves as the first catalog issued: about these, of course, there is no question. In most cases there is little to prove whether the located catalog is the fifth or the twentieth, unless, of course, the date coincides with the date of founding.

c.1886 Detroit   MiU-H
ANGELL, GEORGE R. Art Store and Galleries. Catalog of oil and water colors, brushes, canvas and all artists' materials. 12mo., 40pp., ptd. wrap.

1877 Boston   MH-BA
AVERILL & HUNTING. Successors to H.S. Doane & Co. Est. before 1827. Priced catalog of all kinds of brushes. 24mo., 16pp., wrap.

1895 St. Louis   MoSHi
BAXTER, C.O. & CO. Ill. catalog of mouldings and picture frames, and artists' supplies.

c.1895 New York   NNMM
BELL COMPANY. Catalog of stencil work for home decoration - artistic, fascinating and inexpensive. 24mo., 24pp., stencil designs pp. 8-23, pict. wrap.

c.1900 Chicago   NNMM
CHICAGO SIGN & BOARD CO. Catalog #10. 98pp. of ills., and detailed desc., wrap.

c.1880 Cincinnati   OC
CLOSSON, A.B., JR. Compliments of . . . Ill. prices current of all materials for decorations, canvas on stretchers, frames, brass and glass plaques, tools, etc.

c.1832 Boston
COTTON, N.D. Catalog of drawing materials and stationery, valentines, writing cases and desks, paper weights, pens, ink, wax, drawing papers, boards, etc. Dated by Nicholson's Drawing Book for 1832. 16mo., 32pp., pict. wrap.

1890 Chicago   OrU
DEARBORN ART CO. Catalog and price list of portraits and frames mfg. by . . . Fol., ill.

1878 New York   NNMM
DEVOE, F.W. & CO. Priced catalog of artists' materials. Sq. 12mo., 250pp., ill. throughout, glt. pict. cl. Trademark dated 1852. Plate of first building erected in 1852.

c.1892 New York & Chicago   MdTanSW
DEVOE, F.W. & RAYNOLDS,   NNMM
C.T. CO. Est. 1755. Ill. catalog of artists' materials. 12mo., 320pp., fine ills., cl.

These two listings call for comment. There is no mention of C.T. Raynolds in the 1878 catalog issued by F.W. Devoe at the corner of Fulton & William Sts. in October 1878; yet a very few years later, when C.T. Raynolds was located at 106 Fulton St., New York, a catalog is issued under both names AS ESTABLISHED in 1755.

This statement, found in this c.1892 catalog, is used in Etna M. Kelly's Business Founding Date Directory published in 1954 by Morgan & Morgan.

Seeger & Guernsey's Cyclopaedia of Manufactures and Products of the U.S., published

in 1890, lists these two firms separately.
Was C.T. Raynolds established in 1755?
Obviously F.W. Devoe began business about
1852 when they boast of their first building.
What is the answer?

C. Leander Bishop, in his History of American Manufactures does not mention either
of these gentlemen. He also makes it very
clear that there was very little paint manufactured in the colonies before the Revolution.

It seems quite certain that Devoe &
Raynolds as a firm could not have been established in 1755. Perhaps you don't care.
However, now and then it does seem worth
while to correct a few of the errors that are
used to propagate and multiply incorrect
history.

1897 St. Louis   MoSHi
ERKER BROTHERS OPTICAL CO. Ill.
catalog of artists' materials. Sq. 12mo.,
120pp., wrap.

c.1870 New York   NNMM
FECHTELER, JULIUS. Ill. catalog of
transfer ornaments, designs of decal. representing many objects. 20 lvs. of designs
with price list. Wrap. See Palm & Fechteler.

nd. Cleveland   NNMM
FLEHARTY & WOODRUFF. Ill. catalog and
retail price list for general engravers;
steel letter and stencil cutters. 18pp., wrap.

1875 Boston   NNC
FROST & ADAMS. Est. 1848. Ill. catalog
of artists' materials, paint boxes, brushes,
easels, etc. 8vo., 48pp., pict. wrap.

1878 Boston   NNC
------ Ill. catalog, pocket edition. 16mo.,
133pp., fine ill. ref.

c.1885 Boston   MBSPNEA
------ Ill. catalog. 16mo., 152pp., wrap.

c.1900 Boston
------ Ill. catalog of artists' materials and
pyrography supplies. 158pp., wrap.

1898 Baltimore   NNMM
FURST BROTHERS. Ill. catalog of art supplies, frames, etc. 4to., 48pp., pict. wrap.

1886 Chicago   MnHi
GERTS, LUMBARD & CO. Ill. catalog of
brushes, paints, etc.

1887 Chicago   MnHi
------ Ill. catalog of artists' materials and
supplies.

1876 New York   NSbSM
HANEY, JESSE & CO. Standard   NNMM
scroll book of ornaments for car and
carriage painters. 200 designs, 8vo., ills.,
pict. wrap.

1884 New York   MnHi
HANLON & GOODMAN. Ill. catalog of
paints and brushes.

c.1890 Baltimore   NNMM
HIRSCHBERG, HOLLANDER & CO. Ill.
catalog of materials for designers, decorators, lithographers, sign painters, etc.
4to., 208pp., ill. throughout, pict. wrap.

c.1892 Baltimore   NNMM
------ Ill. catalog of designs for china,
pottery and glass, stencils, tools, etc. 8vo.,
274pp., dec. wrap.

1883 Syracuse   NSyHi
KENYON, POTTER & CO. Ill. trade price
list of paints, brushes and artists' supplies,
including feather dusters and shoe brushes.
Tall 16mo., pict. wrap.

nd. Philadelphia   PHi
KEYSTONE BRUSH CO. Barker, Moore &
Mein. Ill. price list of artists' materials.
12mo., 16pp., pict. wrap.

c.1876 Chicago
LOCKE, A.W. Ill. price list of decal.,
chromos, embossed pictures; complete
workshop for $1.25. 24mo., 16pp., one ill.,
wrap.

c.1876 Chicago
LUEBKER, HENRY. Price list of transfer
ornaments, etc. 24mo., 16pp., pict. wrap.

c.1900 New Haven   NNMM
MALLEY, EDWARD CO. Ill. catalog of
pryrographic supplies. 72pp., fine ills.,
pict. wrap.

1875 Cincinnati & New York
PALM, CHARLES & CO. Issued for
Wadsworth Bros. & Howland. Price list of
transfer ornaments and painters' supplies.
Ornaments for buggies, carriages, wagons,
cutters, sleighs, agricultural implements,
brushes, etc. Sheets of stencils. 8vo.,
48pp., a few ills., wrap.

1877 Cincinnati & New York   NSbSM
------ Sample book of transfer   NNMM
ornaments. 42 pls. of designs for buggy,
coach, carriage, scrolls for sleighs, coats
of arms, gearing, corner pieces, etc.
Large 4to., 42pp., pict. wrap.

c.1880 Cincinnati & Chicago   NNMM
------ Fol. broadside of decal.   MnHi
transfer letters for signs, wagons, carriages, coaches, buggies, etc. Ill.

1887 Cincinnati & Chicago   OC
----- Ill. price list of transfer ornaments
for buggy, coach and carriage.

nd. Cincinnati & Chicago   OC
------ Ill. catalog of Palm's pat. transfer
letters.

1880 New York & Cincinnati   MdTanSW
PALM & FECHTELER. Price list of transfer ornaments, decal. and carriage painters'
supplies; directions for use, etc. 8vo.,
32pp., wrap.

c.1880 New York & Cincinnati   NSbSM
------ Sample book of transfer ornaments,
designs, figures and stencils. 4to., ill.

nd. New York & Cincinnati   NSbSM
------ Price list of transfer ornaments,
etc. 14pp.

1884 New York
PEARL ART CO. 8pp. of art supplies. See
also photography.

1881 Chicago   MnHi
RAYNOLDS, C.T. & CO. Ill. catalog of
brushes, paints and artists' materials. See
F.W. Devoe & C.T. Raynolds for details.

1880 Chicago   NNMM
RICE, C.F. Ill. catalog of mirrors, frames,
mouldings and artists' supplies.

c.1900 Chicago   NNMM
THAYER & CHANDLER MFG. Ill. catalog
of pyrographic supplies. 90pp. of ills.,
wrap.

1877 New York   NSbSM
VALENTINE & CO. Coach and car varnish.
The Tally Ho! 16mo., 28pp. col. pict. wrap.
with a fine col. plate frs. of the regulation
coach built by Brewster & Co. Not a catalog
but a fine piece of brochure advertising.

1874 Boston   NSbSM
WADSWORTH BROTHERS & HOWLAND.
See also Chas. Palm & Co. Price list of

transfer ornaments and supplies for carriage, coach and sign painters, etc. 8vo.,
24pp., fine ills., wrap.

1876 Boston   MH-BA
------ Ill. catalog of artists' and painters'
supplies. Large 12mo., 58pp., wrap.

1883 Boston
------ Ill. catalog for architects, artists
and engravers. 8vo., 144pp., pict. wrap.

1895 Boston   DLC
------ Ill. catalog of colors, instruments,
brushes and supplies. 8vo., 178pp., fine
ref., wrap.

c.1870 Boston
WALKER, A.A. & CO. Catalog of artists'
materials, pocket edition. Instruments,
paint boxes, crayons, shades and decorative
novelties. 12mo., 160pp., fine ills., wrap.

nd. St. Louis   MoSHi
WEBER, F. & CO. Ill. price list #190.
Pyrography and wood burning supplies and
artists' materials.

c.1850 Boston
WHEELER, ASAHEL. Artists' colorman.
Depot of paints. Offers paints and materials, brushes, canvas, paint boxes, tinware,
varnishes, tools, etc. 12mo., 44pp., dec.
wrap.

c.1860 Boston
WHIPPLE, M.J. Ill. catalog of artists'
materials, sketch folios, bds., paint books,
boxes, etc. 16mo., 47pp., wrap.

c.1894 Boston   MH-BA
WHITING, JOHN L. & SON CO. Est. 1864.
Catalog of brushes. 8vo., 180pp., ill.

1874 Philadelphia   MdTanSW
WILSON, HOOD & CO. Ill. catalog of
frames, mouldings, picture nails, etc. and
artistic accessories. 80pp. eye opening
price list. Wrap.

Since paint boxes, brushes, compasses and other artists' tools were sold in the general stores, don't
overlook the chapters General Hardware and House Furnishings. Also, since it is a question in many
minds just when a house painter, car painter or carriage painter becomes an artist, I suggest a hasty
check of Paints, in which grouping many catalogs offer supplies for all painters.

Chapter 5

Automobiles

No creation by Americans for Americans has ever stirred both the souls of contemporary users and the possessive hearts of the antiquarian collectors of the next generation as much as the American automobile. Greeted with open arms - after the first few years, of course - by the travelling minded public as each new model appeared, and treasured by the individual collector and museum as soon as they gathered a good vintage and enough dust, the automobile today stands first in the field of popular Americana.

Although many libraries and museums, both private and public, have hoarded this colorful literature for quite some years, when the time came to count, locate and record it, there was little available. With the help of the curators and librarians of the outstanding collections, I feel that I have listed a fairly complete roll call of catalogs available for research.

The old garages of the first decade of this century are fading into American history with the blacksmith shops and stables. There may still be examples hiding in attics, libraries and private collections that we can smoke out for a revised and more complete edition.

1896 Chicago, Indianapolis & Toledo PP
AMERICAN BICYCLE CO. The Trimoto.
No data available.

1899 Indianapolis NLIAM
------ Ill. catalog of electric vehicles.
12mo., 20pp.

1900 Chicago NLIAM
------ Catalog of electric vehicles. 8vo.,
26pp., ills. throughout, wrap.

1900 Chicago NLIAM
------ Rambler sales dept. catalog showing
two models of Rambler - runabout and
surrey. Gas. 16mo., 8pp., ill. as above.
N.B. This make appears to have no connection with the Rambler built from 1902
on by Thomas B. Jeffrey Co. of Wisconsin.

1900 Indianapolis NLIAM
------ Waverly auto dept. - circular of
Waverly electric cars. 8vo., 32pp., ill.
throughout.

1901 Indianapolis NLIAM
------ Waverly auto dept. Ill. folder of
Waverly electric vehicles. 16mo., 7pp., 7
ills.

1901 Indianapolis NLIAM
------ Catalog of Waverly electrics.
12mo., 16pp., 2 col. drawings on wrap.

1896 Chicago NLIAM
AMERICAN ELECTRIC VEHICLE CO.
Catalog of electric carriages. 8vo., 24pp.,
11 ills. of 8 styles.

1897 Chicago NLIAM
------ 2 sales letters to L.M. Alden.

c.1899 Chicago NLIAM
------ American electric Stanhope and
Run-About-Buggy. 2 lvs., ill., 6x6.

1900 Chicago NLIAM
------ Catalog, 6-1/4x6-1/2, 20pp., 8 ills.

1900 Chicago NLIAM
------ Catalog of electric vehicles. 8vo.,
24pp. with 21 drawings of electrics.

c.1900 Chicago MiD
AMERICAN VEHICLE CO. Twentieth
century movement. 16pp., ills. of models
and styles.

1899 Ardmore, Pa. NLIAM
THE AUTOCAR CO. Catalog of gasoline
carriages. 32mo., 12pp., ill.
N.B. Earliest known catalog of oldest
maker of motor vehicles in U. S. still
in business.

1902 Ardmore, Pa. PP
------ Photostat only of 1902 catalog.

1900 New York   NLIAM
AUTOMOBILE CO. OF AMERICA. Factory
at Jersey City. Catalog of Gasmobile
standard model runabouts. Ills. of cars
under construction in factory. 18mo.,
26pp., wrap.

1900 New York   NLIAM
------ Ill. folder of runabout and surrey.
12mo., 4pp.

1901 New York   NLIAM
------ Gasmobile Stanhope and surrey
models. 12mo., 4pp., ills. of models and
bus.

c.1901 New York   MiDbF
------ Factory at Marion, N. J. Catalog
of the Gasmobile. 16mo., 11pp., fine ills.,
wrap.

c.1900 Cleveland   MiD
BAKER MOTOR VEHICLE CO. Catalog of
Baker vehicles. 16pp., ills. of models.

1895 New York   NLIAM
BARROWS MOTOR VEHICLE CO. Catalog
of Barrow power equipment and electric
vehicles. Earliest catalog in NLIAM. N.B.
This vehicle is described in the Horseless
Age for November, 1895.

c.1899 Indianapolis   MiD
BLACK, C. & H. MFG. CO. The Black
Automobile. 6pp. with ills. of 5 models.
See Horseless Age, June 14, 1899, page 10
for further details.

1900 Buffalo   NLIAM
BUFFALO ELECTRIC CARRIAGE CO.
3 page folder, 24mo., with ill. of Buffalo
Stanhope.

1901 Buffalo   MiDbF
BUFFALO GASOLINE MOTOR CO. Catalog.
12mo., 32pp., ills. of styles, wrap.

1900 Cartaret, N. J.   NLIAM
CANDA MFG. CO. Folder, 4x7, 6pp., ills.
of The Auto-Quadricycle, Model of 1900.

1900 Cartaret, N. J.   NLIAM
------ Catalog, 4x7, 6 ills., 12pp. of Canda
Motor Vehicles; Stanhope, Spider Runabout,
Auto-Quadricycle, A-Q Van and Auto-
Tricycle.

nd. Philadelphia   PHi
CAREY - McFALL CO. Ill. catalog of
automobile body hardware, hearse mountings and lamps.

c.1900 Chicago   MiD
CHICAGO MOTOR VEHICLE CO. Catalog
of Chicago Motor Vehicles. 24pp. with fine
ills. of models and styles.

c.1900 Columbus, O.   MiU-T
COLUMBUS BUGGY CO. Catalog of electrics. 20pp. More complete listing
unavailable.

1900 Buffalo   NBuHi
CONRAD MOTOR CARRIAGE CO. Preliminary catalog of automobiles. Fine ill.
brochure.

1900 Cambridgeport, Mass.   MiDbF
CREST MFG. CO. Circular of 5-1/2 hp.
duplex motors, ill.

1900 Cambridgeport, Mass.   NLIAM
------ Circular of engines, spark plugs
and gas car model. 16mo., 4pp., ill.

1901 Cambridgeport, Mass.   MiDbF
----- Crest vertical motors. 4pp. with
ill. of 3 hp. roadster.

c.1901 Cambridgeport, Mass.   MiDbF
------ Crest Motors - 3, 4, and 5 hp. -
the lightest and cheapest. 12mo., 4pp.,
Model roadster ill.

1891 Steinway, L. I., N. Y.   MiD
DAIMLER MOTOR CO. Ill. catalog and
price list of gas and petroleum motors for
pleasure boats, carriages, street railway
cars, quadricycles and other purposes. Although devoted mostly to boats and motors,
page 15 is headed Daimler Motor Vehicles -
with desc. and ills. of the motor quadricycle,
the motor carriage and a motor bicycle.
Page 14 however, does admit that the company
is not ready to supply definite figures, but
will as soon as they can show them in actual
operation. 16pp., ills., wrap.

c.1892 Steinway, L. I., N. Y.   CU-A
------ The Daimler Motor - safest, most
economical and perfect gas engine existing.
16mo., 18pp., ills. of motors, boats, pict.
wrap. Motor launch - page 8 has been applied
very successfully to propulsion of boats,
street cars, fire engines, road wagons and
carriages. A map with directions for visiting the plant have been added to the 1891 ed.

1901 Brooklyn   MiDbF
De DION-BOUTON   PP   NvRH NNQ
MOTORETTE CO. Catalog of Motorettes.
16mo., 18pp., ills. of styles and models,
spec. and details.

1901 Brooklyn   MiDbF
------ Catalog for 1901 season.   NNQ
8vo., 4pp., ills. of 6 delightful models.

c.1901 Brooklyn   MiDbF
------ Sixteen hundred mile trip   PP
over American roads, etc. 16mo., 24pp.,
pict. wrap. of runabout.

1896 Springfield, Mass.   NLIAM
DURYEA MOTOR WAGON CO. 3 panel
folder, 24mo., 6pp., ills. of Motor Wagons,
Motors and Automobile Vehicles of all kinds.
Note: Catalog of first production run of
America's first gasoline automobile. Also
letter dated 9-30-96 to Wm. Estes, a pros-
pect from George Henry Hewitt, Pres. of Co.

1898 Springfield, Mass.   NLIAM
------ Catalog. 8vo., 20pp., ills.   PP
of 5 models of gasoline cars and one launch.
Also cuts and information of first Duryea,
winners of Chicago Times-Herald Race,
1895, Cosmopolitan Race in N. Y., 1896 and
London to Brighton Run, 1896.

1897 Reading, Pa.   PP
DURYEA POWER CO. America's Leader.

1899 Reading, Pa.   PP
------ See Peoria Rubber Mfg. Co.

1901 Reading, Pa.   NvRH
------ What They Say, or The Voice of the
People on Motor Vehicles. Ills. of mechan-
ism and 3 wheeled Duryea.

1901 Reading, Pa.   MiDbF
       Catalog of Duryea Motor Vehicles,
16mo., 16pp., pict. wrap. of landolet model.

1901 St. Louis   MiD
DYKE, A.L. Catalog #6. Automobile parts
and supplies. 12mo., 47pp., ills. of Dyke's
Automorette #6.

1900 South Easton, Mass.   NvRH
ECLIPSE MOTOR CO. Ill. catalog of
Eclipse Steam Motor Carriages. 12pp.,
wrap.

1896 New York & Philadelphia   NLIAM
ELECTRIC CARRIAGE & WAGON CO.
Sheet, 8vo., 1 page, ill. of Electric Surrey,
designed by Morris & Slallom of Philadelphia. Notation in red at bottom of 5 mile
record set at Narragansett Park, Providence
on 9-11-96.

1900 New York   NLIAM
ELECTRIC VEHICLE CO. Catalog, 8vo.,
30pp., prof. ills. of 20 models of the
Columbia electric automobiles and two
gasoline models.

c.1900 New York   NLIAM
----- Folder of Up-to-date Transportation,
describes electric cab service of the company in New York. 32mo., 4pp., ill.

c.1901 New York   MiD
------ Catalog of Columbia Gasoline Runabouts. 14pp., ills., wrap.

c.1901 New York   MiD
------ Catalog of Columbia & Riker automobiles. 16pp., ills., wrap.

c.1901 New York
------ Columbia automobiles, electric and
gasoline. 30pp., ills., wrap.

1900 Chicago   NLIAM
ELGIN AUTOMOBILE CO. Sheet, 4to., 1 page,
ills. of The Winner Gasoline Wagon and The
Elgin Electric Stanhope.

c.1901 Clyde, O.   MiD
ELMORE MFG. CO. Catalog of Elmore
automobiles. 12mo., ills., wrap.

1900 Akron, O.   OAkF
FIRESTONE TIRE & RUBBER CO. Facts
for the Fall. Firestone side wire tires.
24mo., 12pp., ills. and prices.

1898 Chicago   MiD
FISCHER EQUIPMENT CO. Ill. brochure
on Wood's Moto-Vehicles. 22pp., wrap.

1902   PP
FOSTER AUTOMOBILE MFG. CO. Catalog
of the Foster Steam Wagon.

c.1900 Geneva, O.   NLIAM
GENEVA AUTOMOBILE & MFG. CO.
Folder, 12mo., 8pp. Ills. of Geneva Steam
Vehicles.

1900 Holyoke, Mass.   NLIAM
HOLYOKE AUTOMOBILE CO. Catalog,
8vo., 8pp., one ill. of Gasoline Carriages.
Wrap.

c.1901-2 Kenosha, Wis.   MiDbF
JEFFERY, THOMAS B. & CO. Catalog of
the Rambler Automobile. 12mo., 22pp.,
tinted pict. wrap, ills. of Model C and
photos of blacksmith shop, assembly room,
engine room, etc.

c.1900 Buffalo   NLIAM
KENSINGTON BICYCLE MFG. CO. Booklet:
The Horse and his Successor, Kensington
Automobiles. 8vo., 9pp., no ill. Meager
description of electric vehicles.

1901 New Haven   MiDbF
KIDDER MOTOR VEHICLE CO. Steam the
motive power - 1000 pounds - $1000. Cir-
cular with 2 photo ills. First issued.

1901 Springfield, Mass.   NvRH
KNOX AUTOMOBILE CO. Model 1901.
8vo., 8pp., 2 pls. - Knox delivery, three
wheeler and gas runabout. First car, first
catalog.

c.1901 Springfield, Mass.   MiDbF
------ Knoxmobile Model B. 8vo., 4pp.,
ill. with details and prices.

1899 Everett, Mass.   NvRH
LEACH MOTOR CO. 16 page catalog with ills.
of steam pleasure and commercial cars
with specs.

1899 Boston   MiDbF
LIQUID AIR, POWER & AUTOMO-   NvRH
BILE CO. Prospectus. 4to., 16pp., ills. of
Peerless coupe, trap and model #1; history
of steam vehicles from 1763; ports. of
Code, Knudsen and Chase. Pict. wrap.

1899 New York   MiU-T
LOCOMOBILE CO. OF AMERICA.   NvRH
8 page brochure by Stephen L. Pierce. Three
miles for a cent by motor carriage. Ills.
and detailed desc.

1900 New York   MiU-T
------ Catalog of   TWS   NvRH NLIAM
1900 models of the Locomobile steam automobiles. 12mo., 20pp., ills. of styles 1, 2,
3, 4, 5, 6 -- Stanhope, Locosurrey, Loco-
racer and Lococycle. $700. to $1200.
Fine pict. wrap.

1900 New York   NLIAM
----- Factories at Worcester & Westboro,
Mass. & Bridgeport, Conn. Catalog of
Locomobile Steam Automobiles. 8vo., 30pp.
Ills. of styles 2, 02, 3, 03, 003, 4, 5, and 05.
1901 models.

1900 New York   NLIAM
------ Styles in brief. 4to., 4pp., letter
type desc. with 2 ills., two col. type.

1900 New York   NLIAM
------ Bridgeport factory. Test. booklet.
Some practical tests of the Locomobile.
4to., 8pp., ill., wrap.

1900 Westfield, Mass.   NLIAM
LOOMIS AUTOMOBILE CO. Folder, 8vo.,
4pp., ills. of the Loomis Automobile, gas,
Models 1 , ill., 2 and 3.

1900 Westfield, Mass.   NLIAM
------ 18mo., 8 page catalog with green
cover of Models 1, 2 and 3. Three ills.

c.1900 Everett, Mass.   MiDbF
MILNE, FRANK. Successor to Milne &
Killam Mfg. Co. Catalog of steam automobiles built to order. 8vo., 4pp., ills. of
roadster, burner and boiler, with desc.,
directions and prices.

1900 Milwaukee   NLIAM
MILWAUKEE AUTOMOBILE CO. Catalog
of steam motor vehicles - styles A, B, D,
F, H - passenger - and L - light delivery.

12mo., 32pp., ill. throughout, center spread
engraving, details and test.

c.1900 Milwaukee   MiDbF
------ Catalog of Model C. 12mo., 6pp.,
ill.

1900 Tarrytown-on-the-Hudson   NLIAM
MOBILE CO. OF AMERICA. Folder, 8vo.,
4pp., ill., 2 col. text, mostly tests.entitled:
Points to be Considered in Buying an Automobile. Re Mobile steam cars.

1900 Tarrytown-on-the-Hudson   NLIAM
------ Single sheet, 8vo., 1 page telling of
the exhibition on the roof of Madison Square
Garden where the Mobile was demonstrated
on a 40% grade.

c.1900 LaPorte, Ind.   MiD
MUNSON CO. Mfg. of Automobiles.
Automobiles adapted to all uses. 16pp., ill.
of models.

c.1900   MiDbF
NATIONAL. Model 135. Designed for the
new Edison battery. 1 leaf, ills. with list of
regular models - prices $1250. to $1800.

1901 Detroit   NvRH
NORTHERN RUNABOUT CO. Utility is the
basis of beauty. Manual of specs. with ills.

1899 Greenfield, Mass.   NLIAM
OAKMAN MOTOR VEHICLE CO. Hertel
Motor Carriage. 24mo., 1 page, ill.

1900 Greenfield, Mass.   NLIAM
----- The Hertel Motor Carriage. MiD
24mo., 2pp., ill.

1899 Warren, O.   NLIAM
OHIO AUTOMOBILE CO. Folder, 4to., 4pp.,
one ill. First catalog of the Parkard automobile.

1900 Detroit   MiDbF
OLDS MOTOR WORKS. Est. 1880. Inc.
1890. Reorganized 1900. Catalog of Olds
engines - stationary, marine and automobile. 32pp., ills. of 3 auto models, col. pict.
wrap.   Offers catalog of gas and electric
cars.

1901 Detroit   NLIAM
------ Catalog of gas and electric runabouts, Oldsmobile curved dash, etc. 18mo.,
33pp., ills. of models. Positive photostat
copy. N.B. This appears to be the first
complete Olds automobile catalog. Engines
made in 1891.

1900 New York   NLIAM
OVERMAN AUTOMOBILE CO. Catalog of
Victor steam automobiles. 12mo., 12pp.,
ill., wrap.

1899 Peoria, Ill.   PP
PEORIA RUBBER MFG. CO. Catalog of
Duryea gasoline motor vehicles.

c.1901 Buffalo, N. Y.   MiDbF
PIERCE, GEORGE N. CO. Pierce   MiD
Motorettes, Tried and True. 12mo., 8pp.,
ills. N.B. Forerunner of the Great Arrow
and Pierce Arrow.

1897 Hartford, Conn.   NLIAM
POPE MFG. CO. Catalog of Columbia
Motor Carriage. 8vo., 8pp. with 3 ills. in-
serted. N.B. First Columbia catalog
located.

1897-8 Hartford, Conn.   NLIAM
------ 18mo., 3pp. ills. of Columbia Mark
#III, IV and V.

1898 Hartford, Conn.   NLIAM
------ Catalog of Columbia Motor
Carriage - its relation to the horse. 16mo.,
25pp.

c.1900 Allston, Mass.   MiDbF
PORTER MOTOR CO., INC. Catalog of The
Portermobile. 12mo., 4pp., with one ill.

c.1900 Allston, Mass.   MiDbF
------ Catalog. 16mo., 11pp., one ill.

c.1896 Brooklyn   NLIAM
RIKER ELECTRIC MOTOR CO. Single
sheet about 6 in. sq. showing ill. of Riker
Electric Trap No. 1.

1899 Brooklyn   NLIAM
------ Folder, 18mo., 4pp., 2 ill. of electric vehicles.

1900 Elizabethport, N. J.   NLIAM
RIKER MOTOR VEHICLE CO. Catalog of
all kinds of electric autos, 8vo., 32pp., ills.
throughout, wrap.

1900 Elizabethport, N. J.   MiD
------ Catalog of Riker Electric   PP
Vehicles. 9pp., ills., wrap.

c.1900 Elizabethport, N. J.   MiD
------ Catalog of Riker Electric Vehicles.
28pp., ills., wrap.

1900 Hyde Park, Mass.   NLIAM
ROBINSON, JOHN T. CO. Circular of the
Robinson Automobiles. Style A - Gas. 8vo.,
4pp., one ill.

c.1900 Boston   NLIAM
ROGERS, W.S., Builder. Catalog of Motor
Carriages. 16mo., 23pp., 10 ills., wrap.

1899 Williamsport, Pa.   PHi
RUSH TIRE CO. The Rush detachable tire.
16pp., ills., cover title.

c.1900 St. Louis   NvRH
ST. LOUIS AUTOMOBILE &   MiD
SUPPLY CO. Catalog of running gears,
engines, supplies and complete gasoline and
electric vehicles. 4to., 32pp., ills. of runabout $1200., Stanhope $1800., electric
delivery wagons $1000. Pict. wrap.

c.1900 St. Louis   MiDbF
------ Something about our latest styles -
Rigs that run. 8vo., 5pp., ills.

1899 St. Louis   NLIAM
ST. LOUIS MOTOR CARRIAGE CO. 4to.,
4 page circular with 2 ills. of gasoline motor
carriages.

1900 St. Louis   NLIAM
------ Circular of St. Louis auto runabouts,
traps, Stanhopes and delivery wagons. 8vo.,
4pp., 4 ills.

c.1901 Philadelphia   MiD
SEARCHMONT MOTOR CO. Catalog of
Searchmont Automobiles. 32pp., ills.

c.1901 Buffalo   MiDbF
SPAULDING AUTOMOBILE &   NBuHi
MOTOR CO. Spaulding Automobiles - The
Runabout. 16mo., 4pp., ills. Runabout
$650. - $700.

1900 Springfield, Mass.   NLIAM
SPRINGFIELD CORNICE WORKS. Folder
of the Meteor automobile. 18mo., 4pp., ill.
N.B. A good example of the booby traps of
classification in this field. Some library
lists have come in with nothing but the date
and company name; this might have gone
under architectural building materials but
for Austin Clark's care and time in preparing complete card data for this guide.

c.1900 Boston   MiDbF
STANLEY MFG. CO. Catalog of the Stanley
automobile, ill. 4to., 12pp., fine ills., pict.
wrap.

c.1900 Keene, N. H.   NLIAM
THE STEAMOBILE CO. Catalog of Keene
Steamobiles. 8vo., 10pp., ills.

c.1900 New York   NLIAM
STEAM VEHICLE CO. OF AMERICA.
Catalog of the Reading steam carriages -
models B, C and D. 8vo., 15pp., 5 ills.,
wrap.

c.1901 New York   MiD
------ Catalog. 32pp., fine ills.

c.1900 Syracuse, N. Y.   NLIAM
STEARNS STEAM CARRIAGE CO. Catalog
of steam carriages. 16mo., 15pp. with 7
ills.

1901 Syracuse, N. Y.   NvRH
------ Steam carriages for business and
pleasure. Ill. brochure with detailed desc.

c.1901 Chicopee Falls   MiD
STEVENS, J. ARMS & TOOL CO. Stevens-
Duryea two cylinder gasoline carriage.
16pp., ills.

1900 Cleveland   NLIAM
STRONG & ROGERS. One page ill. of
electric spider Stanhope.

1901 New York   NvRH
TRIPLER LIQUID AIR POWER CO. 24 page
pamphlet with ills. of vehicles and other
manufactures.

c.1899 Attleboro   MiD
UNITED STATES AUTOMOBILE CO.
Preliminary catalog of motor carriages and
appliances. 29pp. with fine ills.

1899 Waltham   NLIAM
WALTHAM MFG. CO. The Orient electric
runabout. 12mo., one leaf.

1900 Waltham   NLIAM
------ Orient automobiles: Victoriette,
three wheeled autogo, four wheel autobo and
motor bicycle and runabout - all gas models.
Ill. folder opening to 9 in. sq. sheet.

1901 Springfield, Mass.   MiDbF
WARWICK CYCLE & AUTOMOBILE CO.
Catalog of Warwick Automobiles. Sq. 12mo.,
fine ills., pict. wrap.

c.1901 Cleveland   MiD
WHITE SEWING MACHINE CO. The White
Steam Carriage. 48pp., ills.

1901 Cleveland   MiDbF
WINTON MOTOR CARRIAGE CO. The Auto
Era, published by . . . Auto Show No.
8vo., 34pp., fine ills. Not a catalog in the
true sense but a fine reference in Winton
models for 1901.

1900 Chicago & New York   NLIAM
WOODS MOTOR VEHICLE CO. Catalog of
Woods electric carriages. 12mo., 33pp.,
fine ills., wrap.

1900 Chicago & New York   NLIAM
------ Catalog of electric vehicles. 8vo.,
24pp., 10 full col. pls.

1901 Chicago & New York   NvRH
------ Catalog. - Slogan Vivida Vis Animi.
Col. pls. of road wagon, game trap, spider,
brake and station wagon. One of the best.

NLIAM writes that their 1895 Barrows Motor Vehicle Co. catalog is the earliest in the collection.
What is a catalog? When did Daimler actually issue a catalog, as promised as soon as we can show
them in actual operation. In this book it isn't a question of when the first American automobile
roamed the streets, but merely a question of when the manufacturer actually offered it in a catalog.

Chapter 6

Barbers' Supplies

To museums with 19th century barber shops, and to many private collectors of barbers' mugs and bottles, this chapter should offer identification and dates of manufacture for almost every once familiar article of the trade. The fact that it is short does not detract from its historical value as many of these catalogs, covering a period from 1860 to 1910, are far more complete than those compiled in other fields.

Those who are familiar with Carl Drepperd's reference books know that he conscientiously tried to cover the field of American industry. The mere fact that in his Pioneer America - Its First Three Centuries he mentions only two barber supply catalogs, indicates that there are few available today. I am lucky to be able to locate catalogs of both J. B. Williams and W. H. Sample, and to offer them with the conviction that Mr. Drepperd thought very well of their contents.

Included are samples of English barbers' supply catalogs from which I believe American barbers and hairdressers ordered during the Civil War period. These are especially recommended for illustrations of some of the first hand-worked mechanical devices to save the barbers' tired fingers and wrists after a long day.

c.1877 Chicago   ICHi
    ALLING, MRS. W.J. Wholesale price list and catalog of domestic and imported human hair goods. 8vo., 4pp., ill.

1849 New York   N
    BALLARD, O.M. Ballard's improved liquid permanent hair dye - grey hair restored to its original color $1.00. 8vo., 8pp., amusing ills., wrap.

1892 Cincinnati   OC
    BERNINGHAUS, EUGENE. Catalog of barbers' furniture and supplies. 4to., 98pp. of fine ills., many in col., wrap.

    Berninghaus claims the invention of the revolving and reclining chair; 8 full col. pls. 19 ill. pp. of chairs, 33 of furniture, 6 of shaving mugs and 2 of poles. Fancy Japanese fans suspended from the ceiling were operated by the customer - only $3.50 each. Bay rum $1.50 per gallon.

1865 Boston   ICHi
    BURGESS, B.F. & Son. Est.1843. Artificial hair work, toilet goods, interesting facts about hair and hair-trade manufactures. 16mo., 16pp., ill. of wig mould, etc. Wrap.

c.1870 Boston   ICHi
    ------ Rich toilet goods, razors, curling irons, pins, combs, soaps, etc. Test. by Harriet Beecher Stowe. 24mo., 16pp., ills., wrap.

1878 Chicago   ICHi
    BURNHAM, ED. Ill. catalog of human hair goods, tools and materials for the hairdresser - curling irons, needle rooting machines, crimping, frizzing, pinching, pressing irons, wig blocks and waving sticks. 12mo., 36pp., ills., pict. wrap.

1895 San Francisco   OrU
    CASPER, SAM. Price list of human hair and mfg. of real hair goods and fancy ornaments. 8pp.

c.1900 Brooklyn, N. Y.
    CENTRAL SUPPLY CO. Catalog of barbers' supplies, perfumes, Bohemian glass bottles, mugs, bowls, paper vases, jars, glazed pottery stands, urns, cuspidors, etc. Catalogs are our salesmen. 8vo., 40pp. of fine ills., mailing wrap.

1908 Pittsburgh, Pa.   MdTanSW
    COVALT & SMITH. Ill. catalog of barbers' supplies. 40 col. pls. of bottles, bowls, furniture, jars, shaving mugs, poles, vases, etc. 4to., 152pp., pict. wrap.

c.1895 New York
    ELLIOTT'S HUMAN HAIR ESTABLISHMENT. Price list of hair goods. Largest stock of first quality in the city - ash, gray, auburn, golden - old hair taken in exchange. 8vo., 4pp., ill.

49

1867 Birmingham, Eng.   NNMM
GOOD, WILLIAM. Est. 1836. Wholesale
catalog of manufactured hair, combs, toilet
mirrors, brushes, cutlery and tools for
barbers. 8vo., 64pp., ills. of hand rotary
brushes. Child's pat. improved suspending
rotary hair brush - in action in the barber
shop - wigs. Not American - true - but -
I'll bet it sold more fancy bottles and rotary
hair brushes to American barbers than to
Englishmen.

1864 London, Eng.   NNMM
HOVENDEN, R. & SONS. Revised catalog
of toilet articles, combs, brushes, human
hair goods, shaving boxes, blocks, shampooing stands and curling sticks. 8vo., IV and
90pp., a few ills., pict. wrap.

1866 London, Eng.   NNMM
------ Ill. catalog. VI and 74pp., pict.
wrap.

1866 London, Eng.   NNMM
------ 16 page supplement with ills. of water
cans, Japanned bowls, shampooing stands,
chairs, furniture and Japanned showers, etc.

1867 London, Eng.   NNMM
------ Ill. catalog. 8vo., 136pp., fine ills.,
wrap.

1874 London, Eng.   NNMM
------ Revised and ill. catalog. The most
complete ill. catalog in this field we can
locate. 8vo., XXII, 204pp., fine ills., pict.
wrap.

c.1885 Boston
HUB FURNITURE CO. Koch's adjustable
barbers' chairs, best for durability, ease,
comfort, quality and style. Over 30,000 in
use! Ill. of swan, duck, elephant and eagle
carved arms, with footrests, bottle and mug
racks, mirrors, fancy glass bottles - hobnail
and overlay - poles, stands, dressing cases,
etc. One of the best. Sq. 8vo. with 16pp.
of ills., wrap.

1906 St. Louis   MdTanSW
KERN, AUGUST BARBER SUP-   MoSHi
PLY CO. Catalog #56. Col. and fld. pls. of
shaving mugs with list of designs for trades,
secret societies, etc. Furniture, bottles,
jardinieres - everything for the up-to-date
barber shop. 8vo., 226pp., fine ills., index,
pict. wrap.

1898 St. Louis
------ There is at least one copy extant
but the location has not been sent in.

1889 St. Louis   MoSHi
KOKEN'S BARBER SUPPLY CO. Spring
catalog of bottles, mugs and furnishings.

4to., 148pp., fine ills., many in col. A fine
American ref., pict. wrap.

1899 St. Louis   MoSHi
------ Catalog #10. Ills. of all manner of
shop furnishings, bottles, mugs, chairs, wash
stands, fancy mirrors, etc. Americana?
Some of the most colorful.

1878 Wetzlar, Germany   NNMM
KRAFFT, GEORG. Also Berlin, Paris, London, Amsterdam & St. Petersburg. Illustrirte
Presisliste. 8vo., 62pp., pict. wrap. Without any question, the best ill. barbers' furnishings catalog for this period. From a
wig block to a complete shop.

c.1876 San Francisco   OrU
MARCHAND, L. Decorator. Price list of
fancy decorated barber mugs, dinner and
chamber sets done to order with monograms,
etc. 3pp.

1887 Chicago
ROLLERT & MELCHIOR FURNITURE CO.
Catalog of barbers' chairs, mug cases,
shelves, fancy wash stands, tool brackets,
mirrors, hat and towel racks, furnished
shop walls complete, etc. 8vo., 34pp., fine
ills., pict. wrap.

c.1893 Albany, N. Y.   NNMM
SAMPLE, W.H. Catalog of barbers' chairs,
mirrors, bottles, mugs and furnishings.
112pp., a fine pict. record.

c.1889 New York   PShipL
SHAW, L. Human hair goods, toilet articles,
bangs and waves, supplies, etc. 8vo., 48pp.,
ills., pict. wrap.

c.1882 New York   NNMM
SIMONSON, A. Catalog and price list of
human hair goods. 34pp., wrap.

1880 New York   ICHi
STEIN, S. & CO. Reduced price list of
human hair, hairdressers' materials and
articles of the trade. 12mo., 8pp., ills. of
irons, curlers and tools.

1876 New York   MiDbF
WILLIAMS, J.B. & CO. Ill. catalog of
barbers' supplies. One of the best. See
Carl W. Drepperd's Pioneer America.

nd. Philadelphia   PHi
ZABLUDOFF, J. & SONS. Ill. catalog of
beauty parlor equipment and supplies.

c.1870 Cincinnati   OC
ZWICK, JOHANNA. Ladies Wig Store.
Catalog of hair jewelry, braids, devices,
curls and wigs. Go to Madame Zwick for
the best. 8vo., broadside.

I suggest a perusal of Glassware if you are hunting illustrations of barbers' fancy glass bottles and bowls. Of course General Hardware and House Furnishings catalogs offer combs, scissors, perfumes and soaps for family use. Also there are a few illustrations of barbers' chairs found under Furniture.

Chapter 7

Beekeepers' Equipment

The fact that four libraries were able to contribute examples in this field, added to requests from private collectors, convinced me that it should not be buried in Agricultural Implements and Machinery. A. I. Root of Medina, Ohio, is of course, the outstanding manufacturer of equipment.

Frankly I have high hopes that many indignant librarians will unearth dozens of earlier and better catalogs for another edition. I am sure they exist in libraries as they do in private collections. For the present, however, I recommend the following examples as evidence of a once popular American occupation and industry.

c.1889 New York
COOK, J.H.M. 3rd annual catalog of bee-keepers' supplies. 8vo., 16pp., ill., pict. wrap.

nd. Guilford, Vt.
COOMBS, F, & SONS. Est. 1860. Price list of queens, Italian bees and bee-keepers' supplies. 16mo., 8pp., ill., wrap.

1883 Borodino, N. Y.   NSyHi
DOOLITTLE, G.M. 1883 Bee-Keepers' Club list - over 400 leading bee journals with price list and catalog of supplies. Palestine Queens! 8vo., 12pp., ill., wrap.

1890 Dowagiac, Mich.
HEDDON CO. Net price list of useful im-plements for bee-keepers. 12mo., 40pp., ill., pict. wrap.

1882 Canajoharie, N. Y.
HOUCK & PEET. Circular and price list of bee-keepers' supplies. 8vo., 20pp., ill., wrap.

1878 Conajoharie, N. Y.
NELLIS, J.H. Circular of Italian bees and apiarian supplies. 8vo., 18pp., ill., wrap.

1891 Beverly, Mass.
PRATT, E.L. Catalog of the Pratt Bee Farm - simplicity hives, queens and sup-plies. 8vo., 28pp., ill., wrap.

1881 Medina, O.
ROOT, A.I. Est. 1870. Catalog of bee-keepers' supplies. 8vo., 12pp., ill., wrap.

1891 Medina, O.
------ Bees and honey. 72nd ed. 8vo., 50pp., ill., pict. wrap.

1892 Medina, O.   MH-BA
------ 75th ed. Ill. catalog of supplies. 8vo., 54pp., ill.

1892 Medina, O.   OHi
------ Gleanings - Vol. 20, #15. House organ but in essence a catalog of supplies.

1896 Medina, O.   OHi
------ Catalog of bee-keepers' supplies. 26th year. 8vo., ill., pict. wrap.

1898 Glen Cove, L. I., N. Y.   NNQ
STRINGHAM, I.J. Catalog of apiarian sup-plies. 8vo., 16pp., amusing ill., pict. wrap.

1902 Glen Cover, L. I., N. Y.   NNQ
------ 11th annual catalog. Ill.

Strangely enough although I have always suspected the agricultural implement manufacturers of making apiarian supplies I have still to find hives or other equipment listed. J. H. Nellis and Alfred H. Newman on the other hand both offer pumps, planers and scroll saw machines in their apiarian supply catalogs! There is a lot more to proper beekeeping than the neophyte might suppose. If you have never seen a direct draft smoker, wax extracting machine, bee feeder or any of the fancy patented hives, take a look -- in your nearest library. Demand an 1878 illustrated catalog. If they never heard of such a thing, an inter-library loan request might stir up this uncataloged hive of unsearched Americana.

Chapter 8

Bells & Bell Founders

A lean section with very few locations. However, as pointed out several times, these chapters or sections have been selected from thousands of catalogs of general merchandise and products to aid in speedy research. It does not mean that American bells for every purpose may not be found in price lists under House Furnishings, Agricultural Implements, Miscellaneous Hardware and other groups. The index will direct you to others wherein fine illustrations of bells may be found for further work.

Although the Massachusetts Historical Society has Paul Revere's manuscript account book listing the bells he cast for New England academies, churches and other public buildings, no printed catalogs of this period have survived - if they ever existed. This chapter offers illustrated catalogs from 1856, which seems to be the earliest example recorded and cataloged by any of our repositories.

These catalogs record and illustrate everything from a huge special casting for a town hall to a mere ting-a-ling for a bicycle.

1863 New York   NR
AMERICAN BELL CO. A catalog of Brown & White's steel composition bells for farm, church, fire alarm, railroad, school and steamboat. 8vo., 35pp., fine ills., wrap.

nd. East Haddam, Conn.   CtHi
BARTON, W.E. Bell Mfg. Successor to Barton & Clark. Improved spring tongue hand bells. 16mo., one leaf, ill.

c.1890 Hillsboro, O.   OHi
BELL, C.S. CO. Catalog #34. Steel alloy church and school bells, etc. 8vo., 32pp., fine ills., wrap.

c.1891 Hillsboro, O.   OC
------ Ill. catalog with tinted lithos.

c.1871
BEVINS BROTHERS BELLS. See Miscellaneous Hardware. Walsh, Coulter & Wilson.

1875 Cincinnati   NHi
BLYMER MFG. CO. Price list of steel composition bells for fire alarms, churches, schools, farms, locomotives, plantations and steamboats. 8vo., 85pp., fine ills., wrap.

1883 Meriden, Conn.   CtHi
CHAPMAN MFG. CO. Ill. catalog and price list of Russian and Swiss chime sleigh bells, Broadway body straps with Dexter bells, etc. 26pp., a fine ref.

1885 Cincinnati, O.   MnHi
CINCINNATI BELL FOUNDRY CO. Successors to Blymer Mfg. Co. Annual catalog of bells for churches, fire alarms, court houses, schools, factories, boats, etc. 16mo., fine ills., ref.

1887 Cincinnati, O.   MnHi
------ Annual ill. catalog.

1889 Cincinnati, O.   MnHi
------ Annual ill. catalog.

1886 East Hampton, Conn.   CtHi
EAST HAMPTON BELL CO. Price list of gong and sleigh bells. 4to., 70pp., fine ills., wrap.

nd. East Hampton, Conn.   CtHi
HALL, J.S. & CO. Price list of bells for all purposes. 8vo., 8pp., ills.

1856 West Troy, N. Y.   CCuMGM
MENEELY'S, ANDREW SONS. Est. 1826. Catalog of chimes, alarms, any weight, for academy, church, depot, factory, steamboat, locomotive, ship, fire engine, etc. 8vo., 32pp., fine ills., wrap.

1857 West Troy, N. Y.   CCuMGM
------ Ill. circular.

c.1858 West Troy, N. Y.   N
------ Ill. catalog of chimes and bells, with notes on clients in many states. 8vo., 58pp., fine pict. ref.

1875 Troy, N. Y.   NHi
MENEELY & CO. Ill. catalog of bells.
8vo., 109pp.,with fine ills.throughout, wrap.

nd. Troy, N. Y.   N
MENEELY BELL CO. Ill. catalog of bells -
plates of bells made for Independence Hall,
Columbian Exposition, USS. New York, USS.
Minneapolis, etc. 16mo., 20pp., wrap.

c.1900 Bristol, Conn.   Ct
NEW DEPARTURE MFG. CO. Ill. circular
with col. spread of ZOO LINE BELLS -
turtles, dragons, serpents, lions, fox, etc.,
with display stands.

1894 Middletown, Pa.   PHi
RAYMOND & CAMPBELL MFG. CO.
Susquehanna Iron Works. Ill. catalog of
Cornwall silver bells, also iron bells, oven
doors and castings.

1878 New Britain   CtHi
RUSSELL & ERWIN MFG. CO. Ill. catalog
of bells, sleigh bells, hand gongs, tea bells,
etc. 8vo., 32pp., wrap.

nd. East Haddam, Conn.   NNMM
STARR BROTHERS BELL CO. Ill., desc.
and priced catalog of bells for doors, tables,
altars, locomotives, boats, depots, etc. 72pp.,
wrap.

nd. East Haddam, Conn.   CtHi
------ Ill. catalog of bells #63.

nd. East Haddam, Conn.   CtHi
------ Ill. catalog of bells for bicycles.

nd. New Britain   CtHi
TAYLOR MFG. CO. Taylor's Russian
sleigh bells, pat. November 1872 - Hurrah
for Russian Sleigh Bells! Sold by all leading dealers. Fol., ill., bds.

1869 Troy, N. Y.   NNU
TROY BELL FOUNDRY. Octavous Jones,
Prop. Catalog of chimes, peals and bells
for fire engines, locomotives, plantations and
steamboats. 8vo., 78pp., fine ills., dec.
wrap.

To supplement this group, be sure to check Agricultural Implements and Machinery. The catalogs
of the Metropolitan Agricultural Works, Parker & Wood, L. M. Rumsey and Strong & Douw all
contain fine woodcut illustrations of bells for farm, railroad and steamboat, as well as for other
buildings and vehicles. Among the many Bicycle and Fire Engine catalogs, for example, are fine
illustrations of special bells that should not be overlooked. If after following the above suggestions
you still can't find the manufacturer or bell in the right period needed, try Hardware.

Chapter 9

Bicycles & Accessories

American bicycle catalogs are among the most colorful examples ever produced, and stand second only to the carriage catalogs of the Gay Nineties, and the automobile catalogs of the 20th century. The manufacturers employed many of the finest lithographers, and their copy writers were tops. Although the high wheelers of the 1870 period are the most interesting from a collecting standpoint, having reached their antique status for museums, the catalogs issued after the advent of the modern wheel are really fine examples of American lithographic art in themselves.

This chapter lists a fine complete record with locations from Massachusetts south and west to Nevada and Oregon. Institutional interest is encouraging and promises to spread to other 19th century American manufacturing developments.

1899 Elkhart   In
ACME CYCLING CO. Catalog of Acme bicycles. 12mo., ills., pict. wrap.

1897 Reading, Pa.   PKsL
ACME MFG. CO. Catalog of Stormer bicycles, with sketches by W. L. Hudson. Fine ills., pict. wrap.

1900 Hartford, Conn.   Ct
AMERICAN BICYCLE CO. Bicycle sundries and fittings from the Columbia sales depot; bells, lamps, etc. 8vo., 52pp., ills., wrap.

1897 Columbus, O.   OHi
AMERICAN MACHINE CO. Catalog of standard grade bicycles - Buy of the maker and save money - mfg. direct to the rider. Models $17.50 to $25., American Special $35. 4to., 8pp., ills.

1895 Chicago   NvRH
AMES & FROST. Catalog of Imperials.

1895 Goshen, Ind.   In
ARIEL CYCLE MFG. CO. Makers of Best American Bicycles. 8vo., 16pp., ill., view of plant, col. pict. wrap.

1896 Goshen, Ind.   In
------ Ill. catalog of models and styles. 8vo., 20pp., pict. wrap.

1897 Syracuse, N. Y.   NSyHi
BARNES CYCLE CO. 3rd annual catalog - the White Flyer, Barnes Special, Road Racer, Superba, Tandem. 12mo., 32pp., tinted ills. and pict. wrap.

nd.   MoSHi
BECK & CORBITT IRON CO. See carriages.

1896 Boston   NvRH
BERLO CYCLE CO. Ill. catalog of Berlo bicycles.

nd BICYCLE BELLS   CtHi
See Starr Brothers Bells.

1897 Boston   NvRH
BIGELOW & DOWSE. Ill. catalog of bicycles.

1894 Erie   MdTanSW
BLACK MFG. CO. Catalog of Tribune cycles and accessories. Racer model. 24pp., ill.

1895 Buffalo, N. Y.   NvRH
BUFFALO WHEEL CO. Catalog of Niagara Cycles.

1894-1900 Chicago   ICHi
CASH BUYERS UNION. Ill. catalogs from 1894 through 1900. A fine reference. Ills. of Arlington, Maywood and Oakwood bicycles. 8vo. and large 8vo., 40pp., pict. wrap.

1895 Indianapolis   In
CENTRAL CYCLE MFG. CO. Catalog of Ben Hur bicycles. Sq. 8vo., 12pp., ill., col. pict. wrap.

1897 Indianapolis   MiU-T
------ 7th annual catalog.   In
Sq. 8vo., 18pp., fine ills. and col. pict. wrap. MiU-T also reports variant of 24pp.

1896 Chicago   NvRH
CHICAGO STAMPING CO. Ill. catalog of United States Bicycles.

1897 Chicago   CLU
CHICAGO TIP & TIRE CO. Ill. catalog of bicycles, bells, seats, wheels and accessories. 8vo., 128pp. with fine ills.

1898 New York   N
COLE, G.C. & CO. Ill. catalog of bicycle
specialties. 16mo., 32pp., pict. wrap.

nd. New Haven   CtHi
COLOPHITE MFG. CO. Catalog of bicycles
and tricycles, supplies, apparatus - aluminum
lacquer, etc. If you own a wheel this will
interest you. Ill.

nd. New Britain   CtHi
CORBIN, P. & F. Catalog of bicycle parts,
Corbin new departure coaster brake, Ramsey
swinging pedals, etc. 8vo., 16pp., ills. and
diag.

nd. New Britain   CtHi
------ Ill. catalog. 8vo., 36pp.

1893 Hagerstown, Md.   NNU
CRAWFORD MFG. CO. Ill catalog of
Crawford bicycles; models 2, 3, 5 - the
Gazelle, etc. 8vo., 16pp., pict. wrap.

1897 Hagerstown, Md.   MdHi
------ Ill. catalog. Sq. 8vo., 32pp., pict.
wrap.

1897 Dayton, O.   NNU MiU-T
DAVIS SEWING MACHINE CO.   OHi
Ill. catalog of Dayton bicycles, models A, D,
H, M and O, tandems, etc. 8vo., 32pp., fine
ills., wrap.

1893 Torrington, Conn.   CtHi
EAGLE BICYCLE MFG. CO. Ill. catalog of
Eagle bicycles. 16pp., view of plant, wrap.

1896 Torrington, Conn.   CtHi
------ Ill. catalog. 4to., 32pp., col. pict.
wrap.

1896 Torrington, Conn.   Ct
------ Ill. catalog with Scientific Research
article on Bicycle Construction by permission of Scientific American. 8vo., 12mo.,
pict. wrap.

1897 Torrington, Conn.   NSbSM
------ Ill. catalog of styles and   MiU-T
models. Large 8vo., 32pp., pict. wrap.

1898 Torrington, Conn.   Ct
------ Book of Cash Prices - Recollection
of quality remains long after price has been
forgotten. 8vo., fine ills.

1898 Torrington, Conn.   Ct
------ Ill. catalog with ill. of plant. 4to.,
24pp., fine ills., pict. wrap.

1895 Beaver Falls, Pa.   PKsL
ECLIPSE BICYCLE CO. Catalog of   PHi
Eclipse bicycles - photo. ills. of plant -
records - 16 men weighing 2448 lbs. on one
wheel - lightest and strongest - best. 12mo.,
32pp., pict. wrap.

1896 Beaver Falls, Pa.   NvRH
------ Ill. catalog. 12mo., ills. of tests.
and records. Pict. wrap.

1899 Buffalo, N. Y.   NBuHi
ELECTRIC CITY WHEEL CO. Ill. catalog
of models for men and women. $45. and
$50. 8vo., 12pp., pict. wrap.

1887 Boston   MH-BA
EVERETT, W.B. & CO. Factory - Singer &
Co., Coventry, England. Catalog of Singer's
Cycles - largest cycle works in the world.
24mo., 32pp., ill., wrap.

1895 Everett, Mass.   NvRH
EVERETT CYCLE CO. Ill. catalog of
McCune Cycles.

1896 Chicago   NvRH
EXCELSIOR SUPPLY CO. Advance catalog
of the Thistle Bicycle. Ill.

1893 Chicago   ICHi
FEATHERSTONE, A. & CO. Annual catalog
of the Road King and Road Queen. 7x10,
24pp., fine ills.

1895 Jamestown, N. Y.   N
FENTON METALLIC MFG. CO. Est. 1888.
Catalog - Fenton bicycles have blue crowns.
12mo., 24pp., fine ills., wrap.

1897 Jamestown, N. Y.   N
------ Preliminary catalog - the Fork crown
is blue. Sketches of plant and models. 12mo.,
16pp., wrap.

1895 Bridgeport, Conn.   Ct
FOLDING BICYCLE CO. Catalog of the
Folding Bicycle. 16mo., 16pp., excellent
photos. of models.

1897 Toledo, O.   OT
GENDRON WHEEL CO. Gendron and
Reliance Bicycles. 8vo., 20pp., ill., pict.
wrap.

1895 Buffalo, N. Y.   NBuHi
GLOBE CYCLE WORKS. Catalog of Globe
and Mascot cycles. Ill., pict. wrap.

1886 Chicago   CHi
GORMULLY & JEFFERY CO. (Osborn &
Alexander, agents, San Francisco.) Catalog
of American cycles. 8vo., 28pp., fine ills.,
wrap.

1887 Chicago   CHi
------ 8vo., ill. catalog - same agent.

1892 Chicago   ICHi
------ Price list of Rambler bicycles.
8vo., 32pp., ill., pict. wrap.

1895 Chicago   NNU-W
------ Ill. catalog of Rambler   NvRH
bicycles. 7x10, 44pp., col. pict. wrap.
Indian leaving pony on Rambler bike.

1896 Chicago   NvRH
------ Ill. catalog. Fine col. pict. wrap.

1892 Hartford, Conn.   CtHi
HARTFORD CYCLE CO. The Hartford
Safeties - patterns A, B, C and D - bells,
seats, pumps, tools, etc. 12mo., 24pp., fine
ills., pict. wrap.

1893 Hartford, Conn.   Ct
------ Ill. catalog of Models for 1893.
12mo., 24pp., wrap.

1893 Hartford, Conn.   CtHi
------ Price list of parts. 4to., 8pp., ill.,
wrap.

1894 Hartford, Conn.   Ct
------ 5th annual catalog. The Hartford.
8vo., 28pp., fine ills., pict. wrap.

1895 Cortland, N. Y.   N
HITCHCOCK MFG. CO. The Hitchcock
Motor Cycle. The Victoria for 2 or 3 persons on 4 wheels! 12mo., 16pp., fine ills.,
pict. wrap.

1894 Peoria, Ill.   IHi
IDE, F.F. The Ide Wheel - high art bicycles, models. 8vo., 24pp., ills. of models.

1895 Peoria, Ill.   ICHi
------ Ill. catalog. Sq. 8vo., 32pp., col.
pict. wrap., tinted ills.

1896 Peoria, Ill.   IHi
------ Ill. catalog of models and parts.
16mo., 24pp., wrap.

1894 Indianapolis   In
INDIANA BICYCLE CO. Catalog of Waverly
bicycles. 16mo., amusing ills., dec. wrap.

1895 Indianapolis   NvRH
------ Ill. catalog.

1897 Indianapolis   MiU-T
------ Ill. catalog with Evolution of the
Bicycle showing model for 1790 and the
Waverly.

1897 Fitchburg, Mass.   NNU-W
IVER JOHNSON ARMS & CYCLE CO. Catalog of bicycles, models and styles. 8vo.,
fine pls., pict. wrap.

1897 Middletown, Conn.   Ct
KEATING WHEEL CO. Keating - 365 days
ahead of them all. Catalog with ills. of models,
marginal sketches, better than C & I. 7x10,
32pp., tinted ills., col. pict. wrap.

1897 New York   NhDY
KENYON, C. & CO. Catalog of bicycle
clothing and accessories. 12mo., 24pp.,
fine ills., col. pict. wrap.

1894 Chicopee Falls   NvRH
LAMB MFG. CO. Catalog of Spalding and
Credenda bicycles.

1895 Chicopee Falls   NvRH
------ Catalog of Spalding bicycles.

1894 Hartford, Conn.   CtHi
LEAGUE CYCLE CO. Public opinion of
League chainless safeties. 16pp.

1894 Bridgeport, Conn.   N
LIBERTY CYCLE CO. The Liberty - A
Thing or Two About Them. Models -
Hummer, Scorcher, Roadster, etc. 32pp.,
fine ills., pict. wrap.

1895 Bridgeport, Conn.   N
------ Ill. catalog.

1896 Bridgeport, Conn.   N
------ 2nd ed. of 200,000 copies.

1897 Bridgeport, Conn.   N
------ Ill. catalog - America's Representative bicycle.

1898 Bridgeport, Conn.   Ct
------ Ill. catalog. 8vo., 24pp., col. pict.
wrap.

1890 Boston   NhHi
LOVELL, JOHN P. ARMS CO. Ill. catalog
of bicycles, tricycles, tandems, safeties,
other models. 8vo., fine ills., wrap.

1891 Boston   NNC-W
------ Ill. catalog of models. 8vo., 40pp.,
wrap.

1895 Boston   NvRH
------ Ill. catalog of styles, etc.

1890 Toledo, O.   OHi
LOZIER & YOST. Catalog of Giant Bicycles -
Utile Dulci, etc. High wheelers. 8vo., 16pp.
Fine ills., pict. wrap.

1894 Toledo, O.   MH-BA
LOZIER, H.A. & CO. Est. 1889. Cleveland
Bicycles. Ill. catalog. 8vo., 32pp., pict. wrap.

1894 Cleveland, O.   NvRH
LOZIER, H.A. & CO. Ill. catalog of Cleveland Bicycles.

1895 Cleveland, O.   PKsL
------ Cleveland Bicycles - models and
styles. Sq. 8vo., 12pp., ills., pict. wrap.

1896 Cleveland, O.   OHi
------ Ill. catalog. Reasons why if
Shakespeare were alive he would choose a
Cleveland. Quotes from Shakespeare.
16mo., 8 delightful col. pls. by J. Ottman,
N. Y. Pict. wrap.

c.1895 New York   N
LYON, AMOS M. CO. Lyon Bicycles - models,
styles and accessories. 16mo., 24pp., ills.,
wrap.

1890 Lyndhurst, N. J.   N
McKEE & HARRINGTON. Agents. Factory
in Lyndhurst. Est. 1879. Lyndhurst - a
special made bicycle. 16mo., 8pp., ills. of
styles, wrap.

1894 Lyndhurst, N. J.   N
------ Special features for 1894. 16mo.,
32pp. of ills., wrap.

1895 Lyndhurst, N. J.   N
------ Models for 1895 with a delightful
ill. from Harper's Magazine.

1899 Lyndhurst, N. J.   N
------ Ill. catalog with pict. wrap.

1890 St. Louis   MoSHi
MEACHAM, E.C. ARMS CO. Annual price
list for May - models, styles and accessories.

1895 Middletown, O.   OHi
MIAMI CYCLE & MFG. CO. Catalog of the
Racycles, models in red and blue. 24mo.,
24pp., ills. in red and blue, pict. wrap.

c.1900 Middletown, O.   OHi
------ Racycle Narrow Treads - Models
#1 to 6, $75. to $100., tandems $150. Ills.,
tinted pict. wrap.

1892 Chicago   ICHi
MONARCH CYCLE CO. Est. 1892. 3rd
annual catalog of models and styles - 6000
in use. 8vo., 24pp., ill., wrap.

1893 Chicago   ICHi
------ High Grade Bicycles by Monarch.
Sq. 8vo., 24pp., fine ills., col. pict. wrap.

1897 Chicago   ICHi
------ Ill. catalog.

1895 Chicago   ICHi
MONTGOMERY WARD & CO. Special ill.
catalog of bicycles and accessories.

1896 Chicago   MiU-T
MORGAN & WRIGHT.   OrU
Catalog of bicycles and accessories, data on
racing and records of League of American
Wheelmen. 130pp., fine ills., ptd. The
Werner Co.

c.1900 Hammondsport, N. Y.   N
MOTORCYCLE EQUIPMENT & SUPPLY CO.
Net price list of motorcycle and bicycle
accessories and supplies. 8vo., 12pp., ills.

1895 New York   N
MYERS, S.F. & CO. Catalog #2. Popular
Columbus high grade bicycles, models and
styles. 12mo., fine ills. with pict. wrap. of
Columbus Landing in America, and marginal
scenes throughout.

1898 Toledo, O.   OT
NATIONAL CEMENT & RUBBER MFG. CO.
Catalog of bicycle supplies, etc. 12mo.,
32pp., ills., dec. wrap.

1899 Toledo, O.   OT
------ Ill. catalog of accessories.

1890 Bay City, Mich.   MiU-T
NATIONAL CYCLE MFG. CO. Ill. catalog
of models. A National rider never changes
his mount. 8vo., ills., wrap.

c.1890 Belvidere, Ill.   ICHi
NATIONAL SEWING MACHINE CO. Bicycle
catalog. Photo Color Type Co. ills. of
models - 200 bicycles daily and 500 sewing
machines. Racers, standards, tandems.
Sq. 8vo., 16pp., floral col. pict. wrap.

nd. Bristol, Conn.   CtHi
NEW DEPARTURE COASTER BRAKE CO.
Ill. catalog.

NEW DEPARTURE MFG. CO. See Bells.

1895 New York   OrU
NEW YORK BELTING & PACKING CO., LTD.
Ill. catalog of bicycle tires, pedal rubbers,
handles, repair outfits, stick and stay sundries. 16pp., wrap.

1899 Syracuse, N. Y.   NSyHi
OLIVE WHEEL CO. Olive Bicycles - pls.
of models, etc. 16mo., 24pp. of ills., dec.
wrap.

1886 San Francisco
OSBORN & ALEXANDER. See Gormully &
Jeffery.

1885 Chicopee Falls
OVERMAN WHEEL CO. Catalog of Victor
bicycles and tricycles. 8vo., 24pp., ills. of
models, pict. wrap.

1896 Chicopee Falls   NvRH
------ Ill. catalog of models with fine pls.
of cycling roads, health hints, laws, etc.
Ptd. on tinted paper, unusual art work.

c.1899 Chicago   ICHi
OXFORD MFG. CO. Catalog of Oxfords -
Absolutely High Grade, Low Price - also

sporting regalia, watches, organs and novelties. 8vo., 28pp., ills.

1897 Reading, Pa.   PKsL
PACKER CYCLE CO.   PHi   MiU-T
Ill. catalog of Packer Bicycles, styles and models. 8vo., 24pp., ill. throughout, col. pict. wrap.

1895 Cleveland, O.   OHi
PEERLESS MFG. CO. Catalog of Peerless and Triangle Bicycles. 8vo., 32pp., fine ills., pict. wrap.

1897 Buffalo, N. Y.   NBuHi
PIERCE, GEORGE N. CO.   NNU-W
Catalog of bicycles, models, styles and accessories. 8vo., ills. of models, pict. wrap.

1879 Hartford, Conn.   MiU-T
POPE MFG. CO. Est. 1877. Ill. catalog of Columbia bicycles and sundries.

1880 Hartford, Conn.   CtHi
------ Ill. catalog of models and styles. 24pp., pict. wrap.

1881 Hartford, Conn.   CtHi
------ Ill. catalog. 24pp., wrap.

1882 Hartford, Conn.   NHi
------ 5th annual ill. catalog. Mfg. at Weed Sewing Machine Co. (N. Y. agent E.I. Horsman.)

1883 Hartford, Conn.   MH-BA
------ Ill. catalog. Sixth Year of Mfg. Models, etc. Tests. 8vo., 34pp., wrap.

1883 Hartford, Conn.   Ct
------ Ill. catalog of high wheelers, parts, accessories, etc. 34pp.

1884 Hartford, Conn.   Ct   MH-BA
------ What and Why! Ill. catalog. 16mo., 72pp., wrap.

1885 Hartford, Conn.   MH-BA
------ 8th annual ill. catalog. Fine ills. 8vo., 50pp., pict. wrap.

1887 Hartford, Conn.   MiU-T
------ 10th annual greeting. Price list of Columbia bicycles, parts, tires and sundries. 8vo., 50pp., fine ills., pict. wrap. of plant.

1888 Hartford, Conn.   MiU-T
------ Ill. catalog. Pict. wrap.

1889 Hartford, Conn.   Ct   MiU-T
------ Only ed. New Boy's High Wheeler. 12th annual catalog, a fine ref. job. 8vo., 54pp., pict. wrap.

1890 Hartford, Conn.   CtHi   MiU-T
------ Ill. catalog. 48pp., col. pls., wrap.

1891 Hartford, Conn.   CtHi
------ Ill. catalog of experts, racers and tandem models, tricycles, tandem tricycles. Only ed. 53pp., fine ills., pict. wrap.

1892 Hartford, Conn.   CtHi
------ Ill. catalog of styles.   Ct

1893 Hartford, Conn.   NvRH
------ Ill. catalog of Hartford Safeties.

1894 Hartford, Conn.   CtHi   MH-BA
------ 17th annual catalog of models and parts. 8vo., 46pp., ills., pict. wrap.

1895 Hartford, Conn.   MiU-T
------ 18th annual ill. catalog.   NvRH

1896 Hartford, Conn.   CtHi
------ 19th annual ill. catalog. 32pp., wrap.

1898 Hartford, Conn.   CtHi
------ Ill. catalog of Columbia bicycles and parts.

1899 Hartford, Conn.   CtHi
------ Ill. catalog of Columbia and Hartford Safeties. 26pp., fine ills., ptd. Orr Press.

1894 Indianapolis   In
PROGRESS MFG. CO. Ill. catalog of bicycles. Models - Crusader, Pathfinder, etc. 8vo.

1894 New York   N
RALEIGH CYCLE CO. Ill. catalog of models with racing champions and records. 8vo., 32pp., fine ills., col. pict. wrap.

RAMBLER BICYCLES. See Gormully & Jeffery.

1895 Reading, Pa.   PKsL
RELAY MFG. CO. Ill. catalog of Relay bicycles, models, seats, accessories, etc. 12mo., 32pp., pict. wrap.

1893 Ilion, N. Y.   N
REMINGTON ARMS CO. Est. 1816. Catalog of bicycles, models, accessories, etc. 8vo., 48pp., fine ills., view of plant, wrap.

1894 Ilion, N. Y.   N
------ Ill. catalog.

1895 Ilion, N. Y.   N
------ 2 ill. catalogs. 1 - Models. 2 - Parts, etc.

1897 Ilion, N. Y.   N
------ Ill. catalog. 32pp. with marginal ills. and pict. wrap.

1900 Ilion, N. Y.   N
------ A Wheel is Known by the Company that Makes it.

1895 Rochester, N.Y.   N
ROCHESTER CYCLE CO. Ill. catalog of
Rochester bicycles. 8vo., 20pp. of models,
accessories, etc. Dec. wrap.

1890 Peoria, Ill.   IHi
ROUSE, HAZARD & CO. Est. 1864. 11th
annual catalog of cycles. High Wheelers -
American, Champion, Columbia, Expert and
Victor, Volunteer, Challenge, Ideal and Star.
8vo., 40pp., fine ills., pict. wrap.

1891 Peoria, Ill.   IHi
------ Price list #71. Second hand cycles,
rock bottom prices. The Vineyard model,
etc. 10pp.

1893 Peoria, Ill.   NcU   ICHi
------ 14th annual catalog of bicycles.
8vo., 50pp. of ills., bells to wheels, wrap.

1894 St. Louis   MoSHi
ST. LOUIS REFRIGERATOR & WOODEN
GUTTER CO. LU-MI-NUM bicycles. Ill.
catalog of models. 8vo.

1892 New York   NNMM
SCHOVERLING, DALY & GALES. Ill. and
desc. priced catalog of bicycles and sundries.
32pp., wrap.

1898 Chicago   ICHi
SEARS ROEBUCK & CO. Cheapest Supply
House on Earth. Bicycles for 1898. Acme
Jewel Models, accessories, parts, etc. Sm.
4to., ill. throughout, pict. wrap.

1887 Smithville, N.J.   PShipL
SMITH, H.B. MACHINE CO. Catalog of
Star bicycles and tricycles. 8vo., 36pp.
Ills. of high wheelers, tricycles, etc. with
fine pict. wrap.

1888 Smithville, N.J.   PKsL
------ Catalog of Star bicycles and tricycles.
High Wheelers, racers, special models,
training machines accessories. Large 8vo.,
36pp., fine ills. throughout, col. pict. wrap.
Litho. by W.H. Butler of a typical Gay Ninety
American Wheelman on a special and a fine
view of the plant.

1899 Smithville, N.J.   PKsL
------ Ill. catalog of bicycles and tricycles.
8vo., 40pp., fine ills., pict. wrap.

1886 Newark, N.J.   MH-BA
SMITH, HOWARD A. & CO. Successor to
Zacharias & Smith. Ill. catalog of bicycles,
tricycles and cycling goods. 8vo., 32pp.

1894 Newark, N.J.   NvRH
------ Encyclopaedia of Cyclers' Wants.
An exhaustive ill. catalog.

1895 Southington, Conn.   Ct
SOUTHINGTON CUTLERY CO. Bicycle
cranks - the guard detachable. 16mo.,
16pp., fine ills., pict. wrap.

1896 Southington, Conn.   Ct
------ Ill. catalog of bicycle specialties.
16mo., 14pp., pict. wrap.

1888 New York   ICHi
SPALDING, A.G. & BROTHER. Ill. catalog
of bicycles and supplies.

1897 New York   NvRH
------ Branches in Chicago & Philadelphia.
Ill. catalog of bicycles.

1890 Boston   PShipL
STALL, W.W. Ill. catalog of bicycles, tricycles and accessories. Models of high
wheels and low. 8vo., 48pp., fine ills. showing the change in style for the years to come.

1894 Syracuse, N.Y.   NvRH
STEARNS, E.C. CO.   N   NSyHi
Stearns bicycles. Supply catalog of models
and parts. The Yellow Fellow. Sq. 8vo.,
18pp., fine ills., wrap.

1895 Syracuse, N.Y.   N   NvRH
------ Ill. catalog of The Yellow Fellow
Bicycle. 36pp., fine ills., wrap.

1897 Syracuse, N.Y.   NNU-W
------ The Yellow Fellow Year Book. A
treatise by E.C. Stearns. Ills. of models,
styles, etc. 8vo., pict. wrap.

1898 Dayton, O.   ICHi
STODDARD MFG. CO.   OHi
Catalog - Greatest Show on Earth - Tiger
and Tigress Specials - Cygnets, Juveniles,
Tandems. Sq. 8vo., 24pp., fine ills. of
models, etc. Col. pict. wrap.

1884 Boston   NNMM
STODDARD, LOVERING & CO.   PPL
Catalog of bicycles - numerous makes -
imported Dinger & Co. gears and D. Rudge
& Co. models, parts, wheels, etc. Specs.
and details. 36pp. with fine ills., wrap.

1885 Boston   MH-BA
------ Ill. catalog with tests., models, etc.
8vo., 48pp., wrap.

1886 Boston   MH-BA
------ Ill. catalog of 42pp., 8vo.

1895 Freeport, Ill.   IHi
STOVER BICYCLE MFG. CO. Catalog of
high grade bicycles - models - the Phoenix,
Paragon, etc. with views of plant. 8vo., 32pp.,
col. litho. pict. wrap. of Cox's famous
Brownies riding their Stover bikes.

1892 Philadelphia   PKsL
SWEETING CYCLE CO. Catalog of models,
Excelsior, Quadrant, Belmont, Phoenix,
U. S., etc. 8vo., 30pp., ills., col.pict.wrap.

1895 Syracuse, N. Y.   N
SYRACUSE CYCLE MFG. CO. Syracuse
Cycles - Spin to Win with the Crimson Rim.
Ill. catalog of models, views of plant, etc.
12mo., 32pp., fine ills., wrap.

1898 Deep River, Conn.   NNMM
TINKHAM STANDARD AMERICAN TRI-
CYCLE CO. Ill., desc. and priced catalog
of styles, etc. 13 lvs., with fine ills., wrap.

c.1895 Nashua, N. H.   NhHi
TRINITY CYCLE MFG. CO. Catalog of
Trinity bicycles - models - standard and
tandem. Sm. 4to., 16pp., fine ills., wrap.

1894 Philadelphia   PHi
TRYON, EDWARD K. JR. & CO. Catalog of
bicycles, models and styles. Tall 8vo., 20pp.,
fine ills., pict. wrap.

c.1895 Paterson, N. J.   N
UNITED STATES CYCLE CO. New York
Office. Catalog of the Builders of High Art
Bicycles, models, styles and accessories.
8vo., 16pp., fine ills. of models, pict. wrap.

1895 Boston   NvRH
VERY CYCLE CO. Ill. catalog of Warwick
Perfection Cycles.

1892 New York   N
VON LENGERKE & DETMOLD. Agents.
Price list of Peregrine Cycles for season.
8vo., 20pp., fine ills.

c.1899 St. Paul, Minn.   MnHi
WAGNER CYCLE CO. Catalog #4. Announcement of our new model Wagner Motor Cycle -
The Best at any Price. 16mo., 16pp., fine
ills., wrap.

1899 Waltham   ICHi
WALTHAM MFG. CO. The Orient Bicycle -
styles, models, tandems, multicycles - The

Decemtuple, built for ten! Tall 12mo., 32pp.
of delightful ills., pict. wrap.

1896 Springfield, Mass.   CSmH
WARWICK CYCLE CO. Ill. catalog of
Warwick Cycles. 32pp., wrap.

1895 Chicago   ICHi
WESTERN WHEEL WORKS.   NvRH
Advance catalog of Crescent Bicycles. Sq.
8vo., 16pp., fine ills. and pict. wrap.

1890 Trenton, N. J.   PKsL
WHITE CYCLE CO. Catalog of bicycles,
tricycles, velocipedes, accessories, clothing,
etc. 8vo., 36pp., fine ills., pict. wrap.

1897 Cleveland   OHi
WHITE SEWING MACHINE CO.   NvRH
The White Bicycle. A Then and Now Portfolio, 1775 to 1897. Sq. 8vo., 36pp., fine
ills. with a col. pict. wrap. and double spread
showing the grand parade with an audience
of Revolutionary Soldiers and horsemen.

1895 Hamburg, Pa.   PKsL
WILHELM, W.H. & CO. Annual Greeting -
with sketches of models, styles and accessories. 8vo., 32pp., fine ills., wrap.

1896 Hamburg, Pa.   PKsL
------ 6th annual catalog of models. 16pp.,
fine ills. with an ill. folder of specials.

1891 Chicago   ICHi
WILKINSON, JOHN CO. Ill. catalog of Rover
bicycles and accessories.

1894 Cleveland   OHi
WORTHINGTON, GEORGE & CO. Catalog
of High Grade Bicycles. 8vo., fine ills.,
pict. wrap.

1885 Newark, N. J.   NNMM
ZACHARIAS & SMITH. Ill. and desc. price
list of bicycles and tricycles. 36pp., fine
ills., index and wrap.

1896 Freehold, N. J.   NvRH
ZIMMERMAN MFG. CO. Ill. catalog of
Zimmy Cycles.

Chapter 10

Boats & Ships, Marine Hardware & Supplies

This classification includes outstanding examples of located catalogs. In one or two cases 20th century specimens have been listed to broaden the field, and to suggest the possibility of earlier issues hidden in uncataloged collections. I would not care to stand in court and swear that 1792 is the correct date of the first American printed list of shipbuilding material. I cannot state that Mr. Annesley's 1816 patent is the first printed record of American built ships. However, until our repositories can study their collections and discover earlier data, this is the best I can offer.

As you will find in every chapter of this guide, there are several great collections easily picked out for search. It is interesting to find as many unusually good pictorial pieces scattered from New England to California in libraries that make no claim to maritime Americana.

As in the case of early textile mill catalogs, the manufacturers of whaleships, whaleboats, whaling gear and equipment apparently did not need any advertising or catalogs. Their job was only to keep pace with the demand. I have listed the few pseudo catalogs, with Frank Brown's broadside catalog under Whaleships, Whaleboats, etc. for obvious reasons.

1892 Miamishore, O.   ViNewM
ACME FOLDING BOAT CO. Ill. catalog.
12mo., 36pp., wrap.

c.1915 Cleveland, O.   TxDaDeG
AMERICAN SHIPBUILDING CO. Catalog,
ill. throughout, from a brass door knob to a
full fledged 500 ft. lake steamer. 4to.,
192pp. Only two catalogs of complete
steamboats have come to light, located in
our repositories. See also Rees - 1913.

1869 Providence, R. I.   MH-BA
AMERICAN SHIP WINDLASS CO.   RHi
Catalog - improved method of handling
anchors and chains. Emerson's pat. double
Windlass marine hardware, etc. 8vo., 40pp.,
fine ills., pict. eagle wrap.

1888 Providence, R. I.   RHi
------ Ill. hardware catalog. 8vo.

1891 Providence, R. I.   RHi
------ Ill. hardware catalog. 8vo.

1897 Providence, R. I.   RHi
------ Ill. catalog of windlass and   DSi
hardware novelties for boat and ship. 8vo.

1816 Albany, N. Y.   MWA
ANNESLEY, WILLIAM. Desc. of William
Annesley's new system of boat and ship
building, pat. in U.S. 11pp., fld. plate.
Ptd. J. Buel.

An important beginning, though not a trade
catalog as we know them today. To the
first who builds in any seaport or any navi-
gable lake, I will give one pat. right with
drawing and pamphlet gratis . . . to all
others, the right of building vessels under
100 tons will be .75 per ton . . . above 100
tons, .50 per ton.

c.1900 Amesbury, Mass.   ViNewM
ATLANTIC CO. Ill. catalog of dories and
small crafts.

1887 Clayton, N. Y.   NCooHi
BAIN, A. Became St. Lawrence MiD
Skiff, Canoe and Steam Launch Co. Ill. catalog of celebrated St. Lawrence River steam
launches, skiffs, canoes and yachts. 8vo.,
32pp., ills. by F.H. Taylor, pict. wrap.

1884 Providence, R. I.   RHi
BAKES & ROBERTS. Night code of signals,
Baker & Roberts' new apparatus. 8vo.,
12pp., col. ills. of apparatus, wrap.

c.1900 Bay City, Mich.   NBmlAM
BROOKS BOAT MFG. CO. Catalog #11.
Pattern system of boat building, knocked
down boats, frames, hardware and equipment. Tall 8vo., 64pp., photo. ills. of St.
Lawrence skiffs with motor or sail, models,
designs, etc.

c.1890 New Bedford   MH
BROWN, FRANK E. Successor to Pierce,
Eben, Mfg. of Pierce Bomb Lances. Ill.
broadside circular offering all types of
whale craft with prices. 16-1/2x31-1/2.

1892 Steinway, N.Y.   CU-A
DAIMLER MOTOR CO. Daimler Motors -
safest, most perfect gas engine, etc. See
Automobiles for complete data. 16mo.,
16pp., plus map with directions for visiting
plant. 5¢ fare! Ills. of motors, launches,
etc. Pict. wrap.

1899 Steinway, N.Y.   NNQ
------ Marine Dept. catalog of launches,
yachts, house boats, etc. 4to., 56pp., tinted
photos.

1792 Bath, Me.   RPJCB
DAVIS, JONATHAN & SON. Broadside.
Kennebec River price current for lumber
delivered at Bath, masts hewed in best
manner, yards hewed 8 sq. of spruce or pine,
bowsprits hewed 8 sq. of pine, timber, planks,
common lumber - as priced. One leaf.

1894 Detroit   MiD
DETROIT BOAT WORKS. Catalog of steam
and sail yachts, electric launches, etc. Sq.
8vo., 72pp., fine ills., pict. wrap.

1887 Waukegan   ViNewM
DOUGLAS, R.J. & CO. Ill. catalog of boats,
canoes, etc.

c.1900 New York   CtMyM
DURKEE, CHARLES D. Complete catalog
of marine hardware and hardware for wet
places. 8vo., 842pp., fine ills.

1889 Boston   ViNewM
FERDINAND, L.W. & CO. Ill. catalog of
ship chandlery boats and marine hardware
and accessories. Sq. 8vo., 130pp., ills. from
an anchor to a windlass, wrap.

1887 Morris Heights, N.Y.   ViNewM
GAS ENGINE & POWER CO. Ill. catalog of
naptha launches.

1890 Morris Heights, N.Y.   ViNewM
------ Ill. catalog of boats, canoes, launches,
etc.

1893 Morris Heights, N.Y.   TxDaDeG
------ Seven years has demonstrated that
the Naptha Launch is the only gentleman's
launch. Ill. catalog of designs, models in
scallop shell design. Col. pict. wrap.
16mo., 16pp.

1896 Morris Heights, N.Y.   NBmlAM
------ Ill. catalog of launches and boats.
4to., 72pp. of designs and models, with list
of owners, diags., plans, etc. Wrap.

c.1890 Boonville, N.Y.   NBmlAM
GRANT, H.D. MFG. Co. Catalog of Adirondack Guides Boats, date supplied by Grant's
son who carried on the business. 4pp. with
blueprint photo.

1899 HEMMENWAY, S. & SON. Sail Makers.
See Sporting Goods.

1872 New York   CtMyM
HIRSCH PROPELLER CO. Morgan Iron
Works. (John Roach & Son, sole agent.)
Ill. catalog of propellers, etc. 16pp., wrap.

nd. Lawrence, Mass.   NBmlAM
HOLMES & ROBERTSON CO. Ill. catalog of
Adirondack portable sporting boats and
canoes. 16pp., wrap.

1884 Glens Falls, N.Y.   NBmlAM
JOINER, F. & Son. Photographic catalog
and price list of boats. 12pp. with 8 photos.
tipped in, wrap.

1880 Chicago   ViNewM
KANE, THOMAS & CO. Ill. catalog of
Racine Boats and Canoes. 12mo., 40pp. of
designs and plans, pict. wrap.

1885 Chicago   ICHi
------ Ill. catalog of Veneer and Lapstreak
boats and canoes - The Racine, St. Paul,
Shadow, Saranac, Michigan, Belle City, Lake
Geneva and other designs and models. Sq.
8vo., 44pp., a fine job, wrap.

1893 Chicago   ICHi
------ Ill. catalog of boats, canoes, hardware and marine accessories.

nd. Lakefield, Ont., Can.   NBmlAM
LAKEFIELD CANOE WORKS. 8 page ill.
circular of boats and canoes.

1836-80 New Bedford   MNbedfOD
          CtMYM   MH   RP   ViNewM
LINDSAY, BENJAMIN, TABER, C. & A., &
TABER, CHARLES & CO. Outfits for a
Whaling Voyage. Printed lists of every
imaginable piece of marine chandlery plus
many used only on whalers - with blanks to
be filled in for each voyage, sometimes four
or five years - quantities and prices. 16mo.,
cf. or mbld. bds., as a rule, pict. title. Ptd.
by J.C. Parmenter to 1840, by Benjamin
Lindsay until c.1845, and from then on by
A. & A. Taber and Charles Taber & Co.

c.1895 Harrison, N.J.   ViNewM
MARINE ENGINE CO. Ill. catalog of steam
launches.

c.1900 Chicago   ICHi
MARINE IRON WORKS. Catalog #14. Boilers, engines, machinery and complete steam
craft. 8vo., 48pp., ills., wrap.

c.1900 Racine, Wis.   ViNewM
MARTIN, FRED W. Ill. catalog of plans for
boats and canoes.

nd. Racine, Wis.   NBmlAM
------ Album of designs for boats, canoes
and yachts. 72pp., ills., pls., drawings and
plans.

1893 Veazie, Me.   ViNewM
MORRIS, B.N. Ill. catalog of canoes.

1893 Veazie, Me.   ViNewM
------ Ill. catalog of boats, canoes, etc.

1888 Baldwinsville, N. Y.   DSi
MORRIS MACHINE WORKS. Est. 1864. Ill.
catalog of centennial marine pumps, engines,
propellers and fittings. 16pp.

c.1900 Salem, O.   OHi
MULLINS, W.H. Catalog #8. Stamped and
embossed sheet metal boats. 8vo., 36pp.,
fine photo. ills., pict. wrap.

1898 South Boston, Mass.   ViNewM
MURRAY & TREGURTHA. Ill. catalog of
launches and engines.

1860 New York   MH-BA
NEFF & MERRILL. Catalog of ship chandlery, stores and provisions. 16mo., 30pp.,
a good complete list for 1860.

1896 New York   DSi
NEWHALL SHIP CHANDLERY CO. 1896
ship chandlers', sailmakers' hardware, boat
blocks, flags, anchors, hawsing beetles,
mallets, harpoons, irons, etc. 32mo.,
148pp. of ills., cl.

1884 New London, Conn.   CtMyM
NEW LONDON VISE WORKS. Joseph Hyde
Sons & Co. Ill. catalog of solid box vises,
iron ship carpenters' clamps and heavy
marine hardware. 8vo., 8pp.

1866 New York   CtMyM
NEW YORK SUBMARINE CO. Improved
buoying apparatus, diving apparatus, etc.
10pp. with 2 fld. pls.

1883 Peterborough, N. H.   NBmlAM
ONTARIO CANOE CO. Catalog of a New
Folding Boat. 4pp., ills.

1880 Battle Creek, Mich.   MiU-T
OSGOOD. Osgood's Portable Folding Canvas Boat. Pat. Feb. 20, 1870. 16mo., 16pp.,
ills. with pict. wrap.

1882 Lockport, N. Y.   MnHi
PENFIELD BLOCK CO. Ill. cata-   DSi
log of wood and wrought iron blocks, dead
eyes, bulls' eyes, hearts and lizards, topmast
trucks, etc. 8vo., 40pp., fine ills., wrap.

1897 Eddystone & Philadelphia   PBS
PENN IRON WORKS. Ill. catalog of Globe
marine engines, launches, yachts, etc.
8vo., fine ills., wrap.

1898 Eddystone & Philadelphia   PHi
------ Ill. catalog of Globe gas and gasoline engines for launches, etc. 8vo., 102pp.,
lists of owners of yachts, fine photos.

1897-1912 Eddystone & Philadelphia   PBS
------ Collection of 5 ill. catalogs, books
of diags. and plans, photos., etc.

1826 Paterson   MH-BA
PHENIX MFG. CO. Catalog of Phenix mill
canvas. 16mo., 10pp., price list. Tests.
from U.S. Navy and various shipbuilders and
ship captains.

1883 Waukegan   ICHi
POWELL & DOUGLAS. Ill. catalog of fishing, hunting and pleasure boats. 8vo., 24pp.,
fine ills., col. pict. wrap.

1884 Waukegan   ViNewM
------ Ill. catalog of pleasure
boats. Litho. ills. by Miller & Umbdenstock.
Staat's hand propeller launch, models and
designs. 8vo., 32pp., ills. throughout, col.
pict. wrap.

c.1875 Providence   RHi
PROVIDENCE TOOL CO. Catalog of heavy
marine hardware, chain links, ship chandlery,
etc. 8vo., 20 fine pls., wrap.

1913 Pittsburgh   OC
REES, JAMES & SONS CO. Ill. catalog of iron
and steel hull freight and passenger steamers,
tugboats, dredge boats, towboats and barges
for inland waters. Light draught river
steamers of every description a specialty,
being the pioneers in the knockdown galvanized steel hull watertight compartment and
composite steamers for foreign trade. 4to.,
60pp., fine ills. See also American Ship
building Co.

1883 Providence   RHi
RHODE ISLAND TOOL CO. Price list of
sailmakers' furnishings and ship chandlery,
marine hardware, etc. 8vo., 74pp., fine ills.,
pict. wrap.

1880 Canton, N. Y.   NBmlAM
RUSHTON, J.H. MFG. Ill. catalog of St.
Lawrence Skiffs, Barnegat Sneak Boats, American Traveler's Canoe - models Stella
Maris, Mohegan, Princess, Grayling - also
equipment, accessories, etc. 12mo., 24pp.,
fine ills., pict. wrap.

1881 Canton, N. Y.   NBmlAM
------ Ill. catalog of Sporting Boats and
Canoes.

BOATS

1882 Canton, N. Y.   NBmlAM
------ Ill. catalog of new designs.

1884 Canton, N. Y.   NBmlAM
------ Ill. catalog. 8vo., 48pp.

1885 Canton, N. Y.   NBmlAM
------ Ill. catalog of   NCooHi ViNewM
new plans and designs.

1886-1890 Canton, N. Y.   NBmlAM
------ Four ill. catalogs with designs and
plans.

1891 Canton, N. Y.   NBmlAM
------ Ill. catalog of   NCaS NCooHi
sporting and hunting boats and canoes.

1881 New York   ViNewM
SAFETY STEAM POWER CO. Ill. catalog.

1900 St. Louis   MoSHi
ST. LOUIS & TENNESSEE RIVER PACKET
CO. Ill. catalog.

c.1884 Boston   MH-BA
STANDARD LIFE-SAVING MATTRESS CO.
Inc. 1884. Ill. catalog and tests. of patent
air cushions and mattresses. 12mo., 16pp.

1881 Rahway, N. J.   NBmlAM
STEPHENS, W.P. Catalog of canoes and
sailing boats. 16pp., fine ills.

1853 Boston   MH-BA
TENNEY & CO. Price list of ship chandlery, naval and ship stores, West India groceries, goods, etc. 16mo., 22pp.

1881 Boston   MH-BA
THAXTER, SAMUEL & SON. Est. 1770.
Oldest nautical warehouse in the country.
Mfg. and importers of nautical and optical
instruments, chart and book publishers and
compass adjusters. 4to., 32pp., ill. Still
under the same sign - Admiral Vernon with
his quadrant.

1894 New York   NN
TIEBOUT, W. & J. Ill. catalog and price
list of brass and galvanized marine hardware, anchors, buoys, lamps, flags, bells,
cannon, oars and life belts. Fine ills.

c.1900 New York   TxDaDeG
TOWNSEND-DOWNEY SHIPBUILDING CO.
Ill. catalog. Builders of steel and wooden

vessels of all types, marine engines, boilers, etc. Photo. of Kaiser Wilhelm's
Meteor, etc. Tall 4to. with fine ills.

1894 San Francisco   CSmH
UNION GAS ENGINE CO. Catalog of stationary engines and launches, etc. 36pp.
with fine ills.

c.1880 Savannah, Ga.   GU
WALTER, JAMES E. Ship Chandler. Check
list of ship stores, rope, cordage, oakum,
paints, dead eyes, whale irons, etc. with
pilotage information, etc. 24mo., brochure
of 18pp., stiff wrap.

1871 Troy, N. Y.   NBmlAM
WATERS, BALCH & CO.   NTR
Mfg. of paper boats. Annual ill. catalog and
oarsman's manual. 4to., 294pp., fine ills.
throughout, wrap. One of the best small
boat references.

1888 Watertown, N. Y.   ViNewM
WATERTOWN BOAT & CANOE CO. Cata-
log of St. Lawrence Skiffs, Barnegat Sneaks,
etc. 8vo., 56pp., fine ills., pict. wrap.

c.1850 Boston   NNMM
WEBSTER & KINGMAN. Carved ornaments
for ships, etc. See Architectural Building
Materials.

nd. Middletown, Conn.   CtHi
WILCOX, CRITTENDEN & CO. Est. 1847.
Catalog #80. Marine hardware and fittings,
from an anchor to a sailmaker's palm and
needle. 8vo., 372pp., fine ills. throughout,
view of shops, a fine reference, cl. See A
Century of Dependability for history of this
firm wherein they ill. other early catalogs
in the company files.

1885 Chicago   ViNewM
WILLARD, CHARLES P. & CO.   ICHi
Ill. catalog of Willard's steam launches, tugboats, yachts, paddle wheel ferry boats, etc.
8vo., 16pp., fine ills., wrap.

1888 Chicago   MnHi
------ Catalog #18 of steam boilers,
engines, launches, etc. 4to., 24pp., ill.,
wrap.

1893 Chicago   MoSHi
------ Ill. catalog of steam launches,
yachts, etc.

Many of our outstanding hardware catalogs list and illustrate marine hardware, especially the very
comprehensive ones issued by Reading, Sargent, Bingham and Simmons (over 5000pp.). Also don't
overlook Montgomery Ward and Sears Roebuck & Co., both semi-annual and special hardware catalogs. Whaling harpoons turn up in the most unexpected pages.

Chapter 11

Books, Booksellers and Publishers

I undertake this chapter with the hope that a short explanation will be read. The utter impossibility of listing and locating the American booksellers' catalogs from the very beginning should be apparent to the initiated. If you have access to such monumental works as Brigham, Evans, McKay and Sabin, brush up a bit on the subject. One of the reasons for history is background. If you don't know that American book auction and sales catalogs were first printed in 1713, you may want to do a little reading before you attempt to use this guide -- and criticize it.

This chapter covers one of the most important subjects in the whole gamut of Americana. Without printed catalogs of books, brochures and pamphlets there would be no records of anything. Use it as a supplement to the exhaustive material already recorded and preserved. Since many of the listings are herein offered as examples of imagination rather than important imprints, I suggest it as a cracker and cheese with brandy dessert -- NOT as a checklist in any way, shape or form.

1886 Philadelphia   MH-BA
ALTEMUS, HENRY. Philadelphia Bible
Warehouse. Est. 1842. Catalog of Bibles,
books and albums. 4to., 28pp., ill., wrap.

1872 Philadelphia & San Francisco   CHi
AMERICAN SUNDAY SCHOOL UNION.
Pacific Coast repository. Catalog of books
and various other publications. 4to., 44pp.,
wrap.

ANDREWS, JOHN S. See Metropolitan.

1863 San Francisco & New York   CtHi
APPLETON, D.E. & CO. John Brown and
The Union Right or Wrong Songster, con-
taining all the celebrated John Brown and
Union songs and desc. book catalog. 16mo.,
64 and 49pp.

1879 Philadelphia   PKsL
BAIRD, HENRY CAREY & CO. Catalog of
practical and scientific books for Dec. 1,
1879. 8vo., 96pp., pict. wrap.

1887 San Francisco   CHi
BANCROFT, A.L. & CO. Catalog of books,
stationery and school furnishings. 8vo.,
ill., pict. wrap.

1887-8 San Francisco   CHi
------ Catalog of the publications of
Porter & Coates of Philadelphia. 8vo.,
ill., pict. wrap.

1892 San Francisco   CHi
------ Spring list and holiday bulletin of
Houghton, Mifflin & Co. 8vo., ill., pict.
wrap.

1890 San Francisco   CHi
BANCROFT-WHITNEY CO. Catalog of law
books, etc. 12mo., 106pp., bds.

1883-4 Hartford, Conn.   CtHi
BARROWS, S.W. & CO. Ill. catalog of
holiday books for Christmas and New Years.
Estes and Lauriat titles. 8vo., 24pp.

1791 New Haven   CtHi
BEERS, ISAAC & CO. Catalog of books
sold by him at his bookstore in New Haven.
12mo., 24pp.

1801 New Haven   CtHi
------ Catalog of books for sale at their
bookstore in New Haven. 12mo., 75pp.

1770 Philadelphia   Evans 11563
BELL, ROBERT. Catalog of old physical
and surgical authors to be sold at the prices
marked therein.

1770 Philadelphia   Evans 11564
------ Catalog of second hand Greek and
Latin classics for sale by Robert Bell.

1778 Philadelphia   Evans 15734
------ Catalog of books in Bell's circulating library, containing about 2000 volumes.

1778 Philadelphia   Evans 15735
------ Jewels and diamonds for sentimentalists now on sale at Bell's bookstore, next
door to St. Paul's Church, Philadelphia.

1786 Philadelphia   Evans 19544
------ Catalog of Jewels and Diamonds
for Sentimentalists! Lately returned from

the Eastward. At the bookstore of the late deceased will begin the sale of a number of said decedent jewels and diamonds for sentimentalists!

1804 Boston   CSmH
BOOKSELLERS.   NN   MH   DLC
A catalog of all books printed in the United States, with prices, where published, etc., annexed. Published by the Booksellers. 79pp.

1889 New York   NNGr
BRADBURN, THOMAS. May catalog of miscellaneous, new and second hand books, rare, scarce and standard. Prices do not include postage. There is really nothing new about our postage troubles today. Large 8vo., 16pp.

1769 Philadelphia   Evans 11189
BRADFORD, THOMAS. Catalog of a circulating library kept by Thomas Bradford.

c.1760 Philadelphia   Evans 8555
BRADFORD, WILLIAM. Catalog of books. Just imported from London and to be sold by W. Bradford at the London Coffee House, Philadelphia. Wholesale and retail, with good allowance for those who take a quantity.

1769 Philadelphia   PHi
BRADFORD, WILLIAM &   Evans 11190
THOMAS. Catalog - imported in the last vessels from London, and to be sold by William and Thomas Bradford, printers, booksellers and stationers, at their bookstore in Market Street adjoining the London Coffee House; or, by Thomas Bradford, at his house in Second Street one door from Arch Street -- a large and neat assortment of books and stationery. Fol., 2pp.

1885 Cookton, O.   NNU
BUCKEYE CLUB AGENCY. Model list of leading periodicals of America. 8vo., 16pp., wrap.

1817 Buffalo, N. Y.   NBuHi
BUFFALO BOOK-STORE. A catalog of the Buffalo Book-Store. Library companies, merchants and others purchasing a considerable amount will have a very liberal deduction. Ptd. S.H. & H.A. Salisbury, Buffalo's first printers. 12mo., 29pp.

1883 New York
BUILDER & WOOD-WORKER. Hints on estimating. A handbook for builders by Chas. D. Lakey - with A Catalog of Valuable Books on Architecture. 16mo., 64pp., ill. catalog, 27-64pp., wrap.

1804 Northampton, Mass.   MBAt
BUTLER, SIMEON & ILIHU. Catalog of books for sale at their store.

1796 Philadelphia   CtHi
CAMPBELL, ROBERT. A catalog for 1796 containing a very extensive and valuable collection of books in the different branches of literature and science. 8vo., 83pp.

1795 New York   Evans 18947
CAMPBELL, SAMUEL. A catalog of a valuable collection of books in elegant bindings, and genuine London and Edinburgh editions. Catalog advertised to be had gratis at place of sale. C.S.Brigham considers this the first example of _real_ American book cataloging.

1827 Philadelphia   PKsL
CAREY, H.C. & LEA L. Catalog of valuable works now preparing and speedily to be published. 12mo., 12pp.

1817 Philadelphia   PKsL
CAREY, M. & SON. Catalog of modern publications for March. 12mo., 24pp.

1886 Cincinnati   OC
CLARKE, ROBERT & CO. Bibliotheca Americana. Catalog of a valuable collection of books and pamphlets relating to America. 8vo., VII, 280 and 251pp., ptd. wrap.

1887 Cincinnati   OC
------ Supplement to Bibliotheca Americana. 8vo., 60pp., ptd. wrap.

1803 New York   NNGr
COLLINS & PERKINS. Printers and importers of books to the College of Physicians and Surgeons. A catalog of medical, chemical and botanical books for sale. 8vo., 16pp., prices in quill and ink.

1805 New York   MWA
COLLINS, PERKINS & CO. A catalog of books and stationery for sale. 24pp.

1882 New York   DAIA
COMSTOCK, WILLIAM T. Publisher. Ill. catalog of practical books on architecture. 8vo., 82pp. with fine ills., pict. wrap. Data about various editions and notes about editions destroyed by fires not available elsewhere to the best of my knowledge.

1818 Hartford, Conn.   CtHi
COOKE & HALE. Catalog of books offered to the public on the most accommodating terms, at wholesale or retail by Oliver D. Cooke and Horatio G. Hale, etc. 8vo., 47pp.

1869 Boston   NNGr
CROSBY & DAMRELL. October tradelist. Large 8vo., 30pp., wrap.

1897 Philadelphia   PKsL
CURTIS PUBLISHING CO. A Year of
Pleasure for One Dollar. 16mo., 32pp.,
ills., pict. wrap. Included because of the
authors listed with notes on their books.

1774 Williamsburg, Va.   DLC
DIXON, JOHN, & HUNTER,   Evans 13252
WILLIAM. A catalog of books to be sold at
the Post Office, Williamsburg. Fol. broadside.

c.1900 Philadelphia   PKsL
ELIOT PUBLISHING CO. New ill. catalog
of books, fine bindings, parlor albums and
novelties. 8vo., 96pp., pict. wrap.

c.1857 New York   NNGr
EVANS & CO. D.W.Evans & J.H.Prescott.
The Original Great Gift Book Establishment.
Desc. catalog of books, catalog of prizes.
The philosophy of a gold watch with every
book is something to be considered and
studied even in this day and age. I wonder
how the Income Tax Lads would handle this
one. 12mo., 60pp., pict. wrap. by Roberts.
N. Y. street scene of store with omnibus and
grand 1857 delivery wagons, etc.

c.1858 New York   NNGr
EVANS, D.W. & CO. Pioneer Gift Book
Store. A descriptive catalog - complete
index - a gift worth from .50 to $100. with
every book purchased for $1.00. Catalog of
Gifts and Scheme of Distribution. Sq.
16mo., 72pp., pict. wrap. of store and interior by J.W.Orr, N. Y.

1860 Philadelphia   PKsL
EVANS, GEORGE G. Formerly Evans &
Co. G.G. Evans Great Gift Book Store.
Est. 1854. Great gift sale with scheme of
prizes, pedlars solicited - the Barnum
period and the Barnum spirit. Sq. 16mo.,
50pp., delightful pict. wrap. of store and
interior by J.Spittall.

1861 Philadelphia   PKsL
------ New improved catalog. 12mo.,
48pp., pict. wrap. Preface about his competitors being wiped out in panic of 1857-8 -
how he survived - good reading.

c.1861 Philadelphia   PKsL
------ Special catalog - special prizes,
etc. Sq. 16mo., 24pp., pict. wrap.

1744 Philadelphia   Evans 5396
FRANKLIN, BENJAMIN. A catalog of
choice and valuable books, consisting of near
600 volumes, in most faculties and sciences,
viz: Divinity, history, law, mathematics,
philosophy, physics, poetry, etc., which will
begin to be sold for ready money only, by
Benjamin Franklin, at the Post Office in
Philadelphia, on Wednesday, the 11th day of

April 1744, at nine a clock in the morning;
and, for dispatch, the lowest price is
mark'd in each book. The sale to continue
three weeks, and no longer; and what then
remains will be sold at an advanced price.
Those persons that live remote, by sending
their order and money to said B. Franklin,
may depend on the same justice as if present. 16mo., 16pp. Divided into sections
entitled - Books in folio, books in quarto,
books in octavo, books in duodecimo - and
one final item a pair of globes, 16in. in
diameter, made by J. Senex.

1886 Chicago   NNMM
GASKELL, G.A. & CO. Ill., desc. and
priced catalog. 4 lvs., wrap.

1769 Philadelphia   Evans 11282
HALL, DAVID. David Hall, at the new
Printing Office, in Market Street, Philadel-
phia, has to dispose of wholesale and retail,
the following books . . . Fol., 2pp. Ptd.
D. Hall and W. Sellers.

1804 Newburyport   MB
HEDMAN, E. A catalog of sea books, etc.

1833 Boston   DeWint
HILLIARD, GRAY & CO. Catalog of books
recently purchased in London and for sale.
8vo., 36pp., wrap.

1818 New Haven   CtHi
HOWE & SPAULDING. A catalog of books
for sale by . . . 8vo., 105pp.

c.1863 New York   NNGr
HURST & CO. Catalog of standard books,
games and stationery. 8vo., ill. throughout,
pict. wrap. A rather pleasant change from
18th century importance to Abe's Jokes,
Incidents of Camp Life, Bottle-Nose Ben,
the Indian Hater, etc.

c.1864 New York   NNGr
------ New catalog of standard books, etc.
8vo., ill., unusual pict. wrap.

1856 Philadelphia   PKsL
JOHNSON, T. & J.W. A catalog of law
books. 8vo., 48pp., wrap.

1772 Boston   Evans 12424
KNOX, HENRY. General. A catalog of
books imported and to be sold by Henry
Knox. 8vo. The Yankee bookseller who
rescued the cannon for General Washington
and trained them on his British customers
and drove them out of Boston.

1896 Philadelphia   PKsL
LEA BROTHERS. Publishers. Special
clearance sale for 1896 medical books, etc.
12mo., 16pp., red and blk. type.

c.1858 Philadelphia   PKsL
LINDSAY & BLAKISTON. Publishers. A
catalog of medical, dental and pharmaceutical books. 8vo., 64pp., wrap.

c.1860 Philadelphia   NNGr
LIPPINCOTT, J.B. & CO. Catalog of medical works for sale by booksellers generally.
8vo., 24pp., woodcut ills., wrap.

1869 Albany, N. Y.   NNGr
LITTLE, W.C. & CO. Catalog of law books.
Sq. 16mo., 132pp., ptd., wrap.

1805 Salem, Mass.   MSaE
MACANULTY, BERNARD B. A catalog of
books, stationery, etc.

1772 Williamsburg   Evans 12441
MacGILL, ROBERT. Catalog of a small
collection of books, consisting of history,
entertainment, new novels, song books,
some law books, and a few divinity books.
For sale by Robert MacGill.

1836 Boston   CtHi
MASSACHUSETTS SABBATH SCHOOL
SOCIETY. Desc. catalog of publications of
Depository #25 on Cornhill. 12mo., 24pp.

c.1860 New York   NNGr
METROPOLITAN GIFT BOOK STORE.
John S. Andrews, Prop. Great sale of
books - a gift with every book from .25 to
$100. - $1000. worth of prizes - Preserve
this catalog - 1300 books listed, cheaper
than anyone else plus prizes. 24mo., 38pp.
of delightfully Barnum blurbery, wrap.

1762 New York   Evans 9222
NOEL, GARRAT. A catalog of books, etc.
sold by Garrat Noel, bookseller and station-
er, from London, at his store next door to
the Merchants' Coffee House, consisting of
history, divinity, law, physics, military,
surgery, miscellany, philosophy, antiquity,
trade and commerce, mathematics, husbandry, gardening and farriery, clasicks and
school books, novels, poems, plays, etc. At
which place will be found a constant supply
of books and stationery of all sorts, with all
the new published articles, and where store-
keepers, pedlars and others may be furnished in a wholesale or retail way, and all
orders directed to him will be punctually
complied with. 8vo., 36pp. My own inter-
pretation would, of course, read: all orders,
mailed with cash or proper recommendation
and address, will be carefully packed and
shipped promptly.

1767 New York   Evans 10718
------ Catalog of books on history, divinity,
law, arts and sciences and the several parts
of polite literature, to be sold by Garrat
Noel, bookseller. 12mo., 23 plus pp.

1771 New York   Evans 12168
NOEL, GARRAT & HAZARD,   CtHi
EBENEZER. A catalog of books sold by
Noel & Hazard at their book and stationery
store, next door to the Merchants' Coffee
House, where the public may be furnished
with all sorts of books and papers. 8vo.,
40pp.

1805 Lansingburg, N. Y.   N
PENNIMAN & BLISS. A catalog of books,
classical, scientific and miscellaneous; also
a variety of stationery which will be sold at
New York prices. 36pp.

c.1870 Philadelphia   PKsL
PETERSON, T.B. & BROTHERS. Ill. catalog of books - portraits of authors, etc.
8vo., 24pp., pict. wrap.

1861 Philadelphia   PKsL
QUAKER CITY PUBLISHING HOUSE. A
catalog of gift books - desc. catalog of
Duane Rulison's gift enterprise. 8vo.,
48pp., ill., pict. wrap.

1761 Philadelphia   Evans 8998
RIVINGTON, JAMES. Catalog of books for
sale by James Rivington.

1762 New York & Philadelphia Evans 9259
------ A catalog of books sold by Rivington
& Brown at their stores in New York and
Philadelphia. 90pp.

nd. St. Louis   MoSHi
ROEDER, PHILIP. Bookseller. Holiday
catalog of books and stationery.

1865 New York   NNGr
SHELDON & CO. A desc. catalog of publications. 12mo., 56pp. and page 57 with
quotation from W. H. Channing. Wrap.

1853 New York
STEARNS & CO. Mammoth catalog of
books, prints, valentines and stationery.
Valentines from .06 to $20., postage free.
8vo., 48pp., ills. in great variety. Pict.
wrap.

1804 Newburyport   MB
STEDMAN, EBENEZER. A catalog of sea
books, pilot's charts, maps, etc. Broadside.

1883 New York & Cincinnati   MoSHi
VAN ANTWERP, BRAGG & CO. Price list
of the eclectic educational series.

1896 Denver   CoD
WESTLEY, CHARLES. Ill. catalog of fine
books, arts and crafts, etc.

1837 Philadelphia   PKsL
WHETMAN, JOSEPH. Bookseller. A
general catalog of new and old books in
various departments. 12mo., 76pp.

1869 San Francisco   CHi
WHITNEY, SUMNER. Catalog of law books.
8vo., 172pp., bds.

1885 San Francisco   CHi
------ Catalog of law books, book cases,

boards, etc. Albums, ledgers, etc. 8vo.,
102 and 52pp., bds.

1772 Philadelphia   Evans 12629
WOODHOUSE, WILLIAM. Catalog of new
and old books for sale by William Woodhouse.

If your grandfather was a bookseller, and you can't find any listing of his catalogs, please refer to my heading. Ask your local librarian, or write to any of the national, state, municipal or university special collections curators, and I am sure they will give you complete details as to the locations of the bibliographies available. If you live near New York City, drop in at the Grolier Club where you will find one of the most outstanding collections in the country. Remember, this is only a guide.

Chapter 12

Carriages, Wagons & Accessories

Individual carriage makers' biographies, histories of American carriages and chapters in volumes covering American transportation have all exploited and recorded the story of the development of this colorful facet of Americana. Although many compilers have used one or two illustrations from catalogs, none have been thoughtful enough to locate the sources so that others could use them.

The completeness of this chapter indicates that our libraries and repositories from coast to coast have recognized these brochures as important Americana, saved them, and cataloged them for research. From about 1850, when Studebaker Brothers realized that newspaper and periodical advertising was not adequate, the new presses started rolling Studebaker catalogs as well as their wagons all over the country. From the smallest 48mo. with only one or two models featured, to the masterpieces of the Gay Nineties, offering the finest styles ever built -- the brougham to carry you down Fifth Ave. with two coachmen and a spanking pair of chestnuts, and the most elegant hearse one can imagine to carry you to the old cemetery, -- this panorama of examples of the carriage maker's art assisted by the designers and lithographers should satisfy the most exacting scholar.

1886 Chicago   MnHi
ABBOTT BUGGY CO. Catalog of buggies, carriages, etc. 32pp., fine ills., wrap.

c.1876 Concord, N. H.   NhHi
ABBOTT-DOWNING CO. Mfg. of coaches, wagons and drays. Catalog of models and styles. Ills. of wagons and four coaches. Ills. called charts.

nd. Concord, N. H.   NhHi
------ Catalog with colored drawings, wrap. 12pp. with 2 and 3 drawings on each page.

nd. Concord, N. H.   NhHi
------ Catalog of wagons only, col. drawings. 14pp., one wagon each page.

c.1880-90 Concord, N. H.   NNMM
------ Catalog of wagons and trucks. 12 lvs., 12 col. pls., each with detailed desc. of models - express, delivery and trucks. Pict. wrap. of plant.

c.1890 Concord, N. H.   MiU-T
------ Catalog of wagons, trucks, etc. Ill.

nd. Kalamazoo   MiU-H
ACME ROAD BREAKING & SPEEDING CART CO. Catalog.

1895 Cincinnati   OC
ALLIANCE CARRIAGE CO. 7th annual triumphal tour for 1895 - the successful salesman on the road. 16mo., 80pp., ills. of models and styles, pict. wrap.

1897 Cincinnati   ICHi
------ Styles for 1897. Honest   OC
work at honest prices - we lead where others follow - best on earth. Capacity 10,000 per year. Sq. 12mo., 168pp., fine ills. throughout, pict. wrap.

1899 Cincinnati   OC
AMERICAN CARRIAGE CO. Catalog #14. 8vo., 48pp., fine ills., some in col. with drivers, etc. Pict. wrap.

1902 Cincinnati   OC
------ Catalog #17. 64 plus 32pp., fine ills., pict. wrap.

nd. Kalamazoo   MnHi
AMERICAN CART CO. Ill. catalog. 8pp.

c.1891 Buffalo, N. Y.   NNMM
AMERICAN GEAR & SPRING CO. Ill., desc. and priced catalog of wagons and springs. 26pp., wrap.

1897 Owensboro, Ky.   KyU
AMES, F.A. & CO. Catalog of pleasure vehicles. 8vo., 32pp., fine pls. of models. Wrap.

1893 Boston   NCooHi
AMES PLOW CO. Catalog of agricultural wagons, farm wagons, dump and road carts, business vehicles, harness, etc. 112pp., ills., 8 fine pls.

1900 Boston   CtY
------ Catalog. See also listings under Agricultural Implements.

75

1877 Amesbury, Mass. MAmPL
AMESBURY CARRIAGE MFG. ASSN. Compliments of . . . Ill. catalog of carriages.
Carriage center of the world! A fine pict.
record.

1892 Amesbury, Mass. MAmPL
------ Joint catalog of exhibitors at world
fair at Chicago. Ptd. Amesbury for exhibition.

1893 Amesbury, Mass. MAmPL
------ Official souvenir issued with other
American mfg. represented. Ill.

c.1890 Cincinnati OC
ANDERSON & HARRIS CARRIAGE CO. Fol.
broadside with 26 ills. of styles, models and
designs - in red type - with 8vo. ill. circular of harness. Prices.

c.1900 Detroit NSbSM
ANDERSON CARRIAGE CO. High school
line of high grade carriages. 4to., 92pp.,
with fine pls. throughout, col. pict. wrap.

c.1900 Detroit MiU-T
------ Catalog of high grade carriages.
8vo., 128pp., fine pls., pict. wrap.

nd. Sidney, O. OC
ANDERSON, FRAZER & CO. Sidney Wheel
Works. Price list. 16mo., 14pp., ills. of
pat. wheels and wooden hubs. Pict. wrap.

1891 Lansing *OREGON?* OrU
ANDERSON ROAD CART CO. (Agent,
Portland, Ore.) Catalog of Anderson road
carts - breaking, speeding, track and physician's. 16mo., 16pp., ill., wrap. 8 ills.
tipped in.

1881 Cincinnati OHi
ASHBROOK, TUCKER & CO. Catalog of
first class buggies, carriage and wagon
hardware, trimmings and wood work, tops
and bodies. 32pp., ills., wrap.

1890 Atlanta
ATLANTA WAGON CO. See Florence
Wagon Co., successors.

1886 Amesbury, Mass. NSbSM
ATWOOD BROTHERS MFG. CO. Catalog of
carriage lamps, mountings, dashes with
eagle finials, brass parts, etc. Fine ills.

1890 Auburn, N.Y. CBKcoM
AUBURN WAGON CO. Catalog of wagons,
bob sleighs for farm and team. 12mo., fine
ills., wrap.

c.1901 Cincinnati OC
AUEL, JOHN. Mfg. of Carriages and Buggies. Catalog #42. 36pp., ills., pict. wrap.

c.1901 Cincinnati OC
------ Catalog #43. 40pp. with 18 page
price list.

c.1902 Cincinnati OC
------ Ill. catalog #44. 64pp. with 32 page
price list. Pict. wrap.

c.1902 Cincinnati OC
------ Ill. circular showing 16 models
with ill. wagon list.

1884 Cincinnati OC
AUFDERHEIDE, WILLIAM & CO. Cincinnati Carriage Works. Ill. catalog. 12mo.,
30pp., pict. wrap. Cont. invoice laid in.

c.1872 Jackson, Mich. MiU-H
AUSTIN, TOMLINSON & WEBSTER MFG.
Est. 1843. The Jackson Michigan Wagon.
6 page 24mo. folder-thimble skein wagons-
one ill.

1889 Amesbury, Mass. MAmPL
BABCOCK, F.A. & CO. Carriage NNMM
builders' catalog for foreign and domestic
use. Ill. catalog of 45 lvs., fine pls.

1882 Watertown, N.Y. PShipL
BABCOCK, H.H. & SONS. Prop. of Jefferson Buggy Co. Catalog and price list of
side bar and side spring buggies, etc. 16mo.,
24pp., fine ills. of models. Pict. wrap.

nd. Watertown, N.Y. NSbSM
BABCOCK, H.H. BUGGY CO. Ill. circular
of models and styles.

1893 Watertown, N.Y. CtY
------ Ill. catalog of buggies.

c.1900 Watertown, N.Y. MiD
------ Ill. catalog. 90pp., fine ref., wrap.

c.1901 Philadelphia Branch NSbSM
------ Ill. catalog of models and styles,
with fine pls. throughout. 4to., 96pp.

BABY CARRIAGES. See Toy and House
Furnishings Chapters.

1882 Amesbury, Mass. MAmPL
BAILEY, S.R. & CO. N.B. One of the
greatest and best remembered American
carriage and sleigh builders - a legend in
his own time. First est. in East Pittstown,
Maine, in 1856, he moved and expanded in
1866, as the S.R. Bailey Sleigh & Carriage
Mfg. at Bath. About 1882 he moved to
Amesbury, Mass. where he built a great
business that is even today making steel
channels for automobiles, and going strong.
See Sun on the River - The Story of the
Bailey Family Business by Margaret S.
Rice. Concord, N.H. 1955.

nd. Amesbury, Mass.   MAmPL
------ Ill. catalog of carriages, sleighs
and poles.

nd. Amesbury, Mass.   MAmPL
------ Ill. catalog of Bailey pneumatic
whalebone road wagons.

nd. Amesbury, Mass.   MAmPL
------ Ill. catalog issued by S.R. & E.W.M.
Bailey.

nd. Amesbury, Mass.   MAmPL
------ Ill. catalog of carriages, sleighs
and poles.

nd. Amesbury, Mass.   MAmPL
------ Ill. catalog of high grade sleighs.

1896 Amesbury, Mass.   MAmPL
------ Ill. catalog of styles and models for
1896.

nd. Amesbury, Mass.   MAmPL
------ Ill. pamphlet. Home of the Whalebone Road Wagon and Remarks concerning
its production.

c.1884 Lunenburg, Vt.   VtSM
BALCH, GEORGE S. & SON. Ill. catalog of
Corning side bar wagons, piano box, booted
buggy, phaetons, sun tops, farm wagons and
express wagons, hearses, round backs,
Portland and Keene patterns, double sleighs
and buckboards, etc.

1890 Cincinnati   MiU-T
BARKLEY, FRANK B. MFG. CO. Catalog
#20. Harness, saddles, road carts and bug-
gies. 8vo., 44pp., fine tinted ills., wrap.

c.1894 Cincinnati   OHi
------ Catalog #24. 8vo., fine ills. of
models, etc., wrap.

nd. Cincinnati   OC
BARNETT CARRIAGE CO. Ill. catalog.

1889 Valparaiso, Ind.   MnHi
BARRY WAGON & CARRIAGE MFG. CO.
Ill. catalog of styles and models. 42pp.,
fine ills., wrap.

1899 St. Louis   MoSHi
BECK & CORBITT IRON CO. Ill. catalog of
carriage hardware, spokes, leather trimmings and wagon materials. 8vo., 932pp.,
fine ref., pict. cl.

1873 West Meriden, Conn.   MiU-T
BEECHER MFG. CO. Ill. catalog and price
list of carriage builders' hardware, trimmings, etc. 40pp., wrap.

1894 Newtown, Conn.   CtHi
BEERS, D.G. & CO. Tops and trimmings -
Eureka styles. 16mo., 38pp., fine ills.,
pict. wrap.

1896 Newtown, Conn.   Ct
------ Tops and trimmings. 16mo., 40pp.,
fine ills., pict. wrap.

1895 Davenport, Ia.   IaHi
BETTENDORF AXLE CO. Desc. catalog
and price list of Bettendorf hollow steel
wagon gears, etc. 16mo., 12pp., litho. ills.,
pict. wrap.

c.1900 Amesbury, Mass.   MAmPL
BIDDLE, W.E. & CO. 1871-1930. Made
auto bodies after carriage trade died out.
Ill. catalog of carriages and carriage wood
work of every desc.

1890 Amesbury, Mass.   NCooHi
BIDDLE & SMART CO. Special catalog of
the celebrated Clarkson carts, etc. Obl.
12mo., 32pp., fine ills., wrap.

nd. St. Marys, O.   MiU-T
BIMEL CARRIAGE & MFG. CO. Ill. catalog
of fine carriages and buggies. 13pp.

1890 Binghamton   NSbSM
BINGHAMTON WAGON CO. Ill. catalog of
wagons and carriages for farm, business
and pleasure.

1897 Binghamton   NNMM
------ Desc. and ill. catalog. 11pp., wrap.

1885 Burlington, N. J.   NjR
BIRCH, JAMES H. LIGHT CARRIAGE MFG.
The American who invented and sold the
famous rickshaws to the Orient. Fol. pict.
broadside with ills. of plant and 16 styles
and models.

nd. Amesbury, Mass.   MAmPL
BIRD & SCHOFIELD. 1895-1913. Ill. catalog of fine carriages.

1876 South Bend, Ind.   In
BIRDSELL CO. Catalog #14. 14th annual
catalog of cast iron and steel farm wagons.
76pp., fine ills.

c.1885 Cincinnati   OC
BOOB, WILLIAM W. Catalog #19 - buggies,
surreys, express and U.S. mail wagons,
harness, etc. 4to., 78pp., fine ills., wrap.

1879 Boston   CtY
BOSTON BUCKBOARD & CARRIAGE CO.
Ill. catalog of high grade carriages. 8vo.,
styles and models, col. pict. wrap.

1880 Boston   CtY
------ Ill. catalog.

c.1890 Boston   Ct
------ Ill. catalog.

1893 Boston   NSbSM
------ Album of styles - unusually fine ref.
8vo., fine pls. and col. pict. wrap.

1870 Syracuse, N. Y.   MiU-T
BRADLEY & CO. Est. 1832. Ill. catalog of
wagons and carts. 12mo., 20pp., wrap.

1881-1886 Syracuse, N. Y.   NCooHi
------ Collection of ill. catalogs, NSyHi
carts, carriages, wagons, also ill. circular
for this period.

1886 Syracuse, N. Y.   MiD
------ Bradley handy wagons, buckboards,
surreys and delivery wagons. 16mo., 16pp.,
fine ills. of above styles.

1888 Syracuse, N. Y.   MH-BA
------ Ill. catalog of two and four   MnHi
wheel vehicles - styles and models. 40pp.
with circular enc.

1890 Syracuse, N. Y.   MdTanSW
------ Price list B - Bradley wagons.
8vo., circular with col. ills. Cable buckboard, Goodrich triple buckboards.

c.1890 Syracuse, N. Y.   ICHi
------ Ill. catalog of two wheel carts, etc.

nd. Syracuse, N. Y.   MnHi
------ Ill. catalog. 52pp., fine ills., wrap.

1877 New Haven   Ct
BRADLEY, W.H. & CO. Ill. catalog of
carriages and wagons.

1863 New York   MH
BREWSTER & BALDWIN. Ill. catalog of
fine carriages. 96pp.

1868 New York   NN
------ Ill. catalog of carriages. 82 lvs. of
pls.

1879 New York   NN
BREWSTER, J.B. & CO. Est. New Haven,
1810 - Est. New York, 1827. Report of pre-
sentation to Brewster & Co. . . . from the
carriage builders and members of accessory
trades, etc. . . . N.B. Not a catalog but
an important piece in the development of
this industry.

c.1880 New York   MiU-T
------ N. Y. improved method of hanging
half-spring wagons. 161 fine diags. and ills.

nd. New York   PU
------ Ill. catalog of carriages. No further data obtainable. What has become of
the catalogs of one of our most important
American carriage builders? According to

Bishop, one of our greatest, second only to
John Cook of New Haven from whom he
learned the trade in 1810.

1883 Bridgeport, Conn.   MH-BA
BRIDGEPORT CART CO. Ill. catalog.
16mo., 16pp.

nd. Bridgeport, Conn.   NSbSM
BRIDGEPORT COACH LACE CO. 8vo. circular with 6 samples and text.

nd. Amesbury, Mass.   MAmPL
BRIGGS CARRIAGE CO. Est. 1866. Ill.
catalog of Briggs high point wagons.
N.B. When the carriage trade slowed down,
this firm built trolley cars until about 1926.
Although I have a colored glass paper weight
in use on my desk with a fine ill. of a Briggs
High Point Golfers' Break that reads at the
bottom under the calendar for 1898 - Send
for Catalog, sadly enough this seems to be
the only copy ever preserved.

1887-9 Chicago   MnHi
BRISTOL & GALE CO. Ill. catalogs of car-
riages, buggies and road wagons. Jan. 1887,
June 1887, March 1889.

1890 Homer, N. Y. & New Haven   CtHi
BROCKWAY, WILLIAM N. Carriage
Builder. Wholesale catalog of carriages,
wagons, etc. 8vo., 56pp., fine ills., lithos.
by L.S. Punderson of New Haven. Wrap.

1891 Homer, N. Y.   NSbSM
------ Ill. catalog. 4to., 68 pls.,   PKsL
pict. wrap.

1892 Homer, N. Y.   N
------ Ill. catalog. 8vo., 76pp., col. pls.,
pict. wrap.

1907 Homer, N. Y.   MiU-T
------ Ill. catalog. 95pp., fine ills., and
pls. with supplement. 11pp. with ills.

c.1860 New Bedford   NSbSM
BROWNELL, GEORGE L. Ill.   MiD
catalog of fine carriages. 16mo., 32pp., 61
fine pls., wrap.

c.1900 Columbus, O.   OHi
BUCKEYE BUGGY CO. Catalog #27 -
Arbiters of fashion in fine vehicles. 8vo.,
120pp. fine pls., pict. frs. and wrap. A nice
touch and a welcome note among thousands
of cut and dried titles.

1898 Buffalo, N. Y.   NSbSM
BUFFALO SPRING & GEAR CO. Catalog X.
Buffalo bike wagons, buggies. 8vo., 16pp.,
fine ills. of models, wrap.

c.1900 Cincinnati   OC
BUOB & SCHEU MFG. Wholesale price list
of tops, cushions, backs, aprons, etc.
24mo., 48pp., fine ills., pict. wrap.

c.1880 Burlington, Ia.   MnHi
BURG, JOHN & SONS. Ill. catalog of carriages. 56pp. with fine ills., wrap.

1879 Amesbury, Mass.   MAmPL
BURLINGAME, CHARLES A. MFG. Broadside catalog of light carriages. Ills. of
styles and models.

nd. Amesbury, Mass.   MAmPL
------ Ill. catalog of fine carriages.

c.1890 Columbus, O.   OHi
CAPITAL CITY CARRIAGE CO. J.M. Scat-
terday & Co. Prop. Ill. catalog of carriages,
buggies, phaetons, surreys, fancy traps and
wagons. 8vo., 32pp.

nd. Philadelphia   NNMM
CAREY & CO. Est. 1864. Ill. and desc.
catalog of carriage lamps. 28pp., wrap.

c.1900 Philadelphia   PKsL
------ Lamps of quality. 36pp. of pls.
showing 29 styles of lamps for runabouts,
buggies, doctor's phaetons, cut-unders,
traps, surreys, rockaways, wagonettes, am-
bulances, patrols, delivery, fancy vans, dead
wagons, hearse, embalming wagons, landaus,
coaches, etc.

1899 Troy, O.   OHi
CARRIAGE SUN SHADE CO. Catalog of
carriage specialties. 4to., 20pp., fine ills.,
pict. wrap.

1899 Troy, O.   OHi
------ Season of 1899. Sq. 8vo., 16pp.,
fine ills. of tops, seats, etc.

1887 Minneapolis   MnHi
CASE, J.I. IMPLEMENT CO. Catalog of
buggies, carriages, surreys, park wagons,
buckboards, etc. 16mo., 44pp., fine ills.

1897 Chicago   NSbSM
CASH BUYERS UNION. Catalog   ICHi
#317. Special catalog of buggies, carriages,
carts, saddles and harness. Sq. 8vo., fine
ills.

1898 Chicago   ICHi
------ Special catalog of buggies. Ill.

1899 Chicago   ICHi
------ Special catalog E-354 for season of
. . . Sq. 8vo., 128pp., ills., col. pict. wrap.

1889 Jackson, Mich.   MnHi
CENTRAL CITY ROAD CART CO. Ill. catalog of road carts. 15pp., pict. wrap.

1891 Flint, Mich.   MiFLi
CHASE, ZACH. Catalog of fine carriages,
carts, wagons, poles, parts, fancy gates and
horse hosiery. 12mo., fine ills., wrap.

1885 Nashville, Tenn.   MiU-T
CHERRY, MORROW & CO. Farmers' almanac and household annual - famous Tenn.
wagons. 32pp., ills., wrap.

1898 Utica, N. Y.   NNMM
CHILDS, CHARLES H. & CO. Catalog of
fine sleighs. Ill. and desc. 12pp., wrap.

c.1894 Yorkville, Ill.   ICHi
CHURCH, W.R. Doctor's carriages, medical cases, rubber goods for physicians. Ill.

1893 Cincinnati   MiU-T
CINCINNATI CARRIAGE EXHIBI-   OC
TORS at Worlds Columbian Exposition.
Cook, Davis, etc. 73pp. of fine ills. of
American vehicles.

1901 Cincinnati   OC
CINCINNATI VEHICLE CO. Ill. catalog for
April. Tall 16mo., 16pp., wrap.

1902 Columbus, O.   OC
CLIMAX BUGGY CO. Catalog #7. 8vo.,
24pp., fine ills., wrap.

1890 Ilion, N. Y.   NIC
COLEMAN CARRIAGE & WAGON CO. Ill.
catalog of fine carriages. 32pp. of ills.
with ptd. wrap.

1895 Ilion, N. Y.   CBaKM
------ Fine carriages for . . . 8vo.,
50pp., swell ills., pict. wrap.

nd. South Bend, Ind.   In
COLFAX MFG. CO. Ill. catalog of pony
carts and fancy vehicles.

1914 Detroit   MiU-T
COLUMBIA BUGGY CO. Ill. catalog of delivery wagons, etc. 188pp.

c.1900 Columbia, Pa.   PKsL
COLUMBIA WAGON CO. Catalog #45.
Commercial bodies. 4to., 40pp., fine pls.,
wrap.

1885 Columbus, O.   MiU-T
COLUMBUS BUGGY CO. Ill. catalog, re-
modeled with additions of new styles. 48pp.
of fine ills.

1886 Columbus, O.   OAkF
------ Ill. catalog of fine vehicles,   OHi
with test. letter from Walt Whitman. 55pp.
with col. pict. wrap.

1886   Columbus, O.   MiU-T
------ Ill. broadside of Columbus Buggy
goods by C. Walker & Bro. of Ann Arbor,
agents.

1888   Columbus, O.   MnHi
------ Ill. catalog of 60pp.

1889   Columbus, O.   OC
------ Ill. catalog with voluntary tests.
from liverymen. 16mo., 16pp., wrap.

1889   Columbus, O.   OakF
------ Ill. catalog of fine carriages.
12mo., 68pp., col. pict. wrap.

1893   Columbus, O.   OAkF
------ Ill. catalog. 95pp., pict.   MiD
wrap.

c.1900 Columbus, O.   MiU-T
------ See Automobiles.

1898   Columbus, O.   NSbSM
COLUMBUS CARRIAGE & HARNESS CO.
Catalog #22, with fine ills., col. chart, etc.
of carriages, harness, etc. by mail. 4to.,
146pp., fine pls., pict. wrap.

1900   Columbus, O.   OHi
------ Catalog #24. 4to., 160pp., fine ills.,
wrap.

1900   Columbus, O.   CBaKM
------ Catalog #29. 4to., 144pp., of pls.
and ills., col. pict. wrap. Fine job.

1886   Columbus, O.   OC
COLUMBUS DASH & WAGON CO. Fine
vehicles and dashes. 12mo., 24pp., fine ills.
with wrap.

1886   Columbus, O.   OC
------ Catalog of fine vehicles, etc. 4to.,
4pp. with ills. and wholesale price list.

1896   Indianapolis   In
CONDE, H.T. IMPLEMENT CO. Ill. catalog
of carriages and other vehicles.

c.1886 Connorsville, Ind.   In
CONNORSVILLE BUGGY CO. Ill. catalog of
stick-body buggies, phaetons, surreys, buckboards, etc. 8vo., 32pp. of models and
styles. Ills. of The Economist, etc.

1887   Cincinnati   MnHi
COOK CARRIAGE MFG. CO. Catalog of
fine carriages, buggies, surreys, wagons,
etc. 12mo., 75pp. of ills., pict. wrap.

1889   Cincinnati   OC
------ Ill. catalog of vehicles. 12mo.,
48pp., pict. wrap.

1860   New Haven   NCooHi
          DLC   CtHi   VtSM NSbSM
COOK, G. & D.   NN   CtY   Ct
Est. 1794. Ill. catalog of carriages and
special business directory. 8vo., 226pp.,
with excellent tinted litho. pls. of every
American carriage of the day.

nd. New Haven   MiU-T
------ Ill. catalog of carriages detailed
desc. 97pp.

1873   Fort Wayne   In
COOMBS & CO. Catalog of hardware, iron
and wood stock for wagons and carriages.
8vo., 152pp., ills. of fancy carriage steps,
braces, bodies, rails and parts. Ptd. cl.

1882   Fort Wayne   InFw
------ Ill. catalog of carriage and wagon
hardware. 8vo., 342pp., fine ills., cl.

1872   Cortland, N. Y.   VtSM
CORTLAND COUNTY CARRIAGE WORKS.
Catalog of carriages - Democrats, platform
spring wagons, sewing machine wagons, and
top and open buggies. Fine ills., wrap.

1890   Cortland, N. Y.   DLC
CORTLAND MFG. CO. Catalog of fine carriages - styles and models. 8vo., 32pp.,
fine ills., pict. wrap.

1890   Cortland, N. Y.   CBaKM
------ Ill. catalog of carriage specialties
and the celebrated May trap, etc. 8vo.,
40pp.

1887   Cortland, N. Y.   N
CORTLAND TOP & RAIL CO., LTD. Catalog of tops, dashes, cushions, railings and
specialties. Sq. 8vo., 32pp., fine pls., pict.
wrap.

1880   Cortland, N. Y.   NCooHi
CORTLAND WAGON CO. Catalog and price
list of platform spring wagons, buggies,
swell bodies and Portland cutters. 48pp.,
fine ills., wrap.

1883   Cortland, N. Y.   MiU-T
------ Ill. catalog.

1884   Cortland, N. Y.   PShipL
------ Catalog of models with lithos. of
styles by Gies of Buffalo. 16mo., 32pp.,
pict. wrap.

1888   Cortland, N. Y.   NSbSM
------ Fine ill. catalog of open and top
buggies.

1900   Delhi, N. Y.   NSbSM
CRAWFORD, G.W. & H.D. MFG. Catalog of
Stiver's patent runabouts. Large 8vo.,
40pp., fine pls. of models, wrap.

1887 Milwaukee   MnHi
CRIBB, GEORGE C. Ill. catalog of carriages. 32pp., fine ills., wrap.

c.1895 Memphis, Tenn.   NSbSM
CRUMP, E.H. BUGGY & HARNESS CO.
Catalog #20. Largest mail order house in
the South. WE make the prices. 8vo.,
64pp., fine pls. of Dixie buggies and fancy
harness.

c.1890 New Haven   CtHi
CRUTTENDEN & CO., Carriage Makers.
Catalog of fine carriages - L.S. Punderson
litho. pls. of styles - fine ill. ref.

c.1890 New Haven   CtHi
------ Ill. catalog of desirable second hand
carriages.

1880 Rochester, N. Y.   NNMM
CUNNINGHAM, JAMES & SON CO. Ill.
catalog of fine carriages and hearses for
children and parents. 16mo. with 12 fine
pls., pict. wrap.

1873 New Haven   CtHi
DANN BROTHERS & CO. Revised   Ct
ill. price list of arms, shafts, bodies and
coats, 16mo., 24pp., fine ills., with doc.
wrap.

c.1886 Cincinnati   OC
DAVIS, GOULD. Mfg. of Carriages. Fol.
ill. broadside with 22 ills. of styles and
models, with a fine cut of plant.

1887 Cincinnati   ViU
DAVIS, HIRAM W. & CO. Ill. catalog of
carriages - every style, etc.

1894 Cincinnati   OC
------ Led the procession in 1893, propose
to continue that position in 1894. Ill. circular, 16mo., nice bit.

nd. Peoria, Ill.   MnHi
DAVIS, LUTHY & CO. The Easy Cart beats
'em All. 1 page ill. circular with a sense of
humor.

1890 Jonesville, Mich.   MiU-H
DEAL, JACOB J. Builders of Fine Carriages. Catalog of buggies, phaetons and
cutters. 12mo., 20pp., fine woodcuts, wrap.

1876 Columbus, O.   OHi
DENIG & FERSON MFG. Ill. catalog of
childrens' carriages. 24pp. of fine ills.,
wrap.

1879 Columbus, O.   OHi
------ Ill. catalog of carriages and velocipedes. 28pp., pict. wrap.

1886 Denver   NSbSM
DENVER MFG. CO. Catalog #2. Wagons,
carriages and harness. 4to., ills. throughout, styles and price list.

1895 Canton, O.   ICHi
DEXTER WAGON CO. Ill. catalog of carriages and wagons.

nd. Flint, Mich.   MiFli
DURANT-DORT CARRIAGE CO. Catalog
#14. Ills. of models, etc. Wrap.

c.1885 Cincinnati   OC
EAGLE CARRIAGE CO. Ill. catalog. 8vo.,
48pp., fine ills., eagle pict. wrap.

1891 East Williston, N. Y.   NSbSM
EAST WILLISTON CART CO. Ill. catalog
of carts and carriages.

1885 Cleveland   MnHi
EBERHARD MFG. CO. Ill. catalog of malleable iron carriage steps, braces, brackets
and hardware.

1883 Salem, O.   NSbSM
EDWARDS, M.L. MFG. CO. Ill. catalog of
fine carriages.

1884 Elkhart   MnHi
ELKHART CARRIAGE & HARNESS MFG.
CO. Catalog #21. Wagons, carriages,
harness. Fine ills., 80pp., pict. wrap.

1885 Elkhart   InELK
------ Catalog #22. Ills. of wagons and
harness.

1886 Elkhart   OrU
------ Catalog #23. 4to., 64pp., fine ills.,
pict. wrap.

1887 Elkhart   MiD
------ Catalog #24.

1890 Elkhart   In
------ Catalog #27. Carriages, saddles
and harness. Ills. throughout, pict. wrap.
With undated circular, 2 ills., price list.

1896 Elkhart   InELK
------ Catalog #36. 4to., 112pp.,   In
ills., pict. wrap.

1897 Elkhart   InELK
------ Catalog #38. 144pp., ills.   In

1899 Elkhart   InELK
------ Catalog #39. Ill.   In

1900 Elkhart   NSbSM
------ Catalog #40. In   VtSM   NNMM
Fine ills. of harness, wagons, axles and
buggies.

1900-1908 Elkhart   NSbSM
------   In   OHi   InELK MiU-T
Catalogs #41 to 61, with fine ills., pls. and
details.

c.1886 Amesbury, Mass.   MAmPL
ELLIS, W.G. & SONS. Ill. catalog of fine
carriages.

c.1887 Amesbury, Mass.   MAmPL
------ Ill. catalog of carriages and wagons.

c.1888 Amesbury, Mass.   MAmPL
------ Ill. catalog by builders of fine light
and heavy carriages.

1885 Cincinnati   OC
EMERSON & FISHER CO. Ill. catalog -
Physicians' buggies - models - My Favor-
ite, etc. 16mo., 36pp.

1888 Cincinnati   MnHi
------ Ill. catalog, 47pp., pict. wrap.

1889 Cincinnati   MnHi
------ Ill. catalog and tests. 28pp., wrap.

1889 Cincinnati   MnHi
------ Ill. catalog with tests. 64pp.

1891 Buffalo, N.Y.   N
EMPIRE STATE WAGON CO., LTD. Ill.
catalog of wagons and carriages with pict.
wrap. of Roman chariot racing. 8vo., 72pp.

1882 Cincinnati, O.   OC
ENGER, GEORGE & CO., Mfg. Ill. catalog
of buggies, carriages, wagons, Brewster &
Tinkham side bars, spring wagons. 8vo.,
12pp., wrap.

1885 Cincinnati   OHi
------ Ill. catalog. 8vo., 28pp.,   OC
wrap.

1886 Cincinnati   MnHi
------ Ill. catalog. 24pp., pict. wrap.

1888 Cincinnati   NSbSM
------ Catalog.   OC

1877 New Haven   CtHi
ENGLISH & MERSICK. Ill. catalog of carriage makers' goods, supplies, carriages,
wagons, etc. 4to., 1366 interleaved, fine pls.

c.1889 Miamisburg, O.   NSbSM
ENTERPRISE CARRIAGE MFG. CO. OC
Est. 1879. Catalog of carriages, carts and
wagons. 8vo., 80pp. with 80 tinted lithos.
by Henderson, Achert-Krebs Co., view of
plant, models, styles, etc.

c.1890 Miamisburg, O.   MiD
------ Catalog #11. Styles in   OC
carriages and sleighs. 24pp., fine ills.,
wrap.

c.1886 Watertown, N.Y.   NSbSM
EXCELSIOR CARRIAGE CO. Catalog #17.
Fine carriages, carts, etc. 68pp. of fine
pls., wrap.

1885 Cincinnati   OC
EXCELSIOR CARRIAGE GOODS CO. Ill.
catalog. 16mo., 12pp., fine ills., wrap.,
mss. order for March 23, 1885 enc.

1888 Cortland, N.Y.   NNMM
EXCELSIOR TOP CO. Catalog and price
list of carriage tops, cushions, backs, rails,
dashes and gears. 32pp., ills., wrap.

1886 Cincinnati   OC
FAVORITE CARRIAGE CO. Ill. circular
with 10 ills. - fancy cart to stage coach.

c.1890 Amesbury, Mass.   MiD
FELTCH, E.S. & CO. Broadside with 29
ills. of styles and models.

1883 Racine   MnHi
FISH BROTHERS. Catalog of carriages,
carts, wagons, etc. 56pp., fine ills., tinted
pict. wrap.

1886 Racine   MnHi
------ Ill. price list. 24pp., fine ills.,
wrap.

1898 Cincinnati   OC
FISHER CARRIAGE CO. Catalog of carriages. 12mo., 40pp., fine ills., pict. wrap.

1898 Rome, N.Y.   N
FITCH GEAR CO. Ill. catalog of gears,
wagons - Winner, Penn, Brewster, Concord,
Banner. 8vo., 48pp.

1866 New Haven   CtY
FITCH, W. & E.T. Mfg. Catalog of carriage sprints, iron castings, steps, braces,
parts and Bristol's pat. curry combs and
harness snaps, etc. Fine ills., wrap.

1870 New Haven   CtY
------ Ill. catalog.

1873 New Haven   CtHi
------ Ill. catalog. 4to., 66pp.,   CtY
fine ills.

1876-1883 New Haven   CtY
------ Ill. catalogs. 4 fine ref. catalogs.

1907 Flint, Mich.   MiU-T
FLINT BUGGY CO. Catalog #13. Ill., wrap

c.1890 Flint, Mich.   MiU-T
FLINT WAGON WORKS. Catalog   MiFli
of old reliable Flint farm, freight and
lumber wagons, carriages and carts. 8vo.,
40pp., ill., wrap.

nd. Flint, Mich.   MiU-T
------ Catalog of high grade vehicles.
8vo., 130pp., ills. and pls., wrap.

1890 Atlanta, Ga.   MiD
FLORENCE WAGON CO. Successors to
Atlanta Wagon Co. Ill. catalog of farm
wagons, etc. 8vo., 40pp., ptd. wrap.

nd. Amesbury, Mass.   MAmPL
FOLGER & DRUMMOND. Est. 1887. Ill.
catalog of fine carriages.

nd. Amesbury, Mass.   MAmPL
------ Ill. catalog of high grade vehicles.

nd. Charleston, S. C.   ViWC
FRANKE, C.D. & CO. Ill. catalog #17.
Carriage and wagon accessories, etc.

1885 Aurora, Ill.   NSbSM
FRAZIER, W.S. & CO. Designers and
Builders. Ill. catalog of superior vehicles,
pat. by . . . 8vo., 32pp., ills. and pls.,
pict. wrap. N.B. When we commenced
manufacturing road carts in 1881, there
were no light, rideable two-wheeled vehicles
in the U. S.

c.1890 Aurora, Ill.   IIli
------ Portfolio of designs. Tall 8vo.,
looseleaf with 24 excellent pls. Litho. by
Globe Litho. Co.

1891 Aurora, Ill.   NSbSM
------ Ill. catalog.

1893 Aurora, Ill.   NSbSM
------ Track sulkies. 16mo., 16pp. of
photos., track records for 1892 - Nacy &
Prompter in action. Globe lithos.

1899 Aurura, Ill.   CBaKM
------ Catalog of superior   CtY
vehicles. 8vo., 32pp., litho. pls., wrap.

nd. Amesbury, Mass.   MAmPL
FULLER BUGGY CO. Ill. catalog of vehicles, issued by agent.

c.1877 Philadelphia   NSbSM
FULTON, WALKER & CO.   VtSM
Centennial omnibusses, half-busses, business and express wagons, wagonettes, etc.
4to., 4pp. with ills.

1878 Homer, N. Y.   NSbSM
GAGE & BISHOP. Ill. catalog of vehicles.

1887 Cincinnati   OC
GAINSFORD CARRIAGE CO. Ill. catalog of
fine carriages. 12mo., 52pp.

c.1900 Cincinnati   OC
GEM BUGGY CO. Ill. catalog of buggies,
etc. 4to., 56pp., fine ills. with col. pict.
wrap.

1886 Toledo, O.   MnHi
GENDRON IRON WHEEL CO. Ill. catalog
of childrens' carriages, velocipedes, goat
and dog sulkies, etc. 46pp. of delightful
ills., pict. wrap.

1899 Toledo, O.   CtY
------ Ill. catalog.

1900 Toledo, O.   CtY
------ Ill. catalog.

1905 Geneva, N. Y.   NNMM
GENEVA WAGON CO. Ill. and desc. catalog
of light wagons and hearses. 40pp., wrap.

1880 Cincinnati   OC
GLOBE CARRIAGE CO. Ill. catalog of
carriages. 8vo., 12pp., fine ills., pict. wrap.
with 4 page price list.

c.1885 Cincinnati   MnHi
------ Ill. catalog. 32pp., wrap.

1881 Minneapolis   MnHi
GOODMAN & CUSHMAN. Ill. catalog of
carriages, buggies, phaetons, farm and
spring wagons. 12mo., 48pp., wrap.

1005 Albany, N. Y.   NSbSM
GOOLD, JAMES & CO. Sleigh circular -
models Box A & B, Square Box 1 & 2, Cutter
1 & 2, pony sleigh, light six, etc. 16mo.,
15pp. with fine woodcuts, pict. wrap. of The
Fashionable Sleigh of 1820. Outstanding
pict. record for 1865.

1897 Goshen, Ind.   NCooHi
GOSHEN BUGGY TOP CO. Catalog of buggy
trimmings and supplies. 64pp. with fine
ills.

1903 Goshen, Ind.   In
------ Ill. catalog of cushions, gears, tops,
etc. 8vo., 56pp., pict. wrap.

1901 Grand Rapids   MAmPL
GRAND RAPIDS ENGRAVING CO. MiU-H
See Printers' Samples of work. Fine litho.
pict. record of carriage mfg. from six
states, showing plants, in the form of an
appreciation of their catalog business.

c.1900 Groton, N. Y.   NNMM
GROTON CARRIAGE CO. Desc. and ill.
catalog of buggies, wagons and speeders,
etc. 96pp., wrap.

1870 Chicago   MiU-T
HALL, KIMBARK & CO. Ill. catalog of
wagon and carriage materials and supplies,
heavy and light hardware, etc. 325pp., cl.

1876 HANEY, JESSE. Designs for carriage
painters, etc. See Artists' Materials.

1888 Albany, N. Y. & Cincinnati   MnHi
HAYCOCK, T.T. CARRIAGE CO. Ill. catalog of fine carriages, etc. 40pp., fine ills.,
wrap.

1889 Albany, N. Y. & Cincinnati   MnHi
------ Ill. catalog. 42pp., wrap.   OC

1889 Albany, N. Y. & Cincinnati   OC
------ Champion C and D grade buggies
and phaetons. 8pp. of ills.

1891 Albany, N. Y. & Cincinnati   MiD
------ Catalog of buggies, phaetons, wagonettes, coupe carts, etc. 12mo., 56pp., fine
ills., wrap.

1884 St. Louis   MnHi
HAYDOCK, D.W. BROTHERS. Catalog of
fine buggies, phaetons, etc. 36pp., fine ills.,
wrap.

1885 St. Louis   MnHi
------ Ill. catalog. 62pp., wrap.

1887 St. Louis   NSbSM
------ Wholesale catalog.   MnHi MoSHi
12mo., 44pp., fine ills., wrap.

1888 St. Louis   NSbSM
------ Ill. catalog.

1900 Cambridge, Mass.
HENDERSON BROTHERS. Ill. catalog of
carriages and wagons for baker, butcher,
milkman, merchant and special businesses.
2700 in stock. 16mo., 24pp., fine ills., dec.
wrap.

1888 Freeport, Ill.   MnHi
HENNEY BUGGY CO. Ill. catalog of buggies, carriages, wagons, etc. 48pp., fine
ills., wrap.

1890 Freeport, Ill.   MdTanSW
------ Ill. circular folded to 16mo., price
list.

1874 Strasburg, Pa.   PHi
HERR, BRACKBILL & CO. Strasburg Spoke
& Implement Works. Price list #3 - wheels,
spokes, handles, shafts, bent felloes, etc.

1900 Wakefield, Mass.   NSbSM
HEYWOOD BROTHERS & WAKEFIELD CO.
Estab. 1826. Catalog of specialties in rattan for the carriage trade. 8vo., 12pp., fine
ills., wrap.

1901 Cincinnati   OC
HIGHLAND BUGGY CO. Catalog #24 of surreys, pony vehicles, buggies, etc. 8vo.,
52pp. of fine pls., col. pict. wrap.

1890 Bridgeport, Conn.   CtHi
HINCKS & JOHNSON. Successors to Wood
Brothers. Ill. 4to. catalog for Spring - by
largest builders of heavy carriages in New
England.

1890 Bridgeport, Conn.   CtHi
------ Ill. catalog of desirable second hand
carriages for the Fall.

c.1890 Bridgeport, Conn.   CtHi
------ Ill. 4 page business stuffer of
Berlin coach, landau, landolet, etc.

1885 Cortland, N. Y.   NCooHi
HITCHCOCK MFG. CO. Catalog of wagons
and sleighs. 16mo., 64pp., fine ills., pict.
wrap.

1887 Cortland, N. Y.
------ Ill. catalog.

1889 Cortland, N. Y.   MiD
------ Ill. catalog of spring wagons, swell
buggies, light bobs, Portland cutters, etc.
8vo., 32pp., fine ills., dec. wrap.

c.1896 HOBSON & CO. See Northampton
Works.

1876 Cincinnati   OHi
HOLLIDAY, THOMAS & CO. Annual catalog of childrens' carriages. Fine 36 page
ill. record.

1890 Cortland, N. Y.   NNMM
HOMER WAGON CO. See also H.M. Whitney
Co., successors. Catalog of open and top
buggies, carriages, surreys, road wagons
and sleighs. 52pp. with fine ills., wrap.

c.1896 San Francisco   MiD
HOOKER & CO. Ill. catalog of fine carriages, #23. 50pp.

c.1898 San Francisco   CHi
------ Catalog #25 of wagons and harness.
Fine 8vo., ill. record.

c.1885 New Haven   NNMM
HOOKER, HENRY & CO. Ill. priced catalog of carriages, etc. 18 lvs., fine ills.,
wrap.

1897 New Haven   NNMM
------ Catalog of carriages with 18 photos.
of general styles and models. Wrap.

1885 Philadelphia   PKsL
HOOPES BROTHERS & DARLINGTON.
Catalog #19. 16mo., 8pp. of ills. of styles,
view of plant, etc.

nd. Philadelphia, New York & Paris PHi
HORSTMANN, WM. H. & SONS. Ill. catalog
of carriage and hearse lace and trimmings
for the trade. Fine record.

1882 Syracuse, N. Y.   NNMM
HUGHSON'S WAGON CO. 5th annual catalog
of carriages and parts, accessories, repairs.
32pp. of fine ills., wrap.

1890 Amesbury, Mass.   MAmPL
HUME CARRIAGE CO. Est. 1857. Ill. catalog of fine carriages.

nd. Huntingberg, Ind.   In
HUNTINGBERG WAGON WORKS. Ill. catalog of carriages and wagons.

1884 Auburn, N. Y.   MdTanSW
HURD, JOHN M., Mfg. Ill. catalog of
childrens' wagons, carts, etc. 8vo., 16pp.
with prices.

nd.   MiU-T
IVERS, F. Ill. catalog of broughams,
landaus, cabriolets, rockaways and the renowned Ivers buggies. 28pp., np.

1878 Rochester, N. Y.   NR
JACOBS & HUGHES. Ill. catalog of
childrens' carriages, carts, express wagons,
etc. 12mo., pict. wrap.

c.1882 Rochester, N. Y.   MnHi
------ Ill. catalog. 10mo., 32pp., wrap.

JEFFERSON BUGGY CO. See Babcock,
H. H. & Sons, Prop.

1940 Waterloo, Ia.   NNMM
JERALD SULKY CO. Ill. catalog of sulkies,
carts, show vehicles and accessories. 32pp.
Wrap. No. 1940 is not a misprint. This
catalog is listed with the express purpose of
impressing the atomic minded with facts:
1. people still use horses and drive horse
powered vehicles for fun and relaxation, and
2. 1940 is already 20 years ago. Today's
news is tomorrow's history. What you read
in today's papers you forget in 24 hours.
Catalogs like this should not be forgotten.

nd. Merrimac, Mass.   MAmPL
JUDKINS, J.B. CO. Ill. catalog of carriages
and auto bodies.

1887 Kalamazoo   MiD
KALAMAZOO WAGON CO. Ill. 32 page catalog of wagons, carts, etc.

1887 Marshalltown, Ia.   MnHi
KETCHUM WAGON CO. Ill. catalog of carriages, wagons, etc.

c.1900 Cincinnati   OC
KEYSTONE BUGGY CO. Catalog #9.
12mo., 72pp., fine ills., wrap.

KIBLINGER. See Republican Publishing Co.

nd. Chicago   ICHi
KIMBALL & CO. Some new and stylish
carriages. Ill. catalog.

1882 Chicago   ICHi
KIMBARK, S.D. Ill. catalog of carriages.

1885 Binghamton   MnHi
KINGMAN, STURTEVANT & LARRABEE.
Ill. 12mo. catalog of 12 ill. pp.

1907-8 Cleveland   NNMM
KIRK-LATTY MFG. CO. Ill. and desc. catalog of juvenile wagons, velocipedes,
barrows, cycle wagons and automobiles.
48pp., wrap.

1878 Philadelphia   ICHi
KNICKERBOCKER ICE CO.   PHi
Est. 1832. Inc. 1864. Desc. price list of
ice wagons. 6x9, blank memo, 11pp. plus
7 col. pls. and many black and white of ice
machinery, tools, etc. A fine pict. record
of a vanished American industry.

1882 Philadelphia   PKsL
------ Ill. catalog. 12mo., 64pp., 18 fine
col. pls. of ice wagons built for towns and
cities all over the USA., plus 7 black and
white pls. Wrap.

1883 Philadelphia   NNMM
------ Ill. catalog of ice wagons, tools,
plows, etc. 66pp., fine pls., many in col.,
pict. wrap.

1884 Philadelphia   PHi
------ Ill. catalog of ice wagons and ice
equipment. 64pp., fine pls., many in col.

1896 Philadelphia   NSbSM
------ Desc. price list of wagons, machinery, tools, etc. 8vo., 64pp. with 25 of the
best col. pls. in the field. Scenic wagons of
Washington crossing the Delaware, Central
Park Skating, etc. A record of a lost art as
well as an American industry. N.B. For
those who want further information about
the ice trade, the Ice Trade Journal, 1877-
1904, profusely ill. throughout, may be
studied at ICJ and NN.

c.1895 Quincy, Ill.   ICHi
KOENIG & LUHRS WAGON CO. Ill. catalog
of wagons, trucks and moving vans.

1890 Toledo, O.   OT
KROH, C.Z. & CO. Ill. catalog of tops and
trimmings, rails, seats, cushions, etc.
16mo., 40pp., pict. wrap. of street scene at
plant with buggies, carriages, wagons and a
wood burning locomotive.

nd. Fond du Lac, Wis.   MnHi
LaBELLE WAGON WORKS. Catalog of the
celebrated LaBelle Wagons. 34pp., fine
ills., wrap.

c.1890 Amesbury, Mass.   MAmPL
LANE, T.W. MFG. CO. Est. 1874. Ill.
catalog of Lane carriages. 4to., 36pp.,

nd. Amesbury, Mass.   MAmPL
------ A few specialties in carriages. Ill.
catalog.

nd. Amesbury, Mass.   MAmPL
c.1925 ------ Ill. catalog of fine carriages -
and the last issued by any carriage mfg. in
Amesbury!

1879 Montréal, Can.   NNMM
LARIVIERE, N. & A.C. Carriage and sleigh
builders. Ill. catalog. 19 lvs., fine pls.,
wrap.

1862 New Haven   OClWHi
            CtY   CtHi   Ct   NSbSM
LAWRENCE, BRADLEY & PARDEE. Ill.
catalog of carriages, sleighs, harness,
saddles, etc. 147pp., frs., fine pls. and
ills. One of the best and earliest pict.
records.

c.1870 New Haven   NNMM
------ Ill. catalog with 200 photos. of
models and styles of carriages and sleighs.

1887 Lexington, Ky.   KyU
LEXINGTON SPOKE & WHEEL CO. New
price list with announcement. 8vo., 4pp.,
ills.

c.1860-65 Merrimac, Mass.   NSbSM
LITTLE & LANCASTER. Est. 1857 by
Little, becoming Little & Lancaster in 1859.
Ill. catalog of fine carriages, introduction
about orders by mail, etc. Tall 8vo., 37
fine pls., pict. wrap.

nd. Amesbury, Mass.   MiU-T
LOCKE & JEWELL. Ill. catalog of wagons
and carriages. 14pp.

1890 Manchester, N. H.   MiU-T
McCRILLIS, J.B. & SON. Broadside 17x22
with 32 ills. of styles, models, etc.

1900 Buffalo, N. Y.   OC
McKINNON DASH CO. Factories at Buffalo
and Syracuse, N. Y. and Cincinnati and Troy,
Ohio. Catalog of dashes, fenders, roll up
straps, block washers and shaft leathers.
8vo., 106pp., fine ills., pict. wrap.

1880 Stoughton, Wis.   MnHi
MANDT, T.G. MFG. CO. Catalog of carts,
carriages, wagons, etc. 40pp., ills., wrap.

1884 Stoughton, Wis.   MnHi
------ Ill. catalog. 48pp., wrap.

1887 Stoughton, Wis.   MnHi
------ Ill. catalog. 16pp., wrap.

1888 Stoughton, Wis.   MnHi
------ Ill. catalog of 32pp. Wrap.

1881 St. Louis   MnHi
MANNY & BAUER. Ill. catalog of farm
wagons and sugar mills and other mill
machinery. See also Milling.

c.1870 New Haven   NSbSM
MANVILLE, B. & CO. Carriage Builders.
Ill. catalog of fine carriages, fine drawings,
excellent job. Wrap.

1881 New Haven   CtHj
------ Manville, Dudley   Ct   CtY
& Co. 8vo., fine ills., dec. wrap.

1884 New Haven   CtY
------ Ill. catalog.

1887 New Haven   CtHi
------ Artistic Almanac and Fund   CtY
of Facts. 16mo., 32pp., fine ills., pict.
wrap.

MASURY - Carriage painting supplies. See
Paint.

nd. Watertown, N. Y.   MnHi
MAUD S. GEAR CO. Ill. catalog of carriages. 24pp., wrap.

nd. Cincinnati   OC
MIAMI BUGGY CO. Special notice to
liverymen and others who have a use for
superior buggies or phaetons at figures very
much reduced. 4to., 4pp., ills.

nd. Kalamazoo   MiU-H
MICHIGAN BUGGY CO. Circular of the
Easy Road Cart. Ills.

1906 Kalamazoo   MiU-T
------ Wholesale price list. 11pp., ills.

1891 Middletown, Va.   ViU
MIDDLETOWN CARRIAGE CO. Ill. catalog
of models, styles, etc. 12mo., 58pp., wrap.

c.1877 Toledo, O.   NSbSM
MILBURN WAGON CO. Ill. catalog of farm
and freight wagons.

1880 Toledo, O.   MnHi
------ Ill. catalog. 32pp., fine ills., wrap.

1886 Toledo, O.   MiU-T
------ Ill. catalog of fine buggies and
phaetons. 48 fine pls.

nd. Toledo, O.   MiU-T
------ Broadside 11x17 with ills. of carriages.

nd. Toledo, O.   MiU-T
------ Catalog of business wagons, trucks,
drags, express wagons, etc. 48pp., ill.

nd. Amesbury, Mass.   MAmPL
MILLER BROTHERS. Est. 1888. Ill. catalog of carriages of wood and iron.

c.1880 Bellfontaine, O. & Muncie, Ind. MiU-T
MILLER BROTHERS. Not in 1890 directory. Broadside of celebrated carriage
works of . . . Ills.

c.1900 Goshen, N. Y.   CBaKM
MILLER CART CO. Ill. catalog of high
grade road carts and sulkies. 8vo., 16pp.,
fine photo. ills., racing records and champions.

c.1883 Cincinnati   OC
MILLER, GEORGE C. & SONS. Book of
styles #3. 12mo., 42pp., with fine ills.

c.1885 Cincinnati   OC
------ Book of styles #5. 12mo., 56pp.,
fine ills.

1893 South Bend, Ind.   CtY
MILLER-KNOBLOCK WAGON CO. Ill. catalog of carriages, wagons, etc.

nd. Mexico, N. Y.   CBaKM
MILLER SPRING FARM & DRAY WAGONS.
Ill. catalog. 8vo., 24pp., pict. wrap.

1898 Racine, Wis.   NSbSM
MITCHELL & LEWIS, LTD. Farm wagon
catalog #50. 8vo., 80pp., col. pls., pict.
wrap. A fine pict. record of Gay Nineties.

1880 Columbus, O.   OHi
MITHOFF, EVANS & HUBBARD, Mfg. Ill.
catalog of childrens' carriages and wagons -
express wagons for dog and goat, etc. 24pp.
of fine ills.

1881 Columbus, O.   OHi
------ Ill. catalog of 32pp.

1889 St. Louis   MoSHi
MOON BROTHERS CARRIAGE CO.   MnHi
Catalog. 8vo., 32pp., fine ills., col. pict.
wrap.

1894 St. Louis   MoSHi
------ Catalog. Fol., 32pp., ill. and pict.
wrap.

1889-92 St. Louis   MoSHi
------ Wholesale price lists, orders, etc.

1893 Syracuse, N. Y.   NSyHi
MOYER, H.A. Designer and maker of high
grade carriages. Catalog of Genteel road
wagons, stanhope, surreys, Corning, Concord and piano buggies. 8vo., 52pp., 39 pls.
of styles, wrap.

1899 Syracuse, N. Y.   NSyHi
------ Ill. catalog. 66pp.

c.1900 Syracuse, N. Y.   DLC
------ Fine ill. catalog.

1902 Syracuse, N. Y.   NSyHi
------ Democrats, road wagons and bikes,
carts with bicycle wheels. 85pp., fine ref.

1903-7 Syracuse, N. Y.   NSyHi
------ Just in case of an exhaustive study.

1904 Syracuse, N. Y.   MiU-T
------ Unusually fine pls., 70pp.   N

1893 Muncie, Ind.   In
MUNCIE WHEEL & JOBBING CO. Ill. price
list #46. Wheels, parts, gears, etc. 16mo.,
64pp., fine ills., pict. wrap.

c.1890 Cincinnati   OC
MURRAY, WILBUR MFG. CO. This catalog
will save you many a dollar - keep it handy.
Everything you need for a horse. 8vo.,
146pp., tinted pls., buggy to saddle, harness
and gear. Pict. wrap.

1893 Cincinnati   OC
------ Kind words never die - a good name
is rather to be chosen than great riches.
8vo., 50pp. of fine ills., pict. wrap.

1902 & 1906 Cincinnati   MiU-T
------ Fine ill. catalogs.   OC

1911 Cincinnati   NNMM
------ Just in case you want to go farther,
and happen to be in NYC.

1886 Chicago   MnHi
NATIONAL TUBULAR AXLE CO. Ill. catalog. 48pp.

1896 Amesbury, Mass.   MAmPL
NEAL & BOLSER. Fine carriages. Ill.
catalog of our novelties.

1882 Boston   NSbSM
NELSON, F.S. & CO. Catalog of carriages
and sleigh woodwork. Fine ills. of bodies,
etc.

1884 Boston   MH-BA
NEW ENGLAND HORSE & CARRIAGE
DEPOSITORY. Est. 1858. Peremptory
sale at Salem of entire sleigh stock of Smith
& Manning. 8vo., 8pp.

c.1900 Cincinnati   OC
NEW EUREKA CARRIAGE & HARNESS CO.
9th annual catalog with price list #22.
12mo., 32pp., fine ills. The Bread Winner,
etc.

nd. Cincinnati   OC
------ A Few Pointers. Circular.

nd. New Haven   CtHi
NEW HAVEN CARRIAGE CO.   Ct
Ill. catalog, 15pp.

nd. New Haven   NNMM
------ Ill. catalog, 24pp., wrap.

1880 Homer, N. Y.   MiD
NEWTON, C.O., Mfg. Catalog of platform
spring wagons - A Great Success. Circular
with 5 ills. of styles.

c.1898 Newton Upper Falls   VtSM
NEWTON RUBBER WORKS. Catalog of
sectional rubber carriage tires and special
clamps, etc. Ills.

c.1890 Buffalo, N. Y.   NSbSM
NIAGARA TOP CO. Ill. catalog of tops and
trimmings. 8vo., fine ills., pict. wrap.

1868 New Haven   CtY
NORTH, O.B. & CO. Ill. catalog of canopy
and carriage tops, narrow lazy backs, wood
seats, cushions and falls, rails, saddlery
and carriage hardware.

1870-91 New Haven   CtY
------ A fine collection of ill. catalogs.
Not complete run, 15 in all, lacking 1890.

1881 New Haven   CtHi
------ Ill. catalog with tinted   CtY
lithos. Pls. by Punderson & Crisland.
84pp.

1889 New Haven   CtHi
------ Fine ill. catalog. Price   CtY
list. 8vo., 32pp., pict. wrap.

c.1890 New Haven   CtHi
------ Price list of canopy tops, etc.
32pp., fine ills., wrap.

c.1896 New York   NNMM
NORTHAMPTON WORKS. Hobson & Co.
Ill. and desc. catalog #86 - carts, wagons
and wheels. 52pp.

1887 Milwaukee   VtSM
NORTHWESTERN SLEIGH CO.   MnHi
Ill. catalog of styles and designs for models,
J.H. Yewdale & Sons lithos. 8vo., 50pp.,
col. pict. wrap.

1889 Milwaukee   MnHi
------ Ill. catalog. 70pp., lithos., pict.
wrap.

1889 New Haven   CtY
OCHSNER, A. & SON. Ill. catalog of carriage locks, styles and carriage parts.

1892 New Haven   CtHi
------ Ill. catalog of coach locks, pattern
and body makers' tools, etc. 8vo., 22pp.

1894 New Haven   CtY
------ Fine ill. catalog.

1896 New Haven   NSbSM
------ Hearse and coach locks.   CtY
8vo., 20pp., ills., wrap.

c.1900 Cincinnati   NSbSM
OHIO CARRIAGE MFG. CO. Ill.   OHi
catalog of fine carriages.

c.1907 Cincinnati   MdTanSW
------ Split hickory vehicles and harness
direct from factory to you. 8vo., 32pp.,
fine ills., wrap.

1909 Cincinnati   OC
------ Annual catalog #35. Split hickory
vehicles - Ohio oak tanned harness. Ports.
of management, views of mfg., tinted and
fld. pls. 4to., 126pp., fine ills., port. pict.
wrap.

c.1909 Cincinnati   OC
------ A Good Buggy and How it is Made.
7x11, 32pp., ills. of craftsmen, systems,
shops, pict. wrap. in col. By H.C. Phelps,
Pres. & Treas.

c.1910 Cincinnati   MiU-T
------ Portfolio of split hickory vehicles.
172pp. with fine ills.

1900 Amesbury, Mass.   NSbSM
OSGOOD, GEORGE W. MFG. Est. 1870.
Catalog of fine carriages and sleighs, with
fine pls. of stanhopes, town carts and
cabrioles, etc. Ptd. Grand Rapids Eng. Co.

1889 Cincinnati   OC
OVERMAN CARRIAGE CO. Ill. catalog of
Overman carriages, 2nd ed. 12mo., 48pp.,
fine ills. of styles and models.

PALM BROTHERS. Supplies for carriage
painters. See Artists' supplies.

c.1885 Amesbury, Mass.   MAmPL
PARRY, A.A. & CO. Est. 1875. Ill. catalog of carriages of the best class.

1885 Indianapolis   In
PARRY MFG. CO. Ill. catalog of Parry
buggies, road and spring wagons, etc.

c.1890 Indianapolis   In
------ Ill. catalog.

c.1900 Indianapolis   NSbSM
------ Ill. catalog. 4to., 52 pls., many in
col. of styles and models and the plant.
Wrap.

nd. Flint, Mich.   MiFli
PATERSON, WILLIAM C. CO. Ill. catalog
of fine carriages.

PHILADELPHIA BABY CARRIAGE CO.
See House Furnishings.

1888 Cincinnati   MnHi
PHOENIX CARRIAGE CO. Ill. catalog of
fine carriages. 20pp.

c.1890 Cincinnati   OC
------ Ill. circular #52.

1892 Columbus, O.   OHi
PIONEER BUGGY CO. Good, better, best -
Superior Vehicles - Beware Frauds - Don'ts
and Remembers. 8vo., 32pp., fine ills. of
styles, col. chart.

1898 Piqua, O.   OHi
PIQUA WAGON CO. Ill. price list, one leaf.

c.1900 Pontiac, Mich.   MiU-T
PONTIAC BUGGY CO. Catalog of Western
Amesbury Vehicles. 8vo., 121pp., fine ills.,
wrap.

1890 Wayne, Mich.   MiU-H
PROUTY & GLASS CARRIAGE CO. Catalog
of carriages and sleighs. 8vo., 16pp., excellent ills., dec. wrap.

1889 Racine   MnHi
RACINE WAGON & CARRIAGE CO. Lead-
ing Styles for 1889. 8vo., 64pp., ills. of
specials for Park Hotel, Jamaica Wagonette,
Express Co. and other delivery vehicles.
Wrap.

1897 Racine   WaMaG
------ Leading Styles for 1897. Fine ills.,
wrap.

c.1874 Dover, N. H.   NhHi
RANDLETT, JASPER H. Ill. and desc. catalog of carriages for sale. 22pp.

c.1890 Cincinnati   OC
RATTERMANN & LUTH. Ill. catalog of
buggies, wagons, carts, etc.

nd. Cincinnati   OC
------ Ill. folder with 6 styles by eastern
branch at Rochester, N. Y.

1899 Mansfield, O.   CBaKM
RICHLAND BUGGY CO. A catalog by
builders of fine vehicles. 4to., 40pp., fine
pls., pict. wrap.

1874 Philadelphia   PHi
ROWLAND, WM. & HARVEY. Catalog of
elliptic, platform wagons and side springs,
Norway and Swedish iron nails, steps, gears,
parts, etc. 16mo., 8pp., wrap.

c.1895 Springfield, O.   CtY
RUBBER TIRE WHEEL CO.   OC
Est. 1894. Catalog of Victoria and trotting

buggies with rubber tires, other styles, etc.
8vo., 12pp., ills., pict. wrap.

1898 Springfield, O.   OC
------ SKI-HI. A message from Mars.
7x10, double wrap. in full col. by the
Winters Press. Text with fine photos. of
Pres. McKinley's Victoria, Prince of Wales'
brougham, Senator Hanna's Victoria and
special styles owned by Astor, Gould,
Lawson and many others. Unquestionably
the most fantastic American carriage catalog located. The message from Mars
relates how the Martians landed in Springfield and after the remains had been cleaned
up, a catalog of rubber tires was found.
The imagination in the col. designs of the
rubber tired creations henceforth used on
Mars are difficult to translate - especially
when written in the Martian tongue. Well
worth the careful inspection of historian or
student.

1890 Hornersville, N. Y.   CBaKM
ST. JULIEN GEAR CO. Catalog of fine carriages. 12mo., 36pp., fine pls., wrap.

1888 St. Louis   MnHi
ST. LOUIS REFRIGERATOR & WOODEN
GUTTER CO. Ills. of childrens' carriages
and sleighs.

c.1860 Boston   NNMM
SARGENT, FRANCIS & CO. Broadside catalog with 24 lithos. of styles and models of
fine carriages by J. Mayer.

1886 Cincinnati   MnHi
SAYERS & SCOVELL CO. Ill. catalog of
carriages and wagons. 30pp., pict. wrap.

1889 Cincinnati   MnHi
------ Ill. catalog. 32pp., fine pls., pict.
wrap.

1889 St. Louis   NNMM
SCHELP WAGON & CARRIAGE CO. Ill. and
desc. catalog of buggies, phaetons, jump
seaters, etc. 32pp., wrap.

1906 Oneida   NNMM
SCHUBERT, AUGUST GEAR CO. Catalog A,
desc. and ill. of all kinds of bodies, seats,
trimmings and tops. 44pp.

1877 Chicago   OrU
SCHUTTLER, PETER. Wagon Mfg. (Agent,
Portland, Ore.) Ill. catalog with fld. plate,
prices and details, bds.

1889 Columbus, O.   MnHi
SCIOTO BUGGY CO. Ill. catalog, 32pp.,
pict. wrap.

1876 Philadelphia   MiU-T
SCOTT & DAY. Ill. price list of carriages
and wagons. 262pp., bds.

1892 Newark, N. J.   NSbSM
SEARLS MFG. CO. Ill. catalog of dashes, dash rails, mountings, trimmings, whips and whip sockets, etc. 8vo., 144pp., fine ref., pict. wrap.

c.1900 Newark, N. J.   NSbSM
------ Catalog #17. Carriage and NjR sleigh goods from dash to whip. 8vo., 170pp., pict. wrap.

1893 Chicago
SEARS ROEBUCK & CO. Special catalog. Vehicles of all kinds, 12 factories represented, all styles and models. 7x10, 144pp., ills. of styles and models, pict. wrap.

c.1876 Cincinnati   OC
SECHLER CO. Col. fld. circular with 30 ills. of styles and models mfg. by . . . Cincinnati Litho., with prices and details on verso. Mighty unusual col. catalog of first water.

1887 Cincinnati   MnHi
------ Ill. catalog. 36pp., pict. wrap.

1888 Cincinnati   MnHi
------ Ill. catalog. 39pp., pict. wrap.

c.1900 Taunton, Mass.   NSbSM
SHARKEY, JOHN T. Ill. catalog   MiD
of styles and models, with a 4 page ill. circular for 1907. 4to., 80pp., fine pls., wrap.

1883 Syracuse, N. Y.   NSyHi
SHORT & SMITH, Builders. To the trade - ill. catalog of carriages and fine sleighs. 16mo., 32pp., fine pls., pict. wrap.

nd. Syracuse, N. Y.   NNMM
SIDE-SPRING WAGON CO. Folder with two ill. lvs.

1884
SMITH & MANNING of Salem. See New England Horse & Carriage Depository.

1874 Plantsville, Conn.   CtHi
SMITH, H.D. & CO. Ill. price list. 74pp., fine ills., wrap. Carriage hardware of all kinds.

1880 Plantsville, Conn.   CtHi
------ Ill. price list. 4to., 103pp. of ills.

1895 Plantsville, Conn.   CtHi
------ Ill. price list of carriage, coach, sleigh and wagon hardware. 4to., 182pp., fine pict. ref.

1884 New York   VtSM
SMITH, ISAAC & SON CO. Wholesale price list of wagon umbrellas, canopies for phaetons, carts, square wagons and also trucks, carts and fishing boats. Delightful ills. for beach and garden artist.

1885 Philadelphia   NSbSM
SMITH, S.A. & CO. Annual catalog of childrens' carriages, for central park with a nurse, models with fringe, plush and velvet styles with stenciled bodies. 12mo., 72pp. of ills., pict. wrap.

c.1881 Rome, N. Y.   NNMM
SPRING WAGON CO. Catalog and price list of Fitch platform and spring wagons. 18pp. with fine ills., wrap.

nd. Cincinnati   OHi
STANDARD WAGON CO. Our platform spring two-wheelers. 8vo., ill., leaflet.

1884 Cincinnati   OHi
------ Ill. catalog of two-wheelers, Fischer bodies, platform spring.

1885 Cincinnati   OHi
------ Ill. catalog.

c.1885 Cedar Rapids, Ia.   MnHi
STAR WAGON CO. Ill. catalog of wagons, carts, etc. 79pp., wrap.

1898 Chicago   ICHi
STAVER CARRIAGE CO. To the trade. Ill. catalog.

c.1882 Lancaster, Pa.   PHi
STEINMAN, GEORGE M. & CO. Ill. and desc. catalog of hardware, iron and steel saddlery, carriage parts and hardware. 4to., a fine ref.

1901 New Haven   CtHi
STEVENS & SACKETT CO. Ill. catalog of coach, carriage and hearse lamps, carriage mouldings, mountings, plated ware, etc. 4to., 62pp.

c.1859 South Bend, Ind.   In
STUDEBAKER BROTHERS. Est. 1852. Catalog #3. Special wagons and fine harness famous for style. 4to., 100pp., fine pls., pict. wrap. Without any question one of the best ref.

1875 South Bend, Ind.   ICHi
------ Ill. catalog. 6pp.

1875 South Bend, Ind.   In
------ Buyers of wagons - a few reasons why - Output in 1852 two wagons, last year 20,000. 48mo. brochure of 8pp. with pict. wrap.

1875 South Bend, Ind.   In
------ (Richmond, Va. agent). 22nd annual price list - retail prices for Studebaker wagons for farm and freight. 16mo., 12pp.

nd. South Bend, Ind.   In
------ Two famous carriages. Lincoln's,
Lafayette's and Harrison's. 12mo., 12pp.,
ills., wrap.

c.1877 South Bend, Ind.   MiU-T
------ Broadside 18x24. Ills. of styles of
buggies, carriages, sleighs and wagons.

c.1880 South Bend, Ind.   NSbSM
------ Ill. catalog with pict. wrap.

c.1883 South Bend, Ind.   ICHi
------ (San Francisco agent). Ill. catalog
of carriages, carts, wagons. 8vo., with
pict. wrap.

c.1891 South Bend, Ind.   MiU-T
------ With nearly 40 years   MiD
experience, etc. 8vo., 96pp., fine ills. of
plant, styles, models, etc. Offers street
sprinklers and special catalogs.

1892-3 South Bend, Ind.   NSbSM
------ Worlds Fair catalog.   MiU-T
128pp., ills., pict. wrap.

1892-3 South Bend, Ind.   MiU-T
------ Spanish edition of Worlds Fair catalog.

1897 South Bend, Ind.   MdTanSW
------ Supplement to catalog A. Harness.
12mo., 18pp., fine ills., wrap.

1897 South Bend, Ind.   MdTanSW
------ Harness dept. price list. Wagons,
carriages, street sprinklers and harness.
12mo., 12pp., pict. wrap.

1897 South Bend, Ind.   MdTanSW
------ Price list of wagons for catalog #88.
16mo., 64pp., wrap.

1897 South Bend, Ind.   NSbSM
------ Catalog #97, superseding   In
#76, 84 and 90. Fine ills. of plant, passen-
ger wagons, carriages, buggies, etc.

1897 South Bend, Ind.   MdTanSW
------ Folder #105. Milk and bakery
wagons. Ills., prices, 10pp., wrap.

1898 South Bend, Ind.   In
------ Ill. catalog. 8vo., 96pp., pict. wrap.

c.1900 South Bend, Ind.   MiD
------ Almanacs. Ill. advertising brochures.

1901-13 South Bend, Ind.   MiU-T
------ vp. ills., fine ref. If you still
thirst for newer and more up to date
models . . .

1896 Binghamton   NSbSM
STURTEVANT-LARRABEE CO.   VtSM
Ill. catalog of sleighs. 8vo., 64pp. with fine
ills. from Milk Sled to the Portland, dec.
wrap.

c.1890 Rochester, N. Y.   NCooHi
SULLIVAN BROTHERS. Catalog of buggies,
cutters, surreys, carts and wagons. 12mo.,
32pp., fine ills., pict. wrap.

c.1905 Rochester, N. Y.   MiU-T
------ Ill. catalog of carriages,   MiD
cutters and sleighs.

c.1890 Boston   MiD
THOMAS, CHAUNCEY & CO. 4 page ill.
folder of fine carriages.

1900 Lynchburg   Vi
THORNHILL WAGON CO. Catalog #37 -
Thornhill wagons. 8vo., ills. of styles and
models.

1884 Jonesville, Mich.   MiU-T
TIFFANY BROTHERS MFG. Catalog of fine
carriages, platform wagons, lumber wagons,
cutters, sleighs and hardware. 16mo.,
16pp., fine ills., wrap.

1907 Tiffin, O.   OC
TIFFIN WAGON CO. Special catalog #4 -
dumping wagons. 12mo., 16pp., ills.

nd. Dover Canal, O.   NSbSM
TOOMEY, S. & CO. Toomey two-wheelers.
12mo., 12pp., ills.

1882 Elyria   OC
TOPLIFF & ELY, Mfg. Est. 1865. Price
list of carriage hardware - bow sockets,
seat risers, connecting rods, etc. 8vo.,
4pp., ills. and view of plant.

1897 Troy, O.   NNMM
TROY CARRIAGE CO. Ill. catalog of
carriages, wagons, etc. 40pp. with fine
desc. and ills., wrap.

1888 Chicago   MnHi
TUDOR BUGGY CO. Ill. catalog. 28pp.,
models and styles, wrap.

1889 Chicago   MnHi
------ Ill. catalog. 22pp., wrap.

1897 Detroit   Mi
TUTTLE & CLARKE. See Horse Goods.

c.1880 Boston   NSbSM
TYLER, GEORGE & CO. Ill. catalog of
carriages.

1895 Boston   CtY
------ Ill. catalog of sleighs for 1895.

1896 Boston   CBaKM
------ Ill. catalog of sleighs. 12mo.,
12pp., wrap.

nd. Cincinnati   OC
UNITED FACTORIES CO. United buggies,
the best money can buy. One leaf, fld.,
4to., fine ills.

1892 Cincinnati   OC
UNITED STATES BUGGY & CART CO.
Catalog of fine vehicles, etc. To purchasers: We here give our customers a catalog
of 133 different styles, containing 54 different kinds of vehicles; also 47 different kinds
of harness, making a record of the greatest
variety ever offered in the U. S. 12mo.,
48pp., fine ills. throughout of styles, etc. as
outlined, with view of plant on Lawrence St.,
pict. wrap. One of the best.

1896 Cincinnati   MiU-T
------ Price list for 1896. 2pp.

1903 Cincinnati   OC
------ For further research #31, 32 and
36 for 1903, 1904 and 1907.

VALENTINE for carriage painters. See
Artists' Materials.

nd. Columbus, O.   NNMM
VEHICLE APRON & HOOD CO. Catalog of
carriage canopies, hoods, - Trademark
Blizzard - blankets, aprons and horse
covers. 24pp., fine ills., wrap.

VERMONT CHILDRENS' CARRIAGES MFG.
CO. See Toys.

WADSWORTH & HOWLAND. Carriage and
wagon painting. See Artists' Materials.

1900 Goshen, Ind.   In
WALKER, EDWARD W. CARRIAGE CO.
Catalog #31. We make all vehicles we catalog. 16mo., 128pp., fine ills. throughout,
wrap.

1891 Waterloo, N. Y.   NSbSM
WATERLOO WAGON CO., LTD. Catalog of
Brewsters, Whitechapels, buggies and buckboards. 12mo., 66pp. of fine ills. of styles,
wrap.

1897 Waterloo, N. Y.   MdTanSW
------ 14th annual catalog. 16mo., 92pp.,
fine ills., wrap.

1900 Waterloo, N. Y.   NCooHi
------ Ill. catalog.

p.1900 Waterloo, N. Y.   NCooHi
------ Later issues for the exhaustive
historian.

c.1879 Watertown, N. Y.   MiU-T
WATERTOWN SPRING WAGON CO. Ill.
catalog and price list. 32pp.

1885 Watertown, N. Y.   MnHi
------ Ill. catalog. 60pp., wrap.

1893 Decatur, Ill.   IHi
WAYNES SULKEYETTE CO. Handy ref.
catalog. Fine ills.

nd. Waynesburg, O.   MiD
WAYNESBURG WAGON CO. Ill. catalog.
27pp., pict. wrap.

1890 Chicago   CBaKM
WEBER WAGON CO. Farm and spring
wagons, harness and blankets. Ill. catalog,
col. pls., 100pp., pict. wrap.

c.1895 Chicago   MnHi
------ Ill. catalog. 58pp., one col. plate,
wrap.

c.1898 Indianapolis   In
WHALEBONE BUGGY CO. Catalog - quantity unlimited and quality unequaled at
lowest prices for the best vehicles made.
8vo., 20pp., fine ills., American flag in col.
wrap.

1876 Bridgeport, Conn.   PHi
WHITE MFG. CO. Ill. folder of Boudren's
pat. adjustable dash lamps, etc.

1886 Bridgeport, Conn.   CtY
------ Ill. price list of carriage lamps.

1889 Bridgeport   NNMM
------ Ill. catalog #3 - carriage lamps,
handles and mountings. 86pp., wrap.

1890 Bridgeport, Conn.   CtHi
------ Ill. supplement.

1891 Bridgeport, Conn.   DLC
------ Catalog and price list of hearse
mountings. Fine ill. record.

1891 Bridgeport, Conn.   MiU-T
------ Hearse mountings, lamps,   CtHi
fringes, tassels, emblems and decorations.
Ill. catalog, 4to., 62pp., wrap.

1895 Bridgeport, Conn.   NCooHi
------ Carriage   CtHi   Ct   MiD
lamps for 1895. 8vo., 74pp., fine ills., wrap.

1897 Bridgeport, Conn.   NCooHi
------ Lamps and   CtHi   Ct   MiD
mountings for hearse and undertakers'
wagon. 70pp. of swell ref. pls. and ills.

1900 Bridgeport, Conn.   NSbSM
------ Catalog   NNMM   DLC   WaMaG
#6. Carriage lamps and mountings. 90pp.
of fine ills. in 4 pts., wrap.

1900 Bridgeport, Conn.   NNMM
------ Ill. catalog. 8vo., 125pp.   DLC
of fine ills., wrap.

1901-2 Bridgeport, Conn.   NCooHi
------   MiD   CtHi   Ct   MiDbF
Lamps for coach   NNMM   MiU-H
and tally-ho. 8vo., 89pp., ills., wrap. All
fine collections running to 1905.

1892 Leominster, Mass.   NNMM
WHITNEY, F.A. CARRIAGE CO. Annual
catalog of childrens' carriages, go-carts,
perambulators, etc. 4to., 72pp. of delightful ills. of parasol and fringed buggy style
tops, of lace and wicker. Startling models
and styles. Wrap.

1902 Leominster, Mass.   NNMM
------ Annual catalog. 126pp. of ills. of
what used to be, wrap. A far cry from the
50 horsepower Go-Carts that now infest the
parking lots and highways for the amusement
of lazy teenagers.

c.1890 Cortland, N. Y.   VtSM
WHITNEY, H.M. CO. Successors to Homer
Wagon Co. Open and top carriages, road
wagons and sleighs. 8vo., 62pp. of fine pls.,
pict. wrap.

1883 Syracuse, N. Y.   MnHi
WHITNEY WAGON WORKS. Ill. catalog.
36pp., wrap.

c.1890 Kalamazoo   MnHi
WINANS, PRATT & CO. Successors to
George H. Winans & Co. Ill. catalog of
carriages and wagons. 20pp., wrap.

c.1885 Winona, Wis.   MnHi
WINONA WAGON CO. Catalog #5 - buggies,
carriages, surreys and spring wagons.
12mo., 32pp., with fine ills., wrap.

c.1885 Michigan City, Mich.   ICHi
WINTERBOTHAM, J.H. & SONS. Catalog of
bent work, seats, carriage and wagon bodies,
gears, etc. Ilis.

c.1890 New Haven   CtHi
WOOD BROTHERS. See Hincks & Johnson,
successors.

1882 Indianapolis   NSbSM
WOODBURN SARVEN WHEEL CO. In
Price list of vehicles for season. 12mo.,
12pp., ills., pict. wrap.

1884 Carmel, Conn.   CtY
WOODRUFF, MILLER & CO. Ill. catalog of
vehicles.

1887 Carmel, Conn.   NSbSM
------ Ill. catalog of fine   CtY
carriages.

1900 Carmel, Conn.   NSbSM
------ Ill. catalog with supplement to 1898
catalog tipped in.

c.1900 Amesbury, Mass.   MAmPL
WORTHEN, C.F. Est. 1896. Ill. catalog of
carriages and wagons. Plant destroyed by
fire in 1904.

nd. York, Pa.   NNMM
YORK SPRING WAGON WORKS. Ill. and
desc. catalog of express, delivery and platform wagons. 70pp., wrap.

In the Agricultural Implement & Machinery section, of course, you will find many of the finest farm wagons illustrated. Also, if you are really interested in the model hearse that carried grandfather to his grave, you'd better check Undertakers' and Funeral Directors' Furnishings & Equipment. Sears Roebuck, Montgomery Ward and other firms listed under the Miscellaneous section offered carriages and wagons, too. If you are hunting for a special design or model, and the familiar name appears in the index, follow through; many an American craftsman has invented and created a car- riage or a fanning mill, but due to financial necessity it can be found only in a general catalog issued by a more successful manufacturer or jobber.

Chapter 13

Celebration, Decoration & Theatrical Goods

A reviewer once described a small collection of verse as a good stew; this chapter is a good stew but it lacks the carrots -- see final comments and suggestions.

Included here you will find everything from a small piece of red, white and blue bunting to the most exotic wig ever created. There are firecrackers to burn the youngsters' fingers, and for Boston's largest and most glorious displays. Included are catalogs of circus tents, camping tents, badges and flags for political rallies, regalia for campaigns and badges for fraternal organizations. Musical bells, stage settings, costumes and wigs may be found in goodly number. The catalog of Norman & Evans Steam Merry-Go-Rounds is the only one that has come to light so far; may its colorful pictorial information excite other librarians to hunt for its cousins and aunts. It isn't possible that we had only one American Steam Merry-Go-Round manufacturer in the 19th century.

c.1890 Boston
BOSTON REGALIA CO. Catalog #11. Ills. of grange badges and regalia, jewelry, working tools, military and theatrical goods, banners, flags, ballot boxes, etc. 16mo., 24pp., wrap.

c.1900 Syracuse, N. Y.
CLANCY, J.C. Catalog #20. Theatrical stage fittings with ills. of props, settings, sets, scenes, hardware, etc. Sq. 8vo., 48pp., wrap.

c.1900   NStIHi
CONSOLIDATED FIREWORKS CO. OF AMERICA. Ill. catalog of latest and greatest novelties, fireworks in the sunshine, Hirayama Japanese day fireworks, displays cheap and easy to offer. Ills. and prices.

1893 New York
DESSART BROTHERS. Mfg. Trade catalog of masks, theatrical hair goods, etc. 8vo., 16pp., fine ills., pict. wrap.

c.1900 New York   ICHi
EMPIRE HARDWARE CO. Est. 1875. Catalog of store furnishings - Japanned cannisters-styles New York, Manhattan, Niagara, Denmark - Buffalo bins, pict. cabinets with mirrors, floor cans, etc. Sq. 8vo., 157pp. of ills., coffee mill to complete store, wrap.

1885 Philadelphia   PKsL
EXCELSIOR FIREWORKS CO. (George Miller & Son, agent.) Price list of exhibition garden pieces, balloons, flags, lanterns, etc. 16mo., 4pp.

1891 Erie, Pa.   NNMM
EXHIBITION SHOW CASE CO. Catalog of show cases and cabinets. Ill., desc. and priced. 16 numbered pp., incl. cvs.

1893 Decatur, Ill.   IHi
FARIES, ROBERT. Catalog of revolving and stationary window display fixtures. Delightful ills. throughout, hats, shoes, gun racks, etc. 16mo., 76pp., pict. wrap.

1889-1909 St. Louis   MoSHi
HEIMANN, MORRIS A. MFG. CO. Catalog. Designer and manufacturer of store fixtures, office fixtures, show cases and display fixtures. 35x48cm. Ill. This catalog was actually published in 1909. We have two others which are undated but which probably are before 1900, designated only as #14, #15.

1904 New York   ICHi
KRIEG, CARL H. & CO. Catalog of shoe retailers' supplies, furniture, furnishings, racks for display, etc. 7x10-1/4, 176pp., ill. throughout, wrap.

1890 New York   ICHi
LEGGETT, FRANCIS H. & CO. Price current of fireworks, ills. of father doing the honors for the kiddies in a derby - brown one? - special rockets, exhibitions, a riot of red and blue ill. action. 16mo., 32pp., pict. wrap.

1884 Chicago   ICHi
LEVY, M.R. & CO. Ill. broadside of patent waterproof openwork banners for circus, politicians, town celebrations, etc.

1833 New York   NHi
LORRILLARD, PETER & GEORGE. George
crossed out in ink, Jr. added. Wholesale
price list of snuff - fine, coarse, brown and
yellow, sweet scented chewing tobacco, fine
cut smoking tobacco. Beware of deceptions!
Fld. leaf, 2pp.

1896 Boston   MBSPNEA
MASTEN & WELLS FIREWORKS MFG. CO.
Trade price list and desc. catalog of pieces,
collections and exhibitions for home, clubs
and towns. 16mo., 84pp., ills.

1897 Boston   NNMM
------ Price list and desc. catalog. 16mo.,
84pp., fine ills., wrap.

c.1900 Boston   MWA
------ Fol. broadside. Desc. price list
through agents Rawson & Simpson Co.

p.1900 Boston   PShipL
------ Various later dates.   ICHi

c.1880 Brooklyn, N. Y.   NNQ
MAYLAND, R.H. Since 1866. (Carl Fischer,
agent.) Catalog of Mayland's musical bells
and theatrical props and specialties. 8vo.,
16pp., ills., wrap.

1898 New York   NNMM
MUNTER BROTHERS. Ill. list of war
novelties. One leaf.

c.1880 Chicago   ICHi
MURRAY & BAKER. Ill. catalog of awnings,
tents, signs and banners for all occasions,
camping, etc.

c.1898 San Francisco   CHi
NEVILLE & CO. Price list #8. Ills. and
prices of awnings, flags, nets, tents, etc.
for camp, store, home and public buildings,
etc. 8vo., 32pp., wrap.

c.1900 San Francisco   CHi
------ Ill. catalog #11.

1879 Boston   MiDbF
NEW ENGLAND FIREWORKS LABORATORY.
(B.T. Wells, agent.) Catalog and price list
of fireworks for home, town and city. 16mo.,
40pp., fine ills.

c.1885 Boston   MBSPNEA
------ Price list of single pieces, collections, exhibitions for town and country. Desc.
of Cottage City displays - has handled Boston
displays for 11 years. Complete from bomb
to banner and flag. 16mo., 48pp., wrap.
N.B. Boston displays since 1861.

c.1898 Lockport, N. Y.   OrU
NORMAN & EVANS, Mfg. A catalog of
Steam Merry-Go-Rounds mfg. by . . .

4to., 8-1/2x11, 3pp., wrap. 4 col. litho. by
Courier of Buffalo of Norman & Evans'
Galloping Horse Steam Merry-Go-Round.
2pp. of text, desc., directions, tools furnished with each outfit, details. Delightful
experience for young and old, latest improved designs of steam engines, tents,
equipment, etc.

1891 Norwich, Conn.   CtHi
NORWICH NICKEL & BRASS WORKS. Display fixtures for all lines of goods. #2.
Supplement #2. 4to., 4pp., ills. Also supplement #3, Sept. 1891.

c.1889 Norwich, Conn.   CtHi
------ Ill. catalog and price list of display
frames, stands, cornice fixtures, specialties and novelties for window and interior
display. 4to., 48pp.

1906 Norwich, Conn.   CtHi
------ Catalog by Norwich Nickel & Brass
Co., successors.

1896 New York   NNMM
PALMENBERG'S, J.R. SONS. Ill. catalog
and price list of display fixtures and forms.
3rd ed. Original paper cvs. Ill. throughout, forms, dummies, heads, Geo. Washington, etc. Lady on bicycle, etc.

1891 Boston   NNMM
RAIT, JAMES. Catalog of metal fixtures
for the display of boots and shoes. Ill. and
desc. 40 numbered pp. Original gray paper
cvs. with design.

nd. Rochester, N. Y.   PKsL
ROCHESTER FIREWORKS CO. Programs
of exhibition assortments, lawn displays for
summer resorts and family use.

c.1900 Boston   NNMM
ROTHE, A. Ill. catalog of theatrical wigs,
etc. 56pp.

1884 San Francisco   CHi
SADLER & CO. Ill. catalog of fireworks,
flags, banners, exhibitions, toy pistols,
crackers, etc. 12mo., 120pp., fine ills.,
wrap.

c.1880 New York
SHANNON, MILLER & CRANE. Ill. catalog
of gold, silver and tinsel trimmings, theatrical goods, flags and banners. 8vo., 40pp. of
ills., pict. wrap. A fine ill. record of fringes,
tassels, spangled stars, eagles, etc., armor
cloth and fancy foil buttons.

1889 Baltimore   NNMM
SHOW WINDOW PUBLISHING CO.   NNU
300 ways to dress show windows. Fine ills.,
12mo., cl.

c.1900 New York   NNMM
THORP, S.S. & CO. Ill. catalog of flags for
all purposes - hotels and public buildings,
stations, steamboats, yachts, etc. 8vo.,
24pp., col. ills., pict. wrap.

c.1888 Baltimore   NNMM
TORSCH & LEE MFG. A catalog of silk
badges, rosettes, stars, etc. for every
organization, fire departments, police balls,
political parades, societies, etc. 4x11, 20pp.
with col. pls., pict. wrap. with sample badge
enclosed in folder.

1885 Staten Island   NStIHi
UNEXCELLED FIREWORKS CO. Net price
list with ills. of crackers, display pieces,

exhibition and display assortments, toy
pistols, penny banks, etc. 16mo., 72pp.,
fine ills., pict. wrap.

1889 Staten Island   NStIHi
------ Ill. catalog of celebration goods,
latest improved displays, novelties, cap
pistols, etc. 16mo., 80pp., fine ills.

c.1898 Newark, N. J.   NjR
WHITEHEAD & HOAG CO. Catalog #20.
Ball and parade badges for fire and police
departments, clubs, lodges, political parties
and other organizations. Tall 4to., 24pp. of
col. and tinted pls. An unusually fine col.
pict. record, pict. wrap.

Jewelry catalogs supplement this section, and in them you will find badges and buttons not apparently
listed by the manufacturers. Again be sure to check the Department, Dry Goods and Miscellaneous
Stores. Sporting Goods Stores also carried banners, flags and tents for all occasions and occupations. In the chapters headed Fire Engines and Clothing you will also find badges, regalia and
uniforms for firemen, policemen and the military. Even Silversmiths produced badges and trophies,
and of course, Montgomery Ward & Co., and Sears Roebuck & Co. shouldn't ever be neglected as a
last resort.

Chapter 14

China & Pottery

The offerings in this chapter, well mixed in the glory hole of American advertising history, are as pure clay as library locations offer. There are a good many in private collections whose eventual disposition I am not at liberty to record; that they are still available is important.

Whereas I can guarantee that the Ballard churns and crocks are pottery of the first water, Higgins & Seiter's pictorial references offer everything from the grandest German steins to the fanciest in American and European glass. Jones, McDuffee and Stratton also are very inclusive and should not be examined with the idea that the wares are necessarily all made by Yankee potters.

1862 Burlington, Vt.   VtSM
BALLARD, A.K. & O.L. Broadside catalog of stone and Rockingham Ware. Ill. by 18 woodcuts of pitchers, jugs, crocks, churns, etc.

1871 Burlington, Vt.   NNMM
------ Broadside catalog with ills. of stone and Rockingham Wares.

1850-1872 Burlington, Vt.
------ Five broadside ill. lists known in private collection, hence not located.

c.1890 New York   NNMM
BERLIN & YEDDO CHROMO CO. Catalog of pottery decorations for cuspidors, vases, umbrella holders, etc. Pls. showing 103 designs. 24mo., 48pp., pict. wrap.

1885 Hartford, Conn.   CtHi
BOSWORTH, S.B., MFG. Price list circular and pict. billhead, with 6 ills. of jugs, jars, churns, pitchers and pots.

c.1900 Cleveland   OHi
BOWMAN, GEORGE H. CO. Catalog #5. For dealers and studios - White China Designs for decorators and artists. 4to., 22pp. with fine pls., pict. wrap.

c.1880 Chicago   MiDbF
BURLEY & CO. Est. 1838. Catalog #15. White China for decorators. Large 4to., 52pp. of pls. of tableware, crockery, lamps, ornaments, vases, etc. with supplement and wrap.

nd. Chicago   NNMM
------ White China for decorating. Ill. catalog and price list separate at back. pp. 1-32, price list pp. 1-30. Original paper cvs.

1809 New York   MWA
CLARKSON, CROLIUS. Ill. broadside with 5 woodcuts of --- Stone Ware for sale at manufactory back of the City Gaol and New City Hall, and opposite Manhattan Wells at the following prices . . . Jars, jugs, vases, crocks, pitchers, etc.

c.1860 Great Bend, Pa.   PKsL
COLSTEN, W.A. Broadside catalog of Rockingham and Yellow Ware. The best goods manufactured in the U. S. Ills. of pottery works - 2 column list of prices of stone ware and 3 columns of vases, flower pots, pedestals, baskets, churns, etc. 1 leaf, both sides.

1840 Nashua, N. H.
CRAFTS, T. & CO. Broadside price list of stone ware, pots, pitchers, churns, ink pots, ice jars and kegs.

1842 Nashua, N. H.
------ Broadside price list of crocks, jugs, etc.

1845 Nashua, N. H.
------ Broadside price list of earthenware jugs, crocks, churns, etc.

1885 Denver   CoD
DENVER FIRE CLAY CO. Catalog of fire bricks, crucibles, mufflers, pots for assayers, chemists, etc. Ill., wrap.

1895 Denver   CoD
------ 5th ed. of ill. catalog.

1910-? Boston   NNMM
EASTERN CLAY GOODS CO. Catalog of clay products, Akron stone ware, etc. 64pp., ills., wrap.

1878 Elizabeth, N. J.   MdTanSW
ELIZABETH POTTERY WORKS.   L. B.
Beerblower & Co., Mfg. 16 page ill. catalog
of white granite CC decorated ware and
druggists' ware, toilet sets, etc.

1851 Fairfax, Vt.
FARRAH & STEARNS. Broadside price
list of earthenware goods.

1840 Exeter, N. H.
FARRAR, G.W. & J.H. Broadside price
list of stone ware.

c.1860 Fort Edward, N. Y.   MdTanSW
FORT EDWARD STONEWARE ASSOCIATION
Messrs. Satterlee & Mory, Ottman Brothers,
George S. Guy & Co. 24mo., 8 page ill.
folder with 27 cuts of jugs, cream pots, bean,
butter, molasses and pudding crocks, churns,
cuspidors and pitchers.

1861 Fort Edward, N. Y.   N
------ Fort Edward Pottery. Broadside
price list with 12 woodcuts.

1861 Fort Edward, N. Y.   N
------ Fort Edward Pottery. Satterlee &
Russell. Ill. broadside price list.

1852 Amesbury, Mass.
HENDRICK & MANN. Price list of Redware.

c.1880 North Cambridge, Mass.   NNMM
HEWS, A.H. & CO. Est. 1765. Advt.: 1890 -
Oldest Pottery in U. S. Catalog and wholesale price list of fancy earthenware. 24pp.,
ills., wrap.

1898 New York   NCornC
HIGGINS & SEITER. Catalog #9.   NNMM
Fine china and rich cut glass. 8vo., 220pp.
of fine ills., pls., some in col., figurines,
steins, jardinieres, tea sets, tobacco jars,
complete line, col. dec. wrap.

1899 New York   NNMM
------ Ill. catalog #10. One of the best
pict. records. 8vo., 250pp., wrap.

1900-1901 New York
------ Ill. catalogs #12 and 13. 8vo. with
260 and 300pp., resp., col. pls., wrap.

1874 Philadelphia   PHi
JEFFORDS, J.E. & CO. Prices current for
pottery. 16mo., ill., wrap.

1882 Boston   MdTanSW
JONES, McDUFFEE &   PPL
STRATTON. Catalog of English, Chinese,
and Japanese dinnerware, English CC,
Yellow and Rockingham, lamps, cuspidors,
vases, fancy crockery, etc. 8vo., ills. and
47 col. pls. of printed wares, fine ref., wrap.

1854 Exeter, N. H.
LAMOAR, ASA B. Price list of Earthenware - jugs, pitchers, crocks, churns, pots,
etc. Also noted for 1862 and 1865.

1856 Fairfax, Vt.   VtSM
LEWIS, BOSTWICK & CADY. Broadside
price list of pottery with ills. of stone ware
bowls, churns, jugs, pots and pitchers.

MAIDA LAMP & CHINA CO. See also
Lighting.

c.1870 Manchester, N. H.
MANCHESTER POTTERY WORKS. Klemke
& Watjen, Props. Earthen, stone, yellow
and Rockingham Ware, plain and fancy
flower pots, cuspidors, jugs, vases, etc. 8
page folder with pict. wrap.

c.1878 Meriden, Conn.   NNMM
MANNING, BOWMAN & CO. Ill. catalog
and price list of Granite Porcelain Finished
Wares - interesting facts folder.

1885 Meriden, Conn.   NNMM
------ Ill. catalog of granite ironware,
decorated agateware, porcelain lined coffee
urns, etc. 146pp., cl.

1892 Meriden, Conn.   NNMM
------ Ill. catalog of Perfection chafing
dishes, urns, sets, dinnerware, etc.
342pp., cl.

1869 Fort Edward, N. Y.   N
NEW YORK STONE WARE POTTERY.
Satterlee & Mory, Props. Broadside price
list with 12 woodcuts of jugs, churns, pots,
etc. Shipping instructions!

1871 Fort Edward, N. Y.   N
------ Broadside price list of Rockingham
Ware - tomato fruit jars! 12 woodcuts of
various pottery of the period for the general
store and the farmer's wife.

1854 Burlington, Vt.   VtSM
NICHOLS & ALVORD. Alford has been
crossed out in ink - draw your own conclu-
sions. Broadside price list with woodcuts
of stone and fancy earthenware.

1855 Burlington, Vt.   VtSM
NICHOLS & BOYNTON. Broadside price
list with ills. of stone ware, fancy and
pressed ware, etc.

1856 Burlington, Vt.   VtSM
------ Broadside list of wares, ills.

1863 Worcester, Mass.
NORTON, F.B. Broadside with list of
prices and ills. (9) of decorated churns,
beer bottles, cuspidors - spittoons to be
exact - jugs, pots, etc.

1855 Bennington, Vt.   NNMM
NORTON, JULIUS & EDWARD. Ill. invoice
with fine engraving of works - with list of
pots, jugs, etc. with prices.

1848 Ashfield, Mass.
ORCUTT, GUELFORD & CO. Price iist of
stone ware churns, jugs, pots and other
household kitchenware.

c.1888 Brooklyn   NNMM
OVINGTON BROTHERS. Ill.   NHi
catalog of blue and white china, art potteries
with a history of Ovington potteries. 12mo.,
64pp., fine ills., wrap.

c.1880 Boston   ICHi
PARKER & WOOD. Seedsmen. There are
times when the wraps. and would-be title
pages of trade catalogs drive one to the very
brink. Ill. catalog of fancy earthenware
flower pots, hanging pots, saucers, ferner-
ies, art pottery, stylish cuspidors, umbrella
stands, etc. 8vo., 32pp., fine ills., pict.
wrap.

c.1895 Trenton, N. J.   PKsL
PROGRESSIVE MFG. CO. A rare opportunity to buy pottery ware of all kinds, the
finest china lamps, tea sets in Cable and
Hampden ironstone, etc. 4to., 4pp., ills.

1874 West Troy, N. Y.   N
RUSSELL, A.J. & J.L. Broadside price
list of every description of stoneware - ale,
beer, blacking, ink and porter bottles, snuff
jars, etc. Fine woodcuts.

1879 Hartford, Conn.   CtHi
SEYMOUR & BOSWORTH, MFG. Price list
circular and billhead with 6 ills. of flower
pots, jars, jugs, pitchers, etc.

1870 Troy, N. H.   NhD
SILSBY, C.M. & CO. Ill. catalog of earthenware flower pots and saucers, garden
vases, hanging pots, jugs, churns, cuspidors, etc. 14 ills. of fine decorated ware.

c.1870 Norwalk, Conn.   NNMM
SMITH, A.E. & SONS' NORWALK POTTERY.
Ill. and priced broadside of stone, brown and
Rockingham Wares.

1842 Sterling, Mass.   MWA
TOLMAN, HENRY & SON. Broadside price
list of jars, jugs, pots, churns, nests, beer
bottles, butter bowls, chambers, etc. 2
columns of wares.

c.1870 Utica, N. Y.   NNMM
WHITE, N.A. MFG. Broadside price list of
pottery for farm and store with 12 ills.

1875 New York
WILSON, WM. H. Mfg. Agent. Reduced
prices of crockery and glassware - in
crates for the country trade - complete
lists of best white ironstone, etc. 16mo.,
24pp., wrap.

nd. Philadelphia   NNMM
WRIGHT, TYNDALE & VAN RODEN. Catalog of porcelain, pottery and glass. 14 lvs.
with fine ills., wrap.

1877 Trenton, N. J.   MH-BA
YOUNG'S, WILLIAM SONS. Est. 1853.
Excelsior Works. Ill. catalog of earthenware, porcelain door knobs, furnishings of
white granite, dipped, blue edge and CC
ware. 16mo., 10pp., view of factory, wrap.

If this chapter seems short, don't give up. The same mixture of pottery creations are to be found
in great variety under Glass, House Furnishings, Lighting and even the old General Store Hardware
Goods section. What good would a fine plate of an 1880 hotel lobby be without a gorgeous spittoon,
a floral design umbrella stand and several huge pottery potted palms? To try to list such elegant
records under both glass and china would be suicide. The catalogs of medical supplies, pharmaceuticals, photographic supplies and silverware would be skeletons without the creations of the potter.
If you can't find what you want here, please roll up your sleeves and do a little hunting on your own.

Chapter 15

Clocks & Watches

If private collections and personal libraries could be counted as permanent repositories, this chapter would be much larger. As it is, the clock and watch associations, clubs, and other organizations of enthusiastic collectors have been more active in acquiring catalogs in this field than the historical societies and other repositories; more power to them for rescuing them from the dump and paper drives. I sincerely hope that before another edition is compiled many of these collections may be pointed at or promised to some national, state, local or university historical society or library.

The American Clock and Watch Museum at Bristol, Connecticut - CtBrAM - has provided us with many important locations for research. Many other repositories have reported fine examples. From Jacob Gorgas designs for clock and watch faces in 1765, to the latest and daintiest creations for 1900, we offer the neophyte a horological education, the historian a pictorial record of which he may not be conscious, and the advanced collector more tools with which to classify and date his holdings.

1865 Chicago & New York
AMERICAN CLOCK CO. (Agents for E. N. Welch Co. and Seth Thomas Clock Co.) Ill. catalog of clocks. A fine pict. record of shelf and steeple styles, painted glass fronts, octagons, Sambo, Topsey and continental figures - the plainest and the fanciest of the period. 24mo., 90pp., pict. wrap.

1869 Chicago & New York   CtBrAM
------ Ill. catalog of clocks.

1876 Chicago & New York   CtBrAM
------ Ill. catalog of clocks.

1890 Waltham   NNU
AMERICAN WALTHAM WATCH CO. Information - a few points in construction of a pocket watch. 12mo., 44pp., ill., wrap.

c.1860 Waltham   PPF   MH-BA
AMERICAN WATCH CO. Desc. brochure, details of business, tests., 8vo., 20pp., wrap.

1884 Waltham   PPF   CtBrAM
------ Ill. price list of watches.

1874-96 Ansonia   CtBrAM
ANSONIA CLOCK CO. Ill. price lists of clocks manufactured by Ansonia for: 1874, 1883, 1885, 1886 and 1896.

c.1898 Chicago   CtMyM
BAIRD CLOCK CO. The Baird Chronograph, the only reliable time stamp. 8pp., ill.

c.1850 Boston   MWA
BEALS, J.J. & CO. Broadside offering 16

ills. of styles and models of parlor, kitchen, banjo and shelf clocks.

1839 New York   DSi
BLISS & CREIGHTON, Mfg. Observations on Chronometers. Sq. 16mo., 9pp., wrap.

1887 Forestville, Conn.   Ct
BRISTOL BRASS & CLOCK CO. Listed here merely for the record. This catalog lists and ills. only lamps and lighting accessories. See Lighting.

c.1890 Springfield, Mass.
BULLOCK, O.W. & CO. Catalog of fine watch tools, parts, etc. 8vo., 85pp., ill., pict. wrap. Plus 4 page supplement for 1891.

1873 New York   CtBrAM
COLLINS GOLD METAL WATCH & JEWELRY FACTORY. Ill. catalog of watches and jewelry.

c.1880 Canton, O.   NNMM
DUEBER WATCH CASE CO. Ill. catalog of watch cases.

c.1890 Canton, O.   NNMM
------ Ill. catalog of the best in watch cases - pls. of styles, designs and movements. 4to., 32pp., pict. wrap.

1888 Chicago   PPF   MH-BA
ELGIN NATIONAL WATCH CO. Ill. catalog of watch parts and materials. 7x10, 144pp.

1890 Sag Harbor, N. Y. & Branches NNMM
FAHYS, JOSEPH & CO. Ill. catalog of watch
cases. 56pp., cl. and bds.

c.1891 Sag Harbor, N. Y. NNMM
------ Ill., desc. and priced catalog #1 -
watch cases, pp. 100 to 156, cl.

1891 New York, Chicago & San Francisco
------ Ill. catalog - Here it is! NNMM
A Jeweler's Dream - Fit for a King.
Monarch #1. 4to., cl.

1889 Boston PPF MH-BA
FANEUIL WATCH TOOL CO. Watch tool
machinery, rivet lathes, attachments, etc.
16mo., 48pp., ills., wrap.

1883 Providence RHi
FLOYD, PRATT & ROUNDS. Ill. catalog of
American watches and jewelry. 16mo.,
20pp., pict. wrap.

1899 Chicago ICHi
FORT DEARBORN WATCH & CLOCK CO.
20th annual ill. catalog. A fine pict. record
of watches, clocks, chains, charms and
ornaments. All styles and models, even to
toothpicks. 4to., 698pp., dec. cl.

1875 Winsted, Conn. CtBrAM
GILBERT, WILLIAM L. CLOCK CO. Est.
1825. Ill. catalog of fine clocks.

1878 Winsted, Conn. CtBrAM
------ Ill. catalog of clocks.

1880 Winsted, Conn. CtHi
------ In May Wm. L. Gilbert and G. B.
Owen consolidated. Ill. catalog of shelf,
banjo and wall clocks. 8vo., 48pp., pict.
wrap.

1881 Winsted, Conn. CtBrAM
------ Ill. catalog.

1885 Winsted, Conn. CtBrAM
------ Ill. catalog, all styles and models.

1887 Winsted, Conn. MH-BA
------ Ill. price list of clocks and clock
materials. 16mo., 20pp., wrap.

1891-2 Winsted, Conn. CtBrAM
------ Ill. catalog of fine clocks. CtHi
Tall, hall, banjo, wall, shelf styles and
models. 8vo., 110pp. of fine ills., plus
20 page price list, pict. wrap.

1892 Winsted, Conn. CtHi
------ Ill. catalog of clocks. 8vo., 12pp.,
wrap.

1895-98 Winsted, Conn. CtBrAM
------ Ill. catalogs of fine clocks, designs,
styles, etc. A fine ref. library 1875-1898.

c.1900 Winsted, Conn. CtHi
------ Showrooms in New York & Chicago.
Where Gilbert Clocks are made. Fol., fine
pls. and ills. with price list. Pict. wrap.

1765 Ephrata, Pa. MiDbF
GORGAS, JACOB. A catalog of figures,
designs and scenes for engraving watch and
clock faces. 8pp., ills. See Treasures in
Truck and Trash by Carl W. Drepperd. 1950.
Pp. 92-97.

c.1895 Cincinnati OC
HERSCHEDE, FRANK. Mfg. & Importer.
Ill. catalog of hall clocks with 15 fine pls.,
plus 26 loose pls., possibly kept together for
another catalog. Large 8vo., 16pp. of text
and desc., wrap.

c.1815 Plymouth, Conn. PPF MWA
HOADLEY, SILAS. Broadside - Clocks
made and sold by Silas Hoadley, warranted
to perform equal to and of the kind made in
the United States, if cased and well used.

c.1815 Plymouth, Conn. MWA
------ Clocks with improvement of boxing
the pivots with ivory, etc.

1868 Boston NNMM
HOWARD WATCH & CLOCK CO. Ill., desc.
and priced catalog of clocks. 38pp. with 32
ills., pict. wrap.

1872 Boston CtBrAM
------ Ill. catalog of watches DSi
and clocks. 112pp.

c.1874 Boston DSi
------ Ill. brochure - Electro-Magnetic
Watch Clock. 4pp.

1889 Boston NNMM
------ Catalog of hall striking PPL
clocks. 5x10, 27pp. with 10 fine pls., wrap.

1881-99 Bristol, Conn. CtBrAM
INGRAHAM, THE CO. A fine collection of
ill. catalogs with pls. and details of styles
and designs. 1881, 1882, 1884, 1886, 1895-6,
1897-8 and 1899.

1882 Ithaca NNMM
ITHACA CALENDAR CLOCK CO. Share
New York Offices with Waterbury Clock Co.
Ills. of Ithaca Calendar Clocks. Designs:
No. O-Bank, No. 1, Regulator, No. 2 Bank,
No. 3 Vienna, also Favorite, Belgrade and
Emerald. Clocks for parlor, office, library,
cottage, farm, etc. 4x8-1/2, 24pp. of fine
ills., wrap.

c.1850 New Haven CtBrAM
JEROME, CHAUNCEY. Ill. catalog of
clocks, etc.

1852 New Haven   CtBrAM
------ Ill. catalog of clocks, new designs
and styles.

1869 New York   CtBrAM
KENNEDY ELECTRIC CLOCK CO. Ill. catalog of electric clocks.

1882 Philadelphia   PKsL
KEYSTONE MFG. CO. How watch cases are
made, history of watch case making, Boss
cases with prices, shops, parts, etc. Fol.,
ills., wrap.

1886-7 New York   CtBrAM
KROEBER, F. CLOCK CO. Ill. catalog of
fine clocks.

1888-9 New York
------ Ill. catalog of clocks for all places
and purposes.

c.1800 Portland, Me.   MWA
LORIS, J. & BROTHERS. Broadside - At
The Sign of the Golden Watch. Inform
customers that they do watchmaking . . .
and have constantly on hand watches, eight
day clocks, watch chains, teaspoons, rings
and fancy work.

1887 New York   MiDbF
LOVEL MFG. CO. Ill. price list of wonderful luminous dial clocks that shine at night,
etc. 8pp.

1875 New York   CtBrAM
MANHATTAN BRASS CO. Ill. price list of
brass and copper goods.

c.1890 Cleveland, O.   OHi
MORSE, J.S. MFG. 9th annual catalog.
Improved American watchman's time detec-
tor. Clocks and recording devices. 8vo.,
40pp., fine ills., wrap.

1885 Philadelphia. Branches in New York
& Chicago   NNMM
MUHR, H. & SONS, Mfg. Catalog of the
watch case department. Fine pls., medals
awarded, etc. 4to., 17pp., pict. wrap.

1886 Philadelphia   NNMM
------ Catalog of watch cases. 17 lvs.,
fine pls., wrap.

1880 New Haven   CtBrAM
NEW HAVEN CLOCK CO. Ill. catalog of
clocks.

1881 New Haven   CtHi
------ Ill. catalog of clocks with fine ills.
of all models and styles. 8vo., 80pp., wrap.

1883 New Haven   CtHi
------ Ill. broadside, 8x11, with cuts of
The Pilgrim, etc.

1888-9 New Haven   PPF CtBrAM
------ Ill. catalog of clocks,   CtHi
special designs: Buffalo, lantern, tennis
clock ink stand, paper weight, bouquet, banjo,
stirrup, lighthouse, mortar and pestle, cigar
lighter clocks, etc. 8vo., 192pp., swell ills.,
pict. wrap.

1889-90 New Haven   NNMM
------ Fine ill., desc. and priced catalog
of standard and novelty clocks. 206pp.,
fine ref.

c.1893 New Haven   NNMM
------ Ill. catalog of special clocks, special designs for hall, mantel, boudoir, 8 day
calendar, marbloid models, plaques, etc.
Large 8vo., 48pp., wrap.

c.1890 New York
NEW YORK WORLD. Publishers. Special
catalog for weekly world subscribers.
Watches of all makes - Elgin, Standard,
Waltham, Dueber-Hampton cases, etc.
16mo., 24pp., ills. of each make, wrap.

nd. New York   NHi
PRENTISS CLOCK IMPROVEMENT CO.
Clocks by Prentiss - 60 day calendar and
program clocks. Tall 16mo. with fine ills.

c.1893 Chicago   PPF ICHi
SEARS ROEBUCK & CO. Catalog - Largest
Watch House in the World. Annual sales
over 100,000, etc. 8vo., ill. catalog and
price list.

1863 Plymouth Hollow, Conn.   CtBrAM
SETH THOMAS CLOCK CO. Est. 1813.
Ill. catalog of clocks.

1864 Plymouth Hollow, Conn.   CtBrAM
------ Ill. catalog.

1868 Thomaston, Conn.   CtBrAM
---- Special catalog of clocks.

1872 Thomaston, Conn.   CtBrAM
------ Ill. catalog of mantel clocks.

1880 Thomaston, Conn.   CtBrAM
------ Ill. catalog.

1883-4 Thomaston, Conn.   CtBrAM
------ Ill. catalog of mantel   NNMM
and shelf clocks. 120pp., wrap.

1884-5 Thomaston, Conn.   PPF CtBrAM
------ Supplement catalog #394.   MH-BA
Ill. catalog of clocks and watches. 8vo.,
20pp., wrap.

1888-9 Thomaston, Conn.   CtBrAM
------ #453. Fine ills.   CtHi   MH-BA
of clocks - desk, alarm, mantel, grandfather and fancy designs. 8vo., 128pp.,wrap.

1889 Thomaston, Conn.   CtBrAM
------ Ill. price list of   CtHi MH-BA
clocks. 8vo., 40pp., fine ills.

1890 Thomaston, Conn.   CtBrAM
------ Ill. catalog. 8vo., CtHi MH-BA
24pp., wrap.

1890-91 Thomaston, Conn. PPF CtBrAM
1896-97 ------ Ill. catalogs offering the
best assortment for the Gay Nineties. Also
note at CtHi if needed, other ill. catalogs
after 1900. Now a division of General Time
Corporation.

c.1894 Worcester, Mass.   MH-BA
WASHBURN & MOEN MFG. CO. Ill. catalog,
interleaved of clock, watch and motor
springs. 16mo., 24pp.

1881 Waterbury, Conn.   CtBrAM
WATERBURY WATCH CO. Ill. catalog of
fine watches.

1883 Waterbury, Conn.   CtBrAM
------ Ill. catalog of fine watches.

1887 Waterbury, Conn.   CtHi
------ The whole story of the Waterbury.
$2.50 but still reliable, ills. of parts and
watches. 32mo., 8pp., pict. wrap.

1889 Waterbury, Conn.   CtHi
------ A Tale of Three Revolutionary
Watches. Ills. of series E, J & L. 64mo.,
8 ill. pp., delightful pict. wrap.

1898 Waterbury, Conn.   CtHi
------ With New England Watch Co.
Pointers for watchmakers and repairmen.
Styles - The Elfin, smallest made in U. S.,
the Cavour, popular ladies' low price watch,
parts and tools. 24mo., 16pp., wrap.

c.1899 Waterbury, Conn.   CtHi
------ Ill. catalog to dealers only. Series
E, J, K, L and N. Fol., 4pp., wrap.

1891-97 Waterbury, Conn.   CtHi
------ The Waterbury, a house organ with
ills. of watches, parts, tools, etc.

1880 Forestville, Conn.   CtBrAM
WELCH, E.N. MFG. CO. Ill. catalog of
clocks.

1886 Forestville, Conn.   MoSHi
------ Ill. catalog of clocks and clock
parts, cases and materials.

1889-93 Forestville, Conn.   CtBrAM
------ Ill. catalogs for 1889-90, 1892-93
and 1893. Fine ref. group.

c.1790-1800 New Brunswick, N. J. NjR
WILLIAMS, JOHN H. Clock & Watchmaker.
Fol. broadside with cont. border - corner of
Albany & Peace Sts., opposite the Whitehall
Tavern - begs leave to return grateful
acknowledgements for past favors at his old
stand - and offers: 2 columns of goods -
musical and common eight day clocks, etc.,
from candlesticks to sleeve buttons.

c.1880 New Haven   CtHi
YALE CLOCK CO. American clocks in
great variety of style and finish, under
F. A. Lane's patents. 16mo., 24pp., pls. of
desk set clock, beauty alarm, Yale bell,
Idol, Companion, Traveler, paper weight,
Yale gem, Brunswick, Yale comet, Yosemite,
Orient, grandfather, etc.

1893 Chicago   NNMM
YOUNG, OTTO & CO. Ill. price list of
watches. 4to., fine ills., cl.

American clocks and watches have been offered and illustrated by hundreds of jewelers and merchants in countless catalogs throughout the 19th century. In both the Jewelry and Silverware
chapters you will find fully as many styles and models illustrated by the jobber and merchant as
you will find in this chapter of manufacturers' price lists. Both the A. C. Becken and Busiest
House in America catalogs are excellent examples. If you can't find an illustration and date of
some American piece in these three spots, try Department, Dry Goods and Miscellaneous Stores,
Hardware - General Goods and Products, and House Furnishings.

Chapter 16

Clothes, Overclothes, Underclothes, Hats, Shoes & All Things in Between. Rogers Peet & Co., 1892

Food, clothing and shelter are still our three primary needs, though Benjamin Franklin would hardly recognize many of them as required by 1900. Human foppery has gone through many periods of strange changes, some commendable and many frightful, in which statement I include the female as well as the male, contrary to the dictionary definition.

In this chapter I have tried to include every raw material and finished product that adorns the human frame on every occasion from ballroom to factory to mountain climbing and back home again. Some catalogs are so all inclusive that, as I have said many times, they refuse classification. In some examples you will find not only shoes but shoe machinery, and perhaps wonder why this isn't placed under machinery and tools. However, this being a democracy, the majority wins, and selections have been made on a basis of the most important illustrations or predominance of description and detail. If you are hunting a simple silk thread or trousseau, it ought to be listed right here.

c.1899 St. Paul, Minn.   MnHi
ALBRECHT, E. & SON. A catalog of fur clothing, fine and fancy furs. 8vo., 48pp., ill., wrap.

c.1900 Fall River   NNMM
AMERICAN PRINTING CO. & FALL RIVER IRON WORKS. Catalog of prints, dress goods, etc in full col. pls., photo. of plant, etc. 4to., cl., American Colortype Co. pls.

1878 New York
ARTHUR, HENRY. Catalog of skins, uppers, lasts and cobblers' tools. Ill.

c.1850 Boston   MBSPNEA
ATWOOD, D.J. Merchant Tailor. Catalog of costumes for many purposes, theatrical, etc. Trimmings. 16mo., 8pp., details of trimmings.

1880 New York   OAkF
BALLARD, STEPHEN & CO. Price list of rubber goods, boots, overshoes, oiled clothing, gloves, etc. 24mo., 48pp., fine ills., wrap.

1890 Denver   CoD
BALLIN & RANSOHOFF. Fall and winter catalog of dress goods, fashions, etc.

1880 St. Louis   MoSHi
BARR, THE WILLIAM DRY GOODS CO. Ill. catalog of domestic fashions for fall.

1892 St. Louis   MoSHi
------ Ill. catalog - The Style - domestic patterns.

1878 Boston   OAkF
BATCHELDER & LINCOLN. Rubber price list of boots, shoes, rubbers, etc. 16mo., 8pp., ills., wrap.

1881 Boston   OAkF
------ Ill. rubber price list. 8pp., wrap.

1878 St. Louis   MoSHi
BATES, REED & COOLEY. Ill. catalog and memorandum book of dress goods.

nd. New York, Chicago & Boston   NNMM
BELDING BROTHERS & CO. Ill. and desc. catalog of silk embroidery, knitting and crocheting. 80pp. with 30 col. pls., wrap.

1902 New York, Chicago & Boston   NNMM
------ Revised ill. and desc. catalog of silk patterns, knitting, etc. 64pp., inter-leaved with col. pls., wrap.

1884 New York & St. Louis   NNMM
BENTLEY, CHARLES E.   MoSHi
Ill., desc. and priced catalog of novelties in art needlework, patterns and lace work. 112pp., wrap.

1883 Denver   CoD
BERNHEIMS, W.S. Cash Store. Ill. catalog of domestic fashions.

nd. New Haven   NNMM
BESSE, RIGHEY & CO. Ill., desc. and
priced catalog of clothes, hats and men's
furnishings. 8pp., wrap.

BICYCLE CLOTHING. See Bicycles -
Kenyon.

c.1890 Cincinnati   OC
BIG STORE. Catalog of mens' clothing,
cheviot suits, scotch mixed, $2.98, with
samples of cloth - like felt. Trade Palace
of the most liberal and progressive retailers
in the world. 8vo., 4pp., ills. and samples.

1893 Allegheny   PKsL
BOGGS & BUHL. Catalog #14. Price list
and fashion book for fall and winter, clothes
and novelties. 4to., 148pp., fine ills., pict.
wrap.

c.1835 South Boston, Mass.   MWA
BOSTON INDIA RUBBER FACTORY.
Broadside - India rubber waterproof goods.
2 columns of rubber clothing, boots, etc.
Dec. border.

1891 Boston   OAkF
BOSTON RUBBER SHOE CO. & BAY STATE
RUBBER CO. Gross price list. 16mo.,
12pp., wrap.

1896 Boston   OAkF
------ Ill. catalog of rubber shoes, overshoes, etc. 16mo., 24pp., wrap.

1860 Boston   NNMM
BOYNTON, N. & CO. Russell Mills Cotton
Duck goods described. One leaf.

1881 New York & New London, Conn. NNMM
BRAINERD & ARMSTRONG CO. Ill. and
desc. catalog of knitting silks, rules for
work, patterns, etc. 40pp., wrap.

1900 New York & New London, Conn. CtNlC
------ Embroidery lessons with catalog of
silks, etc. and fancy work. Ills.

1882 New Yoek
BRIGGS & CO. Catalog of Brigg's patent
transferring papers - a warm iron transfers
these patterns to any fabric. 8vo., 156pp. of
designs, many of them identical to the hand
blocks, pewter, tin and copper on wood, of
the 1830 period and also ill. in Godeys to the
Civil War. See Antiques Magazine, Vol. 37,
#4, April, 1940. Stumbling Blocks. Col.
pict. title, cl.

1872 New York   NNMM
BRINCKERHOFF, WM. & CO. Ill., desc.
and priced catalog of hats and caps for
autumn. 32pp., wrap.

nd. New York   NHi
BROOKS BROTHERS. Various ill. catalogs
of boys' and mens' clothing.

1870 New York   MH-BA
BUTTERICK, E. & CO. Catalog of patterns,
latest fashions for fall 1870. For woman,
child and doll. 8vo., 24pp., fine ills., pict.
wrap.

1871 New York   MH-BA
------ Catalog of prices and ills. PKsL
of patterns. 8vo., 24pp., wrap.

1871-2 New York   PKsL
------ (Baltimore agent.) 8vo., 32pp.,
ills., skating scene wrap.

1873 New York   MoSHi
------ Ill. catalog of patterns for   NNMM
dresses, jackets, coats, etc. for spring.
30pp., fine ills., wrap.

1873-4 New York & Norwich, Conn.   NNMM
------ Catalog of patterns, etc. 30pp.,
fine ills., pict. wrap.

1874-5 New York & Hannibal, Mo.   MoSHi
------ Ill. catalog of patterns.

1880 New York   COCAC
------ Ill. catalog of patterns, woman,
child and doll.

1883 New York   COCAC
------ Ill. catalog of fashions and patterns.
4to., ills. throughout, pict. wrap.

1884 New York   COCAC
------ 4to., pict. wrap.

1885 New York   COCAC
------ Ill. catalog of patterns,   MoSHi
styles and fashions.

1886 New York   COCAC
------ Ill. catalog of fashions,   MoSHi
styles, etc. 4to., fine ills., pict. wrap.

1893 New York   NNMM
------ Metropolitan Fashions - patterns,
desc., ill. and priced. 8 lvs.

1883 Cincinnati   OHi
CALDWELL, JOHN D. Mfg. &   OC
Dealer. Price list of Masonic supplies,
robes and furnishings. 8vo., 40pp., fine
ills., pict. wrap.

1885 Cincinnati   OHi
------ Ill. catalog of Masonic furnishings.

1880 New York   OAkF
CAMMEYER, ALFRED J. Ill. price list of
rubber boots and shoes. 10pp.

1894 New York   NNMM
------ Ill. catalog of boots and shoes -
styles and fashions. 40pp.

1899 New York   NNMM
------ Ill. catalog of footwear. 48pp.,
wrap.

1884 New Haven   OAkF
CANDEE RUBBER CO. Ill. catalog of rub-
ber boots, shoes, etc. 32pp. of styles, etc.
Wrap.

1893 Utica, N. Y.   NNMM
CANFIELD, ROBERT H. Ill. catalog of
spring and summer hats. 32pp., fine ills.,
wrap.

1895 New York   NNMM
CASTOR, GEORGE A. & CO. History of
Male Attire - Evolution of Mens' Clothing.
16mo., 32pp., fine ills., pict. wrap. of Ye
Golden Lion - Modern cutaway compared to
1850 styles.

c.1900 South Pasadena, Calif.   NNMM
CAWSTON OSTRICH FARM. Ill. catalog of
ornaments, boas, plumes, etc. Ostrich
feathers, styles and fashions. 30pp., fine
ills., wrap.

1883 New York   KU
CELLULOID NOVELTY CO. Ill. catalog of
collars, cuffs, short bosoms, waterproof
bosoms, the invention of the age; with verse
and delightful ills. to boot. Sm. 12mo.,
32pp. of swell ills., wrap.

1883 Chicago   ICHi
CHICAGO CORSET CO. Ill. catalog of
styles in corsets, col. pls. of Lillian Langtry,
Moujeska, Maud Granger, all looking pleas-
antly comfortable in Chicago Corsets.
12mo., 15pp., pict. wrap.

c.1885 Chicago   NNMM
------ Ill. catalog of Ball's pat. corsets.
16pp., pict. wrap.

c.1895 Chicago   ICHi
CHICAGO MERCANTILE CO. Millinery
catalog. Ills. of models and styles in hats
with trimmings - birds, plumes, ribbons,
ornaments, etc. 4to., 32pp., delightful ills.,
wrap.

nd. Cincinnati   OHi
CINCINNATI REGALIA CO. Catalog #558.
Ill. catalog of firemens' uniforms, badges,
hats, clothing and equipment.

c.1875 Cincinnati   OC
COAN & CO. Mfg. & Importers. Broadside
catalog of ladies' furs, raw skins, etc.

1876 South Norwalk   NNMM
COMSTOCK BROTHERS. Catalog of cloth-
ing for men, youths, boys and children.
Ill., desc. and priced. 16pp., wrap.

1881 New York   MH-BA
CO-OPERATIVE DRESS ASSOCIATION.
Est. 1881. Catalog of boys' clothing and
general goods. 16mo., 24pp., ills., wrap.

nd. Louisville, Ky.   ViWC
COWAN, ANDREW & CO. Catalog #76, oak
tanned leather, artistic boot and shoe uppers
and lasts. Ills.

1884 Denver   CoD
DANIELS & FISHER. Ill. catalog of patterns, fashions, parasols, Hamburg embroi-
deries, laces, trimmings, etc.

1896 Denver   CoD
------ Ill. catalog of patterns, fashions and
styles for clothing woman, girl and doll.

1876 New York   MoSHi
DEMOREST, MME. A catalog of reliable
patterns for all seasons. 8vo., 16pp., ills.
of patterns for woman, young lady, girl and
sometimes dolls. Pict. wrap.

1878 New York   MoSHi
------ What to wear and how to   NNMM
make it. Full information in every department of dress. 8vo., 158pp. of ills., pict.
wrap.

1879 New York   MoSHi
------ What to wear and how to   NNMM
make it, etc. 8vo., 122pp., ills., pict. wrap.

1880-99 New York   MoSHi
------ I am quite sure it is safe   NNMM
to report ill. catalogs from about 1870-1900
for these two repositories. I am also sure
many have not reported.

1897 Denver   CoD
DENVER DRY GOODS CO. Ill. catalog -
Imperial Fashions for July.

1898-1900 Denver   CoD
------ Ill. catalogs for spring, summer,
fall and winter. Fashions, dry goods and
notions.

c.1880 San Francisco   CHi
DOLLIVER & BROTHER. A catalog of
shoes, leather findings, cobblers' equipment
and shoe machinery. 8vo., fine ills., pict.
wrap.

1878 Boston   OAkF
EDMUNDS & MAYO. Hard-Pan price list
of boots, rubbers and shoes. 16mo., 8pp.,
ills., wrap.

1890 Boston   OAkF
------ Hard-Pan price list, 30 days cash.
16mo., 12pp., ills., wrap.

c.1880 Philadelphia   PHi
EDWARDS & CASTLE. Ill. catalog of shoe
findings and leather, French and American,
boot and shoe uppers, hemlock and oak sole
leathers, calf, sheep and morocco. 8vo.,
ill. throughout, pict. wrap.

1893 New York   NHi
EQUIPOISE CO. The Equipoise waiste -
she can bend, exercise and vacation in perfect posture, in fact she sings! 24mo.,
16pp., col. litho. ills., wrap.

c.1850 Boston   MStOSV
FANEUIL HALL CLOTH & CLOTHING
WAREHOUSE. Milton & Slocum, Tailors,
Prop. Broadside 19x24 with woodcut of
warehouse and lists of clothing and goods.

FIREMENS' UNIFORMS, etc. See Boughton,
Fire Fighting.

1899 Richmond, Va.   V
FLEISCHMAN, MORRIS & CO. Catalog of
old Virginia footwear. 16mo., 8pp., fine
ills., pict. wrap.

c.1885 New York   NNMM
FLETCHER, MRS. A. Ill. catalog of ladies'
and childrens' underwear. Ed's. note: how
in the world did a kid ever get into those
drawers? 32pp., delightful ills., wrap.

c.1900 Huntington, West Va.   Wv-Ar
FLODING, GEORGE A. MFG. Revised desc.
price list #25. IOOF lodge regalia and para-
phernalia, uniforms, robes, colors and furnishings. 12mo., 32pp., fine ills., pict.
wrap.

1722 Boston   Evans 2341
FRANKLIN, JAMES. Printer. Hoop Petti-
coats arraigned and condemned in the light
of nature and law of God. 16mo., 8pp.

c.1890 St. Louis   MoSHi
GAUSS, WILLIAM T. Ill. catalog of waterproof coats and cloaks.

1891 St. Louis   MoSHi
GAYLORD & BARCLAY. What to wear and
where to get it.

1889 Denver   CoD
GOLDEN EAGLE STORE. Fall and winter
catalog of clothing, fashions, dry goods and
notions.

1885 New York   OAkF
GOODYEAR INDIA RUBBER GLOVE CO.
(Lamkin & Foster, agents.) Ill. catalog of
rubber boots, gloves, shoes, etc. 36pp.

1896 St. Paul   MdTanSW
GORDON & FERGUSON. Est. 1871. Ill.
catalog of furs, fur coats, collars, capes,
etc., sketched on models by Ahnelt. 8vo.,
36pp., wrap.

1895 Manchester, N. H.   NhHi
GRANITE STATE SHOE CO. Catalog for
1895. Sandow knit boots, the best ever
made, etc. 8vo., 40pp., fine ills., pict.
wrap.

1886 New York   NNMM
HACKETT, CARHART & CO. Catalog of
mens', boys' and childrens' clothing for
spring and summer. 20pp., ills., wrap.

1893 Sacramento   CHi
HALE BROTHERS & CO. Catalog #19.
Womens' wear for spring and summer.
4to., 100pp., fine ills., wrap.

c.1890 Hillsdale, Mich.   MiU-H
HALL, MARVIN E. Catalog #4. Price list
of Sons of Veterans goods, uniforms, supplies and equipment. 12mo., 32pp., fine
ills., wrap.

c.1894 Hillsdale, Mich.   MiU-H
------ Ill. catalog #7. Price list of military goods, uniforms, trimmings, flags,
swords, arms, etc. 4 col. lithos. by Gugler
Litho. Co. 8vo., 42pp., fine ills., pict. wrap.

1876 Philadelphia   PHi
HANAUER, KOHN & CO. Price list of
clothing mfg. for the fall season. 16mo.,
8pp., ills.

1894 Johnstown, N. Y.   NNMM
HARRISON, A. Catalog of Dr. Warner's
Coraline corsets, delightful ills., some in
col. 8 lvs., wrap.

1876 Philadelphia   PKsL
HART, CLARENCE A. Catalog of society
uniforms, goods, military regalia, etc.
4pp. of ills.

1892 New York   COCAC
HERPICH, CHARLES P. Catalog of furs
for the season, boas, capes, coats, muffs,
robes, etc. 8vo., fine ills., pict. wrap.

1895-97 New York   COCAC
------ 2 ill. catalogs of furs and fur
pieces.

1882 San Francisco   CHi
HERRMANN, THE HATTER. Ill. catalog of
the best in hats. 4to., 64pp., fine ills., wrap.

1896 New York   NNMM
HILTON, HUGHES & CO. Successors to
A.T. Stewart & Co. Catalog of spring and
summer fashions, capes, coats, dresses,
hats, etc. 12 lvs., fine ills., wrap.

1870 Orange, N. J.   NjR
HOFFMAN, DANIEL MFG. Spring catalog,
hats, caps, furs, straw hats and straw goods.
Delightful ills. 8vo., 20pp.

c.1900 Danbury, Conn.   NNMM
HOLBROOK, E. STORE. Catalog of
Patrician shoes for women. 8 lvs., fine ills.

1823 Billerica, Mass.   MWA
HOLDEN, ASA JR. Broadside. Asa Holden
has taken a shop near the Canal Mills where
he mfg. ladies' and gentlemens' boots and
shoes of all kinds.

1856-1900 Philadelphia   PHi
HORSTMANN, WM. H. & SONS. Est. 1816.
Ill. catalogs of costumes, uniforms and
regalia for Odd Fellows, Knights of Pythias,
Masonic Order, etc., hats, coats, notions,
etc. 16mo. to 4to., vp., fine ills. and pict.
wrap. 1856, 1869, 1872, 1873, 1875 to 1883,
1885, 1888, 1889 and 1901.

1883 Boston   OAkF
HOSMER, CODDING & CO. Spring and
summer price list of boots, rubbers and
shoes - styles for 1883. Ills.

nd. Lynn   NNMM
HURLEY SHOE CO. Catalog of Tri-on-fa
ladies' shoes, dist. by E.C. Dawson. 20pp.,
ills., wrap.

c.1878 Lynn
INGALLS, J.F. Ingalls' ill. catalog of
stamping patterns. Price .15. 8vo., 188pp.
of designs, perforated stamping patterns,
NOT Briggs' transfer patterns. Wrap.

c.1880 Lynn   CSmH
------ Catalog of Briggs' transferring
patterns and designs, outfits for stamping
clothing, fancy art work, etc. 252pp. of
designs. Wrap.

1886 New York   NNU
JAEGER, DR., SANITARY WOOLEN
SYSTEM CO. Catalog of sanitary woolen
clothing and bedding, samples of camel's
hair underwear. 8vo., 50pp., ills., dec.
wrap.

c.1887 New York   MH-BA
------ Catalog of sanitary clothing, etc.
8th ed., 60pp., ill., dec. wrap.

1892-3 New York   NNMM
------ Ill. catalog of sanitary woolens, etc.
12mo., ills., price list, etc., cl.

1845 Boston   MH-BA
JEWETT PRESCOTT & CO. Est. 1836.
Price list of the silk and shawl store. 8vo.,
12pp.

1896-7 New York   COCAC
KAYE & EINSTEIN. Furs for fall and
winter, black coney, ermine, mink, sable,
etc. 4to., 16pp., fine ills., pict. wrap.

c.1835 Boston   MWA
KIMBALL, JOHN S. Broadside. Ready
made linens, neckstocks, suspenders,
hosiery and gloves, shirts, cravats, dickies,
bosomettes, drawers, etc. Blue with dec.
border. W.H. Homer, Printer.

c.1885 San Francisco   CHi
KLARENMEYER, S. UNDERWEAR HOUSE.
Ill. catalog of underwear, etc. 8vo., 15pp.

1897 Chicago   OrU
LADIES' SUPPLY CO. Ill. catalog of
ladies' and childrens' wear of all kinds and
styles. 16pp.

1896 New York   NNMM
LANGDON & BACHELLOR. Langdon &
Bachellor's Genuine Thompson's Glove
Fitting Corsets, the perfect fit. Corset
format, 12pp., delightful ills., col. litho.
pict. wrap.

1898 St. Paul   MnHi
LANPHER, FINCH & SKINNER. A catalog
of fur coats with fine ills. Prices added in
ink. 8vo.

1899 St. Paul   MnHi
------ Ill. catalog of furs and coats,
stoles, etc. 8vo. with ptd. prices tipped in.

nd. Cincinnati   OC
LEAVITT & CODDINGTON. C.H.S. Broad-
side price list of the Cincinnati Hosiery
Store. 12mo., one leaf.

1881 New York   MiDbF
LeBOUTILLIER BROTHERS. Catalog of
fashions, laces, trimmings, buttons and
other notions. 8vo., 96pp., fine ills., wrap.

c.1870 New York   MiDbF
LEIBOLD, JOHN. Catalog of leather and
findings, lasts, boots, shoes, harness and
tools. 8vo., 12pp., fine ills., especially of
tools, pict. wrap.

1877 Warehouse Point, Conn.   CtHi
LEONARD SILK CO. Price list of tsatlee
and canton stock, silks, threads and notions.
One leaf.

1886 San Francisco   CHi
LIEBES, H. & CO. 25th annual fashion
plate of sealskin and rich furs for the season 1886-7. 8vo., 15 lvs., fine pls., wrap.

1895 Columbus, O.   MH-BA
LILLEY, M.C. & CO. Est. 1865. Catalog
of military uniforms and supplies with price
list and fine ills. 8vo., 52pp., wrap.

1882 Cincinnati   OC
MABLEY'S MAMMOTH CLOTHING HOUSE.
A review of fashions for spring and summer.
16mo., 36pp., with fine ills., pict. wrap. of
store.

1891 Richmond, Va.   V
McADAMS & BERRY. Correct dress for
fall and winter. 12mo., ills. throughout,
pict. wrap.

1892 Richmond, Va.   V
------ Ill. catalog of fashions and styles.

1850 New York   MH-BA
M'ARTHUR, WILLIAM & CO. Price list of
dress and dry goods. 24mo., 46pp., wrap.

1886 Auburn, N. Y.   NNMM
McCONNELL & ANDERSON. Catalog of
ladies' and misses' cloaks. 5 lvs., fine ills.,
wrap.

nd. St. Louis   MoSHi
McCREERY, ESSEX & CO. A catalog of
hats, caps, bonnets, trimmings, artificials,
white goods, silks, ribbons and notions.
16mo., 38pp., wrap.

1892 St. Paul   MnHi
McKIBBIN, DRISCOLL & DORSEY. 12th
annual catalog of hats, caps, furs, gloves,
etc. 4to., fine ills., wrap.

1893 St. Paul   MnHi
------ Changed to McKibbin Fur Co. Semi-
annual ill. catalog of furs, etc.

1899 St. Paul   MnHi
------ Changed to McKibbin & Co. Ill.
catalog of furs and clothing.

1887 New York   MdTanSW
MAERLENDER BROTHERS. Importers and
Mfg. Catalog of fine furs, ladies' and
gent's coats, hats, muffs, gloves, etc. 8vo.,
16pp., fine fashion pls., pict. wrap.

1879-96 Chicago   ICHi
MANDEL BROTHERS. A fine collection of
ill. catalogs, principally clothing, fashions,
styles, but with house furnishings, notions,
etc. as well. 10 fine pict. records 1879-96.

1880 Philadelphia   NNMM
MARKS BROTHERS. Spring blue book of
fashions and catalog of ladies' hats. 8 lvs.
on fine heavy stock, pls., cl.

1885-86 Boston   MH-BA
MASSACHUSETTS BOOT & SHOE CO. Est.
1865. Catalog of boots, shoes, rubbers, etc.
12mo., 16pp., fine ills., wrap.

c.1888 New York   MdTanSW
MAST, J.B. CO. Ill. price list of hatters'
goods. 8vo., 16pp., ills., wrap.

nd. Philadelphia   PHi
MAXWELL, J.J. & SON. Catalog of fancy
and staple dresses, mantillas and cloak
trimmings. 24mo., ill., wrap.

c.1890 MILBURY ATLANTIC SUPPLY CO.
See Sporting Goods.

1895 New York   ICHi
MILBURY ATLANTIC SUPPLY CO. In the
swim. Catalog of bathing suits. Ill. throughout with pre-Max Sennett bathing beauties.
Sq. 16mo., 16pp., pict. wrap.

1900 Mashawaka, Ind.   In
MISHAWAKA WOOLEN MFG. CO. A catalog of shoes, boots and rubbers with felt and
wool linings. 16mo., 52pp., fine ills., col.
pict. wrap.

1869 Newark, N. J.   NjR
NEWARK INDIA RUBBER CO. Price list of
India rubber boots and shoes. One leaf
circular.

1852 New Haven   CtHi
NEW HAVEN SHIRT MFG. CO. Festival of
. . . Actually a sales brochure of unusual
imagination. 8vo., 25pp., wrap.

1886 Portland, Ore.   OrU
OLDS & KING. Succeeded by Olds &
Summers. Ill. catalog of dry goods,
dress goods, etc. 45pp.

1887-88 New York   NNMM
O'NEILL, H. & CO. Ill. catalog #9 of
fashions for fall and winter. 174pp., wrap.

1895-6 New York   MoSHi
------ Ill. fashion catalog for fall and
winter.

nd. New York   NNMM
------ Litho. ill. catalog of hats. 20pp.,
fine pls., hat format, pict. wrap.

1896 St. Charles, Mo.   MoSHi
PALACE CLOTHING CO. Ill. catalog -
Art in dress for spring and summer.

1892 San Francisco   CHi
PFISTER, J.J. KNITTING CO. 4th ill. catalog of knitted bathing suits and knitted
athletic wear. 4to., 72pp., fine ills. throughout, wrap.

1897 Chicago   OrU
PHELPS, DODGE & PALMER CO. Spring
catalog of boots and shoes with fine ills.
64pp., wrap.

1896 Detroit   COCAC
PORT HURON MFG. CO. Ill.   MiU-H
catalog of Alaska Fibre garments, with
sample of material. 12mo., 24pp., pict.
wrap. of Alaska Fibre.

112

c.1890 Lynn   NNMM
PRAY, W. PRESCOTT. Catalog of premium
specialties, patterns, samples, etc. 16pp.
of patterns, wrap.

nd. New York   NNMM
------ Catalog of materials for fancy work,
patterns, etc. 8 lvs. of designs.

1859 Dover, N. H.   NhHi
PURINGTON & HAM. Ill. catalog of furs,
hats, coats, clothing, uniforms for firemen
and other occupations, buffalo robes, etc.
with delightful woodcuts. 32mo., 24pp. of
above, pict. wrap. of polar bear and fancy
cast iron hat tree loaded with silk toppers.
Is this Americana?

c.1875 New York   RHi
RAYMOND & WHITLOCK. Catalog of
Knights Templar regalia, Masonic and other
fraternal orders' uniforms and parapher-
nalia. 8vo., 32pp., fine ills. throughout,
wrap.

1877-8 New York   MH-BA
RIDLEY, EDWARD & SONS. Fall and
winter catalog of fashions, with price list of
clothing and accessories. 8vo., 158pp., fine
ills., pict. wrap.

1856 New York   MH-BA
ROGERS, P.L. Catalog of one price mens'
and boys' clothing, wholesale and retail.
32mo., 32pp., wrap. If one could track down
P.L. Rogers and find him to have been the
Father of the Rogers in Rogers Peet & Co.,
one might write new history. As we stand
now, Rogers Peet & Co. was est. in 1874.

1888 New York   NHi
ROGERS PEET & CO. Est. 1874. Hints on
dress for 1888. 16mo., 32pp., delightful
ills., pict. wrap.

1888-9 New York
------ The art of dress for fall and winter
with blank measurement forms, etc. 12mo.,
44pp., fine ills., wrap.

nd. New York   NNMM
------ Ill. catalog of fine and fancy livery.
111pp., wrap.

1892-3 New York   COCAC
------ Catalog of clothes, overclothes,
underclothes, hats, shoes and all things between. 16mo., 48pp., delightful ills., pict.
wrap.

1894 New York   NNU-W
------ Catalog of boys' and mens' ulsters,
suits, hats, shoes, etc. Sq. 16mo., 64pp.,
swell ills., pict. wrap.

1898 New York   NNMM
------ A catalog of mens' wear with a
dash of personal advice. 100pp., with fine
ills., wrap.

1900-10 New York   NNMM
------ Just in case you are interested in
following Rogers Peet's styles in the first
decade of this century, NNMM has them for
you.

1894-5 St. Louis   MoSHi
ROSENTHAL, I.B. MILLINERY CO. Ill.
catalog for fall and winter.

1885 New York   OAkF
RUBBER CLOTHING CO. (Issued for New
York agents.) Price list of Goodyear and
other make rubber clothing and goods.
4to., 4pp., fine ills.

c.1897 St. Louis   MoSHi
S AND C COMPANY. Ill. catalog of fine
millinery, etc. 4to. and a fine pict. record.

1888 Boston   OAkF
SAGE & CO. Ill. catalog of rubber boots,
rubbers, shoes and overshoes. 16pp.

1877 Battle Creek
SALISBURY, B. & CO. Ladies' Dress
Reform Mfg. Co. Catalog of special uniforms, bloomers, fits, corsets, etc. with
delightful ills. of Dr. Kellogg Sanitorium
with hist. sketch. 8vo., 16pp., pict. wrap.
See Cornflake Crusade by Gerald Carson,
p. 187, one of the lads who stepped in to
share the fabulous Kellogg gold rush.

1884 New York   OAkF
SAWYER, H.M. Catalog of Cape Ann oiled
clothing, rubber and leather goods, coverings for driver, horse and wagon. 24mo.,
40pp., fine ills., pict. wrap.

nd. New York   NNMM
SHAYNE, C.C. Catalog of new fur fashions
for women and some for men. 32pp., fine
ills. throughout, pict. wrap.

nd. New York   NNMM
------ Ill. catalog of womens' furs. 18
col. pls. with details, wrap.

1845 Boston
SHUTE, WILLIAM M. Catalog of hats, caps,
furs, muffs, capes, etc. and other articles
mfg by . . , 64mo., 32pp., ills. Frontis
map showing store, pict. wrap. of Ma and
darling daughter mincing along with fur
coats and muffs. Almanac for 1844 and 1845.

1850 Boston   MH-BA
SIMMONS, GEORGE W. OAK HALL. A
catalog of mens' and boys' fashions and
clothing for all occasions. Great sale for
the season! Sq. 16mo., 64pp., ill. through-

out, firemens' and other occupational uniforms, fine pict. wrap. of Oak Hall amidst Boston 1850 traffic.

1854 Boston
------ The Oak Hall Pictorial 25th ed. Grown like an acorn, etc. Glowing description and ills. 16mo., 16pp., pict. wrap.

N.B. The 1850 edition announces the California branch, Simmons, Lilly & Co., and calls special attention of ship captains, seamen and those for sailing for California to the complete outfits to be found among the bargains in San Francisco.

Continuing the N.B., there is a very curious and amusing bit, called to my attention by Harold J. Hayes of East Pepperell, Mass. in Thoreau's Maine Woods on pp. 65-66:- Half way over this carry --- we noticed a large flaming Oak Hall hand bill about two feet long wrapped round the trunk of a pine --- this should be recorded among the advantages of this mode of advertising --- that --- the bears and otter and beavers --- and --- the Indian may learn where they can get themselves --- the latest fashions. We christened this Oak Hall carry. Mr. Hayes writes that he used this carry in 1929 but found no remnants of the old hand bill.

1882 Baltimore
SIMON, CHARLES & SON. Ill. catalog of ready made underwear. 16mo., 36pp., wrap.

1874 New York   NNMM
SMITH, A. BURDETTE. Smith's instruction book, being a catalog of patterns. 56pp., ills., wrap.

1848 New York   NNMM
SMITH, JOHN I. Fashionable Umbrella, Parasol & Parasolette Mfg. & Warehouse. Est. 1808. Catalog in form of a letter to visiting trade buyers, 3 column list of prices, 4to., 4pp. Fine engraving of plant, 232 Pearl St.

1850 New York   NNMM
------ 4 page ill. letter with trademarks, styles, price list, etc.

1837 South Bend, Ind.   In
SOUTH BEND TAILORS ASSOCIATION. A bill of prices entered into by the crooks - local name for the tailors - of South Bend, April 19th. Broadside one leaf, 8vo.

1872 New York   NNMM
SPELMAN, J.B. & SONS. Ill. and desc. catalog of standard trimmings for women's costumes. 32pp., wrap.

1870 Boston   MH-BA
SPRINGER BROTHERS. Catalog and price list of cloaks and coats. Sm. 12mo., 10pp.

1889 Boston   NNMM
------ Catalog of fashions for the fall season. 8pp., ills., wrap.

c.1890 New York   F
STANDARD FASHION CO. Ill. catalog - A Big Hit! One of our Drummers. Styles and fashions. 16mo., 12pp., col. pls., col. pict. wrap.

1892 New York   MdTanSW
------ Patterns for ladies' and girls' outer clothing for April. 8pp. of ills. of patterns.

1832 Portsmouth, N. H.   NhHi
STAVERS, WM. & GOODWIN, ICHABOD. Catalog of dry goods, general assortment of woolens, worsteds, cottons and silks. 50pp.

1894 Chicago   COCAC
STEVENS, CHAS. A. & BROTHERS. ICHi Special fall and winter catalog of fine cloaks, silks, peletots and reefers, etc. 12mo., 40pp. with fine ills. of the fanciest and finest. Pict. wrap.

c.1866 New York   NNMM
STEWART, A.T. & CO. Catalog of womens', mens' and childrens' clothes and dry goods. 22pp., ills., wrap.

1868-9 New York   NNMM
TERRY, J.R. Bulletin of fashions in hats and furs for fall and winter. 20pp. with 19 fantastic ills., pict. wrap.

c.1870 New York & Boston   OAkF
TOWER, A.J. MFG. Price list of rubber clothing, boots, rubbers and shoes. 16mo., 32pp., ills., pict. wrap.

1858 New York   MH-BA
UNION INDIA RUBBER CO. Catalog of all kinds of clothes, under the Goodyear patent, and other articles for many industrial purposes. 12mo., 35pp., ills., wrap.

1893 New York   COCAC
UNITED STATES CLOAK & SUIT MFG. CO. Ill. catalog of fall and winter styles for 1893-4. 8vo., 16pp., fashion pls., wrap.

1887 New York   NNMM
VOGEL BROTHERS. Fashion catalog for spring and summer, suits, shirts, etc. 12 lvs. of ills., wrap.

1880-81 Philadelphia   NNMM
WANAMAKER, JOHN. Catalog #8. Mens', youths' and boys' fall and winter clothing. 28pp. with fine ills. and pict. wrap.
N.B. Wanamaker catalogs are scattered in many private collections. I feel sure that further checking would discover other examples in PHi, PKsL and other repositories.

1899 New York   OHi
WARNER BROTHERS CO. Catalog of 20th
century corsets. Ills. of various models
and styles. 4to., 24pp., with delightful ills.

1893 Lynn   NNMM
WEBBER, WALTER P. Webber's ill. catalog of new patterns for fabrics, stamping
outfits and supplies. 44pp. of designs and
ills. in wrap.

1865 New York   NNMM
WEST & CO. West's report of New York
fashions for spring and summer. 8pp. of
text with 5pp. of ills., wrap.

c.1867 London, England   MH-BA
WHITELOCK & SON. Est. 1827. Catalog
of ladies' underclothing, India outfits and
wedding gowns and outfits. Sm. 12mo., 8pp.
Probably used by American importers before our merchants started cataloging in
earnest.

1804 Boston   MHi
WHITMAN, DAVIS. Broadside. Davis
Whitman's Shop, #26 Cheapside, offers
ladies' muffs and tippets.

1828 Boston   MH-BA
WHITWELL, BOND & CO. Sale of boots and
shoes under direction of New England
Society. 8vo., 26pp. Though an auction
sale, a record of styles, lasts, leathers, etc.
of an early period.

c.1895 St. Louis   MoSHi
WILLIAMSON CORSET & BRACE CO. Inc.
1882. Ill. catalog of underskirts, dresses,
corsets, etc. 12mo., 16pp., swell ills. of
styles, etc. Pict. wrap.

1899 St. Louis   MoSHi
------ Ill. catalog of corsets, shirts,
skirts, etc. Under skirts, dress skirts,
styles and models. 12mo., dec. wrap.

1896 Boston   MBSPNEA
WINCH BROTHERS. The Little Drummer,
an ill. catalog of boots, shoes, lasts, uppers,
leather findings, etc. 12mo., 124pp., fine
ills., pict. wrap.

1895 Worcester   MWA
WORCESTER CORSET CO. Ladies' Companion. An ill. catalog of models, styles
and fashions in corsets.

1891 Chicago   ICHi
WORK BROTHERS. Ill. catalog of clothing
for all purposes and occupations.

1892 Chicago   ICHi
------ Clothing - for merchants only. Eye-
opener boys' suits, etc. 12mo., 120pp.,
swell Ills., pict. wrap.

1899 Chicago   ICHi
------ Fall and winter catalog - fashion
plates with sample swatches for each plate.
Fine job. 4to., 70pp. of styles. Pict. wrap.

If you are a woman you will, of course, turn to Miscellaneous - Department Stores and Mail Order
Houses - for aprons, housecoats, or whatever else you can't find on these pages. Gentlemen, please
follow suit. If there are articles I haven't even met on these many pages, maybe you will find them
under House Furnishings or Hardware - General Store Goods. The stretched imagination of some
catalogers is unbelievable, especially after Montgomery Ward and Sears Roebuck set a new pace.
Strange but true, you will find jewelry in fashion catalogs, ice boxes illustrated on the same page
with night gowns, and toys whenever the compiler needed an extra page or so to finish the job.

Chapter 17

Dental Instruments, Furnishings & Supplies

Original plans were to have one medical catalog chapter, but hysterical library voices mingled with professional history convinced me that dentistry was no longer mere medicine. We have come a long way from the good old days when the local blacksmith pulled the community's teeth -- in fact the turnkey is no more, and American dentistry is a great profession, standing alone with as many specialist divisions as medicine.

The examples located in our outstanding libraries provide a fine collection for research in this field, whether for a student's thesis or a real history of American dentistry. The greatest American in this field is, of course, S. S. White. This group alone constitute a library. However, don't overlook John D. Chevelier's 1853 furniture and gold teeth at NNMM, or Otto Kunz' mineral teeth of 1847 at OC. Can you remember those lovely red plush chairs with the walnut swan carved arms -- or haven't you really lived?

p.1900 Two Rivers, Wis.   PU-D
    AMERICAN CABINET CO. Ill. catalogs of dental office furniture. 1906 and 1909.

1871 London & New York   PU-D
    ASH, CLAUDIUS & SONS. Ill. catalog of artificial teeth, dental instruments, furniture, materials and tools. 201pp., cl.

1875 New York & London   MH-D
    ------ Ill. catalog of dental furnishings, instruments, etc. 8vo., 302pp., cl.

1895 New York & London   NNNAM
    ------ Ill. catalog of dental rubbers, tools, materials for impressions and sundries. 44pp.

1899 New York & London   PU-D
    ------ Ill. catalog of dental furnishings.

1897 Buffalo, N. Y.   PU-D
    BUFFALO DENTAL MFG. CO. Catalog and general instructions - dental vulcanizers. Ill., wrap.

1897 Buffalo, N. Y.   NNNAM
    ------ Snow & Lewis automatic pluggers in six styles. Catalog E. Ill., 8pp.

p.1900 Buffalo, N. Y.   PU-D
    ------ Ill. catalogs of dental equipment to 1915.

c.1900 New York (5th Ave., in fact)   PU-D
    CADY, EDWARD EVERETT. Dentistry by specialists and well known people who recommend them. Five branches: Fillings $1. and up; crown and bridge work $20. to $30. per tooth; fashionable work as plates

and artificial teeth of rubber and gold $4. to $15. - 18k gold $50. Delightful letters. Since placing my mouth in your hands, etc. Discount cards for clergymen they bring patients, we lend a hand. 24mo., 44pp., dec. wrap.

1898 Niagara Falls   NNNAM
    CARBORUNDUM CO. Catalog #2. Ill. catalog of carborundum mfg. under Acheson pat. 61pp.

c.1900 Fort Wayne   PU-D
    CENTURY CHEMICAL CO. Catalog of preparations for the teeth, powders, pastes, tablets and mouth washes. 12mo., 8pp.

c.1900 Fort Wayne   PU-D
    ------ Revised price list of dentifrices. 12mo., 6pp.

1853 New York   NNNAM
    CHEVALIER, JOHN D. Catalog of dental instruments, gold teeth, gold, chairs and furniture. 32pp., wrap.

c.1854 New York   NNNAM
    ------ Catalog of dental supplies. 32pp., wrap.

c.1895 Baltimore   NNNAM
    CHLORIDE OF SILVER DRY CELL BATTERY CO. Desc. catalog of chloride of silver supplies. 6th ed. 55pp., ill.

1896 Baltimore   PU-D
    ------ Cataphoresis in dental operations with ill. catalog. 24pp., wrap.

1897 Baltimore   PU-D
------ 2nd edition.

c.1867 Boston   PU-D
CODMAN & SHURTLEFF. To Dentists -
ills. of improved apparatus for anaesthesia.
4pp.

1870 Boston   PU-D
------ Ill. catalog of dental furniture,
implements, instruments and materials;
pats. Snowden & Cowman, Butler, Archer,
White -- fountain spittoons, cabinets, etc.
8vo., 96pp., swell ills., cl.

1875 Boston   DNLM
------ Ill. catalog of dental instruments
and supplies. 8vo., wrap.

1882 Boston   MH-D
------ Catalog of dental furnish-   ADA
ings, foot operated drills, furniture, instruments. 8vo., 228pp., delightful ills., cl.

nd. Boston   DNLM
------ Bound volume of ill. catalogs with
several Codman & Shurtleff examples.

c.1897 New York   ADA
CONSOLIDATED DENTAL MFG. CO. Ill.
and desc. catalog of dental supplies, furniture, engines and instruments.

p.1900 New York   PU-D
------ Ill. catalogs for 1904,   ADA
1908, 1914 and 1915 for further research.

c.1900 Philadelphia   NNNAM
DENTAL MEDICINE CO. Catalog of dental
pharmaceutical preparations, specialties
and instruments. 19pp., ills.

1897 Chicago   NNNAM
DENTAL PROTECTIVE SUPPLY CO. Condensed price list of dental specialties. 32pp.,
ills., wrap.

p.1900 New York   PU-D
DENTISTS' SUPPLY CO. Twentieth
Century Mould Book.

c.1893 Detroit   NNNAM
DETROIT DENTAL MFG. CO. Ill. catalogs
nos. 6, 7, 8 - dental supplies, resp. 15, 16
and 16pp., ills., wraps.

1893 San Francisco   CHi
EDWARDS, JAMES W. Ill. catalog of dental
materials, tools and supplies. 4to., bds.,
fine ills.

1885 Philadelphia   PU-D
GREEN, WILLIAM P. Ill. price list of the
West Philadelphia Dental Depot.

1897 New York
HANAWAY, H.D. Ill. catalog of dental furniture, instruments and materials. 594pp.

c.1900 Hartford, Conn.   PU-D
HARTFORD DENTAL DEPOT. Ill. catalog
of dental furniture, chairs, etc., materials
and instruments. 3rd ed. 808pp. See also
Messinger, W. C.

1881 Boston   MH-D
HOOD & REYNOLDS. Ill. catalog   ADA
of dentists' furniture, tools, instruments
and supplies. 8vo., 302pp., fine ills., cl.

1883 Boston   PU-D
------ Ill. catalog of dental forceps, etc.
to the trade. 8vo., 20pp., ills.

1893 Boston   NNNAM
------ Catalog of gold foil and supplies,
with history of firm, etc. 48pp., fine ills.,
wrap.

c.1890 Boston   NNNAM
HOOD, JOHN & CO. Price list of dental
amalgams, physical properties and history
of, etc. 55pp.

c.1900 Boston   MH-D
------ Dental catalog of gold foil and
other dental supplies; furniture to teeth.
8vo., 675pp., fine ills., dec. cl.

c.1890 Lowell, Mass.   OCP&G.
HOYT, E.W. & CO. Col. pict.   PU-D
circular - Rubifoam Tooth Powder - lovely
smiling teeth that have any modern TV advt.
licked a mile with their 1890 tints.

1871 Philadelphia   PU-D
JOHNSON & LUND. Ill. catalog of dental
materials.

1885 Philadelphia   PU-D
------ Ill. catalog of furnishings.

1888 Philadelphia   PU-D
------ Ill. catalog of instruments, etc.

1900 Philadelphia   DSi
------ Ill. catalog and price list of anvils,
bottles, cutters, wedges, drills, etc. 4to.,
250pp., fine record, dec. cl.

1872 New York & Brooklyn   PU-D
JOHNSTON BROTHERS. Ill. catalog of new
cone socket instruments. Pat. 1872.

c.1880 New York & Brooklyn   MH-D
------ Ill. catalog of new improved OC
cone socket instruments. 8vo., 32pp., wrap.

1881 New York & Brooklyn   NNNAM
------ Preliminary ill. dental catalog of
materials and supplies. 220pp., fine ills.

1880 Philadelphia   PU-D
JUSTI, H.D. & CO. Dental depot - students'
price list of operating and mechanical instruments.

1888 Philadelphia   PU-D
------ Ill. price list of dental materials.
239pp., fine ills.

1901 Philadelphia   PU-D
------ Catalog of supplies. New Columbia
chairs in red plush, brass spittoons, etc.
8vo., 410pp., great ills., cl.

c.1890 Fort Wayne   PU-D
KELLER MEDICINE CO. Ill. catalog of
non-secret dental medicines, Rochester
dental chairs, fixed and socket handled instruments, engines, amalgam alloys, plastic
zinc fillings, furniture, cabinets and laboratory supplies. 4to., vp., a fine ref.

1860 Philadelphia   PU-D
KERN, HORATIO G. A catalog of surgical
and dental instruments.

1877 Philadelphia   DNLM
------ Ill. catalog of surgical instruments
including dental materials.

1885 Philadelphia   DNLM
------ Ill. catalog of instruments for
surgeon and dentist.

1855 Buffalo, N. Y.   PU-D
KING, WILLIAM JR. A catalog of drugs and
chemicals, surgical and dental instruments,
and fancy articles for physicians and dealers.
Seaver's steam press, Buffalo.

c.1847 Pittsburgh, Pa.   OC
KUNZ, OTTO. A guide for dentists to pro-
cure teeth from Otto Kunz, mfg. of mineral
teeth. For search purposes, a catalog of
artificial teeth and plates c.1847. 4to., 6pp.,
with ills.

1858 Philadelphia   DNLM
KURMERLE, J.F. Ill. catalog of surgical
and dental instruments, syringes, etc. 8vo.
with fine ills. for this period.

1874 St. Louis   MoSHi
LESLIE, A.M. & CO. Est. 1856. Ill. catalog of dental and surgical apparatus,
appliances and instruments.

nd. St. Louis   MoSHi
------ Ill. catalog. 8vo., 41pp., pict. wrap.

1879 St. Louis   ADA
------ Ill. catalog of dental instruments.

1897 Philadelphia   PU-D
MARSHALL DENTAL MFG. CO. Ill. catalog of dental furniture, instruments and
supplies. 2nd ed., revised.

1897 Hartford, Conn.   DNLM
MESSINGER, W.C. - Hartford   CtHi
Dental Depot. Ill. catalog of dental furniture,
as well as instruments and materials. 8vo.,
594pp., fine ills., dec. cl.

1848 Camden, N. J.   PU-D
MURPHEY, JOSEPH T. Murphey's Dental
Catalog. At New York Institute, Oct. 1847,
the subscriber received the premium for
his superior gold foil, etc. Ill. catalog.
48mo., 12pp. Photostat copy only.

p.1900 St. Louis   ADA
NOLDE, JOHN T. MFG. CO. Catalog of
dental furniture, instruments and materials.
Ill.

c.1895 St. Paul, Minn.   PU-D
NOYES BROTHERS & CUTLER. Ill. catalog
of surgical and dental instruments.

1900 St. Paul, Minn.   NNNAM
------ Ill. catalog. 4th ed., 1200pp.

c.1880 Philadelphia   NNNAM
PARTRICK & CARTER. Ill.   PU-D
catalog of Dr. W.G.A. Bonwill's dental and
surgical engines, hand pieces, mallets, etc.
16pp.

c.1880 Philadelphia   PU-D
------ Directions for operating Dr.
Bonwill's engines, etc. 12pp.

1894 Toledo, O.   NNNAM
RANSOM & RANDOLPH CO. Merely suggestions. Priced catalog of dental furniture.
24pp., ills., wrap.

1895 Toledo, O.   NNNAM
------ A word to the wise - priced catalog.
15pp. with ills.

p.1900 Toledo, O.   PU-D
------ Ill. catalog of dental specialties.

1898 New York & Rochester, N.Y.   NNNAM
RITTER DENTAL MFG. CO. Ill. catalog of
new Columbia dental chairs, electric dental
engines and appliances. 16pp.

1901 New York & Rochester, N.Y.   DSi
------ Ill. catalog of dental furnishings.
Large 8vo., 675pp., col. pls., dec. cl.

p.1901 New York & Rochester, N.Y.   PU-D
------ Ritter dental equipment, etc.

c.1900 New York   PU-D
ROWAN, EDWARD. Catalog of decimal gold
foil, etc. 24pp.

1870 Philadelphia   PU-D
RUBENCAME & BARKER. Catalog DLC
of dental instruments and materials mfg.

and for sale by . . . 12mo., 184pp., fine ills., wrap.

c.1897 Monrovia, Md.   NNNAM
RUSSELL ELECTRIC MALLET CO. Remco.
Catalog #3 of the Russell electro-magnetic
dental mallet, pat. 1897. 17pp., ills.

c.1898 New York   NNNAM
SCHARMAN, GUSTAV. Catalog of dental
specialties. 16 lvs., ill., wrap.

p.1900 Chicago   PU-D
SEARS ROEBUCK & CO. Special ill. catalog of dental supplies. 4to., 88pp.

nd. Binghamton   PU-D
SHARP, W.M. CO. Catalog C - seamless
crown system supplies, etc. 20pp. Also a
copy in French.

1884 New London, Conn.   CtNlC
SHEFFIELD, LUCIUS T.   PU-D
Artificial teeth without plates - new system,
with catalog of materials, etc. 34pp., ills.

1887 Philadelphia   NNNAM
SIBLEY, GIDEON MFG.   PU-D
Abridged price list of artificial teeth and
dental supplies. 36pp., ill., wrap.

c.1900 Philadelphia   NNNAM
------ Catalog of the Sibley dental chair,
fountain cuspidor, dental engines and other
specialties. 32pp., ills., wrap.

c.1890 Pittsburgh, Pa.   MH-D
SMITH, LEE S. & SONS. Ill. catalog of
dental instruments and materials, furnishings, drills, engines, etc. 4to., 558pp., fine
ills., cl.

1893 Pittsburgh, Pa.   ADA
------ Ill. catalog of furnishings.

1897 Pittsburgh, Pa.   ICHi
------ Ill. catalog. 8vo., 594pp., cl.

c.1900 Pittsburgh, Pa.   PU-D
------ Ill. catalog of dental   PHi
furniture, chairs to spittoons. 3rd ed., cl.

1860 Philadelphia   DNLM
SNOWDEN & BROTHER. Ill. wholesale catalog of surgical and dental instruments.

1886 Philadelphia   PU-D
SPEAKMAN, WILLIAM M. Non-combination price list of dental goods. 16pp., ills.

c.1900 Philadelphia   NNNAM
------ Price list of high standard, low
priced, non-combination dental goods. 83pp.
and 4 lvs., ill., wrap.

c.1889 Cincinnati   PU-D
SPENCER, M.A. & CO. Est. 1871. Condensed price list of dental goods, tooth
extracting forceps, operative department
goods and mechanical department goods.
1871-1889. 4to., 48 plus 32pp., fine ills.

c.1860 Cincinnati   OC
TOLAND, JNO. T. Ill. and priced catalog of
dentists' materials, porcelain teeth, gold and
tin foils, plate, dental instruments, chairs,
cases, lathes, rolling mills, etc. Large
8vo., 72pp., wrap.

1898 Chicago   NNNAM
VICTOR ELECTRIC CO. Ill.   PU-D
catalog of high grade electrical, dental and
surgical specialties. 3rd ed. Diagram of
office equipped with dental engine, ready to
buzz the devil out of anyone's nerves. Sq.
16mo., 48pp., fine ills., pict. wrap.

1898 San Francisco   NNNAM
WHITE, L.I. TOOTH CROWN CO. Ill. catalog for 1898. Ills. of teeth and supplies,
some in col., nice job. 32pp.

1862 Philadelphia   PPSSWhite
WHITE, SAMUEL S; DENTAL   PU-D
MFG. CO. Successors to Jones & White Co.
Est. 1844. Both the company library and
PU-D have very complete collections starting with 1862. Aside from leaflets and
circulars, this 1862 is believed to be the
first catalog. A catalog of porcelain teeth
and dentists' materials, ill. and priced.

1866 Philadelphia   PU-D
------ Instructions in manipulation of hard
rubber for dental purposes, with a price list.
8vo., 48pp., ills., cl.

1867 Philadelphia   MoSHi
           ICHi PU-D PKsL MH-D
------ Catalog of   NNNAM   NStIHi
dental furniture, instruments and materials.
Fine ills. of carved walnut chairs with lions'
feet, claw and swan arms and red plush
seats, fountain spittoons with horse hitching
post stands, bowls, furnishings, etc. 8vo.,
226pp., cl. One of the finest ref. in the field.

1873 Philadelphia   NNNAM
------ Revised ill. price list since 1867
catalog. 80pp.

1876 Philadelphia   NNNAM
------ Ill. catalog of 408pp., cl.

1877 Philadelphia   PU-D
------ Ill. catalog of dental   ADA
supplies.

1878 Philadelphia   NNNAM
------ 1877 ill. catalog   ADA PU-D
with appendix for 1878.

1883 Philadelphia   NNNAM
------ Revised price list of cone socket
instruments. 36pp., ill., wrap.

1885-1900 Philadelphia   PPSSWhite
------ Ill. catalogs, PU-D ADA NNNAM
price lists and circulars were issued regu-
larly and in these four repositories you will
find almost any pict. ref. needed.

p.1900 Philadelphia   ADA
------ Ill. catalogs to 1925. Since the
dateline is 1900, other libraries did not report, and may well have later catalogs to

offer for research if needed. A complete
list of the S.S. White Library has not been
included.

1890 Philadelphia   NNNAM
WILMINGTON DENTAL MFG. CO. PU-D
Ill. catalog of dental materials and supplies.
376pp., cl.

c.1880 Chicago   PU-D
WINEBRENER, M.H. Dentists' price list -
circular offering dental work - plates in
gold and platinum $100. to $150.; ills. of
teeth and tools.

Naturally many manufacturers of medical and surgical instruments and furnishings of the 19th
century produced and offered dental supplies as well. Also, you will find dental instruments and
supplies in the chapter of Drugs and Pharmaceuticals. Even catalogs listed under House Furnishings
will provide tooth powders, brushes, etc.

Chapter 18

Department, Dry Goods & Miscellaneous Stores

Although each of these words might well have a chapter of their own, it seems less confusing to group them under one heading. Herein you will find everything from a miscellaneous cargo dumped at Oregon City in 1850 to the last word in miscellaneous merchandise offered by John Wanamaker in 1900. Perhaps, if it should enter your head to write a tale of the Gold Rush to the Yukon, Barclay and Smith's catalog - On To The Klondike, 1897 - might help. Perhaps too, if wondering what the pioneers settling Fairview, Indiana in 1829 wore, ate and drank, Mr. Berkshire's broadside will give you a picture. I also recommend a trip with Butler Brothers' Drummer throughout the country in 1885.

This chapter includes locations for Montgomery Ward catalogs and Sears Roebuck & Co. offerings as well. From Abernathy of Oregon to Whittelsey of Indiana and B. Altman & Co. to John Wanamaker, this chapter covers about everything one could expect to hunt in the U. S. A. from 1829 to 1900.

1850 Oregon City   OrP   OrU
                         Photostat copies
ABERNATHY, GEORGE & CO. 20.5x31.5
cm. broadside. Entire cargo of barn
Desdemona will be offered at the warehouse
of . . . Cargo listed in 2 columns of 69
lines, small type, large and extensive
assortment of merchandise.

1879-80 New York   MH-BA
ALTMAN, B. & CO. Catalog #34, Fall &
Winter. Dry goods, ladies' clothing, novelties, etc. Large 8vo., 104pp., fine ills.,
pict. wrap.

1886-7 New York   MH-BA
------ Fall & Winter catalog #54. 8x10,
89pp., fine ills., pict. wrap.

1894-5 New York   NNMM
------ Ill. Fall & Winter catalog. Dry and
fancy goods, general house furnishings, etc.
96pp., pict. wrap.

c.1898 Springfield, Mass.   NNMM
BAKER, W.G. 21st catalog and supplement.
Miscellaneous goods. 52pp., fine ills., wrap.

p.1900 Baltimore   MdTanSW
BALTIMORE BARGAIN HOUSE. Collection
of 4to. catalogs, fully ill. throughout, offer
ing nearly everything one can imagine. 1903
to 1911. #471-#578. Catalogs before 1900
are in private collections and will some day
be located for research -- I hope.

1897 San Francisco   DLC
BARCLAY, J. & SMITH, HARPER A. On to
the Klondike; how to go, when to go, where

to go, what to take with you, and where to
get it. General merchandise to take to
Alaska mines - trade with Barclay & Smith.
4to., 12pp.

1829 Fairview, Ind.   In
BERKSHIRE, C. New store. Subscriber
has just opened at his house, eight miles
east of Washington on main road from St.
Louis to Louisville, offers a general assortment of spring, summer and fall goods.
List of goods. Broadside 8-1/2x11-3/4.

1863-4 Springfield, Mass.   MoSHi
BLISS, BENJAMIN K. Spring catalog of
general merchandise.

1843 Philadelphia   PKsL
BROWN, WILLIAM H. & CO.   PHi
Catalog of American and foreign dry goods.

1829 Vincennes   In
BURTCH & HEBERD. Broadside 11x16.
Respectfully inform their friends and the
public in general that they have received
from Philadelphia and Baltimore a large and
general assortment of goods - Oct. 1-

1885 New York & Chicago   MdTanSW
BUTLER BROTHERS. Christmas at Butler
Brothers. 4to., ill. throughout. Glass,
china, fancy goods, novelties and general
merchandise.

c.1887 New York & Chicago   MdTanSW
------ Our Drummer - 86th trip. 4to., ill.
throughout, pict. wrap.

c.1889 New York & Chicago   MdTanSW
------ Our Drummer - 90th trip. 4to., ill.
throughout.

1893 New York & Chicago   MdTanSW
------ Our Drummer - 105th   ICHi
trip. Mid-winter offerings - apples to
whales. Exhaustive.

1895 New York & Chicago   ICHi
------ Our Drummer. 4to., as above.

1900 New York & Chicago   ICHi
------ Our Drummer, as above,   N
adze to zither.

p.1900 New York & Chicago   MdTanSW
------ Our Drummer. N has a   N
fine run 1900 to 1912. MdTanSW has 1912
and 1931. Others still preserved in private
libraries.

1895 Chicago   MoSHi
CARSON, PIRIE SCOTT & CO. The
Shoppers' Economist.

1896-7 Chicago   ICHi
------ The Shoppers' Economist. Bicycles,
clothing, furniture, musical and optical
goods, etc. Well ill.

vd. Chicago   Various
CASH BUYERS' UNION.   locations
Est. 1885. Although this firm undoubtedly
issued complete general merchandise catalogs
like Montgomery Ward and others, we have
only been able to locate special catalogs
which will be found under Carriages, Bicycles,
House Furnishings, Sewing Machines, etc.
The catalogs are 4to., well ill. and fully as
good as any issued in this period.

1883 Philadelphia   PKsL
DARLINGTON, RUNK & CO. Spring &
Summer catalog. Dry goods, dress goods,
clothing, house furnishings, etc. Fine ills.,
wrap.

1900 New York   MdTanSW
DUNHAM, JAMES H. Successors to George
Bliss & Co. The Order Solicitor clothing to
show cases, atomizers to yard goods. 4to.,
454pp. of ills., wrap.

nd. New York   NNMM
FECHTMAN, L. FOREMAN & CO. Trade
catalog of fabrics, furnishings and supplies.
46pp., ill.

1898 Cincinnati   OC
FOLEY & WILLIAMS MFG. CO. Catalog
#38. Ill. catalog of general merchandise.

1899 Winchester, Va.   V
HELLER'S UNDERSELLING DEPARTMENT
STORE. General catalog. 8vo., 14pp., ills.,
wrap.

c.1880 Chicago   ICHi
HOME SUPPLY CO. Ill. catalog of clothes
to carriages.

1879-80 New York   NNMM
JOHNSTON, J. & C. Fall & Winter   MoSHi
catalog of department store articles -
clothes to upholstery, etc. 227pp., fine ills.,
wrap.

1878 Boston   NNMM
JORDAN, MARSH & CO. Spring catalog of
various womens' dept. store purchases.
24pp., fine ills., wrap.

1882 Boston   NNMM
------ Spring & Summer retail   MH-BA
and mail order catalog, wholesale and jobbing, new book dept., etc. 8vo., 96pp., wrap.

1882-3 Boston   NNMM
------ Fall & Winter catalog. 208pp., ill.,
wrap.

1897-8 Boston   MH-BA
------ Fall & Winter catalog. 12mo.,
246pp., fine ills., wrap. I am sure there
are other Jordan Marsh catalogs in other
repositories, but to date they have not been
offered.

c.1880 Chicago   MdTanSW
LINCOLN, L.W. & CO. Est. 1874. Annual
catalog of specialties - gents' furnishings,
guns, hardware, trunks, chemicals, tinware,
etc. 8vo., 40pp., ill., wrap.

1894 Chicago   MdTanSW
LININGTON, C.M. The Silent Salesman.
Dolls and glass to toys and everything in
between. Letters similar to Butler
Brothers. 4to., 178pp., fine ills., index,
wrap.

1879 New York   NNMM
LORD & TAYLOR. Est. 1826. General
catalog of merchandise. 158pp., fine ills.,
wrap.

1882 New York   COCAC
------ Catalog for Spring &   NNMM
Summer. Sq. 8vo., 152pp. and 8 lvs. Fine
clothing and general merchandise. Pict.
wrap.

1889-90 New York   NNMM
------ Catalog for Fall & Winter. 8 lvs.,
ill., wrap. I could locate dozens in private
collections but these are representative of
library examples.

c.1899 New York   MdTanSW
LYNN, J. & CO. Latest catalog and guide
to rapid wealth. For door-to-door salesmen. 8vo., 92pp., ills.

1881 New York   NNMM
MACY, R.H. & CO. Est. 1858. Catalog for
Spring & Summer. General merchandise,
ill., desc. and priced. 128pp., wrap.

1883 New York   NNMM
------ Catalog for Spring & Summer.
Fancy and dry goods, etc. 92pp., wrap.

1880-1910 New York   NNMM
------ General ill. catalogs of   NBB
various dates. Many in private collections.

1888 Chicago   ICHi
MARSHALL FIELD & CO. Ill. catalog -
accordians to soap and even writing materials. 4to., pict. wrap.

1889 Chicago   ICHi
------ Ill. catalog of general merchandise.
4to., a fine pict. record. Wrap.

1901 Brooklyn   NNQ
MATTHEWS' SONS, A.D. Ill. catalog of
house furnishings, notions, dry goods and
general goods. Also other examples after
1901.

nd. Brunswick, Mo.   MoSHi
MERCHANT & BEAZLEY. Ill. catalog of
fall and winter trade - new goods - fine
assortment.

1898 Chicago   MoSHi
MERCHANTS EXCHANGE ASSOCIATION.
Ill. catalog of spring and summer goods.

1872 Chicago   MH-BA
MONTGOMERY WARD & CO. Est. 1872.
#1 *Photostat only. See also One Hundred
Influential American Books Printed Before
1900. Grolier Club 1947.

1876 Chicago   ICHi
------ #16. Ill. catalog of merchandise.

1876 Chicago   ICHi
------ #17. Ill. catalog.

1877-1901 Chicago   ICHi
------ A fine pict. ref. collection.

1882 Chicago   MH-BA
------ Catalog #31. Spring & Summer.

1890-91 Chicago   MH-BA
------ Catalog #48. Fall & Winter.

1891-1904 Chicago   NNMM
------ Catalogs #50 to 73. 4to., fine ills.,
pict. wrap. Fine ref. library in itself.

1894 Chicago   COCAC
------ Catalog #55. Spring &   MH-BA
Summer. 550pp. and pict. wrap. as usual.

1897 Chicago   NSbSM
------ #61. Silver Anniversary   ICHi
1872-1897. History of growth, etc. Silver
pict. wrap.

1891 Chicago   ICHi
NATIONAL MERCHANDISE SUPPLY CO.
Catalog - big savings to farm and home, no
middleman's profits, etc. Apple parer to
wine press - everything. 4to., 272 ill. pp.,
limp lea. cover.

1866 San Francisco   CHi
NEWHALL, H.M. & CO. Catalog of general
goods. 14pp., wrap.

1897 Portland, Ore.   OrU
PACIFIC COAST HOME SUPPLY ASSOCIA-
TION. 6th ill. catalog - for members only.
192pp., with fine ills. of bottles to stoves to
wagons and all way stations. See Peabody
Trading Co. of Boston. There were many
of these associations during this Gay Ninety
period. Possibly it was a better racket than
the trading stamps of recent years.

1893 Boston
PEABODY TRADING CO. Large 4to. catalog issued only to members for two years.
This is #4070. Fine ills. of fine silver,
harness, carriages, furniture, stoves, lamps
and general goods. 246pp.

1858 St. Louis   MoSHi
RICHARDSON, MELLIER & CO. Price list
of goods.

1878 New York   CBevT
RIDLEY, E. & SONS. Spring and summer
fashions, clothes to velocipedes. 8vo.,
184pp., fine ills., wrap.

1878-9 New York   MoSHi
------ Fashions and general merchandise.
Ill. price record.

1888 New York   NNMM
------ Fashions and fancy dry goods, etc.
Fall & Winter. Catalogs #1 and 2 of Vol. IX.
150pp. of ills., wrap.

1897-8 New York   NNMM
------ Fall & Winter catalog #2, Vol. XVIII.
Fashions, dry goods, leather, silver, ranges,
etc. 96pp. of ills., wrap.

1896-7 St. Louis   MoSHi
ROEDER, PHILIP. Holiday catalog of
general goods. Ill.

1897-8 St. Louis   MoSHi
------ Ill. catalog for the holidays.

c.1870 New York   MiDbF
ROUSS, CHARLES BROADWAY. Ill. price
list of advertising novelties, souvenirs,
decorations, etc. 8vo., 8pp. with 64 ills.

c.1900 New York   MdTanSW
------ General goods catalog in great
variety. 4to., 96pp., ills., wrap.

1897 St. Louis   MoSHi
SCRUGGS, VANDERVOORT & BARNEY.
Ill. general catalog.

1886-1926 Chicago   NNMM
          NNC-W ICHi MeBa MH-BA
          TxLT   KU   NBB COCAC
SEARS ROEBUCK & CO. Everyone is
familiar with these 4to., well ill. pict. wrap.
catalogs of every known American product.
Suffice it to say that the nine listed libraries
have reported many locations. The micro-
film set has been given to and purchased by
many more libraries. However, you may
rest assured these listed locations will provide you with representative collections of
the originals.

1898 Chicago   ICHi
SIEGEL-COOPER & CO. Catalog #30 for
Spring & Summer. China, glass, toys - in
fact, from carriage house to parlor, bedroom
and bath. 4to., 176pp., fine ills., pict. wrap.

c.1895 Chicago   ICHi
SMYTH, JOHN M. CO. Smyth's dictionary
of economy #61. World's authority on lowest prices. It costs a dollar to print it.
You know the story about everything but the
kitchen sink - well, we have that too. 4to.,
1224pp., fine ills., pict. col. wrap.

1899 Chicago
------ Ill. money saving book. Everything
to eat, use and wear. 4to., 442pp., fine ills.,
col. pict. wrap.

1882-1940 St. Paul, Minn.   MnHi
SOMMERS, B. & CO. In 1886 changed to
G. Sommers & Co. Known as the Western
Bargain House. Covered the general stores
of the Northwest before Sears, Roebuck &
Co. One of the finest and most complete
runs of any firm in this field. Issued
several times a year, 4to., ill. throughout.
Glass, furniture, fashions, toys, musical instruments, bicycles, wagons, etc. 24 page
average with pict. wraps. OUR LEADER
was the thing to read and still is if you want
to find an 1885 pattern glass tumbler or a
classy surrey.

1882-3 New York   ICHi
STERN BROTHERS. Ill. catalog of general
merchandise - fashions, dry goods and furnishings.

1883-4 New York   ICHi
------ Ill. catalog for Fall & Winter.

1897-8 New York   NNMM
------ Catalog #91 for Fall & Winter.
112pp., ill., pict. wrap.

1898 New York   NNMM
------ Catalog #92 for Spring & Summer.

1899 New York   NNMM
------ Catalog #94. 108pp. of ills. of
furnishings, etc.

1900 Kansas City, Mo.   MoSHi
TAYLOR, JOHN. Ill. catalog of dry goods
and general merchandise.

1892 Philadelphia & New York   PHi
WANAMAKER, JOHN. Formerly A. T.
Stewart & Co. Est. New York 1823 -
Philadelphia 1861. Catalog #32 for Spring
& Summer. Ills. of buttons, china, glass to
novelties, watches and woodenware. Every-
thing. 4to., 132pp., fine ills., 4 col. fashion
pls., pict. wrap.

p.1900 Philadelphia & New York   NNMM
------ Later dates - fine ill.   PHi
records of general merchandise. There are
also private collections.

1887 Brooklyn   NNMM
WECHSLER & ABRAHAM. Catalog of
fashions for Spring & Summer, Vol. V. Dry
goods, notions, furniture, etc. 140pp. with
fine ills. and wrap.

1884 Sacramento   NNMM
WEINSTOCK & LUBIN. Catalog of fancy
and dry goods, clothing, silverware, clocks
and general merchandise. 120pp., fine ills.,
wrap.

1884-5 Boston   MH-BA
WHITE, R.H. & CO. Est. 1860. Catalog of
clothes and house furnishings and general
merchandise. 4to., 176pp. of fine ills.,
pict. wrap.

1829 Carlisle, Ind.   In
WHITTELSEY, ISAAC N. Broadside
8-1/2x11, text with fine border. New store
established in Carlisle - will keep on hand
a handsome assortment of dry goods, groceries, hard and queensware. Lists of
goods. Unusual early record.

Chapter 19

Drugs & Pharmaceuticals

The January 1959 issue of The American Journal of Pharmacy published a very selective check list of early U. S. pharmaceutical trade catalogs. This is, to the best of my knowledge, the only printed record in the field.

This chapter broadens the reference possibilities and locates through the cooperation of the libraries listed, a fairly complete roster. From 1760 to 1900 these examples indicate the interest of the leading repositories throughout the country. You will find a great many of the best American glass bottle, vial and laboratory utensils illustrations that should be of use to the historian and student, as well as a fine pictorial panorama of our colored pills and powders. It may surprise the reader to find that even as far back as 1812 our drug stores advertised and sold dye-stuffs, painters' colors and surgeons' instruments, even though they did not dispense soda water and quick lunches, magazines and bathing caps, etc. If you have no interest in drugs, don't neglect the many other records of American goods sold in these stores during the 19th century. The Lloyd Library and Museum in Cincinnati reports about 240 bound volumes and 200 unbound folders, each containing from five to ten pharmaceutical trade catalogs beginning with 1804. These have not as yet been cataloged and can not be included.

1890 Detroit   MiU-H
ANDERSON MFG. CO. Catalog #2. Pharmaceutical apparatus, machinery and supplies - furniture, equipment, mixers, percolators, stills, etc. 8vo., 32pp., fine ills., wrap.

c.1860 Boston
ATWOOD, CHARLES H. Catalog of chemicals, druggists' goods, medicines, perfumes, glassware, whiskey, toilet articles and sundries. 64mo., 32pp., wrap.

1853 St. Louis   MoSHi
BARNARD, ADAMS & PECK. Prices current of druggists' and apothecaries' supplies, surgical instruments, etc. 12mo., 97pp., fld. chart of ills. by Duval, Litho., Philadelphia. Pict. wrap.

1859 St. Louis   DLC
BARNARD & CO. Price current of drugs and sundries. 132pp.

1865 New York
BARNES, DEMAS & CO. U. S. Medicine Warehouse. Catalog of medicines with approximating prices. 16mo., 28pp., pict. wrap.

1867 New York
------ Cover stamped Barnes, Ward & Co., New Orleans. Catalog of medicines. 16mo., 32pp., wrap.

1868 New York
------ Cover stamped John F. Henry, Successor. Catalog of medicines. 16mo., 32pp., wrap.

1842 Alton   ICHi
BARRY, A.S. & CO. Broadside of Drugs and Medicines.

1884 Boston   DNLM
BAWKER, H.L. & CO. Price list and desc. catalog of extracts, acids and essential oils. 8vo.

1860 St. Louis   MoSHi
BLAKSLEY, HENRY. Patent Medicine Depot. Medicine catalog. 9pp., pict. title.

c.1895 San Francisco   CHi
BOERICKE & RUNYON. Desc. catalog of homeopathic pharmaceuticals. 12mo., 87pp. Ills., wrap.

1876 New York   NNNAM
BOERICKE & TAFEL. Desc. catalog of homeopathic works, with prices of medicines. 16mo., 43pp., ills.

1889 New York and vp.   DSi
------ Ptd. Philadelphia. Drug prices current. 140pp.

1894 New York   NNNAM
------ Physicians' catalog, medicines and books, sundries for physicians. 184pp.

1812 Boston   MWA
BRINLEY, GEORGE. A catalog of drugs,
medicines, dye-stuffs, painters' colours,
surgeons' instruments, etc., to be sold by
George Brinley at his store #3 South Side of
the Old Market House. 16pp. Ms. notation -
1812.

1868 St. Louis   MoSHi
BROWN, WEBBER & GRAHAM. Wholesale
price list of drugs, etc.

c.1900 Worcester, Mass.   NNNAM
BUFFINGTON PHARMACY CO. Catalog
and price current homeopathic medicines
and physicians' supplies.

1833 Hartford, Conn.   CtHi
BULL & METCALFE. Catalog of drugs,
patent medicines, wines, etc. for druggists
and apothecaries at the sign of the Good
Samaritan. 16mo., 18pp.

1852 Philadelphia   PPL
BULLOCK & CRENSHAW. Successors to
Smith & Hodgson. Catalog of drugs, pharmaceutical preparations and medical wares,
apparatus and instruments. 24pp.

1853 Philadelphia   PKsL
------ Ill. catalog of drugs, sundries and
medical supplies for physicians. 8vo.,
56pp., wrap.

1854 Philadelphia   PKsL
------ Ill. catalog of drugs and   PHi
sundries, Queensware funnels and vials,
skeletons in neat boxes with lock and key,
nursing bottles, mortars and pestles, eye
glasses and druggists' glassware. 8vo.,
40pp., swell ills., wrap.

1858 Philadelphia   DSi
------ Catalog of chemicals, pharmaceutical apparatus, Wedgwood ware, furnaces,
lamps, stoves, flasks, tongs, crucibles, etc.
8vo., 96pp., a pict. dictionary, pict. wrap.

1860 Philadelphia   DNLM
------ Catalog of drugs, appara-   DLC
tus, etc. 8vo., 122pp., ills., wrap.

1862 Philadelphia   DNLM
------ Ill. catalog.

1875 Philadelphia   DNLM
------ Ill. catalog. 140pp.

c.1880 Philadelphia   MH-BA
------ Prices current for wholesale druggists and mfg. pharmacists. 16mo., 104pp.,
wrap.

1880 Philadelphia   DNLM
------ Ill. catalog of drugs and sundries.
152pp.

1859 Boston   DSi
BURR, M.S. & CO. Catalog of American,
English and French proprietary medicines,
fancy toilet articles, chemicals, soaps,
herbs, headache pills, balsams, oils - balsams to whiskey. 12mo., 72pp., pict. wrap.

1836 New York   OCL
BUSH & HILLYER. Catalog of drugs and
medicines.

1876 Newark, N. J.   NjR
CANDIT, HANSON & VanWINKLE. A new
catalog of drugs, chemicals, etc. 12mo.
with fine ills.

1831 Philadelphia   NNNAM
        ViRM DAPh DNLM NcU-Ph
CARPENTER, GEORGE W.   PPiU
Essays on some of the most important articles of materia medica - including an all
important list of articles that should be
purchased by a druggist at the outset of his
business - and a catalog of medicines,
surgical instruments, etc. 226pp. A fine
catalog record.

1834 Philadelphia   NNNAM
        DSi   DNLM DAPh MdU-D
------ Essays - to which is added a catalog. 320pp.

1852 Philadelphia   PHi
------ Circular to physicians and druggists of the United States. 8vo., 96pp., ill.

1854 Philadelphia   PHi
------ Ill. catalog and circular to physicians. 8vo., 100pp.

1855 CHAPIN, WHITON & CO. Agents.
See Turner.

1882 Chicago   DLC
CHAPMAN, GREEN & CO. Desc. dose and
price list of drugs, etc. 140pp.

1878 Boston   DNLM
CHENEY & MYRICK. Druggists' Handbook
of American and foreign drugs, etc. 12mo.

vd. Boston
CODMAN & SHURTLEFF. See Medical
Chapter. Some dental supplies listed and
ill.

1878 Peoria   DAPh
COLBURN, BIRKS & CO. Drug prices current. 516pp.

c.1842 New York & Jamaica, L. I.   NNQ
COMSTOCK & CO. A catalog of drugs.
All within named articles sold wholesale and
retail, and most also by our agents at
Lambertson's Jamaica drug store, etc.
30pp., ills. and plate, wrap.

1871 New York
CRITTENTON, CHARLES N. Crittenton's
Central Medical Warehouse. Catalog of
approximate prices of drugs. 16mo., 44pp.,
pict. wrap. of the warehouse.

1876 New York
------ Price list of drugs and sundries.

1877 New York
------ Price list of drugs and sundries.

1899 St. Louis   MoSHi
DAUGHERTY, DANIEL P. Drug Buyers'
Guide with prices and ills.

1771 Philadelphia   PPAmP
DAY, JOHN & CO. Catalog of drugs, chymical and galenical preparations, shop furniture, patent medicines and surgeons' instruments, sold by John Day & Co. Druggists
and Chymists in Second street, Philadelphia.
Ptd. by John Dunlap in Market street. 8vo.,
29pp.

1771 Philadelphia   PHi
------ Sabin #61523. 8vo., 31pp. Also
noted but not located by Evans #12024 as
having 33pp. What happened to this copy?

1771 Philadelphia   DLC
------ Catalogus medicinarum et pharma-
corum quae praeparanur et vanalia prostant.
Ptd. John Dunlap. 20pp.

1868 Detroit   DSi
DUFFIELD, PARKE & CO. Became Parke,
Davis & Co. in 1866. Catalog of Duffield's
medicinal fluid extracts. 16pp. Facsimile
of original.

1869 New York   MBM
DUNG, ALBERT & SON. Catalog of drugs
and chemicals. 14pp.

1810 Philadelphia   WU-Ph
DYOTT, T.W. MD. Dr. Robertson's genuine
patent and family medicines prepared by
sole prop. T. W. Dyott, grandson of late
celebrated Dr. Robertson. At wholesale and
retail and from agents in principal towns in
U. S. 24pp. Ptd. Thomas Town. Photostat
only.

1814 Philadelphia
------ Approved patent and family medicines, drugs, glassware, medicine chests,
etc. 8vo., 28pp. List of drugs and agents,
4pp.

c.1900 Grand Rapids
FINCH, PAUL V. & CO. Cut rate catalog -
drugs, herbs, patent medicines, chemicals,
pharmaceuticals, etc. Tall 16mo., 80pp.;
ills., wrap.

1875 New York   DSi
FOUGERA, E. & CO. Desc. catalog of
standard medicinal preparations and new
remedies. 105pp.

c.1890 New York & Boston
FOX, RULTZ & CO. Catalog of bottles,
corks, druggists' sundries, flint glassware,
colognes, ovals, prescription bottles, etc.
Sq. 8vo., 24pp., fine ills., wrap.

1899 New York   NNNAM
FRASER TABLET TRITURATE MFG. CO.
Catalog of tablet triturates, hypodermic and
compressed tablets, chocolate coated
physicians' private formulae and vial cases.

1872 Chicago   DSi
FULLER & FULLER. Prices current -
chemicals, oils, proprietary medicines,
sundries, furniture, glassware, moulds,
signs, scales, counters, presses and trusses.
8vo., 190pp. with 8 page col. ill., circular, cl.

1894 Chicago   DAPh
------ Prices current. 915pp., ills., cl.

1899 Chicago   DAPh
------ Prices current. 1052pp., ills., cl.

1900 Baltimore
GILBERT BROTHERS & CO. Catalog of
drugs and chemicals, bottles, glassware and
sundries. Even watches. 8vo., 228pp., fine
ills., dec. wrap.

1848 np.   DSi
GLASSBLOWERS' list of prices for druggists' ware. Broadside.

1865 Boston   MBP
GOODWIN, GEORGE C. & CO. Catalog of
patent medicines, toilet articles, perfumery,
etc. 24pp.

1874-5 Boston   MH-BA
------ New England Patent Medicine Warehouse. Pat. medicines and sundries for
druggists. 12mo., 73pp.

1876-7 Boston   CtGreH
------ Catalog of drugs   MBP   MH-BA
and sundries. 12mo., 128pp.

1880 Boston   MBP
------ Catalog of drugs and sundries.
268pp., ills., cl.

1885 Boston   MH-BA
------ Catalog of drugs and sun-   MBP
dries with fine ills. 12mo., 384pp., cl.

1862 Denver   CoD
GRAHAM'S CITY DRUG STORE. Catalog
of medicines, patent medicines, gold scales,
glassware, paints and sundries.

1826 Boston   CtMyM
GREGG & HOLLIS. Medicine chests carefully prepared for all climates with directions - diseases incident to seamen. Ships'
chests replenished - list of medicines and
drugs. 16mo., 20pp., self wrap.

1879 New York   DSi
HAGERTY BROTHERS. Catalog of druggists' glassware, fancy goods and sundries.
272pp., fine ills.

1880 New York   MBP
HALL & RUCKEL. 8th annual catalog -
prices current. 365pp., ill.

c.1879 Philadelphia   DLC
HANCE BROTHERS & WHITE. Priced catalog of sugar coated pills, etc. 44pp.

1806 Baltimore   MdBJ-W
HANNA, JAMES. New and improved directions for use of medical compositions contained in marine medicine chests prepared
by James Hanna. A catalog of medicines.
See also Hollis.

1886 New York   NNNAM
HAYS, DAVID & SONS. Price list of compressed and triturate tablets and standard
pharmaceutical specialties.

1825 Boston   CtMyM
HENCHMAN, DANIEL. Medicine chests of
all kinds with directions suitable to their
contents, carefully put up by . . . medicines
of best quality. List. 16mo., 16pp., wrap.
Mostly for ship captains and seamens' com-
plaints.

1869 New York
HENRY, JOHN F. Successor to Demas
Barnes. Catalog of medicines and druggists sundries. 16mo., 42pp., ills., view of
plant and map pict. wrap.

1871 New York
------ Catalog of medicines and sundries.
16mo., 82pp., pict. wrap.

1872-3 New York & Burlington, Vt.   WU-Ph
HENRY & CO. See Wells   DLC
Richardson & Co.

1835 Boston   OCL
HENSHAW, P. Price list of drugs, pharmaceuticals, etc.

1870 New York   NcU-Ph
HERNSTEIN, ALBERT L. Ill. catalog of
drugs and sundries.

1806 Boston   DNLM
HOLLIS, THOMAS. (Weld) Weld is
crossed out on the title page and Thomas
Hollis written in. Medicine chests of all

kinds, with directions, carefully put up by
- Weld-Hollis - Medicines of best quality
at low prices. 16mo., 10pp., wrap.

1834 Boston   CtMyM
------ A companion to the medicine chest.
List of medicines - advice to rescue drown-
ing persons, etc. 16mo., 8pp.

1851 Boston
JACKSON, EBEN JR. & CO. Prices current - drugs, medicines, dye-stuffs, oils,
flint and green glassware, paints, wines and
brandies, etc. 16mo., 20pp., wrap.

1896 Milwaukee   DSi
JERMAIN, PFLUEGER & KUEHMSTED CO.
Wholesale price list of drugs and pharma-
ceuticals. 1408pp.

1895 St. Louis   MoSHi
JUDGE & DOLPH PHARMACEUTICAL CO.
Cut price list of drugs, hot water bottles,
perfumes and sundries. Large 8vo., 48pp.,
ills., wrap.

KING - See Dental Supplies.

1800 Salem, Mass.   MSaE
LANG, EDWARD S. Medicine chests with
suitable directions, prepared at his shop in
Salem. 12mo., 10pp.

nd. Philadelphia   PHi
LEIDY, ASHER S. List of drugs and medicines at his medical store. One leaf.

1898 Indianapolis   NNNAM
LILLY, ELI & CO. Ill. catalog of formalde-
hyde disinfectors, deodorizers, sterilizers,
chemicals, etc. 32pp.

1891 Cincinnati   OCL
LLOYD BROTHERS. Price list of fluid
extracts.

1892 Cincinnati   OCL
------ Catalog of pharmaceutical preparations.

1897 Cincinnati   OCL
------ Price list of drugs and sundries.

1899-1932 Cincinnati   OCL
------ A fine collection of drug catalogs
issued by Lloyd Brothers.

c.1871 Cincinnati   OCL
LLOYD, J.U. with O.F. Gordon. Price list
of chemical apparatus. Collection being
cataloged.

1804-1900 Cincinnati   OCLloyd
This listing is not according to Hoyle, but
knowing that people do not read prefaces and
introductions, I want this collection noted.

240 bound volumes and 200 unbound folders, containing from five to ten American drug and pharmaceutical catalogs, dating from 1804.

1877 Allentown
LOCHMAN, C.L. See printing samples for drug labels.

1885 Chicago   WU-Ph
LORD, OWEN & CO. Prices current of drugs and sundries.

1888 Chicago   WU-Ph
------ Prices current.

1878 Chicago   WU-Ph
LORD, STOUTENBURGH & CO. Prices current of drugs and druggists' sundries and supplies. Ills. of glassware, etc.

1879 Chicago   WU-Ph
------ Ill. catalog of drugs, etc.

1880 Chicago   NCorniC
------ Ill. catalog.   MBP WU-Ph

1881 Chicago   WU-Ph
------ Ill. catalog, 127pp.

1882 & 1888 Chicago   WU-Ph
------ Ill. catalogs.

c.1870 New York   NjOE
LUHME, J.F. & CO. General desc. catalog of chemical, pharmaceutical and physical apparatus. 160pp. with fine ills.

1896 St. Louis   DSi
LUYTIES HOMEOPATHIC PHARMACY CO. Price list and reference book for druggists. 164pp.

1872 New York   WU-Ph
McKESSON & ROBBINS. Est. 1833. Prices current of drugs and druggists' articles. Ill.

1873 New York   DSi
------ Prices current. Ill. of glassware, fancy and plain, window display bottles, moulds, scales, mortar and pestles, drugs, etc. 8vo., 160pp., wrap.

1874 New York   NCorniC
------ Prices current. Ill. catalog.

1875 New York   WU-Ph
------ Prices current. Ill. catalog.

1876 New York   WU-Ph
------ Prices current. Ill., col. pls.

1877 New York   NCorniC
------ Prices current.   MBP WU-Ph
Ills. of glassware and all druggists' sundries. Col. pls., 174pp.

1878 New York   MBP
------ Prices current of druggists' wares of every desc., ills., 208pp.

1879 New York   WU-Ph
------ Prices current, ill., wrap.

1880 New York   NCorniC
------ Prices current of   MBP WU-Ph
druggists' articles, flint and green glass-ware, implements, fancy moulds, cases, perfumes, etc. Fine ills., pict. wrap. 226pp.

1881 New York   WU-Ph
------ Prices current. Fine ills.

1882 New York   MBP
------ Prices current. Ills.

1883 New York   WU-Ph
------ Ill. catalog with   MBP MnU-B
prices current. Large 8vo., 244pp., fine ills., col. pls., cl.

1884 New York   MBP
------ Prices current. Ill., cl.

1884 New York   NNNAM
------ Catalogo general y precios corrientes de las drogas - including surgical instruments - 472pp., fine ills., some in col., cl.

1885 New York   NCorniC
------ Prices current.   DAPh WU-Ph
Fine ills., cl.

1886 New York   MBP
------ Prices current, ills., cl., 206pp.

1887 New York   WU-Ph
------ Ill. catalog, col. pls., cl. MBP

1888 New York   MBP
------ Ill. catalog, 218pp., ills., cl.

1890 New York   WU-Ph
------ Ill. prices current, cl.

nd. St. Louis   MoSHi
MALLINCKRODT CHEMICAL WORKS. Ill. catalog of druggists' chemicals.

c.1865 New York   MBM
MANDELBAUM, S. Price list of druggists' and chemists' articles. 76pp.

1828 Boston   MBP
MASSACHUSETTS COLLEGE OF PHARMACY. Catalog of materia medica, and of pharmaceutical preparations with uniform prices. 40pp.

1872 St. Louis   WU-Ph
MELLIER, A.A. Ill.   MBP   MBM
catalog and prices current of drugs and
pharmaceuticals. 126pp.

1877 St. Louis   MH-BA
------ Wholesale catalog of drugs, interleaved. 5th ed. 16mo., 178pp., ills., plus
advts.

1892 New York   MdTanSW
MERCK & CO. Merck's Market Report -
Prices of drugs and chemicals, advts.,
index. 4to., 52pp.

1894 Philadelphia   PHi
MERRELL, A.F. & CO. Catalog of pharmacy goods, drugs, glassware, implements,
etc. 4to., 32pp., ill.

1880 Cincinnati   OC
MERRELL, WILLIAM S. & CO. Revised
current price list of drugs and pharmaceuticals for mfg. druggists. 8vo., 20pp.

1881 Cincinnati   MH-BA
------ Catalog of drugs, etc. 16mo., 52pp.

1883 Cincinnati   MH-BA
----- Catalog of drugs, etc. 16mo., 48pp.

1894 New York   NNNAM
MEYER, BERNARD. Ill. catalog of druggists' pill and powder boxes, standard drugs,
etc. 32pp.

1889 St. Louis   WU-Ph
MEYER BROTHERS DRUG CO. Est. 1852.
Annual catalog and prices current. 816pp.,
ill., cl. Also offers soda fountains, glassware, etc.

1885 Philadelphia   NNNAM
MITCHELL, C.L., M.D. & CO. 8th annual
catalog. Physicians' handbook and ill. catalog of soluble medicated gelatin preparations. 48pp.

1889-1900 St. Louis   MoSHi
MOFFITT-WEST DRUG CO. Collection of
drug and pharmaceutical catalogs, well ill.
for research.

1880 Chicago   WU-Ph
                DLC   DSi   MH-BA
MORRISON, PLUMMER & CO. Druggists'
ready reference with ills. and prices of
sundries, etc. 8vo., 334pp., fine ills., cl.

1882 Chicago   WU-Ph
------ Ill. catalog of drugs, etc.

1887 Chicago   WU-Ph
------ Ill. catalog, 736pp., ill.,   MBP
cl.

1899 Philadelphia   MH-BA
MULFORD, H.K. CO. Catalog of pharmaceutical and biological products. 16mo.,
216pp., fine ills., cl.

1878 St. Paul   MnHi
NOYES BROTHERS & CUTLER. Ill. catalog
of drugs and pharmaceuticals, surgical and
dental instruments, galvanic batteries,
artificial limbs, microscopes and sundries.
Large 8vo.

1888 St. Paul   WU-Ph
------ Ill. catalog of drugs and   MnHi
sundries, pharmaceutical and medical.

1890 St. Paul   WU-Ph
------ Ill. catalog. 476pp.,   MnHi
ills., cl.

1885-1889 St. Paul   OCL
------ Ill. catalogs, fine ills., vp., cl. A
fine reference library right here.

1893-1902 St. Paul   OCL
------ Ill. catalogs of druggists' supplies,
surgical and dental instruments, etc. 1893,
1895, 1897-8, 1901-2., vp., fine ills.

1890-1914 St. Paul   MnHi
------ Ill. catalogs. This collection consists of 33 catalogs from 1878 to 1914. A
fine ill. ref.

1888 Lancaster, N. H.   NhD
NOYES, P.J. Mfg. Pharmacist. Price list
of gelatine coated pills and granules, tablets,
extracts, tinctures, etc. Ills. of medical
trunks, bags, cases, etc. 16mo., 76pp., fine
ills., pict. wrap.

1836 New York   OCL
OLCOTT & McKESSON. Catalog of drugs.

1870 San Francisco   CHi
PAINTER & CALVERT. Price list of pharmaceutical preparations. 12mo., 20pp.,
wrap.

1880 Detroit   DLC
PARKE, DAVIS & CO. Est. 1866. Complete
price list of drugs, etc. 176pp.

1893 Detroit   DNLM
------ Complete price list of laboratory
products. 200pp.

1894 Detroit   DLC
------ Desc. catalog of laboratory DSi
products, compressed tablets and tablet
triturates. 48pp.

1868 Philadelphia   PKsL
PARRISH, EDWARD. Priced catalog of
apparatus, pharmaceutical preparations,
new remedies, toilet articles, sundries.
8vo., 32pp., fine ills.

1870 Philadelphia   DLC
------ Annual priced catalog   DSi
of Parrish's Pharmacy. 32pp., ills.

1800 Portsmouth, N. H.   MBHi
PEIRCE, CHARLES. Valuable medicines
just received from Lee & Co.'s patent and
family medicine store in Baltimore and for
sale by . . . list. Fol. broadside.

1874 Portland, Me.   NNNAM
PERKINS, JOHN W. & CO. Catalog of drugs,
chemicals and dyes, druggists' sundries,
paints, artists' materials and oils. 16mo.,
144pp., ill., glt. pict. cl.

c.1875 Louisville, Ky.   OCL
PETER, A. & CO. Catalog of drugs, etc.

1826 Philadelphia   PPPCPh
PPiU   ICJ   DNLM NcU-Ph
ViRM   ICU-M
PHILADELPHIA COLLEGE OF PHARMACY.
The druggists' manual, being a price current
of drugs, medicines, dye-stuffs, paints,
glassware and patent medicines. 8vo., np.

1804 New York   DNLM
POST, JOEL & JOTHAM.   DLC
Directions for use of the medicine chests
to be used with the catalog, etc. Ptd. Wm.
A. Davis. 16mo., 16pp.

1804 New York   DLC
------ Catalog of drugs and chemicals, at
wholesale and retail, at corner of Wall and
William streets. 40pp.

1839 Portsmouth, N. H.   NhD
PRESTON, WILLIAM R. Druggist and
Apothecary. Medicine chests for ships and
families, with lists of medicines and directions. 16mo., 32pp.

1883 Philadelphia   PKsL
QUEEN, JAMES W. & CO. Ill. catalog of
chemical glassware for druggists, chemists,
etc. Ills. of shapes, designs and sizes.
8vo., 50pp., wrap. See also Glass, Optical
and Scientific Goods.

1868 New York   NcorniC
QUINLAN, JEREMIAH. Catalog   PKsL
of druggists' wares, perfumers' green,
black and colored glassware, bottles -
Britannia and porcelain ware - private
moulds made to order, jars, urns, labels,
show globes, carboys, stoppers, etc. 16mo.,
140pp., glt. dec. wrap. Great job.

1870 Pittsburgh, Pa.   DNLM
RADCLIFFE, DR. Dr. Radcliffe's great
family medicines, seven seals, or the golden
wonder, etc. 8vo., 8pp., ills.

1891 San Francisco   CHi
REDLINGTON & CO. Prices current of
druggists' proprietary articles and sundries. 8vo., 345pp., fine ills., bds.

c.1870 New York
REED, CARNRICK & EDWARDS. Prices
current of pharmaceuticals, synthetic preparations and chemicals. 16mo., 24pp., wrap
with cut of trademark.

1873 New York
------ Miscellaneous list of pharmaceutical preparations for the medical profession.
24mo., 48pp., wrap.

1859 Boston
REED, CUTLER & CO. Druggists' glassware, mixed ware, sundries and supplies.
3 columns. Broadside with nice cont.
border.

1858 St. Louis   MoSHi
RICHARDSON, MELLIER & CO. Prices
current and catalog of drugs, dye-stuffs,
chemicals, glassware, paints, etc. 16mo.,
67pp.

c.1870 New York   NjOE
ROHRDECK & GOEDELER. Late J. F.
Luhme & Co. Catalog of chemicals, drugs,
etc.

1836 New York
RUSHTON & ASPINWALL. Druggists.
Companion to the medicine chest, with plain
rules and list of medicines. 64mo., 32pp.,
mbld. bds.

1880 Boston   MBP
RUST BROTHERS & BIRD. Catalog of
drugs and druggists' articles. 164pp., ills.

1834 Albany, N. Y.   OCL
SANDS & SHAW. Catalog of drugs and
pharmaceuticals.

1804 New York   OCL
SCHEIFFELIN, JACOB. Catalog of drugs.

1871 New York   DSi
SCHIEFFELIN, W.H. & CO. Est. 1794.
Oldest drug house in U. S. still alive.
Prices current. 130pp.

1873 New York   MBM
------ General prices current. 140pp.,
ill., wrap.

1876 New York   NCorniC
------ General prices   NNNAM
current of druggists' sundries, glassware,
display bottles, mortar and pestles, lamps.
8vo., 258pp., ill., wrap.

1880 New York   DAPh
------ Pharmaceutical preparations.
32mo., 52pp., wrap.

1881 New York   NCorniC
        MBP   DAPh DNLM WU-Ph
------ General prices current. 8vo.,
427pp., ill., cl.

1883 New York   NCorniC
------ General prices DAPh WU-Ph
current. 8vo., 479pp., ill., cl.

1885 New York
------ General prices current. 8vo.,
554pp., ill., dec. cl.

1887 New York   WU-Ph
------ General prices current. Ill., cl.

1891 New York   NNNAM
------ General prices current. Ill., cl.

1795 Boston   MBP
SMITH & BARTLETT, (Thomas) A catalog
of drugs and medicines, instruments and
utensils, dye-stuffs, groceries and painters'
colours, etc. imported, prepared and sold
by . . . 22pp. Evans reported a copy in
DLC, but Sabin later discovered it could no
longer be located.

1880 Boston   MBP
SMITH, DOOLITTLE & SMITH. Prices
current. 288pp.

1860 Chicago   ICHi
SMITH & DWYER. Price current of drugs,
chemicals and medicines. 4pp.

1832 Boston
SMITH, JOSEPH M. Druggist. Medicine
chests containing necessary medicines and
instruments, distinctly labelled, etc. 12mo.,
12pp., with a list of medicines. Wrap.

1827 Cincinnati   OCL
SMITH, L.W. Catalog of fresh drugs.

1886-1896 Brooklyn, N. Y.   DLC
SQUIBB, EDWARD R. Semi-annual price
lists of standard pharmaceutical preparations and pharmacopoeial reagents. A fine
collection. #56, 57, 59, 61, 62, 63, 64, 65,
66, 67 - 25, 28 and 32pp.

SQUIBB, E.R. & SONS. #68, 69, 71, 73, 74
and 76. 40 to 60pp.

1883-88 Brooklyn, N. Y.   DNLM
------ Collection of catalogs. #50, 51, 52,
53, 54, 55 and 60. 25 to 32pp.

1884-1900 Brooklyn, N. Y.   NNNAM
------ Collection of catalogs. #51, 52, 53,
54, 56, 57, 58, 61, 64, 67, 68, 70, 71, 72, 73,
74, 75, 76, 77, 78, 79 and 84. 25 to 60pp.

1875 Detroit   NjOE
STEARNS, FREDERICK & CO. Catalog #75.
Pharmaceutical products and preparations,
alkatrits, alkametric granules and alkader-
mic pellets. 178pp., ills., wrap.

1883-4 Detroit   ICHi
------ Catalog of popular non-secret medicines. 66pp. with 12p. supplement.

1885 Detroit   ICHi
------ Revised price list. 8pp., ills.

1885 Detroit   ICHi
------ Revised catalog. 16pp., ills.

1886 Detroit   NNNAM
------ Desc. catalog with   ICHi
article on positive medication. 32pp.

1886 Detroit   ICHi
------ Retail druggists' diary and want
book. Text, price list and blanks for notes,
80pp., ill.

1887 Chicago   WU-Ph
STEVENSON, ROBERT & CO. Wholesale
catalog of drugs and druggists' sundries,
pharmaceuticals, etc. 522pp., ills., cl.

1890 Chicago   WU-Ph
------ Ill. catalog of drugs and RU-Ph
sundries.

1876 New York   NjOE
STUTTS, GEORGE O. Price list of druggists' glassware. 68pp., ills.

1880 New York   NNNAM
TARRANT & CO. Mfg. and Imp. Est. 1834.
General prices current of drugs, chemicals,
pharmaceuticals and druggists' sundries.
8vo., 170pp., ill., dec. wrap. Ptd. Francis
Hart. Col. plate.

1882 New York   DAPh
------ General prices current, etc. 8vo.,
192pp., dec. wrap., fine ills.

1857 Cambridgeport, Mass.   DNLM
THAYER, HENRY & CO. Desc. catalog of
fluid and solid extracts in vacuo, also con-
centrations and officinal pills. 16mo.,
24pp., wrap.

1866 Cambridgeport, Mass.   DNLM
------ Desc. catalog.

1879 Cambridgeport, Mass.   WU-Ph
------ Desc. catalog.

1885 Cincinnati   OCL
THORP & LLOYD BROTHERS. Complete
physicians' catalog of prices current for
fine pharmaceutical preparations for Jan.

nd. Cincinnati   OCL
------ 2 other undated catalogs reported
without details.

1888 New York   DAPh
THURBER, WHYLAND & CO. General
prices current. 208pp.

c.1850 New York & New Lebanon, N. Y.
TILDEN & CO. Annual catalog of NNNAM
herbs, medicinal plants, vegetable medicines,
also extracts, ointments, essential oils,
waters - raised, prepared and put up in the
neatest style . . . 24pp.

1852 New York   DNLM
------ Catalog of pure medicinal extracts.
28pp.

1854 New York   DNLM
------ Catalog of . . . 32pp.

1855 New York   NNNAM
          NN   PVI   WTR   DNLM
------ Catalog of pure medicinal extracts
prepared in vacuo, etc. 8vo., 32pp.

1858 New York   NNNAM
------ Formulae for making tinctures, in-
fusions, syrups, wines, mixtures and pills.
162pp.

c.1860 New York   DSi
------ Price list of pure sugar coated
pills. 16pp.

1861 New York   NNNAM
------ List of solid and fluid extracts, etc.
162 and 32pp.

1865 New York & New Lebanon   TxU
------ Prices current of medicinal preparations. 8vo., 8pp., pict. wrap.

1867 New Lebanon, N. Y.   DNLM
------ Prices current. 16pp.   DLC

1874 New Lebanon, N. Y.   DNLM
------ Catalog of pure medicines, etc.

1889 Philadelphia   DSi
TROEMNER, HENRY. Price list of fine
druggists' scales and weights. 68pp., ill.

1855 Boston
TURNER, T.LARKIN, Agent. Dr. Lorraine's
vegetable cathartic pills. Test. letters from
1824 on to date. 64mo., 30pp., wrap.

1760 Newport, R. I.   DNLM
TWEEDY, JOHN. A catalog of   RHi
drugs and of chymical and galenical medi-
cines, sold by John Tweedy at his shop in
Newport, Rhode Island and for him in New
York, at the sign of the Unicorn and Mortar.
np., nd., 28pp. Evans 8753. Ptd. by James
Franklin, 1760. SGO. 32pp.

1873 Harvard, Mass.   MHarvF
UNITED SOCIETY. Shakers. Catalog of
roots, herbs, barks and powdered articles
prepared in the United Society, etc. 16mo.,
24pp., ptd. wrap.

1883 New York   NNNAM
VAN DUZER, S.R. Prices   DAPh
current of drugs, chemicals, pharmaceuticals, paints, oils, etc. 8vo., 108 and 40pp.,
ills., col. plate, wrap. DeVinne Press.

1871 Chicago   ICU-M
VAN SCHAACK, STEVENSON & REID.
Prices current of drugs and pharmaceuticals.

1872 Chicago   ICU-M
------ Prices current.

1873 Chicago   ICU-M
------ Prices current and ill.   OCL
catalog.

1874 Chicago   DSi   OCL   ICU-M
------ Prices current. Ill.   WU-Ph
catalog. 378pp.

1875 Chicago   WU-Ph
------ Prices   DSi   OCL   ICU-M
current and ill. catalog. 404pp., fine ills.

1876 Chicago   ICU-M
------ Prices current. 404pp.   OCL

1878 Chicago   ICU-M
------ Prices current. 404pp.   OCL

1879 Chicago   WU-Ph
                          OCL   ICHi
VAN SCHAACK, STEVENSON & CO. Annual
prices current and ill. catalog. 490pp.

1881 Chicago   WU-Ph
------ Ill. prices current.   OCL

1882 Chicago   WU-Ph
------ Ill. prices current.   OCL

1884 Chicago   WU-Ph
------ Ill. prices current.   OCL

1885 Chicago   WU-Ph
------ Ill. prices current.   OCL

1887 Chicago   WU-Ph
                   OCL   ICHi   NNMM
VAN SCHAACK, PETER & SONS. Ill. catalog of drugs and pharmaceuticals, sundries,
furniture, glassware - a fine pict. record,
pict. cl. 12mo., 739pp.

1889 Chicago   WU-Ph
------ Ill. prices current.   OCL

1890 Chicago   WU-Ph
------ Ill. prices current.   OCL

1890-1908 Chicago   OCL
------ Collection of ill. catalogs.

1872 Philadelphia   PHi
WAMPOLE, HENRY K. & CO. Ill. catalog
of chemicals, drugs, druggists' glassware,
shop furniture, perfumes, etc. 8vo., 50pp.,
fine ills., wrap.

1874 Philadelphia   PHi
------ Prices current. A fine ill. catalog
of druggists' sundries, etc. 378pp.

1879 Philadelphia   PHi
------ Catalog of the best goods at the
lowest prices. Ills. of fancy glassware,
nursing bottles, drugs, etc. 8vo., 56pp.,
wrap.

1871 Philadelphia   PHi
WARNER, WILLIAM R. & CO. Physicians'
catalog and formulary of soluble sugar
coated pills, supplies, etc. 16pp., pict.wrap.

1889 Philadelphia   NNNAM
------ Therapeutic reference book. 119pp.
and 17 lvs.

1890-95 Philadelphia   NNNAM
------ 3 catalogs for 1890, 1894 and 1895.

1879-1881 Rochester, N. Y.   NR
WARNER'S SAFE REMEDIES. 8vo., 32pp.,
ills., pict. wrap. 3 catalogs for 1879, 1880
and 1881.

1883 Rochester, N. Y.   NNU
------ Book of $1000. prize enigmas.
Amusing tests. in a cleverly compiled ill.
pseudo catalog. 8vo., 32pp.

1872 Chicago   ICU-M
WEED, W.A. & CO. Ill.   MBP MBM
yearbook of pharmaceutical information
with prices current. 192pp.

1879 Boston   MBP
WEEKS & POTTER. Ill. catalog of foreign
and domestic drugs, including fancy glass
novelties, druggists' glassware, atomizers
and sundries. 215pp.

1888 Boston   MBP
------ Ill. catalog of druggists' sundries.
Revised prices. 300pp.

1890 Boston   MdTanSW
------ Revised catalog. Ill.   DNLM
throughout, glass and drugs, etc. 12mo.,
131pp., dec. cl.

1890 Boston   DNLM
------ Ill. catalog. 468 and 131pp.

c.1885 New York   NNNAM
WEISMANN & MUELLENBACH. Catalog
#108 and price list. Seven good reasons
why you should buy your drugs, perfumery,
chemicals, etc. here. 16pp., ills.

1806 Boston
WELD . See Hollis.

1872-3 New York & Burlington, Vt. WU-Ph
WELLS, RICHARDSON & CO.   DLC
Late Henry & Co. Annual catalog of prices
of medicines, etc. 240pp. Wells Richardson stamped over Henry.

1851 Madison, Ind.   In
WHEELER & BARCLAY. Successors to
and located at the old stand of Siddall &
Brothers. Price list of drugs, dye-stuffs,
paints, etc. Broadside.

1873 Philadelphia & New York   CBaK
WHITALL, TATUM & CO. Armstrong Cork
Co. Works: Phoenix Flint Glass Works at
Schetterville, N. J. and Green Glass Works
at Millville, N. J. The collection of catalogs
of druggists' wares, chemists' supplies and
medical materials that follow supplies one
of the best American glass references
available. A catalog of druggists' glassware - bottles, candy jars, show vases and
vials, snuff jars, perfume bottles, globes,
laboratory glassware, etc. 12mo., 43pp.,
fine ills., col. pls., dec. cl.

1874 Philadelphia & New York   PLACC
------ Ill. catalog of druggists, chemists'
and perfumers' glassware and sundries.
8vo., 46pp., fine ills.

1876 Philadelphia & New York   PLACC
------ Ill. catalog. 8vo., 48pp., cl.

1877 Philadelphia & New York   PLACC
------ Ill. catalog. 8vo., 96pp., cl.

1878 Philadelphia & New York   PLACC
------ Ill. catalog. 8vo., 96pp.

1879 Philadelphia & New York   PLACC
------ Ill. catalog. 96pp.

1880 Philadelphia & New York   NCorniC
------ Ill. catalog.WU-Ph MiDbF PLACC
Col. pls. of labels and window show bottles.
8vo., 72pp.

1881 Philadelphia & New York   PLACC
------ Ill. catalog. 8vo., 80pp.   MSaE

1882 Philadelphia & New York   PLACC
------ Ill. catalog. MSaE PPL CBaK
8vo., 88pp.

1883 Philadelphia & New York   PLACC
------ Ill. catalog.   MSaE WU-Ph
8vo., 88pp.

1884 Philadelphia & New York   PLACC
------ Ill. catalog.   MSaE   WU-Ph
8vo., 104pp., cl.

1885 Philadelphia & New York   PLACC
------ Ill. catalog. 8vo.,   MSaE
106pp., cl.

1886 Philadelphia & New York   PLACC
------ Ill. catalog.   PKsL   MSaE
8vo., 148pp., cl.

1887 Philadelphia & New York   NCorniC
------ Ill.   MSaE WU-Ph   PLACC
catalog. 8vo., 162pp., cl.

1888 Philadelphia & New York   NCorniC
------ Ill. catalog.   WU-Ph   PLACC
8vo., 172pp., cl.

1889 Philadelphia & New York   NCorniC
------ Ill. catalog. 8vo.,   PLACC
178pp., cl.

1890 Philadelphia & New York   NCorniC
------ Ill. catalog with supple-   PLACC
ment. 8vo., 198pp. and 32p. supplement, cl.

1891 Philadelphia & New York   NCorniC
------ Ill. catalog.   DNLM   PLACC
8vo., 200pp., cl.

1893 Philadelphia & New York   NCorniC
------ Ill. catalog.   NNMM   PLACC
8vo., 206pp., wrap.

1894 Philadelphia & New York   NCorniC
------ Ill. catalog. 8vo.,   PLACC
206pp. cl.

1895 Philadelphia & New York   NCorniC
------ Ill. catalog. 8vo., PPL   PLACC
206pp., cl.

1896 Philadelphia & New York   PLACC
------ Ill. catalog. 8vo., 206pp., cl.

1897 Philadelphia & New York   PLACC
------ Ill. catalog. 8vo., 206pp., cl.

1898 Philadelphia & New York   MdTanSW
      MiDbF NNNAM   NCorniC
------ Ill. catalog. 8vo., 206pp., cl.

1899 Philadelphia & New York   PLACC
------ Ill. catalog. 8vo., 202pp., cl.

N.B. It would be impossible to give a complete listing of all the good ills. and col. pls. in each of these locations. Please refer to the descriptive 1873 listing, adding glass novelties, details, new styles and designs, and col. pls. as each offering grows in size.

1817 Boston   DNLM
WHITE, CHARLES. A catalog of   MBP
materia medica and of pharmaceutical preparations. 35pp.

1857 Boston   DLC
WILSON, FAIRBANKS & CO. Catalog of drugs and medicines, English, French and American chemicals and glassware. 128pp. with ills.

1878 Philadelphia   PHi
WYETH, JOHN & BRO. Mfg. Chemists. Retail circular of pharmaceutical preparations, with list of poisons, their antidotes and directions in emergencies. 16mo., 32pp.

1881 Philadelphia   DNLM
------ Catalog of elegant pharmaceutical preparations.

1883 Philadelphia   PKsL
------ Catalog of fluid extracts, standard formulae, etc. 12mo., 176pp., cl.

1886 Philadelphia   DLC
------ Price list of suppositories, etc. 20pp.

1891 Philadelphia   DNLM
------ Price list of the most elegant pharmaceutical preparations. 90pp.

1892 Philadelphia   DSi
------ Catalog of fluid extracts, etc.

1893 Philadelphia   PKsL
------ Prices current.

1800 Philadelphia
YORKE, SAMUEL. Drugs and medicines at the auction store of Samuel Yorke. May 28. Broadside. Evans 38255.

A great many catalogs listed in the chapters Dental Instruments and Furnishings and Medical and Surgical Instruments also carried fine illustrated references in the drug department. These three are inseparable and should all be consulted in searching any one of a thousand border line products.

Chapter 20

Fences

It may seem odd that such a small group of catalogs should be segregated and put under a separate heading. This has been done because of many requests through the years which indicate definitely that fencing and barbed wire have played an important role in the development of the country's farms and industries. Quality is the password, not quantity.

We hope we have provided material easily found and readily accessible. From the turned wood fences of New England to the barbed wire enclosures for western farms and railroad properties, there are at least a few good specimens. There are also fine illustrations of the fancy ornamental wrought and cast iron fences, railings, guards, etc. that still decorate some of our city parks and fine old estates.

1885 Des Moines   MnHi
BAKER WIRE CO. Ill. catalog of barbed wire fencing.

nd. Philadelphia & Worcester   PHi
BARTLETT, F.J. Agent. Ill. circular of Brinkerhoff Patent metallic fencing.

1885-87 St. Louis   MnHi
BRODERICK & BASCOM ROPE CO. 3 ill. catalogs of barbed wire fencing. 1885, 1886 and 1887.

nd. Chicago   MnHi
CHANNON, H. CO. Catalog #1. Barbed wire fencing.

c.1855 Clinton, Mass.   MH-BA
CLINTON WIRE-CLOTH CO. Formerly Lowell Wire Fence Co. Ill. catalog of power loom wire-cloth, and patent wire fencing. 8vo., 16pp.

vd. DeKalb, Ill. & Springfield, Mass.
ELLWOOD, I.L. & CO. and WASHBURN & MOEN MFG. CO. See Washburn & Moen.

1887-88 DeKalb, Ill.   MnHi
HAISH, J. & CO. Ill. catalogs of barbed wire fencing, etc. 2 catalogs for 1887 and 1888.

1883 Lima, O.   NNMM
LIMA IRON FENCE CO. Ill. and desc. annual catalog of wrought and malleable iron fencing. 18pp., wrap.

c.1887 Minneapolis   MnHi
MINNEAPOLIS FENCE & IRON   MnM
WORKS. Ill. catalog of wood and iron fences, railings, guards, balustrades, fine

turned wood gate posts, hitching posts, stable railings and fencing, fancy iron fences, etc. 8vo., 48pp. of fine ills., pict. wrap.

1886 Minneapolis   MnHi
MINNEAPOLIS WIRE WORKS. Successors to Cargill & Co. Ill. catalog and price list of patent web wire fencing.

1887 Minneapolis   MnHi
------ Ill. catalog of fencing, wire work, etc.

vd. New York
MOTT, J.L. See Ornamental fences, etc.

1895 Adrian, Mich.   ICHi
PAGE WOVEN WIRE FENCE CO. Ill. catalog - photos. of fencing for farms, parks, railroad tracks, city estates, etc. Tall 8vo., 24pp., pict. wrap.

1900 Philadelphia   PKsL
PHILADELPHIA HEDGE CO. Ill. catalog of fences, hedges, shrubbery, wood and iron fences.

c.1885 Minneapolis   MnHi
PRICE, CONDIT & COURTER. Ill. catalog and price list of Thomas perfection fences for lawns, parks, etc. 8vo., 15pp. with 4 page leaflet tipped in.

nd. Pittsburgh, Pa.   MnHi
SCUTT, H.B. & CO. Ill. catalog of barbed wire fencing, etc.

c.1876 Chicago   ICHi
THORN WIRE HEDGE CO. Ill. catalog of Kelly barbed wire fencing. 8pp.

1884 Chicago   MnHi
------ Ill. catalog.

1886 Chicago   MnHi
------ Ill. catalog.

c.1870 Worcester, Mass. & DeKalb, Ill.
WASHBURN & MOEN MFG. CO., TxDaDeG
Worcester. Est. 1831. I.L. Ellwood & Co.,
DeKalb, Ill. Ill. catalog of Glidden Patent
steel barbed wire for fencing livestock,
railroad right of way, etc. 24mo., 24pp.,
graphic ills., pict. wrap.

1877 Worcester & DeKalb   IHi
------ Utility and efficiency of barbed wire
for farmer, gardener and country gentleman.

Ills. of fencing in use on farm, in city, ball
parks, etc. 12mo., 58pp., pict. wrap.

1893 Worcester   MH-BA
------ General catalog wire, iron, steel
and copper wire, wire drawers, galvanizers,
Waukegan barbed wire fence, ropes and
cables. 4to., 84pp., ills., cl.

nd. Worcester   PHi
------ Ill. catalog of Brinkerhoff patent
metallic fencing.

See also Machines & Tools.

Be sure to augment this data by checking Architectural Building Materials and Ornamental Ironwork.
Few American manufacturers of the 19th century could afford to produce nothing but fences, and that
is exactly why these few have been given a special section.

Chapter 21

Firearms

Although Ernest R. Gee, John C. Phillips and Raymond L. J. Riling have contributed invaluable bibliographical volumes for the study and preservation of American inventive genius in this field, as usual the trade catalog has not had a fair share of the credit. Mr. Riling has recognized their value and used them to very good advantage but has not located them for future reference.

In 1940 L. D. Satterlee compiled Ten Old Gun Catalogs which is an actual facsimile reprint of those he considers most important to the history of our development. He states that - These Catalogs are Seldom Found in any of the Larger Libraries, and have practically Disappeared from Circulation. In spite of the fact that many great private collections have rescued these records, and temporarily taken them out of circulation, this chapter provides definite proof that our larger libraries have preserved and cataloged a fine, though conveniently scattered, national store of material.

c.1900 Bridgeport, Conn.
BRIDGEPORT GUN IMPLEMENT CO.
Special catalog of Forstner bits, etc. 16mo., 8pp., ills.

c.1900 St. Louis, Mo. & Ogden, Utah
BROWNING ARMS CO. Est. St. Louis 1831. Ill. catalog of inventions - Browning Sixteen, Wild Mule, etc. 16mo., 20pp., wrap.

1887-8 Cleveland   OCl
CHAMBERLAIN CARTRIDGE CO. Ill. catalog of fixed ammunition, shotguns, clay pigeons, sporting accessories, etc. 8vo., 24pp., fine ills. of game, etc. Wrap.

1894 Cleveland   NSbSM
------ Ill. catalog.

1876 Baltimore   PKsL
CLARK & SNEIDER. The Sneider patent double-barreled breech-loading shotgun, ammunition, shells, etc. 8vo., 22pp., ill., wrap.

1888 Hartford, Conn.   CtHi
COLT'S PATENT FIRE-ARMS MFG. CO. Est. 1856. Ill. catalog of military, sporting and defensive arms. Also Baxter steam engines, marine engines and universal printing presses, derringers, police revolvers, parts, tools, ammunition, etc. Large 4to., 36pp., fine ills., pict. wrap.

1898 Hartford, Conn.
------ Ill. catalog. Business library not available.

1900 Hartford, Conn.   CtHi
------ Colt's revolvers and rifles. New Army, New Navy, New Service, Pocket,

Police and Target. Bisley derringers, lightning magazine rifles, etc. 16mo., 16pp., fine ills. of above models.

1806 Wilmington, Del.   DeWint
DuPONT de NEMOURS, E.I. & CO. Riflemen Attention! GUNPOWDER of the first quality warrented superior to any Dutch or English imported, etc. Broadside. 8vo. Ptd. Wilmington by James Wilson.

c.1820 Wilmington, Del.   DeWint
------ DuPont's superior gunpowder, Eagle gunpowder for sportsmen, balls, flints and shot, etc. 1 column list. Broadside. 8vo.

1891-2 Wilmington, Del.
Ill. catalog. Compliments of . . . Powder and flasks, etc. 4to., 16pp. Ills. of flasks, accessories, etc.

1889 New York
FOLSOM, H.D. ARMS CO. Trade price list for August. 4to., 32pp., ills., wrap.

c.1900 Hartford, Conn.   CtHi
GATLING GUN CO. New model five barreled Gatling gun. 971 lbs. Broadside with ills.

1880 New York
GODFREY, CHARLES J. Trade price list for February. Ills. of the parlor rifle, chap air pistol, spencer rifles, revolvers: Veteran, Defender, Spy, American Princess, Patriot, etc. Fol., 8pp., fine ills.

1881 New York
------ Trade price list. Breech and muzzle loading shotguns, rifles and revolvers.

1884-87 New York
------ Ill. price lists.

c.1892 New York   MdTanSW
------ New England Arms Co. Ill. catalog
of shotguns, rifles, ammunition, powder,
traps, glass target balls, etc. Also sporting goods.

GREAT WESTERN GUN WORKS. See
Johnston.

1897 Worcester, Mass.
HARRINGTON & RICHARDSON ARMS CO.
Est. 1871. Ill. catalog of revolvers. 12mo.,
16pp., fine ills. of models, etc.

1891 New York
HARTLEY & GRAHAM. Ill. catalog of guns,
rifles, revolvers and ammunition. (Agents
for Union, Bridgeport and Remington -
flasks, decoys and equipment.) 4to., 114pp.,
a fine ref.

1891 New York
------ Ill. price list for September.

1891 New York
------ Ill. price list for November.

1890 Dayton, O.   NSbSM
HEIKES & McDONALD. 1st annual tourna-
ment - open to the world - prizes and
purses - rifles and targets. In essence an
ill. catalog of firearms, with ill. advts.

c.1900 Norwich, Conn.   CtHi
HOPKINS & ALLEN ARMS CO. Catalog #2.
Gun stocks, barrels, parts, etc. 8vo., 24pp.,
ills., pict. wrap.

nd. New York   OCl
HOWELL, WILLIAM P. Est. 1797. Ill.
catalog of arms and ammunition; also
pieces for exhibitions, targets, balloons.
16mo., 14pp., ills.

1870 Pittsburgh, Pa.   PKsL
JOHNSTON, J.H. Great Western Gun
Works. Est. 1865. Retail price list of
guns, rifles, etc. 12mo., 32pp., fine ills.,
pict. wrap.

1871 Pittsburgh, Pa.   PKsL
------ Ill. price list of firearms, parts and
ammunition.

1872 Pittsburgh, Pa.   PKsL
------ Ill. catalog of guns, rifles, etc.

1873 Pittsburgh, Pa.   MdBelW
------ 10th annual ill. catalog   PKsL
of firearms and sporting goods. 12mo.,
32pp.

1875 Pittsburgh, Pa.   PKsL
------ 12th annual ill. catalog of sporting
goods.

1877 Pittsburgh, Pa.   MoSHi
------ List #16. Catalog of guns,   PKsL
rifles, revolvers, ammunition and sporting
goods.

1878 Pittsburgh, Pa.   PKsL
------ Ill. price list #20. Firearms.
N.B. We have no office in Chicago, nor any
connection with that swindling concern the
Great Western Gun Works. Send 10¢ for
catalog. 8vo., 48pp., wrap.

1879 Pittsburgh, Pa.   MdBelW
------ List #24. PPi   PHi   PKsL
Wholesale ill. catalog of guns, rifles and
sporting goods. N.B. Correspondents
writing for information for their own benefit
and of no interest to anyone else, please en-
close a 3¢ stamp for answer - our time is
valuable; we simply ask you to pay postage.
8vo., 48pp., fine ills.

1881 Pittsburgh, Pa.   MdBelW
------ #27. Ill. catalog.

1881 Pittsburgh, Pa.   MdBelW
------ #28. Ill. catalog.

1882-3 Pittsburgh, Pa.   MdBelW
------ #32. Ill. catalog.

1884 Pittsburgh, Pa.   PKsL
------ #34. Reduced price list. Shotguns,
rifles, revolvers, ammunition, fishing tackle
and sporting goods. At lowest prices ever
offered to agents, clubs, postmasters and
dealers. One or a dozen. Sq. 8vo., 56pp.,
fine ills., pict. wrap.

1888 Pittsburgh, Pa.
------ Ill. catalog of firearms and sporting goods. Small 4to., 64pp., wrap.

1895 Pittsburgh, Pa.   MdBelW
------ Ill. catalog #46.

c.1875 New Haven   NNMM
KELLOGG, A.A. Ill. and desc. catalog of
guns, pistols and firearms. 4 lvs.

1881 Boston   KyU
LOVELL, JOHN P. & SONS. Est. 1840.
Ill. catalog of firearms - the Champion,
Excelsior - also agents for Parker, Davis
and Remington - ammunition and tackle.
4to., 100pp., fine ills., pict. wrap.

1888 Boston
LOVELL, JOHN P. ARMS CO. Ill. catalog
of sporting goods. 4to., 100pp., fine ills.,
pict. wrap.

c.1890 Boston   OC
------ Ill. catalog of firearms. 4to., 96pp.,
pict. wrap.

1892 Boston   MH-BA
------ Ill. catalog of sporting goods, firearms, bicycles, etc. 4to., 100pp.

1898 Boston   MH-BA
------ Ill. catalog of firearms, etc. 4to.,
180pp., wrap. A comprehensive ref.

1899 Boston   MH-BA
------ Everything the gunner wants. 4to.,
112pp. of ills., pict. wrap.

c.1879 Middlefield, Conn.   CtHi
LYMAN (WILLIAM) GUN SIGHT CORP.
Price list, desc. and letters endorsing
Lyman's patent gun sight. Also a rear sight
for sporting and target rifles. 16mo., 15pp.,
ills.

1884 Middlefield, Conn.   CtHi
------ Lyman's patent combination gun
sights. 12mo., 16pp., ills.

1894 Middlefield, Conn.   CtHi
Lyman's sights and rifles. Ill.
price list and desc. 16mo., 96pp., ills.,wrap.

nd. Middlefield, Conn.   CtHi
------ Ills. and test. letters of Lyman's
rifle and shotgun sights.

c.1897 Middlefield, Conn.   CtHi
------ Ill. price list of sights for all
rifles - Colt to Winchester - models 1873
to 1897. 96pp., wrap.

1891 New Haven   CtHi
MARLIN FIRE ARMS CO. Ill. catalog of
repeating rifles, new models, cartridges,
etc. 16mo., 8pp.

c.1900 New Haven   CtHi
------ Ill. price list of repeating rifles,
carbines, repeating muskets and shotguns -
Marlin's rust repeller, etc. 8vo., 120pp.,
fine ill. ref.

p.1900 New Haven   CtHi
------ Ill. catalogs available.

1872 Chicopee Falls
MASSACHUSETTS ARMS CO. Maynard's
patent breech-loading rifles, sporting rifles
and shotguns. 24mo., 10pp., ills.

c.1860 Chicopee Falls   MH-BA
MAYNARD ARMS CO. Ill. catalog of breech
loading and self priming rifles and shotguns.
8vo., 21pp.

1884 St. Louis   MoSHi
MEACHAM, E.C. ARMS CO. Price list
#319, Nov. 15. Ill's. of models of Baker,

Colt, Greener, Marlin, Remington, Spencer,
Scott, Sharps, Smith & Wesson, Flobert,
Stevens, Whitney and Winchester - shotguns,
rifles, revolvers, powder horns, parts, gun
tools, camping equipment, etc. 4to., 48pp.,
ill. throughout, pict. wrap.

1884 St. Louis   MoSHi
------ Ill. price list #322. Firearms to
decoys, handcuffs and roller skates. 36pp.

1851 St. Louis   MoSHi
MEAD, EDWARD. Mead's ill. catalog of
guns - also jewelry and novelties, with an
ill. treatise on the rifle. An 1851 American
gun catalog? Why not?

1863 New Haven
NEW HAVEN ARMS CO. Business library
not available. Catalog of the Henry rifle
with a diagram and test. 26pp.

1865 New Haven   CtHi
------ Henry's repeating rifle. 8vo., 45,
(2) pp., diagrams.

c.1876 Meriden, Conn.   CtHi
PARKER BROTHERS. Catalog of the
Parker breech-loading, double-barreled
shotgun, best and lowest priced in the world,
endorsed by leading sportsmen - paper or
metal shells, etc. 8vo., 34pp., fine ills.,
pict. wrap.

1881 West Meriden, Conn.   CtHi
------ Ill. catalog of Parker guns. 8vo.,
48pp., pict. title and wrap.

c.1890 Cincinnati   OC
PETERS CARTRIDGE CO. Price list of
Peters' cartridges for trap and field shoot-
ing. 16mo., 8pp., ill.

1874 Cincinnati   OCl
POWELL, P. & SON. Est. 1827. Ill. catalog of rifles, breech-loading shotguns,
improved Colt, Remington and Whitney firearms. 8vo., 50pp., fine ills.

1875 Cincinnati
------ Ill. catalog of firearms.

1876 Cincinnati   OCl
------ New catalog. Rifles for saloons,
picnics - the famous #21. Fine ills., wrap.

1878 Cincinnati   OCl
------ Annual catalog of muzzle and
breech-loading shotguns, etc. 12mo., 56pp.,
fine ills., pict. wrap.

1888 Cincinnati   OC
POWELL & CLEMENT. Late P. Powell &
Son. Catalog #59. Fall and winter sporting
goods. 4to., ills.

1889 Cincinnati   OC
------ Catalog #62. Spring and summer -
firearms, sporting goods, cutlery, skates,
ammunition, etc. 4to., 40pp., ills., wrap.

1890 Cincinnati   OC
------ Ill. catalog of sports-
mens' supplies in all departments, notes on
bargains and how to detect swindlers selling
poor sporting goods. Fine ref.

1866 Providence   RHi
PROVIDENCE TOOL CO. Ill. catalog of
Peabody breech-loading firearms. 8vo.,
12pp., fine ills., wrap.

1871 Providence   RHi
------ Peabody breech-loading firearms
for infantry, cavalry and sporting purposes.
4to., 32pp., swell ills., wrap.

nd. Providence   RHi
------ Peabody- Martini rifles - reprinted
partly from Gen. Norton's work - ills. of
guns and works. 4to., 52pp., ills., wrap.

1866 Ilion, N. Y.   MiDbF
REMINGTON (E. & SONS) ARMS CO.
Reduced price list for Jan. 8vo., 4pp., ills.

1870 Ilion, N. Y.   N
------ Remington's new patterns of firearms - 16 ills. of models - cane rifle, vest
pocket pistols, repeating rifles. N.B. In
these days of robbery and house breaking, etc.
Fol. broadside. A fine pict. record.

1875 Ilion, N. Y.   N
------ Ill. price list of revolving and repeating pistols and rifles, etc. 16mo.,
16pp., wrap.

1876 Ilion, N. Y.
------ Remington #3 revolver, 1875 model.
#1 folder, ills. and list of prices.

1878 Ilion, N. Y.   N
------ Ill. catalog of military, hunting,
target and sporting breech-loading rifles,
etc. 7th ed. Sq. 12mo., 92pp., pict. wrap.

1894 Ilion, N. Y.   N
------ See also Sporting Goods.

1875 St. Louis   MoSHi
RUDOLPH & CO. Ill. circular and price
list of fishing tackle, guns, revolvers and
rifles. 4to.

1895 Utica, N. Y.   MH-BA
SAVAGE REPEATING ARMS CO. Ill. catalog of military, sporting and target rifles
and carbines, smokeless powder, metallic
ammunition, metal jacket bullets, reloading
tools and sights. 8vo., 72pp., fine ills.,
wrap.

c.1900 Utica, N. Y.   MdTanSW
------ Ill. catalog of hammerless military
and sporting rifles, carbines, metallic
ammunition, reloading tools, sights, etc.
4to., 60pp., col. pict. wrap.

1874 New York   N
SCHOVERLING & DALY. Ill. catalog of
Charles Daly guns and revolvers, Martin's
vest pocket pistols, the OK, Never Miss and
Victor - J.C. Clabrough, Birmingham,
Adirondack, Wesson & Harrington - also
gunsmiths' implements, powder horns, game
bags, powder pouches, etc. 8vo., 95pp., ill.
throughout, pict. cl.

1864 New York   CtHi
SCHUYLER, HARTLEY & GRAHAM. Ill.
catalog of arms and military goods, regulations for uniforms of army, navy, marine
and revenue corps of U. S. Ills. of badges,
swords and appurtenances and small arms,
models from 1849 to date. Fol. 142 (6) pp.,
frs., fine ills. and col. pls. N.B. Raymond
L. J. Riling in his Guns and Shooting, A
Bibliography, believes this to be the first of
the large and elaborate American catalogs
in this field published in this country.

1876 Chicago   MiDbF
SHARP'S RIFLE CO. (E.E. Eaton, agent.)
Sharp's Creedmore rifle - Twenty five years
of use - best in the world! High scores, etc.
4to., 4pp., ills.

c.1865 Boston (?) & Hartford (?)   MH-BA
SPENCER REPEATING RIFLE CO. Catalog
of repeating rifles, sporting rifles, with
Civil War ref., test. 8vo., 28pp., ills.

1880 Springfield, Mass.
SMITH & WESSON. Superior Revolvers -
Excellence of workmanship, force, accuracy,
simplicity. Medals 1867, 1873 - Vienna,
Philadelphia. 8vo., 24pp. of fine tinted
lithos. by Major & Knapp, N. Y. Pls. of new
models, double action revolving rifle, fld.
plate, pocket pistols.

c.1880 Springfield, Mass.
------ 9x12 loose bd. tied catalog of pls.
of: New Model Army #3; Navy #3; 38 #2;
Double action; 32 #1-1/2 and 32 double
action - finest pls. engraved by John A.
Lowell, in any catalog in this field. No
text, no prices.

1883 Springfield, Mass.
------ Smith & Wesson Revolvers - for
March - models and reloading tools, etc.
Ill. folder.

1892 Springfield, Mass.
------ Single shot target pistols with
automatic shell extractor, rev. lock, adjustable sight. Ill. folder for Nov.

1899 Springfield, Mass.
------ Superior Revolvers - Military,
Pocket, Target. Large 8vo., 68pp., fine pls.
throughout. Models from 1880 to 1899 with
new action and pat. ammunition.

1890 New York   NHi
SQUIRES, HENRY C. Desc. price list and
catalog of Sportsmens' supplies, everything
for forest, field and stream - with ills. by
Beard, Shilde-Hassam, Gibson, Smedley and
Fred Remington. 4to., glt. dec. imm. vel.,
VIII and 164pp. One of the most outstanding
catalogs in the whole field of American advertising.

1898 Chicopee Falls, Mass.   MiDbF
STEVENS, J. ARMS & TOOL CO. Fine
single shot target and sporting rifles, sights,
pistols, parts, etc. 16mo., 80pp., swell ills.
Wrap.

1867-99
TRYON (EDWARD K.) BROTHERS. Guns,
revolvers, rifles, etc. See Sporting Goods.

1878 Boston   MH-BA
TURNER, G.W. & ROSS. Quarterly price
list for April. Colts, Smith & Wescons,
Winchesters - The Empress, Prairie Queen,
Mountain Eagle, etc. Large 8vo., 32pp.,
fine ills., wrap.

1879 Boston
------ Price list of firearms. 8vo., 32pp.,
ills., wrap.

nd. Torrington, Conn.   CtHi
UNION HARDWARE CO. Catalog # 1. Gun
implements and police goods. 16mo., 35pp.,
fine ills.

1875 Lowell, Mass.   MH-BA
UNITED STATES CARTRIDGE CO. &
WALLACE & SONS. Ill. catalog of rim and
central fire pistols and rifles, military cart
ridges, etc. 8vo., 48pp. plus 27pp. listings
by Wallace & Sons for Feb. Fine ill. record.
See also Wallace & Sons, Ansonia, Conn.

c.1883 New York   NNQ
VON LENGERKE & DETMOLD. Est. 1882.
Ill. catalog of guns, ammunition and sports-
mens' goods, gun club supplies, etc. Also
National American rules for trap shooting,
Old Long Island rules, Jersey City Heights,
etc. Large 4to., 24pp., fine ills., wrap.
See also Sporting Goods.

1887 New York   MH-BA
------ Ill. catalog of guns, ammunition,
etc. 4to., 28pp., fine ills.

1875 Ansonia, Conn.   CtHi
WALLACE & SONS. Est. 1848. See U. S.
Cartridge Co. - joint catalog. Wallace &
Sons, Machinery & Tools.

1900 St. Louis (East Alton, Ill.)   MoSHi
WESTERN CARTRIDGE CO. Factory at
East Alton. July price list of shotgun
ammunition. 16mo., 20pp., ills., wrap.

1873 New Haven   PKsL
WINCHESTER REPEATING ARMS CO. Now
a division of Olin Mathieson Chemical Corp.
First catalog issued 1863. Ill. catalog of
firearms. N.B. The Olin Mathieson
Chemical Corp. have a complete collection
from 1863 to date in their historical library.
The collection is not available for public
use, quite understandably, but reserved for
company business research.

nd. New Haven   CtHi
----- Metallic ammunition, paper and
brass shot shells, gun wads, primers, percussion caps, celebrated Winchester and
Hotchkiss repeating rifles. Broadside, fol.,
with fine ills.

1881 New Haven   CtHi
------ Rifles, cartridges, moulds, etc.
2,000,000 cartridges a day! Broadside, fol.,
with ills.

1881 New Haven   CtHi
------ Repeating firearms, rifled muskets,
carbines, hunting and target rifles, etc. and
Hotchkiss magazine firearms for military
and sporting use. 8vo., 48pp., fine ills.,
pict. wrap.

1886 New Haven   CtHi
------ Winchester repeating firearms,
single shot rifles, etc. 8vo., 76pp., fine
pict. record, pict. wrap. showing the works.
N.B. To Postmasters: Should this package
be misdirected, notify this company, we will
at once forward postage stamps required.

1888 New Haven   CtHi
------ Ill. catalog of rifles, muskets, carbines and cartridges, etc. 8vo., 78pp., fine
ills.

1894 New Haven   CtHi
------ Catalog #52. Ill. 8vo., 100pp.,
desc., wrap.

1896 New Haven   CtHi
------ Catalog #57. Ill. in great detail,
all products. 8vo., 128pp., fine ills. N.B.
One of the many catalogs from which a
guide to the quantities issued in the 19th
century -- if anyone ever finds time.
Many, as in this case, are keyed with or
near the printer's slug: 9/97/150M. What
has become of the other 149,999 copies of
this record?

p.1900 Both CtHi and Olin Mathieson have ill.
catalogs. Perhaps some day the latter will

FIREARMS

open its library to the public, or make arrangements to photostat material for research.

1893 Boston
WOOD, JOHN JR. Firearms. See Sporting Goods.

This chapter covers firearms, both military and sporting, but please be sure to search Sporting Goods. Cap pistols and toy guns will, of course, be found under Celebration, Decoration and Theatrical Goods and Toys.

Chapter 22

Fire Engines

The history of fire fighting is surely one of the most glamorous chapters in any Americana volume. If this has never occurred to you, read Kenneth H. Dunshee's As You Pass By, Hastings House, 1952, and then trot down to Maiden Lane and visit the Home Insurance Company's H.V. Smith Museum's library, or, if more convenient, any of the other locations listed from Boston to St. Louis. Here again private collectors have accumulated while public libraries have been hampered by financial support and inadequate staff problems.

This section includes a fine representative mass of material limited as far as possible to fire fighting equipment and supplies. From the hand pumps of c.1815 to the monster steamers of the Gay Nineties we hope you will find the identifying illustration you need.

c.1900 Cincinnati OC
AHRENS-FOX FIRE ENGINE CO. Est. 1868. Ill. catalog of modern steam fire engines, hoators and fire department supplies. 8vo., 64pp., fine ills.

p.1900 Cincinnati OC
------ Ill. catalogs for 1915 and c.1917.

1869 Boston MH-BA
AMERICAN CONSOLIDATED FIRE EXTINGUISHER CO. Catalog of new pat. fire engines. List of purchasers, tests. 12mo., 50pp., pict. wrap.

1892 Seneca Falls, N. Y. & Cincinnati, O.
AMERICAN FIRE ENGINE CO. OC
Inc. 1891. A consolidation of: Button Fire Engine Co., Waterford, N. Y., Ahrens Mfg. Co. of Cincinnati, O., Clapp & Jones Mfg. Co. of Hudson, N. Y., Silsby Mfg. Co. of Seneca Falls, N. Y. Ill. catalog of Ahrens, Button, Clapp & Jones, and Silsby steam fire engines, hand fire engines, pumps, carts, hose carriages, wagons and fire department supplies. 4to., 106pp. of fine ills., frs. plate of works, dec. cl. One of the best pict. records located today.

1893 Seneca Falls & Cincinnati TxDaDeG
------ To the public. OC
Exposition of 1893. Ill. catalog of steam fire engines, pumpers, hose carts, carriages, etc. 16mo., 24pp., fine ills., pict. wrap.

1902 Seneca Falls & Cincinnati OC
------ The Metropolitan fire engine. 8vo., 32pp., fine ills.

1903 Seneca Falls & Cincinnati OC
------ The Cosmopolitan steam fire engine especially adapted to use of villages, public institutions, private estates, warehouses and factories. 8vo., 24pp., ills.

1867 Boston MH-BA
AMERICAN FIRE EXTINGUISHER CO. A new pat. fire engine - the extinguisher portable, always ready. 8vo., 58pp., tests., ills.

c.1900 Elmira, N. Y. NNHome
AMERICAN La FRANCE FIRE ENGINE CO. Est. 1875 as the La France Fire Engine Co. The story of the chemical fire engine - a history and a catalog with fine ills. 64pp., pict. wrap.

p.1900 Catalogs still extant in private collections. See also La France Fire Engine Co.

1874 Manchester, N. H. MH-BA
AMOSKEAG MFG. CO. Est. 1859. First engine built in 1859. Ill. catalog of fire engines and hose carriages, with a list of engines and dates of mfg. from #1 to #503, the clients and when delivered! A great industrial record, and ill. at that. 8vo., 50pp. plus 16pp. of suggestions to engineers, etc. See also Manchester Locomotive Works.

1887 Boston DLC
BOSTON WOVEN HOSE CO. Catalog of fire department supplies with ills. of fire engines, hose, helmets, horns and other equipment. Sq. 8vo., 142pp., wrap.

1890 Boston OAkF
------ Ill. catalog of rubber hose for fire departments, belting, etc. 44pp.

1886 Troy, N. Y.   N
BOUGHTON, E.W. & CO. Headquarters for
firemens' uniforms, caps, helmets, etc.,
with a history of the Chas. Eddy Steamer Co.
and Troy Fire Department, 1808 to 1886.
24mo., 8pp., with pict. wrap. of steamer and
team in action and Mr. Boughton's emporium
in col. This really isn't a trade catalog, but
it's worth studying.

c.1876-7 New York   NNMM
CAIRNS & BROTHER. Successor to H. T.
Gratacap, est. 1836. Largest mfg. of firemens' equipment in U. S. A. Ill. circular -
Our aim is to . . . gold and red ills. of
helmets, fancy and derby style, crests, rims,
red shirts, belts, buckles, buttons, tasseis,
badges, lanterns, torches, etc. A wonderful
pict. record. 12mo., 24pp., pict. wrap.

c.1877 New York   NNMM
------ Ill. catalog of firemens' equipment.
12mo., 21 numbered pp., pict. wrap.

p.1900 New York   NNMM
------ Catalog #28. 1836 to 1935. Ill.,
desc. and priced catalog of firemens' equipment. 8vo., 36pp., fine ills., wrap. A careful study of two of these pict. records, side
by side at NNMM, will prove to the most
stubborn Americana collector that today's
news is tomorrow's history - and that trade
catalogs ARE Americana.

1878 Chicago   DLC
CASWELL FIRE DEPARTMENT SUPPLY
CO. Ill. catalog of fire apparatus of every
desc., fine ills. of engines, carts, hose,
uniforms and accessories. 8vo., 40pp., wrap.

1887 Hudson, N. Y.
CLAPP & JONES MFG. CO. Est. 1862. Ill.
catalog, new ed. In 25 years we have now
500 engines in use in 6 models and sizes,
for any community. Ills. of models by Moss
Eng. Co. of Boston. 4to., 16pp., pict. wrap.

c.1890 St. Louis   MoSHi
COONEY, P.J. CO. Ill. catalog of fire department equipment.

1853 Seneca Falls, N. Y.   NNHome
COWING & CO. Ill. catalog of pumps,
sleds, branding irons and garden fire
engines, etc. 8vo., 28pp., fine ills., pict.
wrap.

1868 Seneca Falls, N. Y.   MH-BA
------ Ill. catalog - abridgement #2 - of
fire engines, hydraulic rams, pumps, etc.
8vo., 68pp., wrap.

1887 Hartford, Conn.   NNHome
DOUGLAS, W. & B. Pumps. Ill. catalog of
pumps for fire apparatus, engines, etc.
318pp. with fine ills.

1883 Concord, N. H.   NhD
EASTMAN, SAMUEL & CO. Treatise on
fire hose, different weaves and mfg., quali-
ties, etc. 8vo., 32pp., wrap.

c.1895 New York   NNHome
FABRIC FIRE HOSE CO. Catalog of fire
apparatus, ills. of nozzles, valves, hose,
extinguishers, life belts, hose reels, carts,
bells, hats, horse collars and hames, etc.
8vo., 111pp., wrap.

1884 Chicago   MdTanSW
FIRE EXTINGUISHER CO.   PPL
Price list of the Harden Star Hand Grenades
with directions and desc. 16mo., 64pp., ill.,
wrap.

1895 New York   NNHome
GAMEWELL FIRE ALARM TELEGRAPH
CO. Ill. catalog of fire and police telegraph
boxes, alarms, patrol wagons, etc. 20pp.

1868 Lowell, Mass.
GATES, JOSIAH & SONS. Lowell Fire
Engine Hose Factory. Broadside -
9-1/2x12-1/2 - fine ill. of steam fire
engine, wire spoked wheels and firemen on
the double with a fine team of horses. All
kinds of fire hose of oak leather, fire
buckets, blunderbusses, couplings, etc.

c.1895 New York   NNHome
GLEASON & BAILEY. Ill. catalog #58 of
fire apparatus. Ills. of fire engines, hose
carts, extinguishers, etc. 44pp., a fine ref.

1881-2 Seneca Falls, N. Y.   PKsL
GOULD MFG. CO. Est. 1848. Ill. catalog
of pumps, hydraulic rams, water systems;
new model fire engines - Swan Neck Village,
Warehouse or Plantation piano styles, etc.
8vo., 240pp., fine ills., pict. wrap.

1885 Seneca Falls, N. Y.   ICHi
------ Ill. catalog of pumps for fire
engines and all purposes - engines, hose
carts, etc. 8vo., 264pp., pict. wrap.

1892 Seneca Falls, N. Y.   PKsL
------ Ill. catalog of pumps, hydraulic
machinery, rams, fire engines, etc. 300pp.,
ills., dec. cl.

1895-6 Seneca Falls   ICHi
------ Ill. catalog as above. 8vo., PKsL
356pp., dec. cl. See also B. S. Nichols,
Gould Steam Fire Engines.

1872 New York   NNHome
GUTTA PERCHA & RUBBER MFG. CO. A
circular desc. improved patent for carbon-
ized fire fighting hose for steam fire
engines. Price list of hose, couplings, etc.

1893 New York   NNMM
HAYWARD, S.F. & CO. Ill. and desc. catalog of fire apparatus and specialties. 86pp.,
fine ills., wrap.

c.1880 Philadelphia   NSbSM
HENDERSON & CO. Ill. and desc. catalog
of firemens' uniforms and equipment. 8vo.,
with fine ills. throughout.

1869 Lockport, N. Y.   MH-BA
HOLLY MFG. CO. Ill. catalog of fire protection machinery and equipment, and
water supplies for villages and cities. 3rd.
ed. 8vo., 32pp.

c.1845 Boston
HUNNEMAN, W.C. & CO. Est. 1792. Circular of pat. fire engines listing 3 sizes:
$800., $850. and $900., with equipment;
2 pipes, side lamps, 4 buckets, bell and 28
feet of hose each. Tests. dated 1841 to 1844.
Engraving of engine by Morse, Tuttle & Co.
More powerful than the N. Y. engines and
less cumbersome than Philadelphia models.
8x11, 4pp.

1887 New York   DSi
JACKSON, A.S. Ill. catalog and price list
of fire department supplies - ills. of hook
and ladder trucks, hose carts, etc. 8vo.,
32pp., pict. wrap.

1874 Boston   NNHome
JOHNSON'S MFG. CO. Johnson's pat.force
pumps as fire extinguishers. Ills. of . . .
in use at fires. 8vo., 20pp., wrap.

1891 Kansas City, Mo.   MoSHi
KANSAS CITY FIRE DEPARTMENT
SUPPLY CO., and HALE PATENT FIRE
HARNESS CO. Ill. catalog of Hale Water
Tower, Hale swinging harness, Hale automatic horse cover and halter strap, electric
wire cutters and nozzles. Ill. water tower
in action, complete uniforms and accessories. 8vo., 50pp. of ills., fld. plate, pict.
wrap.

1884 Elmira, N. Y.   NNHome
La FRANCE FIRE ENGINE CO. Est. 1875.
Ill. catalog showing La France's pat. rotary
steam fire engines in 6 sizes. 40pp., fine
ills. and fine job. Pict. wrap.

1895 Elmira, N. Y.   NNHome
------ Ill. catalog of piston steam fire
engines, rotary steam fire engines and
Haye's pat. aerial extension hook and ladder
trucks. 8vo., 70pp. See also American
La France Fire Engine Co.

1860 Cincinnati   OC
LATTA, A.B. & E. Built first successful
steam fire engine in U. S. for Cincinnati in
1852. See King's history. Ill. catalog of
steam fire engines and perhaps the first and

earliest American steam fire engine catalog
still preserved. 4to., 51pp. of ills., wrap.
N.B. As Latta sold out to Lane & Bodley in
1863, there were very few catalogs issued.

1868 LOWELL FIRE ENGINE HOSE
FACTORY. See Josiah Gates & Son.

1877 Manchester, N. H.   CSmH
MANCHESTER LOCOMOTIVE WORKS. Ill.
catalog of steam fire engines and fire fighting equipment - Amoskeag steamers, etc.
68pp. with full page pls.

1903 Manchester, N. H.
------ Catalog of Amoskeag Steam Fire
Engines and hose carriages. 8vo., 54pp.,
fine pls. of single and double steam in different sizes, two and four wheeled fancy
hose carriages. Pict. wrap.

MANNING, MAXWELL & MOORE. See
Hardware - Miscellaneous Machinery.

c.1815 Philadelphia   PKsL
MERRICK, S.V. & CO. Pat. Jacob Perkins.
Desc. of pat. improved fire engines and
other hydraulic machines mfg. by . . .
8pp. with 2 ills.

1875 New York   NNMM
MILLER, FRED J. Miller's ill. catalog of
fire apparatus and fire department supplies,
fine ills. of hook and ladders, engines, hose
carts, buckets, lanterns, uniforms, badges,
belts, horns, lamps, torches, etc. Even a
toy steam fire engine! 8vo., 64pp., pict.
wrap. A swell job.

1880 Boston   MiDbF
MITCHELL, A.W. & CO. Claims to be oldest mfg. of firemens' badges in U. S. I
cannot sustain the statement any more than
Montgomery Wards's. Ill. catalog of firemens' badges for hats, coats, chief to hose-
man, insignia, etc. Maine, Mass., R. I.,
Ill., Ga., New York, Colo., Ky., Del., Tenn.,
Va., etc. Badges mfg. 8vo., 18pp., pict.
wrap.

c.1900 Chicago & New York   NNNHome
NEW YORK BELTING & PACKING CO., LTD.
Fire department catalog #12, showing fire
apparatus of every desc. - hoses, engines,
carts, nozzles, uniforms, pumps, etc.
190pp., ill. throughout.

1878 Burlington, Vt.
NICHOLS, B.S. Probably an agent. The
Gould Steam Fire Engine. 8vo., 28pp., one
ill. of steam fire engine.

c.1900 Minneapolis   MnHi
NOTT, W.S. & CO. Ill. catalog of fire
department equipment. 8vo., 96pp., fine ref.

Concord, N. H.
PAGE BELTING CO. See Machinery,
Tools & Supplies.

PERKINS, JACOB - Patentee. See Merrick,
S. V. Mfg.

1868 Seneca Falls, N. Y.   NNHome
RUMSEY & CO. Est. 1840. Special ill.
catalog of life and force pumps, garden and
fire engines - #1 piano styles, etc. 8vo.,
20pp., fine ills., pict. wrap.

1880-81 Seneca Falls, N. Y.   MnHi
------ Desc. catalog and price list of
pumps, hydrants, rams, fire engines, hook
and ladders, bells, hose carts, hardware,
etc. Fine ill. ref.

1881-2 Seneca Falls
------ Ill. catalog of bells, engines, hose
carriages, pumps, equipment and hardware.
Large 8vo., 229pp., dec. cl.

1886 Seneca Falls   NSbSM
------ Ill. catalog and desc. price list of
pumps, hydrants, rams, models and styles
of new fire engines and fire department supplies. 8vo., 176pp., fine ill. ref. 46th ed.
Preface boasts of 46 years of experience.

RUMSEY & SIKEMEISER CO. See Hardware - Miscellaneous Machinery, etc.

1876 Seneca Falls, N. Y.
SILSBY MFG. CO. Est. 1845. Silsby rotary
steam fire engines mfg. at Island Works.
Fol. 4 page ill. pseudo catalog. Fine view of
plant, ills. of two steam fire engines and two
hose carriages. List of 500 engines now in
operation all over the U. S. A., with complete details of fire engines.

1885 Seneca Falls, N. Y.   TxDaDeG
------ Ill. catalog of Silsby steam fire en-
gines, hose carts and carriages, improved
Holly rotary pumps, Silsby heaters and all
fire department supplies. 4to., 90pp., fine
albertypes of engines by Forbes Co. of
Boston and Gies & Co., Litho. of Buffalo.
One of the best.

1858 New York   MH-BA
UNION INDIA RUBBER CO. Catalog . . .
also conducting hydrant engine and steam
hose, etc. See also Clothing.

nd. Philadelphia   PHi
WIRT & KNOX MFG. CO. Ill. catalog of
fire fighting equipment.

Be sure to check the cross references. In the sections devoted to Machinery and Supplies, Pumps,
and even General Hardware Goods, you will find many engines, hose carts and other products used
by the fire fighter. You may even find uniforms under Clothing, and parade decorations, badges,
etc. are listed under Celebration, Decoration and Theatrical Goods. Also it must be admitted that
many a hand pump and garden or village fire engine will be found among the more general Agricultural Implement and Seedsmens' catalogs from about 1830 to 1860. The best reference in this field
is William T. King's History of American Steam Fire Engines, Philadelphia, 1883.

Chapter 23

Food & Drink

A tea bag to the most ornate Gay Ninety soda water fountain might be a fairly complete analysis of this chapter. For years Soda Water held a separate file because of the library interest in the plates of these creations of American imagination, and whiskey and beer were scattered in confusion. At last soft drinks and food have come together, and that demon rum has teamed up with tobacco. The locations are far from complete as noted several times before, but this selected group should represent a good working collection in this primary department of life, liberty and the pursuit of happiness. From groceries offered by Abraham & Straus to canned meats and fancy foods offered by George Woodman & Co., one should be able by examining a few of these selected catalogs to catch a glimpse of our eating habits during the 19th century.

c.1900 Brooklyn, N. Y.   NNQ
ABRAHAM & STRAUSS. Ill. grocery catalog.

C.1885 Akron, O.   OHi
AKRON MILLING CO. What to buy and how
to use cereals by T. J. Murray. A colorful,
tempting - catalog? 16mo., with suggestions, col. ills., and col. pict. wrap.

c.1900 Boston & vp.   PShipL
AMERICAN SODA FOUN-   NHi   MiDbF
TAIN CO. American soda book of recipes
and suggestions. 100 formulas for installing
and operating fountains. Ills. of plain and
fancy fountains, counter glass and equipment,
etc. 8vo., 264pp., pict. cl.

1881 New York   MH-BA
AMERICAN SWISS MILK PROD-   OC
UCTS CO. Catalog of Dr. N. Gerber's celebrated milk foods, chocolate milk in powder
and new process condensed milks. Sm.8vo.,
32pp., handsome col. pict. wrap. of allegori-
cal representatives of America and Switzer-
land, and birdseye view of New York City
and Brooklyn Bridge. Chocolate milk in
1880?

1893 Chicago   DSi
ARMOUR & CO. Souvenir with sketches of
plants, glue factory and special packing
rooms, etc. 12mo. brochure, ills., col.
pict. wrap.

c.1880 Washington D. C.   KyBardBM
BARBOUR & HAMILTON. Est. 1850. Ill.
catalog of groceries and provisions - apples
to whiskey. Sq. 12mo., 14pp., glt. dec. wrap.

1872 Philadelphia   PHi
BLATCHLEY, CHARLES G. Blatchley's
ill. and desc. catalog of Tingley's horizontal
ice cream freezers and air tight oyster
buckets, etc. 8vo., 8pp., pict. wrap.

c.1886 Columbus, Ind.   In
CEREALINE CO. Ill. catalog of cerealine
flakes with 200 recipes from professional
cooks - 3rd ed. 8vo., 32pp., ills., pict.
wrap. See Gerald Carson's Cornflake
Crusade, N. Y. 1957, pp. 127 and 201. Dr.
Kellogg took such things very seriously.

c.1872 Madison, Ind.   NNMM
CHAPMAN, J.W. & CO. Ill., desc. and
priced portable soda fountains.

1854 Philadelphia   PHi
CLARKE, A.R. Catalog of choice teas, foreign fruits, groceries, segars and wines.
24mo., 14pp.

1861-2 Boston   MH-BA
CUMMINGS, A. Catalog of groceries at
retail. 16mo., 18pp., wrap.

c.1875 Cincinnati   OC
ERKENBRECHER, ANDREW. Price list of
various brands of starch for culinary,
laundry and mfg. purposes. 16mo., 6pp.
N.B. Erkenbrecher is known as father of
the Cincinnati zoo.

1900 Jersey City   NNU
FRANCO-AMERICAN CO. Col. ill.
brochure - Franco-American soups and
specialties. Sm. 4to. with col. pls. and col.
wrap.

c.1880 Lockport, N. Y.   MH-BA
FRANKLIN MILLS CO. Ill. brochure and
price list of entire wheat flour. 8vo., 12pp.

1882 Boston   NNMM
FREEMAN, K. & S.A. Fish Wharves. Price
list of mackerel. One leaf.

c.1870 San Francisco   CHi
GHIRARDELLI, DOMINGO. One leaf eagle
dec. advt. and price list of chocolates and
candies. Possibly this is a printer's proof.
The Ghirardelli chocolate name in San
Francisco is almost as important as
Hershey is in the U.S.A. CGi note.

1876 Glen Cove, N. Y.   NNQ
GLEN COVE STARCH MFG. CO. Prices
and recipes for cooking with Duryea's improved corn starch.

1864 New York   NHi
GREAT AMERICAN TEA CO. Price list of
teas - at their Large Marble Stores, in
original packages and 30 pound boxes. 4to.,
4pp., ills.

1876 New York   NHi
GREAT ATLANTIC & PACIFIC TEA CO.
Est. 1859. A & P Food Stores of today.
Centennial almanac, with lists of teas and
chromo premiums, and plans for the future.
12mo., ills., and pict. wrap.

1891-2 Boston   MH-BA
GREAT LONDON TEA CO. Price list and
premiums - teas, coffee, spices, extracts -
with premiums of dinner and tea sets,
silverware, etc. Club sales began in 1877.
8vo., 136pp., fully ill. with 4 col. ills.

1888 St. Louis   MoSHi
GREELY-BURNHAM GROCERY CO. A
brief history - on 50th anniversary. A catalog in essence, and a good trade ref.

1895 Philadelphia   PHi
HEINZ, H. J. CO. The spice of life -
visitors' view of the famous 57. 12mo., col.
ill., pict. wrap.

nd. Lowell, Mass.   NNMM
HOOD, C.I. & CO. A booklet of sarsaparil-
la - 8 lvs., pict. wrap. in flower format.

c.1891 Cincinnati   NHi
KINGERY MFG. CO. Est. 1876. Kingery's
crystal flake ice cream improving hokey-
pokey, automatic fountains, polar shavers,
star milk shake squeezer. 16mo., 27pp.,
delightful ills., wrap.

1899 Cincinnati   OC
------ To our patrons and the trade in
general - our 1899 catalog - ills. of steam
peanut roasters, corn poppers, hokey-pokey
machines, etc. 8vo., 32pp., pict. wrap.

1893 Oswego   NSyHi
KINGSFORD, T. & SON. Columbian souvenir -- Forbes lithos. of Indian maiden
feeding American eagle corn and 4 col. ills.
of T. Kingsford packages of finest starches,
etc. 16mo., 12pp., wrap. as above.

c.1890 New Britain   MoSHi
LANDERS, FRARY & CLARK. Catalog of
the universal bread mixer.

1890 San Francisco   CHi
LEBENBAUM BROTHERS. Ill. catalog for
May - teas and wines of the best quality,
domestic and imported. 8vo., 40pp., ills.,
pict. wrap.

c.1890 Philadelphia   MiDbF
LIPPINCOTT, CHARLES & CO.   PHi
Ill. catalog of apparatus for making and dispensing soda waters, fancy fountains, counter
glass and plated wares, etc. 8vo., 218pp.,
fine ills., pict. wrap. Fountains $150. to
$3000. Bathing beauties, icebergs and
fancy statuary.

c.1880 Manchester, N. H.   NhHi
MANCHESTER TEA CO. Price list for
general ref. 3rd year in business - promises lowest values and best service for cash.
16mo., 30pp., wrap.

1866 New York   OC
MATTHEWS, JOHN. Mfg. Ill. catalog of
Matthews' machines for making and dispensing soda water, new recipes, materials for
bottling, drawing, etc. 12mo., 19pp., price
list, wrap.

1867 New York   NNMM
------ Ill. and priced catalog of soda water
apparatus - ornate fountains and counter
ware, etc. 64pp., wrap.

1875 New York   CSf
------ Ill. catalog #1 of apparatus for cool-
ing and dispensing soda water and other
beverages. Fine ills. of glass bottles,
counter ware, fountains, etc. 4to., 112pp.,
pict. wrap.

1879 New York   OC
------ Ill. catalog of fountains and accessories for dispensing soda waters, sparkling
liquors, etc. The Avalanche, for example,
was made of 3 kinds of marble and 57 jewels,
measured 32x105x118 inches, dispensed 10
beverages and 24 sirups and cost $4000.
The Water Sprite Tumbler Washer was
adorned with 36 jewels - the works covered
with a crystal glass dome - $300. If you
are really interested you had better see a
copy. The locations are at your service
from coast to coast.

1897 St. Louis   MoSHi
MOLL, A. GROCER CO. Price list for 1897.

1859 Providence   RHi
NORTH AMERICAN EATING HOUSES. Est.
1856. Bill of Fare. A catalog of menus,
each facing a plate of an eating house or
restaurant, with an index. A fine record of
prices and eating houses for 1859. 4to.,
76pp., dec. cl.

c.1895 Portland, Ore.   OrU
NORTHROP & STURGIS CO. Mfg. Chemists. Portland Soda Works. Ill. price list
and catalog of Matthews' soda water fountains, apparatus, etc.

c.1880 New York & Paris   NHi
PARK & TILFORD. A catalog of ales,
wines, spices and condiments, with price
lists. 12mo., 68pp., pict. wrap.

1876 Philadelphia   PHi
PENNSYLVANIA SALT MFG. CO. Catalog
of bi-carbonates, etc. 16mo., 24pp., ills.,
col. pict. wrap.

1886-7 Boston   MH-BA
PIERCE, S.S. & CO. Est. 1831. Catalog
and price list of groceries, condiments,
liquors and wines, tobacco, etc. 8vo., 48pp.,
wrap.

1889-1900 Boston   KyBardBM
------ The Epicure. A monthly organ that
served as catalog for many years. The
Barton Museum has examples, and the
S.S. Pierce Co. has a good file. Ill. through-
out with pict. wrap.

1879 Boston   MBSPNEA
PUFFER, A.D. & SONS MFG. CO. Ill. catalog of Puffer's frigid soda and mineral
water apparatus, with fine ills. of fountains -
The Astor, Glaciate, Tower, Bonanza,
Vienna, etc., glassware, etc. 16mo., 144pp.,
pict. cl.

1890 Boston   NNMM
------ Advance circular of the frigid soda
water apparatus. 8 lvs., fine ills.

c.1890 Boston
------ Ill. catalog of frigid soda water
apparatus, fountains, etc. 4to., 307pp. of
swell ills., dec. cl.

1897 Cincinnati   OrU
PURE FOOD CO. Price list and premium
lists of teas, spices, extracts, baking powder
and soaps mail order dept. with fine ills.
24pp., wrap.

1897-8 Providence   RHi
ROSE, R.L. CO. Souvenir price list of
groceries and spices, fancy foods, etc. -
the best of everything. 8vo., 56pp., col.
pict. wrap.

1895 Philadelphia   PHi
SHOWELL & FRYER, LTD. Priced and ill.
catalog of imported groceries, spices, wines,
etc. 8vo., 88pp.

c.1830 Providence   MBSPNEA
SLEEPER'S TEA WAREHOUSE. Price list
of green teas, black teas. 16mo., 14pp.,
self-wrap.

1847 New York   NHi
TEA AT AUCTION. A 12 page catalog of
teas just received from ship Zenobia, with
prices written in margins.

1876 Boston
TUFTS, JAMES W. CO. Ill. and desc. cata-
log of Tufts Arctic Soda Water Apparatus.
Ills. of fountains as Texan, Rio Grande,
Golden Gate, etc., counter glass, etc. 4to.,
176pp., fine ills., cl.

1876 Boston   OC
------ Tuft's automatic crystal fountains.
8vo., 4pp., ills. Also offers child's tea sets
and centennial paper weights.

1877 Boston   NNMM
------ Ill. catalog. Fine ills. of   ICHi
equipment, delightful statuary fountains with
equally delightful names, counter glass, etc.
16mo., 48pp., pict. wrap.

1884 Boston   N
------ Ill. catalog of fountains, equipment,
glassware, furnishings and fancy ware. 4to.,
256pp. of fantastic ills., glt. pict. wrap.

1887 Boston   MdTanSW
------ Ill. catalog of fountains and furnishings. 4to., 32pp., fine ills., wrap.

c.1890 Boston   NHi
------ Apparatus book of directions with
ill. catalog of furnishings. 4to., 276pp.,
dec. cl.

c.1890 Boston   MH-BA
TUFTS, JAMES W. MFG. Fine Silver
Plated Ware. 12 page ill. brochure of table
ware, fancy dishes, shaving mugs and soda
fountain supplies. Other located catalogs
are mostly soda water fountains and equipment.

c.1892 Boston   NNMM
------ Ill. catalog supplement of arctic
soda fountain apparatus and furnishings.
302pp. and a complete job, pict. cl.

1864 Boston   MiDbF
WALKER, F.A. CO. Ill. catalog of Masser's
five-minute freezer, improved for home and
parlor. 16mo., 16pp., ills., wrap.

FOOD & DRINK

c.1880 Savannah, Ga.   GU
    WALTER, JAMES E. Ship Chandler and
Grocer. 24mo. booklet, listing stores-
groceries. Beef, pork, flour, potatoes, etc.
Ptd. wrap.

1892 Boston   PShipL
    WEEKS & POTTER CO. Useful information
and price list of soda waters and fountains,

also equipment. 12mo., 48pp., fine ills.,
pict wrap. See also Drugs & Pharmaceuticals.

1884 Philadelphia   PPL
    WOODMAN, GEORGE B. & CO. Price list
of sugar, coffee, tea, flour, canned meats
and fancy foods.

Don't neglect the wellknown grocery catalogs of Montgomery Ward & Co. and Sears Roebuck & Co. Some of the catalogs offering House Furnishings, in the kitchen department, also provide recipes and equipment that throw light on 19th century culinary enthusiasm. Then, too, under Alcohol and Tobacco, the S. S. Pierce offerings do include fancy foods and groceries. By following the index and using your head you ought to be able to get together a pretty good 19th century dinner.

154

Chapter 24

Furniture

To separate furniture from house furnishings may seem a ridiculous straw splitting proposition. This chapter includes everything from an acorn carved gentleman's chair to a walnut what-not. It also includes many well illustrated catalogs that offer apple parers and wall brackets, but the most important records lie in the designs and styles of pure furniture.

Unfortunately such lists as William Lawrence's offerings in 1833 are not illustrated, but after the Civil War you will find references that will lead you to a scattered collection of American furniture that should please the most exacting student and historian. Such catalogs as Morton Bank's even offer barbers' chairs as well as the usual line of marble top walnut creations and stenciled suites for grownups and children. If you will search and then follow the nearest location, you should be able to find a good description and contemporary illustration of everything from a stenciled Boston Rocker to a brass bedstead with both half and full canopy.

1883 Philadelphia   PPL
ALLEN, F. LOUIS. Ill. catalog of bric-a-brac, racks, tables, chairs, couches, etc. 16pp.

1873 New York   NNMM
AMERICAN DESK MFG. Kehr, Kellner & Co. Ill. catalog of furniture for home, bank and counting houses, desks, stools, etc. 16mo., 54pp., fine ills., pict. wrap.

1875 New York   NNMM
------ Ill. catalog of designs for writing desks, secretaries, tables, etc. 16mo., 36pp., pict. wrap.

1886 Chicago & New York   NNMM
ANDREWS, A.H. & CO. Ill. and desc. catalog of opera chairs. 26 lvs., fine ills.

1899 Baltimore   NNMM
BAGBY FURNITURE CO. Ill. catalog of furniture, mattresses, chairs, tables, etc. 8vo., 56pp., pict. wrap.

c.1900 Baltimore   NdTanSW
------ Ill. catalog of bureaus, hat racks, couches, church furniture and wicker chairs, etc. 8vo., 56pp., pict. wrap.

1878 Baltimore   NNMM
BANKS, MORTON C. Ill. catalog of chamber, parlor and dining room furniture - fine pls. of stenciled sets for children and grownups, piano stools, barbers' chairs, carved parlor suites in walnut, fancy marble topped stands, etc. Elegant! Fol., 130pp., fine pls., frs. of plant.

c.1890 New York   NNMM
BAUMANN, LUDWIG CO. Catalog of section 43 for complete house furnishers. Fine ills. 356pp., wrap.

BENT, SAMUEL S. & SON. Iron furniture - See Ornamental Ironwork.

c.1890 New York   NNMM
BHUMGARA, F.P. & CO. Ill. catalog of furniture for all rooms in the home, lanterns, etc. 12pp., wrap.

1886 New York   NNMM
BONNER & PAEPKE. New Ill. catalog of cribs and cradles with price list supplement. 16pp., wrap.

1884 Boston   MdTanSW
BOSTON FANCY CABINET CO. Ill. and priced catalog of towel racks, what-nots, hat trees, etc. 8vo., 28pp., wrap.

c.1887 New York   NNMM
BOWMAN, J.R. Ill. and desc. catalog of Bowman's scroll saw designs for brackets, what-nots and ornamental woodwork. 28pp., wrap.

c.1894 Cincinnati   NNMM
BROOKE, J.C. Ill., desc. and priced catalog of church and school furniture and accessories. 38pp., pict. wrap.

c.1873 Brooklyn, N. Y.   NNMM
BROOKLYN FURNITURE CO. Ill. catalog of furniture - chairs, stands, tables, beds, bureaus, sofas, etc. 8vo., 64pp., bds.

c.1890 Oshkosh, Wis.   MnHi
BUCKSTAFF-EDWARDS CO. Ill. catalog of
cane and wood seat chairs, plush and leather
upholstered, etc. 8vo., 170pp., fine ills.

1886 St. Louis   MoSHi
CARONDELET AVE. FURNITURE MFG.
CO. Ill. catalog of furniture.

c.1885 Baltimore   MdTanSW
CHIPMAN, GEORGE & SON. Ill. catalog of
chairs of all desc. - childrens' high chairs,
swivel chairs and stools, cane seats, upholstered, etc. 8vo., 140pp., ill. with each
page.

c.1880 Boston   NNMM
CLARK, CARROLL W. & CO. Ill. catalog
of furniture specialties, beds, elastic mattresses, desks, chairs, tables, etc. 8vo.,
32pp., pict. wrap.

c.1890 Cincinnati   OC
CLARKE BROTHERS & CO. Fol. broadside
with over 150 ills. of fancy cabinet ware,
brackets, what-nots, carved wall pockets,
checker tables, music stands, hat stands,etc.

nd. Westwood, N. J.   MdTanSW
COLLIGNON BROTHERS. Pat. & Mfg. Ill.
catalog of folding rockers, settees and
Stowe's canvas cots. 22pp., dec. wrap.

nd. Boston & New York   NNMM
COMINS, GEORGE T. MFG. Ill. catalog of
cradles. 24pp., wrap.

1880 Camden, N. J.   NNMM
CONNANT'S, F.H. SONS. Ill. catalog and
price list of chairs, rockers, stands, tables,
etc. 36pp., pict. wrap.

c.1875 New York   NNMM
COOGAN BROTHERS. Ill. catalog of parlor,
library and chamber furniture - rose and
grape carved walnut, marble topped tables,
parlor sets that make you squirm to look at
the ills. even. 8vo., 40pp., pict. wrap.
Street view of shop showing busy traffic, etc.

1875 New York & Canton, O.   ICU
COOGAN, JAMES J. Warehouse Canton, O.
Ill. catalog of parlor and chamber suites,
carpeting, spool beds $2., ladies' and gents'
chairs $7., carved walnut sets - 7 pieces
$25. 8vo., 32pp., pict. wrap.

c.1876 Philadelphia   MdTanSW
COOPER, JAMES W. & BROTHERS, MFG.
Ill. catalog and price list of fancy cabinet
ware, tables, jardinieres, stands, parlor
easels, music stands, wall pockets, racks,
etc. 60pp., pict. wrap.

1883 St. Louis   MoSHi
CRANE, J.H. CO. Ill. catalog of furniture.

nd. North Bennington, Vt.   NNMM
CUSHMAN, H.T. MFG. CO. Est. 1879. Ill.
catalog of mission furniture of many designs
decorative screens, etc. 62 lvs., wrap.

nd. Detroit   NNMM
DEINZER, F. & SON. Ill. catalog of upholstered furniture, mattresses, etc. 20pp.
dec. wrap.

c.1890 Boston   DeWE
DERBY & KILMER DESK CO. 16th ill. catalog of Derby's roll top desks and office
furniture. Sq. 12mo., 20pp., fine ills., pict.
wrap.

1893 Somerville, Mass.   MdTanSW
DERBY, KILMER & POND DESK CO. Successors to Derby & Kilmer Desk Co. 17th
ill. catalog of roll top desks, bank and office
furniture, typewriter desks, etc. 8vo., 36pp
Pict. wrap.

1889 Black River, N. Y.   MH-BA
DEXTER, H.C. CHAIR CO. Formerly
Dexter & Scott & Poor. Ill. catalog of fancy
plush and carpet upholstered rockers, etc.
8vo., 60pp.

1884 Baltimore   MdTanSW
EAGLE FURNITURE WORKS. D. Wilfson &
Son. Ill. catalog of walnut and poplar
chamber suites, buffets, wardrobes, beds,
stands, tables, desks, etc. 24pp. and price
list.

1897 Milford, N. H.   PBS
EMERSON & SON. 8th annual catalog -
housekeeping outfits - beds, chairs, buffets
for parlor, bedroom and bath. 7x10, 64pp.
of ills. of bargains, wrap.

1874 Cincinnati   OC
EXCELSIOR SCHOOL FURNITURE MFG.
CO. Ill. catalog of school, office and church
furniture, school apparatus and supplies, etc
8vo., 86pp., pict. wrap.

c.1898 Boston   MdTanSW
FRENCH, WILLIAM C. Mfg. Ill. catalog of
hardwood cottage and French bedsteads,
patent bow cradles, folding cribs, etc. 8vo.,
37pp., pict. wrap.

1884 New York   MdTanSW
GARDNER & CO. Ill. catalog of patented
veneer seats, chairs, settees, lodge chairs,
railroad station settees, etc. with price list.
68pp.

c.1860 Boston   NNMM
GEAR, A.S. & J. & CO. Broadside 32x46
with fifty odd woodcuts of designs of furniture for home, school, office and railroad
car - and the machines to make them.

c.1900 Grand Ledge, Mich.   NNMM
GRAND LEDGE CHAIR CO. Ill. catalog of
chairs. 80pp. N.B. Several p.1900 ill.
catalogs of chairs, desks, beds, tables, etc.
also available to 1907.

1886 Richmond, Ind.   In
GRANT, GEORGE H. & SWAIN. Richmond
Church Furniture Co. To pastors and
church building committees - ill. catalog of
chairs, pews, pulpits, settees, tables, etc.
Sq. 8vo., 32pp., wrap.

c.1870 Philadelphia   PKsL
HALE & KILBURN MFG. CO. Ill. catalog of
Champion folding beds and cribs, Hale's
flexible bed springs, chairs, mirrors, rocking and tilting chairs, settees, etc. Folding
beds $33. up. 64mo., ill. fld.

1870 Boston   DLC
HASKELL, WILLIAM O. & SON. Ill. catalog
of the Boston school furniture mfg. Ills. of
furniture and supplies, apparatus, etc. 8vo.,
101pp., fr. plate.

1891 Williamsport, Pa.   NNMM
HEILMAN, A.H. & CO. Ill. catalog and
price list of chamber furniture, chiffoniers,
bedside tables, stands, etc. 33pp., pict.
wrap.

c.1880 Buffalo, N. Y.   NNMM
HERSEE & CO. Est. 1836. Fol. circular
with 21 ills. of sideboards, mirrors, tables
with marble tops $4. extra, stands, etc.

1883-4 Gardner, Mass.   NNMM
HEYWOOD BROTHERS & CO. Ill. catalog
of cane, rattan and reed furniture, chairs,
childrens' wagons and carriages, etc.

1886 Gardner, Mass.   OHi
------ Ill. catalog of rattan and reed
furniture, childrens' carriages with cockle
shell designs and fringe on top. Sq. 8vo.,
96pp., pict. wrap.

1893 Gardner, Mass.   NNMM
------ Ill. catalog. 144pp. N.B. Later
ill. catalogs also available at NNMM.

1893 New York   DLC
HEYWOOD, WALTER CHAIR CO. Ill. catalog for Sept. Stenciled rockers, childrens'
high and low, Gem folding carriage and
chair, etc. Large 4to., 92pp. of pls. with
16pp. price list. Pict. wrap.

1874 Indianapolis   In
HIGGINS FURNITURE MFG. CO. Ill. catalog of Higgin's bent wood school furniture.
8vo., 32pp., pict. wrap.

c.1895 New York   NNMM
HOSKINS & SEWELL. Ill. catalog of brass
and iron bedsteads. 16pp., pict. wrap. in
shape of flag.

1874 Philadelphia   PKsL
HUTCHINS & MABBETT. (Agents) Ill. catalog of Gardner patent chairs and seats for
railroad cars, stations, offices and libraries,
nursing and sewing rockers, settees, swivel
chairs and stools, childrens' desks, etc.
12mo., 16pp. of ills. One shows seats in
Central RR. of N. J.

1868 New York   NNMM
JOHNSON, NATHANIEL. Ill. catalog of
school furniture. 24pp., pict. wrap.

1883 New York   PKsL
JORDAN & MORIARTY. Ill. catalog of
furniture and carpets, parlor and bedroom
suites, cribs, sofas, carved walnut and
marble tops, etc. 8vo., 36pp., delightful pict.
wrap.

c.1885 New York   NNMM
------ Ill. catalog. 32pp., pict. wrap.

1886 New York   PU
------ Ill. catalog of furniture in all depts
8vo., 36pp., pict. wrap.

nd. Chicago   ICHi
KANE, THOMAS & CO. Ill. circular of
revolving desks, combination bookcases,
secretaries, desks for ladies or lawyers in
cabinet, Gothic or cylinder designs of ash,
cherry, maple, mahogany and walnut - solid
or veneered. 4to., 4pp.

c.1884 New York   NNMM
KELLNER, JOHN A. Ill. catalog of desks,
writing desks, tables, secretaries, etc.
24pp., wrap.

1876 Boston   NNMM
KIMBALL, J. WAYLAND. Book of designs,
furniture and drapery drawings with price
list appended. 29pp. of text with 27pls., cl.

1889 Denver   CoD
KINDEL, GEORGE J. Bedding House. Ill.
catalog of box spring mattresses, brass and
iron bedsteads, etc.

c.1865 Philadelphia   PKsL
KNELL, GEORGE. Ill. catalog of upholstered
furniture, 21 woodcuts of physicians' chairs,
parlor sofas, beds, lounges, chairs in the
Spanish, Victorian, Antoinette, shield and
medallion designs, Spanish smoking chair!
etc. 8vo., 24pp.

1883-4 West Gardner, Mass.   MdTanSW
KNOWLTON, A. & H.C., MFG. Ill. catalog
of cane and wood seat chairs, high chairs,

Boston rockers, stenciled arm and side
chairs, etc. 38pp. plus price list.

nd. New York   NNMM
KOHN, JACOB & JOSEF. Depot for U. S. A.
Ill. catalog of massive bent wood furniture.

1876 Chicago   ICHi
KRAUSE, F.W. Ill. catalog of patent Gothic
chairs, 16pp. of designs, etc. Librarian's
comment:- ugly and would break your back
in ten minutes.

c.1880 Laconia, N. H.   NNMM
LACONIA FURNITURE CO. Ill. catalog of
Rickert's perfect soft center bed lounges -
various designs. 8vo., 38pp., pict. wrap.

1876 New York   NNMM
LAMB, J. & R. Ill., desc. and priced catalog of ecclesiastical furnishings. 56pp.

1886 New York   NNMM
------ Ill. catalog of church furniture. 72pp.

1878-95 St. Louis   MoSHi
LAMMERT, MARTIN. After 1890 Lammert
Furniture Co. Ill. catalogs of furniture for
parlor, bedroom and bath, kitchen, club, etc.
1878 8vo.,   160pp., pict. wrap.
1882 8vo.,   298pp., wrap.
1894 Large 4to.,   204pp., wrap.
1895 Large 4to.,   176pp., wrap.
A fine ref. collection.

c.1833 Portsmouth, N. H.   MWA
LAWRENCE, WILLIAM E. Furniture Warehouse. Ill. broadside with swan woodcut -
list for sale:- Feathers - French, Russian,
Sicilian, birds', ducks', sea fowl, common,
southern, northern live geese, etc., ticking,
webbing, sacking, tassels, fringes, beds and
furniture. Ptd. T.H. Miller.

c.1880 Pittsburg (sic) Pa.   PBS
McLEAN, W.B. MFG. CO. Est. 1878. Ill.
catalog of designs, couches, lounges, etc.
12mo., 20pp. of pls., wrap., ptd. in script.

c.1880 Pittsburg (sic) Pa.   PBS
------ Catalog of pls. of designs - 26pp.
with 3 extra pls., pict. wrap. Couch #52.

c.1880 New York   NNMM
MANHATTAN RECLINING CHAIR CO. Ill.
catalog of patent foot rest reclining chairs,
reclining lounges and couches, and specialties in parlor furniture, the Morris chair.
4to., 12pp., fine ills., wrap.

1884 Marietta, O.   MdTanSW
MARIETTA CHAIR CO. Mfg. Ill. catalog
of cane and wood seat chairs, stands,
tables, bedsteads, kitchen safes - tin pan-
elled. 98pp. and price list.

1886 Montoursville, Pa.   NNMM
MONTOURSVILLE MFG. CO., LTD. Ill.
catalog and price list of wood furniture
designs and styles - in ash, imitation mahogany
and walnut. 25pp., pict. wrap.

1880 Philadelphia   NNMM
MOYER, TUFTS & CO. Ill. catalog of beds
with price list. 24pp., pict. wrap.

c.1900 Detroit   NNMM
MURPHY CHAIR CO. 35th annual ill. catalog of chairs. 184pp., wrap. This is really
1907 but I didn't want to leave the famous
Mr. Murphy out.

1884 Grand Rapids, Mich.   MdTanSW
NELSON, MATTER & CO., MFG. Ill. catalog of furniture - bedroom suites, sideboards,
hall racks, furnishings, etc. 24pp., plus
price list, wrap.

1906 Grand Rapids, Mich.   NNMM
------ Ill. catalog. 47th annual. 158pp.
of fine ills. - for comparison.

1874 New Haven   CtHi
NEW HAVEN FOLDING CHAIR CO. Est.
1863. Ill. price list of childrens' carriages,
baby furniture, etc. 8vo., 4pp.

1880 New Haven   CtHi
------ Ill. price list of folding chairs for
invalids. 8vo., 16pp., pict. wrap.

1884 New Haven   CtHi
------ Ill. price list of folding chairs, etc.
8vo., 24pp., pict. wrap.

1885 New Haven   CtHi
------ Ill. catalog of folding chairs for
invalids, etc. 8vo., 86pp., pict. wrap.

c.1880 Boston   NNMM
OSGOOD & WHITNEY. Ill. catalog of furniture, carpets, crockery, ranges, chamber
suites, painted and stenciled platform rockers, grained sets, oriental sofas, ladies,
gents and students' chairs, etc. with ice
boxes and ranges, etc. to boot. Tall 4to.,
48pp., pict. wrap.

c.1878 Boston   NNMM
PAINE'S FURNITURE MFG. CO. Ill. and
priced catalog of furniture designs. 27pp.

c.1880 Boston   NNMM
------ Ill. catalog of walnut suites in Gothic
and Roman styles, etc. 16mo., 28pp., pict.
wrap.

1885 Boston   N
------ Ill. catalog of mfg. and imported
furniture, upholstery and decorations. 12mo.,
356pp., pict. wrap.

1893 Boston   MdTanSW
------ Ill. catalog of furniture NNMM
for home, bank and office, parlor bedroom
and bath. 16mo., 288pp., fine ills., fine ref.

c.1890 Meriden, Conn.   CtHi
PARKER, CHARLES CO. Ill. catalog of
piano and organ benches, stools, etc. 8vo.,
36pp., pict. wrap.

1876 Brooklyn, N. Y.   NNMM
PEARSON, A. Ill. catalog of black walnut
suites, Turkish suites, and furniture for
dining room, bedroom and study. 8vo., 32pp.
Wrap.

c.1900 Glendale, L. I., N. Y.   NNMM
PRAIRIE GRASS FURNITURE CO., INC. Ill.
catalog of Crex grass furniture for parlor,
porch and lawn, etc. 78pp.

1883 Detroit   NNMM
RAYL, T.B. & CO. Ill. price list of artificial and natural wood ornaments, carved
panels, handles and finials for sideboards,
bureaus, desks, secretaries, etc.

nd. Chicago   MnHi
REVELL, ALEXANDER H. & CO. Ill. catalog of desks, chairs, high desks, tables,
stools, etc. for offices.

c.1884 Boston   MdTanSW
ROBINSON, C.H. & CO. Ill. catalog and
price list of the Good Luck Parlor Mantel
Bed. Fol. folder to 24mo., 20pp., fine ills.

1890 Boston   ICU
------ Everything to furnish a home. Ill.
catalog of parlor suites in walnut and mahogany, furniture designs, and everything including hand painted Gone With The Wind Lamps.
8vo., 192pp., pict. wrap.

1892 Rockford   NNMM
ROCKFORD CO-OPERATIVE FURNITURE
CO. Ill. catalog of furniture designs for
every room in the home. 4to., 30 plus 40pp.
Fine ills., pict. wrap.

nd. Rockford   NNMM
ROCKFORD UNION FURNITURE CO. Ill.
catalog of furniture. 40pp.

1884 Boston   NNMM
ROSS, TURNER & CO. Ill. and priced catalog of hammocks, fancy and plain, with
attachments. 22pp., pict. wrap.

1889 Chicago   MH-BA
SALTER & BILEK, Mfg. Ill. catalog of
fancy music stands, cabinets, desks, tables,
clock shelves, what-nots, towel racks and
brackets. 4to., 48pp.

1893 Piqua, O.   OHi
SANITAL MATTRESS CO. Ill. brochure
about Sanital mattresses and operations of
company. 12mo., 32pp., ills.

1871 New York   NNMM
SCHERMERHORN, J.W. Ill. catalog ICHi
of school materials - desks, bells, clocks,
globes and general furniture. 8vo., 160pp.,
wrap.

1873 Chicago   NNMM
SENG, W. & CO. Spring price list of bed
lounges and upholstered furniture. 8vo.,
8pp., ills.

1880 Boston   NNMM
SHAW, APPLIN & CO. Ill. catalog of lodge
furniture. 10 lvs., wrap.

1888 Jamestown, N. Y.   NNMM
SHEARMAN BROS. LOUNGE FACTORY &
UPHOLSTERY WORKS. Ill. and desc. catalog of lounges and chairs with price list supplement. 34pp., pict. wrap.

1890-91 Sheboygan   NNMM
SHEBOYGAN CHAIR CO. Ill. catalog of
chairs of all designs and styles of the period.
166pp., cl.

nd. Grand Rapids, Mich.   NNMM
SLIGH FURNITURE CO. Ill. catalog of
furniture for the bedroom, styles for any
home. 95pp., wrap.

1883 Boston   MiDbF
SMALL, S.C. & CO. Ill. catalog of fine furniture, opening April 9. 8vo., 8pp., pict.
wrap.

c.1890 Boston   MiDbF
------ Ill. catalog of Paine's artistic furniture, etc. 16mo., 48pp., pict. wrap.

1882 St. Louis   MoSHi
SMITH-DAVIS MFG. CO. Ill. catalog of
spring beds, woven wire mattresses, wire
and canvas cots, and iron bedsteads.

c.1865 New York   NNMM
STEIN, ALEXANDER. Mfg. Ill. catalog of
fine parlor furniture.

1875 Chicago   NNMM
SUGG & BEIERSDORF FURNITURE MFG.
CO. Ill. catalog and price list of styles -
spool beds, fancy base walnut marble top
tables, heavy carved bedsteads, chairs,
stands, etc. Lithos. by Chas. Shober. Sq.
8vo., 70pp., pict. wrap.

1886 Hartford, Conn.   CtHi
TAFT CO. Ill. catalog of natural and artificial wood carved ornaments for furniture.
8vo., 24pp., fine ills., pict. wrap.

1887 Hartford, Conn.   CtHi
------ Ill. catalog. 8vo., 30pp.

1886 New York   NNMM
TEEPE, J. CHARLES. Ill. catalog of plain
and fancy hardwood woodenware and cabinet
work for furniture and furnishings. 48pp.,
wrap.

c.1884 Boston   MdTanSW
TUCKER MFG. CO. Ill. price list of mantel
and wardrobe beds.

1892 Mottville, N. Y.   NNMM
UNION CHAIR WORKS. F.A. Sinclair, Prop.
Ill. catalog of chairs, rockers, sewing and
childs', tables, etc. 8vo., 20pp., pict. wrap.
of Bill Nye on Rockers.

1886 Albany, N. Y.   N
UNION SCHOOL FURNITURE CO. Ill. catalog of school furniture and furnishings.

c.1870 Mt. Lebanon, N. Y.   MiDbF
UNITED SOCIETY OF SHAKERS. Ill. circu-
lar of chair designs with prices in pencil.
(R.M. Wagan, agent.) 5-1/2x10, 7 ills.

1874 Mt. Lebanon, N. Y.   MHarvFM
------ Ill. catalog and price list of Shaker
chairs, foot benches, floor mats, etc.
16mo., 29pp., frs. of factory, several ills.,
hand col. Ptd. Albany.

1876 Mt. Lebanon, N. Y.   NOCSM
------ Ill. catalog of furniture.   N
16mo., 32pp., wrap.

1876 Mt. Lebanon, N. Y.   NNMM
------ Ill. catalog and price list of chairs,
foot benches, mats, etc. 33pp., plus 4 lvs.,
wrap.

1876 Mt. Lebanon, N. Y.   NNMM
------ Centennial catalog of chairs and
furniture. 38pp., wrap.

N.B. For further data check:
MacLean, J.P. A Bibliography of Shaker
        Literature. Columbus, O. 1905
Andrews, E.D. New York State Museum
        Handbook #15. The Community
        Industries of the Shakers. 1933

Both of these works list important furniture,
house furnishings and seed catalogs in detail.

Locations of large Shaker collections that
might also provide examples of these records,
when recognized and properly cataloged are:
CtY, DLC, MWiW, NhD, NN and OHi.

1878 Boston   MdTanSW
WAKEFIELD RATTAN CO. Price list of
reed and rattan chairs and tables for all
rooms and all purposes. 24mo., 24pp., pict.
wrap.

c.1890 Boston   NNMM
------ Ill. catalog for Chicago and San
Francisco agents. 77pp., wrap.

nd. Boston   MH-BA
------ Ill. catalog. 4to., 96pp., wrap.

WAYNE, J.L. & SONS. See Hardware -
General Goods for furniture ornaments and
trimmings.

1877 Chicago   NNMM
WENTER, F. Ill. catalog of brackets, carved
tables, stands and shelves. 8vo., 36pp.
pict. wrap. See also Hardware.

1889 New York   MoSHi
WILD, H.L. Ill. catalog of scroll saw designs for fine and fancy furniture.

c.1894 New York   MdTanSW
WILLARD MIRROR & FRAME MFG. CO.
Ill. catalog of Willard's patent cloak and
clothing triplicate mirrors, looking glasses,
cloak and clothing racks, hangers, fancy hat
trees for bar and hallway. 12mo., 12pp.,
pict. wrap.

1886 Williamsport, Pa.   NNMM
WILLIAMSPORT FURNITURE MFG. CO.
Ill. catalog of ash, cherry, maple, antique
oak, oak, imitation mahogany and walnut
furniture, finished and in the white, with
MANKEY patent stencil decorations for
parlor, bedroom and kitchen. Fol., 36
numbered lvs. of pls., pict. wrap., also
price list of chamber furniture for July.
22pp., wrap. - and price list for Jan. 1887.

1892 Baltimore   MdTanSW
WILSON & HECHINGER.   NNMM
Ill. catalog of chairs in the best manner, all
styles and designs. 80pp., wrap.

As suggested, house Furnishings' offerings include many catalogs of bureaus, chairs and tables,
literally buried among masses of butter churns and washing machines; in these cases the churns,
crockery and ranges are in the majority. Use the Hardware chapter too where you will find catalogs
of cabinetmakers' goods with illustrations of the furniture to which they are necessary conveniences.

Chapter 25

Glassware

Conferences and correspondence with librarians of outstanding collections would seem to indicate that American glass manufacturers issued very few catalogs before 1860, or, IF they did, printed only very small editions for their best customers. Whatever the reason, these records have not been preserved. Jobbers' and merchants' catalogs have been included, and references added from other fields for their glass illustrations.

In using this chapter, please bear in mind the many occupations and trades to which glass production was, and still is, indispensable. The reference you are hunting may be in the chapters on Barbers' Supplies, Drug and Pharmaceutical Sundries, Household Utensils, Lamps and Lighting, and even on Silverware, for as you know, many fancy silver pieces held the best of American glass containers. Though the index is fairly complete, don't forget that some of the best Gay Ninety glass novelties were illustrated only in Sears, Roebuck, Montgomery Ward, Butler Brothers and other general merchandise catalogs.

1894 Hulton, Pa.   PKsL
AGNEW, THE CO., LTD. Flint Glass
Bottle Mfg. Ill. catalog and prices current
of bottles and flasks in different styles of
finish for various purposes. 16mo., 38pp.,
glt. ptd. wrap.

ATWOOD. See Drugs.

1880 Baltimore   N
BAKER BROTHERS & CO. Est. 1790.
Baltimore Glass Works. Ill. catalog of
bottles, plain and fancy, ink to tooth powder
and including glass target balls for sportsmen. 12mo., 60pp., pict. cl.

c.1870 Pittsburgh, Pa.
BAKEWELL, PEARS & CO. Folded in 1884.
Catalog of plates. 4-1/2x9-1/2, glt. ptd. cl.
2 fld. lithos. by Armor, Feurhake & Co. 49
numbered pls. This catalog is in a private
library. For reprints of patterns, etc. see
Ruth Webb Lee.

c.1880 New York   NNMM
BASSETT, GEORGE F. & CO. Ill. catalog
of china, crockery, glassware and kerosene
goods. 130pp., fine ills., wrap.

c.1890 np. Probably Bellaire, O.   WvWO
BEAUMONT GLASS CO. Ill. catalog of
glassware.

c.1860-70 Sandwich, Mass.   MSaHi
BOSTON & SANDWICH GLASS CO. List of
wares - tableware, fancy pieces, bottles,
vases, epergnes - in plain and ornate patterns, ale mug to wine glass. 16mo., 68pp.,
referring to ill. catalog, pls. 1 to 80.

c.1865 Boston   MiDbF
BRIGGS, RICHARD. Est. 1798.   DLC
Catalog of articles for sale by . . . This
corner has been occupied for the sale of
glass and chinaware for upwards of 70 years.
Austrian and Bohemian glass, fancy and student lamps, tableware of the finest. 32mo.,
32pp., ptd. wrap.

BROOKLYN FLINT GLASS WORKS. Taken
over by Amory Houghton in 1864, moved to
Corning, N. Y. and became the Corning
Glass Works in 1875. Unfortunately, no
catalogs located.

c.1875 Philadelphia   PKsL
BURNHAM, CHARLES & CO., Mfg. Ill.
price list of Banker's patent boxed demijohns, faucet safety containers for alcohol,
jugs for general stores and druggists. Pats.
1862-1873. 24mo., 8pp. with 5 ills., tests.,
wrap.

c.1900 Philadelphia   PPL
CALDWELL, J.E. & CO. Ill. catalog with 5
pls. of types and styles of cut glass, bowls,
pitchers, etc.

1881 Wheeling   WvWO
CENTRAL GLASS CO. Ill. catalog of flint
glassware.

1866 Pittsburgh   PKsL
CHAMBERS, A. & D.H. Pittsburgh Glass
Works. Est. 1843. Prices current of drug-
gists' glassware, black bottles, demijohns
and window glass, flasks - Pike's Peak and
Union patterns. 24mo., 30pp. Oct. 1, wrap.

1872 Pittsburgh, Pa.   PKsL
------ Prices current - railroad coach and
car glass, sky-lights, gas lamps, flasks,
soda bottles, etc. 40pp.

DYOTT, T.W. Dyottsville Glass Works.
See Drugs.

nd. Morgantown, West Va.   NCornC
ECONOMY TUMBLER CO. Catalog#14 -
tumblers and general glassware. Fol., fine
ills., wrap.

1881 Pawtucket   NNMM
ELLIS, A.L. & CO. Circular, price list and
sizes for glass eyes, separate lvs. for each
with ill.

nd. New York   NNMM
FALCK, OTTO F. STAINED GLASS WORKS.
Ill. catalog of stained glass for many uses.
12 col. pls., wrap.

1870 St. Louis   MdTanSW
FILLEY, CHAUNCEY I. Catalog of imported glassware, Queensware, coal oil lamps,
chandeliers, looking glasses, fruit jars, etc.
40pp.

1884-5 New York   NCornC
FITZPATRICK, J. & CO. Price list of window and picture glass. Sept. 1884 - 16mo.,
8pp., ills. Aug. 1885 - 12pp. plus 16 pls. of
designs in red and black.

FOSTER-MUNGER CO. Stained glass win-
windows. See Architectural Building
Materials.

1899 Moundsville, West Va.   WvWO
FOSTORIA GLASS CO. Catalog #1. DLC
Ill. catalog of flint glassware and decorated
lamps. 4to., 16pp., col. pls.

c.1900 Moundsville, West Va.   NCornC
------ Ill. catalog - apparently also #1 -
table glassware and novelties. 4to., 123pp.
with many fine pls.

c.1900 Moundsville, W. Va.   DLC
------ Catalog #2. Lamps for the season.
40pp., fine pls., wrap.

c.1901 Moundsville, West Va.   DLC
------ Ill. catalog #3 of fine decorated
lamps, price list with 3 ill. circulars.

nd. Philadelphia   PHi
FOX, HENRY C. Flint Glass Mfg. Ill. catalog of blank stock for decoration.

FOX, RULTZ & CO. See Drugs.

FRENCH, W.A. & CO. Windows. See
Architectural Building Materials.

1886 Philadelphia   PHi
GILLINDER & SONS. Revised ill. catalog of
Franklin window glass for railroad cars,
coaches, picture, etc. For July - designs
for stained glass windows, etc. 16mo., 32pp.
Wrap.

c.1890 Philadelphia   NCornC
------ Ill. catalog of glassware for illumi-
nating purposes. #12. 4to., 48pp., fine ills.
of lighting fixtures.

1873-74 Cincinnati   OC
GLENNY, WILLIAM & CO. Est. 1851.
Prices of American window glass, also
English and French. Enameled, cut and
col. for churches, etc. 1 page circular.

GLEASON, E.P. See Lighting.

c.1880 Philadelphia   PKsL
HERO GLASS WORKS. Ill. catalog of the
Hero Glass Works. Gem self-sealing butter, fruit and oyster jars, coffee and tea
jars, lightning Gem beer bottle fastener,
eagle designs, etc. 8vo., 8pp., pict. wrap.
of plant and works.

1898 New York   NCornC
HIGGINS & SEITER. See also   NNMM
China and Pottery. Catalog #9. Ill. 8vo.
with 220pp. of ills. and some col. pls. of
stemware, cordials, wines, whiskey sets,
silver mounted bottles and tableware of the
finest and fanciest.

1899-1901 New York
------ See China and Pottery.

1868 Boston & New York   NNMM
HILLS, TURNER & HARMON. Price list of
French and German window glass set at
meeting of agents in New York.

1883 Philadelphia   NNMM
HIRES & CO. Revised ill. price list of window and picture glass, etc. 40pp., wrap.

1880 New York   NCornC
HOGG & PATTERSON.   ICHi NNMM
Ill. catalog of plain and decorated opal goods
for Aug. 1. Col. pls. of lamp shades, bowls,
cones, chimneys, domes, globes, smoke
bells, etc. Tall. 4to., dec. bds., - without
any question one of the best col. pl. records
of American glass of the 19th century. 55
lvs., 47 pls. of which 29 are in col.

1874 New York   NCornC
HOLBROOK, E.F. & BROTHERS. Ill. catalog of ornamental glass for railway cars,
dwellings and churches. Imported French
windows - railway, picture, polished and
rough plate glass. 4to., 2 and 29pls., cl.

1883 New York   MnHi
------ Ill. price list of French picture
glass for all purposes, enameled glass, etc.

1898 Alton, Ill.   MoSHi
ILLINOIS GLASS CO. Ill. catalog of bottles
and containers of every type for every purpose - ink, perfume, liquor, flasks, displays,
window vases, col. labeled bottles, etc. Sq.
8vo., 174pp., dec. lea.

nd. Bellaire, O.   NNMM
IMPERIAL GLASS CO. Ill. catalog #200.
Iridescent novelties, crystal table lines and
other staple ware. 150pp., wrap.

JACKSON. See Drugs.

c.1900 Follansbee, West Va.   WvWO
JEFFERSON GLASS CO. Ill. catalog of
glassware.

c.1900 Zanesville, O.   OT
KEARNS-GORSUCH BOTTLE CO. Ill. catalog of packers' ware, machine made and
hand blown bottles - St. Nicholas, Albion
and Dayton jars, etc. 12mo., 104pp., pict.
wrap.

1876 Zanesville, O.   OHi
KEARNS, HERDMAN & GORSUCH. Zanesville City Glass Works. Prices current of
druggists' green glassware, black bottle
ware, demijohns, flint vials, window glass,
flasks in Eagle and Union Pocket ovals,
Gothic, Octagon and square salts, etc.
24mo., 40pp., glt. dec. wrap.

1870 Pittsburgh, Pa.   NCornC
KING, SON & CO. Cascade Glass Works.
Ill. catalog of crystal glassware, tableware,
blue and white ring jars, bar ware, patent
candy jars, preserve and jelly jars, etc.
26pp. with fine pls., wrap.

c.1880 New York   NNMM
LAMB, J. & R. Ill. catalog of artistic
stained glass, ecclesiatican and domestic,
col. pls. 16pp. plus 4 lvs., wrap.

LAMPS, lanterns, chimneys, globes, street
lights, chandeliers, signs, etc. See Lighting.

c.1888 Boston   NCornC
LIBBEY, W.L. & SON. New England Glass
Works. Ill. catalog and price list of blown
and rich glassware. 4to., 16 fine pls.

LOVELL, F.H. CO. See Lighting.

nd. Pittsburgh, Pa.   MdTanSW
MACBETH-EVANS GLASS CO. Founded
1869 at Charleroi, Pa. Ill. catalog #38 -
Glassware for gas and electric fixtures,
globes, reflectors, shades, etc. 12mo.,
128pp., fine pls., cl.

nd. Pittsburgh, Pa.   NCornC
------ Export catalog #103.   PKsL
Glassware for lighting fixtures, chimneys,
globes, etc. 8vo., 34pp.

1897 Pittsburgh, Pa.   PKsL
MACBETH, GEORGE A. & CO. The Way
Out of All Lamp Chimney Troubles. Ill.
catalog of different styles of chimneys.
24mo., 40pp.

1901 Pittsburgh, Pa.   PKsL
------ Price list #11. Macbeth pearl
glass and pearl top lamp glasses. 16mo.,
12pp.

c.1890 Chicago   NNMM
McCULLY & MILES. Ill. catalog of stained
glass for church and public and private
buildings, and for decorators. Tall 4to.,
24pp., with col. pls. by Shober & Carqueville,
dec. wrap.

1868 Pittsburgh, Pa. & Pittsburgh Haven
McKEE & BROTHERS. Prices of   NhD
glassware for April 1868. 24mo., 16pp.,
fine ills. Ptd. Pittsburgh Haven.

c.1900 Jeannette, Pa.   NCornC
McKEE GLASS CO. General catalog #G 23.
Ills. of pressed tableware, tumblers, stemware and fine cut glass. Sm. fol., 92pp. of
ills.

19-- Jeannette, Pa.   NCornC
------ Ill. catalog of pressed tumblers,
beer mugs, stemware, bar novelties. Fol.,
112pp. of pls.

1876-1885 McKESSON & ROBBINS. Fine ill.
catalogs of glassware. See Drugs for complete listings.

c.1890 Honesdale, Pa.   NNMM
MAPLE CITY GLASS CO. Ill. catalog #10 -
cut glass tableware, patterns Devonshire,
Rosamond, Falkirk, Newport, Martini, etc.
Tall 4to., 48pp., wrap.

1886 New York   NCornC
MATTHEWS, JOHN. Ill. catalog of
Matthews' decorative glass and transparent
signs - executed by Tighlman sandblast and
other patent processes. 8vo., 48pp. of fine
ills.

1889 St. Louis   WU-Ph
MEYER BROTHERS DRUG CO. Est. 1852.
Annual catalog, ills. and col. pls. of soda
fountains, counter glassware, bottles, vases,
shaving mugs, jars and cigar lighters.
8vo., 816pp., fine ills., pict. cl.

1884 St. Louis   MoSHi
MILLER & STEPHENSON. Ill. catalog #5 -
glass and china wares.

MORRIS, THEO. W. & CO. See Schancks.

c.1885 New Bedford   NCornC
MT. WASHINGTON GLASS CO. Ill. catalog
of chandeliers, crystal gas fixtures, brackets
and hall lights, cut tableware, lamps and
shades, vases, globes and art glassware.
Fol., 22 fine pls. of chandeliers for church,
home, hotel, theatre, etc., cl. $50. to $350.

1854 Philadelphia   PHi
MOWBRAY, W. & CO. Plain and ornamental
stained glass. 8vo., 24pp., fine ills.

c.1880 Boston   NNMM
NEW ENGLAND GLASS WORKS. W. L.
Libbey & Son. See also Libbey. Ill. catalog
of blown and rich cut glass. 12 fine photo.
pls. showing 138 patterns. Albertype -
Forbes & Co. A swell job. Fol. 1/2 lea.
and cl. 2 copies located in private libraries.

1872 Ottawa, Ill.   IHi
OTTAWA GLASS CO. (J. Alston, agent,
Chicago.) Catalog of glass for windows,
store fronts, railroad cars, skylights, show
cases, etc. 24mo., 34pp., dec. wrap.

1880 New Bedford   MiDbF
PAIRPOINT MFG. CO. Ill. catalog #17.
Glass containers in finest plated silverware,
tea sets, water sets, covered dishes, bowls,
fancy glass novelties, cake baskets, nut dishes,
cribbage boards, epergnes, etc. Large 4to.,
56pp., excellent pls., wrap.

1886 New Bedford   NHi
------ Ill. catalog and price list of castor
sets, cake dishes, bottles, paper weights,
glass fireman's horn. 4to., 144pp., wrap.

PALMER, FULLER & CO. Colored glass
windows. See Architectural Building
Materials.

c.1860 Brooklyn, N.Y.   NNMM
PARDESSUS, S.J., Mfg. Ill. catalog of glass
shades, globes for fancy clocks, scales, wax
flowers and stuffed birds, fluted, silvered,
enameled reflectors, etc. 16mo., 28pp., one
of the earliest catalogs in this field.

1873-1900 Philadelphia & New York   NNMM
MSaE   MiDbF   MdTanSW   PKsL
CBaK   PLACC   NCornC   DSi
NNNAM   WU-Ph   PPL
PHOENIX FLINT GLASS WORKS at Schet-
terville, N. J. and GREEN GLASS WORKS at
Millville, N. J. A remarkable collection of
catalogs well located in twelve scattered re-
positories. Since many of these have
recently been located in a check list of
pharmaceutical catalogs in the American
Journal of Pharmacy - Vol. 131, Jan. 1959 -
I feel it is reasonable to place the complete

list in the Chapter of Drug and Pharmaceutical Catalogs. They do however represent
to the student a fine glass research library.

PITTSBURGH GLASS WORKS. See Chambers.

c.1901 Pittsburgh, Pa.   NNMM
PITTSBURGH PLATE GLASS CO.   PKsL
Catalog A - glass, paints, oils and painters'
sundries, col. pls. of shades, globes of all
styles. 12mo., 254pp. plus 16 lvs., dec. cl.

PLUNKETT, F. & CO. See Wheeling Flint
Glass Works.

QUEEN, JAMES W. See Optical and Scientific Instruments.

QUINLAN, JEREMIAH. See Drugs and
Pharmaceuticals.

1889 New York
REED GLASS CO. Price list of French,
beveled and plain looking glass pls., etc.
16mo., 64pp., wrap.

1875 New York   NNMM
RUSSELL, HENRY & CO. 20th semi-annual
circular of table glassware, chandeliers,
kerosene lamps and brackets. 8pp., ills.

1884 New York   NCornC
RUSSELL & NATHAN. Ill. cata-   NNMM
log #11 - hanging and table lamps, handy
painted shades, pattern glassware, political
plates and novelty glass. 4to., 20pp., ills.

1878 New York   NNMM
SCHANCK'S GLASS DEPOT. Est. 1837.
Theo. W. Morris & Co., successors to
Morris, Delano & Co., D. S. Schanck's Sons
and Schanck & Downing. Catalog, 1837-1878
polished plate glass, French, English and
American window glass, crystal and rough
plate, enameled, colored and ornamental.
24mo., 8pp., wrap.

SCHIEFFELIN, W.H. Est. 1794. See Drugs.
Catalogs - 1876 to 1883.

1884 Philadelphia   NCornC
SHOEMAKER, BENJAMIN H. Philadelphia
Depot of French Plate Glass. Price list of
plain and beveled silvered plates for August.
16mo., 39pp.

SNEATH GLASS CO. See Lighting Chapter.

SOMMERS, G. & CO. See Department
Stores. Fine ill. ref. for pattern glass and
glass novelties from 1882 on.

STUTTS, GEORGE O. See Drugs.

nd. New York   NCornC
SUTPHEN & MYER. Price list of polished
plate glass, beveled and plain looking glass
plates. 16mo., 64pp., wrap.

c.1888 Baltimore   NCornC
SWINDELL BROTHERS. Price list of
Baltimore window glass and bottles. 16pls.
of designs and patterns. Tall 24mo., 40pp.,
plus. pls.

TARRANT & CO. Est. 1834. See Drugs.
1880 and 1882.

1893 New York   MdTanSW
TIFFANY GLASS & DECORATING CO.
Exhibit at World's Fair, Chicago with appendix of Tiffany windows and where they may
be seen. 8vo., 32pp., fine ills.

1896 New York   MdTanSW
------ Ill. catalog of Tiffany Favrile Glass.
3pp. plus 6 photo. ills., 16mo., plus chron.
hist. of glass.

1896 New York   NNMM
------ Ill. catalog of Favrile   BeBa
Glass made under supervision of Mr. Louis
Tiffany. History of . . . 2nd ed. Sq.
16mo., text and 8 fine pls., pict. wrap.

1899 New York   NCornC
------ Tiffany Favrile Glass - relation to
other glass, use in decorative arts, vases
for collectors, wedding presents, etc. Sq.
16mo., 28pp. plus 10 fine tinted pls., 5th ed.,
dec. wrap.

c.1875 Somerville, Mass.   NNMM
UNION FLINT GLASS CO. Founded 1851.
Amory Houghton sold his interest in 1864,
continued under Julian de Cordova until 1924.
Ill. catalog of kerosene lamps, fixtures, etc.
38pls. showing patterns: Boston Beauty,
Rose, New York, Gem, Baltimore, Lomax,
Pillar, - Table lamps - Vienna, Arizona,
Utah, Grant, Canada, Sprig, Trenton - peg
lamps, Troy-smoke bells, cones, globes,
shades and reflectors. 4to., 38pls., price
list wrap.

c.1900 Somerville, Mass.   NCornC
------ Ill. catalog of blanks - 260 pls. of
shapes, designs, styles in baskets, bowls,
bottles, vases, etc. Fol., looseleaf lea.,
excellent pls.

1902 Somerville, Mass.   MStOSV
------ Ill. catalog of vases, bowls and all
styles of blanks for decorating.

c.1891-5 Pittsburgh, Pa.   NCornC
UNITED STATES GLASS CO.   NNMM
Founded Tiffin, O., 1891. Subsidiary com-

panies: Columbia Glass Co., Gillinger &
Sons, O'Hara Glass Co. and Ripley & Co.
Ill. catalog of glassware - pressed tumblers
and beer mugs, etc. Fol., 36pp.

nd. Pittsburgh, Pa.   NNMM
------ Ill. catalog of glassware of factories
J, M, N, R and subsidiaries; also factories
F, G, H, K, L, P. Pat. dates from 1873 to
1890. Fine pict. ref. N.B. NNMM also
has catalogs #106, 107, 109 and 111 after
1900.

VAN DUZER, S.R. See Drugs - 1883.

VAN SCHAACK, PETER. See Drugs.

1877 New York   MH-BA
WALKER GLASS IMPORTING, SILVERING
& MFG. CO. Ill. catalog of looking glass
plates and crystal mirrors. 8vo., 16pp.

1872 Philadelphia   PHi
WAMPOLE, HENRY K. & CO. Ill. catalog
of druggists' glassware, fancy glass for
railroad cars, bottles, candy jars, church
windows and even mere lamp chimneys.
8vo., 50pp., wrap. See also Drugs.

1837 Wheeling   WvWO
WHEELING FLINT GLASS WORKS.
F. Plunkett & Co. Price current of glass-
ware mfg. by . . . at their glass works at
Wheeling. Broadside ptd. Oct. 12, 1837.
The earliest list of American glass recorded
to date.

c.1900 Brooklyn, N. Y.
WILLIAMSBURGH FLINT GLASS CO. Ill.
catalog of flint and colored glass, lamp
chimneys, plain and etched, hand lamps in
Polka, Tulip, opalescent twist, etc., candy
jars, fish bowls, etc. 24mo., 52pp., fine
ills., dec. wrap.

1872 Pittsburgh, Pa.   MnHi
WOLFF, HOWARD & CO. Prices current of
druggists' and window glass. Ills. of glassware. 16mo., 46pp., pict. wrap.

ZANESVILLE. See Kearns.

1872 Philadelphia   PHi
ZIEGLER & SMITH. Prices current for
glass. September.

1873 Philadelphia   PHi
------ Circular of revised price list with
ills.

1874 Philadelphia   PHi
------ Prices current of glassware.
March.

Chapter 26

Hardware—Builders' Hardware
& General Hardware Goods

In 1800 Samuel Broome's catalog of hardware in broadside form offered barlow, panknives and other sorts of knives, jews harps, H & L hinges, flatware, horse whips and half hunters, razors, scissors, curling tongs, snuffers, buckles and even watches. In 1838 William H. Carr's catalog of American Manufactured Hardware included literally everything from an adze to a window spring. In between this A and W, for comparison, we find blacksmiths' bellows, cutlery, hollow ware, hoes, kettles, locks, mills, presses, rifles, soaps, tomahawks, and vises. These goods are listed with their sixty odd American makers. In 1859 Mr. Adams published a clothbound catalog with fine illustrations covering the alphabet from apple parers to warming pans. I believe that these three examples outline the contents of this chapter.

In other words this section of the guide attempts to cover hardware goods rather than machinery and tools, though of course many small hand tools and a few of the early labor saving devices are represented as well. I realize the conflict with not only other hardware catalogs but with House Furnishings. My advice is to use all three Hardware chapters. If you start with a manufacturer's name or a product that has generally been considered hardware since 1800, you should be able to find the necessary date and illustration to fit.

1859 New York - Nueva-York
ADAMS, JOSEPH H. Jose H. Catalago Illustrado de Ferreteria Americana, Herramientas, Maquinas Y Otros Articulos. Ill. catalog of American hardware and many other articles. 8vo., 296 and X pp., plus supplement of 292 and IV pp., with from one to a dozen ills. to each page, cl. Ptd. Nueva York, S. Hallet.

N.B. The most outstanding American illustrated trade catalog of the 1850 to 1860 decade, and an excellent example, by comparison to Wm. H. Carr's 1838 offering, of the development and progress in the field during the twenty years between them. If you could put them side by side, and study them item by item, you might be surprised to find that the only real difference was in the printing presses that produced them! Mr. Adams has very little more to offer in American hardware than Mr. Carr, except perhaps the new square seated flush, and a few other creations, but the illustrations make one realize the truth of the old Chinese proverb. This copy is gold stamped J. I. De Cordova, and Mr. Adams has written on the title page - for Mr. Cordova's own private use. JHA.

1879 New York   MH-BA
AIKMAN, JAMES & CO. Catalog of tinware, brass, copper, iron and britannia goods. 8vo., 128pp., fine ills., wrap.

c.1882 Boston   MBSPNEA
ALARM BELL DOOR KNOB CO. Burglars, Tramps and Entry Thieves - every bell knob warranted - $2. to $3., installation 25¢. Circular, one leaf, 3 ills.

c.1894 Boston   NNMM
ALLEN & LOTTS. Catalog #10 - ills. of cabinet hardware, brass goods, clock ornaments, claw and ball feet for furniture, bureau brasses - designs George Washington, Eagle, bee hive, lion, etc. Sm.4to., 100pp. of ills. A fine ref.

1810 Boston   MWA
ALLEN, ANDREW J. A catalog of account books, cutlery, fancy goods, notions and novelties. 8vo., 8pp., woodcut on title.

1886 Waterbury, Conn.   NNMM
AMERICAN RING CO. Ill. catalog of drop handles, drawer pulls, desk knobs and cabinetmakers' supplies with supplement #3. Fine ills., cl.

1887 Waterbury, Conn.   NNMM
------ Ill. catalog with supplement #4.

1889 Waterbury, Conn.   NNMM
------ Ill. catalog of handles, etc. 89 numbered pp., fine ills., cl.

1883 Providence   PPF
AMERICAN SCREW CO. Catalog   RHi
and price list, ill. throughout, many labels
in full colors, fine job. 4to., 124pp., glt.
pict. wrap.

1892 Providence   RHi
------ Ill. catalog of screws and boxes
with labels, etc.

1887 Chicago   MnHi
ANDREW BROS. & CO. Catalog of wares.

1897 Hartford, Conn.   CtHi
ARMS POCKET BOOK CO. Price list of
specialties, fancy leather goods, novelties,
etc. 8vo., 12pp., ills., wrap.

1884 Winchendon   MnHi
BACKUS, I.S. Catalog of patent combination
portable cabinets, cabinet hardware, etc.

BARKER, ROSE & GRAY. See House Furnishings.

c.1895 Philadelphia   PKsL
BERGER, L.D. BROTHERS, MFG. Ill. catalog of hardware, stove hardware, tinners'
and plumbers' supplies.

1900 Philadelphia   PKsL
------ Ill. catalog of hardware, supplies
for plumbers and tinsmiths, including roofing ornaments and weathervanes.

N.B. PKsL also has later issues to 1918.
See also Tinsmith's Tools.

1884 Chicago   MnHi
BLAIR, WILLIAM & CO. Wholesale prices
current for hardware, tinners' stock, etc.

1884 Brooklyn, N.Y.   NNQ
BOHANNAN, WILSON. Catalog of drawer
and combination locks, patent catches, etc.

1882 Chicago   MnHi
BOOTH, JOHN. Ill. catalog of iron and
wire goods.

1865 Branford, Conn.   CtHi
BRANFORD LOCK WORKS. Revised price
list for June. Ill. catalog of builders' hardware. 4to., 4pp.

1869 Branford, Conn.   CtHi
------ Ill. catalog of locks, knobs, keys,
escutcheons, etc. Fine ills. and plate of
works. 4to., 154pp., cl.

1886 Branford, Conn.   Ct
------ Ill. catalog of 443 ill. pages, cl.

nd. Boston   NNMM
BRICKMAN, ALBERT H. Ill. catalog of
distinctive furniture hardware, fireplace
equipment, etc. 44pp., fine ref., wrap.

c.1895 Bridgeport, Conn.   MH-BA
BRIDGEPORT CHAIN CO. Est.1887. Catalog #9 - wire and flat metal chains, saddlery and shelf hardware, metal stamping
and fastener goods. 8vo., 40pp., fine ills.

1885 Brooklyn, N.Y.   NNQ
BROOKLYN WIRE NAIL CO. Ill. catalog of
nails, tacks, screws, etc. Revised prices.
16mo., wrap.

c.1800 New York   NjR
BROOME, SAMUEL & CO. Samuel Broome
& Co. have the following goods on reasonable
terms: dry goods, cinnamon, nutmegs, hose,
knives - panknives, barlow and other sorts -
H & L hinges, jews harps, latches, handles,
necklaces, horse whips and half hunters,
carpenters' tools, powder and shot, flatware,
etc. Broadside - 8-1/2x13, 3 columns of
goods - hardware predominates.

1882 San Francisco   MH-BA
CALIFORNIA WIRE WORKS. Ill. catalog of
wire and wire goods, useful and ornamental.
12mo., 172pp., cl.

1885 San Francisco   MH-BA
------ Ill. catalog of all kinds of wire,
rope, garden, lawn and ornamental wire
work, traps, cages, etc. 84pp., cl.

p.1900 Canton, O.   NNMM
CANTON CUTLERY CO. Ill. catalog of designs of knives and cutlery. Listed for the
fine pls., even though c.1910.

1878 Philadelphia   MH-BA
CARR, CRAWLEY & DEVLIN. Philadelphia
Hardware & Malleable Iron Works. Ill.
catalog of all kinds of hardware - hinges to
dish pan handles, and drawer pulls to
carriage steps. 4to., 264pp., cl. A fine
pict. ref.

1899 Philadelphia   PHi
CENTRAL HARDWARE CO. Ill. catalog and
price list of all manner of hardware. 8vo.,
24pp.

1817   MWA
CHARLESTOWN IRON & STEEL STORE.
See Wyman.

c.1895 Chicago   ICHi
CHICAGO HARDWARE MFG. CO. Catalog
#6 - Price list of high grade hardware for
all purposes, trades, etc. Sm. 4to., 240pp.,
fine ills., cl. and mor.

1830 Cincinnati   NNMM
CINCINNATI CABINET-MAKERS. Book of
prices covering the manufacture of cabinetmakers' hardware. pp.1 - 108, bds.
N.B. This book is actually not a catalog of
goods and products but since it controls the
prices of manufacture it might be very handy
to have located to use in conjunction with an
unpriced broadside list of this same date.

1888 New York   NNMM
CLAFLIN, GEORGE W. & CO. Our Man on
the Road Representative. An ill. catalog of
guns, toys, novelties and general store merchandise, firearms to watches, but mostly
hardware. 8vo., ills., wrap.

1882 Windsor Locks   CtHi
CLARK, GEORGE P. Catalog and price list
of pat. rubber rolls, wheels, castors, trucks,
etc. 24mo., 24pp., fine ills., wrap.

1883 St. Paul, Minn.   MnHi
COLBERT, HILL & CO. Ill. catalog of
wooden and willow ware, cordage, paper bags,
axle grease, brooms, etc. 8vo., 92pp., fine
ills., wrap.

1895 New Britain   NNMM
CORBIN, P. & F. Ill. catalog of Hardware
mfg. by . . . A complete encyclopaedia of
American hardware of the Gay Ninety period.
4to., 678pp. plus supplement #1, 112pp., cl.

1895 New Britain   MnU
------ Ill. catalog of   DSi   ICU
hardware. 678pp. plus supplements, 122
and 129pp. as above.

1859 Albany, N. Y.   MH-BA
CORNING, ERASTUS & CO. Catalog of
domestic and imported hardware - nails,
rivets, spikes, etc. 16mo., 54pp., annotated.

nd. Philadelphia   PHi
CRAWFORD CO. Ill. catalog of adjustable
steel pipe hangers, hanger parts and other
forged specialties.

nd. Philadelphia   PHi
De ARMOND & CO. Catalog #59 - Upholstery goods, cabinet hardware, oval tube
track accessories, etc.

nd. Montgomery, Pa.   Phi
DECKER, J.C., INC. Mfg. Ill. catalogs of
dog furnishings, suitcases and trunks, fancy
leather goods and specialties. Catalogs #32,
36 and 37.

1883 Brooklyn, N. Y.   NNQ
DIETZ, ALONZO E. Ill. catalog of tubular
rim night latches and locks, cast bronze
padlocks, etc. 4to., 22pp., fine ills.

nd. Terryville, Conn.   CtHi
EAGLE LOCK CO. Ill. catalog #45 - locks
and latches, catches and builders' hardware.

1862 Boston   MiDbF
EATON, LOVETT & WELLINGTON. Ill.
catalog of woodenware, fishermens' outfits,
general hardware - axes to Yankee notions.
16mo., 62pp., fine ills., wrap.

1874 Brooklyn, N. Y.   NNQ
EDDY, GEORGE M. & CO. Ill. price list of
measuring tapes, brass cased surveyors'
and tailors' tapes, tapes of asses' skin and
all varieties. 8vo., 10pp.

1878 Philadelphia   PHi
ENTERPRISE MFG. CO. Ill. catalog of pat.
hardware specialties. See House Furnishings for complete listings.

c.1900 Boston   ICHi
EVANS, McEVOY & CO. Ill. catalog of brass
goods, cabinet hardware, furniture trimmings
and tools. 8vo., 98pp. and index. Fine ills.
Pict. wrap.

c.1867 New York   MoSHi
EVANS, W.M. & CO. Brown's pat. combined
carpet stretcher and tack driver.

1878 St. Paul, Minn.   MnHi
FARWELL, GEORGE L. Catalog #3 - ills.
of stoves, hardware, tinners' stock, agricultural implements, etc. with discount sheet.
4to., wrap.

1858 Philadelphia   PKsL
FAUST, WINEBRENER & CO. Catalog of
hardware, cutlery, saddlery, tools, guns,
spectacles, fireplace tools, anvils, sleigh
bells, etc. 16mo., 58pp., wrap.

1885 Meriden, Conn.   NNMM
FOSTER, MERRIAM & CO. Ill. and priced
catalog of cabinet hardware and builders'
and cabinetmakers' supplies. 87pp., wrap.

1892 Meriden, Conn.   NNMM
------ Revised catalog of cabinet hardware.
239pp. with fine ills. in orig. wrap.

1884 Freeport, Ill.   MnHi
FREEPORT HARDWARE MFG. CO. Ill.
catalog of hinges, pat. spring hinges and
builders' hardware.

1818 Cambridgeport, Mass.   MWA
FULLER, ROBERT. Catalog of the New
Iron Store - anvils, vises and tools of old
sable and Russia iron and steel, etc. Circular with a fine example of period border.

1872 Chicopee Falls, Mass.   N
GAYLORD MFG. CO. Ill. catalog of Gaylord's chest, cupboard, drawer, piano and
wardrobe locks. 4to., 45pp. of pls. in glt.
and silver tint. Dec. cl. An unusual job
and fine ref.

1884-87 Milwaukee   MnHi
GEUDER & PAESCHKE MFG. CO. 4 ill.
catalogs for 1884, 1885, 1886 and 1887. Ills.
of lanterns, coal hods, stoves, stove boards,
tea and coffee pots, pans, shovels, waffle
irons, etc. Fine ref. collection.

nd. Brooklyn, N. Y.   NNQ
GLIDDEN, W.L. Ill. catalog of scaffolding,
ladders, rope, pulleys, flags, flag poles and
supplies. 14pp.

1884 Antrim, N. H.   NhHi
GOODELL & CO. Ill. catalog and desc.
price list of cutlery - table cutlery and knives
for butchers, hunters and cooks - skinning,
sticking, shoeworkers, cigar cutters, also
for cheese, steak, putty and bread. 16mo.,
24pp. - an unusual ref.

1875 Chicago   ICHi
GOULD, BRIGGS & CO. Ill. catalog of nails,
screws, sieves, curry combs and general
hardware.

1888 New York   MH-BA
GOULD, ROBERT S. CO. Revised price
list of general hardware. Large 4to., 8pp.,
fine ills.

1801 New York   MH-BA
------ Ill. price list of carpet hardware.
4to., 68pp., wrap.

1888 New Haven   MnHi
GRILLEY CO., THE. Ill. catalog of silver,
bronze and brass pat. screws and other
hardware.

1870 Chicago   MH-BA
HALL, KIMBARD & CO. CBaK   MoSHi
Ill. catalog of anvils, carriage bodies, wheel
barrows, yokes, keys and general hardware.
Railway and machinists' supplies. 8vo.,
325pp., well ill., pict. cl.

c.1860 New York   NHi
HALSTEAD, A.L. & SONS. Ill. catalog of
general hardware, housekeeping articles,
Japannery, hollow ware, brass, bronze, copper, iron and tin goods, sporting goods,
fishing tackle, etc. 16 plus 16pp. of mss.
notes of orders with prices. Wrap.

c.1886 Worcester, Mass.   MH-BA
HAMBLIN & RUSSELL MFG. CO. Inc. 1884.
Ill. catalog of hardware specialties and
standard wire goods and novelties. 8vo.,
60pp., wrap.

c.1888 Worcester, Mass.   MH-BA
------ Ill. catalog. 8vo., 92pp.

1888 New York   MdTanSW
HAMMACHER, SCHLEMMER & CO. Ill.
catalog of cabinet and piano hardware, upholstery goods and metal work of all kinds.
92pp., fine ills., wrap.

1889 New York   MdTanSW
------ Ill. catalog of drawer pulls, brasses
and fancy cabinet hardware. 96pp.

1890 New York   MH-BA
------ Ill. catalog of cabinet and upholsterers' hardware, tools, supplies, etc. 4to.,
210pp., fine ill. ref., cl. See also Machinery
and Tools.

1886 Boston   NNMM
HARRINGTON, GEORGE S. Ill., desc. and
priced catalog of cabinet hardware and furniture mfg's. supplies. 140pp., cl.

1883 Minneapolis   MnHi
HARRISON & KNIGHT. New ill. catalog of
hardware for every household and for every
trade. 8vo., 358pp., cl.

1888 Beaver Falls, Pa.   MnHi
HARTMAN MFG. CO. Ill. catalog of wire
and iron goods.

1884-86 Augusta, Me.   MnHi
HARVEY, H.H. & CO. Ill. catalogs and
price lists of hardware - hammers, sledges,
all manner of tools, wedges, anvils - also
sleds for lumbermen, etc. For 1884-5 and
1886.

HIBBARD, SPENCER, BARTLETT & CO.
See House Furnishings.

1871 Philadelphia   PKsL
HILLEBRAND & WOLF. Formerly Lieb-
rich, Hillebrand & Wolf. The Star Lock
Works. Ill. price list of trunks and padlocks, dead latches, bells and bell pulls,
keys, locks, springs and pat. hardware for
builders. 4to., 3pp. plus 27 pls. in gold and
silver tinted lithos. One of the very few
catalogs that show, ill. and explain the old
door pull-bells.

1876 New York   NNMM
HOLDEN, C.F. & G.H. Holden's New York
Bird Store. Holden's Book on Birds - with
a complete ill. catalog of cages and accessories and supplies. 12mo., 128pp., large
fld. plate of cages, gadgets, etc. and complete
price list, pict. wrap.

1896 Lakeville, Conn.   CtY
HOLLY MFG. CO. Ill. catalog and price
list of cutlery, scissors, razors and knives
for all trades and purposes.

nd. Lakeville, Conn.   CtHi
------ Ill. catalog of American cutlery, etc.

p.1900 Lakeville, Conn.   CtY
------ Ill. catalogs to 1907 for further
work.

1874 Darlington, N. J.   NNMM
HOPKINS & DICKINSON MFG. CO. Ill. catalog of hand made locks and bronze hardware for all purposes, builders' hardware,
etc. 137pp., gold ptd. wrap.

1888 St. Paul, Minn.   MnHi
HORTON & CO. Ill. wholesale catalog of
general hardware.

1884 Pittsburgh, Pa.   MnHi
HUBBARD, BAKEWELL & CO. Ill. catalog
of general hardware tools, etc. Axes, saws,
shovels, hoes, drainage equipment, etc.

1888 Cincinnati   OC
IRELAND MFG. CO., THE. Ill. catalog #5.
Builders' hardware. 4to. with fine ills., cl.

1883 Buffalo, N. Y.   NBuHi
JEWETT, JOHN MFG. CO. Ill. catalog of
holiday goods - coal hods and vases, brass,
iron and silver plate novelties, cuspidors,
kettles, wine coolers, umbrella stands and
stenciled tinware. 8vo., 64pp., fine ills.,
pict.wrap.

1890 Buffalo, N. Y.   NBuHi
------ Ill. catalog of holiday goods, etc.

c.1896 Jersey City   NNMM
KATO MFG. CO. Ill. catalog of ash trays,
ink stands, pedestal lamps, etc., stands and
novelties. 36 lvs.

1883-87 Chicago   MnHi
KEITH, BENHAM & DEZENDORF. Ill. catalogs for 1883, 1884, 1885, 1886, 1887 of
cutlery, hardware, nails, metal stocks, tinners' stocks, agricultural implements, etc.
Well ill. throughout all 5 catalogs. Nos.1-4
paged continuously - bound.

nd. Philadelphia   PHi
KEYSTONE BRUSH CO. Price list of general house furnishings and hardware.

1873 Philadelphia   PKsL
KEYSTONE WORKS. George Griffiths,
Prop. Ill. catalog and price list revised;
ills. of pans, pipes, wash boilers, shovels,
pokers, coal hods, coffee roasters, etc.
16mo., 18pp., pict. wrap.

1874 Philadelphia   PKsL
------ Revised ill. price list. 16mo., 16pp.

1883 Philadelphia   PHi
------ Ill. price list of coal hods, scoops,
spades and all manner of hardware.

1883 Manchester, N. H.   NhHi
KIMBALL, EZRA W. Desc. catalog and
price list of harness, trunks, luggage and
general hardware. 16mo., 38pp., fine ills.,
wrap.

nd. New York   NNMM
KRAUSE, G.C. A collection of designs for
fancy cabinet hardware. 48 pls., portfolio
in bds.

1898 Lancaster, Pa.   PKsL
LANCASTER MACHINE & KNIFE WORKS.
Catalog of brace and bits, butchers' cleavers
and knives, etc. 8vo., 22pp., ills., wrap.

1883 New York   NNMM
LINDEMANN, O. CO. Ill. catalog of bird
cages, accessories, cups, feeders, stenciled
trays - fancy and plain - architecturally -
Doric, Gothic, Corinthian and Colonial. Fol.
Pict. wrap.

1874 New York
LITTLE, CHARLES E. Successor to
Charles S. Est. 1760. Ill. catalog and price
list of hardware, cutlery, edged tools for
coopers, slaters, carpenters, etc. Discount
sheet enc. 16mo., 24pp., fine ills.

1869 Philadelphia   PHi
LLOYD, SUPPLEE & WALTON. Ill. catalog
of English, German and American hardware.
Ills. of locks, latches, strap and fancy hinges,
ladles, scoops, pans, coolers, lanterns,
irons, stands and novelties. 8vo., 248pp. Cl.

1885 Burlington, Ia.   MnHi
McCOSH IRON & STEEL CO. Ill. catalog of
bolts, nails, screws, wagon and carriage
hardware and heavy machine hardware.

1886 Burlington, Ia.   MnHi
------ Ill. catalog of hardware.

nd. Cleveland   MnHi
McCURDY & CO. Ill. catalog of stock and
standard hardware.

1900 Denver   CoD
McFADDEN, W.R. & SON. Ill. catalog of
curios, game heads, rugs and wall pieces,
fur robes, etc.

1882 New Haven   NNMM
MALLORY, WHEELER & CO. Ill. catalog
of locks, knobs, padlocks, marine hardware
and general hardware. 332pp., cl.

1891 New Haven   NNMM
------ Ill. catalog of hardware. 296pp., cl.

1884 Philadelphia   PHi
MANLY & COOPER MFG. CO. Price list
of wrought iron goods for May. 8vo., 8pp.

1788 New York   Evans
MARTIN, JOHN. New invented friction rollers made and sold . . . #207 Queen street
near the corner of Golden Hill. Fol. broadside, woodcut, colophon.

1886 Toledo, O.   OHi
MATHER & GROSH CUTLERY CO. Ill. catalog of hand forged razor steel pocket
cutlery, axes, butchers' knives, scissors,
razors, etc. 12mo., 56pp., wrap.

1890 Toledo, O.   OT
------ Ill. catalog - How to choose a good
razor and the best pocket knives. 12mo.,
32pp.

1891 Toledo, O.   OT
------ Ill. catalog. 8vo., 80pp., fine ills.

1894-5 Toledo, O.   OHi
------ List #9. Ill. catalog. 80pp.

1883 New York   NNMM
MEDFORD FANCY GOODS CO. Ill. catalog
of furnishings, hardware, with an unusual
assortment of dog collars, plain, fancy, tiny,
and huge, studded, silver ornamented,
leashes, etc. 12mo., 48pp., pict. wrap.

1887 Chicago & New York   MnHi
MERCHANT & CO. Ill. catalog of brass
and copper specialties, metals and general
hardware.

1867 New York   NHi
MILES & CO. Miles' ill. catalog of improved Challenge meat cutters, butchers'
tools, etc. 8vo., 16pp., fine ills., wrap.

1894-5 Cincinnati   MoSHi
MILLER, DuBRUL & PETERS. Ill. catalog
of cigar moulds.

c.1880 Philadelphia   PHi
MILLER LOCK CO. Catalog #7 - Champion
locks for every trade, home and office, padlocks, etc. 8vo., 20pp. with ills. throughout.

c.1898 San Francisco   CHi
MILLER, SLOSS & SCOTT. Catalog #7 -
fine ills. of hardware, tools, brass goods,
cutlery, sporting goods, iron and steel, pipe,
etc. 4to., 1236pp., an exhaustive ref., cl.

1885-9 Milwaukee   MnHi
MOORE MFG. & FOUNDRY CO. Ill. catalogs of hardware specialties, builders' hardware, door hangers, etc. for 1885, 1886,
1887, 1888 and 1889. 8vo., cl.

1879 Nashua, N. H.   N
NASHUA LOCK CO. Ill. catalog of locks,
latches, hinges, silver glass knobs, bell
pulls, locks and keys in swell designs -
silver and glt. tint pls. 4to., 180pp., outstanding, cl.

1883 Nashua, N. H.   NhHi
------ Supplementary catalog #3 - locks
and latches - builders' hardware. 4to., 4pp.

1859 New Britain   MH-BA
NEW BRITAIN BANK LOCK CO. The great
American, or key register bank locks. 8vo.,
32pp., fine ills., wrap.

NEW ENGLAND BUTT CO. See also House
Furnishings.

nd. New Haven   CtHi
NEW HAVEN WIRE CO. Ill. price list of
wire nails, Copeland's improved nails, plain
and barbed wire, brads and tacks.

1873 New York   NHi
NEWTON, D.A. (Mfg. agent.) Ill. price
list of hardware specialties - American meat
and vegetable choppers, Silver's pat. sausage
stuffer, bench vises, carpenters' tools, etc.
16mo., 12pp., fine ills., wrap.

nd. New York   MnHi
NEW YORK STAMPING CO. Ill. price list
of specialties in ironware and general hardware.

1890 Greenfield, Mass.   DLC
NICHOLS BROTHERS. American Tap & Die
Co. Ill. catalog #21 - Cutlers to American
butchers - ills. of scimiters, sticking, boning,
fish, oyster, tobacco, skinning and masticat-
or knives. 8vo., 132pp., pict. wrap.

1876 Norwalk   CtHi
NORWALK LOCK CO. Ill. and desc. catalog
of builders' hardware, plain and ornamental,
locks, latches, hinges, knockers, glass knobs,
etc., a veritable encyclopaedia. 4to., 488pp.

1877 Norwalk   CtHi
------ Ill. price list of knobs and special
builders' hardware. 4to., 22pp., pict. wrap.
of plant.

1899 Norwalk   CtHi
------ Ill. catalog of builders' hardware -
locks, latches, hinges, fancy glass knobs,
keys and key plates, brass knockers, etc.
4to., XVI and 234pp. of ills., cl.

1886 Oak Hill, N. Y.   NHi
OAK HILL MFG. CO. Ill. catalog of builders' and tinners' hardware, rests, sad irons,
coffee pot stands, foot scrapers, latches,
bolts, boot jacks, mincing machines, etc.
8vo., 68pp., wrap.

1855 Philadelphia   PKsL
OGDEN, E. HALL. Philadelphia Malleable
Iron Works. Ill. catalog of general hardware, saddlery, iron castings, bed keys,
door buttons, beef steak pounders, coffee

roasters, mills, horse combs, candlesticks, dog irons, gridirons, coopers' vises, etc. 16mo., 44pp., purple glazed glt. ptd. wrap.

c.1900 New York & vp.   ICHi
OPPENHEIMER, S. & CO. Est. 1868. Sausage Casings & Butchers' Supplies, cover title. 4to., 240pp. of ills. of tools, scales, rollers, spice mills, special machinery, garments, market fixtures, etc. Hand tools such as hog scrapers. Fine ref., cl.

1884 San Francisco   CHi
OSBORN & ALEXANDER. Ill. catalog of hardware, tools, machinery, machine tools, engines, bicycles, etc.

1886 San Francisco   CHi
------ Ill. catalog of bicycles and general hardware. Probably ptd. for Osborn and Alexander by Pope Mfg. Co. 8vo., ills.

1887 San Francisco   CHi
------ Ill. catalog of general hardware.

c.1890 San Francisco   CHi
------ Ill. catalog of hardware - all branches.

1876 West Meriden, Conn.   CtHi
PARKER & WHIPPLE CO. Ill. catalog of door knobs, locks, builders' hardware of all sorts. 8vo., dec. cl.

1853 New Britain   CtHi
PECK & WALTER MFG. CO. Ill. price list of builders' and home owners' furnishings, hardware, coach and cabinetmakers' hardware, also brass, iron and German silver castings to order. 12mo., 48pp., fine ills.

1883 Southington, Conn.   MnHi
PECK, STOW & WILCOX CO. Ill. catalog of general hardware - meat choppers, brass andirons, fireplace tools, traps and a fine assorted line. See also Tinsmiths' Tools and Supplies for other catalogs. 1871-88.

1888 Southington & New York PKsL
------ Ill. catalog of tinsmiths' NHi tools and machines, teapot handles, sad irons, stands and supplies. Sq. 8vo., 128pp. Wrap.

1877 Cincinnati   OC
PERIN & GAFF MFG. CO. Factories: Camp Washington, O. and Jeffersonville, Ind. Ill. catalog and price list of general hardware and agricultural implements, etc. Andirons, cow bells, boot jacks, lanterns, piano stools, foot scrapers, tinware, etc. 4to., 400pp., mor. and cl. with discount. Nos. 9 and 10, 32 and 12pp., pict. wrap.

nd. Philadelphia   PHi
PETERS, JAMES & SON. Ill. catalog of fire protection hardware, wrought iron, and general blacksmithing tools and products.

c.1830 Boston   MWA
PICKENS & LITTLEHALE. Prices of iron hollow ware, kettles, spiders, skillets, basins, wagon boxes, etc. Broadside with 2 columns of goods listed.

1883-4 Boston   NNMM
PITKIN BROTHERS. Ill. catalog of cabinet hardware. 50pp., fine ills., wrap.

1855 Pittsburgh, Pa.   PKsL
PITTSBURGH NOVELTY WORKS. Livingston, Copeland & Co. - formerly Livingston, Roggen & Co. Ill. catalog and price list of scales, paint mills, Kaughphy mills, copying presses, rim locks, latches, hinges, wrenches, etc. 16mo., 52pp., fine ills., glt. ptd. wrap. N.B. Quality not quantity - one of the best pict. ref. of the cast iron rim locks with brass knobs, of this period.

1884 New York   MiDbF
POPE & STEVENS. Ill. catalog of skates, dog collars, tools for wig-makers, tinners, cigar makers, trunk makers, upholsterers, etc. 8vo., 80pp., pict. wrap.

c.1880 Norwich, Conn.   CtHi
PRESTON BROTHERS. Annual catalog of fine pocket cutlery, skates, mouse traps, bird cages, etc. 8vo., 55pp., fine ills., pict. wrap.

1866 Reading, Pa.   PksL
READING HARDWARE WORKS. Harbster Brothers & Co. Ill. catalog and price list of builders' hardware, Japanned and bronzed household furnishings, sad irons, tobacco cutters, foot scrapers, boot jacks, cabinet hardware, coffee mills, fancy cork squeezers, etc. 8vo., 62pp. of fine ills., dec. cl.

1876 Reading, Pa.   PHi
------ Ill. catalog of builders' hardware - fancy locks, knobs, etc. 4to., 72pp., wrap.

1877 Reading, Pa.   PHi
------ Ill. catalog of all manner of hardware for builders and home owners, and for all trades.

1878 Reading, Pa.   PHi
------ Special catalog of hardware for Sept. Ill.

1885 Reading, Pa.   PKsL
------ Ill. catalog and price list of general hardware, fine ills. of bells and boot jacks to novelties, general hardware and so to waffle irons. 4to., 272pp. and XII, index, calf and cl.

1891 Reading, Pa.
------ Ill. catalog of hardware for all purposes and for all trades. 4to., 460pp., index
768 items, fld. plate of works, a fine job,
dec. mor. and cl.

1897 Reading, Pa.   PKsL
------ Ill. catalog of plain and   PBS
fancy hardware - builders' hardware, household furnishings - gadgets, inventions, novelties, apple parers, bells, bird cages,
waffle irons and even toy penny banks. 4to.,
calf, 672pp., an American hardware dictionary, and ill. to boot. See also Lighting.

nd. Lancaster, Pa.   PHi
REESE PADLOCK CO. Ill. catalog of padlocks and hardware specialties.

1836 Hartford, Conn.   MWA
RIPLEY, ROBERTS & CO. Circular with
list of offerings for the iron trade - files,
rasps, anvils, vises, scythes, crowbars,
book safes, scales, caldrons, carriage
springs, etc.

1888 St. Paul, Minn.   MnHi
ROBINSON & STRINGHAM CO. Ill. catalog
and price list of pieced tinware, sheet iron
goods, stamped and japanned ware. 4to.,
14pp.

1892 Patchogue, L. I., N. Y.   NNQ
ROE, JUSTUS & SONS. Price list of measuring tapes of all kinds, linen, metallic and
steel - for all trades. 8vo., 8pp., fine ills.

1874 New Britain   Ct
RUSSELL & ERWIN MFG. CO. Ill. catalog
and desc. price list of hardware - anvils,
bells, nails, etc. 8vo., 32pp., fine ills.,
wrap.

1878 New Britain   CtHi
------ Ill. catalog of hardware for all purposes - builders, home owners, trades, etc.
8vo., 32pp., wrap.

1886 New Britain   Ct
------ Ill. catalog of hardware.

1887 New Britain   CtHi
------ Ill. catalog of hardware, Vol. VII,
fine pls., ills. of works, etc., adze to wringer and anvils to Texas cow bells. 4to.,
XXII and 1012pp., bkrm.

1887 New Britain   MnHi
------ Revised catalog of wire   CtHi
nails, bolts, screws, brass machine screws,
etc. 12pp., ill.

1897 New Britain   CtHi
------ Ill. catalog of hardware.   Ct
4to., 998pp. of fine ills., bkrm.

1773 Boston & Worcester   MWA
SALISBURY, SAMUEL & STEPHEN. A
large and complete assortment of hardware
goods, imported from London, Bristol,
Birmingham and Sheffield, very cheap by
wholesale and retail at their shops. Fol.
broadside. N.B. It was 99 and a fraction
years before A. Montgomery Ward offered
such a diversified list of American or any
other hardware.

1852-88 New Haven   CtY
SARGENT & CO., MFG. One of the finest
collections in the field, covering a long and
important - almost - half century. Ill. catalogs of various sizes in bds., cl. and wrap.
All ill. throughout, from an academy bell to
a zinc ornament. 1852, 1856, 1857, 1871,
1874, 1877, 1880, 1881, 1884, 1886, 1887 and
1888. See listings for other locations.

1866 New Haven   Ct
------ Ill. catalog of general hardware.
8vo., 296pp., fine ills. of goods from their
factories in Mass., N. H., N. Y., and Vermont.

1869 New Haven   CtHi
------ Appendix to ill. catalog - ills. of
wall brackets, fireplace equipment, and
hardware. 8vo., 48pp.

1871 New Haven   CtHi
------ Ill. catalogs of padlocks,   CtY
col. tinted pls. in glt. and silver.

1874 New Haven   CtHi
------ Ill. catalog of hardware.   CtY
4to., 812pp. of fine ills., from builders'
hardware to house furnishings.

1880 New Haven   MdTanSW
------ Price list and ill.   CtY
catalog of hardware - bells, scale beams,
hooks, twine holders, harness snaps, boot
jacks, meat cutters and stuffers, coffee and
other mills, ornamental iron novelties,
pinking irons, etc. 4to., 981pp., thumb
index, cl.

1896-98 New Haven   NNMM
------ Ill. catalog and price list of general
hardware for builders' and an assortment of
novelties and necessities for households.
1089pp., cl.

1876 New York & Portland, Conn.   MH-BA
SCHEIDER, JOSEPH & CO. Ill. catalog of
plain, stamped and japanned tin ware. 8vo.,
84pp., wrap.

1878 Lowell, Mass.   MH-BA
SEWALL & CO. Ill. catalog of wire goods.
16pp.

1879 Philadelphia　　　　　NNMM
SHANNON, J.B. & SONS. Ill. catalog and
price list of art metal work for furniture
decoration, and fine cabinet locks, etc.
32pp., pict. wrap.

1884 Philadelphia　　　　　PPL
------ Ill. Christmas catalog of cutlery,
ironwork, skates and general hardware with
prices. 16pp.

1888 Philadelphia　　　　　PPL
------ Ill. price list of builders' hardware,
house furnishings and general hardware.
287pp., a fine pict. ref.

1883-99 St. Louis　　　　　MoSHi
SHAPLEIGH, A.F. HARDWARE CO. Ill.
catalogs of builders' hardware and general
hardware. 1883, 1892 and 1899. All well
ill.

1875 Royer's Ford, Pa.　　　PHi
SHEELER, BUCKWALTER & CO. Supplemental ill. catalog of new goods for 1875 -
new model stoves and general hardware.
4to., 8pp.

c.1880 Detroit　　　　　OHi
STANDART BROTHERS WHOLESALE
HARDWARE. Est. 1863. Ill. catalog of
house furnishings and general hardware,
bells to washing machines, some col. pls.
4to., 836pp.

1885 Syracuse, N. Y.　　　MnHi
STEARNS, E.C. & CO. Ill. catalog of hardware specialties.

1882 Lancaster, Pa.　　　PHi
STEINMAN, GEORGE M. & CO. Ill. catalog
of hardware, iron, steel, saddlery and carriage hardware, stoves, house furnishings,
building materials, etc. Large 8vo., 240pp.,
pict. wrap.

1899 Davenport, Ia.　　　MoSHi
STERNBERG MFG. CO. Ill. catalog of
cigar moulds, etc.

1873 Reading, Pa.　　　PKsL
STERNBERGH, J.H., Mfg. Reading PHi
Bolt & Nut Works. Ill. price list of hot
pressed bolts, machine bolts, etc. 16mo.,
8pp.

c.1900 Philadelphia　　　PKsL
STEWARD & ROMAINE MFG. CO. PHi
Ill. catalog and price list of expansion bolts,
pat. parallel expansion bolts in iron and
brass, etc.

1885 New York　　　　MnHi
STODDARD LOCK & MFG. CO. Ill. catalog
of tumbler locks, etc.

1888 St. Paul, Minn.　　　MnHi
STRONG-HACKETT HARDWARE CO. Ill.
catalog of seasonable goods and hardware
specialties. 36pp., wrap.

c.1890 Indianapolis　　　In
SULLIVAN-GEIGER CO. Ill. catalog #8 -
tinware, enameled ware, sheet metal goods.
To the trade, cookie cutters, lanterns,
mouse traps, japanned ware, toys, etc. 4to.,
220pp. of fine ills., stiff wrap.

1847 Terryville, Conn.　　　CtHi
TERRY, JAMES & CO. Price list of American trunk locks, carpet bag frames, etc.
Folder 8x13, one page price list and one
page mss. order.

1884 Portland, Ore.　　　OrU
THOMPSON, DeHART & CO. Price list and
ill. catalog of general hardware. 876pp. of
fine ills., wrap.

c.1873 Indianapolis　　　In
TUCKER & DORSEY. Tucker's alarm till -
$36. a dozen, one free with first order, and
other goods. 24pp., ills.

c.1832 Sheffield, Eng.　　　MH-BA
TURNER, THOMAS & CO. Catalog of table
and pocket knives, files, tools and general
steel hardware. 16mo., 29pp. N.B. Undoubtedly these same goods were listed in
American catalogs for this period - so, why
not?

1886 St. Louis　　　　MnHi
UDELL & CRUNDEN. Ill. catalog of step
ladders, ladders, etc.

1873 Wolcottville, Conn.　　　CtHi
UNION HARDWARE CO. Ill. catalog and
price list of skates, straps, buckles, tool
handles, muzzles, dog collars, parlor skates,
fluting irons, etc. 12mo., 48pp., pict. wrap.

1884 Indianapolis　　　MoSHi
UNITED STATES WIRE NAIL WORKS. Ill.
price list of wire nails.

1855 New York　　　　IHi
UPSON MFG. CO. (Scofield, Farnum & Co.,
agents.) Price list of hardware, Griswold
& Co.'s augers and bits, Watson's cotton,
wool, horse, curry and Jim Crow cards.
1 page circular.

1887 Brooklyn, N. Y.　　　MoSHi
VOGEL, WILLIAM & BROTHERS. Price
list of sheet metal screws and tinware.

nd. Indianapolis　　　NNMM
VONNEGUT, CLEMENS. Ill. catalog and
price list of builders' hardware, locks,
knobs, hinges, latches and escutcheons, etc.
208pp., fine ills., gold lettered cl.

1873 New York   NHi
WALSH, COULTER & FLAGLER. Prices
current of American and foreign hardware -
lists tools for all trades as well as general
hardware. 12mo., 102pp., wrap.

1870 New York   NHi
WALSH, COULTER & WILSON. Prices
current of American and foreign hardware -
a fine complete list. 12mo., 80pp. American firms recommended.

1877 Troy, N. Y.   MH-BA
WARREN, J.M. & CO. Troy Stamping
Works. Price list for 1876. Ill. catalog -
hardware, iron, steel, nails, tin, copper,
etc. 12mo., 24pp.

1879 Troy, N. Y.   MH-BA
------ Price list E. Ill. catalog of stove
trimmings and specialties. 12mo., 8pp.

1875 Chicago   NNMM
WAYNE, J.L. & SONS. Ill. catalog for
builder, cabinetmaker and upholsterer - designs of trimmings for fine furniture -
carvings, brackets, handles for coffins, etc.
and general hardware. 4to., 96pp., pict.
wrap.

1882 Providence   RHi
WEAVER, GEORGE E. Ill. catalog of hardware supplies for builders, painters, farmers, etc. - bird cages to locks and latches,
mouse traps and tools. 8vo., 206pp., pict.
wrap.

nd. Chicago   MnHi
WELLS & NELLEGAR CO. Ill. catalog of
hardware, cutlery, nails, tinners' stock,
barbed wire goods, etc.

1877 Chicago   NNMM
WENTER, F. Successor to Smith & Wenter.
Ill. catalog of fancy cabinet hardware. 36pp.
Wrap.

1817 Boston   MWA
WILBY, FRANCIS. Catalog of hardware
goods at public auction. 8vo., 29pp. - a fine
list of contemporary general hardware.

1853 New York   NHi
WILLETTS & CO. Catalog of American,
English and German hardware - sperm,
whale and lard oil for lamps, bed keys,

saws, nails, pumps, sad irons, well wheels -
a fine reminder of many conveniences of
1853 that most of us never heard of before.
24mo., 18pp., pict. ptd. wrap.

1883 Brooklyn, N. Y.   NNQ
WILSON, BOHANNAN MFG. CO. Catalog of
pat. drawer and combination locks. 8vo.,
4pp. with 3 ills.

1882 Chicago   MnHi
WILSON, EVANDEN & CO. Ill. catalog of
hardware, cabinet and round oil tanks and
cabinets, etc.

1817 Charlestown, Mass.   MWA
WYMAN, WILLIAM & THOMAS B. The
Yellow Store. Price list of Sable, Archangel,
Russia and Swedes Iron, wagon tires, plough
shares, moulds, spindles, sleigh shoes, anvils, oven doors and glass. Broadside -
7-1/2x10-1/2 on yellow stock with border.
List of goods - mss. order on back to Captain Woodbury, Boston, Oct. 15.

1871 Stamford, Conn.   CtHi
YALE LOCK MFG. CO. Est. 1851. Catalog
#3 - Price list and discount sheet for Feb.
8vo., 32pp.

1876 Stamford, Conn.   NNMM
------ Ill. catalog and price list of locks.
223pp., a fine ref. in gold stamped cl.

Established in 1851, the Yale Lock Mfg. Co.
became the Yale & Towne Mfg. Co. in 1883.
With this 1884 catalog we find that they
swung into production of heavy machinery,
hoisting machinery, cranes, etc., creating
and helping the development of American
industrial supremacy.

1884 Stamford, Conn.   MH-BA
YALE & TOWNE MFG. CO. Cata-   CtHi
log #10. Only 30 miles from New York!
Large 4to., 384pp. of fine ills., cl.

1894 Stamford, Conn.   CtHi
------ Catalog #15, with supplement #14.
Ills. of art metal work, fancy latches, new
designs in brass knockers, brasses, escutcheons, reproductions of 17th century, the
last word in American locks. 12mo., 140
plus 60pp., fine pls. N.B. CtHi also has
#16 and #18 available for research.

I had considered including a chapter of General Store Goods, but decided such a classification might
only prove confusing. Even a tiny sparable may be hidden in some 1899 catalog with plates of
mining machinery, though of course it should be in a catalog under Cobblers' Tools in the next
chapter.

1838   CARR, WILLIAM H. & CO., Philadelphia   PKsL

American Manufactured Hardware

8vo., 32pp., Ptd. and Dec. Wrap.

I have singled out this extraordinary example of American cataloging for special treatment. Although the Joseph H. Adams illustrated catalog for 1859, noted at the beginning of this chapter, offers an even greater variety of goods, it is twenty years later and only a record of Joseph Adams. Mr. Carr printed a record of sixty odd American firms, many of whom never issued catalogs, at least according to present reports. For this reason I have indexed the following manufacturers and jobbers in spite of the fact that they are represented only in the Carr catalog.

It would be interesting to know whether or not this may have been an early co-operative plan brochure. Perhaps the answer will be found in an old ledger or day book of expenditures at some future date. For the present we can at least list these gentlemen and their goods for reference.

ADAMS, Daniel & Co. Sand papers.

AGSMORE, John. Tools.

AIKEN, Herrick. Leather splitting machinery.

ALRICK, H. & S. & Co. Sand papers.

AMES, N. P. Knives and tools.

AMES, Oliver. Shovels and spades.

ATWOOD, A. Sieves and wire goods.

BACON, Nathaniel. Shadeless lamps.

BACON, William W. Tinware, plain and Japanned, for kitchen, bath and parlor, toys, spittoons, candlesticks, spice and tea boxes, etc.

BATES, Moses Jr. Cobblers' tools and lasts.

BEATTY, John. Axes, and tools for all trades.

BELDEN & LEE. Sleigh and cow bells, waffle irons, surveyors' instruments and tools.

BEMIS, S. C. & Co. Knives and small tools.

BREED, Joseph. Ropes and lines - the Norwich line.

CARR, William H. Forks and tools for farmers, tanners, etc.

CLARK & RANKIN. Rifle and gun barrels.

COE, Israel. Brass kettles and hollow wares.

CONANT, Joseph. Hatchets, axes and tools.

CUMMINGS, Charles. Glue for all jobs.

DEAN, Barney. Andirons, brads, mills, etc.

DEEP RIVER Mfg. Co. Shipwrights' tools.

DOUGLAS AXE Mfg. Co. Broad and shingling axes, adzes, tomahawks, also Yankee, Kentucky, Georgia, New Jersey and Spanish axes.

ENOS, Edward J. Bed keys, vises, gimlets, carpenters' tools.

FAIRBANKS, E. & T. Scales, hoisting screws, presses for bookbinders, clothiers and factories, etc.

FIELD, Albert. Sparables and cobblers' tools.

FOOTE, Homer & Co. Patent coach wrenches, hammers and tools.

FOSTER, Merriam & Co. Casters of horn, brass, iron, etc.

HAMMOND, S. & L. W. Latches, locks and builders' hardware.

HOWARD. E. & Co. Brads and tacks for segar boxes, etc.

HYDE, F. & Sons. Fancy soaps.

ISBELL, M. M. & Co. Patent shutter fasteners.

KEITH, Scott & Co. Tacks, pumps, etc.

KING, J. M. Wilson's stamp, dies, stock, etc.

LAMSON, N. & Co. Scythe snags and tool handles.

LANGDON, Upson & Co. Fine, super-fine, super-super-fine and Ne Plus Ultra ivory combs.

M'KEE, Lewis & Co. Locks and latches, builders' hardware, etc.

MANSFIELD & DARLING. Corn and grass scythes, cutters, knives, etc.

MERRIAM, Marcus. Window springs, cupboard fasteners, etc.

MASON, James S. Challenge blacking.

MOORE & STUART. Tea kettles, hollow ware, shutter fasteners, etc.

NASON, Leonard. Axes, hoes and implements.

PARKER & MILE. Sad irons, coffee mills, implements and tools.

POOLE, J. & J. H. Surveyor's instruments, levels, etc.

RICHARDSON, Asa. Joiners' and Engineers' rules and bevels, etc.

ROCKWELL & HINSDALE. Axletrees, crowbars, scythes and implements.

ROWLAND, Jonathan. Shovels and spades.

ROWLAND, William. Mill saws.

SNYDER, David. Shovels and spades.

STANLEY, Callendar P. Co. Superior plate locks.

STEPHENS & THOMAS. Rolled and sheet brass and wire goods.

STILLMAN, W. Patent saw knives.

TIBBALS, Brooks & Co. Augers and bits.

TOMLINSON, William H. Pocketbooks, wallets and leather goods.

WADSWORTH, Platt & Sprague. Springs, locks, latches, bolts, etc.

WASHBURN, Philander. Shovels, scoops, spades, etc.

WILSON, Increase. Coffee mills, gridirons, jack screws, pokers, door knockers, shutters and tools for all trades.

WOOD, Harrison & Manvel. Coach hinges and hardware, carriage steps, etc.

ALSO SUNDRIES by various manufacturers.

Chapter 27

Hardware—Tools & Machine Tools,
by Trades & Industries

This chapter has been created to try to help the historian, collector and student find dates and manufacturers of tools and machine tools built for specific purposes and used by the craftsmen of the 19th century. From the catalog standpoint it is impossible to classify hand tools separately: I tried it. By 1860 some catalogs included brads for segar boxes as well as machinery and engines weighing many tons.

Try to remember that the American blacksmith of the last century was a manufacturer of many goods; he was not a mere shoer of horses. He made wagons and even pulled teeth to help his suffering neighbors in many small communities. His tools, as late as the turn of the 20th century, were not just bellows, anvil and hammer. He was the most versatile craftsman of them all. No machine shop, manufacturing plant, mill or mine was ever developed without him. When the first automobile appeared the real American blacksmith slowly began to fade from the scene. Today he is practically extinct, but his workmanship lives on in what we call a mechanic. Don't forget him.

Millers' tools catalogs, for instance, as listed are not devoted necessarily to tools and machines for mills exclusively. They have been selected and segregated to save the searcher time, because tools and supplies in this field predominate. A few are really one craft or trade catalogs, but even before the Civil War, American craftsmen and manufacturers could not afford to produce one single product. The cost of living isn't a 20th century invention.

My father's advice of many years ago is still good. When I forgot some chore or left the switch on in the old Autocar c.1906, ruining the battery, my favorite excuse was I didn't think. His answer was THINK. I pass it along to you. Don't tell me that you looked for oil well drills ONLY under Oil Well Supplies. I have explained carefully that the firm that made rock drills made them for good drinking water, coal, gold and silver as well as oil. Try Miners' Tools to round out your research problem. Carry this philosophy through this chapter and I think you'll find what you are looking for.

BLACKSMITHS' TOOLS & SUPPLIES

1888 Newark, N. J.   NjR
ATHA TOOL CO. Ill. price list of tools -
blacksmiths, ironers, carriage builders,
farriers - excelsior hammers, tongs, etc.
Sm. 4to., 146pp., fine pls., pict. cl.

1883 Buffalo, N. Y.   NBuHi
BUFFALO FORGE CO. Ill. cata-   CSmH
log of portable forges, bellows, anvils, blowers, fans, tools. 16mo., 40pp., pict. wrap.

1890 Buffalo, N. Y.   NBuHi
------ Ill. catalog of portable forges and
blacksmiths' tools. 48pp., pict. wrap.

1895 Buffalo, N. Y.   NBuHi
------ Ill. catalog of forges and all blacksmith shop furnishings. 12mo., 48pp.

1896 Buffalo, N. Y.   NBuHi
------ General ill. cat-   ICHi   CSmH
alog of apparatus, anvils, bellows, blowers,
fans, engines - with fine ills. of blacksmith
shops all over the USA. - buildings and
equipment. 4to., 398pp., dec. cl., a great ref.

1897 Buffalo, N. Y.   NBuHi
------ General ill. catalog of blacksmith
supplies. 8vo., 308pp., swell ills., dec. cl.

1894 Lancaster, Pa.   PKsL
CHAMPION BLOWER & FORGE CO. Ill.
catalog of anvils, bellows, lever and crank
blowers, portable forges and blacksmiths'
drills, tongs and tools.

nd. Lancaster, Pa.   PHi
------ Ill. catalog #44. Blacksmiths'
supplies. 8vo.

177

nd. Cleveland   MnHi
CLEVELAND STEAM GAUGE CO. Ill. catalog of Watson's portable forges, etc.

1883 St. Louis   MnHi
EVENDEN, J.W. Ill. catalog of bellows, etc.

1875 Philadelphia   PHi
KEYSTONE PORTABLE FORGE CO. Desc.
catalog and price list of portable forges, fan
blasts, fan blowers, anvils and general supplies. 8vo., 42pp., fine ills., pict. wrap.

1887 Chicago   MnHi
KIMBARK, S.D. CO. Ill. catalog of blacksmiths' and wagon makers' tools and supplies.

1886 Chicago   MnHi
PARKHURST & WILKINSON. Ill. catalog of
blacksmiths' anvils, bellows, tools, iron,
steel supplies, nails and hardware.

1882
TALLMAN & McFADDEN. See Carpenter
& Woodworkers' Tools for ills. of black-
smiths' tools.

1889 San Francisco
VAN WINKLE, I.S. & CO. See Hardware -
Miscellaneous Machinery, Tools & Supplies.

BOOK BINDERS' MACHINE TOOLS

1874 Philadelphia   PKsL
CHAMBERS BROTHERS & CO. Ill. catalog
and price list of book folding machines,
pasting and covering machines, etc.

1879 Philadelphia   NNC
------ Complete catalog and price list of
book and newspaper folding machines, printers' and binders' machinery. 8vo., 80pp.,
pls. and photos., pict. cl.

c.1889 Philadelphia   CSmH
------ Catalog of folding and book binders'
machinery. 8vo., 69pp., ill., dec. cl.

c.1900 Harrisburg, Pa.   PKsL
HICKOK, THE W.O. MFG. CO. Ill. catalog
of stamps and rolls for finishing dept. of
book binderies - ills. of roll and stamp patterns. 8vo., 24pp., wrap.

c.1900 Harrisburg, Pa.   PKsL
------ Catalog #81. Ill. price list of book
binders' machinery and tools.

c.1900 Brooklyn, N. Y.   NNQ
HOOLE MACHINE & ENGRAVING WORKS.
Catalog #79. Ills. of paging, numbering
machines, end-name printing machines,

book binders' tools, etc. Sq. 8vo., 46pp.,
pages 1 -29 pls. of designs for binding
decorations, etc. Dec. wrap.

p.1900 Brooklyn, N. Y.   NNQ
------ Ill. catalog #91. Tall 16mo., 44pp.,
pages 3 - 37 pls. of designs, wrap.

c.1889 Brooklyn, N. Y.   NNQ
McADAMS, JOHN & SONS. Ill. catalog of
disk and pen ruling machines, paging
machines, strikers, attachments, etc.

vd.   vp.   NNC
It is reasonable to suggest that more ill.
catalogs of book binders' tools and machinery may be found in Columbia University's
American Typefounders collection of American printing material.

BRICK MAKING TOOLS & MACHINERY

c.1884 Anderson, Ind.   In
ANDERSON FOUNDRY & MACHINE WORKS.
Ill. catalog of The Chief brick machines,
pat. Jan. 1, 1884. To brick makers, block
layers, builders and contractors - the greatest achievement of the 19th century - brick
machine and celebrated portable engines
and kilns. 8vo., 8pp., pict. wrap.

1878 Philadelphia   PKsL
CHAMBERS BROTHERS & CO. Catalog of
the new brick machine. 8vo., 51pp., ills.,
pict. wrap.

c.1894 Philadelphia   PPF
------ Catalog #15 - brickmaking machines.
119pp., fine ills., wrap.

c.1892 Centinela, L.A. County, Calif.   CHi
CENTINELA BRICK-KILN & DRIER CO.
Ill. brochure with ills. of 7 models with full
details of each, pict. wrap. 8vo., 7pls., -
model pat. 1892.

1881-84 Lancaster, Pa.   MnHi
MARTIN, HENRY. Inventor, prop. and mfg.
Ill. catalogs for 1881, 1882, 1883 and 1884.
Ills. of latest and best improved brick making
machinery. 4to., fine ills., wrap.

1886 Lancaster, Pa.   PHi
------ Ill. catalog of newest brick machines.
8vo., 32pp., pict. wrap.

1890 Wellington, O.   OHi
WELLINGTON MACHINE CO. The new
Quaker brick machine. 4to., 36pp. with fine
ills., pict. wrap. An industrial monster of
1890, but a mere toothpick in today's roster
of atomic giants.

1885 Woodland, Pa.   MH-BA
WOODLAND FIRE BRICK CO., LTD. Est.
1870. 4to., 48pp. with fine ills. and apparently the first catalog issued.

CARPENTER, CABINETMAKER & WOOD-
WORKERS' TOOLS & MACHINE TOOLS

1871 Trenton, N. J.   PKsL
AMERICAN SAW CO. Ill. price list for Jan.
Ills. of Emerson's pat. saws made at Beaver
Falls, Pa. 16mo., 16pp., pict. wrap.

1874 Trenton, N. J.   PKsL
------ Ill. catalog of movable-toothed circular saws, perforated cross cuts, etc.
8vo., 40pp., fine ills., pict. wrap.

1885 Trenton, N. J.   PKsL
------ Ill. price list of circular, mill,
Mulay, gang and cross cut saws. 8vo., 48pp.

1894 Trenton, N. J.   PKsL
------ Ill. catalog of emery grinding and
buffing machines, new improved saws, etc.
4to., 32pp., pict. wrap.

1881 New York   PC
AMERICAN TOOL CO. Price list and catalog of carpenters' tools, tool chests - for
gentlemen, boys, youths, farmers and planters. 75¢ to $225. 8vo., 30pp., fine ills.,
wrap. This is the type of reference catalog
that I hope may tempt librarians to check
their holdings. It seems a shame to list
this only in a private library.

1898 New York   DSi
AMERICAN WOOD WORKING   N
MACHINERY CO. Ill. catalog of new and
improved machinery. Large 4to., 364pp. of
fine pls. of moulders, planers, etc. - noted
as their first catalog, dec. cl. One of the
best.

1866 Indianapolis & Chicago   In
ATKINS, E.C. & CO. Est. 1857. Sheffield
Saw Works. Ill. catalog of saws. 16mo.,
fld. plate, wrap.

c.1870 Indianapolis   In
------ Ill. catalog with suggestions to
lumbermen and sawyers in use and care of
saws and tools. 16mo., 168pp., wrap.

1883 Indianapolis   In
------ Ill. price list of improved saws and
tools. 12mo., 24pp., fine ills., wrap.

1851 Griswoldville, Conn.   CtHi
BAILEY, A Prices of edged tools mfg. by
. . . Broadside 10x12, ptd. Wethersfield.

1857 Middletown, Conn.   CtHi
BALDWIN TOOL CO. Owners of The
Arrowmammett Works. Ill. catalog and invoice price list of bench planes, moulding
tools, etc. 8vo., 26 lvs., pls. of wood planes
and knives for every curve. Fine pict. wrap.
of plant.

1858 Middletown, Conn.   CtHi
------ Ill. catalog and invoice price list of
bench planes, moulding planes, gentlemens'
tool chests, etc. 12mo., 28pp. of pls.,
planes, knives, etc. Pict. wrap.

c.1870 Laconia, N. H.   NhHi
BALDWIN, N.H. Ill. catalog of   NhD
Baldwin's celebrated foot lathes, fittings,
knives - complete work shop outfits. 16mo.,
48pp. with 24pp. of pls. of machines, one fld.
Pict. wrap.

1877 Rockford, Ill.   IChi
BARNES, W.F. & JOHN CO. Desc.   DSi
price list of Barnes pat. foot power machinery, ills. of velocipede scroll saw, and other
models, patterns for builders, examples of
work, lathes, etc. - and American books
recommended for architects. 24mo., 64pp.,
fine ills., pict. wrap.

1893 Rockford, Ill.   IChi
------ Catalog #35. Ill. price   DSi
list of metal woodworking machinery, hand
power and foot power machines. 8vo., 40pp.
Wrap.

c.1880 Philadelphia   PHi
BARNETT, G. & H. BLACK DIAMOND
FILE WORKS. Catalog of hand cut files,
rasps, etc. Fol., 18pp., pict. wrap.

1876 Battle Creek,   MiU-H
BATTLE CREEK MACHINERY CO. Ill. catalog of Boult's carving, panelling, moulding
and dovetailing machines and dimensional
saw machines. Sm. 4to., 32pp. plus 3 ill.
circulars. Ill. examples of cigar moulds,
coffins, furniture, etc. Pict. wrap.

c.1877 Battle Creek   NNMM
------ Ill. catalog of Boult's carving,
moulding and panelling machines. 30pp.
with fine ills., wrap.

nd. Brooksville, Vt.   MH-BA
BROOKS EDGE TOOL CO. Est. 1825. Successors to Brooks Bros. and N. C. Brooks
& Co. Ill. price list of axes and edged tools.
16mo., 4pp.

c.1850 Middletown, Conn.   CtHi
CHAMBERLAIN, LEWIS & CO. Price list
of rules, levels, bevels, squares, gauges,
etc. Broadside 8x13 with cont. border.

c.1876 New York   DSi
CHASE, W.L. & CO. New ill. catalog of
eagle foot lathes and appurtenances. 24mo.,
40pp., pict. wrap.

1838 Fredonia, N.Y.   NHi
CROSBY, PEARSON. Pearson Crosby's
portable prairie saw-mill. Broadside with
woodcut ills. of models, details, pat. rights,
etc. Installed complete for $200.

1877 St. Louis   MoSHi
CURTIS & CO. Est. 1854. Empire Saw
Works. Ill. price list of Empire Saws.
24mo., 30pp., fine ills., glt. pict. wrap.

1892 Defiance, O.   OHi
DEFIANCE MACHINE WORKS, THE. Est.
1850. Ill. catalog of part of the 300 classes
of wood working machinery we manufacture.
Ills. of machines for wagon parts, etc. also
tire setting machines and ironwork machinery. 24mo., 68pp. of ills., pict. wrap.

1884 Philadelphia   MnHi
DISSTON, HENRY & SONS. Ill. catalog of
files, saws and tools.

1886 Philadelphia   MnHi
------ Ill. catalog of best saws made.

1887 Philadelphia   PKsL
------ Pocket catalog. Ills. of saws, files,
saw tools, etc. 16mo., 64pp., pict. wrap.

nd. Philadelphia   PKsL
------ The Saw and How to Use it, with
ill. catalog. Ills. of plant, 58 buildings and
3500 workers. 16mo., 40pp., pict. wrap.

c.1890 Philadelphia   PKsL
------ Ill. catalog of pat. saw   PHi
grips and handles, new blades, files, etc.
Fol., 8pp. This catalog is under the name
of Henry Disston & Sons File Co.

c.1900 Philadelphia   PKsL
------ Handbook for lumbermen -   PHi
with an ill. catalog. 8vo., 175pp., ills., wrap.

1877 East Douglas & Boston   ICHi
DOUGLAS AXE MFG. CO. Ill. catalog of
axes of every type for every craftsman -
some ill. in col. views of plant, pls. 8vo.,
113pp., dec. cl.

c.1900 South Shaftsbury, Vt.   VtHi
EAGLE SQUARE MFG. CO. Est. 1817. A
carpenter is known by his tools. Complete
line of steel squares, with a short history of
Company. 4x8, 32pp., fine ills., wrap.

c.1895 Cincinnati   OC
EGAN, CO., THE. Broadside 24x38 with
132 engravings of models and styles of wood
working machines, hand and power - not

thought of as a catalog today, but a piece of
pict. Americana with more ills. than many a
brochure type catalog. A fine record.

c.1880 Plantsville, Conn.   CtHi
ELLRICH, CO., THE. Ill. and desc. catalog of first quality tools and hardware for
carpenters. 16mo., 16pp., fine ills., wrap.

1893 Beaver Falls, Pa.   PKsL
EMERSON, SMITH & CO., LTD. Ill. catalog
of premium saws - Great contest - $100 in
gold, with the Sawyers' Own Book added.
24mo., 128pp., red and glt. pict. wrap.

c.1880 Hartford, Conn.   Ct
FLEETWOOD & POMEROY. Complete ill.
price list of designs, tools, saws, scroll
saws and equipment. 4to., 24pp. of ills.,
pict. wrap.

c.1888 Chicago   ICHi
FOLDING SAWING MACHINE CO. The folding sawing machine - convenient as a pocket
knife - folds up as complete as a pocket
knife too - tests. 1885-1887. 8vo., 32pp.
with fine ills., pict. wrap.

nd. New York   MnHi
FRANCIS AXE CO. Ill. catalog of hatchets,
axes, picks, etc.

1889 Philadelphia   PKsL
GOODELL & WATERS. Est. 1860. Ill. catalog of wood working machinery. 4to.,
128pp., fine ills. throughout, wrap.

1872 Greenfield, Mass.   WHi
GREENFIELD TOOL CO. Ill. catalog of
joiners' bench planes, moulding tools, irons,
handles, blades, etc. A fine pict. record.

1880 New York   OHi
HAMMACHER, A. & CO. Ill. catalog of
cabinetmakers' hardware trimmings, upholsterers' materials. 8vo., 242pp., ills. of
adze to yardstick.

1883 Hartford, Conn.   CtHi
HARTFORD HAMMER CO., THE. Ill. catalog of tools forged from solid cast steel -
for many trades - carpenter and builder,
etc. 8vo., 16pp., fine ills., wrap.

c.1850 Middletown, Conn.   CtHi
HUBBARD, C. & F. Price list of rules,
try-squares, T bevels, gauges, etc. 8x10
broadside.

1885 Millers Falls, N.Y.   MnHi
MILLERS FALLS HARDWARE CO. A work-
man is known by his tools. Ill. catalog of
hand tools, with fine ills. of carpenters'
equipment. 8vo., 24pp., wrap.

1886 Millers Falls, N.Y.   N
------ Ill. catalog of tools. 8vo., 32pp.,
ills., dec. wrap.

1887 Millers Falls, N.Y.   N
------ Ill. catalog of tools. 8vo., 64pp., a
fine ill. record, pict. wrap.

1884-5 Chicago   MnHi
MONARCH MFG. CO. Monarch   ICHi
Lightning Sawing Machine - 8,785 test. letters offered on request - col. lithos. by
Shober & Carqueville: Winter in the Piner-
ies of Michigan - Civilized Choctaws Sawing - Life of Horace Greeley - Get rid of
that backache. A delightful pict. job worthy
of Currier & Ives popularity. 8vo., 24pp.,
col. pict. wrap.

c.1890 Rochester, N.Y.   CBaK
NEIDLINGER, GEORGE. Revised   NR
price list of augers, rimmers (sic) for mfg.
pumps, gutters, hubs for wagons, etc.
16mo., fine ills., wrap.

1878 Pawtucket, R.I.   RHi
NEW AMERICAN FILE CO. Ill. price list
of files and rasps. 4to., 9pp. details and
prices with 13 pls. and 2 ills., pict. wrap.

c.1890 Columbus, O.   OHi
OHIO TOOL CO. Ill. catalog of high grade
mechanics' tools. Ills. of draw knives,
bench planes, benches, screws and vises,
etc. 16mo., 20pp., wrap.

1900 Cincinnati   OC
PARKS BALL BEARING MACHINE CO.
Parks improved single and combination belt
power wood working machines, with fine ills.
throughout. 8vo., 82pp., pict. wrap.

1880 Hartford, Conn.   MdTanSW
POMEROY, A.H. Ill. priced catalog of
fancy woods, scroll saw materials, Brower's
designs, etc. 16pp.

c.1890 Hartford, Conn.   CtHi
------ Ill. catalog of lathes, scroll saws,
pocket cutlery and clock movements - ills.
of designs - Weeden toy steam engines, toy
locomotives and steamers. 8vo., 38pp.,
pict. wrap.

c.1850 Deep River, Conn.   CtHi
PRATT, N.B. Circular of handles, mallets,
scratch-awls, ice-breakers, blades, etc.
4to., 4 page price list.

1882 St. Louis   MoSHi
ROBERTS, WILLIAM S. & CO. Ill. catalog
of wood working machinery.

1876 Norwich, Conn.   CtHi
ROGERS, C.B. & CO. Ill. catalog of wood
working machinery.

1888 Buffalo, N.Y. & Portland, Ore.   OrU
ROSS, JOSIAH. (J. M. Arthur, agent.) Ill.
catalog of wood working machinery. In pre-
senting my catalog for 1888 . . . 8vo.,
16pp., fine ills. and grand pict. wrap. of
plant.

1884 Stratford, Conn.   CtHi
RUSSELL, L.H. Russell's designs for
lathes and scroll saws. Ills. of designs by
Bowman, Fleetwood, Hope and Ware. 4to.,
fine ill. ref., pict. wrap.

1870 Sandusky, O.   CBaK
SANDUSKY TOOL CO. Ill. catalog of planes,
bench and hand screws and clamps, blades,
knives and mechanics' tools. 16mo., 32pp.,
glt. pict. wrap. of plant.

c.1880 Rochester, N.Y.   N
SHIPMAN ENGINE MFG. CO. Amateur and
mechanics' manual and ill. catalog of lathes,
scroll saws, designs and tools for wood
working. 8vo., 36pp., pict. wrap.

1887 Smithville, N.J.   DSi
SMITH, H.B. MACHINE CO. Ill. catalog of
pat. improved wood working machinery - a
fine ref. Sq. 8vo., 122pp, plus 20 page circu
lar. Fine ills. with pict. wrap. of plant.

1862 New Britain, Conn.   CtHi
STANLEY WORKS. Est. 1842. Price list
of hardware - bolts, barrel and square neck,
carpenters' tools, etc. 4to., 4pp., fine ills.

1872 New Britain   CtHi
STANLEY RULE & LEVEL CO. Price list
of U.S. Standard boxwood rules and ivory
rules, planes, mallets, shaves, drivers, etc.
4to., 46pp., fine ills., wrap.

1879 New Britain   CtHi
------ Ill. price list of rules, planes,
mallets, etc. 8vo., 66pp., wrap.

1888 New Britain   MnHi
------ Ill. catalog of carpenters' tools and
equipment.

1900 New Britain   MoSHi
------ Catalog #26. Ill. price list of carpenters' and cabinetmakers' tools.

nd. New Britain
------ Ill. catalog of improved labor-
saving Bailey's pat. adjustable carpenters'
tools.

1882 Syracuse, N.Y.   NSyHi
STEARNS, E.C. & CO. Ill. catalog   MnHi
of goods and tools. Ills. of spoke shaves,
clamps, vises, augers, etc. 8vo., 32pp.,
pict. wrap. of tools.

c.1898 Detroit   NNMM
STRELINGER, CHARLES A. & CO. Ill. and
desc. price list of wood workers' tools.
Special ill. catalog, pages 604-999 cl.

1877 Philadelphia   PHi
TALLMAN & McFADDEN. Ill. catalog of
lathes, scroll saws, tools and tool chests and
ills. of designs and patterns. 8vo., pict.
wrap.

1878-9 Philadelphia   PPL
------ Ill. catalogs for 1878 and   PHi
1879. Ills. of scroll saws, lathes, etc. with
designs as above, also ills. of blades, drills,
chisels and even skates. 8vo., wrap.

1882 Philadelphia   PKsL
------ Ill. catalog.

1867 Hartford, Conn.   CtHi
THRALL, WILLIS & SON. Desc. price list
of rules, squares, bevels, levels and gauges.
4to., 4pp.

c.1876 Wilmington, Del.   PKsL
TRUMP BROTHERS. Ill. catalog of Fleetwood scroll saws, pat. 1872, lathes, designs,
etc. 16mo., 16pp., pict. wrap.

c.1890 Philadelphia   PKsL
WALTER'S, WILLIAM P. SONS. Est. 1831.
Catalog #9. Ill. price list of wood workers'
tools and foot power machinery, lathes, designs, blades, etc. 12mo., 244pp., fine ills.,
wrap.

c.1892 Philadelphia   PKsL
------ Ill. catalog of wood workers' tools
and hand and foot power machinery, etc.

1885-6 Chicago   ICHi
WILKINSON, THE JOHN CO. Ill. catalog
and price list of scroll saws, veneers, edged
tools and cutlery.

c.1880 New York   WHi
WILLIAMS & CO. Ill. catalog of Williams'
ornamental designs for fretwork, scroll
saws and fancy wood carving. 8vo., fine
pict. ref.

1880 Valley Falls, R. I.   PKsL
WOOD, W.J. & RICE, T.D. Ill.   CBaK
catalog of hand and bench screws, carvers'
mallets, wood clamps, etc. 8vo., 18pp.,
fine ills., pict. wrap.

1876 South Boston, Mass.   MH-BA
WOODS, S.A. MACHINE CO. Est. 1854.
Ill. catalog of planing and moulding machin-
ery. 4to., 38pp., fine ills., wrap.

COBBLER & SHOEMAKERS' TOOLS
AND MACHINERY

c.1870 New York   NHi
LEIBOLD, JOHN. Ill. catalog of leather and
findings, calf, lasts, harness and shoemakers' tools. One of the best ill. cobblers'
tools ref. 8vo., 24pp., fine ills., pict. wrap.

1871 Canton, Mass.   MWA
REED, FRANKLIN, MFG. Ill. catalog and
price list of hardware, with a fine section
of shoemakers' tools, as well as agricultural
and other trades. 8vo., 28pp., glt. pict. wrap.

1884 Cincinnati   OC
ROSS, MOYER MFG. CO. Ill. catalog of
boot and shoe machinery, cobblers' tools,
materials and supplies. 8vo., 236pp. and
over 500 ills. Pat. dates run 1864 to 1884.
Dec. cl., a swell ref.

COOPERS' TOOLS & MACHINERY

nd. Jersey City   ViWC
COLWELL COOPERATE CO. Catalog #26.
Ill. price list of tools, stock supplies for
barrels, containers. tubs, pails, etc.

1867 Glens Falls, N. Y.   MH-BA
COOL, FERGUSON & CO.   N
Thompson's pat. barrel machines. 16mo.,
8pp. with a plate, pict. wrap.

1881 Rochester, N. Y.   N
GREENWOOD, JOHN & CO. Rochester
Barrel Works. Ill. catalog of Greenwood's
pat. stave, heading and barrel and keg
machines. 8vo., 26pp., fine ills., pict. wrap.

c.1885 Buffalo, N. Y.   N
HOLMES, E. & B., MFG. Ill. catalog of
machinery and tools for mfg. barrels, kegs,
etc. 8vo., 20pp., pls., pict. wrap.

c.1900 Buffalo, N. Y.   NBuHi
------ Catalog M - Cooperage machinery,
tools and equipment. 4to., 169pp., ill., wrap.

1890 Boston   N
LANG & JACOBS. Catalog of coopers' supplies, stock, oil cabinets, coopers' tools,
etc. 8vo., 65pp., fine ills., pict. wrap.

1874
LITTLE, CHARLES E. See Builders'
Hardware Section.

1854 Elmira, N.Y.   NStlHi
TRAPP, WILLIAM CO. Elmira Barrel
Factory. Desc. and ill. catalog of Trapp's
pat. barrel machinery. 12mo., 32pp., with
fine tinted pls., glt. dec. wrap.

c.1870 Lockport, N.Y.   N
TREVOR MFG. CO. Catalog A. Ills. of
machinery for kegs, barrels, drums - bark-
ers, staves, cutters, packers. Large 8vo.,
48pp., fine ills., pict. wrap.

1887 Chicago   ICHi
WINNIE MACHINE WORKS. 14th annual
catalog of barrel hoop machinery, cooperage
tools and goods, stave and heading machines.
8vo., 16pp., fine ills.

1894 Chicago   ICHi
------ 20th annual catalog of tools and
hoop machinery, and a full line of money
making machinery and supplies. 8vo.,
32pp., fine ills., pict. wrap.

TOOLS FOR THE ICE MAN

1875-1900 Arlington, Mass.   MH-BA
WOOD, WILLIAM T. & CO. Est. 1834.
Oldest ice tool establishment in U.S. Ill.
catalog of ice tools, machinery, elevators,
ice houses and wagons - in fact every tool
and machine connected with this once active
and prosperous industry.

The collection at MH-BA is without question
one of the most complete in any field of
American production in the 19th century,
covering both hand tools, horse power, delivery, machinery through its development
for 25 years.

The following are available for study:
1876, 1878, 1879, 1881, 1882, 1886, 1888,
1889, 1890, 1891, 1892, 1893, 1894, c.1894,
1896, 1897, 1898, 1899. All 12mo. and 8vo.,
from 32 to 48pp. of fine ills. with ptd. and
pict. wrap.

1900 Arlington, Mass.   MH-BA
------ Ill. catalog, revised   ICHi
prices, hand and machine tools, elevators,
wagons, etc. of finest quality. 8vo., 48pp.
wrap.

MILLERS' MILLS, SUPPLIES & TOOLS

1881 Chicago   MnHi
AMERICAN GRINDING MILL CO. Ill. catalog of mills and supplies.

1874 Cincinnati   MnHi
BLYMER MFG. CO. Ill. catalog of sugar
cane mills, evaporators, farm machinery,
bells, etc.

1880 Cincinnati   OHi
------ 21st annual ed. of the Sorgo hand
book. Desc. and ills. sugar making tools
and machinery. 8vo., 24pp.

c.1885 Cincinnati   OC
BRADFORD, THOMAS & CO. Est. 1840.
Bradford portable under runner mills for
corn, wheat, stock feed, etc. - furnishings,
belts, stones, pulley and geared mills. 8vo.,
4pp., ills.

1898 Hyde Park, Mass.   MH-BA
BRAINARD MILLING MACHINE CO. Ill.
price list of milling machines, gear cutters,
mill and tool grinders, tools, etc. Pocket
catalog. 16mo., 104pp., fine ills.

1900 Cincinnati   OC
CINCINNATI MILLING MACHINE CO.
Treatise on milling and milling machines.
8vo., 151pp., fine pls. and ills., lea.

1774 Philadelphia   Evans #13201
CLARKSON & BONSELL. Millstones to be
sold by Clarkson & Bonsell, Philadelphia.
Ptd. by Robert Aitken.

1859 Cincinnati   OHi
CLARK SORGO MACHINE CO. Ill. price
list of cane mills. 12mo., 24pp., ills., wrap.

1864 Cincinnati   OHi
------ Ill. catalog of cane mills, etc.

1866 Cincinnati   OHi
------ Ill. catalog of cane mills   OC
and handbook to Cook's evaporator, etc.
12mo., 13 and 23pp., fine ills., pict. wrap.

1888 Cleveland   MnHi
CLEVELAND STONE CO. Ill. price list of
grindstones for all purposes, mounted for
hand and power use in mills, scythe stones,
etc. 8vo., fine ills.

1876 New Haven   CtHi
HARRISON, EDWARD STANDARD MILL CO.
Est. 1847. Ill. price list of Harrison's celebrated burr stone mills, flouring mills, etc.
8vo., 16pp., pict. wrap.

1097 New Haven   DeWE
HARRISON, LEONARD D. MFG. CO. Est.
1847. Ill. catalog of Harrison's standard
vertical and horizontal burr stone mills and
mill machinery and tools. 8vo., 40pp., pict.
wrap.

MANNING, H.S. & CO. See Hardware -
Miscellaneous Machinery.

1881 St. Louis   MnHi
MANNY & BAUER MFG. CO. Ill. catalog
of farm machinery, but also showing fine
ills. of sugar cane mills. See also Agricultural Machinery.

1887 Philadelphia   DeWE
MILLBOURNE MILLS CO. Est. 1814.
Antecedents and present operations. Ills.
of procession at Centennial and display at
Philadelphia, Sept. 15, 1887. 1814 to date.
8vo., fine photos. Labels in col.,fld. plate,
cl.

1875 Philadelphia   PPL
MITCHELL, J.M., agent. Ill. catalog of
belting, mill supplies, pulleys, tools, etc.
with prices and instructions. 27pp.

1886 Utica, N. Y.   NSyHi
MUNSON BROTHERS. Est. 1825. Annual
catalog of portable mills and mill machinery - fine ills. of standard, double geared,
long column, 4-run mills, soap stones,
spindles, also drawings and plans. 8vo.,
64pp., pict. wrap.

1873 Richmond, Ind.   MH-BA
NORDYKE MARMON & CO. Est. c.1850.
Moved to Indianapolis in 1876. Ill. price
list of mill furnishings, flour mills, belting
mills, water wheels, shafting and belting.
Sm. 8vo., 118pp.

c.1888 Indianapolis   In
------ Ill. price list of portable grinding
mills. 6pp., tests., pict. wrap.

1893 Indianapolis   MH-BA
------ Catalog of books on mills and milling, etc. 8vo., 68pp., ills., wrap.

c.1900 Indianapolis   MnHi
------ Price list of flour and cereal mills
and machinery, and mill supplies. 4to.,
560pp., fine ills.

1880 Buffalo, N. Y.   DeWE
NOYE, JOHN T. & SONS. Ill. and desc. circular of portable mills, flouring and grist,
plantation corn mills, Niagara sheller, lead
and paint crushers, mill stones and furnishings. 8vo., 56pp., pict. wrap.

1887-8 St. Louis   MnHi
OYLER, GEORGE K. Ill. catalog of sorgo
and sugar mills, furnaces and evaporators.

1888-9 St. Louis   MnHi
------ Ill. catalog of sugar mills, etc.
See also Agricultural Implements and
Machinery.

1849 Baltimore
PAGE, GEORGE. Inventor, Machinist and
Manufacturer. Ill. and very desc. brochure
of mills and powers - hand, horse and wind -
stationary and portable - corn, planing, saw,
etc. with delightful woodcuts of Blair's mill,
near Washington City - also thrashing
machines, post hole borers and model mills.
8vo., 32pp. and 8 page appendix, pict. wrap.
N.B. The pity of it is that it is still in a
private library and can't be located.

1850 Baltimore
------ Ill. catalog of grist, saw and wind
mills and supplies. 8vo., 56pp., pict. wrap.
The Prairie Cottage mill is a gem.

1874 Winona, Wisc.   NNC
PORTER, L.C. MILLING CO. Ill. catalog
of model mills made by Still & Bierce of
Dayton, Ohio. Fol., 8pp., fine pls.

1884 Richmond, Ind.   In
RICHMOND CITY MILL WORKS. Ill. catalog of flouring and roller mills, mill stones
and supplies. 8vo., 180pp., a great pict.
ref., wrap.

1885 St. Louis   MnHi
RUMSEY, L.M. MFG. CO. Ill. catalog of
sorgo and sugar mill machinery, cider and
wine mills and presses.

1887 St. Louis   MnHi
------ Ill. catalog of mills and supplies.

1884-5 Chicago   MnHi
STOVER MFG. CO. Ill. catalog of grinding
mills, etc. Largest line of grinding mills
in the world.

1888 Chicago   MnHi
------ Ill. catalog of mills.

1895 Chicago   IHi
------ Ill. catalog of grinding mills and
supplies. 12mo., 64pp., pict. wrap. See
also Bicycles.

1874 St. Louis   MoSHi
TODD, G. & W. Ill. catalog and pattern
price list of mill furnishings of every kind.

c.1899 Essex Junction, Vt.   VtHi
TRUAX, J.W. MFG. Eagle Mill Picks -
best and cheapest for all work on burr mill
stones. Ills. of picks and mill stones. Sq.
16mo., 24pp., pict. wrap.

nd. Appleton, Wis.   MnHi
VALLEY IRON WORKS MFG. CO. Ill. catalog of mill supplies.

1886 Chicago   MnHi
VICTOR GRINDING MILL CO. Ill. catalog
of mills for many purposes.

c.1876 Winona, Wis.   DeWE
WINONA MFG. CO. Ill. catalog #20. Ills.
of cob, grist, grinding and saw mills, cutters,
hullers, presses and shellers. 8vo., 64pp.,
pict. wrap.

MINERS' TOOLS, MACHINERY & SUPPLIES

1865 San Francisco   CHi
BANDMANN, NIELSEN & CO. Nobel's pat.
blasting oil. 8vo., 33pp., 5 ills. with 8p.
supplement.

N.B. Although the meticulous may question
this listing, I maintain that because of the
importance of Alfred Nobel's discovery, and
the fact that his blasting oil must be offered
in hundreds of trade catalogs before 1900 of
which we have no record, this 1865 ill. desc.
belongs here as a sale catalog recording
his triumph in finding a backer and starting
production.

c.1900 Denver   CoD
BLAKE MINING & MILLING CO. The
Blake Morooher electrical ore separator
with diags. and ills. and mining data. 16mo.

1866 San Francisco   CHi
BOOTH, H.J. & CO. Union Iron Works.
Circular and pattern list of pumps and
mining machinery. 8vo., 146pp., fine ills.,
wrap.

1865 Boston   PPL
BOSTON MILLING & MFG. CO. Ill. and
desc. brochure with tinted pls. of some of
the best mining and ore working machinery
of this decade.

1876 Boston   CSmH
BURLEIGH ROCK DRILL CO. Ill. price
list and catalog of Burleigh's rock drills and
mining machinery. 36pp.

c.1883 Santa Cruz & San Francisco, Calif.
CALIFORNIA POWDER WORKS.   PKsL
Price list of Santa Cruz Gun-   CHi
powders. Ills. of labels:- Cabinet, Eureka,
California Sporting, Duck, Pacific Rifle,
Quail, - Hercules blasting powder, etc.
8vo., pict. cl. - without question, the best
pict. record of both blasting and sporting
and military powders of this period. See
also Sporting Goods.   N.B. See Van Gelder
& Schletter - History of Explosive Industry
in America. Columbia Univ. Press 1927.

Eventually bought out by duPont, this group
of men headed by Captain John H. Baird
saved the day for the California miners and
the Union when the Confederacy threatened

to cut off all powder and explosive shipments
from the Atlantic coast manufacturers.

c.1890 Emporium, Pa.   PKsL
CLIMAX POWDER MFG. CO. Climax powders for blasting and mining purposes - and
how to use it. 24mo., 16pp., ill., pict.wrap.

1882 Denver   CoD
COLORADO MINING WORKS. Ill. catalog
of boilers, engines, bolts, forgings, car
wheels, etc.

c.1893 Cleveland   OHi
CUMMER, F.D. & SON CO. Ill. price list of
Cummer's drying machines, ore roasters,
calcining machinery, kilns, etc. 8vo., 72pp.
Plans, drawings and ills. Wrap.

1889 Denver   CoD
DAVIS, F.M. Mining & Milling Machine Co.
Ill. catalog of Davis' pat. horse powers, etc.
for mining and milling machinery.

c.1892
DIAMOND PROSPECTING CO. See Oil Well
Machinery and Tools.

c.1890 Ansonia, Conn.   CtHi
FARREL FOUNDRY & MACHINE CO. Est.
1868. Ill. catalog of Bacon & Farrel's ore
and rock crushing machinery. 4to., 74pp.,
pict. wrap.

c.1892 Ansonia, Conn.   CtHi
------ Ill. catalog of Bacon's hoisting
engines for mining machinery. 4to., 132pp.,
fine ills., wrap.

1885-1900 Chicago   ICHi
FRASER & CHALMERS. CoD DSi CHi
Ill. catalogs of steam engines, mining
machinery, air compressors, ore concen-
trators and other mining apparatus and
equipment. 8vo., vp., fld. pls., diags.,
plans of mining machinery, ptd. and pict.
wrap. DSi has a bound volume of examples
1885-1900 numbering 800pp.; CoD and ICHi
have fine runs, and CHi reports several.

HENDY, JOSHUA MACHINE WORKS. See
Hardware - Miscellaneous Machinery.

1876 New York   MH-BA
INGERSOL ROCK DRILL CO. Pat. 1872.
Ill. price list of rock drills, tests. 12mo.,
32pp.

c.1900 San Francisco   CHi
MERRALLS MILL CO. Ill. catalog of
Merrall's rapid stamp mill tension quartz
mill, rock breakers, etc. Tests. from
Hudson Mining Co., etc. 8vo., 8pp., pict.
wrap.

c.1895 San Francisco   CHi
PARKE & LACY CO. Ill. catalog of hoisting
and pumping machinery for prospectors.
4to., 12pp., pict. wrap.

c.1896 San Francisco   CHi
------ Ill. catalog of Lidgerwood Mfg's.
hoisting engines. 4to., 12pp., wrap.

1899 San Francisco   CHi
------ Ill. catalog of hoisting, pumping and
crushing machinery. 8vo., 38pp., wrap.

1878 San Francisco   CHi
PRESCOTT, SCOTT & CO. Ill. catalog of
mining machinery, smelting furnaces, boilers, engines, pumps, etc. in 10 sections.
8vo., 120pp., wrap.

1886 New York   MH-BA
RAND ROCK DRILL CO. Ill. catalog of
rock drills, improved air compressors and
all kinds of mining machinery. Sm. 4to.,
128pp., fine ills.

1889 New York   DSi
------ Ill. and desc. catalog of rock drills
and air compressors. 190pp.

1884 San Francisco   CHi
RISDON & LOCOMOTIVE WORKS. Ill. catalog of hangings, pulleys, shaftings and
mining equipment. 8vo., pict. wrap.

1885 San Francisco   CHi
------ Handbook and catalog of water
powers for mining, with tables, etc. 8vo.,
ill., wrap.

c.1886 San Francisco   CHi
------ Ill. handbook and price list of the
Heine safety boiler. 8vo., wrap.

1890 San Francisco   CHi
------ Ill. catalog of Cornish pumping
engines and mining appliances. 8vo., wrap.

1895 San Francisco   CHi
------ Ill. catalog #7. Mining Machinery.

c.1900 San Francisco   TxDaDeG
------ Catalog #12. Gold mill-   CHi
ing machinery. 8vo., 90pp., fine ills., pict.
wrap.

1881 Boston   CHi
SAMPSON'S, GEORGE H. New England
Agency. Ill. catalog of Atlas powder, nitro-
glycerine, fuses, etc. 8vo., 16pp., wrap.

1894 Sacramento, Calif.   CHi
SCHAW, INGRAM, BATCHER & CO. Ill.
catalog of sheet steel, iron pipe and mining
supplies. 8vo., wrap.

c.1900 Harrisburg, Pa.   PHI
STAUFFER, B.G. Stauffer's cata-   PKsl
log of prospectors', Miners' and Treasure
Seekers' Instruments - Valuable Details -
Do Not Lose! Ills. of mineral rods, dipping
needles, earth mirrors, goldmeter and
guide manual. Tall 4to., 16pp., - circular
enc. - pict. wrap. N.B. Probably issued
to catch the Alaska gold rush neophytes and
enthusiasts.

1898 Denver   CoD
UNION PUBLIC ORE SAMPLERS CO. Ill.
catalog of hoisting machinery, Diamond core
drills, etc.

1876 New York   MH-BA
UNION ROCK DRILL CO. Consolidation of
Winchester Rock Drill Co., G. H. Reynolds
and Delameter Iron Works. Ill. catalog of
steam and compressed air rock drills, complete outfits for tunneling, mining and rock
working. 8vo., 7pp.

nd. Cleveland   OHi
WELLMAN-SEAVER-MORGAN CO. Desc.
and ill. catalog of ore and coal handling
machinery. Fol., 103pp.

1899 San Francisco   CHi
WHITE, ROGERS & CO. Catalog #1. Mining
machinery, hoisting and pumping works, etc.
8vo., 18pp., ills., wrap.

OIL WELL SUPPLIES
See also MINING.

c.1885 Bradford, Pa.   MH-BA
BOVAIRD & SEYFANG. Central Iron Works.
Ill. catalog of oil, gas and artesian well supplies, price list of drilling tools. 8vo.,
24pp. and 4 page folder.

c.1890 Bradford, Pa.   PKsL
------ Engines and boilers, drilling tools,
oil well supplies. 8vo., 40pp. fine ills.,
pict. wrap., view of plant, etc.

c.1900 Lawrenceburg, Ind.   In
COOK, A.D. MFG. CO. Ill. catalog of improved tube well supplies, steam pumps,
etc. 16mo., 50pp.

1889 Chicago   MH-BA
DIAMOND PROSPECTING CO. Ill. catalog
of drills, tools and supplies. 8vo., 56pp.

1891 Chicago   MH-BA
------ Ill. catalog #7. 8vo., 72pp.

c.1892 Chicago   ICHi
------ Ill. price list of Sullivan Diamond
prospecting drills; sizes B, E, M and R.
8vo., 10pp., pict. wrap.

1870 Oil City, Bradford, and later Pittsburgh.
EATON & COLE. Ill. catalog   TxDaUSS
of oil well supplies. 47pp.

See E. B. Swanson's Petroleum Bibliography - A Century of Oil and Gas in Books,
Appleton, 1960.

John Eaton was one of the flock that
swarmed Oil City in August 1859. In 1862
he started the first oil well supply business
as a broker, and in 1867 as a manufacturer
with Mr. Cole. In 1875 the firm name was
Eaton, Cole & Burnham. In 1878 the name
was changed again to the Oil Well Supply Co.
Ltd.

In 1886 the business was moved to Pittsburgh and by 1889 was the largest producer
in the world. Incorporated in 1891, the
business was taken over by United States
Steel in 1930. The Oil Well Supply Division
in Dallas, Texas now preserves an almost
complete collection of catalogs and price
lists from its beginning under the firm name
of Eaton & Cole in 1870. Mr. Swanson believes this to be the outstanding library - of
catalogs - in this field.

The following are all located at TxDaUSS
with other locations added in one or two
cases:-

1872 New price list for Oct. - 29pp.

1872 New price list for Nov. - 42pp.

1873 Price list of oil well supplies.

1874 Oil well price list. 44pp.

1875 Eaton, Cole & Burnham price list.
142pp.

1876 Oil Well price list #8. 133pp.

1876 Oil Well price list #9. 34pp.

1877 Price List. 26pp.

1878 Oil Well wholesale price list. 39pp.

1879 Eaton, Cole & Burnham price list.
47pp.

1879 Ill. wholesale catalog. 140pp.

1879 Wholesale price list. 42pp.

1880 Oil Well price list. 48pp.

1881 Oil Well price list. 50pp.

1882 Oil Well price list. 50pp.   PKsL

1883 Oil Well price list. 52pp.

1884 Oil Well catalog. 160pp.

1885 Oil Well ill. price list. 78pp.

1886 Oil Well ill. price list. 83pp.

1887 Oil Well price list. 108pp.

1888 Eaton, Cole & Burnham price list.
88pp.

1888 Oil Well ill. general catalog. 244pp.

1890 Eaton, Cole & Burnham revised
price list. 15pp.

1892 Oil Well ill. catalog of artesian well
supplies for oil, gas, water or minerals.
4to., 374pp., cl.   MH-BA

1893 Oil Well catalog, pocket edition.
207pp., cl.   DSi

1894 Oil Well price list, ill. 330pp.

1896 Cipher code of Eaton, Cole & Burnham and Oil Well Supply Co. with price list.
192pp.

1899 Eaton, Cole & Burnham Co. ill. catalog and price list. 336pp.

1900 Oil Well general ill. catalog. 463pp.

N.B. The complete firm name Oil Well
Supply Co. Ltd. has been reduced to Oilwell,
as reported to me by Mr. Swanson, to save
time and space. It is interesting to note
that the catalogs use both Eaton, Cole &
Burnham and Oil Well Supply Co. Ltd. right
up to 1900; also, as the business grew, so
grew the catalogs, from 29 and 47pp. to 463.
It is my understanding that TxDaUSS, Oil
Well Supply Co. Div. also has saved and
cataloged its many offerings during the 20th
century.

1883 Erie, Pa.   PKsL
ERIE CITY IRON WORKS. Ill. catalog of
steam engines, boilers, saw mills, and portable engines. 4to., 20pp., pict. wrap.

c.1885 Erie, Pa.   PKsL
------ Compliments of . . . Ill. catalog of
engines for all purposes, stationary and
mounted on wheels for oil fields, etc. 8vo.,
20pp., fine ills. For complete listings see
Hardware - Machinery, Engines & Supplies.

nd. Chicago   MnHi
GARDEN CITY OIL CO. Catalog.

1886 Buffalo, N. Y.
HARDWICKE & WARE, Mfg. Ill. price list
of oil and salt well supplies. See Hardware -
Miscellaneous Machinery, Engines and Supplies.

1792 Philadelphia   PPL
HIRTE, TOBIAS. Listed as the earliest
possible broadside printed to sell oil for
medicinal purposes. Included here to list
the oil mining equipment for 1792:- one
feather which carefully swept over the sur-
face of the water in the spring collects the
oil. The price of feathers is not given. See
also Medical and Surgical Instruments.

1877 Cincinnati   OC
MIAMI OIL WORKS. Price list of oils.
8vo., 4pp., pict. wrap. of works.

c.1878 Boston   MH-BA
NATIONAL PETROLEUM GAS CO. Associated with Swampscott Machine Co. and
George K. Paul & Co. Hanlon process for
making gas from petroleum. 8vo., 14pp.,
ill.

1865 New York   MH-BA
NEW YORK STEAM ENGINE WORKS. Ill.
price list of portable mining and petroleum
engines. 8vo., 8pp.

1878-9 Philadelphia   PHi
PEIRCE WELL EXCAVATOR & PROSPEC-
TING MACHINE CO. Ill. catalog of oil well
machinery. 8vo., 56pp., fine ills., pict.
wrap.

c.1874 Pottsville, Pa.   DSi
PENNSYLVANIA DIAMOND DRILL CO.
Desc. price list of Diamond drilling appara-
tus. 32pp.

1876 Rochester, N. Y.   N
PLUMBAGO OIL WORKS. Circular #2 -
French's plumbago oil - greatest achievement in science of lubrication for railroads,
sewing machines, all machines. 12mo.,
30pp., wrap.

1883 St. Joseph, Mo.   MoSHi
RUST, O. EAGLE WELL DRILL CO. Old
Reliable well augers from 1875-1883. Ills.
of drills, augers, engines, rigs, etc. 8vo.,
16pp., fine ills., pict. wrap.

Erie, Pa.
SKINNER ENGINE CO. See Hardware -
Miscellaneous Machinery, Engines and
Supplies.

1866 New York   MH-BA
UNITED STATES BLASTING OIL CO. Ill.
price list of nitroglycerine products, etc.
8vo., 56pp., wrap.

1886 Rochester, N. Y.   MnHi
VACUUM OIL CO. Ill. price list.

1873 Phoenixville, Pa.   PKsL
VICTOR ROCK DRILL CO. Ill. price list of
the Victor Rock Drill. Pat. 1873 for well
borers and prospectors. 24mo., 12pp., pict.
wrap.

1879 Phoenixville, Pa.   PKsL
------ Ill. catalog of drills of all sizes and
for any angle - for borers and prospectors.
Centennial award, etc. 12mo., 14pp., tests.,
pict. wrap.

c.1886 Goshen, Ind.
WALKER, EDWARD W. CARRIAGE CO.
See Hardware - Miscellaneous Machinery,
Engines and Supplies.

PLUMBERS' TOOLS & MACHINERY
c.1860-1900

As explained in many other cases, plumbers'
tools are usually found in catalogs listing,
describing and illustrating everything from
a scenic bowl to a hand painted tub. To
avoid double listings and confusion I recommend the following, cataloged under Plumbing, for complete details of plumbers' tools.
There is only one example that is exclusively tools.

1885 Bridgeport, Conn.   MH-BA
ARMSTRONG, F. Ill. catalog of water, gas
and steamfitters' tools. List of customers.
12mo., 57pp., wrap.

See under Chapter on Plumbing:-

Fuller, Albert. New York
Gilbert, J. F. New Haven, Conn.
Harrison, Charles. New York
Meyer, Henry C. & Co. New York
Mott, J. L. Iron Works. New York
Providence Lead Co. Providence, R. I.
Simmons, John. New York
Walworth, James J. & Co. Detroit, Mich.

BERGER BROTHERS. See Tinsmiths'
Tools.

SURVEYORS' INSTRUMENTS

1895 St. Louis   MoSHi
ALOE, A.S. & CO. Ill. catalog of surveying
and mathematical instruments.

1884 Boston   NN
BUFF & BERGER. Handbook and ill. catalog of engineering and surveying instruments.
8vo., 150pp., pict. wrap.

1896 Boston   NNU
------ Ill. catalog with additional pls. of
instruments - measuring currents, for
water power, for mining, etc.

1874 EDDY, GEORGE M. & CO. See Hardware - General Merchandise.

1885 Washington, D. C.   MH-BA
FAUTH & CO. Ill. catalog of astronomical,
engineering and surveying instruments.
8vo., 104pp.

1868 Troy, N. Y.   NR
GURLEY, W. & L.E. CO. A manual N
of instruments for American engineers and
surveyors. Fine ills. 12mo., 164pp., pict.
cl.

1870 Troy, N. Y.   CtY
------ Manual of instruments. Pls. by
Benson. 12mo., 180pp. N.B. We have
handled 28 editions of this manual and ill.
catalog. There are probably a dozen locations that have not as yet been reported.

c.1885 Cincinnati   OC
HERM, PFISTER & CO. Ill. catalog and
price list of surveying and engineering instruments. 8vo., 16pp., pict. wrap.

c.1894 Philadelphia   PKsL
KNIGHT, F.C. & CO. Ill. catalog of engineering and surveying instruments and
materials mfg. by . . . 4to., 64pp., pict.
wrap.

1898 San Francisco   CHi
SALA, J.C. Ill. catalog and manual of civil
engineers' and surveyors' instruments.
8vo., 167pp., fine ills., wrap.

1788 Philadelphia   MBAt
WALL, GEORGE JR. A description with instructions for the use of a newly invented
surveying instrument called the Trigonometer. For the making and vending of which
the inventor hath obtained an exclusive right
for twenty one years from the Legislature
of Pennsylvania . . . etc. 8vo., plate and
32pp.

nd. Philadelphia   PHi
YOUNG & SONS. Mfg. Ill. circular of
engineering, mining and surveying instruments. 16mo., 12pp.

1892 Philadelphia   PHi
------ Ill. catalog of instruments for surveyors, etc. Also the American transit instrument, etc. 8vo., 85pp.

TEXTILE MFG. MACHINERY & SUPPLIES

1881 Providence, R. I.   MH-BA
BROWN BROTHERS & CO. Successor to
Butler Brown & Co. Ill. catalog of supplies
for cotton, woolen, jute, silk and flax mills.
8vo., 252pp., fine ills., cl.

c.1892 Racine   MH-BA
CASE, J.I. THRESHING MACHINE CO. Est.
1842. Catalog of machinery for harvesting
cotton - gatherers, leaf cleaners and separators. 16mo., 32pp., wrap. N.B. It is
ironic that the only catalog before 1900 reported for this mighty producer of American
agricultural machinery must be listed under
cotton picking. There must be dozens hidden on dusty, unchecked library shelves.

1871 Philadelphia   PKsL
CHAMPION COTTON GIN CO. OF PA.
Champion cotton gin and cotton huller, pat.
1867. 8vo., 16pp., ill., pict. wrap.

1861 Worcester, Mass.   MH-BA
CLEVELAND, E.C. Ill. price list of cloth
finishing machinery. 8vo., 12pp.

1876 Worcester, Mass.   MH-BA
CROMPTON LOOM WORKS. Ill. centennial
catalog of looms for cotton and woolen manufacturers. 7x10, 21pp., wrap.

1874 Providence, R. I.   RHi
HOPE COTTON CO. Price list of Joe
Ralston Plantation Machinery, Lone Star Gin
Feeder & Cotton Cleaner, etc. 8vo., 16pp.,
tests., wrap.

1876 Silver Creek, N. Y.   NCooHi
HOWES, BABCOCK & CO. Ill. price list of
Eureka smut and separating machines and
mill furnishings generally. 50pp.

1853 Bridesburg, Pa.   MH-BA
JENKS, ALFRED & SON. Ill. catalog of
textile machinery. 16mo., 86pp., cl.

1882 Lowell, Mass.   MH-BA
LOWELL MACHINE SHOP. Inc. 1845. Ill.
catalog of paper and cotton machinery. 4to.,
36pp., wrap.

1882 Lowell, Mass.   TxDaDeG
------ Ill. catalog. Large 4to., frs. and
fine pls. 76pp., glt. pict. cl.

1883 Lowell, Mass.   MH-BA
------ Ill. catalog of cotton machines.
4to., 20pp., wrap.

1886 Lowell, Mass.   MH-BA
------ Ill. catalog. 4to., 36pp., wrap.

1897 Lowell, Mass.   MH-BA
------ Ill. catalog of improved cotton
machinery. 4to., 104pp., cl.

1899 Lowell, Mass.   MH-BA
------ Ill. catalog of ring frames, ring
twisters, etc. 4to., 96pp., wrap.

1900 Lowell   MH-BA
------ Ill. catalog of looms, slashers and
warpers. 4to., 144pp., cl.

1876 Taunton, Mass.   TxDaDeG
MASON MACHINE WORKS. Builders of
Locomotives and Cotton Machinery. Est.
1842. Ill. catalog of cotton machinery. 4to.,
64pp., fine pls. and details, glt. pict. cl.

1898 Taunton, Mass.   TxDaDeG
------ Ill. catalog of cotton   MH-BA
machinery. Fine pls. of mills throughout
the U.S.A. showing machinery in use. 8vo.,
352pp., cl.

1870 Philadelphia   PKsL
MATTHEWS, C.W. & CASE, J.G. Ill. catalog of reversed motion Champion cotton
gins. 8vo., 13pp., plate, wrap.

c.1880 Springfield, O.   OHi
REED MFG. CO. Desc. loom book. Ill.
catalog of the Weavers' Friend and the Ideal
Looms. 16mo., 16pp., wrap.

c.1899 Reading, Pa.   MH-BA
THUN & JANSSEN. Est. 1892. Ill. catalog
and price list of braiding machinery. 8vo.,
78pp., wrap.

1883 Whitinsville, Mass.   MH-BA
WHITIN MACHINE WORKS. Ill. catalog of
cotton machinery. 4to., 80pp., cl.

1868 Utica, N.Y.   MH-BA
WILLIAMS, J.H. & N.A. Est. 1831. Ill.
catalog and price list of cotton and woolen
machinery, dye stuffs and supplies. 16mo.,
64pp., wrap.

TINSMITHS' TOOLS & SUPPLIES

c.1885 Philadelphia   PKsL
BERGER, L.D. BROTHERS. Mfg. Ill. catalog of tinners' and plumbers' ware, tools,
equipment and supplies. 12mo., 64pp., fine
ills., pict. wrap.

1892 Philadelphia   PKsL
------ Ill. catalog of tinners' tools, etc.
12mo., 48pp., wrap.

1893 Philadelphia   PKsL
------ Ill. catalog of crimpers,   PHi
crests, machines and tools. 12mo., 64pp.,
pict. wrap.

1879 New York & Tarrytown, N.Y.   NNU
BROMBACHER, CHARLES. Pocantico Tool
& Machine Works. Ill. catalog and price
list of tinsmiths' tools and machinery, paper
box machines, produce triers, etc. 24mo.,
36pp., fine ills. of tools, pict. wrap.

1892 Baltimore   CSmH
LYON, CONKLIN & CO. Ill. catalog of tinsmiths' tools and machines. 84pp. of fine
ills., wrap.

c.1880 Philadelphia   PKsL
MERCHANT & CO. Ill. price list of tinsmiths' tools, tables of gauges for tinners,
etc. 16mo., 64pp., wrap.

1871 Southington, Plantsville & East Berlin,
Conn.   MH-BA
PECK, STOW & WILCOX. Est. 1870. Suc-
cessors to Peck, Smith Mfg. Co., S. Stow
Mfg. Co., Roys & Wilcox Co., A.W. Whitney
& Sons, J.E. Hull & Co., and Woodruff &
Wilcox. Ill. catalog of tinsmiths' tools,
machines, supplies and general hardware.
8vo., 112pp., pict. wrap.

1880 Southington, Conn.   NNMM
------ Ill. catalog and price list of tin-
smiths' tools and machines. 735pp., lea.
One of the best tool catalogs located.

nd. Newport, Ky.   MnHi
ROTHWEILER MFG. CO. Ill. catalog of
tinners' tools and machines.

ST. LOUIS STAMPING CO. See also House
Furnishings.

1873 Philadelphia   PHi
TAYLOR, N. & G. CO. Ill. price list of tinsmiths' tools and machines.

1878-9 Philadelphia   PHi
------ Ill. catalog of tinsmiths' tools.

c.1890 Philadelphia   PHi
------ Ill. catalog of tin plate, iron, tools,
machines and stamped ware. 8vo., 80pp.,
wrap.

Chapter 28

Hardware—Miscellaneous Machinery, Engines & Supplies

At the risk of having the reader feel I am belittling the average intelligence and common sense, I will attempt to outline the contents of this chapter. My interest is your interest and the best index errs least in being too complete.

Tools and machinery for the blacksmith, cabinetmaker, carpenter, etc. must, as explained, be also included here. The following catalogs have been corralled separately because they date, describe and illustrate what was known generally before 1900 as heavy hardware. Here you will find catalogs that contain tools and machinery for all crafts and trades under two covers. Also, this is the section for information on brass supplies, cranes, electric dynamos, elevators, engines for a small lathe or a city lighting plant, iron and steel, gears and parts, steam engines for all purposes, and, in short all goods and products that kept and still keep American industry at top level. Keeping that small word think in mind, remember to use the index. It may seem logical that locomotives and fire engines appear under this heading; however, the general collecting interest warranted separate chapters.

I repeat, if hardware is your problem, use all three chapters. If you bought your last bird cage in a hardware store, don't assume that all bird cages are considered hardware by the world at large. There are lots of them illustrated in catalogs under House Furnishings, Department Stores and even Jewelry.

1888 Rochester, N. H.   NR
ACME CO. Rochester Machine Tools Works. Ill. catalog of machine tools, still leads, etc., proven by five years production. 8vo., 24pp., pict. wrap.

1881 Boston   OAkF
ADAMS, THOMAS B. Ill. catalog of oak tanned leather belting for mill and other machinery.

1898 San Francisco   CHi
ALEXANDER - YOST CO. Ill. catalog of hardware, mechanics' tools, workshop machinery, improved novelties, inventions, etc. 4to., 106pp., pict. wrap.

1879 Milwaukee, Wis.   CSmH
ALLIS, EDWARD P. & CO. Ill. catalog of Reynold's improved Corliss engines. 36pp.

1852 Waterbury, Conn. & vp.   CtWAB
AMERICAN BRASS CO. Est. 1812. Earliest printed record reported. Issued by:
Ansonia Brass Co.   Brown & Elton
Benedict & Burnham   Wm. Stephens & Son
Brown & Brothers   Wallace & Sons
            Waterbury Brass Co.

Tariff of prices of brass wire for mfg'rs. high brass, low brass, gilding and copper wire. July 1, 1852. One leaf.

1853-75 Waterbury, Conn. & vp.   CtWAB
AMERICAN BRASS CO. Reported by . . . Collection of price lists of brass wire for manufacturers issued by 13 Conn. firms during this period.

Ansonia Brass Co.   Bristol Brass & Clock
Brown & Brothers   Co.
Brown & Elton   Benedict & Burnham
Hoppock & Jacobs   Scoville Mfg. Co.
Samuel Crofts   Wm. Stephens & Son
James G. Moffet   Waterbury Brass Co.
Wallace & Sons   Wolcottville Brass Co.

1884 Waterbury, Conn.   CtWAB
AMERICAN BRASS ASSOCIATION. Price list of German silver sheet. Jan. 17.

1889 Waterbury, Conn.   CtWAB
------ List #2. Catalog of sheet and roll brass, tubing, etc. May 20.

1882 Waterbury, Conn.   CtWAB
AMERICAN COPPER RIVET ASSOCIATION. Price list of copper rivets and burs. Jan. 1.

1900 Cincinnati   OC
AMERICAN TOOL WORKS CO. Ill. catalog
of special machines for bicycle parts, etc.
12mo., 436pp., fine ills., lea.

1879 Boston   MH-BA
AMERICAN TUBE WORKS. Seamless brass
and copper tubing, locomotive, marine and
stationary boilers. 8vo., 20pp., wrap.

1873 Woonsocket, R. I.   NjOE
AMERICAN TWIST DRILL CO. Ill. catalog
of Diamond soled emery wheels and general
machinery. 12mo., 20pp., wrap.

1870 Jersey City   MH-BA
AMERICAN WATER & GAS PIPE CO. Price
list of wrought iron and cement pipe. 8vo.,
26pp.

c.1895 Worcester, Mass.   DSi
AMERICAN WHEELOCK ENGINE CO. Price
list of Greene-Wheelock steam engines.
20pp.

1881 Oswego, N. Y. & Chicago   MnHi
AMES IRON WORKS. Ill. catalog of stationary and portable steam engines, etc. 4to.,
24pp., pict. wrap.

1887 Oswego, N. Y. & Chicago   DSi
------ Ill. catalog with fine pls. of engines.
8vo., 28pp., wrap.

c.1870 Chicopee Falls, Mass.   DSi
AMES MFG. CO. Catalog and price list with
fine ills. of swing tool makers' engine lathes,
boring, drilling, milling and sinking machinery, pulley turners, gear cutters, planers
and improved brick machines, etc. 12mo.,
20pp. plus 7 extra pls. and pict. wrap.

1876 Chicopee Falls, Mass.
------ Catalog and price list of special
machinery for gun stocks, sewing machines,
special tools. 24mo., 36pp., ills., pict. wrap.

AMOSKEAG MFG. CO. See Fire Engines.

1900 Ansonia, Conn.   CtWAB
ANSONIA BRASS & COPPER CO. Ill. catalog of general products.

1877 London, Eng.   DSi
APPLEBY BROTHERS. Ill. handbook of
hoisting machinery. 158pp.

1885 Providence, R. I.   RHi
ARMINGTON & SIMS ENGINE CO. Ill. cat-
alog of A & S engines, tests. by Thomas
Edison and others. 8vo., 58pp., wrap.

c.1880 Philadelphia   PHi
ARNY, C.W. & SONS. Ill. catalog of leather
and oak leather belting for mills and machinery, fire hose, reels, industrial rubber
parts, etc. 12mo., 40pp., wrap.

c.1883 Boston   PPL
ASHTON VALVE CO. Ill. price list of safety valves for pumps, steam engines, boilers,
etc. 10pp.

1881 Indianapolis   PPL
ATLAS ENGINE WORKS. Ill. and desc. price
list of engines, parts for repairs, dimensions, etc. with diag. 86pp.

1887 Indianapolis   MH-BA
------ Catalog of steam engines and boilers. 8vo., 24pp., ills., wrap.

c.1890 Indianapolis   CHi
------ Catalog #104. (Henshaw, Buckley &
Co., agents.) Ill. catalog of engines, boil-
ers, etc. 8vo., 48pp., wrap.

nd. Cleveland   MnHi
AVERY, W.G. MFG. CO. Ill. catalog of
hardware, milling and elevator specialties,
etc.

1889 New York   PKsL
BABCOCK & WILCOX CO. Steam: its generation and use, with a catalog for users of
boilers - list of users, etc. 8vo., 120pp.,
fine ills., cl.

1896 New York   MH-BA
------ 29th ed. Large 8vo., 184pp., ills.

1888 Erie, Pa.   DSi
BALL ENGINE CO. Ill. catalog of automatic
cut-off steam engines. 40pp.

1882 New York   MnHi
BALLARD, STEPHEN & CO. Ill. catalog of
oak tanned leather belting, lace leather belting and mill supplies.

1891 Rockford, Ill.   MoSHi
BARNES, W.F. & JOHN CO. Ill. catalog of
metal working machinery.

c.1890 Joliet, Ill.   IHi
BATES MACHINE CO. Ill. catalog of heavy
wire machinery, Corliss engines, wire nail
rumblers, etc. 8vo., 64pp., fine pls., wrap.

1894 Providence, R. I.   MH-BA
BEAMAN & SMITH. Catalog C - machinery
and tools, spindle drilling and boring machines,
milling machines, engine lathes, pat. safety
drill and tap holder, etc. 16mo., 48pp., ill.

1899 St. Louis   MoSHi
BECK & CORBITT IRON CO. Ill. catalog of
heavy hardware, iron, steel and leather trimmings, bicycle machines, etc. 8vo., 932pp.

1876 Philadelphia   MH-BA
BELFIELD, H. & CO. Ill. catalog of cast
and wrought iron pipe, etc. 8th ed. 8vo.,
80pp., cl.

1884 Waterbury, Conn.   CtWAB
BENEDICT & BURNHAM MFG. CO. Catalog of general products. Brass wire, etc.

1901 Waterbury, Conn.   CtWAB
------ Catalog of general products in
brass wire, tubing, etc.

1898-1912 Waterbury, Conn.   CtWAB
------ Price lists of general products in
brass wire and tubing. #6, 7, 8 and 9.

BIGELOW & DOWSE. See House Furnishings.

1890 Hartford, Conn.   Ct
BILLINGS & SPENCER MFG. CO. Ill. catalog
and price list of machinists' tools, drop
forgings, etc.

1892 Hartford, Conn.   CtHi
------ Ill. catalog of machinists' tools,
machine parts, castings, etc. 8vo., 90pp.,
pict. wrap.

1900-1 Hartford, Conn.   Ct
------ Ill. cat.

1894 Cleveland   ICHi
BINGHAM, THE W. CO. Ill. and desc. catalog of Hardware - Railway, architects',
miners', engineers', machinists' and tinners' tools and supplies - also table and
pocket cutlery, etc., adze to yoke, match
safes and house gadgets. 8vo., full cf. with
strap, 1476pp., interleaved with correspondence, folders, ill. circulars, brochures of
special tools and ms. notes of price changes
by salesman, fine ills. throughout, 52 page
index. One of the best.

c.1900 Toledo, O.   OT
BISSELL, F.B. CO. Catalog #19 - ill. price
list of electric supplies and power apparatus
for home and factory. 8vo., 887pp., pict. wrap.
The frog on the front cover indicates Frog-
town of long ago when the swamps among
which Toledo was built chuggarummed day
and night.

1884 St. Louis - Branch   MoSHi
BLACK DIAMOND STEEL WORKS & LAKE
SUPERIOR COPPER MILLS. Park Bros. &
Co. Price list for February.

BLACK LEAD CRUCIBLE WORKS. See
Phoenix Mfg. Co.

1896 Worcester, Mass.   MH-BA
BLAISDELL, P. & CO. Ill. catalog of machinists' tools. 8vo., 28pp.

1883 New York & Boston   DSi
BLAKE, GEORGE F. MFG. Ill. catalog of
Blake's improved steam pumps, engines,
etc. 12mo., 80pp., lea. For brewery,
tannery, wells, etc.

1887 Chicago   MnHi
BLATCHFORD, E.W. & CO. Ill. catalog of
mixed metal goods.

1873 Brooklyn, N.Y.   MH-BA
BLISS & WILLIAMS. Ill. catalog of power
presses, dies, etc. 8vo., 44pp.

1876 Brooklyn, N.Y.   MH-BA
------ Ill. catalog of power tools and
presses. 3rd ed. 8vo., 60pp.

1878 Brooklyn, N.Y.   MH-BA
------ 4th ed. - in French. 4to., 90pp.

nd. Brooklyn, N.Y.   MH-BA
------ E.W. Bliss, successor. Ill. catalog of special machinery, presses, dies, etc.

1900-1 Brooklyn, N.Y.   NNQ
------ & Stiles & Parker Press Co. Ill.
catalog of heavy machinery, presses, slit-
ting mills, shear, crimping and seaming
machines and dies.

nd. Philadelphia   PHi
BOND, CHARLES CO. Ill. catalog of stock
gears, sprockets, speed reducers, etc.

1886 Philadelphia   MnHi
BONNEY VISE & TOOL CO. Ill. catalog of
vises, machinists' tools and hardware specialties.

1886 Boston   MnHi
BOSTON & NEW YORK RUBBER CO. Ill.
catalog of belting, steam packing, fire hose,
etc.

1872 St. Paul, Minn.   MnHi
BOUTELL, PAUL D. Successor to Coon &
Boutell. Ill. catalog of tin plate, wire, nails,
sheet iron, all metals, grindstones, cutlery
and domestic hardware. Large 8vo.,
228pp., cl.

c.1890 San Francisco   CHi
BOWERS, W.F. & CO. Ill. catalog of rubber
goods, hose, belting, booting, tubing, etc.
8vo., 54pp., wrap.

1879 St. Paul, Minn.   MnHi
BRADEN, J.B. & BROTHER. New ill. catalog of malleable iron for carriage steps,
wagon and plow parts, etc. Large 8vo.,
88pp.

1892 New Haven   NNMM
BRADLEY & DANN. Ill. catalog and price
list of tools for every trade. 92pp., stiff
wrap.

nd. Philadelphia   PHi
BREWER BROTHERS CO. Ill. catalog of
hardware for mfg., machinists and forgers.

1899 Reading, Pa.   PKsL
BRIGHT & CO. Ill. catalog of machine supplies, machine tools, shaftings, belting,
steam specialties. 8vo., 238pp., cl.

vd. Providence, R. I.   RHi
BROWN & SHARPE MFG. CO. Est. 1833.
A fine collection of ill. catalogs, 16mo.,
12mo., 8vo. and 4to., with pict. wraps., and
fine ills. and pls., from 1867 to 1950.

1891 Providence, R. I.   MH-BA
------ Treatise on uses of grind-   RHi
ing machines with ill. catalog. 8vo., 148pp.

1900 Cleveland   MH-BA
BROWN HOISTING & CONVEYING   OHi
MACHINE CO. Ill. catalog of Brownhoist
pat. automatic hoisting and conveying
appliances. 4to., 144pp., fine ills., cl.

1876 Salem, Ore.   MH-BA
BUCKEYE ENGINE CO. Successors to
Sharps, Davis & Bonsall. Est. 1847. Ill.
catalog of steam engines for all purposes,
saw mills, flouring mills, Hall's shingle and
heading machines, etc. 8vo., 28pp.

1858 Mt. Vernon, O.   MH-BA
BUCKINGHAM, UPTON & CO. Kokosing
Iron Works. Catalog of saw and grist mills,
stationary steam engines, threshing
machines, etc. 8vo., 16pp., 1 plate, wrap.

1880 New York   OAkF
BUCKLEY, JOHN W. Ill. price list of rubber goods for mechanical and industrial
purposes. 12pp.

1885 New York   MnHi
------ Ill. catalog of rubber goods.

1896 South Milwaukee   PHi
BUCYRUS STEAM SHOVEL & DREDGE CO.
Advance catalog with 31 pls. of dredges.
8vo., parts 2 and 3.

1900 Cincinnati   MH-BA
BULLOCK ELECTRIC MFG. CO. Bulletin
#32a. Ill. price list of direct current multi-
polar motors for all purposes. 8vo., 12pp.

1890 New York   MH-BA
C & C ELECTRIC MOTOR CO. 4th year.
Forms for fan motors, list of users.
5-1/2x7, 24pp., ill.

c.1895 San Francisco   CHi
CALIFORNIA WIRE WORKS. Catalog #12.
Ill. price lists of wire strands, cables, etc.
4to., 41pp., pict. wrap.

1860 South Groton, Mass.   MH-BA
CALORIC ENGINE CO. Ericsson's caloric
engine, list of users, prices, tests. 8vo.,
40pp., ills.

CAMPBELL & ZELL CO. See Enterprise
Iron Works.

1881 Pittsburgh, Pa.   DSi
CARNEGIE BROTHERS & CO. Pocket companion, with prices, of rolled iron shapes,
beams, etc. 177pp., ills.

1890 Pittsburgh, Pa.   DSi
CARNEGIE, PHIPPS CO. Pocket companion
with prices of rolled iron and steel shapes,
beams, etc. Tinted pls. 282pp.

1893 Pittsburgh, Pa.   MH-BA
CARNEGIE STEEL CO., LTD. Ill. catalog
of shapes, beams, angles, structural steel,
wire nails and rope, etc. 16mo., 84pp.,
tinted pls.

1864 Boston   MH-BA
CARSLEY BALL MACHINE CO. Ill. bro-
chure of new machines for turning true
spheres - working model, etc. Prospectus.
8vo., 20pp., wrap.

St. Louis
CENTRAL IRON WORKS. See Fritz,
George J.

1875 New York   MH-BA
CHALMERS-SPENCE CO. 7th annual circular pat. non-conductor boiler and pipe coverings. 16mo., 60pp.

1888 Troy, N. Y.   MH-BA
CHAMBERLAIN, BOTTUM & CO. Successor
to Holland & Thompson. Outer cover added
later reads: Lee, Chamberlain, successor
to C. B. & Co. 1889. Ill. catalog of wrought
iron and lead pipe, valves and fittings,
plumbers', engineers' and machinists' supplies, steam heating apparatus and automatic
fire sprinklers. 8vo., 214pp., fine ills., cl.

c.1885 Duluth   MnHi
CHAPIN, A.B. & CO. Ill. catalog of wholesale hardware, mill and lumbermens' supplies, tin plate and tinners' stock, heavy
hardware. 4to., 40pp.

1853 Pine Meadow, Conn.   CtHi
CHAPIN, HERMAN - Union Factory. Catalog and price list of rulers, planes, gauges,
castings for machinery, puddled iron bands,
bars, blooms, axledrafts, car axles, bunters,
crowbars. 8vo., 8pp. Ptd. Hartford.

1891 Indian Orchard, Mass.   MH-BA
CHAPMAN VALVE MFG. CO. Special circular and ill. catalog of valves with bronze
seats, etc. Tall 12mo., 52 and 12pp., ills.

c.1900 Orange, Mass.   DSi
CHASE TURBINE MFG. CO. Ill. catalog of
saw mill machinery. 25pp.

1891 Chicago   DSi
CHICAGO ENGINEER SUPPLY CO. Ill. catalog of mill and general supplies. 200pp.,
fine ills., cl.

nd. Seymour, Conn.   CtHi
CHURCH, STEPHEN B. Ill. catalog of air
cooled engines.

1874 Cincinnati   MH-BA
CINCINNATI BRASS WORKS. Ill. catalog of
brass goods and fittings, needle valve oil
feeders, steam fittings and castings. 8vo.,
34pp.

1892 Belmont, N. Y.   DSi
CLARK BROTHERS. Ill. catalog B - automatic cut-off engines for all purposes.
8vo., 58pp., pls., wrap.

1894 Torrington & Wolcottville, Conn.
COE BRASS MFG. CO. Catalog   CtWAB
of general products.

1863 San Francisco   CHi
CONROY & O'CONNOR. Catalog and tables
of hardware, metals and miscellaneous
goods. 8vo., 132pp., ills.

1874 New York & Trenton, N. J.   DSi
COOPER, HEWITT & CO. Ill. catalog of
rolled iron beams in shapes for all purposes.
50pp.

c.1857-8 Providence, R. I.   MH-BA
CORLISS STEAM ENGINE CO. Est. 1856.
Catalog of the Corliss steam engines, instructions, regulations of power and economy,
experiences of 11 mfg. users. 8vo., 40pp.,
cl.

1898 Providence, R. I.   CtHi
------ Handbook of Corliss engines by
F.H. Shillitto, Jr. 12mo., 224pp., ill., dec.
cl. Ptd. Hartford.

1874 Chicago   MH-BA
CRANE BROTHERS MFG. CO. Ill. catalog
of wrought iron pipe, steam and gas fittings,
brass and iron goods, elevators, hoisting
machines and plow devices. 4to., 104pp., cl.

1895-6 New York   MH-BA
CRANE, WILLIAM M. & CO. Ill. catalog of
gas appliances and fittings, heating, lighting
and cooking machinery and supplies. 12mo.,
32pp., wrap.

c.1890 Cape May, N. J.   PKsL
CROCKER-WHEELER CO. Catalog of perfected electric motors.

1892 Newark, N. J. Works. N. Y. Office.
CROOK, W.A. & BROTHERS. Ill.   PKsL
catalog of standard hoisting engines, boilers,
bridge construction and dredging apparatus,
pile drivers, etc. 4to., 65pp., pict. wrap.

1889 Syracuse, N. Y.   NSyHi
CURTIS MFG. CO. Catalog and price list of
leather belting, rubber and cotton belting,
lace leather, mill supplies, etc. 8vo., 56pp.,
ills., wrap.

1892 Syracuse, N. Y.   NSyHi
------ Ill. catalog of industrial supplies.
12mo., 84pp., glt. pict. wrap. of the Wise
Old Owl waiting patiently for orders.

1873 Boston   MH-BA
DAY & COLLINS. Ill. catalog of hydraulic
cement drain pipe, chimney tops and well
tubing. Tests. 8vo., 25pp., wrap.

1887 St. Louis   MoSHi
DAY RUBBER CO. Price list and catalog of
rubber products for all industries.

1887 Shelton, Conn.   CtHi
DODGE, HALEY & CO. Est. 1840. Ill. catalog of heavy hardware, machinists', railway,
steamship supplies, tools and equipment.
8vo., 290pp., fine ills., cl.

c.1895 Shelton, Conn.   DSi
------ Ill. catalog of machinists', railway
and steamship supplies.

1898 Mishawaka, Ind.   PKsL
DODGE MFG. CO. Circular of Dodge pat.
American rope transmission systems.

1869 Janesville, Wis.   WiU
DOTY MFG. CO. Ill. catalog of pat. machines
for industrial plants. 12mo., 20pp., wrap.

c.1885 San Francisco   CHi
DUNHAM, CARRIGAN & CO. Ill. catalog of
hardware, tools, machine tools, machines,
engines, iron and steel. 4to., a fine ill.
record, pict. wrap.

c.1895 San Francisco   CHi
------ DUNHAM, CARRIGAN & HAYDEN
CO. Successors. Ill. catalog of iron and
steel, mining and milling machinery, engineers' and machinists' supplies, etc. 4to.,
bds.

DUNKIRK IRON WORKS.   See Sellew,
Popple & O'Connel.

1885 Boston   MnHi
EASTERN RUBBER CO. Price list of rubber belting for plants, factories and shops.

1891 New York   MH-BA
EDISON GENERAL ELECTRIC CO. Ill.
circular I.D. #1 of electric percussion drills.
16mo., 20pp.

1890 Baltimore   PKsL
ENTERPRISE IRON WORKS. Campbell &
Zell Co. Ill. catalog of founders', manufac-

turers' and engineers' supplies and equipment. 4to., 54pp., col. litho. frs. with pls. of explosions and experiments. Glt. pict. wrap.

1878-1897 Erie, Pa.   DSi
ERIE CITY IRON WORKS. An unusual collection from 1878 to 1897. 8vo., and 4to., well ill., some pls. and pict. wrap. as follows:

1878   Ill. catalog of portable and stationary engines and circular sawmills. 11pp.

1879   Ill. catalog. 16pp.

1880   Ill. catalog. 20pp.

1881   Ill. catalog of steam engines and boilers. 22pp.

1881   Ill. catalog of mill machinery. 22pp.

1883   Ill. catalog of steam engines   PKsL
and boilers - for the oil fields - and manufacturers, saw mills, etc. 4to., 20pp., pict. wrap.

c.1885 Ill. catalog. Compliments   PKsL
of . . . Engines both stationary and portable, mounted on stands and wheels. 8vo., 20pp., fine ills.

1885   Ill. catalog of engines, etc. 30pp.

1888   Ill. catalog of engines and boilers. 25pp.

1894   Ill. catalog of steam engines, boilers for all plants, etc. 22pp.

1897   Ill. catalog of boilers and engines. 44pp.

1869 Philadelphia   PHi
EVANS, CHARLES & SON. Ill. catalog of screw presses, iron and brass castings and machinery in general. 8vo., 28pp.

1873 Waterbury, Conn.   MH-BA
FARREL FOUNDRY & MACHINE CO. Ill. catalog of rolling mill machinery and power presses. 8vo., 19pp. Photocopy only.

nd. Waterbury, Conn.   CtHi
------ Special catalog of power presses and machine tools for gunsmiths, etc.

1880 Cincinnati   MiU-T
FAY, J.A. & CO. Special ill. cata-   OC
log of heavy pat. wood working machinery designed for car and railroad shops, government arsenals and navy yards with photos. and fld. pls. Fol., 61pp., fine litho. pls., wrap.

c.1880 Philadelphia   MH-BA
FERRIS & MILES. Ill. price list of slotting machines and other machine tools and machinery. 8vo., 12pp.

nd. Fitchburg   MH-BA
FITCHBURG MACHINE WORKS. Circular of the lo-swing lathe. 8vo., 26pp., ill., wrap.

1881 Fitchburg   MH-BA
FITCHBURG STEAM ENGINE CO. Est. 1870. Ill. price list of steam engines and boilers, etc. 8vo., 20pp.

c.1880 Hoboken   NjR
FOCHT, GEORGE IRON WORKS. Ill. catalog of heavy machinery, railroad accessories such as wheels, rails, etc., construction equipment, etc. 4to., 80pp., pls., lithos. steel and photo engravings. A fine job. Wrap.

1896 Miamisburg, O.   OC
FRANKLIN ELECTRIC CO. General catalog of electric supplies for machine shops and plants. Sq. 8vo., 48pp., fine ills. of machines, dynamos, engines, etc. Wrap.

nd. Miamisburg, O.   OHi
------ Desc. and ill. catalog of dynamos and engines for all purposes. 8vo., wrap.

1883 Waynesboro, Pa.   MnHi
FRICK & CO. Ill. catalog of Eclipse traction and portable steam engines - price list tipped in. 4to., 60pp., plus advts., fine ills., wrap.

1885 Waynesboro, Pa.   MnHi
------ Ill. catalog of engines and boilers, etc.

nd. St. Louis   MoSHi
FRITZ, GEORGE J. Central Iron Works. Ill. catalog and price list of steam engines, boilers and supplies for mfgr's. 12mo., 124pp.

c.1900 Minneapolis   DSi
GLOBE IRON WORKS CO. Ill. circular of the White gasoline engines. 64pp.

1867 San Francisco   CHi
GODDARD & CO. Pacific Iron Works. Ill. pattern list and circular for 1867. Ills. of founding, machining, boilermaking, forging and smithing depts., pattern and wood working rooms, drawing and library. 8vo., 96pp., bds. This is a real catalog.

nd. Philadelphia   PHi
GOLD, WALTER C. Ill. catalog of grinding, polishing and plating machinery and materials.

1897 Columbus, Ga.   GU
GOLDEN'S FOUNDRY & MACHINE CO.
Price list #13. Ills. of pulleys, hangers,
shaftings and all mill supplies. 8vo., 70pp.,
red mor.

1878 Boston   DSi
GOODNOW & WIGHTMAN. Price list of
tools for mechanics, pattern makers, founders, mfgr's. 8vo., 80pp., fine ills., wrap.

1887 Newark, N. J.   MH-BA
GOULD & EBERHARDT. Est. 1840. Ill.
catalog of universal automatic gear cutters.
12mo., 16pp.

1897 Newark, N. J.   MH-BA
------ Ill. catalog of machine tools. 8vo.,
40pp.

1899 Newark, N. J.   MH-BA
------ Ill. catalog of high class machine
tools, presses and machines. 8vo., 177pp.

1899 San Francisco   CHi
GRIFFIN, J.J. (Agents for Brown & Sharpe
Mfg. Co.) Ill. catalog of machinists' tools,
squares, rules, calipers, gauges, test tools,
etc. Catalog #101. 4to., 148pp., wrap.

c.1900 Long Island City, N. Y.   NNQ
GUERRLICH, FREDERICK C. Ill. catalog
of hoisting machinery and conveying engines
and machines. 8vo., 32pp., ills. of cranes,
pict. wrap. showing plant.

1871 Philadelphia   DSi
GUNPOWDER PILE DRIVE CO. Ill. circular of Shaw's patent gun powder pile driver.
4pp.

1890 Philadelphia   PKsL
HARRINGTON, EDWIN, SON & CO. Ill. catalog of Harrington hoists, overhead railways,
traveling cranes, etc. 16mo., 84pp., pict.
wrap. of plant.

1888 Providence, R. I.   DSi
HARRIS, WILLIAM A. STEAM ENGINE CO.
Ill. catalog of Harris-Corliss steam engines.
56pp.

1881 Hartford, Conn.   CtHi
HARTFORD ENGINEERING CO. Ill. circular of automatic cut-off steam engines. 4to.,
24pp., pls., wrap.

1887 Torrington, Conn.   CtHi
HENDEY MACHINE CO. Ill. catalog of
machinists' tools and special machinery for
all trades. 8vo., 40pp., pict. wrap.

c.1883 San Francisco   CHi
HENDY, JOSHUA MACHINE WORKS. Ill.
catalog of marine and hoisting engines and

boilers, smelting, mining, hydraulic, quartz
and saw mill machinery. 12mo., 64pp.,

c.1895 San Francisco   CHi
------ Ill. catalog of milling and mining
machinery, boiler, pumps, etc.

1897 Boston & Chicago   MH-BA
HILL, CLARKE & CO. Machinery blue book
of machine tools. 8vo., 400pp., fine ill. ref.,
cl.

1869 San Francisco   CHi
HINCKLEY & CO. Fulton Foundry & Iron
Works. Ill. circular and pattern list of
shaftings, wheels, steam engines, etc.
12mo., 62pp., wrap.

c.1885 Houghton, Mich.   MiU-H
HODGE, SAMUEL F. Est. 1857. Riverside
Iron Works & Lake Superior Iron Works.
Ill. catalog of patterns for wheels, gearing,
steam engines, mining and milling machin-
ery, etc. 16mo., fine pls., glt. pict., cl.

1892 New Haven   CtHi
HOGGSON & PETTIS MFG. CO. Catalog
and price list of Sweetland chucks, standard
chucks, Porter's belt clamps, etc. with tel.
code, etc. 48pp., fine ills.

nd. Erie, Pa.   PHi
HOLLANDS MFG. CO. Ill. catalog #2 -
vises and mechanics' tools.

1868 Waterbury, Conn.   MH-BA
HOLMES, BOOTH & HAYDEN CO. Price
list of sheet brass, copper, nickel and silver
wire, tubing, rivets and silver pls. materials. 16mo., 18pp.

1898 Waterbury, Conn.   CtWAB
------ Price list #6 - Catalog of general
products.

1905 Waterbury, Conn.   CtWAB
------ Catalog of seamless brazed tubing.

nd. Philadelphia   PHi
HOOD BROTHERS. Ill. catalog #8 of high
grade mechanics' tools.

1873 Buffalo, N. Y.   DSi
HOWARD IRON WORKS. Ill. catalog of
hoisting machinery and mill supplies. 27pp.

1885 West New Brighton, S.I., N.Y. MH-BA
HUNT, C.W. CO. Ill. catalog of conveying
machinery, cars, tracks, hoisting equipment,
plant locomotives and coal handling apparatus. 8vo., 38pp.

1900 West New Brighton, S.I., N.Y. NStIHi
------ Catalog #0011. Hunt's noiseless
conveyors, and other machinery and apparatus for coal, ashes, etc. -cars, etc. 4to.,
40pp., fine ills., pict. wrap.

1884 San Francisco   CHi
HUNTINGTON, HOPKINS & CO. Ill. catalog
of hardware, machinery for handling iron,
steel, coal, etc. 4to., bds.

c.1900 Brooklyn, N. Y.   NNQ
JACOBS, GEORGE P. & CO. Ill. catalog
and price list of cast iron parts and fittings,
iron pipe, oil cups, gauges, flanges, etc.

nd. Hartford, Conn.   CtHi
JACOBS MFG. CO. Ill. catalog of Jacob's
improved drill chucks for mechanics,
machine shops, etc.

1825 Vincennes   In
JAMES & McARTHUR. The Iron Store.
James & McArthur are now receiving direct
from their furnaces a large and general
assortment of castings - and will keep on
hand, etc. iron and castings - etc. Broadside 6-1/4x6-3/4, May 11, 1825.
N.B. These castings were probably gears
and wheels for machinery mills, etc., but
there could have been pots and kettles for
the kitchen too.

c.1887 Boston   DSi
JARVIS ENGINEERING CO. Ill. catalog of
complete steam plants for power stations,
etc. 8vo., 68pp., pict. wrap.

1895 Columbus, O.   OHi
JEFFREY MFG. CO. Est. 1877. Ill. catalog #42. Chain belting, elevating, conveying and power transmission machinery,
steel cable conveyors, labor saving appliances. 12mo., 144pp.

1896 Columbus, O.   OHi
------ Ill. catalog #43. Jeffrey labor saving appliances. 50pp.

c.1900 Columbus, O.   OHi
------ Ill. catalog #57.

1883 Pawtucket   MH-BA
JENCKES, E. MFG. CO. Ill. catalog of
manufacturers' supplies, ring travellers,
etc. 12mo., 120pp.

JERSEY CITY CRUCIBLE MFG. CO. See
Phoenix Mfg. Co.

1885 Pittsburgh, Pa. & Chicago   MnHi
JONES & LAUGHLINS, LTD. Ill. catalog of
nails, spikes, iron, heavy hardware and
machinery.

1888 Pittsburgh, Pa.   MH-BA
------ Catalog D. Ills. of shafting, job
cranes, iron and steel wheels and trucks,
etc. 16mo., 40pp.

1867 Pittsburgh, Pa.   PHi
JONES & NIMICK MFG. CO. Catalog #5,
general circular and price list revised.
Heavy hardware and machine tools, etc.
16mo., 48pp., fld. pls., col. pict. wrap.

1888 Anamosa, Ia.   IaHi
KIMBALL BROTHERS. Catalog B. Improved safety elevators. 8vo., 8pp., ills.
and diags., wrap.

1897 San Francisco   CHi
KLEIN'S, JOHN M. ELECTRICAL WORKS.
Catalog #17. Ills. of batteries, bells, annun-
ciators, signals, bulbs, plants, etc. 8vo.,
wrap.

c.1882 San Francisco   CHi
KROGH, F.W. & CO. Ill. catalog and price
list of windmills, horse powers, tanks,
pumps, steam engines. 8vo., 24pp.

1883 Lambertville, N. J.   PKsL
LAMBERTVILLE IRON WORKS. A. Welch,
Prop. Ill. catalog of pat. cut-off engines.
4to., 30pp., 21pls. and figs., wrap.

c.1893-4 Waynesboro, Pa.   MH-BA
LANDIS BROTHERS. Est. c.1890. Ill.
price list of machine tools, grinding machinery, etc. 8vo., 48pp.

c.1880 Cincinnati   OHi
LANE & BODLEY CO. Ill. catalog of circular saw mills and machinery. 8vo., 30pp.,
fine ills., wrap.

c.1885 Cincinnati   DSi
------ Ill. catalog of hydraulic and belt
driven elevators and machinery. 20pp.
Photostat copy only.

1888 Lansing   MiU-H
LANSING IRON & ENGINE WORKS. Ill.
catalog of mill supplies, machinery, engines,
etc. 8vo., 248pp., cl.

1884 Columbus, O.   OHi
LECHNER MFG. CO. Ill. price list for
1884. Ills. of chain belting, improved
elevating machines for tanneries, mills and
mfg. plants. 4to., 16pp., fine ills., pict.
wrap.

LEE, CHAMBERLAIN & CO. See Chamberlain, Bottum & Co.

1883 Springfield, O.   OHi
LEFFEL, JAMES & CO. Desc. and ill. catalog and handbook of Bookwalter engines,
with prices, for mills, plants, printing
presses, other presses, laundries and
machine shops. Pls. of plants in operation.
12mo., 48pp., pict. wrap.

1887 Springfield, O.   MnHi
------ Ill. catalog of boilers and   OHi
steam engines. 8vo., 32pp., pict. wrap.
N.B. For complete listings, see Pumps and
Water Wheels.

1884 Mauch-Chunk, Pa. Works-Weissport.
LEHIGH VALLEY EMERY WHEEL   PKsL
CO. Ill. catalog of emery and curundum
wheels for all purposes, emery wheel
machinery, etc. 8vo., 32pp., plate of plant,
pict. wrap.

1886 Brooklyn, N. Y.   DSi
LIDGERWOOD MFG. CO. Ill. catalog and
price list of improved hoisting boilers,
engines, machinery. 4to., 72pp., pls., pict.
wrap.

1885 Chicago   ICHi
LINK-BELT MACHINERY CO. Ill. catalog
of improved elevating and conveying machinery, clocks, pulleys and wheels, etc. 12mo.,
160pp., pls., litho. pict. wrap. by Wilson
Wagner of Chicago.

1885 Chicago & New York   MH-BA
LOCKWOOD, H.T. & BROTHER. Price list
and tables of square and special sized tin
and iron plate, etc. 10mo., 62pp.

c.1890 East Boston   MH-BA
LOCKWOOD MFG. CO. Est. 1880. Ill.
catalog of binder twine and rope machinery
for mills, factories, etc. Sq. 8vo., 28pp.

1895 Ridgway, Pa.   CHi
McEWEN, J.H. MFG. CO. (Agents Henshaw,
Duckley & Co.) Ill. catalog of automatic
cut-off engines. 8vo., ptd. wrap. for agents.

1871 New York   MH-BA
McKILLOP, SPRAGUE & CO., Dist. Formerly Johnston & Co. Trade list of importers and mfg'rs. of iron, steel and metal
goods. 4to., 40pp.

1886 Hartford, Conn.   DSi
McMURRAY, C.F. Ill. catalog of gears for
all purposes, manufactories and machine
shops. 258pp.

1874 New York   MH-BA
MANNING, H.S. & CO. Ill. catalog of
machinist, railroad, mill and mine supplies.
8vo., 188pp., cl.

1884 New York   TxDaDeG
MANNING, MAXWELL   NhHi   MH-BA
& MOORE. Ill. catalog of railway and
machinists' tools and supplies - locomotive
headlights, rolling stock furnishings, station
equipment, engines, forges, etc. 4to.,
440pp., swell ills., dec. cl.

1897 Marion, O.   DSi
MARION STEAM SHOVEL CO. Ill. catalog
of steam shovels and dredges. 172pp.

1890 Boston   DSi
MASON REGULATOR CO. Ill. price list of
steam regulators and governors. 16pp.

1889 St. Louis   MoSHi
MEDART PATENT PULLEY CO.   MnHi
Est. 1879. Ill. catalog of wrought iron rim
pulleys, pillow blocks, shaftings, couplings,
hangers, etc. 8vo., 36pp., pict. wrap.
Largest pulley works in the world.

1891 St. Louis   MoSHi
------ Ill. catalog of pulleys, hangers,
shaftings, etc. Sq. 8vo., 36pp., pict. wrap.

nd. St. Louis   MnHi
------ Ill. catalog.

1894 St. Louis   MoSHi
------ Ill. catalog. 78pp., pict. wrap.

1876 Philadelphia   MH-BA
MIDDLETON, C.W. & H.W. Catalog of iron
and steel railway and mine supplies. 8vo.,
146pp., fine ills., cl.

c.1894 Brooklyn, N. Y.   NNQ
MILLER, WILLIAM P. Ill. catalog of
Ingersoll Improved Presses for baling rags,
paper stock, cotton waste, hay, hair, hides,
wool, moss, broom corn, manure, hemp, tin
scrap, cork and leather. 32pp., pict. wrap.

1883 St. Louis   MoSHi
MISSISSIPPI IRON WORKS. Pullis Brothers.
Ill. catalog of gears, wheels and machinery.

nd. Garrett, Ind.   In
MODEL GAS ENGINE CO. Ill. catalog of
model gas and gasoline engines. 8vo., 16pp.

1870 New York   N
MONTGOMERY & CO. Ill. catalog of
machinery and tools for blacksmiths, model
makers, jewelers, engravers, silversmiths,
etc. 4to., 332pp., dec. cl.

1884 Pittsburgh, Pa.   MoSHi
MOORHEAD & CO. Soho Iron Mills. Price
list of machine tools, machines, parts, etc.

1836 Philadelphia   PHi
MORRIS, LEVI & CO.'S IRON FOUNDRY.
Price list of wheel patterns, gears, etc.
16mo., 16pp.

1860 Philadelphia & New Castle, Del.
MORRIS, TASKER & CO. Est. 1821.MH-BA
Pascal Iron Works, Philadelphia & Tasker
Iron Works, Newcastle. Ill. catalog of pat-
terns, gears, wheels, etc. 4to., 86pp.

1874 Philadelphia   PHi
------ Ill. catalog of wheels and patterns
for castings, etc. 4to.

nd. Burlington, Ia.   IaHi
MURRAY IRON WORKS. Ill. catalog of
heavy hardware and machinery.

c.1881 Salem, Mass.   MH-BA
NAUMKEAG BUFFING MACHINE CO. Ill.
price list of buffing machines, with list of
users. 16mo., 16pp., pict. wrap.

1897 Providence, R. I.   MH-BA
NEW ENGLAND BUTT CO.   RHi
Est. 1842. Ill. catalog of braiding and
cabling machinery and special machinery
for electrical wire. 8vo., 52pp., wrap.

1900 Dayton, O.   OHi
NEW ERA IRON WORKS CO. Ill. catalog of
New Era gas and gasoline engines, details
and tests. 8vo., 36pp.

1888 Philadelphia   MnHi
NEWKIRK, RITCHIE & BELL. Ill. catalog
of Ritchie's Champion vises and hardware
specialties.

1889 Philadelphia   PKsL
NEWTON MACHINE TOOL WORKS. Ill.
catalog of lathes. 12mo., 80pp., index with
fine ills., wrap.

1869 New York   OAkF
NEW YORK BELTING & PACKING CO. Oldest manufacturer of . . . in Country. Ill.
catalog of patent solid emery vulcanite
wheels, fabrics, etc. adapted to all mechanical purposes. 8vo., fine ills., wrap.

1895 New York   OrU
------, Ltd. Ill. and desc. catalog and price
list of wheels and fabrics. 8vo., 96pp., cl.

1885 Buffalo, N. Y.   NBuHi
NIAGARA STAMPING & TOOL CO. Ill. catalog of ironwork, tools, machine tools and
hardware for all trades. 6th ed. 60 and
44pp., pict. wrap.

1878 Providence, R. I.   PKsL
NICHOLSON FILE CO. Treatise   RHi
on rasps and files for master mechanics and
manufacturers. 4to., 80pp., fine pls.
throughout, dec. cl. Plate of plant and
works. A fine job.

1894 Providence, R. I.   RHi
------ Ill. catalog of rasps and files, tools
and machine tools for mfg'rs. Tall 4to.,
fine pls., limp calf. N.B. The Nicholson
File Co. also has a fine reference library.

1891 Hamilton, O.   OHi
NILES TOOL WORKS. Ill. catalog of tools
and machine tools.

1889 South Norwalk   MH-BA
NORWALK IRON WORKS CO. Ill. price
list of the Norwalk air compressors. 8vo.,
64pp.

c.1870 Norwich, Conn.   CtNlC
NORWICH IRON FOUNDRY. A. H.   DeU
Vaughan & Sons. Ill. catalog and price list
of castings for machinery, mills, etc. 12mo,
40pp., pict. wrap.

c.1890 Buffalo, N. Y.   DSi
NOYE, JOHN T. MFG. CO. Ill. price list of
Rice automatic engines. 8vo., 16pp., pls.,
dec. wrap.

1891 Lansing   OrU
OLDS, P.F. & SON. Celebrated one-horse
power gasoline engines. See ills. and data
in catalog of Anderson Road Cart Co. in
chapter on Carriages.

1884 Albany, N. Y.   DSi
OSGOOD DREDGE CO. Ill. and desc. catalog of steam dredges and hoists. 44pp.with
7 fine pls.

1896 Albany, N. Y.   PHi
------ Ill. catalog. 8vo., 40pp., pls.

nd. Philadelphia   PHi
OTTO ENGINES CO. Directions for using
the Otto engine, etc. 2 ill. price lists, 16
and 20pp.

c.1888 San Francisco   CHi
PACIFIC ELECTRICAL STORAGE CO. Sole
licensee of Electric Accumulator Co. of New
York for Calif., Oregon, Arizona, Washington, Nevada and Idaho. Ill. catalog. 4to.,
fine ills., ptd. New York.

1886 San Francisco   CHi
PACIFIC ROLLING MILL CO. Ill. catalog
of bar and railroad iron, girders, bolts,
nuts and hardware. 6th ed. 8vo., fine ills.

1890 San Francisco   CHi
------ Ill. catalog.

1882   MoSHi
PADDOCK-HAWLEY IRON CO. Ill. catalog
of castings, gears, etc. for mills, mines and
railroads.

1889 St. Louis   MoSHi
------ Catalog and price list.

nd. St. Louis   MoSHi
------ Catalog #104.

1873 Concord, N. H.   NhHi
PAGE BELTING CO. Ill. catalog of tanned
leather belting for all purposes. All We Ask
is a Fair Trial. 16mo., 24pp., pict. wrap.

1883 Concord, N. H.   NhD
------ Ill. catalog of leather and rubber
belting, lace leather, grades, etc. 8vo.,
32pp., pict. wrap.

1889 Concord, N. H.   MnHi
------ Ill. catalog of rubber and leather
belting.

nd. Concord, N. H.   NhHi
------ 24mo. catalog with col. plate
leather samples of 14 grades of tanned
leather belting, wrap.

1894 Concord, N. H.   NhHi
------ Ill. catalog of belting and mechanical goods, grades, etc. Photos. of plants,
link belts, mill strappings, buffalo pelt
fasteners, mats and hose for fire depts. and
brewers. 12mo., 96pp., cl. Fine job.

PARK BROTHERS. See Black Diamond
Steel Works.

1859 West Meriden, Conn.   MWA
PARKERS, SNOW, BROOKS & CO. Fol.
broadside with 5 ills., hand and power punch-
ing and shearing presses, with prices.

1855 Philadelphia   MH-BA
PARRY, GEORGE T. John Rice & Co.,
Mfg. Ill. price list of Parry's pat. anti-
friction boxes. 8vo., 12pp., one ill.

Philadelphia
PASCAL IRON WORKS. See Morris,
Tasker & Co.

c.1890 Corning, N. Y.   DSi
PAYNE, B.W. & SONS. Est. 1840. Ill. catalog of Payne's automatic engines. 4to.,
24pp., pls., pict. wrap.

1890 Detroit   DSi
PENBERTHY INJECTOR CO. Ill. catalog
of steam boiler injectors. 16pp.

1897 Detroit   DSi
------ Ill. catalog of steam boiler injectors and steam specialties. 32pp.

1896 Philadelphia   DSi
PENCOYD IRON WORKS. Handbook of
rolled iron and steel shapes, angles and
rails, etc. 232pp. with 39 fine tinted pls.

1898 Philadelphia   DSi
------ Handbook. 346pp. with 35 pls.
N.B. Later p.1900 catalogs may be found
at PKsL.

c.1876 Philadelphia   MH-BA
PENNSYLVANIA STEEL CO. Ill. catalog of
hammered steel rails, blooms, billets,
slabs and forgings for manufacturers. 8vo.,
68pp., dec. cl.

1884 Philadelphia   MH-BA
------ Ill. catalog. 4to., 118pp., cl.

1883 Philadelphia   DSi
PHOENIX IRON CO. Handbook of rolled
iron and steel shapes. 146pp., tinted ills.

1839 Providence, R. I.   PKsL
PHOENIX IRON FOUNDRY. Eddy's Point.
Pattern book and catalog of castings, gears,
wheels, mill castings, etc. Sm. 4to., 16pp.,
wrap.

1869 Providence, R. I.   RHi
------ Pattern book of gears, wheels,
castings, etc. 4to., 32pp.

1878 Providence, R. I.   RHi
------ Pattern book and price list.

1876 Taunton, Mass.   MTaOC
PHOENIX MFG. CO. & JERSEY CITY CRU-
CIBLE MFG. CO. Owners of Black Lead
Crucible Works. Est.1844. Valuable re-
ceipts and details with ills. of crucibles,
etc. Tests. 16mo., 32pp., medals and mfg.
details.

c.1900 Portland, Conn.   DSi
PICKERING GOVERNOR CO. Price list of
steam engine governors. 24pp.

POPE & STEVENS. Miscellaneous tools.
See General Hardware Goods.

1888 New York   CU-A
PORTER MFG. CO. Ill. catalog of engines
and boilers for saw mills, tractors and
machinery. 8vo., 42pp., pls. and diags.

1880 New York   DSi
------ Ill. catalog of steam engines and
boilers. 48pp.

1900 Philadelphia   PHi
POWELL & MADDOCK. Ill. catalog and
price list of tools, belting machinery and
supplies for mills, engineers, factories, etc.
12mo., 132pp., pls. and charts.

1886 Hartford, Conn.   CtHi
PRATT & WHITNEY CO. Ill. catalog of
tools, machine tools and machinery.

1893 Hartford, Conn.   MH-BA
------ Ill. catalog of tools,   Ct
machine tools for forge, foundry and
machine shops. 12mo., 39pp.

1900 Hartford, Conn.   MH-BA
------ Ill. catalog for International Exhibition at Paris. 8vo., 48pp., wrap.

PRENTICE, A.F. & CO. See F. E. Reed.

1887 Elizabethport, N. J.   PKsL
PROGRESS MACHINE WORKS. Est. 1854.
A. & F. Brown. Ill. catalog and price list of
shaftings, hangers, pulleys and couplings.
12mo., 72pp., view of works, pict. wrap.

PULLIS BROTHERS. See Mississippi
Iron Works.

1899 Fitchburg   MH-BA
PUTNAM MACHINE CO. Est. 1836. Consolidated with Putnam Tool Co. Ill. catalog
and price list of machine tools and metal
working machinery. 8vo., 198pp., cl.

1865 New York   MH-BA
RACHETTE IRON FURNACE CO. New and
improved furnaces for manufacture of iron.
8vo., 12pp., fld. plate.

1888 Racine   MnHi
RACINE MALLEABLE & WROUGHT IRON
CO. Catalog of malleable and grey iron
castings.

READING HARDWARE CO. See Miscellaneous Hardware Goods.

1876 Worcester, Mass.   MWA
REED, F.E. Successor to A. F. Prentice
& Co. Ill. catalog of machinists' tools from
new improved patterns with 30 pls. of
machines. 16mo., 30pp., glt. dec. wrap.

c.1885 Chicago   MnHi
REEDY, J.W. MFG. CO. Ill. catalog of
J. W. Reedy elevators, passenger and
freight - steam, hydraulic and hand power.
Sm. 4to., fine ills.

1883 Boston   OAkF
REVERE RUBBER CO. Ill. catalog of India
rubber goods for mechanical purposes, etc.
28pp.

RICE, JOHN & CO. See George T. Parry.

1836
RIPLEY, ROBERTS & CO. See General
Hardware Goods.

RIVERSIDE IRON WORKS & LAKE SUPE-
RIOR IRON WORKS. See Samuel F. Hodge.

1880 San Francisco   CHi
RIX & FIRTH - Phoenix Iron Works. Ill.
catalog of national drill and air compress-
ers. 8vo., 14pp., pict. wrap.

1884 St. Paul, Minn.   MnHi
ROBINSON & CARY. Supplemental catalog
#10, heavy machinery, etc. 8vo., fine ills.

1877 Trenton, N. J.   MnHi
ROEBLING'S, JOHN A. SONS CO. Ill. catalog of wire ropes - new method of trans-

mitting power, hoisting machinery for construction of bridges, wire for railroads, etc.

1886 Trenton, N. J.   MnHi
------ Ill. catalog of wire rope, etc.

1896 Trenton, N. J.   NjR
------ Ill. catalog and desc. of new methods, etc. 13th ed. 8vo., 40pp., pict. wrap.

1896 Trenton, N. J.   CHi
------ Pacific Coast ed. Ill. catalog of
cables, fencing, etc. 12mo., 84pp., fine ills.,
pict. wrap.

c.1869 New York   OC
ROOT, JOHN B. Reduced price list of
Root's wrought iron boilers, records of
boiler explosions in U. S. - advantages of
Root's. 8vo., 28pp., fine ills.

1874 Connersville, Ind.   DSi
ROOT, P.H. & F.M. Ill. catalog of rotary
blowers for mfg., machine shops, etc. 57pp.

1885 Connersville, Ind.   DSi
------ Ill. catalog. 79pp.

c.1876 Fulton, N. Y.   MH-BA
ROSS, E.W. & CO. Ill. catalog of the best
sawmill in the world. Gridley pat. automatic circular sawmill, mill supplies, feed
cutters, horse rakes, paddle churns, shoe
calking dies, paper mill machinery knives,
plows and cultivators. 8vo., 40pp., a fine
pict. ref.

1886 Philadelphia   MH-BA
RUE MFG. CO. Ill. price list of injectors,
boiler testing apparatus, steam valves and
checks. 8vo., 12pp.

c.1890 St. Louis   MoSHi
RUMSEY & SIKEMEISER CO. Catalog #80-
Ill. catalog of supplies for mfg'rs., blacksmiths, fire companies, city lighting and
water supplies, foundries, etc. - park fountains to street lamps, buggies to trolleys
and fire engines. 12mo., 986pp., great ills.,
dec. cl.

RUMSEY, L.M. MFG. CO. See Agricultural Implements.

RUSSELL & ERWIN MFG. CO. See Hardware - General Goods.

1885 St. Louis   MoSHi
SAFETY HATCH DOOR CO. Ill. catalog of
the Thackston automatic hatch doors and
safety bars for passenger and freight elevators.

1898 St. Louis   CHi
ST. LOUIS IRON & MACHINE WORKS.
(Agents, Henshaw, Buckley & Co., San Fran-

cisco). Ill. catalog of Corliss engines.
8vo., fine ills., pict. wrap.

1852-98
SARGENT & CO. See General Hardware.

1887 St. Louis   MoSHi
SCHERPE & KOKEN IRON WORKS. Ill. cat-
alog of iron castings for tools and machinery.

1875 Waterbury, Conn.   NjOE
SCOVILL MFG. CO. Est. 1802. Pioneer,
with American Brass Co., in the development of the brass and wire industry. Made
buttons for U. S. Army and Navy in 1812 and
branched into the photographic field when
the dry plate boom got under way. Ill. catalog of brass and copper goods. 12mo.,
54pp., wrap. See also American Brass Co.

1888 Cincinnati   OC
SEBASTIAN, MAY & CO. Ill. catalog and
price list of machinery and machine tools
and mfg'rs. supplies. 8vo., 58pp., pict.
wrap.

1876 Philadelphia   PHi
SELLERS, WM. & CO. A treatise on
machine tools, etc. 3rd revised ed. One of
the best ill. catalog-books in the field.
12mo., 264pp., pls., 3 fld., cl.

1874 Dunkirk, N. Y.   DSi
SELLEW, POPPLE & O'CONNELL.
Dunkirk Iron Works. Ill. catalog of engines
and boilers for mills, machine shops, steam
tugs, etc. 8vo., 16pp., fine ills., pict. wrap.

c.1890 Seneca Falls, N. Y.   N
SENECA FALLS MFG. CO. Ill. catalog
#25 B. Lathes, engine gears, screw cutting
and turning machines and engines, etc.
8vo., 56pp., pls., pict. wrap.

1867-69 Philadelphia   PHi
SHARPE & THOMPSON, Iron Founders.
Ill. catalogs of castings for mills, railroads
and mfg'rs.

1893 Muskegon, Mich.   DSi
SHAW ELECTRIC CRANE CO. Instruction
book and ill. catalog of electric cranes -
#86. 24pp.

c.1880 Cincinnati   OC
SHEPARD, H.L. & CO. Ill. catalog of foot
and power lathes, drill presses, engines,
etc. $150-250. 10mo., 66pp., pict. wrap.

1882 St. Louis   MoSHi
SIMMONS HARDWARE CO. Ill. catalog of
tools, machine tools, light machinery and
supplies. 4to., cl., 302pp. of tools for every
trade, dec. cl.

1887-93 St. Louis   MoSHi
------ Ill. catalogs, ill. throughout in cl.
for 1887 and 1893. As complete catalogs as
any in this field. N.B. Simmons catalog
for c.1905 contains 5000pp. of desc. and ills.

1885 New York   NNNAM
SIMMONS, JOHN. Ill. catalog #3 - malle-
able and cast iron gas, steam and water fittings, brass valves and cocks, brass goods
for engine builders, plumbers' and gas
fitters' tools and supplies. 243pp.

c.1888 San Francisco   CHi
SIMONDS SAW CO. Ill. catalog of saws,
pulleys, shafting, etc. 8vo., 42pp., wrap.

c.1885 Erie, Pa.   PKsL
SKINNER ENGINE CO. Est. 1865. Ill. catalog of portable and stationary engines for
all purposes, governors, locomotive boilers,
etc. 4to., 64pp. with ill. circular enc.

1891 St. Louis   MoSHi
SLIGO IRON STORE. Ill. catalog of iron
supplies. Also, three undated ill. catalogs
being #60, #87 and nd.

1872 New York   NjOE
SMITH & GARVIN. Ill. catalog of drill
presses, milling machines, lathes, gun and
sewing machine tools and machinery. 32pp.,
pict. wrap.

1876-1883 St. Louis   MoSHi
SMITH, BEGGS & CO. Ill. catalogs of
engines and steam pumps, portable and
stationary engines, and Corliss engines.

1877 New York   DSi
SNYDER BROTHERS. Ill. price list of
Snyder Brothers' Little Giant steam engines.
8vo., 36pp., pls.

1846 Boston   MBAt
SOUTH BOSTON IRON CO. Cyrus Alger &
Others, Props. List of patterns revised and
corrected to Nov. 1. Lists include gears,
mill wheels, oven doors, etc. Also soap
kettles and hollow ware. 16mo., 88pp., cl.
with label.

c.1883 Philadelphia   DSi
SOUTHWARK FOUNDRY & MACHINERY CO.
Ill. and desc. price list of Porter-Allen
steam engines. 54pp.

1876 Worcester, Mass.   MII-DA
SPENCER WIRE CO. Est. 1820. Pioneer
wire drawer in America. Ill. catalog of
strip steel, drill rods, clock and motor
springs, piano tuning pins, specialties for
all trades. 8vo., 48pp.

1889 San Francisco   CHi
STALLMAN, CHARLES. Ill. catalog and
price list of taps, dies, screw plates, tap
wrenches, die stocks, etc. 8vo., 24pp.

nd. Philadelphia, Altoona & Pittsburgh, Pa.
STANDARD SUPPLY & EQUIPMENT PHi
CO. Ill. catalog B of mill, mine, railroad,
tinners', machinists' and foundry supplies.

1888 Cleveland   MnHi
STANDARD TOOL CO. Ill. catalog of twist
drills, sockets, chucks and machinists' supplies.

1884 Erie, Pa.   TxDaDeG
STEARNS MFG. CO. Est. 1855. Ill. catalog of saw mill machinery, engines, boilers,
pulleys, shafting, etc. 4to., 64pp., fine pls.,
pict. wrap.

nd. Chicago   MnHi
STEEL KEY DRIVE CHAIN CO. Ill. catalog
of detachable link belting for elevators, conveyors, etc.

1874 Middletown, Conn.   MH-BA
STILES & PARKER PRESS CO. Est. 1857.
Charles Parker, 1853 - N. C. Stiles 1857 -
Stiles & Parker 1871. Ill. price list of drop
presses, punch and trimming presses, cutting, forging and die forging machinery.
8vo., 49pp.

1890 Middletown, Conn.   MH-BA
------ Ill. catalog. 12mo., 264pp., cl.

c.1895 Philadelphia   PKsL
STONE & DOWNEY. Catalog #101. Ill.
price list of hardware, implements and
machinery, specialties, tools, cutters, grindstones, etc. 4to., 80pp., pict. wrap.

1870 New York   MH-BA
STORRS, J.W. & CO., Agents. Ill. catalog
of fine machinists' tools and hardware.
8vo., 78pp.

1891 Syracuse, N. Y.   DSi
STRAIGHT LINE ENGINE CO. Ill. price
list of Straight Line Engines. 32pp.

1895-97 Detroit   MiU-H
STRELINGER, CHARLES A. & CO. 3 ill.
catalogs: 1895, 1896 and 1897.
1895 - A Book of Tools. 12mo., 526pp., cl.
1896 - Catalog of Tools and Tool Chests.
1897 - Catalog of wood workers' tools.
400pp., all ill. throughout, and very comprehensive pict. records.

nd. Warren, Pa.   PHi
STRUTHERS, WELLS & CO. Price list of
Warren gas and gasoline engines. 8vo.,4pp.

1894 Boston   PKsL
STURTEVANT, B.F. CO. General catalog
#61. Ills. of blowers, exhausters, portable
forges, hot blast heating apparatus, steam
engines.

1899 Boston   MH-BA
------ Catalog #96. Steel plate, steam
pulley and electric fans, motors. 8vo.,
132pp.

1899 Boston   MH-BA
------ #103. Steam engines for electric
plants. 8vo., 45pp., ill.

1900 Boston   MH-BA
------ Catalog of steam engines, motors
for electric plants, etc. 8vo., ill., 50pp.

1901 Boston   MH-BA
------ Catalog #117. Ills. of steam electric motors and generators and generating
sets. 8vo., 49pp.

1881 Philadelphia
TALLMAN & McFADDEN. Ill. catalog of
tools and hardware for metal workers. 8vo.,
212pp., pict. wrap.

1869 Richmond, Va.   DSi
TANNER, WILLIAM E. & CO. Ill. catalog
of portable engines and supplies. 30pp.

1886 San Francisco   CHi
TAYLOR, JOHN & CO. General catalog and
price list of assayers' materials, mine and
mill supplies, chemicals and chemical
apparatus. 8vo., 200pp., fine ills., wrap.

1873 Philadelphia   PHi
TAYLOR, N. & G. CO. Est. 1810. U. S.
Tin Plate House. Ill. catalog of tin plate
patterns and continuous roofing, etc. 8vo.,
16pp., pict. wrap.

1874 Philadelphia   PHi
------ Catalog of patterns. 4to., fine pls. of
plant in 1810, 1832 and 1874. Cl.

1875 Philadelphia   PPL
------ Price list of tin plate   PHi
patterns and sizes. 4to., 84pp., pls.

1878 Philadelphia   PHi
------ 68th annual greeting. Price list of
tin plate, sheet iron and sheet metals.
12mo., 52pp., ill., pict. wrap. of plant.

1882 Horseheads, N. Y.   MnHi
TERRY MFG. CO. Ill. catalog of Terry
tracks and other hardware specialties.

c.1890 Milwaukee   MnHi
THOMAS & WENTWORTH MFG. CO. Ill.
price list of brass and iron goods for
mechanics and general mill supplies.

nd. Boston   MH-BA
THOMSON-HOUSTON ELECTRIC CO. Catalog of electric motors for all purposes.
8vo., 16pp., pict. wrap.

1887 Toledo, O.   DSi
TOLEDO FOUNDRY & MACHINERY CO.
Ill. catalog of dredging and hoisting machin-
ery. 58pp.

nd. Albany, N. Y.   NNMM
TOWNSEND'S FURNACE & MACHINE SHOP.
Ill. catalog of steam engines, mill gearing
and machinery. 16pp.

1890 Trenton, N. J.   PKsL
TRENTON IRON WORKS. Ill. catalog of
wire rope, tramways, quarry hoists, etc.
with pls. of mines using Trenton materials.
12mo., 36pp.

1891 Cincinnati   OC
TRIUMPH COMPOUND ENGINE CO. Ill.
catalog of Triumph valveless compound
engines under Eickershoff pat. Sq. 8vo.,
37pp., pls.

1870 Boston   MH-BA
UNION STONE CO. Ill. circular #30 - pat.
artificial stones and emory wheels for
machinists. 8vo., 32pp.

c.1884 Peoria, Ill.   MnHi
VAN EPS, H.R. Ill. catalog of wire and iron
goods for manufacturers.

1889 San Francisco   CHi
VAN WINKLE, I.S. & CO. Ill. catalog of
iron, coal, steel and blacksmiths' supplies.
4to., 72pp., wrap.

VAUGHAN, A.H. & SONS. See Norwich
Iron Foundry.

c.1886 Goshen, Ind.   In
WALKER, EDWARD W. CARRIAGE CO.
Revised ill. catalog of wood suction and
chain pumps, wheel barrows, carts, well
drilling machinery and horse powers.
12mo., 46pp.

1875 Ansonia, Conn.   NjOE
WALLACE & SONS. Est. 1848. Ill. catalog
of brass and copper goods, wire, metallic
cartridges, rolled sheet brass tubing, etc.
8vo., 48pp., pict. wrap.

1878 Ansonia, Conn.   NjOE
------ Ill. price list of brass and copper
tubing, wire, etc. 8vo., 37pp., wrap.

1891 Ansonia, Conn.   CtWAB
------ Ill. price list of tubing, rivets,
burs and chain, etc.

1870 Boston   MiLSU
WALWORTH, JAMES J. & CO. Ill. catalog
and price list of pipes, valves, tools, washing machines, hydrants, lamps, fans, forges,
mangles, sprinkler systems, gas and steam
tools, etc. 8vo., 64pp., cl.

1878 Boston   MiLSU
------ Ill. catalog. 8vo., 162pp., glt. dec.
cl. N.B. 1883 and 1887 also available.

1868 New Haven   CtHi
WARNER, G.F. & CO. Price list of malleable iron castings, gears and wheels for
mills, etc. 4to., 4pp.

1894 Worcester, Mass.   TxDaDeG
WASHBURN & MOEN MFG. CO. Ill. catalog
of springs for railroads, mills, manufactories, upholsterers, etc. 16mo., 32pp., pict.
wrap. N.B. For complete listing, see
Fences.

1868 Waterbury, Conn.   CtWAB
WATERBURY BRASS CO. Catalog of rolled
sheet brass and German silver; wire and
tubing. Jan. 15.

1899 New York & Brooklyn, N. Y.   MH-BA
WATERBURY ROPE CO. Est. 1816. Ill.
catalog of rope and rope machinery, binders
twine, special rope for transmission and
hoisting machinery, etc. 8vo., 48pp.

c.1886 Philadelphia   DSi
WATSON & McDANIEL. Ill. price list of
steam traps and machine specialties. 50pp.

c.1890 Paterson, N. J.   MH-BA
WATSON MACHINE CO. Ill. price list of
rope machinery. 8vo., 54pp.

1886 Newark & Passaic, N. J.   DSi
WATTS-CAMPBELL & CO., Agents.
Passaic Machine Works. Ill. catalog of
Corliss steam engines. 8vo., 16pp., pls.

1884 Lebanon, Pa.   ViU
WEIMER MACHINE WORKS CO. Ill. catalog of blowing engines, blast furnace appliances, etc. View of plant.

1886 Little Ferry, N. J.   PKsL
WELLS RUSTLESS IRON WORKS. Catalog
and price list of improved Bower-Barff
apparatus for pipe, ironware, plumbers'
goods, hollow ware, etc. 8vo., 36pp., ills.

1889 Baltimore   PKsL
WENSTROM CONSOLIDATED DYNAMO &
MOTOR CO. Catalog A. Ill. price list of
motors and engines, etc.

1889 Pittsburgh, Pa.   DSi
WESTINGHOUSE MACHINE CO. Ill. price
list and desc. pamphlet of Westinghouse
compound engines. 73pp.

1884 Chicago   MnHi
WHELPLEY, R.T. Hamilton Rubber Co.
Ill. catalog of rubber and leather belting,
rubber goods and heavy hardware.

c.1893 Rochester, N. Y.   DSi
WHITMAN & BARNES MFG. CO. Ill. price
list of automatic steam engines. 16pp.

c.1885 Boston   DSi
WHITTIER MACHINE CO. Ill. catalog of
elevators - high speed, safety, hydraulic,
steam and belt - hand, freight and passenger.
4to., 52pp., pls., ptd. wrap.

1868 Philadelphia   OC
WIARD BOILERS.

c.1885 Philadelphia   PHi
WILBRAHAM BROTHERS. Special ill.
catalog of Baker rotary pressure blowers.
8vo., 42pp.

1888 Minneapolis   MnHi
WILEY & RUSSELL MFG. CO. Catalog of
pat. screw-cutting machinery and tools.

1873-4 Boston   NjOE
WILKINSON, A.J. & CO. Ill. catalog and
price list of hardware, tools and supplies.

1870 Philadelphia   PHi
WOOD, R.D. & CO. Factories: Millville,
Florence and Camden, N. J. Ill. catalog of
cast-iron gas and water pipes, fittings, lamp
posts. 40pp., charts.

c.1900 Philadelphia - and as above - PKsL
------ Ill. catalog of water and gas appli-

ances, pumping machinery, etc. 6th ed.
8vo., 175pp., ill. and fld. charts, cl.

1887 Rochester, N. Y.   DSi
WOODBURY ENGINE CO. Ill. price list of
the new Woodbury automatic, self-contained
high-speed engines - 15 to 200 h.p. 4to.,
14 pls., pict. wrap.

1881 Boston   MH-BA
WOODBURY, MERRILL, PATTEN & WOOD-
BURY. Ill. price list of differential high-
pressure air engines. 8vo., 14pp.

c.1885-99 San Francisco   CHi
WOODIN & LITTLE. Ill. catalogs #12, 16,
23 and 31. Ill. and pls. of hardware, lawn
mowers, stoves, pumps, windmills and
machinery, etc. 8vo., wrap. A fine ref.

c.1883 Newburgh, N. Y.   DSi
WRIGHT, WILLIAM. Ill. price list of steam
engines for water works and manufacturing
plants. 8vo., 24pp., pls., pict. wrap.

1884 Stamford, Conn.   MH-BA
YALE & TOWNE MFG. CO. Est. 1851.
Formerly known as the Yale Lock Mfg. Co.
Ill. catalog #10. Locks, cranes, hoisting
machinery, weighing machinery, etc. 4to.,
384pp., pls., 5 in col., dec. cl.

1887 Stamford, Conn.   DSi
------ Album of crane designs - 89 pls.
and diags. of cranes for every purpose.
24mo., 40pp., pict. wrap. A fine job.

Chapter 29

Horse Goods

Accepting a chapter heading or fact as gospel from what others have written and compiled is a very bad habit. The little story that someone told someone else at the post office grows. One small error in a contemporary 18th century history can destroy an army or a nation by the time it reaches its twenty fifth edition in the 20th. However, I shall take a chance and select the catalogs designated c.1890 as Horse Goods for a separate chapter, hoping you will also search Carriages, wagons and Accessories.

When Edwin Valentine Mitchell wrote The Horse and Buggy Age in New England, like most authors he does not locate the catalogs to which he refers. Speaking about the famous old Smith-Worthington Saddlery Co., established in 1794, he tells about a fat little leather-bound volume, used in connection with the firm's southern trade. This was (or is) a hand-made catalog full of hand water color scale drawings of all the different types of saddles produced, I would gather, about 1840; the catalog is undated. In 1954 Smith-Worthington was still going strong. I suspect this unique pictorial record is still preserved in the company's archives.

From Bessemer steel horse shoes to Uwantum saddles and whips for the most fastidious, this small section should satisfy the ardent horseman-student of the 19th century. Remember the horses who wore straw hats and ornamented nets, or didn't you ever have a chance to snitch a ride on the back step of the grand old ice wagons, or drive your parents crazy riding the sleigh runners behind the jingle of the melodious belled real leather harness? Take a look - they are all in here and located where you can see them in catalogs.

c.1900 Galesburg, Ill. ICHi
ADAMS & JOHNSON CO. Ill. circular of Uwantum harness, saddles, etc.

c.1893 Philadelphia NSbSM
AYRES, WILLIAM & SONS. Something New in Horse Blankets - color pictorial circular and price list. 16mo., 15 col. pls., plush robe, pict. wrap.

1899 Buffalo, N. Y. CBaK
BECKER & WICKSER CO. Ill. catalog of harness, appointments, aprons, whips, foot-warmers, furnishings for stables, etc. 4to., 160pp., pls., pict. wrap.

1892 Boston NSbSM
BROAD GAUGE IRON STALL CO. Ill. catalog of iron stalls and stable fittings. 4to., fine ills., pict. wrap.

1891 Boston MH-BA
CHASE, L.C. & CO. Ill. catalog of carriage robes and horse clothing. 16mo., 40pp.

1893 Boston MiD
------ Chase's three head horse blankets. 16mo., 16pp. of col. designs with amusing comment, col. pict. wrap.

c.1900 Boston NNMM
------ Ill. catalog of robes and blankets. 32pp., col. ills.

c.1890 Chicago ICHi
CHICAGO HORSE SHOE CO. Price list of horse shoes, mud shoes, mule shoes, etc.

1875 Cleveland OHi
CLEVELAND ROLLING MILL CO. Ill. circular of Hale's pat. Bessemer steel horse shoes. 8vo., 16pp.

c.1900 Richmond, Va. Vi
COTTRELL DASSLERY CO. Ill. catalog of Clark carriages, wagons and sleighs - goods for cold days, Brussels carpet covered heaters, carbon bricks of concentrated coal, auto heaters.

1744 Boston MB
CRANCH, ROBERT G. Broadside - 3 column list of goods - Robert G. Cranch, saddlers' ironmonger and bridle-cutter, on the Exchange just imported on last ship from Bristol, etc., sells on lowest terms. Ptd. I. Thomas.

1893 Boston, New York & London NSbSM
CROSS, MARK W. & CO. Ill. cat- VtSM alog of harness and stable furnishings -

stable tools and fixtures, spreaders and hob-
blers, stallion shields, whips, carriage
robes, blankets, mats, etc. 12x16, 45pp. of
pls., swell job.

1883 Denver   CoD
DENVER MFG. CO. Ill. catalog of harness,
whips, lashes, saddles, stable hardware,
boots, dusters, bells for shaft and harness,
etc.

1886 Denver   NSbSM
------ Catalog #2. Price list of harness,
saddles, stable appointments, etc. 4to., a
fine pict. record.

1899 New York   CBaK
EAGLE WINKER MFG. CO. To Horsemen
of the World - Boots of the 20th century.
Ill. catalog of horse boots and furnishings.
16mo., 36pp., col. ills.

c.1892 Cincinnati   MoSHi
ELLIS, G.S. & SON. Ill. catalog of harness
and saddlery.

c.1899 Cincinnati   OC
------ Ill. catalog of horse furnishings.

c.1890 Chicago   CBaK
FENTON, J.H. Ill. catalog of fine turf
goods - everything for the race horse. Ill.
from comb to whip. 8vo., 98pp., pict. wrap.

c.1895 Ransom, West Va.   PKsL
GOETZ, A.D. CO. Ill. catalog of harness,
collars, saddles with fld. pls. - unusual pict.
job. 4to., 212pp. of ills., dec. wrap.

c.1890 Cincinnati   OC
GRAF, MORSBACH & CO. Ill. catalog of
harness and saddlery, with col. pls. 4to.,
168pp. One of the finest col. plate records
in the field. Col. pict. wrap.

1890 Cincinnati   OC
GROSSMAN, SCHLEUTKER & CO. Ill. cat-
alog of saddles, trimmings, harness, etc.
Tall 4to., 164pp. plus 16pp. ill. advts.

c.1894 Chicago   VtSM
HAUSSMANN & DUNN. Ill. catalog of boots,
caps, leggings, jockey uniforms, veterinar-
ian instruments, harness, etc.

1899 New York   NHi
HEMMENWAY. See Sporting Goods.

1879 Concord, N. H.   NhHi
HILL, JAMES R. & CO. Price list and desc.
catalog of the Concord harness, collars, etc.
56pp., ills.

c.1885 Oswego, N. Y.   N
KING HARNESS CO. Est. 1881. Catalog
#27. Ills. of custom made oak tanned leath-
er harness. Sq. 8vo., 88pp., pict. wrap.

c.1890 Oswego, N. Y.   MH-BA
------ Ill. catalog of harness. Large 8vo.,
146pp.

c.1885 Minneapolis   MnHi
LOYE, S.B. & SONS. Ill. catalog of harness,
saddles, collars, whips, blankets, fly nets
and furnishings. 8vo., 20pp.

c.1805 Philadelphia   PPL
McALLISTER, JOHN. A desc. and   PHi
priced catalog of whips mfg. by . . . 4to.,
2pp.

1886 Cincinnati   OHi
McCLAIN & ANDERSON. Ill. catalog #132.
Sweat collars, etc. 8vo., 112pp., pict. wrap.

1895 Greenfield, O.   MH-BA
McCLAIN, E.L. MFG. CO. Ill. price list of
unbranded sweat pads, etc. 24mo., 24pp.,
wrap.

1889 San Francisco   CHi
MAIN & WINCHESTER. Ill. catalog #8.
Bridles, collars, harness, saddlery of the
best leather, etc. 8vo., 318pp. of ills., an
outstanding catalog with 14 col. pls., pict.
wrap.

1882 St. Louis   NNMM
MEYER, BANNERMAN & CO. Catalog of
bits, spurs, harness, saddles, etc. 240pp.,
fine ills. throughout.

1882 New York   NCooHi
MOORE, JOHN. John Moore's ill. catalog
and price list of robes, horse blankets,
carriage rugs, buffalo robes, harness, etc.
16mo., 24pp., pict. wrap.

1879 New York   WaMaG
        NNMM VtSM ICHi NSbSM
MOSEMAN, C.M. & BROTHER. Moseman's
ill. guide for horse furnishings. Fine col.
pls. of jockey costumes, monograms, novelties, stable appointments, saddles, plumes,
weathervanes, hitching posts, rosettes, the
finest harness, carriage ornaments, whips,
etc. The most outstanding record ever
issued. Large 4to., dec. cl. Offices in
New York, London, Moscow, Paris and
Berlin. You can't beat this one with 5 tons
of manuscript material.

1887 New York   NNMM
MOTT, J.L. IRON WORKS. Ill. catalog F.
Stable fittings, ornaments, stalls, plans,
buggy brackets, crestings, weathervanes,
etc. 4to., 224pp., pict. wrap.

1889 New York   ICHi
------ Ill. catalog F with supplement.
Large 8vo., 240pp., pict. wrap. See also
Architecture, Ornamental Ironwork and
Weathervanes for other Mott catalogs.

1897 Sweetwater, Texas   CoD
MYRES, S.D. Ill. catalog of art leather
goods, bits, saddles, ranch supplies, spurs,
etc.

1900 New Brunswick, N. J.   VtSM
NEVERSLIP MFG. CO. Catalog of self
sharpening horse shoe calks, hand taps,
drilled shoes.

1901 New Brunswick, N. J.   VtSM
------ Ill. catalog.

c.1891 San Francisco   NNMM
O'KANE, J. Ill. catalog of fine and fancy
harness, and all manner of turf goods.
74pp., wrap.

1877 Providence, R. I.   RHi
RHODE ISLAND HORSE SHOE CO. Ill.
price list of Perkins pat. machine steam
hammered horse and mule shoes of U.S.
standard. 8vo., 16pp., glt. pict. wrap.

1898 Newark, N. J.   MH-BA
RUBBER & CELLULOID HARNESS TRIM-
MING CO. Ill. catalog #7. Fasteners,
rosettes, etc. 8vo., 72pp.

1800 Boston
SABIN, CHARLES H. Ill. catalog and price
list of harness and saddles. 8vo., 52pp.,
fine pict. wrap.

1871 Springfield, Vt.   VtHi
SMITH, BURR & CO. Est. 1798. First
mfg. of hames in America. Ill. catalog of
pat. hames - bolt, hook, clipse and standard
hames. 12mo., 4pp. of ills with details.
See Toys - bound with others in Burke catalog.

1885 Boston   VtSM
SNOW, W.A. & CO. Successor to Oakes
Mfg. Co. Ill. catalog of cast and wrought

iron stable fittings, hitching posts, feed
boxes, gutters, brass fixtures, etc. See
also Ornamental Ironwork.

nd. South Bend, Ind.   In
SPRING CURRY COMB CO. Merciful is
Man to his Beast. Ill. price list. 16mo.,
4p. col. ill. circular.

c.1898 Decatur, Ill.   ICHi
STARR, J.G. & SON HARNESS CO. Est.
1856. Ill. catalog #37. Harness, horse
gear, carriages, etc. 8vo., 12pp., pict.wrap.

1897 Detroit   MBSPNEA
TUTTLE & CLARK CO. Ill. catalog of
horse goods - carriages, wagons, harness,
stable appointments, racing gear, jockey
furnishings, etc. 4to., 226pp., fine col. pls.

p.1900 Detroit   Mi
------ Ill. catalogs #27, 30, 40, 50, 51 and
55. 1904 to 1917.

nd. Columbus, O.   NNMM
VEHICLE APRON & HOOD CO. Trademark
- Blizzard. Ill. catalog of carriage canopies,
hoods, blankets, aprons and horse covers.
24pp.

1888 Wellsville, Pa.   PHi
WELLS' WHIP CO. Ill. price list of leather
fly nets, light, heavy, western, Houston and
other whips. 16mo., 24pp., pict. wrap.

WESTERVELT. See Ornamental Ironwork.

1891 Cleveland   NSbSM
WORTHINGTON, THE GEORGE CO. Ill.
price list of horse goods - harness, saddlery,
ornaments, rosettes, etc. 4to., 278pp. with
many fine pls., cl. Issued to customers -
label No. 7320.

Chapter 30

House Furnishings

House Furnishings as a heading covers practically the whole gamut of human interests. If a carpenter's hammer is in his back pocket, or on the work table in his shop, it is most certainly hardware in any language. If it is in the kitchen closet of a home with the brooms, dust pans and vacuum cleaner, what is it? There seem to be thousands of articles whose classification depends on nothing but where they happen to be in use. A silver tea set, scattered among several workmen in a factory, is most decidedly silverware. Now comes the time to decide whether I have already written myself into a corner. If this same tea set is gracing a fine Sheraton sideboard in your home, isn't it an important item of furnishing?

This chapter will guide you from andirons to woodenware. I have provided you with cross references to the hardware catalogs whose offerings fit both of these groups. The responsibility of using them puts the burden on you.

1874 Erie, Pa.   PHi
ADAMS, F.F., Mfg. Ill. price list of
Lovell's step and extension ladders. Jan. 1.

1886 Erie, Pa.   PHi
------ Ill. catalog of wringer, clothes
horses, mouse traps, ladders, etc. 16mo.,
40pp., fine ills., pict. wrap.

1856 Boston   MH-BA
ADAMS, JOHN J. Price list of house furnishings and goods. 2pp.

1897 Buffalo, N.Y.   NNMM
ALDRICH & RAY MFG. CO. Ill. catalog of
kettles, urns, pots and pans, wash boilers,
etc. 88pp., wrap.

1875 Amherst, Mass.   MA
ALLEN, L.H. Ill. price list and catalog of
wire goods - mouse and rat traps, baskets,
broilers, novelties. 16mo., 16pp., pict.
wrap.

c.1895 Providence, R.I.   RHi
ANTHONY, COWELL & CO. Est. 1872.
Compliments of . . . facts and figures.
Ill. catalog of baby carriages, cabinets,
rugs, secretaries, etc. 16mo., 82pp., wrap.

c.1894 Pittsburgh, Pa.   PKsL
BAIRD, W.H. & CO. Household   OrU
necessities! Simplicity, cheapness and
durability. Ill. catalog of improved city
iron dish washer, gadgets, novelties, washing machines. Sm. 4to., 18pp. with 4 page
ill. circular enc.

1888 Elmira, N.Y.   N
BARKER, ROSE & GRAY. Price list and
ill. catalog of hardware - acorn hinges to
western cow bells, locks, latches, fire sets,
boot jacks - a swell dictionary of American
gadgets. 4to., 1082pp. of ills., dec. cl.

1876 Philadelphia, New York & Boston
BARTLETT, H.A. & CO. Catalog   MH-BA
of blacking, stove polish, bluing, inks, plumbago, German lead, etc. 16mo., 12pp.

c.1896 Dayton, O.   NNMM
BEAVER SOAP CO. Leaflet price list of
Grand Pa's Wonder Soap. 8pp., delightful
desc.

c.1887 Chicago   MnHi
BERG, JOHN & BROTHER. Ill. catalog of
step and extension ladders.

c.1895 Boston   DLC
BIGELOW & DOWSE. Est. 1839. Ill. catalog of general hardware - very literally,
everything but the kitchen sink. 4to.,
1228pp. of ills., 1/2 mor.

BINGHAM, THE W. CO. See Hardware -
Miscellaneous Machinery.

nd. Grand Rapids, Mich.   MnHi
BISSELL CARPET SWEEPER CO. Ill. catalog of carpet sweepers, styles and models.

BLAISDELL & BURLEY. See Refrigeration.

1893 Chicago   ICHi
BLAKESLEE, G.S. CO. Ill. circular of the
Columbia Dish Washer. 8vo., tests., wrap.

A Guide to

1864 New York   NSbSM
BLIVEN, MEAD & CO. Ill. catalog of
American, German, English and French
hardware - andirons, brackets, sad irons,
pot rests, sewing birds, foot scrapers,
lanterns and sleds. 8vo., 500pp., swell ills.,
dec. cl.

1884 Detroit   MnHi
BOLLES, J.E. & CO. Ill. catalog of wire
and iron goods.

nd. New Haven   MdTanSW
BRADLEY, ROBERT B. & CO. Price list
of Japanese paper ware, wooden ware, mats,
brooms, spittoons, basins, commodes, pails,
etc. Ill. 12mo. folder.

1859 St. Louis   MoSHi
BRAINERD, S.S. Biddy and the Old Domin-
ion - an ill. brochure to sell household goods.

c.1860 St. Louis   MoSHi
------ Catalog of housekeeping articles.

1854 New York
BRIDGE & REMINGTON. American fancy
goods - buttons, brushes, combs, clocks,
watches, jewelry, carpet bags, paper hangings, looking glasses, etc. 16mo., 48pp.,
pict. wrap.

c.1855 Chicago   IHi
BRIGGS & WHITE. Catalog of plain and
painted wooden, willow and cedar ware -
8 sizes of ice boxes, etc. 1 page circular,
4 column.

1876 Cincinnati   OC
BROMWELL MFG. CO. Reduced price list
of feather dusters. 8vo., 2 lvs.

1837 London, England   MH-BA
BROWN, J. Price list of perfumes and
select articles for the toilet. 12mo., 36pp.,
wrap. Included since many of this type of
English catalog were intended for the American trade.

1872 Philadelphia   PKsL
BUEHLER, BONBRIGHT & CO. Ill. price
list of plain, turned, tinned and enameled
iron hollow ware, maslin kettles, waffle
irons, spiders, etc. 16mo., 12pp., glt. ptd.
glazed wrap.

1873 Philadelphia   PHi
------ Ill. price list of coal hods, stove
shovels, pokers, coffee roasters, novelties.
16mo., 8pp., wrap. See also Sporting Goods.

BUFFALO STAMPING WORKS. See Sidney
Shepard & Co.

1874 Boston   MBSPNEA
BURTON, FELLOWS & CO., MFG. Trade
price list of every brush for every trade,
feather dusters for parlor and carriage,
tooth brushes, etc. 16mo., 48pp., ill., wrap.

c.1850 Philadelphia   PKsL
CARRYL, E.W. Ill. catalog of house furnishings - cutlery, flatware, sad irons, tubs,
fireplace irons, furniture, bird cages and
mouse traps, etc. 64mo., 32pp., pict. wrap.

1855 Boston   NNMM
CHASE BROTHERS & CO. Ill.   PBS
catalog of useful and ornamental bronzed
iron goods - bedsteads, hat, coat and umbrella stands, tables, chairs, fireplace tools,
mantels, fountains, gateways and lawn animals and even armed piano stools! 8vo.,
62pp., woodcuts throughout, one of the best
located pict. ref. in the field. Pict. wrap.
See also Ornamental Ironwork.

1889 & 1896 San Francisco   CHi
CLAIRE, JUSTINIAN. Ill. catalog of Assayers' materials, hardware, novelties and
fancy goods. 8vo., pict. wrap.

1875 New York   NNMM
CLARK, JAMES B. Ill. price list of Grand
Central Mills for coffees and spices. 2 lvs.

1897 New York   OCP&G
COLGATE & CO. Est. 1806. Spring List -
laundry soaps, flavoring extracts, new styles
of perfumed candles, etc. 16mo., 12pp., ill.,
pict. wrap.

1880 New York   OCP&G
------ New styles and recipes. 24pp.

c.1884 San Francisco   CHi
COMMERCIAL SOAP CO. Price list of new
flavors, perfumes, etc. 12mo., 16pp.

nd. Philadelphia   PHi
CRAIN PUMP & SUPPLY CO. Ill. catalog
of Buckeye ladders for every purpose, in
the home and out.

c.1886 New York   NSbSM
CRANDELL & GODLEY MFG. Bakers',
confectioners' and hotel supplies. Ill. catalog of fancy tin moulds, glass jars, silverware, whipping machines, kitchen ware for
mass production and for the home. 4to.,
260pp., excellent ills., cl.

1899 New York   OCP&G
CROFTS & REED. Retail price list of
soaps and perfumes.

c.1850 Providence, R. I.   RHi
CUNNINGHAM, B.P. Catalog of Cunningham's Emporium - ills. of furniture, glass
and china ware, stoves, pottery, japanned

ware, Brittania, fancy carved gent's chairs, etc. 16mo., glt. dec. wrap, 120pp., index.

c.1850 Haverhill, Mass.   MWA
CURRIER, W.A. W. A. Currier's kitchen, house furnishings and stove warehouse. Woodcuts of Victorian fancy carved furniture, misc. glassware, stoves, novelties, etc. 16mo., 36pp.

1875 Worcester, Mass.   MH-BA
DEAN, LEWIS. Est. 1857. Ill. catalog of wire goods - sieves, egg beaters, broilers, corn poppers, etc. 24mo., 8pp.

1773 Boston   MWA
DEBLOIS: GILBERT. At his shop near the late Rev. D. Sewall's Meeting House, imports . . . a fine list of goods: buttons to tammies, bearskins, blankets, English, India, Scotch and Dutch dry goods, shoes, rugs, lute strings, feathers, hose, buckles, arms, etc. Broadside 6-1/2x8-1/2 with a fine border. N.B. Lowest rates for ready money only - but no abatement made on prices first asked. Think that one over - no favors for politicians - no stamps and no discounts to anyone.

c.1890 New York   MdTanSW
DENNING, E.J. & CO. Successors to A. T. Stewart & Co. Ill. catalog of furnishings for homes, hotels, steamboats, railroads, apartment houses and institutions. Baby carriages, bicycles, furniture, refrigerators, glass, lamps, china, etc. 8vo., 48pp.

c.1893 St. Paul, Minn.   MnHi
DONALDSON, OGDEN & CO. Ill. catalog of crockery, glassware, lamps, silverware, pocket and table cutlery, holiday goods, etc. 4to., 160pp.

EASTERN BROOM & WOOD WARE MFG. CO. See Rowe.

1888 Ansonia, Conn.   DSi
ELECTRIC SUPPLY CO. Catalog #645. Electrical house goods. 8vo., 50pp., fine ills., wrap.

1892 St. Louis   MoSHi
EMERSON ELECTRIC MFG. CO. Ill. catalog of home and kitchen novelties, etc. Also bulletins of merchandise to 1910.

1878 Philadelphia   PHi
ENTERPRISE MFG. CO. Ill. catalog of patent hardware - food grinders, meat choppers, kitchen implements - even penny banks. 16mo., 40pp., fine ills., pict. wrap.

1882 Philadelphia   PKsL
------ Ill. catalog for 1882.

1883 Philadelphia   PHi
------ Ill. catalog of hardware - food mills and household novelties, etc. 8vo., 32pp., pict. wrap.

1884 Philadelphia   PKsL
------ Ill. catalog - from coffee mills and roasters to mouse traps and penny banks. 8vo., 40pp., pict. wrap.

1887 Philadelphia   MdTanSW
------ Ill. catalog, as above, including sad irons, toasters, etc. plus special recipes, etc. 64pp.

c.1890 Philadelphia   PHi
------ Ill. catalog #27. Food processing machines, etc.

1880 St. Louis   MnHi
EXCELSIOR MFG. CO. Ill. catalog of granite ware, also price list for 1887.

1839 Exeter, N. H.   MWA
EXETER BOOKSTORE & PRINTING OFFICE. F. Grant, Prop. List of books, musical instruments, paints, spectacles, paper hangings, brushes, pat. medicines, blacking, confectionery, Shaker garden seeds, etc. Broadside with a nice list of goods.

1858 Boston   MH-BA
FARLEY, BLISS & CO. Catalog of dry goods. 4to., 8pp., pict. wrap.

c.1885 San Francisco   CHi
FEIGENBAUM & CO. Ill. catalog of fancy goods, cutlery, notions, smoking pipes, toys, etc. 8vo., fine ills., bds.

1854 Buffalo, N. Y.   NBuHi
FLERSHEIM, LEMUEL H. Est. 1840. Catalog of fancy goods from Lem Flersheim's Emporium, #195 Main st., next door to the Metropolitan Theater. Buttons, combs, notions, wooden and willow ware, clocks, crockery, toys, etc.

1888 Henniker, N. H.   NhHi
GAGE & CO. Est. 1863. Ill. catalog and desc. price list of dry measures, bowls and wooden ware of all kinds for the housewife. 8vo., 16pp., wrap.

1887 Chicago   MnHi
GARDNER LADDER CO. Ill. catalog of ladders for all purposes.

1884 Milwaukee   MnHi
GEUDER & PAESCHKE MFG. CO. Ill. catalog of kitchen utensils.

1880 Georgetown, Conn.   CtHi
GILBERT & BENNETT MFG. CO. Ill. catalog of iron wire twist fences, sieves, safes, covers, muzzles, ash sifters and household gadgets. 8vo., 40pp., wrap.

1887 Georgetown, Conn. (Chicago Agent)
------ Ill. catalog of kitchen wire   MnHi
ware.

1852 Philadelphia   PHi
GLENN & CO. Ill. price list of Glenn's
emporium of European fancy and toilet
goods. 8vo., 4pp.

1860 Philadelphia   PHi
GRAYBILL & CO. Ill. catalog of carpets
and oil cloths, wood and willow ware, grocers' outfits, stationery and general merchandise. Tall 16mo., 22pp., fine ills., pict.
wrap.

1784 Newburyport, Mass.   MWA
GREENOUGH, JOSEPH JR. Just imported -
and to be sold at his Cheap Store a little
below Ferry Way - a fine selection of merchandise. List of . . . 7-1/2x12 broadside
ptd. John Mycall with a characteristic
border.

1873 Philadelphia   PKsL
GRIFFITHS, GEORGE. Keystone Mfg.
Works. Est. 1855. Ill. price list of coal
hods, pokers, wash boilers, fire carriers,
muffin pans, coffee roasters, etc. 16mo.,
18pp., pict. wrap.

1874 Philadelphia   PKsL
------ Revised price list for 1874.

1893 Chicago   ICHi
GROSS, J.P. & CO. Ill. price list of broom
corn, broom handles, brushes, twines,
broom tools and machines, etc. 16mo., 8pp.
14 ills.   N.B. I have a hunch Gross may
have been a Shaker agent but can find no
proof of this.

1860 New York   OAkF
GUTTA PERCHA MFG. CO. Ill. catalog
and trade price list of vulcanized gutta
percha goods, clothing and industrial supplies. 12mo., 20pp., fine ills., wrap.

1856 Boston   NNMM
HALL, HENRY A. & CO. Ill. and priced
catalog of India-rubber and Gutta-Percha
goods. 47pp., wrap.

nd. New York   NNMM
HARTFORD CARPET CO. Ill. catalog of
the Hartford Saxony rug. 32pp., fine col.
ills.

c.1886 Philadelphia   PHi
HASLET, FLANAGEN & CO. Ill. catalog of
plain, stamped and japanned tinware, house
furnishings goods, tinmans' supplies, trimmings, stenciled toilet ware, apple corers
and agate ware to whips and ringers. 8vo.,
100pp., pict. wrap.

c.1900 Philadelphia   PKsL
------ Ill. catalog of house furnishings.
Fine col. pict. record.

1887 Boston   NNMM
HATCH, N.M. Ill. catalog of Japanese novelties - baskets, furnishings, screens, etc.
with 5¢, 10¢, 15¢ and 25¢ novelties - tea
cups, sets, etc. 8vo., 16pp., pict. wrap.

1842 Ashford, Conn.   MiDbF
HIBBARD & ALMY. New Firm and New
Goods - crockery, glass, paints, looking
glasses, dry goods, etc. Fol. broadside with
a long list of goods.

1884 Chicago   MnHi
HIBBARD, SPENCER, BARTLETT & CO.
Ill. catalog of general hardware - apple
parers, fly traps, slicers, kitchen ware, pat.
novelties and tools.

1885 Chicago   MnHi
------ Ill. catalog of wire and iron goods.

1983 Chicago   NNMM
------ Ill. catalog of hardware, wire goods
and house furnishings. 88pp.

1887 New York   OAkF
HODGMAN RUBBER MFG. CO. Est. 1838.
Ill. catalog of rubber goods. Ills. of clothing, druggists' supplies, hardware, shoes,
overshoes, saddlery, air beds, toys, etc.
12mo., 123pp., fine ills., pict. wrap.

HOGG & PATTERSON. See Glass Chapter.

c.1870 Cincinnati   OC
HOWDEN'S SONS, MFG. Excelsior cooking
utensils pat. by Worden 1863 and 1865. For
sale by Cincinnati Tin & Japan Co. Ill.
broadside, 4to.

nd. Brooklyn, N. Y.   NNMM
HUEBEL & MANGER. Ill., priced catalog
of popular and useful novelties. 24pp., wrap.

1883 Cincinnati   MnHi
HUNTER SIFTER MFG. CO. Est. 1877.
Ill. catalog of kitchen utensils.

1886-7 Cincinnati   OC
------ Ill. catalog and price list of special
cooking machinery and kitchen equipment,
etc. 8vo., 32pp., lithos. by Weisbrodt, fld.
plate, pict. wrap.

1886 Cincinnati   OHi
INNES & CO. Ill. catalog of brass goods,
fenders, fire sets, coal hods, andirons, etc.
96pp.

1890 New York   NHi
JACKSON, W. & SON. Est. 1827. Ill. catalog of grates and fenders, fireplace sets,

andirons, grates, hods, etc. Fol. 48pp., of
fine pls.

c.1860 Boston   NNMM
JACOBS, ELISHA & CO. Ill. cat-   MiDbF
alog of fancy goods and general   merchandise - buttons, cutlery, silver novelties and
other articles. 32mo., 16pp., woodcuts,
pict. wrap.

1887 Minneapolis   MnHi
JANNEY, SEMPLE & CO. Ill. catalog of
wholesale hardware, agate ironware, hollow
ware, kitchen equipment and furnishings.

c.1892 New York   ICHi
JANUSCH, F.G. Ill. catalog of brass goods
for the fireplace - frames, fenders, and -
irons, etc. Tall 4to., fine pls., pict. wrap.

1884 New York   NNMM
JUDD, H.L. & CO. Ill. catalog of fancy
goods. 108pp., wrap.

nd. Wallingford, Conn. & Brooklyn, N. Y.
JUDD MFG. CO. & H.L. JUDD &   NNMM
CO. Ill. catalog of fireplace furniture,
fenders, andirons, fire sets, screens, coal
hods and stands. 16pp.

Philadelphia
KEYSTONE WORKS. See Hardware -
General Goods.

1829 Vincennes, Ind.   In
KURTZ & LODWICK. Respectfully inform
their friends that they have just received
from Cincinnati a new and splendid assortment of fall goods. List of merchandise.
Broadside 10-1/2x16-1/2.

1878 New York   NNMM
LALANCE & GROSJEAN MFG. CO.   MnHi
Ill. catalog of kitchen utensils, brass and
copper ware, agate iron ware series D.
150pp. of fine ills., pict. wrap.

1884 New York   NNMM
------ Ill. catalog of planished brass and
copper ware, agate ware, enameled ware,
deep stamped and japanned tableware, toys.
16mo., 218pp., ills. throughout.

1890 New York   NNQ
------ Ill. catalog. 350pp., dec. cl.

c.1878 Lancaster, Pa.   PKsL
LANCASTER COPPER WORKS. John P.
Schaum. 4 page ill. folder - trademarks
and list of prices. Kettles, dippers and
warming pans.

1887 New York   MnHi
LANDERS, FRARY & CLARK. Ill. catalog
of table cutlery, etc.

1895 Buffalo, N. Y.   NBuHi
LARKIN SOAP CO. You Must Have Soap -
ill. catalog of soaps and premiums, etc.
4to., pict. wrap.

c.1898 Buffalo   NBuHi
------ The Larkin Idea - Factory to
Family. 4to., ill., pict. wrap. in col.

c.1887 Grand Rapids, Mich.   MdTanSW
LEONARD, H. & SONS. Est. 1844. Ill.
price list of staple goods. Ills. of crockery,
glassware and lamp goods, silver, Britannia
tableware and flatware, etc. 8vo., 160pp.,
index.

1893 Chicago - Port Sunlight   OCP&G
LEVER BROTHERS. Windsor Castle at
Chicago. The home of sunlight soap by
G. A. Sala. Sq. 16mo., 32pp., tinted ills. of
plant, etc. Not a price list but good example
of Gay Ninety sales promotion.

1896 Sacramento   CHi
LEWIS, L.L. & CO. Ill. catalog and price
list of stoves, refrigerators, sewing
machines, ice cream freezers, bicycles,
hardware and kitchen ware. 8vo., 90pp. of
ills., wrap.

1873 Pittsburgh, Pa.   PKsL
LINDSAY, STERRIT & CO. Price list of
double seamed coal hods, etc.

LLOYD, SUPPLEE & WALTON. See also
Hardware - General Goods.

1870 New York   MH-BA
LOCKE, JOHN D. & CO. Est. 1827. Catalog of tinware, Japanned ware, kitchen ware,
stamped ware - candlesticks to toys. 8vo.,
32pp., wrap.

1884 Troy, N. Y.   MdTanSW
LOCKWOOD & BUELL. Ill. price list of
iron agate ware. 16mo., 88pp.

c.1900 New Brighton, Pa.   PKsL
LOGAN & STROBRIDGE IRON CO. Brighton
Coffee Mills. Ill. catalog of new models and
styles. 20pp., pict. wrap.

1887 New York   NNMM
LONDON TOILET BAZAAR CO. Ill. catalog for the house on the art of human decoration. 28pp., pict. wrap.

1893 Chicago, Ill.   ICHi
LORD, OWEN & CO. Ill. catalog of mirrors,
fancy jewel and decorated boxes, novelties,
etc.

nd. Philadelphia   PKsL
McLOUGHLIN & DIFFENDERFER. Successors to Jno. Bell Robinson & Co. Ill.
catalog of brooms, clocks, looking glasses,

floor and table oilcloths, brushes, fancy hardware, Japanned tin ware, wood and willow ware, window shades, etc. 24mo., dec. wrap.

MARIETTA CASTING, Hollow Ware and Enameling Co. of Marietta, Pa. See Buehler, Bonbright & Co.

1854 New York   MiDbF
METROPOLITAN SOAPSTONE CO. 8vo., 17pp. Report from Middlefield, Mass. No further data available.

1890 Baltimore   MdBE
MILLER, DANIEL & CO. Ill. catalog of dry goods, notions, small wares - compliments of . . . fine photos. of contemporary stores and counters with Miller goods displayed. Tall 4to., pict. wrap.

1881 Meriden, Conn.   NNMM
MILLER, EDWARD & CO. Ill. catalog of bronzed parlor ornaments. 60pp. of ills., cl.

c.1890 Cincinnati   NNMM
MITCHELL, ROBERT FURNITURE CO. 3 ill. catalogs of mantels, grates, and fireplace furnishings, etc. #21, 24 and 25 with fine ills. and pp. 78, 80 and 81 respectively. Wraps.

1871 New York   NNMM
MULLER, NICHOLAS. Ill. catalog of bronzes, vases, inkstands, statuettes, paperweights, novelties. 8vo., 40pp. plus 4 page supplement. Wrap.

1880 Winchendon, Mass.   NHi
NASH, M.T. Est. 1825. Ill. catalog of wooden ware - styles of butter churns, etc. 12mo., 12pp., pict. wrap.

1876 Philadelphia   PKsL
NATIONAL NOVELTY CO. Ill. catalog of comb cleaners, knife sharpeners, kitchen utensils, general furnishings. 12mo., pict. wrap.

nd. Philadelphia   PHi
NELMS & BROWN, INC. Ill. catalog of brushes for all purposes.

c.1890 New York   MdTanSW
NEVINS CO. Ill. catalog and price list of desk fitments, table furnishings, brass, silver and leather ornaments and novelties. New things and old things. 80pp., index, cl.

nd. New Albany, Ind.   In
NEW ALBANY BOX & BASKET CO. Ill. catalog #20, plain and fancy boxes and baskets for all purposes. 32mo., 48pp., wrap.

1883 Providence, R. I.   RHi
NEW ENGLAND BUTT CO. Ill. catalog of house furnishings, boot jacks, match safes, sad irons, hitching posts and general hardware. 8vo., 20pp., fine ills.

NEWTON, D.A. Agent. See also Hardware-General Goods.

nd. New York   NNMM
NEW YORK WOOD TURNING CO. Ill. and desc. catalog of curtain poles with fixtures, cornices, etc. 15pp., wrap.

OGDEN, E. HALL. See Hardware - General Goods.

1886 Portland, Ore.   OrU
OLDS & KING. Ill. catalog of dry goods, notions and novelties. Bound with Olds & Summers - see next entry.

1886 Portland, Ore.   OrU
OLDS & SUMMERS. Successors to Olds & King. Ill. catalog of crockery, glassware, lamps, chandeliers, trimmings, cutlery, tableware, etc. 80pp. and noted as their first catalog.

c.1825 Boston   MWA
OLIVER, WILLIAM B. Circular of furnishings and tinware, sperm oil, planished ware, patented lamps, lanterns, mills for various purposes, bellows, tankards, flatware, safes, stoves, coal hods, sifters, pokers, Britannia ware - and - BATHING TUBS to sell or let!

c.1890 Newark, N. J.   ViWC
OSBORNE, C.S. & CO. Ill. catalog #70. High grade tools, cheese scoops, knives, slicers, can openers and kitchen furnishings.

1876 Oswego, N. Y.   OCP&G
OSWEGO STARCH FACTORY. Est. 1848. Kingsford & Son. Ill. catalog of starches for all purposes. 16mo., 16pp., pict. wrap. in col.

1827 Boston   MWA
PAGE, EDWARD. Catalog of crockery, glass and china ware, carpeting hearth rugs, ring neck decanters, pattern glass, tea sets, gold band and lustre landscapes, etc. 16mo., 16pp., dec. wrap.

PAINE FURNITURE CO. See Furniture.

1890 Philadelphia, Pa.   PHi
PARKE, JOHN Y. & CO. A Light Without a Match - by the Biddle & Smart Advt. Co. An ill. catalog of notions and novelties. 16mo., 24pp., pict. wrap.

PECK, STOWE & WILCOX CO. See Hardware - General Goods.

c.1850 Philadelphia   PKsL
PENNSYLVANIA FARINA CO. Berdan's
mechanical bakery apparatus. 4to., 4pp. of
desc. and details of . . .

1857 Wakefield, R. I.   RHi
PERRY, JOHN G. Desc. and ill. catalog of
Perry's premium meat cutters and sausage
stuffers - with directions, medals won, etc.
8vo., 24pp., pict. wrap. - deeelightful.

c.1900 Philadelphia   PKsL
PHILADELPHIA BABY CARRIAGE CO.
Style Book of Bloch Go-Carts and baby carriages, etc. 12mo., 16pp., swell pls. of
models.

nd. Philadelphia
PHILADELPHIA COAL HOD MFG. CO.
Price list of pokers, stove shovels, pipe and
elbows, wash boilers, tea kettles, coffee
boilers, etc.

1856 Oswego, N. Y.   NNU
PLATT & HULL. Everybody's scrap-book.
An ill. catalog of ambrotype and daguerrian
stock, glass, dyes, brushes, canes, wooden
ware, pipes, segars, etc. 16mo., 16pp.
N.B. A simple country Liggetts of 1856!

1816 Lancaster, Mass.   MWA
PLUMMER, FARNHAM & CO. Circular -
Selling off stock - subscriber closing his
business in Lancaster, which consists of
. . . 2 column list of crockery, glassware,
drugs, paints, hardware, etc. One leaf,
August 2nd.

c.1880 Norwich, Conn.   Ct
PRESTON BROTHERS. Anniversary catalog of cutlery, knives for all uses, bird
cages, mouse and rat traps, novelties, etc.
8vo., 55pp. with good ills.

1883 Cincinnati   OHi
PROCTOR & GAMBLE CO. What   OC
a cake of soap will do. Ill. price list with
Palmer Cox Brownie story. 8vo., 24pp.

1890 Cincinnati   OCP&G
----- The Ivory Calendar with fine col. ills.
N.B. The Proctor & Gamble Co. have a research library containing all of their own
price lists, etc. after 1879.

c.1900 Chicago   NNMM
QUAKER VALLEY MFG. CO. Premium
catalog - How to Furnish a Home - Ill. catalog of home furnishings. 48pp.

READING HARDWARE CO. See Hardware -
General Goods.

nd. Baltimore   OCP&G
RESINOL CHEMICAL CO. Beauty Album -
col. ills. - fine teeth and fine complexions.
Amusing brochure.

1888-9 Chicago
REVELL, ALEXANDER H. & CO. Catalog
of household goods and goods for personal
use - The Buyers' Cost Book. From cuspidors to wine glasses, candlesticks to tin
stenciled washbowls, baskets to trunks and
washing machines, furniture and silverware.
4to., 64pp., fine pict. record, pict. wrap.

1880 Chicago   NNMM
RICE, C.F. Ill. catalog of mirrors, mouldings, frames, brackets, cornices, etc.
128pp., fine pls., wrap.

1804 Concord, Mass.   MWA
RICHARDSON & WHEELER. Concord
Variety Store kept by . . . English goods
cheaper than in Boston! Crockery, glass
and china ware, W. I. Goods, iron, nails and
all manner of hardware. Broadside - 2
column list of goods - and a catalog in every
sense of the word. Ptd. Gilbert Dean.

1800 Boston   MHi
RICHARDSON, WILLIAM. A large assortment of lustrings, imported by . . . directly from the mfg. and for sale by . . .
Small circular.

1889 New York   OCP&G
RICKSECKER & CO. Ill. catalog of toilet
goods.

c.1843 Boston   MWA
ROBERTS, FRANCIS R. Attention All! Tea
sets for $1.50, all colors, dining, tea and
coffee ware, glass, china, furniture and
wicks for camphene lamps. N.B. Ware
loaned to Pic Nic parties on reasonable
terms.

nd. Buffalo, N. Y.   NBuHi
ROBERTSON ELECTRIC CO. Catalog #11.
Electric furnishings and supplies.

1888 Minneapolis   MnHi
ROBINSON & STRINGHAM MFG. CO. Ill.
catalog and price list of tea and coffee pots,
kettles, pans, pots, dippers, pails - stamped
and pieced tin wares. Sm. 4to., 14pp., dec.
wrap.

c.1883 Boston   MdTanSW
ROBINSON, C.H. Consolidated and ill.
price list of furniture, carpets, stoves,
ranges and kitchen furnishings goods. 4to.,
96pp., fine ills. throughout.

1879 Philadelphia   PHi
ROHRMAN, J. HALL & SON. Ill. catalog of
plain, Japanned and pressed tinware - coal
hods, grocers' cannisters, tea boxes, trays
and novelties with fine stencils. 8vo., 22pp.,
pict. wrap.

1886 Philadelphia   PHi
------ Ill. catalog of household tinwares.
12mo., 12pp., pict. wrap.

1889 Toledo, O.   MiDbF
ROSS, E. & CO. Catalog of rug patterns.
16mo., 35 col. pls. of designs - cats, dogs,
deer, lion, floral, etc. Pict. wrap. The
best hooked rug ref. in col. we have been
able to locate.

c.1850 Philadelphia   PKsL
ROWE, M. & J.M., Mfg. Ill. catalog PHi
of brooms, buckets, brushes, cedar wood
and other willow wares. Cash paid for
broom corn. 64mo., 16pp., pict. wrap. of
factory. Addressed to country merchants
and city grocers.

ST. LOUIS REFRIGERATOR & WOODEN
GUTTER CO. See also Refrigerators.

1877 St. Louis   MoSHi
ST. LOUIS STAMPING CO. Ill. catalog of
granite ware, cutlery, tinware, stenciled
utensils, etc.

1878 St. Louis   MnHi
------ Ill. catalog of granite iron ware for
all purposes.

c.1880 St. Louis   OCP&G
------ Granite Iron Ware Cook Book and
catalog. 16mo., 54pp., ills., wrap.

1890 St. Louis   MdTanSW
------ Ill. catalog and price list of granite
ware, dripping pans, spoons, sieves, trimmings, tinners' supplies and tools, and all
manner of household equipment. 12mo.,
316pp. of ills., index, cl.

1897 St. Louis   MoSHi
------ Ill. catalog of kitchen granite ware,
etc.

1841 Philadelphia   MH-BA
SAVERY & CO. FOUNDRY. Price list of
hollow ware. Large 12mo., 12pp., wrap.

1883 Chicago   ICHi
SCHLESINGER & MAYER. Ill. price list
for spring and summer - fashions, novelties, gadgets from buttons to napkin rings
and toys. 4to., 104pp., fine ills., dec. wrap.

nd. Zanesville   OHi
SCHULTZ & CO. Price list of Star soaps -
booklet with col. pict. wrap. Little Red Riding Hood.

c.1870 Cincinnati   OC
SCHWAN'S, PETER. Pet Shop. If You
Want a Good Singing Bird, Go To Peter
Schwan. Broadside, one leaf. N.B. Is a
canary house furnishings? Why not? Where

else would you expect one to sing but in some
homey kitchen, parlor or music room? If
you have a bird without a cage, see Lindemann under General Hardware Goods.

1885 Boston & Cambridgeport, Mass.
SEAVEY & CO. Ill. catalog of deep stamped,
retinned and common Japanned ware, kitchen
furnishings - in short, everything from a
toy penny bank to a revolving mouse trap.
12mo., 104pp., thumb index, about 8 ills. to
the page. Swell.

1889 Philadelphia   PHi
SHANNON, J.B. & SONS. Ill. catalog of
household goods in the hardware line.
12mo., 33pp., wrap.

c.1868 Detroit   MiU-H
SHELDEN, ALLAN & CO. Ill. catalog of
staple and fancy dry goods, white goods,
gloves, cloths and Yankee Notions! Ada-
mantine pins to watch chains. 16mo., 12pp.
Marginal dec.

1878 Buffalo, N. Y.   NBuHi
SHEPARD, SIDNEY & CO. Est. 1836.
Buffalo Stamping Works. Ill. catalog of pat.
granite iron ware for every household.

1879 Buffalo, N. Y.   NNMM
------ Ill. catalog of coal vases. 20pp.,
fine ills., wrap.

1881 Buffalo, N. Y.   NNMM
------ Ill. catalog of tinware - tollware -
utensils, vases, tin toys and banks, etc.

1887 Buffalo, N.Y.   MnHi
------ Ill. catalog of deep stamped ware,
fry pans, coal hods, vases and domestic tinware.

nd. Buffalo, N. Y.   MdTanSW
------ Ill. catalog of tinman's supplies,
and house furnishings hardware. 16mo.,
126pp., fine ills., index, wrap.

1888 Buffalo, N. Y.   MiDbF
------ Ill. catalog of Buffalo Stamping
Works. 55pp., wrap.

1890 Buffalo, N. Y.   NNMM
------ Ill. catalog of aluminum   MiDbF
ware, tinware, stamped and stenciled, galvanized ware, refrigerators, etc. 4to.,
236pp., a fine ill. record, pict. wrap.

c.1885 South Orange, N. J.   NNMM
SHEPARDSON, E.B. New ill. and   NjR
desc. catalog of fancy goods, jokes, penny
banks, novelties, toys, tricks, etc. 4to.,
16pp., amusing ills.

nd. Chicago   MnHi
SILLS, W.H. Ill. catalog of kitchen utensils
and metal specialties.

c.1890 New York   N
SPELMAN BROTHERS. A new book - the
coming Bazaar store. Ill. catalog of china
and glass novelties, Japanned tinware, pattern glass to toys. 4to., 26pp., pict. wrap.

nd. Batavia, Ill.   MnHi
SPERRY, D.R. & CO. Ill. catalog of caldrons, sugar kettles, hollow ware for various
trades and household use.

1874 New York   NNMM
SPETH, K.L. Ill. catalog of parlor brackets, flower stands and tables, easels and
fine carved ornaments and furnishings.
45pp., pict. wrap.

1893 St. Louis   MoSHi
STANDARD STAMPING CO. Ill. catalog of
tinware for many places and purposes.

c.1800 Salem, Mass.   MWA
STONE & BREWER. At the sign of the
Coffee Pot. Has constantly for sale English
goods, crockery, glass, china, etc. Broadside offering 3 columns of goods.

1870 New York   NNMM
STRATTON'S WAREHOUSE. Ill., desc. and
priced catalog of china, glassware and house
furnishings. 16pp., pict. wrap.

1898 Denver   CoD
STRUBY-ESTABROOK MERCANTILE CO.
Ill. catalog of woodenware, lightning cheese
cutters, house furnishings and kitchen ware.

1886 Denver   CoD
TAMMEN, H.H. Ill. catalog of clocks,
arrowheads, polished far west agate and
mineral ornaments, charms, etc.

1894 Denver   CoD
------ Ill. catalog of curios, stamp and
jewel boxes, match safes, table ornaments
and jewelry.

c.1870 Cincinnati   OC
TAYLOR & FAULKNER MFG. CO. Ill.
price list of new pat. automatic step ladders
for every shop and home. 16mo., 4pp.

1898 New York   NNMM
TEXTILE NOVELTY CO. Ill. catalog of
tapestry, fancy pillow covers, satin etchings
and decorations for the home. 32pp., wrap.

nd. New York   NNMM
VANTINE, A.A. & CO. Est. 1870. Ill. catalog of household articles, decorative and
ornamental. 123pp., fine ills.

c.1900 York, Pa.   PKsL
VICTOR CLEANER CO. The Victor vacuum
cleaner - Broomall's patent - photos. of
machines for parlor, bedroom and kitchen,

with suggestions for cleaning the carriages,
etc. Dust tank in cellar - a sanitary
machine. $300. Sq. 16mo., 16pp., plus
4 page insert.

1871 Boston   CCuMGM
WALKER, F A. & CO. Ill. cat-   NNMM
alog of useful and ornamental goods for dining room, kitchen, laundry and parlor -
planished, Japanned, stenciled ware in tin,
brass and copper - wooden ware, apple peal-
ers, sugar cutters, Britannia. Sq. 8vo.,
130pp. of fine ills., pict. wrap.

c.1872 Boston   MiDbF
------ Ill. supplement - choice   N
house and kitchen furnishings - bird cages,
cat teasers, Shaker swifts, cooky moulds.
106pp.

c.1875 Boston   N
------ Ill. catalog of heavy hotel and home
kitchen tinware, etc. 8vo., 10pp., fine ills.,
dec. wrap.

WALWORTH, JAMES J. & CO. See Hardware - Miscellaneous Machinery.

c.1845 Worcester, Mass.   MWA
WHEATON & HICKOX. The Housekeepers'
Own Book - A catalog of cutlery, silver and
Britannia ware, tin and wooden, willow,
stone and earthen wares and housekeeping
articles. Ill. throughout - hip-baths, shower
baths, tinned and Japanned plunge baths 6 ft.
long, all patterns, etc. Sq. 32mo., 36pp.,
ptd. wrap.

c.1890 Nashua, N. H.   NhHi
WHITE MOUNTAIN FREEZER CO. Desc.
catalog and ill. price list of Sand's patent
triple motion White Mountain freezers. Ten
patents bought, what we haven't brains to
invent, we buy, etc. 24mo., 12pp., pict.
wrap. of plant.

c.1891 Nashua, N. H. Chicago Agent.   MnHi
------ Ill. catalog.

1889 Boston   MH-BA
WHITNEY, T.D. & CO. Ill. catalog of household and art linens. 4to., 56pp.

c.1891 Boston   MH-BA
------ Catalog of linens and dry goods -
supplies for hotels, yachts, restaurants and
institutions. 8vo., 48pp., pict. wrap.

1890 Cortland, N. Y.   ICHi
WICKWIRE BROTHERS, MFG. Catalog and
price list of wire cloth and wire goods, figures, screens, sieves, bird nests, etc.
8vo., 24pp. of ills., pict. wrap.

1892 New York   NNMM
WIGGINS', H.B. SONS. Ill. catalog of fixtures, fringes, decorations and home ornaments. 32pp., wrap.

1882 Philadelphia   PPL
WILER, WILLIAM. Mfg. of Brass Goods.
Ill. price list of stair rods, fasteners, upholsterers' supplies, fireplace sets and
fenders. 64pp.

c.1895 San Francisco   CHi
WILL & FINCK CO'S. BAZAAR. Ill. catalog of silver and kitchen ware, brushes,
clocks, musical instruments, toys, etc.
4to., 156pp., pict. wrap.

1896 New London, Conn.   CtNlC
WILLIAMS, THE G.M. CO. Pictures of
things you want - anglers' supplies, patent
churns, lamps, guns, baby carriages, bicycles and coats for men and general furnishings for the home. 8vo., 64pp., ills.

1883 Newark, N.J.   NjR
WILLIAMSON, C.T. MFG. Ill. catalog of
cork screws, wood and metal handles with
brush and knife, plain and fancy, or with
power press. Sq. 12mo., 34pp., pict. wrap.

1887 Newark, N.J.   MnHi
------ Ill. catalog of patent wire novelties,
cork screws, baskets, etc.

1884 Worcester, Mass. & Providence, R.I.
WILLIAMSON, W.B. & SONS.   MH-BA
Works at Providence. Ill. catalog of tinware of all sorts - baths, boxes, toilet
ware, vases, trays and bright stamped
goods. 4to., 288pp.

1893 Worcester, Mass.   MH-BA
WIRE GOODS CO. Ill. catalog of bright
wire goods, house furnishings, novelties
and specialties in wire. 4to., 142pp.

1881 New York
WITTE, FRANCIS T. Successors to King,
Briggs & Co. Price current of cutlery,
guns, hardware and house goods. Sq.
12mo., 61pp., index, wrap.

1880 Lowell, Mass.   NNMM
WOODS, SHERWOOD & CO. Ill. catalog
and price list of wire ware for kitchen,
home and shop. 56pp., wrap.

c.1888 New Haven   MdTanSW
YALE SILK WORKS. Catalog of specialties -
popular designs - crazy patchwork and
flower making, materials, flower outfits,
etc. 8vo., 32pp., ills.

The 19th century woodworker who turned out bowls for the kitchen and handles for shovels, also
carved dolls' heads and toys. He might also have carved a fine figurehead for a merchantman, and
a bow and arrow, and a copy of a heavy Chippendale style arm chair. House Furnishings may be
found in twenty five different chapters!

Chapter 31

Jewelry

In 1788 Mr. Hubley of Philadelphia offered prints, plate, plated ware, jewelry, etc for sale. In 1804 Mr. Farley of Salem, Mass. offered jewelry, silver, plated and Britannia hardware, etc. at very low prices. In 1886 Allen, Benk & Co. offered 608 pages of jewelry, novelties, silver plated ware, etc. The only real difference is in the type, illustrations, variety and format. A careful examination and comparison will outline the tremendous growth in this one field from a single sheet broadside list to a 600 page illustrated full fledged catalog as we know the word today. Perhaps Mr. Hubley had one tray of rings in 1788. I wouldn't care to even guess the number of rings illustrated in the Allen, Benk catalog for 1886.

In the offering in this chapter you can find everything from buttons to tools for the jeweler and watchmaker. Illustrated with them you will also find fine colored glassware fitted in silver and gold vases and tableware. Novelties include campaign badges, table ornaments, clocks and watches Masonic emblems and ornate toothpicks as well as the usual run of rings and baubles. S. F. Meyers, for instance, even includes music boxes and talking machines.

1883 New York   NNMM
ALLAN, THOMAS & CO. Ill. catalog of gold and silver jewelry representing winter and summer sports of Canada. 16mo., 34pp., fine ills.

1891 Chicago   MiDbF
ALLEN, BENJAMIN & CO. Annual NHi ill. price list of watches, clocks, diamonds, glass, buttons, lamps, silverware, tools and novelties, trade signs, etc. 4to., 760pp., pict. cl.

1886 Chicago, Ill.   ICHi
ALLEN, BENK & CO. Ill. catalog of jewelry, novelties, etc. 8vo., 608pp., cl.

c.1900 Providence, R. I.   NNMM
BAIRD-NORTH CO. Ill., desc. and priced catalog of diamonds, jewelry, silverware, sewing sets, jewel boxes and cases and novelties. 224pp. of ills., wrap.

c.1900 Baltimore   N
BALTIMORE BADGE & NOVELTY CO. Catalog #95. Ills. of badges for trades, firemen, police, etc. Mardi-Gras, conventions, portrait buttons, souvenir match safes and table ornaments, etc. 4to., 44pp., 20 col. pls. and ills.

1892 Chicago   ICHi
BECKEN, ALBERT C. Trade Mark Monogram ACB. Ill. price list of jewelry, diamonds, clocks, watches, silverware, pens, novelties and jewelers' tools. 4to., 768pp., dec. cl.

1899 Chicago   NNMM
------ Ill. price list of jewelry and novelties, etc. 596pp., dec. cl.

1870 New York   NNMM
BERNHARD, A. & CO. Ill. catalog of hair ornaments and fancy jewelry for hairdress. Tall 4to., 89 lvs., bds.

c.1880 New York   MdTanSW
------ Ill. catalog of diamond and ornamental jewelry, Masonic emblems, chains, charms, etc. Tall 8vo., 48 pls. Litho. by S. Benedicks & Co., with 16mo., 32 page price list - monogram hairwork, dec. cl.

c.1890 New York   NNMM
BRAXMAR, C.G. World's leading mfg. Ill. catalog of badges for firemen, police, sports, politicians with designs for every state and territory. 4to., 90pp., fine ills., dec. wrap.

1887 Chicago   MiDbF
BUSIEST HOUSE IN AMERICA. Copies usually printed for dealers throughout the country. Ill. catalog of diamonds, clocks, watches, jewelry, novelties for bureau and parlor, ornamentation to sportsmens' lodge. 4to., 368pp., monogram cl., San Rafael, Cal.

1889 Chicago   ICHi
------ Ill. catalog of jewelry, novelties, silverware, etc. 4to., cl., 472pp.

c.1890 Chicago   NNMM
------ Ill. catalog #13. 584pp., dec. cl.

c.1874 Chicago   ICHi
CLAPP, W.B. & CO. Ill. trade price list of
jewelry, watches, clocks and fancy goods
and novelties. 8vo., 116pp., fine pls., cl.

1880 Chicago   ICHi
CLAPP, W.B.,YOUNG & CO. Ill. catalog
of jewelry. 8vo., 12pp.

nd. Middletown, Conn.   CtHi
CLARK & TRUE. Ill. catalog of jewelry
and gifts.

1896 New York   MdTanSW
EARL PEARL WORKS. Fall catalog - ills.
of pearl paper cutters, collar buttons, mani-
cure sets, pens, horn combs, whitestone
jewelry, imitation diamonds, silverplate,
etc. 8vo., 16pp. plus circular of card
cases, ornaments, fraternity pins, charms,
etc. Pict. wrap.

1883 New York   NNMM
FAIRCHILD, LEROY W. CO. Ill., desc.and
priced catalog of pens, cases, toothpicks,
match boxes, table ornaments, novelties,
etc. 26 lvs., wrap.

c.1885 New York   NNMM
FAIRCHILD, LEROY & SONS. Supplement -
ills. of charms, pens, jewelry and novelties.
4 lvs.

1804 Salem, Mass.   MSaE
FARLEY, EDWARD. Price list of jewelry,
silver - plated and Britannia hardware,
looking glasses - at very low prices.
Broadside.

nd. Philadelphia   PKsL
FRANKLIN JEWELRY CO. Ill. catalog of
jewelry and novelties.

c.1865 New York   MH-BA
GARLAND, C.H. & CO. Lottery catalog -
gifts, jewelry and watches, etc. 4to., 4pp.,
ills. of store.

1850 Boston   MBSPNEA
GEER & TURRILL. Price list - Great
Novelty! No April fooling this time! List
of jewelry, novelties, watches, etc. Broadside with woodcut ills.

c.1885 Chicago   ICHi
GILES, BROTHER & CO. Ill. catalog of
jewelry. 8vo., 18pp.

1886 Boonville, Mo.   MoSHi
HANNACA, S.S. Ill. catalog of jewelry.

c.1890 Columbus, O.   OHi
HOFMAN SUPPLY CO. Ill. catalog and
manual of engravers', jewelers' and watch
repairers' tools and materials - movements,
examples of work with 2 ill. circulars.
4to., 186pp.

1788 Philadelphia   Evans 21153
HUBLEY, A. & CO. Catalog of prints,
plate, plated ware, jewelry, etc. to be sold,
etc. Ptd. Dunlap & Claypoole.

c.1900 Providence, R. I.   NNMM
IRONS & RUSSELL. Ill. catalog of solid
gold and rolled gold plate society emblems,
pins, buttons, charms, watch fobs, etc. 8vo.,
170pp., fine col. pls., dec. cl.

1886 St. Louis   MoSHi
JACCARD, E. Ill. catalog of jewelry for
Fall of . . .

1887 St. Louis   MoSHi
------ Ill. catalog of jewelry with some
Christmas stories.

nd. New York   NNMM
JOHNSON, E.S. & CO. Ill. catalog of gold
pens, pen holders, cases, toothpick and ear
picks in gold, silver, pearl, ivory, rubber
and celluloid. 53pp., cl.

1898 New York   NNMM
KAUFMAN, LOUIS & CO. Est. 1885. Ring
Makers. Most Complete Ring Catalog Ever
Published. Ills. of designs, styles, sizes,
etc. Tall 4to., 46pp., dec. wrap.

1896-7 New York   MH-BA
KAYTON, H.H. Importers. Ill. catalog of
watch tools, materials, jewelers' findings
and optical goods. 4to., 454pp., exhaustive.

1877 Chicago   ICHi
MARSHALL FIELD & CO. Special catalog
of jewelry, novelties and silver specialties.
4to., 240pp., ills.

1899 St. Louis   MoSHi
MERMOD & JACCARD CO. Ill. catalog and
wholesale price list of jewelry.

1885 New York   NNMM
MEYERS, S.F. & CO. New York Jeweler
and Trade Price List. Vol. 1, #1. Ills. of
clocks, watches, novelties, optical goods,
findings, plated and sterling ware, jewelry
of all styles. Price $1.00. Tall 4to.,236pp.

1895 New York   MoSHi
------ Ill. catalog #39. Clocks,   N
jewelry, novelties, music boxes, talking
machines. 4to., 400pp., dec. cl.
N.B. Others located in private libraries.

c.1886 Philadelphia   NNMM
MUHR'S, H. SONS. Ill. catalog of the jewelry department. 16 lvs., wrap.

1893 Boston   MdTanSW
NEW ENGLAND JEWELER.   NNMM
2nd annual ill. catalog of diamonds, clocks,
watches, jewelry, silverware, bronzes,

gold pens, prize cups, etc. 8vo., 542pp., index, dec. cl.

1872 Chicago   ICHi
NORRIS, B.F. & CO. Ill. catalog of jewelry, silver novelties, flatwear, watches and clocks, etc. 8vo., 66pp.

1892 Chicago   ICHi
NORRIS, B.F., ALLISTER & CO.   N
Annual price list of jewelry, eye glasses, clocks, watches, tableware, charms and novelties. 4to., 392pp., fine ills., dec. cl.

1895 Chicago   ICHi
------ 32nd annual catalog of jewelry, novelties, canes, shaving mugs, souvenir spoons, watches, etc. 4to., 498pp., dec. cl.

nd. New York   NNMM
PECKHAM MERRILL FITCH & CO.   Ill. catalog #17 of fine jewelry and ornamental hair work. 32 pls., ptd. cl.

1881 New York   NNMM
PETTIBONE, G.W. & CO. Ill. catalog of jewelry and watches, etc. 16pp., wrap.

1885 vp.   MdTanSW
PHOENIX LEVER CO. Jan. 1. Ill. wholesale price list of collar buttons, charms, necklaces, vest chains, rings, etc. 24mo., 28pp., wrap.

1879 Chicago   ICHi
PRATT & MYERS. Ill. catalog of fancy goods, dishes, toys, jewelry, musical instruments, etc.

1889 Providence, R. I.   NHi
PROVIDENCE JEWELRY CO. The Fountain Head for jewelry supplies. Ill. catalog of clocks, watches, jewelry, novelties. 8vo., 314pp., fine ills., cl.

1893 Providence, R. I.   RHi
------ Ill. catalog of jewelry, etc. Music boxes, mechanical singing birds in cages, hanging lamps, novelties in jewelry. 4to., 1000pp., a swell ref., cl.

1880 New York   MdTanSW
RIDEOUT, E.G. & CO. Ill. catalog of clocks, watches, fancy jewelry, silverware, notions, tricks, quassia cups. 32pp. of ills., 8vo.

c.1880 St. Louis   RHi
RIDER, S.A. & CO. Ill. catalog of silver vest chains. 8vo., 8 fine litho. pls., wrap.

1900 Attleboro, Mass.   MdTanSW
ROBBINS, CHARLES M. CO., Mfg. Ill. catalog of silver college and school emblems, society pins, col. chart, etc. 32pp. of photo. ills.

1879 Chicago   MdTanSW
RODDIN, E.V. & CO. 23rd annual   ICHi
catalog of jewelry, watches, clocks, silverware and glass novelties. 8vo., 76pp., fine ills., pict. wrap.

1866 Providence, R. I.   RHi
SALISBURY BROTHERS & CO. Est. 1855. 11th ill. catalog of jewelry, clocks, watches, gold, silver and oreide novelties, etc. 18mo., 16pp., fine ills.

c.1900 San Francisco   MdTanSW
SHREVE & CO. Ill. catalog of precious stones, jewelry, watches, plated ware, cutlery, glass, clocks, bronzes, china and art ware. 8vo., 222pp., pls., cl.

c.1886 Chicago   ICHi
SHURLY WATCH & JEWELRY MFG. CO. Ill. catalog of corps badges, cap ornaments, bar pins, rings, sharpshooters, etc. Motifs as The Country is Safe, All Quiet on the Potomac - for Grand Army, Knights Templars, etc. 16mo., 64pp., wrap.

c.1880 New York   NR
STAFPRIT, ARTHUR. Ill. catalog of German-silver badges. 8vo., 16pp. of pls., wrap.

c.1873 Cincinnati   NNMM
STEINAU, JOSEPH & CO. Whole-   NHi
sale catalog of jewelry, watches, clocks, silverware and fancy goods. 4to., 150pp., fine ills. and col. pls., dec. cl.

TAMMEN, H.H.   See House Furnishings.

1878 New York   MH-BA
TIFFANY & CO. Catalog of jewelry, silverware and fine watches. 16mo., 65pp., wrap.

1879 New York   MH-BA
------ 2nd ed. Catalog of jewelry, etc. 16mo., 03pp., wrap.

1881 Providence, R. I.   RHi
TILDEN, THURBER & CO. Our best effort - Season of 1881. Ill. catalog and price list of art specialties in jewelry, silverware and novelties. Large 4to., 12 lvs., fine pls.

1895-6 Providence, R. I.   RHi
------ Ill. catalog of silverware. Sq. 12mo., fine ills., pict. wrap. of plant.

c.1900 White River Junction, Vt.   MdTanSW
UNITED STATES JEWELER. Ill. catalog #7 - to the trade - ills. of clocks, diamonds, jewelry, silverware, etc. 24th year. 290pp. of ills., col. plate of Sessions clock.

c.1900 Portland, Me.   MdTanSW
WARREN MANSFIELD CO. Ill. price list
of jewelry, spoons, tableware, watches, etc.
16pp. of ills.

c.1897 Newark, N. J.   NNMM
WHITEHEAD & HOAG CO. Ill. catalog
137 B - the Multiple Badge. 16pp., fine
ills., wrap. See also Celebration, Decoration, etc.

1893 Chicago   NNMM
YOUNG, OTTO & CO. Ill. price list of
watches, silverware, diamonds, jewelry and
optical goods. 450pp., fine ills., cl.

1895 Chicago   ICHi
------ Ill. catalog of jewelry and silver
novelties, etc. 4to., 464pp., dec. cl.

Just as these jewelry catalogs include silverplate, Britannia ware and tableware, the silverware
catalogs include jewelry. The Jewelry and Silverware catalogs should be used as a team because
of the overlap of offerings. Also note that in 1788 Britannia hardware was a common term, and
don't neglect the Hardware and House Furnishings chapters for what you might consider jewelry
today.

Chapter 32

Lighting by Candle, Oil, Gas & Electricity

When you list a catalog of the Bristol Brass & Clock Co. you sort of involuntarily expect to find at least one clock illustrated therein. However, after a careful examination, you find that this offering for 1887 contains only hall, vase and sewing lamps, kerosene burners, trimmings and accessories. When the title of a book reads Murder in the Kitchen, you can safely expect murder, and probably in a kitchen. The American catalog, however, is more of a challenge; you never know what's in it until you have finished reading and studying it.

From Connecticut to Oregon this chapter can guide you to illustrated records of the development of lighting from wax to electricity, and from the small hand lamp for the bed chamber to the brilliant arc street lights of the Gay Nineties. Plain and fancy, sooty and clean, these catalogs tell the story. They also include ornate chandeliers, curious looking electric bulbs, novelty signs for hotels and bars, colored shades, locomotive headlights, telephones and even tools for the early electrician. I have said that the bicycle, carriage and automobile catalogs were the most colorful in any field, but I must renege. The color plates in the E. P. Gleason and the Hogg & Patterson catalogs should really go in first place.

1877 Chicago   ICHi
ADAMS & WESTLAKE MFG. CO. Est. 1857.
Ill. catalog of metal work, tinware and lamps and lanterns.

1881 Chicago   MiDbF
------ Ill. price list of lanterns - The Farmers' Pet, Railway King, Giant Steamboat, and also for barn, house, shop and factory. 16mo., 16pp., pict. wrap.

1885 Chicago   NNMM
------ Ill. catalog of railway lamps and headlights, etc. 64pp., wrap. See also Railway Equipment special catalog. TxDaDeG

1897 Cleveland, O.   OrU
ADAMS-BAGNALL ELECTRIC CO. Ill. catalog of the A.B. 100 hour incandescent arc lamp. 10pp. with dating correspondence.

1867 Ansonia, Conn.   CtHi
ANSONIA BRASS & BATTERY CO. Ill. price list of coal oil lamps, burners, shades, tubes, collars, clock trimmings. 24mo., 12pp.

c.1876 New York   NNMM
ARCHER & PANCOAST MFG. CO. Catalog of pls. of gas fixtures, globes, lamps, etc. 110 fine pls., cl.

1880 New York   MH-BA
------ Series of 7 ill. circulars of globes, shades, lamps, lighting fixtures, brackets,

chandeliers, harps, pendants, etc. with revised price list offering plate books #12 to 17. One of the finest ref.

1850 Philadelphia   NNMM
ARCHER & WARNER. Familiar   PHi
treatise on candles, lamps and gas lights. 8vo., 16pp.

nd. Philadelphia   NNMM
ARCHER, WARNER, MISKEY & CO. 44 lvs., pls., cl.

c.1864 Boston   MH-BA
AUTOMATIC GAS MACHINE CO. Est. 1864. Catalog of Deak's pat. automatic gas light apparatus. Pat. 1862. List of users, etc. 8vo., 16pp., pict. wrap.

c.1880 Canton, O.   MiDbF
BEST STREET LIGHT CO. Ill. circular of incandescent vapor gas lamps. 16mo., 24pp., pict. wrap.

c.1900 Canton, O.   NNMM
------ Catalog #37 - gas lamps, etc. 40pp., fine ills. and desc., wrap.

c.1889 New York   NNMM
BHUMGARS, F.P. & CO. See Furniture.

1898 Boston   N
BIBBER-WHITE CO. Ill. catalog of electric merchandise - bulbs, lamps, lights, novelties and tools. 8vo., 132pp., cl.

1877 Meriden, Conn.   NNMM
BRADLEY & HUBBARD MFG. CO. Factory
West Meriden. Catalogs #21 and 23 - fine
ills. of lamps, kerosene lighting fixtures,
etc. 77pp. of ills., wrap.

nd. Meriden, Conn.   CtHi
------ A few words about the celebrated
B. & H. lamps. An ill. catalog, some in
col., 12mo., 48pp., pict. wrap.

1885 Meriden, Conn.   NNMM
------ Ill. catalog #43 - polished brass and
rich gold metal oil fixtures, chandeliers,
hanging lamp domes with jeweled ornaments,
brackets, standards. 76pp., a fine pict. ref.

c.1890 Bridgeport, Conn.   CtHi
BRIDGEPORT BRASS CO. Simplest and
surest and handsomest search light gas lantern - simple as primitive oil - for bicycles
and tricycles, etc. 16mo., ills., pict. wrap.

1887 Forestville, Conn.   Ct
BRISTOL BRASS & CLOCK CO. Net price
list of kerosene burners, lamps, trimmings,
vase, hall and sewing lamps, etc. 16mo.,
16pp., wrap. See also Clocks and Watches.

c.1885 Cleveland, O.   OHi
BRUSH ELECTRIC CO. Ill. catalog of
dynamo electric machines - Motors, supplies, plants - pls. of lighting in Detroit,
Los Angeles, Cleveland, etc. - locomotive
and steamship lamps, etc. 4to., 36pp., wrap.

1887 Cleveland, O.   OCl
------ Ill. catalog. Brush systems for
ocean steamers, electroliers, supplies, etc.
8vo., 18pp., wrap.

c.1887 Cleveland, O.   OHi
------ Ill. catalog. 16mo., 34pp., pict.
wrap.

1893 Bridgeport, Conn.   Ct
BRYANT ELECTRIC CO. Ill. price list of
electric specialties for incandescent lighting. 8vo., 44pp., pict. wrap.

1867 New York   MH-BA
BUTLER, JOHN. Ill. catalog of Butler's
pat. rosin gas generator, portable gas apparatus, gas fixtures and supplies. 8vo., 18pp.,
wrap.

1868 New York   MH-BA
------ Light! Light! Give us light. Read
this and you have it. Butler's gas cate-
chism. 12pp.

1880 San Francisco   CHi
CALIFORNIA ELECTRICAL WORKS. Ill.
catalog of lighting fixtures and supplies.
8vo., ills., pict. wrap.

CAREY & CO. See Carriages, Wagons and
Accessories.

CARR, A. MFG. See Plumbing, etc.

c.1896 Chicago   ICHi
CLARK, ALFRED C. Ill. catalog of gas
machines, cheaper light and fuel, etc.

c.1873 Cleveland, O.   MH-BA
CLEVELAND NON-EXPLOSIVE LAMP CO.
Ill. catalog of Perkins & House pat. metallic
kerosene or coal oil safety lamps and filling
cans. 24mo., 32pp., wrap.

1876 Cleveland, O.   OHi
------ Ill. catalog of lamps, filling NHi
cans, chandeliers, fixtures, etc. for the
home. 16mo., 16pp., pict. wrap.

nd. Cleveland, O.   OHi
CLEVELAND VAPOR LIGHT CO. Ill. catalog of lamps, street lights, etc. and lights
for many places.

c.1885 Fitchburg   MH-BA
COBURN, I.W. & CO. Price list and handbook of systems of arc and incandescent
lighting, electro-plating machines, electric
dynamos - vest pocket ed. 64mo., 124pp.,
fine ills., cl.

c.1900 New York   PKsL
COLT, J.B. MFG. CO. Catalog #6. Ills. of
Colt's fixtures, acetylene lighting, lamps,
supplies, chandeliers, etc. 4to., 34pp., wrap.

1899 St. Louis   MoSHi
COMMERCIAL ELECTRIC SUPPLY CO.
Ill. catalog of everything electrical - lamps,
lights, shades, gadgets, novelties, lamps for
railroads, trolleys, buildings, street, etc.
4to., XVII and 511pp., dec. cl.

nd. Philadelphia   PKsL
CONSOLIDATED ELECTRIC STORAGE CO.
Circular #1. Julien storage batteries.

c.1900 Coraopolis, Pa.   MdTanSW
CONSOLIDATED LAMP & GLASS CO. Ill.
catalog of parlor lamps, globes, shades and
Welsbach gas goods - col. pls. of decorated
globes, night lamps, sewing and table lamps,
gas portables, hall and library lamps. 44pp.
with 16 page price list.

1858 Philadelphia   PHi
COOPER GAS REGULATOR CO. Ill. circular of . . . 8vo., 16pp.

c.1850 Philadelphia   PHi
CORNELIUS & SONS MFG. Est. 1809. Ill.
catalog of fixtures for homes, churches,
stores, hotels, public buildings, etc. Tall
4to., title and 22 full col. pls.

1845 New Hampshire   MiDbF
CRESSEY & HANSON. Agents for N. H.
Great Improvement - extra special notice to
all who wish for light. Jones new valuable
lamps for tallow, grease or oil. At half
usual expense to home or church. Broadside.

c.1880 New York   NHi
DIETZ, R.E. CO. Est. 1840. Ill. catalog of
celebrated No. O tubular lanterns, baby lanterns for all purposes. 24mo., 32pp., 16
ills. Pict. wrap. showing more lanterns.

c.1880 New York   NHi
------ Ill. catalog of N. Y. street lamps,
railroad and farm lamps and lanterns.
24mo., 32pp., comic pict. wrap. of the
culled boy and the mouse trap.

1883 New York   NNQ
------ Ill. catalog of lamps and lanterns
for all places and purposes.

1894 New York   DSi
------ From 1840 to 1894. Ill. catalog of
lamps and lanterns for barn, parlor, streets,
stores, surreys, ships and locomotives.
24mo., 64pp., pict. wrap.

1870 Janesville, Wis.   MoSHi
DOTY & CO. Ill. catalog of Doty's hydro-
carbon gas generators.

c.1862 Boston   PKsL
DRAKE. Ill. price list of Drake's pat. automatic gas apparatus for lighting dwellings,
factories, churches, hotels and public buildings. Pat. 1862 - imprint 1682, pict. wrap.,
8vo., 16pp.

nd. New York   MH-BA
EDISON GENERAL ELECTRIC CO. Edison
dynamos. Ills. and instructions for operating, etc. 8vo., 64pp., wrap.

1891 New York   MH-BA
------ Ill. circular-lighting system. 16mo.,
10pp. 2 copies, both ill.

1891 New York   MH-BA
------ Ill. circular of small slow speed
motors. 16mo., 14pp., wrap.

1882 Orange, N. J. & New York   PKsL
EDISON MFG. CO. Incandescent electric
lights with particular ref. to the Edison
lamps at Paris Exposition. Ill. brochure.

1882 Orange, N. J. Boston Agent. MBSPNEA
------ J. Borden, Jr. The Edison Light.
16mo., 28pp., fine ills., wrap.

1883 Orange, N. J. & New York   NNMM
------ Ill. catalog of Edison   NjOE
system, with ill. catalog and price list of
fixtures. 85 and 82pp., bds.

1890 Orange, N. J.   NjOE
------ Catalog #14. Ill. price list of decorative light fixtures. 30pp. of fine ills.,
pict. wrap.

1891 Orange, N. J.   NjR
------ J. H. Bunnell, Agent. Ill. catalog
of Edison-Lalande batteries, jars, cells,
etc. 8vo., 16pp.

nd. Chicago   NNMM
EDWARDS, W.S. MFG. CO. Ill. and priced
catalog #8. Electric fixtures, gas and combination fixtures, etc. 36pp., fine ills., wrap.

c.1872 Warren, Mass.   MH-BA
EXCELSIOR GAS MACHINE CO. Excelsior
gas machines described and compared.
8vo., 24pp., ills., wrap.

1886 Cleveland, O.   MnHi
FOREST CITY NAPTHA CO. Ill. catalog of
fuel and lights.

c.1885 New York   NNMM
FRINK, I.P. Patentee. 2 ill., desc. and
priced catalogs of reflectors for lighting
churches, halls, theaters and public buildings. 1. 16pp., wrap. 2. 8 lvs., pict. wrap.

nd. Brooklyn, N. Y.   NNMM
GAITES, PEACE & CO. Ill. catalog #1 of
gas, electric and combination fixtures, etc.
28 swell col. lithos., cl.

1900 Schenectady   PKsL
GENERAL ELECTRIC CO. Edison incandescent lamps for all places and purposes.
12mo., 110pp., history, fine pls., pict. wrap.

c.1880 Dayton, O.   OHi
GIBBONS, M. J. Est. 1876. Catalog #4.
Ills. of electric fixtures. 4to., 48pp., pict.
wrap. of plant.

GILLETT LIGHT MFG. CO. See Standard
Gas Lamp Co.

c.1880 New York & Brooklyn, N. Y.   NNMM
GLEASON, E.P. MFG. CO. Fol. sheet with
8 ills. of new line of ivory candles and
bobeches - the sunflower, flint opal, standard, etc. Prices on application.

1885 New York   DeWint
------ Ill. catalog of pat. lever   NNMM
Argands, gas burners, street and fancy lanterns, col. pls. of the Manhattan, Turkish,
Beer Keg, hotel, bar, special stores as
segars, beer, fancy globes, shades, smoke
bells, etched and cut in col. 8vo.,
300pp., col. pls., dec. cl.

1893-4 New York   NNMM
HAIDA LAMP & CHINA CO. Catalog #7.
Ill., desc. and priced. Lamps and shades,
etc. for all occasions. 48pp., wrap.

1887 Rochester, N. Y.   NR
HAM, C.T. MFG. CO. Ill. catalog of lanterns, street lights, lanterns for barn, farm,
locomotive, ship, fire engine also fancy oil
cans, pict. labels, etc. 8vo., 40pp., pict.
wrap.

nd. Meriden, Conn.   CtHi
HANDEL, THE CO. Ill. catalog of Handel
lamps and fixtures. 16pp., wrap.

1888 Chicago
HIBBARD, SPENCER BARTLETT CO. Catalog of Rochester Lamps. Mammoth Extension, Parlor, stand lamps with floral hand
decorated shades, study and library lamps,
hanging with prisms, piano lamps, lanterns
for all purposes - barn, railroad and street.
4to., 28pp., excellent ills., pict. wrap.

1887 Watertown, N. Y.   NNMM
HITCHCOCK LAMP CO. Ill. catalog of
Hitchcock's mechanical lamps and fixtures
with 6 col. pls. and text in 4 languages. 25
lvs., pict. wrap.

nd. Southington, Conn.   CtHi
HOBART, CRAIG & CO. Bartholdi central
draft burner lamps - the model light. 16mo.

HOGG & PATTERSON, LTD. See Chapter
on Glass.

1873 Waterbury, Conn.   NNMM
HOLMES, BOOTH & HAYDENS. Ill. price
list of burners and lamp trimmings, brass
parts, fixtures, etc. 48pp., fine ills., wrap.

1867 New York   NNMM
IVES, JULIUS & CO. Ill. catalog of Ives'
pat. lamps and attachments. 32pp., pict.
wrap.

nd. New York   NNMM
KOJAN, D. CO. Ill. catalog of hand wrought
lighting fixtures. 8 lvs., wrap.

1892 New York   MH-BA
LEONARD, H. WARD & CO. Electricity in
a modern residence. 16mo., 20pp.

1898 New York. Factories: Waterbury,
Conn. & New Haven, Conn.   CtHi
LOVELL, F.H. & CO. Ill. catalog of the improved Hitchcock Lamp. Sq. 8vo., 56pp.,
col. pls., with data in 4 languages. Pict.
wrap.

c.1900 Arlington, N. J.   PKsL
LOVELL, F.H. CO. Ill. catalog of railroad
lighting supplies and specialties. Hanging
and wall lamps for cars and coaches, cabs,
desk chandeliers, fancy globes, table glassware, water coolers, etc. 8vo., 96pp., pict.
wrap., view of plant.

MACBETH-EVANS GLASS CO. See Chapter
on Glass.

MACBETH, GEORGE A. & CO. See Chapter
on Glass.

1893-4 New York   NNMM
MAIDA LAMP & CHINA CO. Catalog #7.
Our latest designs in banquet, piano, library,
newel post, hall, princess, boudoir, night
and mammoth lamps- silk and satin shades,
etc. 4to., 48pp., swell ills., pict. wrap.

1876 New York   MiDbF
MANHATTAN BRASS CO. Ill. catalog of
perfection lamps, student lamps, mammoth
and night lights, stands, hall, hanging, bracket lamps - cheapest and best - hurricane,
storm and IXL lanterns, etc., etched and
painted shades. 8vo., 16pp., col. ill., pict.
wrap.

c.1852 Boston   NNMM
MARSHALL, J.P. & BROTHER. Ill. catalog
of lamps with 57 fine pls. Cl. Fine ref.

c.1862 Boston   OHi
MARTINE'S PATENT KEROSENE BURN-
ERS. Full col. pict. broadside showing
lights and lamps. Evans litho.

1855 Baltimore   MH-BA
MARYLAND PORTABLE GAS CO. Price
list and circular of portable gas apparatus,
lights, etc. 8vo., 16pp., pict. wrap.

c.1887 Manchester, Conn.   MH-BA
MATHER ELECTRIC CO. Ill. catalog of
electric lighting and transmission of power,
incandescent systems, lamps and appliances.
8vo., 40pp.

1889 Manchester, Conn.   CtHi
------ Practical thoughts of practical men.
Practical results of Mather system. Sq.
12mo., ill. price list, wrap.

1891 Denver   CoD
MIDLAND ELECTRIC CO. Ill. catalog of
bulbs, lights, lamps, novelties in lighting
fixtures, tools and telephones. Sq. 8vo.,
220pp., dec. wrap.

1868 Meriden, Conn.   MH-BA
MILLER, EDWARD & CO. Price list of
coal oil burners, lamp trimmings and tinmans' ware. 24mo., 24pp., wrap.

c.1895 Meriden, Conn.   NNMM
------ Ill., desc. and priced catalog of
lamps. 96pp., fine ills., cl.

c.1900 Meriden, Conn.   CtHi
------ Ill. catalog #79. Electrolite - most
beautiful reading light known - lamps, etc.
24mo., 12pp., wrap - red and black type.

1876 New York   NNMM
MITCHEL VANCE & CO. Centennial catalog of chandeliers, gas fixtures, bronze
ornaments, clocks, etc. 4to., 12pp., fine
ills., pict. wrap.

nd. Philadelphia   PHi
PARKE, JOHN Y. & CO. Catalog #2. Ills.
of electric lighting apparatus. A light without a match. 16mo., 24pp., fine job.

nd. New York   NNMM
PETRY BROTHERS & CO. Ill. catalog and
price list of reflectors and lanterns. 70pp.

c.1900 Reading, Pa.   PKsL
READING HARDWARE CO. Catalog #1.
Gas, electric and combination fixtures and
chandeliers. Fol., 325pp. with salesmens'
pictures tipped in, fine pls. and excellent
ref., limp mor. For complete line see
Hardware.

1891-2 Rochester, N. Y.   MiDbF
ROCHESTER LAMP CO. Ill. catalog -
largest mfg. in the world, Pompeii to Rochester - lamps for all purposes - hall, parlor,
hanging, prism, chandeliers - and for all
places. 8vo., 32pp., pict. wrap.

1882 New York   KyU
RORKE, EDWARD & CO., Mfg. Ill. catalog
of glassware, kerosene lamps, lighting fixtures, crockery - hanging, hand and table
lamps, fancy etched globes. 4to., 4pp.,
wrap.

1875 New York   NNMM
RUSSELL, HENRY & CO. 21st semi-annual
circular of table glass, lamps, chandeliers
and lighting fixtures. 12pp., fine ills.,wrap.

1883 Philadelphia   NNMM
SIEMENS LUNGREN CO. Successors to
Siemens Regenerative Gas Lamp Co. Ill.
and desc. catalog of lighting and ventilating
apparatus. 18pp., wrap.

c.1900 Hartford City, Ind.   In
SNEATH GLASS CO. Ill. catalog of lantern
globes, lamps, lamp founts - for library,
parlor or machine shop - bracket, cast iron
bases, patterns crescent, mascot, etc.,hand
or footed founts. 12mo., 40pp., dec. wrap.

c.1867 Springfield, Mass.   MH-BA
SPRINGFIELD GAS MACHINE CO. Catalog
of portable gas machines and carbureting
apparatus, gas works for lighting, etc. 8vo.,
8pp.

c.1900 Chicago   ICHi
STANDARD GAS LAMP CO. Gillett Light
Mfg. Co. Ill. catalog of Marvel lamps -
fancy globes, hanging, hall, extension and
chandeliers. Tall 16mo., 48pp., wrap.

1882 Rochester, N. Y.   NSyHi
STEAM GAUGE & LANTERN CO. Ill. catalog of lamps, lanterns and lights for streets,
public buildings, dwellings, locomotives,
steamboats, signals, etc. - river boats,
fire engines, etc. 8vo., 80pp. of the finest
ills., wrap.

1893 Rochester, N. Y. & Chicago   ICHi
------ Ill. catalog of tubular street lights,
safety lanterns, for all purposes. Exhibit
at Worlds Fair - reflectors and all fixtures
and accessories. 16mo., 64pp.

STEVENS & SACKETT CO. See Chapter on
Carriages, Wagons and Accessories.

1892 Boston   MH-BA
THOMSON-HOUSTON ELECTRIC CO. Circular #7006. Ill. price list of arc lighting
apparatus.

c.1900 Toledo, O.   N
TOLEDO CHANDELIER MFG. CO. Ill. catalogs of gas, electric and combination fixtures, chandeliers and lights. Litho. pls. by
the Werner Co. Fol., 165pp. of pls., cl.

c.1880 Brooklyn, N. Y.   NNQ
TUCKER, CHARLES A. Price list of electric goods, gas lighting apparatus, etc.
16mo., dec. wrap.

UNION GLASS CO. See Chapter on Glass.

1883 Newark, N. J.   DSi
UNITED STATES ELECTRIC LIGHTING CO.
Ill. catalog of arc lamps, bulbs, fixtures,
steamboat lighting, etc. 8vo., 24pp.

1874 Boston   MH-BA
WALWORTH MFG. CO. Ill. price list of
solar gas generators. 4to., 24pp.

c.1875-6 Boston   MBSPNEA
WATKINS, A.H. Watkin's pat. portable gas
attachment. Brilliant light! Greatest economy! Ills. of street lamps, chandeliers,
table and bracket lamps. 8pp., ill. folder.

1888-9 Philadelphia   PKsL
WELSBACH INCANDESCENT GAS LIGHT
CO. Desc. of invention, details, reports -
street lights, etc.

c.1900 Philadelphia   PKsL
------ Welsbach Street Lighting Co. of
America. History of Street Lighting - ills.
of lamps, globes, styles, etc. 8vo., 48pp.,
pict. wrap.

1898 New York   N
WESTERN ELECTRIC CO. Est. 1869. Ill.
catalog of lighting supplies. 12mo., 555pp.,
cl.

1894 Pittsburgh, Pa.   PHi
WESTINGHOUSE ELECTRIC & MFG. CO.
The Westinghouse Stopper Incandescent
Lamp. Ill. catalog of . . . Sq. 12mo., 28pp.,
fine ills., wrap.

1885 Boston & Chicago
WHEELER REFLECTOR CO. Ill. catalog
of Wheeler system - Lighting streets - ills.
of lamps and lanterns for railway cars,
stations, styles 3, 9, 10, 110, 434 for railroads, porches, stables - postal cars, libraries - also chandeliers, show windows, etc.
12mo., 40pp., pict. wrap.

1885 Boston & Chicago
------ Ill. catalog of chandelier reflectors,
styles, models, for all places. 12mo.,
20pp., fine ills.

1870 Philadelphia   PKsL
WHIPPLE & DICKERSON. Whipple & Dickerson's liquid fuel machine - col. plate of
lights for locomotives, steamships, etc. Pat.
1869. 8vo., 24pp., litho. pict. wrap.

WHITE MFG. CO. See Chapter on Carriages, Wagons and Accessories.

c.1900 Chicago   ICHi
WILLIAMSON, R. & CO. Catalog   NNMM.
#15. Ills. of electric fixtures, lamps, com-
bination chandeliers, brackets, globes, lanterns, etc. Tall 4to., fine col. pls., cl.

1870 Philadelphia   PHi
WOOD, R.W. & CO. Ill. catalog of cast iron
gas and water fittings, fancy street lamp
posts, etc. 12mo., 40pp., cf.

The best known and best loved picture in American history is the one in which Abe Lincoln sprawls
on the floor reading by the light from the open fire. Light to play, read, study and work by has
always been one of mankind's problems; this is an important record. Hundreds of lighting fixtures
illustrated in catalogs must be found under Glass, Hardware and House Furnishings. Many I have
cross indexed. Others you will have to hunt for in logical places.

Chapter 33

Livestock

There seems to be no way of classifying a horse or cow under Agricultural Implements. They won't fit in the chapter Seedsmen & Nurserymens' catalogs. However, they are a product of American farming, as are hens and other poultry and must be recognized. One of the purposes of this guide is to show what records are available, and though this list is a very small sampling, it does prove that our libraries and historical societies have preserved them.

We can offer the finest horses from Harry Belmont's Stud Farm, the best pigeons and sporting dogs Mr. Boyer produced, and some of Long Islands' tasty Pekin ducks. I hope they will pique many librarians into listing other catalogs of American livestock from every state in the Union.

1885-6 Indianapolis   MH-BA
ACKERMAN, HOWARD U. & CO. Seedsmen
and poultry breeders, household convenience,
farm and garden tools. 6x9, 16pp., ill.

c.1891 Babylon, L. I., N. Y.   NNQ
BELMONT NURSERY STUD FARM. Cata-
log - reprint - and account of sale and dis-
persion of nursery stud. 200pp., pls.

1878 Coatesville, Pa.   PHi
BOYER, N.P. & CO. Ill. catalog of blooded
stock, pigeons, sporting dogs, etc. 8vo.,
16pp., ill., pict. wrap.

1895 Coatesville, Pa.   PKsL
------ Ill. and desc. catalog. 32pp., ill.
throughout, pict. wrap.

c.1893 Speonk, L. I., N. Y.   NNQ
HALLOCK, A.J. Atlantic Farm. Ill. brochure - largest Pekin duck farm in America.
Eggs from thoroughbred hens. Price list.
4pp.

c.1900 Speonk, L. I., N. Y.   NNQ
------ Pekin ducks, barred and white
Plymouth Rocks. Price list. 8pp., ill.

1882 Rye, N. Y.   MH-BA
HALSTED, A.M. New centennial incubator.
Tests. 5-1/2x8-1/2, 8pp., not ill.

1893 Oakdale, N. Y.   NNQ
INDIAN NECK STOCK FARM. Catalog of
stallions. Ill. wrap.

1890 Buffalo, N. Y.   NHi
JEWETT STOCK FARM. Ill. catalog of
standard bred trotting horses. 142pp., pls.,
lea. cvs.

1891 Buffalo, N. Y.   NHi
------ Catalog. 146pp., pls., cvs.

1892 Buffalo, N. Y.   NHi
------ Catalog. 205pp., pls., cvs.

1893 Buffalo, N. Y.   NHi
------ Catalog. 133pp., pls., cvs.

c.1889 Philadelphia   PKsL
JOHNSON & STOKES. Seed and Poultrymen.
Catalog of poultry supplies offered at Flora
Croft's Yards. 8vo., ill.

1881-2 Fredonia, N. Y.   MH-BA
JOSSELYN, GEORGE S. Thoroughbred land
and water fowls. 6x9, 6pp., not ill.

1878 Cincinnati   OC
KITTREDGE, E.W. Ill. catalog of trotting
horses. 12mo., 16pp., ill., wrap.

1877 Castleton, N. Y.   MH-BA
LEWIS, ROBERT. Est. 1871. Advance
Poultry Yards and Hope Hill Gardens.
Seeds and plants, eggs of pure bred poultry.
Price list. 6x9, 8pp.

1891 Huntington, L. I., N. Y.   NNQ
LEWIS, W.H. Hillside Poultry Farm. Ill.
catalog of standard poultry from highest
scoring hens. 32pp.

1885 Oakland, Calif.   CHi
OAKLAND POULTRY YARDS. Price list of
fowls, breeding stock, eggs, incubators, etc.
4to., 41pp., ill., wrap.

c.1887 Brooklyn, N. Y.   NNQ
PARKVILLE FARM. Annual catalog of
trotting stock. Ill.

LIVESTOCK

1894 Islip, L. I., N. Y.   NNQ
THOMPSON, SAMUEL L. The Thompson
Farms. Catalog of trotting stock. 32pp.,
ill. wrap.

1899 Triangle, Broom Co., N. Y.   N
WHITNEY BROTHERS. Est. 1876. Annual
circular and price list of fancy poultry,
hatching eggs, etc. 8vo., 8pp., ill., wrap.

If you are interested in woodcuts and engravings of work horses, don't forget they supplied the power for many agricultural machines. Naturally anyone with average horse sense will comb the Horse Goods chapter and realize that many of the best plates of carriages in action must show the best horses. If you are a real livestock enthusiast, there are bull, cow, horse, dog, sheep, pig, rooster and other animal weathervanes listed under Weathervanes too.

Chapter 34

Magic Lanterns, Stereoscopes & Stereopticons

In 1890 Seeger & Guernsey's Cyclopaedia of American Manufactures only listed four firms under Magic Lanterns and Slides. Others, however, whose catalogs are now preserved for 21st century study and amusement, were listed under Optical Goods and Photographic Apparatus. I have chosen the best illustrated and segregated them because of the collector and library interest.

From the earliest hand viewers to the magnificent double lens, triple power Metropolitan stereopticons, this short list will supply you with locations for study. By 1898 McAllister's catalogs offered some of the best illustrations of Edison's Kinetoscopes and Animated Picture Machines on the market. Politicians who knew not of TV used these powerful lanterns to shoot election returns ALL THE WAY ACROSS A STREET and flash them on a blank wall to the amazement of the walking public. Even in 1862 an enthusiast could sit in his own parlor, thanks to the American Stereoscopic Co. and the Anthonys, and march to the front with the Blues and Greys without anyone knowing he had purchased himself a draft substitute.

1858-62 Philadelphia   PKsL
AMERICAN STEREOSCOPIC NN   DLC
CO. See Photographic Apparatus, etc.

1850-98 New York   MANY
ANTHONY, E. & H.T. & CO.   LOCATIONS
See Photographic Apparatus, etc.

1890 Chicago & New York   NSyHi
BURKE & JAMES. Ill. catalog of magic lanterns, stereoscopes, stereopticons, adapters, machines, slides and pictures, also supplies. 8vo., 32pp., pict. wrap. Catalog #8.

CHAMBERLAIN, N.B. See American Stereoscopic Co. under Photographic Apparatus, etc.

1899 Chicago   NHl
CHICAGO PROJECTING CO. Ill. catalog #110 - Magic lanterns, views, gramaphones, stereoptic viewers, slides and motion picture machines. 12mo., 224pp., pict. wrap.

1891 New York   PKsL
COLT, J.B. MFG. CO. Ill. catalog of optical lanterns and accessories, slides, eye glasses, etc. 4to., 144pp., pict. wrap.

c.1900 New York   NHi
------ Ill. catalog of stereopticons and accessories with tests. from Williams, Princeton and other educational institutions. 8vo., 32pp., ills. of models, etc.

1897 Orange, N. J.   NjOE
EDISON MFG. CO. The Edison stereo. - projecting kinetoscope. Ill. 8 page price list.

1898 Orange, N. J.   NjOE
------ 6 page price list of kinetoscopes. Ill.

1898 Orange, N. J.   NHi
------ World's latest sensation - Edison's startling invention - Moving pictures. 4pp., ill.

1900 Orange, N. J.   NjOE
------ Ill. price list. 20pp., pict. wrap.

1891 Philadelphia   PKsL
FELLOWS PHOTOGRAPHIC CO. Ill. catalog of magic lanterns, lantern slides, stereopticons and views, etc. 8vo., 26pp., wrap.

1880 Philadelphia   MiDbF
HALL, JAMES F. Hall's ill. catalog of magic lanterns for the parlor and town hall, schools and all occasions as well as toy lanterns. 8vo., 86pp., fine ills., pict. wrap.

1887 Philadelphia   PKsL
------ Supplementary list of optical lanterns, photo. transparencies and colored views for luminous projection. 8vo., 16pp.

1860 New York   MH-BA
LONDON STEREOSCOPIC CO. Catalog of instruments, slides and views of American and European scenery. 12mo., 50pp., wrap. Fine ref.

c.1857 Philadelphia   MStOSV
McALLISTER & BROTHER. Est. 1783. Ill. catalog of mathematical, optical and philosophical instruments, magic lanterns and stereoscopes and views.

1861 Philadelphia   PPL
------ Catalog of magic lantern pictures, stereoscopic views and microscopic photographs.

1880 Philadelphia   NSyHi
------ Ill. catalog of magic lanterns, scopes and slides.

1882 Philadelphia & New York   NNCoo
McALLISTER, T.H. Mfg. Optician. Ill. catalog of magic lanterns and stereopticons, views, slides, etc. 8vo., fine ills.   N.B. For complete listing of McAllister catalogs, See Optical and Scientific Apparatus.

1894 New York
------ Ill. catalog of stereopticons, magic lanterns apparatus and list of views. 8vo., 42 and 150pp., fine pict. wrap. See also Optical and Scientific Apparatus.

1898 New York
------ Catalog of stereopticons, magic lanterns, dissolving views, apparatus and views. 8vo., 256pp., ill. throughout, pict. wrap. Also shows Edison's animated picture machines, Cosmorama lenses, park camera obscura, etc.

1889 Chicago   MiDbF
McINTOSH BATTERY & OPTICAL CO. Ill. catalog of lamps, magic lanterns, stereopticons, slides and views. 8vo., 240pp., fine ref., wrap. N.B. For complete listing - See Optical and Scientific Apparatus.

1874 Philadelphia   NSyHi
MARCY, L.J. Optician. Sciopticon manual and Marcy's new magic lanterns, slides, views and accessories. Ill. catalog of apparatus. 12mo., 180 plus 64pp., fine ills., pict. bds.

1886 Philadelphia   NHi
------ Priced and ill. catalog of sciopticon apparatus, magic lanterns and slides. 12mo., 118pp. of ills., wrap. N.B. See Optical and Scientific Apparatus for complete listings.

MEYROWITZ BROTHERS. See Optical and Scientific Apparatus.

1884 Philadelphia   PKsL
MILLIGAN, T.C. Successor to McAllister & Brother. Est. 1783. Ill. catalog of stereo-panopticons, sciopticons, exhibition lanterns, slides, accessories, apparatus. 8vo., 120pp., wrap.

1893 Philadelphia   PHi
------ Ill. catalog of first class magic lanterns, stereopticons and apparatus, colored and uncolored slides and views, etc. 8vo., 50pp., pict. wrap.

c.1900 Chicago   NSyHi
MOORE, HUBBALL & CO. Ill. catalog of magic lanterns and slides, chemical and scientific apparatus, stereoscopes and stereopticons, etc. 224pp. of ills., fine ref.

1848 PIKE, BENJAMIN JR. See Optical and Scientific Apparatus.

QUEEN, JAMES W. See Optical and Scientific Apparatus.

1894 Philadelphia   PKsL
RAU, WILLIAM H. Ill. catalog of   PHi
lantern slides, photographs, views of all parts of U.S.A. and World, for magic lanterns, stereopticons, lectures and education. 8vo., VIII, 226 and 30pp., fine ills., advts. of equipment and accessories, pict. wrap.

1898 New York   CCuMGM
RILEY BROTHERS. Ill. catalog. Largest and best house in the trade - magic lanterns to hire, stereopticons, accessories, slides, animated pictures, etc. 8vo., 32pp., pict. wrap.

1888 Philadelphia   PHi
ROBERTS & FELLOWS, Mfg. & Pub. Ill. catalog of optical lanterns and slides, accessories, etc. 8vo., 136pp. of fine ills.

1875-6 Philadelphia   PKsL
WILSON, EDWARD L. MFG. Wrap. reads Benerman & Wilson. Ill. and desc. catalog of magic lanterns, sciopticons, equipment and appliances, slides. Prof. Morton's new chromatrope, etc. 12mo., 103pp., wrap.

1873 Philadelphia   PHi
WILSON, HOOD & CO. Annual ill. catalog of stereoscopes, views, equipment, lamps, frames, etc. 12mo., 148pp., ills., pict. wrap.

c.1876 Philadelphia   NSyHi
WOODBURY'S. The Sciopticon - models, slides for history educational work, comics, travel, etc. 12mo., 56pp. of ills., wrap.

1875 Rochester, N. Y.   NR
WOODWARD, C.W. Catalog of stereoscopic views of local scenes, Genesee Valley, etc. 16mo., 8pp., wrap.

There are references to both the Optical and Scientific Apparatus, and Photographic Supplies chapters to round out the field. The line between a camera and a stereopticon in 1876 was not too clear classification wise. Today the photographer doesn't want to be mixed up with optical and scientific goods, mathematical supplies and philosophical instruments. Here he is.

Chapter 35

Medical & Surgical Instruments & Supplies

When this guide was first considered as a possible library tool, American Medicine was the all inclusive heading in mind. Correspondence with the Smithsonian, the American Journal of Pharmacy, Harvard and Pennsylvania Schools of Dentistry and the ADA soon convinced me that medicine is no longer merely medicine. For the convenience of the historian and student we offer three chapters based on predominance of catalog material. Ophthalmology is still buried in this general group with surgery and physicians' instruments, appliances and supplies.

If you have never read a history of the Massachusetts General, or other works picturing surgery and hospitalization back in the dark ages of the 19th century, find one and read it. If you can't imagine a surgeon sawing a live human leg, NOT on the field during the Civil War, but in an American hospital, without anesthesia, and in a top hat and frock coat to boot, you haven't lived. The tools with which these gentlemen worked, and the knowledge without which they had to work, should make you appreciate the age in which you are privileged to live. Artificial limbs, operating chairs and tables, spectacles, trusses and bandages, various contrivances for the invalid as well as general hospital supplies are all in here waiting for your attention. A tin hearing horn for the deaf or the first X-ray machine - where else can you find them?

1900 Indianapolis   In
ALLISON, W.D. & CO. Ill. catalog of the Allison line of physicians' appliances, operating tables, chairs, cabinets, etc. 12mo., 42pp., tinted ills. with full col. litho. wrap. by Hollenbeck.

c.1893 St. Louis   NNNAM
ALOE, A.S. CO. Aloe's ill. and priced catalog of superior surgical instruments, supplies and hospital furnishings. 6th ed. 1069pp., fine ill. record, cl.

1879 St. Louis   DNLM
ALOE & HERNSTEIN. Ill. catalog of surgical instruments, apparatus and furnishings. 8vo., wrap.

1879 Cincinnati   OC
AMERICAN DENTAPHONE CO. The Dentaphone - a new invention - the deaf hear through vibrations on the teeth - the dumb to speak. 12mo., 24pp., ills. with prices. $10. to $15. Pict. wrap. N.B. See also Richard Rhodes.

1894 Baltimore   NNNAM
ARNOLD, F. & SONS. Desc. circular and price list of Howard A. Kelly's new instruments. 4to., 21pp., ills.

AUDIPHONE, THE. See Rhodes.

1881 New York   NNNAM
BERGE, J. & H. Est. 1850. Latest Improved Holtz Electrical Machines - see page 7

for medical machines. Franklinism - insulated tables, etc. Dr. Morton's Address. 8vo., 12pp., ills., pict. wrap.

1891 New York   DNLM
BESELER, C. MFG. New ill. catalog of compressed air atomizers, laryngoscopes, gas receivers, oxygen and compounds. 16mo., ills., wrap.

c.1890 Hammond, Ind.   In
BETZ, FRANK S. Ill. catalog of ear trumpets, trusses, surgical instruments, apparatus, etc. offered after twenty years' experience and growth. Fol., 16pp., pict. record.

c.1896 Hammond, Ind.   In
------ Special 30 day bulletin of instruments and furnishings. Ills.

1893 Philadelphia   NNNAM
BOEKEL, WILLIAM & CO. Ill. catalog of surgical goods and chemical apparatus. 54pp.

c.1888 Brooklyn, N. Y.   NNQ
BROOKLYN VACUUM CURE CO. Ill. catalog of vacuum apparatus, pneumatic equalizer, etc. with nature of treatment, etc. 23pp., wrap.

BULLOCK & CRENSHAW. See Drugs and Pharmaceuticals.

1874 New York   NNNAM
CASWELL, HAZARD & CO.   DNLM
W. F. Ford, Mfg. Ill. catalog of surgical
instruments and appliances. 8vo., 130pp.

1880 New York   NNNAM
------ Ill. catalog. 8vo., 227pp.

c.1894 Yorkville, Ill.   ICHi
CHURCH, W.R. Physicians' cases, carriages and rubber goods.

c.1859 Boston   MH-BA
CODMAN & SHURTLEFF.   DNLM
Est. 1838. Ill. catalog of surgical and dental instruments and druggists' supplies.
8vo., 32pp.

1860 Boston   DNLM
------ Ill. catalog of surgical and dental
apparatus and supplies. 8vo., 36pp.

c.1870 Boston   TxDaDeG
------ Ill. catalog - from breast pumps
and dress protectors to silver hearing
trumpets - surgical instruments, etc. 32pp.

1875 Boston   TxDaDeG
------ Ill. catalog. 8vo., 88pp., cl.

1877-8 Boston   DNLM
------ Ill. catalog of surgical furnishings.

1879 Boston   NNNAM
------ Ill. catalog of   DSi DNLM
surgical and dental instruments and furnishings. 4to., 136pp., cl.

c.1881 Boston   MH-BA
------ Ill. catalog of surgical   DNLM
appliances and supplies. 4to., 24pp.

1886 Boston   NNNAM
------ Ill. catalog. 140pp.

1890 Boston   NNNAM
------ Ill. catalog. 144pp.

N.B. See also Drugs and Pharmaceuticals.

1886 Cincinnati   DNLM
CROCKER, SAMUEL A. & CO. Ill. catalog
of surgical instruments, orthopaedic apparatus and physicians' supplies. 8vo., fine
ills., cl.

nd. Cincinnati   OHi
------ Ill. catalog. 3rd ed. 560pp., cl.

1893 Jerseyville, Ill.   IHi
CUTTING & STEELE. Ill. brochure - the
invalid lifter. Fine photos. of lifter in
action - before and after - a child can
handle it! Sq. 16mo., 16pp., pict. wrap.

c.1870 Boston   PPL
DAVIDSON RUBBER CO. Ill. catalog of
breast pumps, syringes, urinals, bed pans
and all manner of invalid equipment. 64pp.,
wrap.

c.1876 Boston   OAkF
------ Ill. price list of medical rubber
goods for home and hospital. 96pp., wrap.

1884 New York   DNLM
DeGARMO, G. J. Catalog of medical and
surgical appliances.

c.1899 Orange, N. J.   NjOE
EDISON MFG. CO. Ill. catalog of Edison's
X-Ray apparatus, cautery transformers and
Edison electro-medical appliances. 36pp.,
wrap.

1895 Pittsburgh, Pa.   NNNAM
FEICK BROTHERS. Advance sheets of ill.
catalog and price list of surgical instruments, artificial limbs, deformity apparatus,
etc. 104pp., fine ills.

1874 New York   DNLM
FORD, W.F. Ill. catalog of surgical instruments and medical appliances. 8vo., wrap.

c.1891 New York   NNNAM
------ Ill. catalog of orthopaedical apparatus and surgical instruments. 182pp.

c.1892 New York   NNNAM
------ Ill. catalog - instruments for New
York Cancer, Bellevue and all city hospitals.
Gibson battery, etc. 216pp.

1893 New York   DNLM
------ Ill. catalog of instruments and hospital furnishings.

c.1897 New York   NNNAM
------ Ill. catalog of orthopaedical apparatus, etc. 57pp.

c.1867 Cincinnati, O. & Detroit, Mich. OC
FOSTER, JAMES A. Foster's pat. union
artificial limbs - best substitutes ever invented, etc. 8vo., 36pp., fine ills. Mr.
Foster goes on to say that the demand has
forced him to move to a more central city
than Detroit, and that he will personally
supervise manufacture and sales at new
quarters in Cincinnati.

c.1887 New York   NNNAM
FREES, C.A. Inventor & Mfg. Est. 1866.
Ill. catalog of artificial limbs and apparatus.
83pp., fine ills.

c.1892 New York   NNNAM
------ Ill. catalog of arms and   CtY
legs for invalids - from the surgical to the
mechanical art. 8vo., 50pp., port. and ills.
with pict. wrap.

1880 Portland, Me.   DNLM
FRYE, G.C. Ill. catalog of surgical instruments, appliances, orthopaedic supplies,
electric batteries, etc. 8vo., wrap.

1883 Portland, Me.   DNLM
------ Ill. catalog of hospital and surgical
supplies.

1878 New York   NNNAM
GALVANO-FARADIC MFG. CO. Manual of
medical electricity and ill. catalog of standard electrical apparatus for medical uses.
107pp.

1883 New York   NNNAM
------ Ill. catalog. 86pp. of ills.

1887 New York   MoSHi
------ Manual and ill. catalog.

1891 New York   NNNAM
------ Ill. catalog of 48pp.

1895 New York   NNNAM
------ Ill. catalog. 27th ed. 111pp.

1880 Minneapolis   DNLM
GARDINER, T. Ill. catalog of surgical instruments and apparatus. 8vo., ills., wrap.

c.1890 Boston   MBSPNEA
GEAR, FRANK J. Ill. catalog of invalid and
sick room supplies, also surgical and electric apparatus and physicians' supplies -
solid panel walnut beds and brass beds
rigged for invalids, converted roller chairs,
etc. 8vo., 44pp.

c.1878 Philadelphia   DNLM
GEMRIG, J.H. Ill. catalog of bandages,
apparatus for deformities, fractures, dislocations, trusses and surgical instruments.
8vo., ill.

1882 Philadelphia   DNLM
------ Ill. catalog. 5th ed.

1887 Philadelphia   NNNAM
------ Ill. catalog. 6th ed. 192pp.

1897 Harrison, N. J.   NNNAM
GENERAL ELECTRIC CO. Edison decorative and miniature lamp dept. Price list of
Roentgen ray apparatus, X-ray tubes with
automatic regulators, etc. 50pp., fine ills.

1899 Geneva, N. Y.   NNNAM
GENEVA OPTICAL CO. 26th annual ill.
catalog of Geneva prescriptions and optical
stock for oculists and opticians. 134pp.

1897 New York   NNNAM
GEORGEN, W.T. Ill. price list of modern
ophthalmological apparatus for physicians
and hospitals. 16pp.

1897-8 San Francisco & Naugatuck, Conn.
GOODYEAR RUBBER CO. Ill.   CHi
catalog of physicians' rubber articles and
supplies, from a glove to a mackintosh.
12mo., pict. wrap.

1850 Hartford, Conn.   MH-BA
GRAY, JOHN W. & CO. Price list of belting, packing, hose and rubber goods for
medicinal purposes. 16mo., 10pp.

1870 Boston   DSi
HALL, THOMAS. Mfg. Ill. catalog of
electro-medical instruments. 7vo., 48pp.
with 76 ills., pict. wrap. See also Optical
and Scientific Apparatus.

1895 San Francisco   CHi
HATTEROTH, WILLIAM. Ill. catalog of
surgical instruments and hospital supplies.
8vo., bds.

1880 New York   NNNAM
HAZARD, HAZARD & CO. Ill. catalog of
surgical instruments and every desc. of
appliances, mfg. by W. F. Ford. 179pp.

1889 New York   DNLM
HERNSTEIN, A.L. Ill. catalog of superior
surgeons' instruments. 2nd ed. 8vo., ills.

1792 Philadelphia   PPL
HIRTE, TOBIAS. (Translated) Indian-
French-Creek-Seneca-Spring-Oil. A short
report. One teaspoonful helps Tuberculosis,
rheumatism, sprains, dislocations, tumors,
headaches, ringworm and venereal diseases.
Tests. Lists 13 dealers where oil may be
purchased. Ptd. Samuel Sauer, Chestnut
Hill.

c.1877 St. Louis   MoSHi
HOLMAN LIVER PAD CO. Lecture and
tests. and a good sales story.

1860 Philadelphia   PU-D
KERN, H.G. Catalog of surgical and dental
instruments, elastic trusses and medical
appliances.

1877 & 1885 Philadelphia   DNLM
------ Ill. catalogs for 1877 and 1885;
surgical, dental and medical supplies.

1873 New York   NNNAM
KIDDER, JEROME MFG. CO. Electricity
to cure diseases. 14pp., fld.

c.1883 New York   NNNAM
------ Ill. and desc. catalog of superior
electro-medical apparatus. 60pp.

c.1887 New York   NNNAM
------ Researches in electro-allotropic
physiology, including instruments and prices.
18pp. and 10 lvs.

KIRSTEIN, E. & SONS. Eye glasses. <u>See</u>
Optical and Scientific Apparatus.

1895 New York   DNLM
KNAUTH BROTHERS. Ill. catalog of surgical instruments and physicians' supplies,
electric and orthopaedic apparatus. 4to.

1894 New York & Berlin, Germany   DNLM
KNY, R. & CO. Ill. catalog of surgeons' and
physicians' supplies. Fol. with 8vo. price
list.

1900 New York   DNLM
KNY-SCHEERER CO. Ill., desc. price list
of surgical and orthopaedic apparatus and
appliances, artificial limbs, trusses, supporters, crutches and invalid furniture.
192pp.

1879 Philadelphia   DNLM
KOLBE, D.W. & SON. Ill. catalog of surgical instruments 8vo.

1858 Philadelphia   DNLM
KURMERLE, J.F. Ill. catalog of surgical
and dental equipment, syringes, etc. 8vo.

nd. New York   DNLM
LANE, C.W. & BROTHER. Catalog and
price list of surgical supplies.

nd. Boston   DNLM
LEACH & GREENE. Ill. catalog of surgical
instruments.

1891 Conshohocken, Pa.   PKsL
LEE, ELLWOOD J. CO. 8th annual retail
catalog - metallic splints, trusses, electric
batteries, orthopaedic supplies, etc. 24mo.,
88pp., ills.

1892 Conshohocken, Pa.   NNNAM
------ Wholesale catalog of specialties.
72pp.

1897 Conshohocken, Pa.   NNNAM
------ Ill. catalog of medical and surgical
plasters. 94pp.

1900 Conshohocken, Pa.   NNNAM
------ 17th annual ill. catalog. 136pp.

1884 Philadelphia   DNLM
LENTZ, C. Ill. price list of medical supplies.

c.1890 Philadelphia   DNLM
LENTZ, C. & SONS. Ill. catalog of orthopaedic apparatus, surgical instruments and
medical supplies.

1874 St. Louis   MoSHi
LESLIE, A.M. & CO. Ill. catalog   DNLM
of surgical instruments and appliances,
bandages, trusses, etc. 8vo.

1876 St. Louis   MoSHi
------ Ill. catalog of medical supplies.

1884 St. Louis   NNNAM
------ Ill. catalog of medical   MoSHi
and surgical apparatus and supplies. 320pp.

1900 New York   NNNAM
LINCOLN & LUCHESI - formerly with J.
Reynders. Ill. catalog of orthopaedic instruments, trusses, supporters, crutches,
elastic stockings and hospital supplies.

1887 New York   NNNAM
LORENZ, P.C. Ill. catalog of surgical instruments, physicians' supplies, etc. 32pp.

1871 New Haven   CtHi
McNEIL & WASHBURN. Ill. catalog of
trusses, supporters, braces, crutches and
instruments. 16mo., 18pp.

c.1880 New York   DSi
MANHATTAN SURGEONS' SUPPLY CO.
Ill. catalog of medical articles including ear
trumpet canes. 15 to 30 ills. per page of
things one never finds in hospitals today.
4to., 48pp., pls.

1886 New York & Albany, N.Y.   NNNAM
MARKS, A.A. Ill. catalog of Mark's pat.
artificial limbs with India rubber hands and
feet. 160pp., fine ills., pict. wrap.

1894 Albany, N.Y.   N
------ Ill. catalog and reasons why Mark's
are best. Tall 8vo., 32pp., pict. wrap.

1894 Albany, N.Y.   CCuMGM
------ Treatise on Mark's artificial limbs
with ill. catalog of limbs for every trade
and ills. of folks at work. Cripples building
furniture, using lathes, playing pool and telephone linemen acting like monkeys. 8vo.,
445pp., one of the best - pict. wrap.

1896 Albany, N.Y.   NNNAM
------ Special catalog - treatise on artificial limbs - similar to 1894.

1895 New York   NNNAM
MEYROWITZ, E.B. Ill. catalog   DNLM
of surgical instruments, ophthalmological
apparatus, and eye, ear, nose and throat instruments, compressed air receivers,
pumps, spray tubes, atomizers and illuminat-
ing apparatus. Pts. 2 and 3, 8vo., 153pp.,
wrap.

1898 New York   NNNAM
------ 4th ed. Ill. as above, 281pp.

1892-1900 New York   NNNAM
------ A fine collection of the famous
Meyrowitz Price List Bulletins:-

#10	February	1892	2 lvs.
#11	May	1892	2 lvs.
#13	March	1893	2 lvs.
#14	November	1893	6 lvs.
#17	February	1895	4 lvs.
#18	March	1896	4 lvs.
#23	October	1900	11 pp.

See also Optical and Scientific Apparatus.

c.1895 St. Paul, Minn.   PU-D
NOYES BROTHERS & CUTLER. Ill. catalog of surgical and dental apparatus, artificial limbs, eyes, deformity apparatus, elastic stockings, etc.

c.1900 St. Paul, Minn.   NNNAM
------ Ill. catalog as above - from artificial eyes to trusses. 4th ed. 1200pp. See also Dental Instruments.

nd. New York   DNLM
OTTO & REYNDERS. Desc. catalog of aspirators and other apparatus for physicians and surgeons. 8vo.

c.1875 New York   DNLM
OTTO, F.G. & SONS. Ill. catalog and price list of surgical and orthopaedical instruments, bandages, etc. 24mo., wrap.

1884 New York   NNNAM
------ Ill. catalog of surgical instruments, electric batteries, orthopaedic appliances, etc. 244 and 46pp.

nd. New York   DNLM
------ Ill. catalog.

1859 New York   NNNAM
PALMER & CO. The surgical adjuvant - report on artificial limbs. #IX. 48pp.

1878 Philadelphia   DNLM
PENFIELD, E.C. & CO. Ill. catalog of abdominal supporters, shoulder braces, elastic stockings, trusses, etc. 8vo., pict. wrap.

1885 New York   MH-BA
POND'S EXTRACT CO. Est. 1838. Wisdom in Fable. 12mo., 16pp., ill., pict. wrap.

c.1884 New York   CtY
PORTABLE HYGIENIC VAPOR & DISENFECTOR CO. The Home Vapor and Shower Bath - perfect luxury for the sick - in use at Bellevue and Hahnemann hospitals. Delightful ills. 8vo., 8pp.

1877 Cincinnati   OC
PULVERMACHER GALVANIC CO. Electricity nature's chief restorer - self application. Apparatus ill. and priced. 12mo., 16pp.

1878 Cincinnati   OC
------ Ill. catalog of apparatus. 12mo., 32pp., wrap.

nd. Philadelphia & New York   DNLM
QUEEN, JAMES W. & CO. Condensed list of clinical thermometers, hydrometers, urinometers, etc. 8vo., ill.

1875 Philadelphia & New York   PKsL
------ Priced and ill. catalog of optical and medical instruments.

1883 Philadelphia & New York   DNLM
------ Ill. catalog of precision instruments used in physiology and medicine. 8vo. See Optical and Scientific Apparatus for complete listing.

1887 New York   NNNAM
REICHARDT, F. ALFRED & CO. Price list #40. Surgeons' instruments and physicians' supplies. 54pp. and one leaf.

1893 Chicago, Ill. & Bristol, England
REINIGER, GEBBERT & SCHALL. NNNAM
(John Wright & Co., agent.) Electromedical instruments and ill. catalog of apparatus. 5th ed. 101pp.

1875 New York   NNNAM
REYNDERS, JOHN & CO. Ill.   DNLM
catalog and price list of surgical instruments, orthopaedical apparatus, etc. 8vo., 184pp., wrap. Also 2nd and 3rd ed. of this.

c.1880 New York   TxDaDeG
------ Ill. catalog of   DNLM NNNAM
operating furniture, etc. 8vo., 286pp., pict. wrap.

1884 New York   NNNAM
------ Ill. catalog of medical   DNLM
supplies, etc. 386pp., pict. wrap.

1889 New York   NNNAM
------ Ill. catalog. 6th ed.   DNLM
398pp.

1895 New York   NNNAM
------ Ill. catalog. 7th ed. 617pp.

1898 New York   NNNAM
------ Combination trade cash price list and ill. supplement. Ills. of spectacles, optical goods, etc.

1879 Chicago   PU-D
RHODES, RICHARD S., & McCLURE. The Audiphone - enables the deaf to hear through the teeth, and the dumb to speak. 8vo., 15pp. See also American Dentiphone.

c.1900 New York   NNNAM
RIKER'S DRUG STORE. Talks on rubber.
Appliances and apparatus for medical purposes, sick room furnishings, etc. 144pp.,
ills.

1874 New York   NNNAM
ROWE TRUSS CO. Ill. catalog of trusses,
supporters, elastic stockings and deformity
instruments. 17pp.

1865 Salem, Mass.   MBSPNEA
SALEM MEDICAL LEG CO.   MSaE
Circular #6 - The Salem Leg - under
patronage of the U.S. Government. 8vo.,
32pp., frs. and pict. wrap.

1894 Battle Creek   NNNAM
SANITARY SUPPLY CO.   Price list of
sanitary and invalid supplies. 32pp.

1883 Boston   NNNAM
SARGENT INVALID FURNITURE CO.
Price list of beds, chairs, operating tables,
etc. 16pp.

1888 Boston   NNMM
------ Ill. catalog of invalid beds, chairs,
tables, etc. 96pp., wrap.

1897 Boston   CCuMGM
------ Ill. catalog of invalid supplies.
8vo., 48pp., pict. wrap.

1856 Utica, N.Y.   DNLM
SAWENS, W. CO. Dr. Matchisi's uterine
catholicon - dedicated to mothers and
daughters of our country. 8vo., 16pp., ills.,
tests., wrap.

1890 Philadelphia   NNNAM
SEELEY, I.B. & CO. Ill. catalog of Seeley's
hard rubber specialties - mechanical treatment of hernia, etc. 7th ed. 94pp.

c.1875 New York   OC
SEIBERT, E.J. (Max Wocher, agent.)
Voltaic armadillo, electric bands and soles.
Reliable remedy for nervous diseases. For
sale by . . . 16mo., 15pp., ills., wrap.

1889 Chicago   DNLM
SHARP & SMITH. Ill. catalog of artificial
limbs, deformity apparatus, eyes, crutches,
supporters, galvanic batteries, etc.

1894 Chicago   CSmH
------ Ill. catalog of surgical and veteri-
nary instruments, medical appliances and
supplies. 8vo., 172pp., wrap.

1873 New York   NNNAM
SHEPARD & DUDLEY. Desc.   DNLM
catalog of surgical instruments for January.
2 lvs., 121pp., 4 lvs.

1878 New York   NNNAM
------ Ill. catalog.   DNLM

1886 New York   NNNAM
------ Ill. catalog of surgical   DNLM
instruments and deformity apparatus, etc.

1883 New York   ICHi
SMITH WHEEL CHAIR CONCERN. Herbert
S. Smith, Prop. Ill. catalog of hospital fur-
niture, etc.

1878 Syracuse, N.Y.   DNLM
SNOW, C.W. & CO. Ill. catalog of instruments and appliances, galvanic batteries,
trusses, etc.

1860 Philadelphia   DNLM
SNOWDEN & BROTHER. Wholesale ill.
catalog of surgical and dental instruments
and supplies.

1866 Philadelphia   DNLM
------ Ill. catalog of supplies for invalids,
hospitals, etc.

1890 New York   DNLM
TAYLOR, G.H. Ill. catalog of remedial
apparatus.

1872 New York   NNNAM
TIEMANN, GEORGE & CO. Ill. catalog of
surgical instruments. VIII and 64pp.

1874 New York   NNNAM
------ Ill. catalog of surgical   DNLM
and dental supplies. VI and 116pp.

1875 New York   NNNAM
------ Ill. catalog and price   DNLM
list. 144pp.

1876 New York   NNNAM
------ Ill. catalog. VIII and   DNLM
124pp.

1879 New York   NNNAM
------ The American   PU-D DNLM
armamentarium chirurgicum - a pictorial
dictionary with prices - vp. - 134, 102, 126,
136, 32 and 36pp. in 6 parts, covering every
branch of medicine.

1889 New York   TxDaDeG
------ American   PU-D NNNAM
armamentarium. One of the most complete
located. XVI and 846pp.

1893 Chicago   TxDaDeG
TRUAX, CHARLES, GREENE   NNNAM
& CO. Ill. price list of physicians' supplies,
surgical instruments and drugs. 6th ed.
8vo., 1568pp. of ills., cl.

1894 New York   NNNAM
UNDERWOOD, G.B. & CO. Price list of
pulmonary inspirators with desc. account,
treatment, etc. 34pp. and 2 lvs.

1897 New York   NNNAM
------ Treatise and directions - heat
medicated air, etc. Desc. of apparatus, no
prices. 40pp.

1898 New York   NNNAM
VAN HOUTEN & TEN BROECK. The
Morton-Wimshurst-Holtz influence machine
for x-ray purposes, etc. 15pp.

1893 New York   NNNAM
VETTER, J.C. & CO. Ill. catalog of the
Vetter galvanic and faradic batteries and
standard electro-medical apparatus. 56pp.

VICTOR ELECTRIC CO. See Dental
Instruments, etc.

c.1875 Cincinnati   OC
VOLTA BELT CO. Ill. brochure and catalog - electro chain belts and bands - medicine rendered useless. Let nature restore
your nerves. 12mo., 40pp., pict. wrap.

1889 New York   NNNAM
WAITE & BARTLETT MFG. CO.   DNLM
Ill. price list of electro-medical and
electro-surgical instruments. 8vo., 64pp.,
wrap.

1890 New York   NNNAM
------ Ill. price list. 48pp., wrap.

1890 New York   DNLM
------ Ill. price list. 8pp., wrap.

1893 New York   NNNAM
------ Ill. price list. 47pp., wrap.

c.1876 New York   NNNAM
WALES, WILLIAM. Optician. Condensed
price list of microscopes, histological and
first quality objectives. 6 lvs.

c.1900 Philadelphia   NNNAM
WALL & OCHS. Physicians' net price list
of ophthalmological and laryngological
apparatus. 24pp.

c.1860 Springfield, Vt.   VtHi
WATKINS, C.A. & CO. Ill. catalog of surgi-
cal apparatus, orthopaedical appliances, etc.
Ills. of invalids stepping lively, etc.

c.1893 Brooklyn, N.Y.   NNNAM
WIESNER, OSCAR E.A. New ill. catalog of
white porcelite enameled steel aseptic hospital furniture, operating room equipment -
six highest awards at Chicago 1893. 38pp.

c.1900 Baltimore   NNNAM
WILLMS, CHARLES SURGICAL INSTRU-
MENT CO. Ill. and desc. catalog of surgical
instruments, orthopaedic appliances, trusses,
microscopes, static machines, hospital supplies, etc. 506pp.

1900 New York   NNNAM
WILLYOUNG, ELMER G. Price list of in-
duction coils, x-ray machines and accessory
apparatus. 2nd ed. 32pp.

1889 Philadelphia   DNLM
YARNALL, E.A. & CO. Ill. catalog of surgical and orthopaedical appliances, acoustic
apparatus, etc.

1892 Philadelphia   NNNAM
------ Ill. catalog of medical   PKsL
supplies. 344pp.

1894 Philadelphia   DNLM
------ Ill. catalog of surgical and medical
apparatus and supplies. 2nd ed. 8vo.

Just in case I haven't made it clear, be sure to check Drugs and Pharmaceuticals, Dental Instruments, and Optical and Scientific Apparatus. It wasn't too long ago that one or two manufactures supplied the mathematician, the school teacher, the dentist, the physician and the surgeon with practically everything he needed to start off in business.

241

Chapter 36

Musical Instruments & Accessories

With the strains of Yankee Doodle only just fading after the 4th of July parade, I am tuned to explain what this chapter offers. Although our high school band had no piano-fortes from Silas Allen's 1836 catalog, or musical merchandise from Mr. Parker's offerings in 1820, there were cornets and drums that are not too different from those shown in Lyon & Healy's 1880 illustrated price list. From a jews harp to the fanciest uniforms for the swellest bands with the last word in equipment and instruments this chapter lists the best examples from about 1820. It does not pretend to list every manufacturer and jobber, but it does claim a fine list of samples available for research.

Lyon & Healy often combined their illustrated catalogs with such come-ons as Major Putnam's Duties of the Drum Major, and McCosh's Guide to Amateur Brass Bands. Mason & Hamlin offered their melodeons, harmoniums and organs in 1860 in one of the earliest illustrated catalogs located. Rudolph Wurlitzer's catalogs offered everything one could dream of in 1898 from a grandfather's clock music box to a musical castor set that played as you mixed your French dressing at the table. From the smallest jews harp to the grandest grand piano the manufacturers represented in this chapter present you with every tool needed to write about and record the American musical scene in the 19th century.

c.1875 Philadelphia   PKsL
ALBRECHT & CO. MFG. Ill. catalog of
grand, square and upright pianos.

1836 Boston   MBSPNEA
ALLEN, SILAS JR. Pianofortes mfg. by
Brown & Hallett for sale at lowest prices,
etc. Broadside.

1898-99 New York   NjOE
AMERICAN GRAPHOPHONE CO.

1898 Price list of Columbia records. 38pp.
                                        Wrap.
1898 Price list of Columbia records. 26pp.
                                        Wrap.
1899 Price list of Columbia records. 16pp.
                                        April.

1882 Dolgeville, N. Y.   NNU
AUTOHARP CO. The Autoharp and how it
captured the family. Ill. catalog of styles.
Harp format, 12mo., tinted ills., col. litho.
wrap.

1891 Boston & Chicago   MBSPNEA
BACON, FRANCIS. Late Raven & Bacon.
Est. 1789. J. Howard Foote's ill. catalog of
Francis Bacon's Pianos. Western depot -
Chicago. 8vo., 12pp., pict. wrap.

1868 Providence, R.I.   RHi
BAKER & RANDALL, MFG. Ill. price list
of models and styles of melodeons - Book-
case model, etc. 6 page folder, telling of
20 years' experience, etc.

c.1880 Boston   MBSPNEA
BATES, G.H.W. & CO. Est. 1863. Ill. catalog and price list of musical instruments -
Paginini violin outfit free, orguinettes,
organinas, accordions, banjos, box meloa-
eons, etc., also toys. 8vo., 32pp., pict. wrap.

c.1875 New York   ICHi
BAUER, J. & CO. Ill. catalog of Agraffe
square and upright pianos.

1882 Hiram, O.   OHi
BEAMAN'S. Beaman's musical bulletin #21,
published occasionally. Ill. catalog of styles,
models of horns, house organs, pianos, etc.
Fol., 4pp.

1881-2 Washington, N. J.   PKsL
BEATTY, DANIEL F. Ill. catalog of
Beatty's world renowned organs and pianos.
Latest prices. 16mo., fld. col. pict. calen-
dar.

1883 Washington, N. J.   NNMM
------ Ill. catalog of Beatty's Beethoven
Organs. 16pp., wrap.

c.1897 Chicago   ICHi
BENT, GEORGE P. Ill. catalog of Crown
pianos, with fine ills. of models and styles.
24mo., 16pp., col. pict. wrap.

c.1884 Freeport, Ill.   ICHi
BENTLEY, H.D. Ill. catalog of piano and
organ stools, music cabinets, etc.

1850 Albany, N. Y.   MH-BA
BOARDMAN & GRAY, MFG. Ill. catalog of
pianofortes, pat. dolce campana attachment,
music and musical instruments, etc. Tests.
24mo., 48pp., pict. wrap.

1879 Bridgeport, Conn.   CtHi
BRIDGEPORT ORGAN CO. Ill. catalog of
organs. 12mo., 24pp., fine ills., pict. wrap.

1890 Boston   MBSPNEA
BRIGGS, C.C. CO. Ill. catalog of Brigg's
grand and upright pianofortes. Fine pls.
4to., 16pp., pict. wrap.

BROWN & HALLETT. See Silas Allen, Jr.

c.1876 Chicago   ICHi
BURDETT. Ill. price list of Burdett's
organs. 34pp.

1881 Worcester, Mass.   MWA
CARPENTER, EDWIN P. Ill. catalog of the
celebrated Carpenter organ actions - models
The Companion - portable, with handles -
Library Organ, built in clock and bookshelves models. Large 8vo., 96pp., pict.
wrap.

c.1889 Chicago   ICHi
CHICAGO COTTAGE ORGAN CO. W. D.
Thayer. Ill. catalog of Kingsbury pianos
and organs. Large 8vo., 24pp., pict. wrap.

c.1890 Chicago   ICHi
------ Ill. catalog of organs and pianos.
Sq. 8vo., 8pp., pict. wrap.

1857 Boston   MH
CHICKERING & SONS. Est. 1823. Chickering & Sons' pianofortes at the exhibition of
1856. 8vo., 18pp., ills.

1863 Boston   NNMM
------ A catalog of the new scale pianofortes. Ill. and desc. with price list. 11 lvs.,
wrap. bnd. in.

1869 Boston   NNMM
------ Ill. catalog of grand, square and upright pianofortes. 4to., 16 pls., wrap.

1874 Boston   NNMM
------ Ill. catalog of new styles and models. 38pp., pict. wrap.

1876 Boston   MBSPNEA
------ Ill. catalog of Chickering models at
Centennial exposition. Sm. 4to., 24pp. of
fine ills., wrap.

1889 Boston
------ Ill. catalog, pict. wrap.

CHRISTIE PIANO CO. Ill. catalog of
Christie pianos - styles, models and new
designs. 8vo., 24pp., dec. wrap.

1889 Detroit   MiD
CLOUGH & WARREN. Ill. catalog of grand
and cabinet combination pianos. 12mo.,
40pp., fine ills. of models. Wrap.

c.1890 Philadelphia   PKsL
COLEMAN, HARRY. New price list of
Misserharter's American excelsior solo
and military band instruments. 8vo., 32pp.,
fine ills.

1890-91 Washington, D.C.   NjOE
COLUMBIA PHONOGRAPH CO.

List of records November 1890 4pp.
                                      Wrap.
List of records November 1891 16pp.
                                      Wrap.

1896 Chicago   ICHi
CONKEY, W.B. American Musical N
Association - Member's catalog of nearly
40,000 selections and ill. catalog of instruments, musical boxes, horns, harmonicas,
accordians, etc. 4to., 182pp., pict. wrap.

1880 Washington, N. J.   NjR
CORNISH & CO. Ill. catalog of high grade
pianos and organs for parlor, barroom and
cathedral. 4to., 24pp., col. pict. wrap. Pip!

c.1890 New York   NNMM
DALE, BENJ. B. Special circular. Dale's
cornets and complete violin outfits. Prices
net cash. One leaf with 12 ills.

c.1865 New York   NNMM
DECKER & SON. Est. 1856. Later became
Decker Brothers. Desc. catalog of piano-
fortes. 8vo., 32pp., fine ills., wrap.

1875 New York   NHi
------ Ill. catalog. 8vo., 28pp., pict. wrap.

1880 New York   TxDa
------ Ill. catalog of Decker Brothers'
grand, square and uprights - models and
styles - $660. - $1500. 12mo., 24pp., pict.
wrap.

1886 New York   NjR
------ Ill. catalog for November. Sm. 4to.,
32pp. of models, pict. wrap.

1891 New York   N
------ Ill. catalog. 16pp., fine pls.

EDISON PHONOGRAPHS. See American
Graphophone Co., National Phonograph Co.,
New York Phonograph Co., North American
Phonograph Co. and Rudolph Wurlitzer Co.

1895 Boston   MH-BA
EMERSON PIANO CO. Est. 1849. Ill. catalog of grand and upright pianos. 65,000 now
in use, etc. 8vo., 25pp., wrap.

1871 Brattleboro, Vt.   NNMM
ESTEY, J. & CO. Est. 1846. Ill., desc. and
priced catalog of cottage organs. 40pp., col.
pict. wrap.

1875 Brattleboro, Vt.   NNMM
------ Ill. catalog of Estey organs. 44pp.,
col. pict. wrap.

1876 Brattleboro, Vt.   CtHi
------ Ill. catalog of Estey NhD NNU
organs. 4to., 24pp., col. pict. wrap.
Account of largest factory in world.

1880 Brattleboro, Vt.   NhD
------ Ill. catalog. 4to., pict. wrap.

1882 Brattleboro, Vt.   NNMM
------ Ill. catalog, desc. and priced -
models and styles. 36pp., pict. wrap.

c.1900 New York   N
FISCHER, CARL. Carl Fischer's new competition catalog of musical merchandise.
Ills. of banjos, guitars, music boxes, violins,
etc. 4to., 120pp., fine ills., pict. wrap.

1883-4 New York   N
FOOTE, J. HOWARD. Ill. catalog of musical merchandise - musical boxes, band
lamps, band equipment and instruments.
8vo., 108pp., pict. wrap.

1893 New York   ICHi
------ Ill. catalog and price list of
Courtois band instruments. 4pp. See also
Francis Bacon.

c.1880 Fort Wayne   MH-BA
FORT WAYNE ORGAN CO. Est. 1871. Ill.
catalog of Packard organs. 8vo., 24pp.

1891 Newark, N. J.   NjR
GABLER, ERNEST & BROTHER. Est. 1860.
Ill. catalog of Gabler pianos and plates - over 32,000 in use, one a relic of
the Civil War, tests. with a partial list of
customers. 4to., 32 plus 12pp., pict. wrap.

1870 New York   NHi
GALENBERG & VAUPEL PIANO CO. Ill.
catalog of pianofortes, models, Bijou,
Separable, Square, etc. Sq. 16mo., 16pp.,
pict. wrap.

c.1874 Boston   MBSPNEA
GUILD, CHURCH & CO. Successors to
George M. Guild & Co. Ill. catalog of
Grand and Square pianofortes. 6th ed. with
test. letters 1865-1873. 8vo., 40pp., pict.
wrap.

c.1890 Boston
------ Ill. catalog of pianofortes.

1890 Rochester, N. Y.   NR
HAINES BROTHERS MFG. Ill. catalog of
pianos, organs, etc.

1882 Boston   ICHi
HALLETT & CUMSTON. Ill. catalog of
grands and uprights.

1894-5 New York   N
HASSE, WM. E. Successor to T.F. Kramer
& Co. Ill. catalog of Symphonion, Polyphone
and Regina music boxes. Fine ills. of
models, also hall clock model, etc. 8vo.,
24pp., pict. wrap. of Regina.

nd. Boston, New York & Philadelphia NNMM
HAYNES, JOHN C., C.H. DITSON & CO., &
J.E. DITSON & CO. Ill. catalog of guitars,
banjos, mandolins, zithers, etc. 40pp.

nd. Philadelphia   MH-BA
HENDERSON & CO. Ill. style journal of
band uniforms and equipment now worn by
Sousa's band. 8vo., 24pp., wrap.

c.1890 Boston   MiTanW
HOWE, ELIAS. Catalog of old violins,
violas, cellos and parts. Medal at 15th Exhibition of Massachusetts Charitable
Mechanics' Association in 1884. Old and
new instruments. 32pp.

1890 Boston & Cambridgeport, Mass.
IVERS & POND PIANO CO.   MBSPNEA
Inc. 1880. Ill. catalog of pianofortes. 4to.,
98pp., pls. of models, pict. wrap.

1873 Dedham, Mass.
IVERS, WILLIAM H. Ill. catalog of Ivers'
pianofortes, models and styles. 16mo., 16pp.
Fine ills., pict. wrap.

c.1890 New York   N
JACOT MUSIC BOX CO. Ill. catalog of
Stella music boxes. 12mo., 16pp., col. pict.
wrap.

1893 New York   NNMM
------ (Jacot & Sons, agents.) Ill. catalog
of ideal interchangeable cylinder musical
boxes. 24pp., wrap.

c.1900 New York   NNMM
------ Catalog of musical boxes   N
with list of tunes. 24pp.

1893 Bridgeport, Conn.   TxDa
KELLER BROTHERS & BRIGHT. Est. 1882.
Keller Brothers' pianos at the Columbian
Exposition - fine ills. of styles and models.
Sq. 12mo., 20pp., col. pict. wrap.

c.1881 Chicago & New York   ICHi
KIMBALL, WILLIAM WALLACE. Ill. catalog of pianos and organs.

1883 Chicago & New York   ICHi
------ Ill. catalog of models and styles of
Kimball pianos and organs.

1887 New York & Baltimore   NjR
KNABE, WILLIAM & CO. Ill. catalog of
grand, square and upright pianofortes -
4 pls. of styles. 4to., 18pp. plus 4pp., pict.
wrap. Ptd. The DeVinne Press.

1891 New York   NHi
KRAKAUER BROTHERS. Est. 1870. Ill.
catalog of pianos, fine pls. 4to., 16pp.,
pict. wrap.

c.1880 Philadelphia   PKsL
LESTER PIANO CO. F. A. North & Co.,
salesrooms. Ill. catalog of improved upright pianos, view of plant and various
models. 8vo., 4pp.

1891 Philadelphia   PHi
------ Ill. catalog of Lester uprights. 4to.,
fine ills., dec. wrap.

1866 New York   TxDa
LINDEMAN & SONS. Ill. catalog of the new
pat. Cycloid pianofortes - gold premium
awards, etc. with fine pls. of styles, etc.
Sq. 12mo., 40pp., pict. wrap.

1880-89 Chicago   ICHi
LYON & HEALY. An unusually fine ref.
collection:

1880 Ill. catalog of musical instruments
      with McCosh's Guide to Amateur
Brass Bands. 8vo., 188pp., col. pls., col.
pict. wrap.

1880-2 Ill. catalog, including uniforms, etc.
       8vo., 148pp., ills. of hats, laces,
plumes, epaulettes - with Maj. Putnam's
Duties of the Drum Major.

c.1883 Ill. catalog of instruments in brass
        and accessories.

1884 Ill. catalog of pianofortes.

c.1887 Ill. catalog of orguinettes, cabinet-
        tos, musical cabinets, etc.

1889 Ill. catalog of piano stools, covers,
      music accessories, small instru-
ments, etc.

1889 Chicago   ICRRD
------ Ill. catalog of Washburn guitars,
mandolins, zithers, etc. 8vo., 64pp., wrap.

1892 Chicago   NHi
------ Ill. catalog of band instruments,
trimmings, accessories, uniforms, etc.
with a guide for bands. 4to., 110pp.

c.1890 New York   NNMM
LYON BROTHERS. Ill. broadside catalog
of Regina musical boxes with 19 ills. of designs and styles.

nd. Albany, N. Y.   NNMM
McCAMMON PIANO-FORTE CO. Styles and
models of McCammon pianos. Ill., 16pp.

c.1880 Rochester, N. Y.   NR
MACKIE & CO. Bell Treble Piano & Organ
Maker. The Bell Treble - Vol. 3, #1 - Our
new ill. catalog of models and styles, medals
won, etc. 4to., 32pp., fine ills., pict. wrap.

1890 Cleveland, O.   OHi
McMILLIN, H.E. Ill. catalog of musical instruments and musicians' supplies. Fol., 8pp.

nd. Worcester, Mass.   NNMM
McTAMMANY ORGANETTE CO. Ill. brochure on automatic organs, organettes and
melopaens. 4 lvs.

1860 Boston   PKsL
MASON & HAMLIN ORGAN CO.   NNU
Ill. and desc. catalog of melodeons and harmoniums - styles $60. to $400. 8vo., 32pp.,
swell ills., dec. wrap.

1870 Boston   NNU
------ Ill. catalog of cabinet organs, etc.
4to., fine ills., pict. wrap.

1874 Boston   NNU
------ Ill. catalog of melodeons and organs.

1876 Boston   N
------ Ill. catalog of 9 new models from
new plant at Cambridgeport, Mass., key-
boards, etc. Fol., 4pp.

1880 Boston   ICHi
------ Ill. catalog of cabinet organs for
December. 33pp.

1881 Boston   NNU
------ Ill. catalog of organs for October.

1889 Boston   NHi
------ Ill. catalog of pianofortes. 8vo., 24pp.

nd. Worcester, Mass.   MWA
MASON & RISCH. The Mason & Risch Vocal-
ion - why hailed as greatest invention of
musical world in 19th century. 8vo., 8pp., 2 ill.

c.1890 New Haven   CtHi
MATHUSHEK PIANO MFG. CO. Ill. catalog
of models and styles.

1894 New York   CSf
MEISEL, C. & CO. Ill. catalog of musical
merchandise - banjos, horns, mandolins,
violins, musical boxes, etc. 4to., 210pp. of
excellent ills., dec. cl.

c.1900 Boston   NNMM
MILLER, THE HENRY F. & SONS PIANO
CO. Ill., desc. and priced catalog of piano-
fortes. 20pp.

1897 Orange, N. J.   NjOE
NATIONAL PHONOGRAPH CO. Ill. price
list of parts for Edison phonographs. 16pp.,
wrap.

1898 Orange, N. J.   NjOE
------ Ill. catalog of Edison phonographs
and supplies. 24pp., wrap.

1898 Orange, N. J.   NjOE
------ Ill. price list of phonographs and
records for September.

1899 Orange, N. J.   NjOE
------ Ill. price list of parts and machines
for February.

1899 Orange, N. J.   NjOE
------ Catalog of Edison records for May.
48pp., wrap.

1899 Orange, N. J.   NjOE
------ Ill. catalog of Edison phonographs,
accessories and records for June. 37pp.,
wrap.

nd. Orange, N. J.   NNMM
------ Ill., desc. and priced cat-   NjR
alog of phonographs, outfits and supplies.
24pp.

1900 Orange, N. J.   NjOE
------ Ill. catalog of phonographs and supplies. 48pp., wrap.

1903 Orange, N. J.   NjOE
------ A Lasting Impression -   NjR
tinted ills. Edison Gem $10., Standard $20.,
Home $30., Edison Triumph $50., Concert
$75., Edison Opera $85. and Edison Victor
$60. 16mo., 32pp., tinted Gibson Girl wrap.

1887 Boston   TxDa
NEW ENGLAND ORGAN CO. Ill. catalog of
designs of cabinet organs. 8vo., 38pp., dec.
wrap.

1888 Boston   MBSPNEA
------ Ill. catalog of latest styles. 74pp.,
wrap.

c.1890 Boston   MH-BA
NEW ENGLAND PIANO CO. Ill. catalog of
New England pianofortes, grand, square and
upright. List of users. 8vo., 48pp.

1895 Chicago   ICHi
NEWMAN BROTHERS. Ill. catalog of
organs.

1835 New York   NNMM
NEW YORK BOOK OF PRICES FOR MANU-
FACTURING PIANO-FORTES. 98pp. and
index, bds. N.B. This may not be a trade
catalog but it surely controlled any price
list issued.

1889 New York   NjOE
NEW YORK PHONOGRAPH CO. Mfg. under
authority of North American Phonograph Co.
Ill. catalog of phonographs and phonograph-
graphophones - styles and designs, also cabinets and directions for new type Edisons.
Sq. 16mo., 32pp., 4 pls. N.B. This would
seem to be the earliest printed catalog located.

c.1898 New York & Chicago   NjOE
NORTH AMERICAN PHONOGRAPH CO.
Music for every home - Form 535 - ill. circular, models of Edison Gem, Standard, etc.
4pp.

1899 New York & Chicago   NjOE
------ Ill. catalog of Edison phonographs
for November. 36pp.

c.1900 New York & Chicago   ICHi
------ Ill. catalog - domestic, commercial
models, nickel in the slot barroom type, etc.
8vo., 16pp., pict. wrap.

c.1900 New York & Chicago   NNMM
------ Instructions for setting up Edison
Standard with ills. and catalog of educational
records. 2 circulars and 10 lvs., wrap.

c.1885 New York   N
PAILLARD, M. J. & CO. Ill. catalog of the
Capital music box, models A, B, C, D and E,
harp attachment, all triumphs of American
skill. 16mo., 8pp., pict. wrap.

PARKER, CHARLES CO. Piano and Organ
Benches. See Furniture.

1820 Boston   MWA
PARKER, JOHN R. A catalog of music and
musical instruments, comprising every species of musical merchandise for sale at
Franklin music warehouse, etc. 16mo.,
54pp. Ptd. Thomas Badger, Jr.

c.1876 New York
PARSONS, CHARLES H. Ill. catalog of band
instruments - the best in the world, etc.
16mo., 48pp., pict. wrap. of Cox's Brownies
forming a band.

1893 Philadelphia & Chicago   PHi
PEPPER, J.W., MFG. Souvenir of World's
Columbian Exposition. Ills. of band instru-
ments, etc. Large 8vo.

1895 Philadelphia   PHi
------ Ill. catalog of musical instruments
for all occasions. 4to., pict. wrap.

1898 Philadelphia   PHi
------ Complete ill. catalog of musical
instruments, trimmings, uniforms and accessories. Large 4to., 90pp., pict. wrap.
One of the best.

1899 Philadelphia   PKsL
------ Complete ill. catalog of   PHi
everything for the musician, amateur and
professional. 4to., 130pp., pict. wrap. Another of the best.

c.1892 Indianapolis   In
PIERCE TONE AGING CO. Catalog of
facts and tests. with a fine litho. of the
plant and instruments. Sq. 12mo., 16pp.,
fine pict. wrap.

c.1881 Concord, N. II.   NhIIi
PRESCOTT ORGAN CO. Est. 1836. Ill.
catalog of Prescott organs, models and
styles - Cottage, Favorite, Cabinet, Chapel,
Boudoir, Orchestral and Standard. 8vo.,
24pp., pict. wrap. of factory.

1876 Buffalo, N. Y.   NBuHi
PRINCE & CO. Ill. catalog of melodeons
and organs.

PRATT & MYERS. See Jewelry.

PROVIDENCE JEWELRY CO. See Jewelry.

c.1890 Rahway, N. J.   ICHi
REGINA, THE CO. Ill. catalog of   N
new styles in Regina musical boxes, novelties, etc. 12mo., 12pp., pict. wrap.

c.1893 New York   PShipL
REGINA MUSIC BOX CO. Ill. catalog of
Regina Corona and Orchestral models with
special lists of tunes. 24mo., 32pp., pict.
wrap. Fine job.

1867 New York   N
SCHRIEBER CORNET MFG. CO. (M. J.
Paillard, agent.) Ill. catalog of musical instruments in brass, German silver and
other metals with short history of company,
models, styles and mfg. data. Sq. 16mo.,
16pp. plus 12 litho. pls. of uniformed players, price list, ptd. wrap. N.B. Quality -
not quantity.

1893 New York   NHi
SCHUBERT PIANO CO. A Visit   N
to the Warerooms and Factory - in 20 col.
tinted lithos. by Donaldson Bros. - room by
room - designs and models, with history of
. . . 8vo., 20pp., col. pict. wrap. Unusual
litho. catalog.

1886 New Haven   CtHi
SHONINGER, B. ORGAN CO. Supplementary
catalog of new styles with latest improvements. Ills. of models - Grand Cymbella
Organ, etc. View of plant. 8vo., 8pp. with
7 ills.

nd. New York   NNMM
SMITH, BERNARD N. PIANO WOOD NN
WORKING FACTORY. Ill. catalog of legs,
carved ornaments, pilasters and trusses for
pianos.

c.1855 Boston   MBSPNEA
SMITH, S.D. & H.W. MELODEON MFG.
Attention of the public invited to superior
melodeons, price list $60. to $225., wood-
cut of plant, opinions of Chickering, etc.
Fol. broadside.

c.1890 New York   NHi
SOHMER & CO. Ill. catalog of celebrated
Sohmer pianos - styles, models, plant, etc.
12mo., 34pp., pict. wrap.

1892-3 New York   NHi
------ A souvenir from Puck, Judge &
Leslies recalling Sohmer pianos. A well
ill. clever piece of sales work. Sq. 16mo.,
12pp.

1889 New York   N
SONNTAG, HERMAN. Ill. catalog of musical instruments - brass, stringed, every
style, supplies, musical novelties, music
boxes, etc. Sm. 4to., 288pp. of ills., wrap.

1893 Chicago   ICHi
STARCK & STARCK PIANO CO. Ill. catalog of styles and models of high grade
pianos. 8vo., 16pp., pict. wrap.

c.1900 Richmond, Ind.   In
STARR PIANO CO. 36 pict. mounted cards
with details of models, in slip case. For
purposes of research a catalog in essence
though not bound with pict. wrap.

1873 New York   N
STECK, GEORGE & CO. Ill. catalog of
Steck's grand, square and upright styles and
designs. Large 8vo., 24pp., pict. wrap.

1878 New York & Astoria, L. I., N. Y.
STEINWAY & SONS. Est. 1853. MH-BA
Ill. catalog of Steinway's grand, square and
upright pianofortes. 8vo., 24pp.

1882 New York   ICHi
------ Ill. catalog of grands and uprights,
styles and models.

1883 New York   N
------ Ill. catalog of piano cases, woodwork and ornaments - view of works at

Astoria, saw mill, iron foundry, etc. 8vo., 24pp. Unusual record.

1888 New York   NHi
------ Ill. catalog of designs and styles of Steinway pianofortes. 8vo., 24pp., fld. pls., wrap.

1892 New York   NNQ
------ Ill. catalog of pianofortes. 12mo., pict. wrap.

1882 Derby, Conn.   CtHi
STERLING ORGAN CO. Ill. catalog of Sterling high grade grand and upright organs. 16mo., 22pp., col. pict. wrap. by Gies Litho. Co. of Buffalo.

1887 Derby, Conn.   CtHi
------ Ill. catalog of models and styles. Sq. 8vo., 24pp., litho. pict. wrap. by Buffalo Litho. Co.

c.1887 Derby, Conn.   CtHi
------ Ill. catalog of parlor grands, etc. 4to., 32pp., Ketterlinus lithos. and ptd.

nd. Derby, Conn.   NNMM
------ Ill. catalog of styles and models. 32pp., pict. wrap.

c.1890 Derby, Conn.   MH-BA
------ Ill. catalog of high grade pianos, uprights and parlor grands, etc. 8vo., 24pp. Wrap. N.B. It is interesting to realize that this small Connecticut piano mfg. turned to such outstanding lithographers as Ketterlinus of Philadelphia and the Gies Litho. Co. of Buffalo for ill. catalogs of this period.

1886 Philadelphia   PKsL
STEWART, S.S. Ill. price list of Stewart's parlor, concert and orchestra banjos - the banjo as an art. Famous players in action. 4to., 40pp., pict. wrap.

1887 Philadelphia   PKsL
------ Ill. price list of celebrated Geo. Bauer's mandolins, guitars and banjos, with banjo philosophy, construction, evolution, capabilities - Huntley & Lee, Mr. Weston as Uncle Tom, etc. 4to., 12 and 24pp., pict. wrap.

1882 St. Louis   MoSHi
STORY & CAMP, INC. Ill. catalog of improved organs.

1882 New York   N
STRATTON, JOHN F. & CO. Ill. catalog of holiday goods for November. Musical cigar boxes, miniature theater and sheep farm music novelties, musical decanters, albums, toys, jewel cases, penny banks, toy pianos -

as well as a thousand other musical creations. 8vo., 52pp., pict. wrap.

c.1890 New York   N
------ Special price list of fine music boxes, new models, novelties, etc. 8vo., 8pp., wrap.

1891 New York   PKsL
STRAUCH BROTHERS, MFG. Ill. catalog of pianoforte actions, parts, models, rise and development, etc. 12mo., 62pp., col. pls. and photos., shop interiors, etc., lea.

1887 New York   NHi
STRICH & ZEIDLER CO. Ill. catalog of grand and upright pianos, new models and styles, with a flyer of the Chef D'Oeuvre - the most ornate creation of the century. 4to., 24pp., pict. wrap.

1890 Worcester, Mass.   MWA
TABER ORGAN CO. Ill. and desc. catalog of Taber organs. Sq. 12mo., 20pp., dec. wrap.

c.1898 Chicago   NjOE
TALKING MACHINE CO., THE. Ill. catalog of talking machines, records, kinetoscopes and films. 12mo., 48pp., pict. wrap.

c.1899 Chicago   NjOE
------ Ill. catalog of phonographs, graphophones, polyphone attachments and records. 12mo., 64pp., pict. wrap.

1877 Worcester, Mass.   MWA
TAYLOR & FARLEY. Ill. catalog of Taylor & Farley organs, new styles and models for 1877. 12mo., 30pp., pict. wrap.

1892 New York & Chicago   ICHi
TONK, WILLIAM & BROTHER. Ill. catalog of musical merchandise for season 1892-3; accordions, jews harps, band instruments, musical boxes and zithers. 8vo., 208pp., pict. wrap.

c.1900 Camden, N.J.
VICTOR TALKING MACHINE CO. See Dr. Deakins Cylinder Records check list. This company was developed from the Berliner Co., first to make and sell disc records.

c.1893 Waterloo, N.Y.   MH-BA
WATERLOO ORGAN CO. Est. 1861. Ill. catalog of melodeons and pianos. 8vo., 24pp., pict. wrap.

1876 New York   MoSHi
WATERS, HORACE PIANO CO. Ill. catalog.

1874 New York   NHi
WEBER, A. Ill. catalog of Weber grand, square and upright pianofortes with fine pls. of models. 4to., 32pp., dec. wrap.

1880 New York   NNMM
------ Ill., desc. and priced catalog. 34pp.
with fine ills., pict. wrap.

1891 New York   N
------ Weber Pianofortes. Tinted pls. of
new styles. Tall 4to., 24pp., with pict.wrap.

1881 Meriden, Conn.   Ct
WILCOX & WHITE ORGAN CO. Est. 1876.
Ill. catalog of models for 1881. 16mo., fine
ills., pict. wrap.

1895 Meriden, Conn.   CtHi
------ Ill. catalog of automatic organs,
melodeons and organs for chapel, parlor and
schools - models Imperial, Perfection, etc.
Sq. 8vo., 24pp., pls., pict. wrap.

1897 New York   PKsL
WING & SON. Complete Book of Information about Pianos with ills. of parts, designs,
models and their mfg. Sq. 12mo., 117pp.,
dec. cl. N.B. An unusually complete combination of mechanics' guide and catalog.

1877 Cambridgeport, Mass.   PShipL
WOODS, GEORGE & CO. Ill. catalog and
price list of parlor organs. 12mo., 16pp.,
fine ills., pict. wrap.

1881 Cambridgeport, Mass.   NNMM
------ Ill. catalog of parlor and chapel
organs. 20pp., wrap.

c.1890 Cincinnati   OC
WURLITZER, RUDOLPH THE CO. Greatest offer ever made - Thomas A. Edison
phonograph - World's fastest selling
machines. 4to., 4pp., ill., wrap.

c.1890 Cincinnati   OC
------ Wurlitzer's holiday specialties
bulletin - ills. of musical clocks, jugs, bottles, books, instruments and novelties. Fol.,
8pp. with fantastic ills., pict. wrap.

1898 Cincinnati   OC
------ Wurlitzer's Band Journal #22. Ills.
of band instruments, music, uniforms, novelties and accessories for November. 4to.,
24pp., pict. wrap.

1898 Cincinnati   PP
------ 38th desc. and ill.   N   OC
price list of musical instruments and novelties. Musical boxes, steins, castor sets,
grandfather clocks, bar and hotel bar slot
machines, albums, decanters for bar, club,
or home parlor. 4to., 48pp. of ills., pict.
wrap.

A piano or melodeon is a musical instrument but it is also a rather swell to-be-bragged-about piece
of House Furnishing too - or rather it was back along; today the story is My dear, it belonged to
Uncle Joshua, and, I simply can't GIVE it away. Smaller musical instruments may also be found
under Hardware, of course again, last but not least, many of the Department and Miscellaneous
Store catalogs.

Chapter 37

Optical & Scientific Apparatus

This chapter is a sort of attic or catch-all. I believe that many of the goods and products offered so nearly fit the average person's definition of what might be listed under Drugs and Pharmaceuticals, Experimental Dentistry, Medical and Surgical Appliances, Hospital Equipment and even Photographic Supplies, that this segregation may prove confusing. On the other hand the librarians concerned with those very classifications disown them as mongrels. Don't forget that many of the best judges of dogdom prefer them to the blue ribbon variety.

A skeleton outline of the contents of these catalogs includes chemicals other than drugs, chemical glassware and apparatus, laboratory equipment, fixtures and furniture, accoustical, astronomical, electrical, mathematical, meteorological, optical and philosophical instruments, machines and supplies, as well as surveying equipment, scales and other precision measuring tools. In common collectible terms they offer glassware, apothecary scales, early precision instruments, dentists' implements and furnishings, curious experimental apparatus and even toys. The records and illustrations offered by Carpenter, Davis Dexter, Queen and Wightman from 1838 to 1900 are to my mind all important in having created the definite professional divisions we recognize today. Without them, medicine might still be one great big mongrel laboratory experiment.

1894 Southbridge, Mass.
AMERICAN OPTICAL CO. Est. 1833. Ill. catalog of eyeglasses and spectacles, lenses, frames, etc. 1833-1894. 4to., 96pp. of fine pls., dec. cl. See also Scoville Mfg. Co., Photographic Apparatus.

1855 Buffalo, N. Y.   NBuHi
ANDREWS & SON, Opticians. At the sign of the spectacles - a catalog of optical instruments, glasses, spectacles, microscopes, transits, mathematical instruments, quadrants, sextants, theodolites, barometers, etc. 12mo., 18pp., fine ills., ptd. wrap.

1897 London, England   MH-BA
BAIRD & TATLOCK. Ill. catalog of chemical and scientific apparatus, etc. with supplement. 8vo., 488pp., dec. cl.

1882 Rochester, N. Y.   MH-BA
BAUSCH & LOMB. Est. 1853.   DNLM
7th ed. Ill. catalog of microscopes and optical instruments. 8vo., 48pp., wrap.

1884 Rochester, N. Y.   MH-BA
------ 9th ed. Ill. catalog of microscopes, objectives and accessories. 8vo., 64pp.

1886 Rochester, N. Y.   MH-BA
------ 10th ed. Ill. catalog of optical supplies, etc. 4to., 96pp., pict. wrap.

1887 Rochester, N. Y.   MH-BA
------ 11th ed. Ill. catalog of optical goods, glasses, photographic lenses, etc. 4to., 98pp., wrap.

1895 Rochester, N. Y.   NNNAM
------ Ill. catalog of microscopes and optical supplies. Columbian ed. 48pp.

1900-12 Rochester, N. Y.   NRGE
------ A fine collection of ill.   NR
catalogs.

1874 Philadelphia   MH-BA
BECK, R. & J. Ill. catalog of scientific instruments and optical goods.

1879 Philadelphia   DNLM
------ Ill. catalog of microscopes and mathematical instruments.

1880 Philadelphia   PKsL
------ Condensed price list of microscopes, telescopes, thermometers, barometers, mounting implements, etc. 8vo., 32pp., pict. wrap.

1881 Philadelphia   MH-BA
------ Ill. catalog of optical goods.

1882 Philadelphia   DNLM
------ Ill. catalog of microscopic apparatus, etc. 11th ed., 8vo., pict. wrap.

1884-1900 Philadelphia   MH-BA
------ Other ill. catalogs, as above.

1872   New York   DNLM
BENJAMIN, E.B. American handbook of
chemical and physical apparatus with ill.
and desc. catalog of appliances and supplies.
8vo., wrap.

c.1877   New York   NHi
------ American handbook and catalog.
8vo., 226pp., index, ills., cl.

1881   New York   NNNAM
BERGE, J. & H. Est. 1850. Catalog of
latest improved Holtz electrical machines.
16pp. See also Medical and Surgical.

1879   Boston   MH-BA
BOSTON OPTICAL WORKS. Ill.   DNLM
catalog of microscopes, telescopes, etc.
16th ed. 8vo., 24pp.

1878   Chicago   MH-BA
BULLOCK, W.H. Est. 1866. Ill. catalog of
optical instruments, microscopes and accessories. 8vo., 24pp., pict. wrap.

1882   Cambridge, Mass.   DNLM
CAMBRIDGE SCIENTIFIC INSTRUMENT
CO. Ill. circular and price list. Fol.

1844   Boston   DSi
CHAMBERLAIN, N.B. & D. Ill. catalog of
pneumatic instruments, laboratory appliances for scientific experiments. 4, 56, 8
and XIVpp., 8vo., ptd. wrap. Excellent ills.

1878   Philadelphia   PHi
CHEYNEY, JESSE S. Ill. catalog of microscopic objects, mounting apparatus and
supplies. 8vo., 32pp.

1876   London, England & Philadelphia
CROUCH, HENRY. (James W.   MH-BA
Queen & Co., agent.) Ill. catalog of stu-
dents' microscopes at British Centennial
Exhibition. 8vo., 8pp.

1879   London & Philadelphia   MH-BA
------ Ill. catalog. 8vo., 32pp. with 2 page
insert.

1848   Boston   DSi
DAVIS, DANIEL. Magnetical Instrument
Maker. Succeeded by Palmer & Hall in
1849 and became Thomas Hall in 1857. Ill.
catalog of apparatus to magnetism, galva-
nism, electro-dynamics and thermo-electric-
ity. 12mo., 46pp. One of the earliest.

1846   Albany, N. Y.   N
DEXTER, GEORGE. Ill. catalog of philosophical apparatus for experiments in the
physical sciences - mathematics, pneumat-
ics, hydrostatics, hydraulics, optics, electricity, etc. 8vo., 24pp., 8 woodcuts.

1899   Orange, N. J.   NjOE
EDISON MFG. CO. Ill. catalog of Edison-
Lalande batteries, motor and fan outfits,
stereo-projecting kinetoscopes and X-ray
outfits. 72pp., wrap., for April.

1887   New York   NNNAM
EIMER & AMEND. Est. 1851.   PKsL
Ill. wholesale catalog of chemicals and
assay apparatus, etc. 281 and X pp., cl.

1890   New York   NNNAM
------ Supplementary catalog of chemical
and physical apparatus. Fine ill. record.
With prices current. 58pp.

1896   New York   NNNAM
------ Ill. catalog. 72pp., wrap.

1897   New York   NNNAM
------ Ill. wholesale catalog of apparatus
and assay goods, etc. 418pp., cl.

1899   New York   NNNAM
------ Ill. catalog of bacteriological apparatus, etc.

1899   Geneva, N. Y.   NNNAM
GENEVA OPTICAL CO. See Medical and
Surgical Instruments and Supplies.

1857   New Haven   CtHi
GRUNOW, J. & W. CO. Ill. catalog of
scientific achromatic microscopes and
scientific apparatus. 8vo., 104pp., 52 ills.,
pict. wrap.

1885   Rochester, N. Y.   MH-BA
GUNDLACH OPTICAL CO. Ill. catalog of
microscopes and accessories, camera
lenses, telescopes, etc. 8vo., 40pp., pict.
wrap. See also Photographic Supplies for
further listings.

1879   New York   OCP&G
HALL & BENJAMIN. Complete   CtY
ill. catalog of chemical and physical apparatus - glass and porcelain laboratory equipment and supplies. 8vo., 216pp., pict. wrap.
N.B. Bottles to magic lanterns, lamps and
scales.

1876   New York   NjOE
HALL & HARBESON. Ill. and desc. DNLM
catalog of chemical and physical apparatus
and instruments for chemists, physicians,
lecturers, school and college laboratories,
etc. 8vo., 123pp., dec. wrap.

c.1873   Boston   NjOE
HALL'S OF BOSTON. Hall's ill. catalog of
electro-plating batteries, chemicals and
supplies. 30pp., pict. wrap. Quote: Having
lost all of our equipment in the great fire of
1872, we are obliged to issue a new edition,
etc.

1882 Boston   NNU
------ Ill. catalog of new pat. batteries
for physicians and families - amusing tests.
8vo., 50pp., dec. wrap.

1880 New York   MStOSV
HAMMEL, L. & CO. Ill. catalog of optical
goods, jewelers' and watchmakers' supplies
and apparatus, watch cases, glasses, etc.
8vo., 308pp., pict. wrap.

1882 New York   NHi
------ Ill. catalog of optical supplies.
8vo., 332pp., pict. wrap.

1882 Cincinnati   PPL
HELLEBUSH, CLEMENS. Ill. price list of
lenses, spectacles, glasses, watch parts,
jewelers' tools, optical apparatus and supplies. 332pp. offering thousands of items.

1888 New York   MH-BA
JAEGER, H.J. & CO. Ill. catalog of scientific apparatus and optical instruments, etc.
8vo., 56pp.

1895 Cincinnati   OC
JONES BROTHERS ELECTRIC CO. Ill.
catalog of models for experimental work -
fancy lights, globes, bells, telephones - supplies. 8vo., 346pp. and XVII, pict. wrap. of
plant.

1855 New York   DSi
KENT, EDWARD N. Practical Chemist.
Ill. and desc. catalog of chemical apparatus,
laboratory equipment in glass, iron and
pottery. 8vo., 62pp., pict. wrap. A fine bit.

nd. Rochester, N. Y.   NR
KIRSTEIN, E. & SONS. Ill. catalog and
price list of eye-glasses, spectacles, spec-
tacle cases, styles of lettering, dies, etc.
Tall 12mo., 20pp., pict. wrap.

nd. New York   NNNAM
KLEINE, CHARLES B. Ill. price list of
microscopes and scientific instruments.
40pp.

1887 Cambridgeport, Mass.   MoSHi
LAMB & RITCHIE. Price list of Ritchie's
corrugated expanding conductors.

c.1878 New York   MH-BA
McALLISTER, T.H. Ill. catalog of optical
goods. 8vo., 24pp.

1881 New York   NNNAM
------ Ill. price list of microscopes and
apparatus, lenses, etc. 40th ed., 87pp.

1887 New York   NNNAM
------ Ill. catalog of optical goods. 49th
ed., 96pp.

1865 Philadelphia   PHi
McALLISTER, WILLIAM Y. Formerly
McAllister & Brother. Ill. catalog and
price list of mathematical instruments.

nd. Philadelphia   PHi
------ McAllister & Brother, Opticians.
Collection of ill. catalogs of optical, mathematical and philosophical instruments. 8vo.
and 12mo., wrap.

1867 Philadelphia   MH-BA
------ Ill. catalog of mathematical and
optical instruments. 8vo., 46pp.

1885 Chicago   DNLM
McINTOSH BATTERY & OPTICAL CO. Ill.
catalog of McIntosh combined galvanic and
Faraday battery, electro-therapeutical
appliances, electric bath equipment, etc.
8vo., 64pp., pict. wrap.

1897 Chicago   NNNAM
------ Electro-therapeutical catalog of
apparatus and appliances. 288pp., exhaustive ill. ref., cl. See also Medical and Surgical Supplies.

1880 New York   NHi
MEYROWITZ BROTHERS. Opticians. Ill.
catalog of optical goods - lamps, magic lanterns, stereopticons, eye-glasses, opera
glasses, microscopes, etc. 4to., 134pp.,
pict. wrap.

1885 New York   N
------ Ill. catalog of spectacles, eye-
glasses, lenses, lorgnettes, fancy stenciled
cases and optical goods. 4to., 46pp., index,
col. plate, pict. wrap. See also Medical
& Surgical Supplies.

Chicago
MEYSENBURG & BADT, Agents. See
Weston Electrical Instrument Co.

1885 New York   NHi
OLESCHLACHER BROTHERS . (Agents for
McIntosh Battery & Optical Co.) Ill. catalog
of microscopes, objects and accessories in
the optical department. 8vo., 72pp., wrap.

1848 New York   DNLM
PIKE, BENJAMIN JR. Optician.   DSi
Pike's ill. and desc. catalog of optical,
mathematical and philosophical instruments
with upwards of 750 engravings, designed as
an aid to professors of colleges, astrono-
mers, chemists, draughtsmen, surveyors,
etc. - ills. of microscopes, optical apparatus of every kind. 2 vols., 346 and 292pp.
with 66pp. priced catalog. The best catalog
of the period.

1856 New York   NNNAM
------ 2nd ed., 2 vols., pict. cl.   DNLM

1884 New York   NNU
PRENTICE, JAMES & SON. Ill. and desc.
catalog of optical, meteorological, mathematical apparatus, instruments, etc. Eye-
glasses, opera glasses, hour glasses, microscopes, transits, etc. 8vo., 192pp., pict.
wrap.

c.1876 Cincinnati   OC
PRINCE, L.M. Optical Instrument Maker.
Perfect sight, how to retain it - imperfect
sight, how to restore it. 8vo., 12pp., ills.,
wrap.

c.1882 Cincinnati   OC
------ 3 catalogs as follows, nd., c.1882.
Series #2 - Meteorological instruments,
                                    44pp.
Series #3 - Spectacles and eye-glasses,
                                    40pp.
Series #4 - Microscopes and optical appa-
                            ratus, 60pp.
3 good ill. records. Still in business and
currently supplies spectacles for OC.

1856 Philadelphia   PHi
QUEEN, JAMES W. & CO. Est. 1853. Ill.
catalog of mathematical, optical, philosophical and school apparatus and furnishings.

1860 Philadelphia   PKsL
------ Ill. catalog. 10th ed. 8vo., 88pp.

c.1868 Philadelphia   PKsL
------ Ill. catalog of globes, optical supplies, opera glasses to stereopticons. 27th
ed. 8vo., 116pp., dec. wrap.

1870 Philadelphia   PHi
------ Ill. catalog and price list of optical
apparatus, etc. 32nd ed.

1872 Philadelphia   DNLM
------ Ill. and priced catalog of optical
instruments.

1873 Philadelphia   PKsL
------ Ill. catalog of optical   NjOE
apparatus, magic lanterns, stereopticons,
dissolving view equipment and machines,
etc. 8vo., 90pp.

1874 Philadelphia   NjOE
------ Ill. catalog of   PPL NNC
physical apparatus, air pumps, rotary
forces, electricity, etc. 8vo., 151pp., wrap.
3395 items offered.

1874 Philadelphia   NNC
------ Ill. catalog of mathematical instruments. 106pp.

1875 Philadelphia   PKsL
------ Ill. catalog of physical   NjOE
apparatus. 107pp.

c.1875 Philadelphia   PKsL
------ Ill. catalog of drawing instruments.
8pp., wrap.

1875 Philadelphia   PKsL
------ Ill. catalog of optical instruments.
8vo., 120pp., pict. wrap. Price 10¢.

1876 Philadelphia   DNLM
------ 39th ed. Ill. catalog of optical
goods.

1877 Philadelphia   PKsL
------ Special reduction in prices for all
apparatus. 8vo., 16pp., wrap.

c.1878 Philadelphia   PHi
------ Ill. catalog with supplement. 8vo.,
43 and 18pp.

1880 Philadelphia   PKsL
------ Desc. manual and ill. catalog of
mathematical instruments. 8vo., 180pp.

1881 Philadelphia   PKsL
------ 47th ed. Ill. catalog. 8vo., 186pp.

1882 Philadelphia   NNNAM
------ Special ill. catalog of school laboratory apparatus. 8vo., 32pp.

1882 Philadelphia   MH-BA
------ 50th ed. Ill. catalog of optical instruments. 8vo., 188pp.

1883 Philadelphia   DNLM
------ Ill. catalog of chemical and PKsL
druggists' glassware, mathematical instruments, etc. 8vo., 50pp., wrap.

1883 Philadelphia   NNNAM
------ Ill. catalog of instruments for phys-
iology and medical purposes after Verdun,
Marey, Regnard and Boudet. 51pp., wrap.

1886 Philadelphia   PKsL
------ Ill. catalog showing ophthalmological instruments, spectacles, Busy-Bodies,
opera glasses, lenses, etc. 8vo., 140pp.

1887 Philadelphia   MH-BA
------ Photographic lenses and how to
choose them - ill. price list, etc. 8vo., 40pp.

1888 Philadelphia   NNNAM
------ Ill. catalog of chemical apparatus.
8vo., 229pp.

1889 Philadelphia   NNNAM
------ 71st ed. Ill. catalog. 107pp.

1887-1889 Philadelphia   MH-BA
------ 4 ill. bound catalogs, 1500pp. with
ills. throughout, photography, lanterns,
optical apparatus, etc.

1891 Philadelphia   PKsL
------ Ill. catalog of electrical testing
apparatus, etc. 124pp., pict. wrap.

1893 Philadelphia   NNNAM
------ 78th ed. Ill. catalog of   PKsL
microscopes and microscopical accessories,
etc. 112pp.

1897 Philadelphia   NNNAM
------ Ill. catalog of ophthalmological instruments and apparatus, etc. 90pp.

1898 Philadelphia   NNNAM
------ Ill. catalog of optical supplies.

20th century Queen catalogs at PKsL.

1875 Boston   NjOE
RITCHIE'S. Ill. catalog of Ritchie's philosophical apparatus. 57pp.

1875 London, England   MH-BA
ROSS & CO. Est. 1830. Ill. catalog of
optical supplies, microscopes and accessories. 8vo., 48pp.

1878 New York   NNNAM
BUHRAUER, T. Ill. price list of microscopes and apparatus. 16pp.

c.1879 Philadelphia   MH-BA
SENTMAYER, JOSEPH. Est. 1863. Ill.
catalog of microscopes and optical apparatus. 8vo., 38pp.

1895 Philadelphia   MH-BA
------ Ill. catalog. 15th ed. 8vo., 48pp.

1882 Rochester, N. Y.   MH-BA
SEXTON, L.R. Agent. Gundlach's new and
improved optical apparatus. 12mo., 24pp.,
ill.

1881 Lancaster, Pa.   NNNAM
SIDLE, JOHN W. Condensed price list of
Acme optical goods and supplies. 3rd ed.
16pp.

1893 Chicago   PPL
SWARTCHILD & CO. Ill. price list of optical goods, parts, jewelers' findings and
tools, watchmakers' supplies, etc. Thousands of ills. 641pp., dec. cl.

c.1870 Rochester, N. Y.   NR
TAYLOR BROTHERS. Ill. catalog of barometers, hydrometers, thermometers, etc.
10pp., dec. wrap.

c.1885 New York & Vienna   NHi
WALDSTEIN, H. Optician. Est. 1840. Ill.
and desc. catalog of optical and mathematical instruments. 8vo., 62pp., wrap.

c.1876 New York   NNNAM
WALES, WILLIAM. Optician. See Medical
and Surgical Instruments and Supplies.

1876 Chicago   NjOE
WESTERN ELECTRIC MFG. CO. Catalog
#VI - electro-medical and surgical appara-
tus. 77pp., ill., wrap.

1899 Newark, N. J.   NNNAM
WESTON ELECTRICAL INSTRUMENT CO.
Est. 1888. Desc. circular and complete cat-
alog of electrical instruments. 60pp., 6 lvs.

1838 Boston   MH-BA
WIGHTMAN, JOSEPH M. Est. 1830. Successors to Claxton & Wightman. Ill. catalog
of philosophical chemical, astronomical and
electrical apparatus. 12mo., 32pp., wrap.

1846 Boston   MH-BA
------ Ill. catalog. 12mo., 84pp.

c.1890 Philadelphia   PKsL
WILLIAMS, BROWN & EARLE. (Agents for
R. & J. Beck.) Ill. catalog of microscopes,
objects and supplies for college and laboratory. 8vo., 100pp., pict. wrap. Fine job.

1865 Peterboro, N. H.   NhD
WOODRUFF. Woodruff's pat. portable
barometer. 4to., 2pp., 2 woodcuts, tests.

c.1879 New York   DNLM
WOOLMAN, G.S. Priced and ill. catalog of
microscopes and optical instruments. 8vo.

c.1876 Philadelphia   NNNAM
ZENTMAYER, J. Ill. price list   DNLM
of microscopes, apparatus and optical instruments. 8vo., 40pp., wrap.

The complicated introduction naturally implies the necessity of using Drugs and Pharmaceuticals,
Dental Instruments, Furnishings and Supplies, Medical and Surgical Instruments and Supplies, and
last but far from least, Photographic Apparatus and Supplies. If you can't find a price record or
an illustration of an American product that should be classified under any or all of these headings
in Pike's two volume catalog for 1848, I'll bet it was never offered in any catalog during the 19th
century.

Chapter 38

Ornamental Ironwork

The purpose of this chapter, as explained in several others, is to segregate the outstanding examples in this field for the convenience of the historian and student. It makes no attempt whatever to compile an all-inclusive section. In many instances the reader is referred to other catalogs listed under Architectural Building Materials, Hardware, House Furnishings, Statuary and Weathervanes - and in one case even to Agricultural Implements.

This group of catalogs represent as completely as possible ornamental brass, bronze, iron, tin and zinc workmanship. They illustrate those pieces of art metal work about which we have been asked most often through the years by collectors and librarians. On its pages one should be able to find references to wrought and cast examples of garden furniture and ornaments, fancy cemetery gates and fences, ornate hat trees, summer houses, hitching posts and the many small pieces time has taught the American collector to value.

c.1874 Chicago   ICHi
AMERICAN WIRE WORKS. Ill. catalog of iron and wire products, plain and ornamental.

c.1890 Lafayette, Ind. & Chicago   ICHi
BARBEE, W.T. WIRE & IRON WORKS. Ill. catalog of elegant designs in iron and wire work - flower holders, gates, fences, garden furniture, vases, fountains, etc.

1894 Lafayette & Chicago   In
------ #B-55. Ill. catalog of wrought steel and wire gates and fences, posts, crestings, summer houses, hitching posts, etc. 4to., 80pp., fine pls., pict. wrap.

nd. Lafayette & Chicago   MnHi
------ Ill. catalog of wire and iron work.

1887 Detroit   MnHi
BARNUM, E.T. Ill. catalog of ornamental iron and wire work - builders' wire cloth, crestings, railings, gates, weathervanes, jail work, etc. 4to., 36pp., pict. wrap.

1888 Detroit   MnHi
------ Ill. catalog of iron work - garden fences, vases, chairs, settees, stable appointments, weathervanes, etc. 4to., 48pp., pict. wrap. See also Architectural Building Materials.

c.1884 Chicago   ICHi
BENNER, M. & CO. Ill. catalog of ornamental ironwork.

1884 Detroit   MnHi
BOLLES, J.E. & CO. Ill. catalog #3 of roof crestings, iron fencing, bank railings, tower ornaments, stable fittings and weathervanes. 4to., 64pp., pict. wrap.

1889 New York & Brooklyn   NNQ
CABBLE, WILLIAM. Excelsior Wire Mfg. Co. Est. 1848. Ill. catalog #42 - railings, wire rope, flower stands, porch and garden furniture, vases, urns, trellises, cylinder moulds, scenic screening, etc. 8vo., 80pp., fine pict. wrap. of plant.

1880 Kenton, O.   OAkF
CHAMPION, THE CO. Champion fences, jockey and horse hitching posts, urns, vases, garden furniture, tree guards, cemetery gates and fences, etc. Fol., 34pp., fine ref.

c.1856 Boston   MdTanSW
CHASE BROTHERS. Ill. catalog with 16 pls. of fancy gates and railings, hitching posts, etc. 4to., dec. wrap. See House Furnishings for fancy hat trees, umbrella stands, garden furniture, etc.

c.1860 Lancaster, Pa.   NNMM
DILLER, WILLIAM. Ill. catalog with tinted pls. of ornamental cast iron railings, gates, fences, etc. 4to., a fine job.

c.1890 St. Louis   MoSHi
EXCELSIOR WIRE & IRON CO. Ill. catalog #19. Art metal work.

1891 New York   ICHi
FISKE, J.W. Ill. catalog of artistic wrought
iron, brass and bronze - gate guards, posts,
grills, railings, crestings, weathervanes,
garden furniture and ornaments, etc. Fol.,
182pp. of pls. - unquestionably one of the
best pict. records located, pict. bds. See
also Architectural Building Materials and
Miscellany - Statuary.

c.1875 Chicago   ICHi
GOULD BROTHERS & DIBLEE. Ill. catalog
of ornamental ironwork, statuary, garden
furniture and ornaments, weathervanes, etc.

1884 Philadelphia   PHi
MANLY & COOPER MFG. CO. Ill. price
list of ornamental wrought ironwork.

1894 Grand Rapids, Mich.   NNMM
METAL STAMPING & SPINNING CO. Ill.
catalog of ornaments in brass, copper, iron,
tin and zinc - pls. of weathervanes, finials,
crestings, fancy ornate railings, fencing,
gates, etc. Tall 4to., 80pp., pict. wrap.

MINNEAPOLIS FENCE & IRON WORKS.
See Fences.

1873 New York   MiDbF
MOTT, J.L. IRON WORKS. Ill. catalog of
fountains, statuary, garden furniture, vases,
animal lawn ornaments, street lamps, hitching posts - chinaman,"nigger boy," etc. Fol.,
fine pls. throughout, pict. wrap.

1875 New York   ICHi
------ Ill. catalog of ornamental ironwork.
Fol., 132pp. of pls., pict. wrap.

nd. New York   NNMM
------ Special catalog A - Garden Furniture. 4to., 64pp., pict. wrap.

1882 New York   NNMM
------ Ill. catalog of artistic grates, fire
irons, fenders, andirons, etc. 4to., 167 lvs.
Pict. wrap. Fine pls. of andiron to weathervane.

1890 New York   NNMM
------ Ill. catalog and price list M of
statuary, lawn animal ornaments, garden
furniture, etc. 4to., 64pp., pict. wrap.

1897 New York   NNMM
------ Ill. catalog A. Cast iron garden
furniture, lawn ornaments, etc. 4to., 64pp.,
wrap.

1905 New York   ICHi
------ Fountains - Catalog H. 16x22,
132pp. of the finest pls. - for the country
estate or the largest city park, grand pict.
wrap. Copyright 1883, 1889, 1893, 1896 and
1905. This company issued many of the
finest pict. catalogs of ornamental ironwork,
but this elephant fol. devoted entirely to
fountains, is to my mind, the masterpiece.
See also Architectural Building Materials
and Plumbing.

NEW ENGLAND BUTT CO. See also House
Furnishings.

1857 New York   NHi
NEW YORK WIRE RAILING CO. Ill. catalog
of iron railings, fancy fences, gates, porch
and garden furniture, verandahs, summer-
houses, tree guards and boxes, urns, vases,
hitching posts, etc. With price list and history of iron founding, etc.

PECK BROTHERS & CO. See Plumbing.

1890 Spokane   OrU
SPOKANE ORNAMENTAL IRON & WIRE
WORKS. Ill. catalog of hitching posts, signs,
weathervanes, grills, fences, gates, railings,
ornamental stairways, crestings, etc.
16mo., 176pp., pict. wrap.

STANDARD MFG. CO. See Plumbing.

STRONG & DOUW. See Agricultural Implements.

nd. Philadelphia   PHi
WERNER, GEORGE F. Art Metal Works.
Ill. catalog of brass and bronze ornaments.

WOOD, R.D. & CO. See Plumbing.

What you can't find here will be found in those chapters suggested in the introduction. Iron match
safes, corner wall brackets, spittoons, andirons, flower holders and vases, urns, fancy cooking
utensils and a thousand other metal creations were often best illustrated in the most general catalogs.
By using this section in conjunction with others, you should be able to cover this facet of creative
Americana thoroughly.

Chapter 39

Paint—Covering Many Trades & Industries

As Mr. Bishop pointed out in 1860, there was very little paint manufactured in the Colonies. (See Artists' Materials and Supplies - Devoe & Raynolds). This chapter presents a small scattered collection for research that indicates historic and library interest. Established dates of the firms will give further information, but for our catalog purposes what we show here must suffice for the present.

1864   Chicago   IHi
ALEXANDER'S. Ill. catalog of Alexander's Four Ace preserving paints for railroads, steamboats, architects and builders. 8vo., 16pp. with a delightful pict. wrap. of a Showboat gambler in a topper holding four aces.

c.1880   Allentown, Pa.   PHi
ALLENTOWN MFG. CO. Col. ill. catalog of Breinig's ready mixed paints - col. samples and prices.

c.1865   Newburgh, O.   OHi
AVERILL & CO. Est. 1860. Averill's pat. water-proof varnish-paint. A Plain Statement of Fact - for tin roofs, bridges, steamboats, railroad cars and all buildings. 12mo. with a pict. wrap, and probably their first.

1888-89   Chicago   MnHi
CHICAGO WHITE LEAD & OIL CO. Ill. price lists for 1888 and 1889.

nd.   Cincinnati   OC
DAY, THE J.H. CO. Ill. catalog #26 of special machinery - paste and paint mixers and mills, the Pony Mixer - other models. 16pp.

1896   New York   NNMM
EGYPTIAN LACQUER MFG. CO. Ill., desc., and priced catalog of transparent and col. lacquers for all purposes, etc. 60pp., wrap.

c.1890   Philadelphia   PKsL
FELTON, SIBLEY & CO. Card price list with fld. col. chart of ready mixed paints made only by . . . best for buggy, carriage and sleigh.

1887   Gibsboro, N. J.   NjR
GIBSBORO COLOR VARNISH CO. John Lucas & Co., Distributor. Price list - for the trade. 8vo., 24pp., col. chart, ptd. wrap. See also Lucas.

1896   Chicago   MH-BA
JOHNS, H.W. MFG. CO. Ill. catalog with col. samples - paints for exterior decoration, dwellings and commercial buildings. 12mo., 12pp.

1897   Chicago   MH-BA
------ Color chart. 12mo., 12pp.

1885   Brooklyn, N. Y.   NNQ
LONGMAN & MARTINEZ. Ill. catalog and price list of pure colors, oils, varnishes and paints. 8vo., 19pp., col. charts, samples, wrap.

1886   Brooklyn, N. Y.   NNQ
------ Color plate price list.

1870   Baltimore   PHi
LUCAS, JOHN & CO. Est. 1849. Prop. of Gibsboro Paint Works. Desc. of improvement in apparatus for preparing lakes and painters' colors with price list, fld. pat. and samples. 16mo., 11pp. October 25.

1870   Baltimore   PKsL
------ Ill. catalog and price list of colors, paints and varnishes. 16mo., 27pp., col. chart, pict. wrap. of plant.

1878   Baltimore   PHi
------ Price list of white lead, color samples and paints for all purposes. 4to.

c.1870   New York   MH-BA
MASURY & WHITON - Globe White Lead & Color Works. Est. 1835. Succeeded by John W. Masury & Son. Ill. price list of railroad colors, ready made, and color samples for all purposes. 8vo., 32pp., pict. wrap.

1871   New York   NSbSM
MASURY, JOHN W. & SON. Successors to Masury & Whiton. Est. 1835. Ill. price list and catalog of pure white lead, zinc and

colors for artists, grainers, decorators and painters of carriages, railroad cars, coaches and dwellings, and all ornamental work. 12mo., 24pp., ill. of labels, plant and samples. Pict. wrap.

1872 New York   NSbSM
------ Ill. catalog for painters, etc.

c.1875 New York   NNMM
------ Sample book of fine colors for carriage, coach and car work. 11 pls., pict. wrap.

1880 Watson, N. Y.   NNQ
MOLLER & SCHUMANN. Coach varnishes, copals, furniture fillers and paints for interior and exterior. Ill. price list on fld. col. map. 16mo.

1881 Watson, N. Y.   NNQ
------ Large fld. col. map of Brooklyn with Moller & Schumann's price list, etc. 16mo., case.

nd. Cincinnati   NNMM
MOSER, CHARLES & CO. Color ill. price list of economy paints with house plans and directions, etc. 20 lvs., fine ills., pict. wrap.

1888 St. Paul, Minn.   MnHi
NOYES BROTHERS & CUTLER. Ill. price list and catalog of brushes, oils, paints and varnishes. 4to., 52pp.

c.1884 New York   NNMM
PIERCE, F.O. & CO. Color ill. catalog of paints with practical suggestions for house painting - paints and varnishes for architects. 31 lvs. with 24 fine col. pls. of homes painted with fantastic flashes of period imagination. Pict. wrap.

PITTSBURGH PLATE GLASS CO. Painters' Sundries. See Glass.

1887 New York   PKsL
RAYNOLDS, C.T. & CO. Sample book and price list of quick drying coach colors, ground in Japan - gold sizing - color chart, etc. See also Artists' Materials and Supplies - Devoe and also Raynolds, and Devoe & Raynolds.

c.1880 New York   NNMM
SEELEY BROTHERS, Mfg. of Averill Paint. In submitting this book . . . to show effect

of different colors on exterior of buildings. #1513. Loaned to . . . 4to., 8pp. and col. chart and 20 col. pls., litho. Sackett, Wilhelms & Betzig, of fine mansard roofed mansions and cottages with rooster and horse weathervanes depicting the last word as to what one should do with paint. c.1880, plus 2 more col. charts about the new Alabastine products. A catalog in essence.

1867 Philadelphia   PHi
SHOEMAKER, ROBERT & CO. Ill. catalog and price list of brushes, oils, paints and varnishes for painters - and all painters' supplies. 12mo., 40pp., wrap.

1858 New York & Manhattanville, N. Y.
TIEMANN, D.F. & CO. Tiemann's   NHi
colors, dry and ground, with oil and water - zinc and lead whites and color paints for June. 16mo., 26pp. with pict. wrap. of works at Manhattanville.

1889 New York   TxDaDeG
VALENTINE & CO. Ill. catalog with color samples of coach and railroad car varnishes and paints - none but the best - all colors. 12mo., 40pp., pict. wrap. of plant.

1882 Brooklyn, N. Y.   NNQ
WADSWORTH, MARTINEZ & LONGMAN. Ill. catalog and price list with homes and buildings in various combinations of garish colors for the most imaginative home owner. Sq. 16mo., 20pp. with 8 fine col. pls. and a swell pict. wrap.

1883 Brooklyn, N. Y.   NNQ
------ Ill. catalog with col. pls. and col. charts. 56pp., pict. wrap.

1872 Philadelphia   PHi
ZIEGLER & SMITH. Ill. catalog of white leads, zincs, colors, putty and supplies. Col. pls. of stained glass windows, etc. 8vo., 50pp., pict. wrap.

1873 Philadelphia   NNMM
------ Ill. catalog of paints and supplies, stained glass windows, homes, etc. 48pp., wrap.

1874 Philadelphia   PHi
------ Ill. catalog of paints and supplies - col. pls. and ills., col. pict. wrap.

Please use this section in conjunction with Artists' Materials and Supplies, Architectural Building Materials and last, but far from least, Drugs and Pharmaceuticals. Although there were no color charts, plates of painted buildings or fancy labels, the drug stores and general stores handling drugs, glass and household goods offered oils and paints as early as 1800. They do not give very much information about colors or ready-mixed paints of American manufacture until about 1850. They do, however, point out the probable manufacturing centers -- or at least the spots where the imported paints were available.

Chapter 40

Photographic Apparatus & Supplies

To the neophyte, or perhaps I should say to the average human being with no interest in this subject, photography is a profession to some and a hobby for many. If, however, you will start with an old family album, continue with a Photographic History of the Civil War, go through your bookshelves, stop in at a movie house or try an illustrated lecture, and then end up in front of your own TV set you will realize that photography influences your whole life --- it isn't just someone else's business or hobby. It dogs your every step from the daily newspaper to the Saturday Evening Post.

The catalogs offered in many repositories trace the history from about 1850. The George Eastman House in Rochester, N. Y. has the most complete collection for research --- and for the critic I will add, to the best of my knowledge. There are illustrated catalogs located from Boston to San Francisco. With the invention of the dry plate, the American camera became popular. Millions who couldn't understand and manage the complicated, messy wet plate process, swarmed to buy the new apparatus. Manufacturers of buttons, bicycles and sewing machines quickly jumped on the photographic band wagon. From about 1870 on this chapter offers a good solid sampling of the available pictorial record.

c.1885 Detroit   NRGE
  ALLEN BROTHERS. Ill. price list of photographic materials and supplies. 4to., 170pp.

1858 New York   DLC
AMERICAN STEREOSCOPIC CO.   NN
First catalog 1850 - not located. Catalog of
American and foreign slides and pictures,
and instruments. 12mo., 34pp.

The following agents are listed who also
issued catalogs for them:

Chamberlain, N. B.	Boston
Emmerick, F. J.	
Langenheim, W.	Philadelphia
McAllister & Bros.	Philadelphia
Pike, Benjamin & Son	New York
Queen, James W.	Philadelphia

1861 Philadelphia   PKsL
------ Catalog of Langenheim's new and
superior style col. photo. magic lantern
pictures, also dissolving view and stereopticon apparatus - microscopic photos. on
glass and paper, etc. 12mo., 36pp., wrap.

1861 Philadelphia & Boston   PKsL
------ Issued N. B. Chamberlain. 12mo.,
36pp., wrap. Magic lanterns with oil lamps
$35. Superior styles with calcium light $85.
List of pictures of the Civil War.

1862 Philadelphia   PKsL
------ Catalog of col. magic lantern pic-
tures of the American Civil War. Sold by
N. B. Chamberlain. 12mo., 16pp., wrap.

1898 San Francisco   CHi
  ANDREWS, T.P. Ill. catalog of photographic
  apparatus. 8vo., pict. wrap.

c.1850 New York   NHi
  ANTHONY, E. & H.T. & CO. Price list of
  apparatus for the ambrotype daguerrean and
  photographic business. Depot for C. C.
  Harrison's celebrated cameras. 8vo., 12pp.

N.B. The George Eastman House reports
that Eastman sold his early photographic
supplies through Anthony before he issued
his own catalogs.

1854 New York   NSyHi
       OrU   NNC   DLC   NN   NRGE
------ See also Snelling. A Dictionary of
the photographic art, forming a complete
encyclopaedia, etc. 8vo., IX, pl., 236pp.,
errata (1), and a complete and systematic
catalog of photographic apparatus and materials sold by . . . 56pp. and 13 pls. The
most outstanding catalog in the field in this
period.

1868 New York   CCuMGM
------ New catalog of stereoscopes and
views and photographic supplies. 8vo.,
44pp., wrap.

1877-99 New York   NRGE
------ The most outstanding collection at
any location, as follows:

1877 - Ill. catalog of photographic materi-
       als and supplies. 8vo., 72pp., wrap.

1881 - Ill. catalog of albums, easels, velvet frames, stereoscopes, plaques, graphoscopes, transparencies, etc. 4to., 80pp., wrap.

1884 - Ill. catalog of photographic apparatus. 4to., 138pp., fine ills.

1885 - Ill. catalog of amateur equipment and supplies. 72pp.

1886 - The Ferrotype - by Edward M. Estabrook - with a 16pp. ill. catalog of cameras and supplies. Pub. Anthony - 5th ed. 12mo., 176pp., cl.

N.B. Another fine example of using a popular work to catalog advantage.

1888 - Ill. catalog of amateur photography equipment. 8vo., 79pp.

1891 - Ill. catalog. 4to., 128pp.

1894 - Ill. price list. 4to., 185pp.

1896 - Desc. catalog and price list. 4to., 190pp.

1898 - Ill. catalog of cameras, lamps, tools, magic lanterns, etc. Large 8vo., 158pp., pict. wrap.

1899 - Ill. catalog of photographic equipment for amateurs. 4to., 135pp.

1886 New York   MBSPNEA
------ Ill. catalog of magic lanterns, lamps, cameras, bicycle camera, etc. 12mo., 80pp. of ills., pict. wrap.

1891 New York   NNNAM
------ Ill. catalog of photographic equipment for amateurs. 132pp.

1895 New York   NSyHi
------ Desc. and ill. catalog of photographic apparatus, studio furniture, original birdie, cameras, etc. for March.

1889 Boston   NRGE
BAKER & STARBIRD. How to make photographs, with desc. price list of apparatus and materials. Sm. 4to., 123pp., pict. wrap.

c.1876 New York   NRGE
BALDWIN, ANDREW H. Ill. catalog of reduced prices of all photographic stock. 8vo., 48pp., wrap.

1900-1912 Rochester, N.Y.   NRGE
BAUSCH & LOMB. NRGE has a fine collection starting with 1900 but too late for this guide.

BAUSCH & LOMB. Photographic lenses, etc. See Optical and Scientific Apparatus.

c.1883 Boston   MBSPNEA
BLAIR TOUROGRAPH & DRY PLATE CO. Annual catalog - ills. of Blair cameras, tripods, ruby lanterns, drying racks, etc. 16mo., 24pp., fine ills., pict. wrap.

1886 Boston   MBSPNEA
BLAIR CAMERA CO. Successors to Blair Tourograph & Dry Plate Co. Ill. catalog of cameras and supplies, detective and concealed cameras, etc. Sq. 12mo., 40pp., pict. wrap.

c.1888 Boston   MH-BA
------ Ill. catalog of the Lucidograph camera and attachments and supplies. 8vo., 8pp.

1891 Boston   NRGE
------ Ill. catalog of photographic apparatus. Large 8vo., 64pp., wrap.

1893 Boston   NRGE
------ Ill. catalog. 4to., 45 and 4pp.

1897-99 Boston   NRGE
------ 5 ill. catalogs of cameras and supplies.

1863 London, England   NRGE
BLAND & CO. Ill. catalog of apparatus and chemical preparations used in photography. 8vo., 112pp. with fine ills.

c.1900 Chicago   ICHi
BOSWELL ELECTRICAL & OPTICAL CO. Est. 1892. Ill. catalog of photographic materials and accessories, stereoscopes, views, improved optograph - apparently a stereopticon converted into a moving picture machine. 8vo., 56pp.

COOKE LENSES. See Taylor, Taylor & Hobson, Ltd.

c.1900 St. Louis   MoSHi
CRAMER, G. DRY PLATE CO. Catalog of isochromatic lighting and non-halatan pls., etc. 16mo., 32pp., pict. wrap.

c.1897 New York   NRGE
CULLEN, WILLIAM C. Ill. catalog and price list of lenses, photographic outfits, supplies, etc. 4to., 144pp., fine ills.

nd. Rochester, N.Y.   NRGE
DEFENDER PHOTOGRAPH SUPPLY CO. Ill. catalog of Defender products. 16mo., 20pp., wrap.

c.1886 Rochester, N.Y.   NRGE
EASTMAN DRY PLATE & FILM CO. -- NOW Eastman Kodak Co. How to make paper negatives with an ill. catalog and price list of Eastman Dry Plate and Film Co. 4to., 48pp. Eastman sold his apparatus and supplies through Anthony before this.

1886-1900 Rochester, N. Y.   NRGE
------ Ill. catalogs of various dates and
sizes with a complete line. Also about 30
catalogs from 1900 to 1925.

1890-1900 Rochester, N. Y.   NR
------ Collection of ill. catalogs as above.

1898 New York   NNNAM
FOLMER & SCHWING MFG. CO. Ill. catalog and price list of photographic apparatus,
magic lanterns and supplies. 80pp. and 2
lvs., fine ills.

c.1898 Chicago   ICHi
FOWLERS' - Opticians. Ill. catalog of
cameras and supplies for amateurs. 8vo.,
66pp., pict. wrap.

1895 Boston   NRGE
FRENCH, BENJAMIN & CO. Ill. catalog of
photographic materials of every description.
8vo., 63pp.

c.1896 Berlin, Germany & New York   N
GOERZ, C.P. OPTICAL WORKS. Ill.price
list of double-astigmatic lenses for cameras.
8vo., 20pp., pict. wrap. of plant.

1899 Rochester, N. Y.   NRGE
GUNDLACH OPTICAL CO. Ill.   NR
catalog of Korona cameras, lenses and
photographic supplies, etc. 8vo., 36pp.,
fine ills., wrap. Also several ill. circulars.

1885 Detroit   NRGE
HARRIS & KITTLE. Ill. catalog of cameras
and supplies. Large 8vo., 186pp., wrap.

c.1900 Philadelphia   PHi
HELIOS CHEMICAL CO. Ill. catalog of
Helios electrical flashlight lamps for photog-
raphers. 16mo., 24pp., pict. wrap.

HELIOTYPE PRINTING CO. See Printers'
Samples.

c.1898 San Francisco   CHi
HIRSCH & KAISER. Ill. catalog of cameras,
plates, papers, apparatus and supplies. 2nd
ed. Also have 4th, 5th and 9th ed.

1894 Boston   MH-BA
HORGAN, ROBEY & CO. (Agents for Eastman Kodak Co.) Ill. catalog of kodaks and
cameras and accessories. 8vo., 60pp.

1847 New York   NRGE
HORSLEY, P.N. Prices of daguerreotype
apparatus and supplies. 2 page circular.
Prices supplied in ink and mailed to South-
worth & Co. June 18, 1847.

HOSMER - Agent. See Rochester Optical
Co.

1870 San Francisco   CHi
HOUSEWORTH, THOMAS & CO. Ill. catalog
of photographic views of scenery on Pacific
Coast. 16mo., 70pp., pict. wrap.

c.1890 New Haven   CtHi
HOWE & STETSON. Cyclone cameras -
how they are made. Ills. of models 1, 2, 3
with examples of work. 16mo., 22pp., pict.
wrap. Ptd. Chicago. Possibly Cyclone
cameras were made by the Western Camera
Mfg. Co. See also Western.

1856 New York   NRGE
HUMPHREY, S.D. Comm. dealer. Retail
price list of ambrotype, daguerrean and
photographic chemicals, apparatus, plates,
cases, glass, paper, etc. Reported by NRGE
as an 18 page appendix to W. H.Thornwaite's
Guide to Photography.

1899 Pittsburgh, Pa.   NRGE
JOHNSTON, WM. G. & CO. Simplified
photography, revised. 4to., 50pp., ill.

nd. New York   NN
KENT, EDWARD N. Desc. catalog of
daguerreotype apparatus and photographic
chemicals for sale by . . .

1900 Boston   NRGE
LLOYD, ANDREW J. & CO. Lloyd's MCM
photographic encyclopaedia of cameras,
apparatus and supplies. 4to., 384pp., pict.
wrap.

1856 New York   NHi
LUHME, J.F. & CO. Prices current of
chemicals, apparatus and utensils for
photographers, daguerreotypists and elec-
trotypists. 8vo., 16pp., early ills., for July.
See also other listing under Drugs.

1855 Philadelphia   PHi
M'CLEES, JAMES E. Elements of
Photography - with a 4 page ill. catalog of
supplies for sale by . . . 16mo., 36 and
4pp.

1881 Philadelphia   NRGE
McCOLLON, THOMAS H. Price current of
photographic goods. 4to., 14pp.

1882 St. Louis   MoSHi
MALLINCKRODT CHEMICAL WORKS.
Photographic memoranda. Facsimile only
reported.

1896 Cresskill, N. J.   PKsL
MANHATTAN OPTICAL CO. Ill. catalog of
photographic lenses, cameras and supplies.
8vo., 32pp. - with Baby Wizard Camera ill.
circular tipped in. Pict. wrap.

1897 Cresskill, N. J.   NjR
------ Ill. catalog of lenses and supplies.
12mo., 48pp., pict. wrap.

1893-1900 Chicago   MoSHi
MARSHALL FIELD & CO. 2 catalogs reported:

    1893-4 - Ill. catalog of holiday goods with a
    fine section of cameras and sup-
    plies.

    1900 - Ill. catalog of cameras and appara-
    tus.

1882 New York   NRGE
MORAN, RICHARD H. Central Stock House.
Ill. price list of photographic supplies and
materials. Large 8vo., 36pp., wrap.

c.1899 London, England   NRGE
NEGRETTI & ZAMBRA. Encyclopaedic ill.
and desc. ref. catalog of optical, photographic etc. instruments, apparatus and supplies.
4to., 602pp., fine ills.

1886 New York   NRGE
OBRIG CAMERA CO. (Agent for Scovill
Mfg. Co.) How to make photographs with a
desc. price list, well ill. Large 8vo., 106pp.

1884 New York   NN
PEARL, EUGENE ART CO. Jobber for
Scovill Mfg. Co. How to make photographs
with ill. catalog of art specialties, amateur
photo. outfits, accessories, supplies, plus
40pp. of Scovill camera requisites. Pict.
wrap.

1900 Minneapolis   MnHi
PECK, O.H. Ill. catalog and price list of
amateur and professional photographic supplies. 8vo., 226pp.

PLATT & HULL. Ambrotype and daguerrian stock. See House Furnishings.

QUEEN, JAMES W. & CO. See Optical and
Scientific Apparatus.

c.1900 Yonkers, N. Y.   N
REFLEX CAMERA CO. Desc. catalog and
price list of pat. reflex hand cameras. 8vo.,
33pp., ills.

1886 Milwaukee   NRGE
REIMERS & KATZ. Price list of photographic stock. 8vo., 48pp., ill.

1892 Rochester, N. Y.   MnHi
ROCHESTER CAMERA MFG. CO. Ill. catalog and price list of photographic apparatus. 4to., 16pp.

1893 Rochester, N. Y.   NR
------ Ill. catalog. 8vo., 56pp., wrap.

1897 Rochester, N. Y.   N
------ Ill. catalog. 8vo., 80pp., pict. wrap.

1885 Rochester, N. Y.   NRGE
ROCHESTER OPTICAL CO. Ill. and desc.
catalog and price list of photographic apparatus. 8vo., 24pp.

1886 Rochester, N. Y.   NRGE
------ Ill. catalog. 8vo., 30pp., wrap.

c.1890 Rochester, N. Y.   NRGE
------ Ill. catalog of Premo cameras.
32pp., pict. wrap.

1893 Rochester, N. Y.   MNBedf
------ Ill. catalog of cameras - models,
Handy, Katch, Midget, Premier, etc. 8vo.,
56pp., pict. wrap.

1894 Rochester, N. Y.   NRGE
------ Ill. catalog and price list. 64pp.

1895 Rochester, N. Y.   NRGE
------ Ill. catalog of 68pp. Pict. wrap.

1898 Rochester, N. Y.   NRGE
------ The Premo camera. 12mo., 79pp.,
wrap.

1899 Rochester, N. Y.   CHi
------ (Agent, H. B. Hosmer of San
Francisco.) Ill. catalog.

1878 Waterbury, Conn. & New York   NRGE
SCOVILL MFG. CO. Est. 1802. SCOVILL
& ADAMS CO. c. 1890, New York. Desc.,
ill. catalog and price list of photographic
apparatus mfg. by American Optical Co.
8vo., 35pp., wrap.

1887 New York   NRGE
------ How to make photographs with ill.
catalog. 8vo., 106pp. See also two others
for 1887.

c.1887 Waterbury, Conn. & New York NRGE
------ Ill. catalog of photographic albums,
publications and apparatus. Issued for C.H.
Codman & Co., agent, Boston. 8vo., 42pp.,
pict. wrap.

1887 New York   NHi
------ How to make pictures by H.C. Price,
with a 38 page ill. catalog of Scovill photographic apparatus and supplies. 8vo., 88pp.,
pict. wrap.

1888 New York   NRGE
------ Ill. catalog of photographic supplies
and apparatus made by American Optical Co.
Large 8vo., 78pp., pict. wrap.

1888 New York   N
------ The photographic negative by W.H.
Burbank with an ill. catalog of Scovill supplies for the cameraman. 8vo., 198pp.,
pict. cl.

1892 New York   NN
SCOVILL & ADAMS CO. Picture making in
the studio by H.P. Robinson with an ill. catalog of Scovill products. 8vo., 62pp., pict.
wrap.

1893 New York   NRGE
------ How to make photographs with ill.
catalog. 152 and VIIpp., pict. wrap.

1898 New York   NRGE
------ How to make photographs, etc. with
ill. catalog. 109pp.

SCOVILL. See also Obrig Camera Co. and
Pearl Art Co.

1858 New York
SEELEY & GARABANATI, Photographic
Chemists. Catalog of apparatus, materials
and pure chemicals mfg. expressly for the
photographic art. 33pp. with ills. Reported
by NRGE.

1849   CSmH
SNELLING, HENRY HUNT. See   NRGE
Anthony, E. & H.T. & Co. Editions for 1849,
1850 and 1851 did not include the Anthony
catalog.

c.1883 St. Louis   MoSHi
SOULE PHOTOGRAPH CO. Catalog of art
reproductions.

1865 Ravenna, O.   OHi
STEIN BROTHERS. Photographers' improved glass decanters for treating nitrate
of silver baths. 4to. broadside.

1899 Rochester, N.Y.   NRGE
SUNART PHOTO CO. Ill. catalog. 8vo.,
56pp.

1890 Chicago   ICHi
SWEET, WALLACH & CO. Ill. catalog of
Puck cameras for cyclists, tourists and
sportsmen, with price list of materials and
supplies. 12mo., 16pp., order blanks, pict.
wrap. of Puck at work on a bike.

c.1890 Chicago   NRGE
------ Catalog of studio apparatus and
supplies. 4to., 128pp., fine ills.

c.1892 Chicago   NRGE
------ Price list of apparatus. 8vo. with
112pp., well ill.

c.1900 New York & Leicester, England NR
TAYLOR, TAYLOR & HOBSON, LTD. Ill.
price list of Cooke lenses for photographers.
8vo., 20pp., wrap.

1887 Chicago   NRGE
THAYER, N.C. & CO. Ill., desc. and priced
catalog of photographers' supplies. 4to.,
203 and XXIXpp.

1897 Chicago   ICHi
VIVE CAMERA CO. Ill. catalog of Vives,
the perfect cameras, also photo. supplies.
Sq. 8vo., 12pp., pict. wrap.

1899 Chicago   MnHi
------ Ill. catalog of Vive daylight tourist
and MPC cameras and supplies. Sq. 8vo.,
50pp., index, pict. wrap.

1896 Walpole, Mass.   NRGE
WALPOLE CHEMICAL WORKS. About hypo,
useful hints from the Walpole Dye & Chemical Works. 24mo., 64pp.

c.1875 Baltimore   NRGE
WALZL, RICHARD. The photographers'
friend - 4th ed. Reduced price list of stereoscopic goods and photo. supplies. 12mo.,
128pp., fine ills.

1882 Baltimore   NRGE
------ 7th ed. Fine ills., 4to., 127pp.

1897 Chicago   ICHi
WESTERN CAMERA MFG. CO. Ill. catalog
and price list of photographic apparatus,
Cyclone cameras, etc. Tall 12mo., 20pp.,
pict. wrap.

c.1900 Chicago   PShipL
------ Ill. catalog of Cyclone cameras and
photo. supplies. 8vo., 72pp., col. pict. wrap.

c.1898 Philadelphia   PKsL
WILLIS & CLEMENTS. Platinotype process
for permanent printing with photo. frs.
18mo., 18pp., wrap.

nd. Baltimore   DLC
WISONG, WILLIAM A. Catalog and price
list of daguerreotype materials and supplies
for sale at Wm. A. Wisong's daguerreotypists' furnishing establishment. 1 page, reported by NRGE. Damaged copy from the
notebook of George S. Cook.

1870 Portland, Ore.   OrHi
WOODWARD & QUIVEY. Woodward &
Quivey's Oregon depot for photo. goods and
artists' supplies. 16mo., 27 and 5pp.
McMurtrie #604.

1899 Chicago   NRGE
YALE CAMERA CO. Ill. catalog and price
list of cameras and kodaks and photographic
apparatus of every desc. 8vo., 96pp.

PHOTOGRAPHIC APPARATUS

Naturally the catalogs located in the chapters Magic Lanterns and Stereopticons - Medical & Surgical Supplies, and last but far from least - Optical & Scientific Apparatus, all contain illustrations of photographic chemicals, lanterns, slides, materials and supplies. I have selected those that are pure photography and those pages are mostly in this field. Time and space will not permit complete cross indexing, so please consult these three sections as well.

Chapter 41

Plumbing—Wood, Lead, Brass & Chromium

Many currently used words when applied to the 19th century change strangely in meaning. Although we at Weathercock House on our 35 acres still listen for the pump to stop before drawing water for a shower or filling the pool in the garden, it would never occur to most of our spoiled 20th century city dwellers. When our well here went dry as it did many times before we drove the artesian, you just didn't take a shower - and that was that. The old one family two-holer still stands just south of the barn. The cast iron hand pump still guards the home carpentered cover to the hand stoned twenty-eight foot well that never went dry until we put in the bathroom. I even rather like the old tub with its claw and ball stubby legs even though it's the devil and all to clean under and behind. If you live in New York City or some other great melting pot of humanity you can never understand the pleasantness of a place like this.

I am really having fun putting this chapter together. The illustrations in these 19th century catalogs are real and have meaning. To most collectors and historians they are almost antiques to be stored away and stared at in a museum. If you really want to thoroughly appreciate your hot and cold running water, your built in showers, tiled bath and chromium fittings, look up one of Hayden, Saunders' catalogs for 1860, then one of J. L. Mott's for 1894 and then a Rundle-Spence for 1900; those three should do it. From the outhouse for 1850 to the drawing room bawth at the turn of the century, this chapter provides material for amusing and interesting research. If you remember them and used them, they're great -- If you never saw such contraptions before, they are just as fascinating.

1878 New York   DeU
ADEE, FRED. Ill. catalog of specialties in plumbing and sanitary goods - most approved styles in toilets, tubs and fancy plumbing. 12mo., 64pp.

1894 New York   DeU
------ Ill. catalog #28. Plates of gold rimmed claw feet seat and foot tubs, embossed closets, Hyde's pat. fancy tubs. 4to., 90pp.

1877 San Francisco   CHi
AMERICAN PIPE CO. Catalog of wood pipe for water and gas. 12mo., 60pp., wrap.

c.1870 Philadelphia   PKsL
BLESSING, C.A. Late Mulligan, Feather & Co. Ill. catalog of plumbers' metal work, copper tubs, oak frames, shower heads, etc. 12mo., 22pp., pict. wrap. Preface states that this is the only ill. catalog of plumbers' copper ware in print. Quite up to date -- more people drink, drive, eat and use more Hopsey-Popsey than any other brand in the United States.

1873 New York   NHi
CARR, A. Ill. catalog of brass work and supplies for plumbers - tubs, showers, fau-

cets, sinks, washstands, pumps - also lanterns for street, opera house, etc. Tall 4to., 192pp., dec. cl.

1866 New York   MH-BA
COLWELLS, SHAW & WILLARD. Price list with tests. of pat. lead-encased block tin pipe for plumbers. 8vo., 58pp.

1877-98 Chicago   ICHi
CRANE CO. Est. 1855. Three fine ill. catalogs for 1877, 1878 and 1898.

1897 Baltimore   DSi
CUYLER & MOHLER. Ill. catalog of plumbers' general supplies. 284pp., fine pict. record.

1870 Boston   MH-BA
DALTON-INGERSOLL CO. Price list of plumbers' supplies. 8vo., 100pp., cl.

1891 Boston   MH-BA
------ Ill. catalog of plumbers' supplies and sanitary specialties. 4to., 124pp., dec. cl.

1881 Chicago   ICHi
DAVIS, JOHN & CO. Ill. catalog of plumbers' supplies.

1885 San Francisco   CHi
DAY, THOMAS & CO. Agent. Ill. catalog
and price list of brass goods, wash basins,
stands, tubs, pipe, etc. 4to., 600pp., fine
pict. record, bds., with 12 fine col. pls. of
hand painted tubs, etc. to boot.

1881 North Dighton, Mass.   MTaOC
DIGHTON FURNACE CO. Ill. catalog of
plumbing and sanitary goods, traps, hoppers,
sinks, etc. 12mo., 40pp., wrap.

1890 Philadelphia   PHi
FLECK BROTHERS. Ill. catalog and price
list of water, gas and steam supplies - tubs,
bowls, sinks, stands, kitchen sinks, etc.
4to., 300pp., dec. cl.

c.1890 Grand Rapids, Mich.   MiU-H
FOUNTAIN BATH BRUSH CO. The fountain
way - tinted ills. of shower brush for tub or
bedroom. Simple as rolling off a log. Sq.
12mo., 16pp., pict. wrap.

1865 New York   ICHi
FULLER, ALBERT. Ill. catalog of plumbers' goods - fancy faucets, shampoo shower,
tubs, etc. - promises catalog with full new
line soon. 8vo., 40pp., bds.

1896-7 San Francisco   CHi
GARRATT, W.T. & CO.

  1896 - Rev. price list #2. Ills. of brass and
  iron bells, pumps and castings. 8vo.,
  32pp., dec. wrap.

  1897 - Rev. price list #4. Ill. catalog of
  plumbers' findings, etc. 8vo., 40pp.,
  dec. wrap.

c.1881 New Haven   CtHi
GILBERT, J.F. & CO. Ill. catalog and price
list of heaters, regulators, pipes, joints,
traps, tools, etc. 16mo., col. pict. wrap.

c.1882 New Haven   CtHi
------ Ill. catalog of plumbers' fittings,
etc. The Gooding pressure regulator, etc.
32mo., 8pp., pict. wrap.

1876 Akron, O.   NHi
GOODYEAR RUBBER CO. The carpet bag
bath, a bath for the millions. Ills. of portable bath for parlor, bedroom and kitchen.
16mo., 8pp., pict. wrap.

1890 Philadelphia   PHi
HAINES, JONES & CADBURY CO. Ill. catalog of plumbers', gas and steam fitters'
supplies, heaters to tubs, etc. 4to.

1878 New York   DSi
HARRISON, CHARLES & CO. Ill. catalog of
copper, iron and earthenware apparatus,

hand painted bowls, basins, tubs, walnut
wash stands, foot baths in iron, etc. 4to.,
412pp., 8 col. pls. with other pls. throughout, dec. cl.

1879 New York   NNMM
------ Ill. catalog of bowls, flushes and
tubs of the fanciest imagination. 16mo.,
74pp., pict. wrap. Grand!

nd. Hartford, Conn.   CtHi
HARTFORD SANITARY PLUMBING CO.
The Glass Water Closet - most perfect
closet in the world - one ill. of this charm-
ing creation. 4 page, 16mo. folder.

1877 New York & Haydenville, Mass. MoSHi
HAYDEN, GERE & CO. (Stamped L. M.
Rumsey & Co., St. Louis, agent.) Ill. catalog of wash bowls in color, steamboat and
railroad toilets, etc., flushes and pumps.
8vo., fine ills.

1860 New York   ICHi
HAYDEN, SAUNDERS & CO. Ill. price list
of plumbers' brasswork, cocks, sinks,
basins, marble slabs, stands, fancy showers.
4to., 102pp., bd.

c.1878 New York   DSi
JAMER, JACOBS & CO. Ill. catalog of iron
pipe and plumbers' supplies. 56pp.

1885 New York   NHi
LEWIS & CONGER. A list of portable bathing apparatus, delightful ills. 8vo., 8pp.,
pict. wrap. Little, but Oh Mi.

1899 Trenton, N. J.   PKsL
MADDOCK, THOMAS & SONS. Ill. catalog
of sanitary earthenware, and specialties pertaining to the plumbing business. 12 col.
pls. of bowls and tubs with hand painted
roses and posies, wild birds in profusion -
the fanciest ever printed. Tall 4to., 72pp.
of imagination for the Gay Ninety bath.

1893 New York   DSi
MAYOR, LANE & CO. Ill. catalog of plumbing supplies. 616pp., a fine exhaustive ref.

1875 New York   NHi
MEYER, HENRY C. & CO. Ill. catalog of
brass work and plumbers' materials -
French jets, walnut wash stands, carved
corner stands, bowls, tubs, etc. 8vo., 232pp.
Fine ills., dec. cl.

1877 New York   N
------ Ill. catalog of plumbing supplies -
the fanciest and best. 8vo., 187 plus 51pp.,
ill. throughout, wrap.

1892 Chicago   ICHi
MOSELEY FOLDING BATH CO.   NHi
Bathing made easy - the comforts of -

delightful ills. of folding tubs, etc. 8vo.,
16pp., pict. wrap. These would inspire a
TV program - The Mosely Murder. They
had it all over the Murphy Folding bed for
fooling the detectives.

1881 New York   DeWint
MOTT, J.L. IRON WORKS. NBB NNMM
Ill. catalog of plumbing supplies, fancy bathrooms, hand painted bowls, tubs, etc. and
ornamental ironwork for home and stable.
8vo., 248pp., dec. cl.

1884 New York   ICHi
------ Catalog D -- the bathroom, laundry,
kitchen and butlers' pantry. 4to., 82pp. of
ills. and col. pls., dec. cl.

1888 New York   DSi
------ Catalog G - Sanitary Plumbing
Department. Plumbing supplies - fine col.
pls. of bowls, basins, stands, tubs and on to
pipes, faucets, etc. 4to., 277pp., dec. cl.

1872 Hartford, Conn.   CtHi
MOULE & CO. Moule's pat. earth   MiD
closet - the dry earth system - cheap,
simple and very effective. Fine ills.
throughout. 16mo., 26pp., swell pict. wrap.

1897 St. Louis   MoSHi
NELSON, N.O. MFG. CO. Catalog B - #25.
Ill. catalog of plumbers', gas and steam fit-
ters' supplies.

1900 St. Louis   MoSHi
------ Catalog C - #27. Plumbers' supplies. 12mo., 648pp. of prices and ills.

1895 Philadelphia   PHi
OWEN & SALTER. Ill. catalog and price
list of plumbing goods and supplies, also for
gas and steam fitters. 4to., 313pp. - 13 of
which are supplies for beer works and breweries, dec. cl.

1893 New Haven   CtHi
PECK BROTHERS & CO. Ill. catalog of
plumbing and sanitary supplies. Architects'
ed. Pls. of basins, bowls, tubs, etc. also
ironwork. 4to., XVI and 328pp., dec. cl.

1893 New Haven   N
------ Plumbers' ed. of our ill. catalog of
plain and fancy plumbing fixtures, bowls,
hand painted basins, etc. Col. pls., 4to.,
588pp., dec. cl. Exhaustive ref.

1893 New Haven   NNMM
------ Ill., desc. and priced general catalog of plumbing and sanitary work. Excellent pls., col. pls. with details. 4to., 598pp.,
golf stamped cvs.

1893 New Haven   MH-BA
------ Ill. catalog of pneumatic syphon
water closets. 4to., 38pp., pict. wrap.

N.B. A good example of the mass of ill.
catalogs flooding the market by 1893. Some
firms issued dozens in one year, all quite
different - and in this case 4 preserved in 4
different locations.

c.1877 Rochester, N. Y.   MH-BA
PNEUMATIC WATER APPARATUS CO. Ill.
brochure of water works supplies for village
and country homes - swell ills. of pumps
and apparatus. 8vo., 8pp.

1888 Providence, R. I.   RHi
PROVIDENCE LEAD CO. Ill. catalog of
plumbers' specialties and general supplies,
fancy baths, etc. 4to., 20pp., pict. wrap.

RUMSEY, L.M. & CO. See Hayden, Gere &
Co.

1900 Milwaukee   NHi
RUNDLE-SPENCE MFG. CO. Catalog D -
ills. of drawing room type baths 15 x 20,
frescoed walls, stained glass windows, gold
decorated basins, bowls, tubs, etc. The new
look for 1900. 4to., 602pp., dec. cl.

1885 Pittsburgh, Pa.   NNMM
STANDARD MFG. CO. Ill. catalog of plumbers' ware, supplies and fixtures - desc. and
priced - hand painted and luxurious - the
last word. 4to., pp. 1-7, 8-218 and 217, glt.
ptd. cl.

1888 Pittsburgh, Pa.   PHi
------ Plumbing and Sanitary Dept. Ill.
catalog of sanitary plumbing goods. Over
250pp. of ills. and pls., some in full col. of
floral and scenic tubs on cast iron ball and
claw feet, delightful ceramic closets as The
Securo, sitz baths, silver pipes, oak tanks,
etc. A fine pict. record. 4to., 250pp., cl.

1893 Pittsburgh, Pa.
------ Ill. catalog of sanitary plumbing
goods. 4to., 204pp., ills., pls. and col. pls.,
cl.

1898 Pittsburgh, Pa.   NNMM
------ Catalog S - 12 col. pls. for scenic
and floral hand painted tubs, basins, bowls,
etc. Swell job. 4to., 342pp. of pls. and ills.
Ptd. cl.   N.B. PHi has a copy of the 1909
issue. Practically up to date, with suggestions to builders or those about to remodel
present dwellings. How about yours?

1884 Springfield, Mass.   PPL
STEBBINS, E. MFG. CO. Ill. catalog of
plumbers' supplies - pipes, faucets, fittings,
showers, tubs, etc. 84pp. with 182 ills.

UNITED BRASS CO. See Thomas Day,
agent.

1895 Schenectady   VtSM
VAN VRANKEN AUTOMATIC FLUSH TANK
CO. Ill. catalog and price list of the Van
Vranken automatic flush. 8vo., 24pp., de-
lightful pict. wrap.

1889 Detroit   MiU-H
WALKER, JAMES & SON. Ill. catalog and
price list of brass, copper and iron plumbers goods and tools - corner wash stands,
sinks, tubs, etc. 8vo., 167pp., dec. cl.

WALWORTH, JAMES J. & CO. <u>See</u> Hardware - Miscellaneous Machinery.

1870 Philadelphia   MH-BA
WOOD, R.D. & CO. Ill. price list of cast-
iron pipes, fittings, etc. and even fancy lamp
posts, etc. 12mo., 40pp., wrap.

Architectural Building Materials, Pumps and Water Wheels and Windmills, all fit the Plumbing
picture of this day before yesterday - use them in conjunction with the following listings and maybe
you'll come to understand why I still paint the old outhouse by the barn and the iron hand pump over
the well.

Chapter 42

Printers' Specimens, Presses & Equipment

If there had been no type founders or printers there could have been no trade catalogs; ipso facto, this chapter and its running mate which follows are two of the most if not the most important chapters in this volume. Trite but true. Consequently I have done my best to make this gathering of locations as representative as possible. I am indebted to Mr. Ralph Green of Chicago for the privilege of using his Check List of American 19th Century Type Specimen Books privately printed in 1951. Mr. Green listed only specimen books by type founders, and covered the collections of only fourteen institutions, as well as a dozen private collections. The latter have been noted as PC. This chapter covers locations in forty institutions, and includes printing presses, tools, materials and supplies. It also includes broadside lists of type and ornaments from the 18th century not generally considered catalogs by gentlemen of the old school.

From the type specimens of the famous White family c.1812, to the then fabulous Hoe printing machines of 1899, the student ought to be able to find records of almost every American type, ornament and press.

NNC has a collection of printing equipment catalogs, presses, stamps, stencils, cuts, etc. Though it numbers probably two thousand, it has not been possible to include a complete list. Outstanding records have been set down.

PC - used to make copies extant known.

RG - used for Ralph Green's Check List. 1951.

1874 New York & Boston   ICN
ADAMS PRESS CO. Ill. price list of presses, type, cuts and borders. 8vo., 32pp., wrap.

c.1004 Cincinnati   CSmH
ALLISON & SMITH. Condensed specimen book and price list of wood type and printers' materials. See also Franklin Type Foundry.

1895-1900 New York   Locations
AMERICAN TYPEFOUNDERS   as follows
CO. Est. 1892. A merger of 23 type foundries. Type specimens, printing materials, and presses. 16mo. to fol., as follows: Pls. and ills., some in col.

1895	4to.	752pp.	PC	NNC
c.1895	4to.	292pp.		NNC
1896	16mo.	625pp.		PC
1896	8vo.	488pp.	PC	NNC
1896	4to.	810pp.	RP	ICN	NNC

c.1896	4to.	766pp.	ICN	NNC
1897	16mo.	934pp.	ICN	NNC
1897	8vo.	714pp.		RG
1897	8vo.	507pp.	PC	NNC
1898	16mo.	946pp.	ICN PC	MWA RG
1898	16mo.	934pp.	PC	MoU
1898	8vo.	522pp.		RG
1898	12mo.	6 lvs. and 1024pp.	NNC PC	MiD
1899	16mo.	918pp.		NNC
1899	12mo.	674pp.		NNC
1899	12mo.	1024pp.	PC	RG
1900	8vo.	950pp.		CSmH

1883 South Windham, Conn.   ICN
AMERICAN WOOD TYPE CO. Specimens for 1883.

c.1885 South Windham, Conn.   CSmH
------ Specimens of wood type.

1878 Philadelphia   MH-BA
AYER, N.W. & SON. Est. 1841. Manual for advertisers, publishers and advt. agents in U.S. and Canada. 5th ed. Large 8vo.,

164pp., cl. N.B. This does not fit here, but where would you put it? These are the folks who used the printers and their type.

1881 Philadelphia   CSmH
------ Ill. price list of printing machines and supplies. 56pp.

1886 New London, Conn.   CtNlC
BABCOCK PRINTING PRESS CO. Ill. catalog of drum cylinder two revolution Babcock presses with desc. for printers and publishers. 4to., 12pp., 2 ills.

1804-1892 Baltimore   Locations
BALTIMORE TYPE FOUNDRY. as follows
Merged with American Typefounders 1892.
Type specimens as follows.

1832 - F. Lucas, Jr. 12mo., 113 lvs.			NNC
1851 - F. Lucas, Jr. 8vo., 240 lvs.			NNC
1854 - Lucas Brothers. 8vo., 229 lvs.			NNC
1879 - H. L. Pelouze & Son. 8vo., 96pp.			NNC
1883 - Chas. J. Carey & Co. 4to., 138 lvs.			NNC MH
1884 - ------ 16mo., 192pp.		MH	CSmH
1886 - ------ 8vo., 179pp.			NNC
1888 - ------ 8vo., 368pp.		ICN	NNC

1873-1900 Chicago   Locations
BARNHART BROTHERS &   as follows
SPINDLER. Formerly Great Western Type
Foundry. Later merged with American
Type Foundry. Type specimens.

1873	8vo.	213 lvs.	PC	NNC
1880	4to.	210 lvs.	PC	
1881	4to.	219 lvs.	PC ICN	NNC
c.1883	4to.	214 lvs.	NN MH	NNC
1885	16mo.	113 lvs.	MH	NNC
1888	8vo.	96 lvs.		MH
1889	12mo.	443 lvs.	ICN PC	NNGr NNC
1893-4	16mo.	494 lvs. Pony specimen book.	NNC	MWA
1893-4	16mo.	550 lvs.	PC	CtMK

c.1895	4to.	323 lvs.	PC	RP
c.1895	16mo.	578 lvs.		NNC
c.1896	4to.	323 lvs.		NNC
1898	16mo.	563 lvs.	RP NNC	ICN and 6 in PC
nd.	4to.	124pp.		NNMM
1900	4to.	880pp.	OrU MWA	CSmH

- Just in case you want to go this far -
1930 4to.   708 and 11pp. #25.   MnHi

1889 New York   CSmH
BARTRAM, F.S. & C.B. Specimens of modern types. Large 8vo., 78 lvs., dec. cl.

1874-93 Milwaukee   Locations
BENTON, GOVE & CO. and   as follows
BENTON, WALDO & CO. Merged with
American Type Founders 1893. Type specimens as follows:

c.1883	4to.	120pp.	NNC
c.1884	8vo.	192pp.	MH
1888	8vo.	190pp.	MH
c.1888	8vo.	166pp.	NNC
c.1890	8vo.	190pp.	NNC
1893	8vo.	272pp.	ICN CtMK

1809-16 Philadelphia   Locations
BINNY & RONALDSON.   as follows
Succeeded by James Ronaldson. Specimens
from the foundry of . . .

1809	12mo.	23 lvs.	NNC
1812	16mo.	126 lvs.	NNC CSmH
1812	12mo.	41 lvs.	PPAmP
nd.	16mo.	44 lvs.	NNC
c.1810	12mo.	261 lvs. and 3.	NNC

1839-41 Philadelphia   NNC
BINNY, JOHN. Archibald   RP   MH
Binny's son.

1839   Bullen's 1933 catalog.

1841   4to.   50 lvs. MH RP   NNC

1884-86 Philadelphia   ICJ
BLANC, A. Type specimens for 1884 and 1886.

1894	Boston		MWA

BOSTON GLOBE. Specimen book of display types.

1896	Boston		MWA

------ Specimen book of display types.

1820-45 Boston   Locations
BOSTON TYPE & STEREOTYPE as follows
FOUNDRY. (John G. Rogers, agent.) 1817
to c.1850. Type specimens:

1820, 1825 and 1826 from Bullen's 1933 catalog. RG reports no longer at NNC.

1827	8vo.	(Updike Collection)	RP	
1828			NNC	NNMM
1829				MWA
1832	8vo.	183 lvs.		NNC
		PC	ViU	ICN
1837	8vo.	7 lvs.		NNGr
			MWA	NNC
1841	8vo.	254 lvs.		ICN
1845	8vo.	540 lvs.		NNC
		PC	RP	MH

1853-92 Boston
BOSTON TYPE FOUNDRY. c.1850-1892.
Merged with American Typefounders Co.
Type specimens:

1853	4to.	139 lvs.		NNC
1856	4to.	95 lvs.		NNC
			ICN	MWA
1857	4to.	32 lvs.		NNC
1860	4to.	60 lvs.		NNC
			PC	MWA
1861	8vo.			MH
c.1862	4to.	42 lvs.		PC
1864	4to.	49 lvs.	MH	NNC
1867	4to.	112 lvs.	PC	NNC
1869	4to.	293 lvs.	ICN	NNC
1871 sq.8vo.	153 lvs.		NNC	
			PC	ICN
1874 sq.8vo.	117 lvs.		CtMK	
			MWA	NNC
1874 sq.8vo.	65 lvs.		NNC	
c.1875	32mo.	64pp.		NNC

1876	4to.	141 lvs.		ICN
		PC	MH	NhD	MWA
1877	4to.	64 lvs.		ICN
1878	4to.	120 lvs.	PC	NNC
1880	4to.	123 lvs.	RP	NNC
1881	4to.	52 lvs.		RP
1883	4to.	100 lvs.		NNC
1883 sq.12mo.	121 lvs.		ICN	
1884	4to.	132 lvs.		NNC
1884	12mo.	152 lvs.		NNC
			RP	ICN
1885	4to.	113 lvs.		CSmH
		PC	NNC	MWA	NhD	ICN
1885	12mo.	50 lvs.		ICN
1886				MH
1887 sq.12mo.	fragment		PC	
1888	Listed in Bullen 1933 catalog.			
1889	4to.	302pp.		NNC
			PC	MWA
1890			MH	MWA
1892	4to.	304pp.		CtMK
		PC	NNC	NhD	MWA	MH

Specimen book containing complete price list of printing presses and supplies.

1892	Catalog of body type for	MWA

daily papers mfg. by . . .

c.1857-96 New York   Locations
BRESNAN TYPE FOUNDRY. as follows
Walker & Pelouze - 1857. Later Walker &
Bresnan, succeeded by P. H. Bresnan.

c.1857	4to.	38 lvs.		NNC
1882	4to.	44 lvs. Bullen 1933 catalog.		
1890	12mo.	11 lvs.		NNC
1896	4to.	180pp. Bullen 1933 catalog.		

1882	Providence, R. I.	RHi

BRIGGS PRINTING MACHINE CO. Ill. circular of Briggs' printing machine presses, November 1. 8vo., 8pp., col. pict. wrap.

1871	Boston	CSmH

BROWN, ORREN L. Brown's pat. type setting and distributing machinery and types. 8vo., 48pp., ill., fld. plate, wrap.

1813-92	New York		Locations	
	BRUCE'S NEW YORK TYPE		as follows	
	FOUNDRY. George Bruce and George			
	Bruce's Son & Co.			

c.1813	18mo.	11 lvs.		NNC	
1815	8vo.	15 lvs.		NNC	
1816 sq.8vo.		22 lvs.		NNC	
1818	8vo.	31 lvs.		NNC	
1818	8vo.	33 lvs., 4 fld.		MWA	
1820	8vo.	62, 53, 50 lvs.	NHi	NNC	
1820	8vo.	33 lvs.		PC	
1821	8vo.	75 and 59 lvs.		NNC	
1824 sm.4to.		31 lvs.		NNC	
1828	8vo.	177 lvs.	RP	NN	
1831	8vo.	121 lvs.		NNC	
1837	8vo.	354 lvs.		NNC	
1841	8vo.	311 lvs.		NNC	
1842	8vo.	298 lvs.		NNC	
1845				MH	
1848	8vo.	224 lvs.	ViU ICN	NNC	
1853	8vo.	333 lvs.		NNC	NNGr
1855		Bullen 1933 catalog.			
1858	4to.	Specimens of business cuts.		NjN	
1861	4to.	26 lvs.		NNMM	
1865	4to.	76pp.	PC	NNC	
1865	4to.	120pp.	RP ICN	NNC	
1867	4to.	76pp.		NNC	
1868		3rd supplement to 1865 spec'n.		CSmH	
1869	4to.	166pp. plus 1-XIV price list of presses and supplies. RP PC MWA ICN ViU NN NHi NNC OrU		CSmH NNMM	
1870-75	4to.	1st to 5th and 7th to 10th supplements.		CSmH	
1870-82	4to.	9 supplements.		MWA	
1870-81	4to.	19 supplements.		NNC	

1874	4to.	reduced and revised prices.		MWA
1876	4to.			NHi
1878	4to.	372pp.	NNC	NNGr
1881	4to.	90 lvs. RP NNC		ICN
1882	4to. ICN	362 and 168pp. MH NNC NHi PC ViU		NNGr MWA RP
1882		reduced price list.		CSmH
1883-92	4to.	various supplements. pp. 353 to 376 PC MH		CSmH ViU
c.1892	8vo.	608pp.	PC	MiD

N.B. One of the best research records located. Very few other manufacturers' catalogs have been as carefully saved and properly filed by our libraries for future use.

1841-89	Buffalo, N. Y.			NNC
	BUFFALO TYPE FOUNDRY.			ICN
	Nathan Lyman d.1873 - Lyman's Sons, W.E.			
	& C.M. Lyman. Type specimens as follows:			

1841	8vo.	160 lvs.		NNC
1853	4to.	140 lvs.		NNC
1871-2	4to.	220 lvs.		NNC
1879	4to.	144 lvs.		NNC
1889	4to.	178 lvs.	ICN	NNC

See also Nathan Lyman, Albany. Est. 1835.

c.1868-94	San Francisco (?)		NNC
	CALIFORNIA TYPE FOUNDRY.		CHi
	(William Faulkner & Son, agent.) Type		
	specimens as follows:		

c.1868	4to.	16 lvs. Specimen book.	CHi
1894	8vo.	240pp.	NNC
1894	16mo.	240pp.	NNC

N.B. There are times in work like this when you have to record what someone else has discovered without proper details - or, leave out an important date.

1874 Williamsburgh, L.I., N. Y. & New York
CAMPBELL PRESS WORKS. Ill. NNQ
catalog of printing presses and sup- NNC
plies. Sq. 8vo., 28pp., wrap.

CAREY, CHARLES J. & CO. See Baltimore
Type Foundry.

1870	New York		ICN

CAULON & ADEE. Specimen book for 1870.

1883-95 St. Louis   Locations
CENTRAL TYPE FOUNDRY.   as follows
Originally a branch of Boston Type Foundry.
Merged with American Type Foundry. Type
specimens as follows:

1883	Specimens - blank for		CSmH

names of agents and jobbers - new designs.

1884	sm.12mo.	320pp.			RP
1885		382pp.			MH
1886	4to.	192pp.			NNC
		RP	MH	MWA	
1889	4to.	314pp.			NNC
1890	4to.	309pp.			NNC
		PC	ICN	MoSHi	
1891	Specimen book brass				MoSHi

type, for book binders.

1892	16mo.	73 lvs.	PC	ICN
1895	16mo.	727pp.		NN

1820	New York		PPAmP

CHANDLER, A. & CO. Specimen book of
types, borders, etc. 8vo., 22 lvs.

1822	New York		NNC

------ Specimen book. 8vo., 21 lvs.

c.1890	St. Louis		CSmH

CHESMAN, NELSON & CO. Specimen book
of enameled wood type.

c.1890	St. Louis		ICN

------ Ill. catalog of specimens, inks, cabinets and furniture for printers.

CHICAGO TYPE FOUNDRY. See Marder,
Luse & Co.

1827-93 Cincinnati   Locations
CINCINNATI TYPE FOUNDRY.   as follows
Originally a branch of Elihu White. Speci-
men books:

1827	12mo.	94 lvs.		NNC
1829	12mo.			OHi
1834	sm.8vo.	177 lvs.		NNC
1844	lg. 8vo.	300 lvs.		NNC
1851	4to.	184 lvs.		NNC
1852	4to.	197 lvs.		NNC
1853	Bullen 1933 catalog.			OHi

1856	4to.	230 lvs.	ICN	NNC
1857	4to.	230 lvs.		NNC
c.1860	4to.	78 lvs.		NNC
1862	4to.	100 lvs.		NNC
1864	lg.4to.	131 lvs.		NNC
c.1867	8vo.	88pp.		ICN
1868	fol.			NN
1870	lg4to.			NN
1874	lg.4to.	100 lvs.		NNC
1876	lg. 4to.	120 lvs.	NN	NNC
1878		138pp.		OrU
1880	fol.	158pp. 13th book.		NNC
				PC NhD
1881		15th book.		CSmH
1882	8vo.	148pp. PC NN		NNC

(Also given as 16th book ?)

1885	sm4to.	291pp. 16th book.		PC
1888	lg. 8vo.	1 1/8" thick.		MH
1888	sm4to.	182 and 186pp.		NNC
		17th book.	PC	ICN
1893	lg.8vo.	188 and 96pp.		NNC
		18th book.	PC	ICN

1880-95 Cleveland, O.   Locations
CLEVELAND TYPE FOUNDRY.   as follows
H. H. Thorpe Mfg. Co. Type specimens:

1880	8vo.	176pp. NN	ICN	NNC
1883	8vo.	38pp.		NNC
c.1883	12mo.	116, 316 and 188pp.		NNC
1885	12mo.	316pp.		NNC
1890	12mo.	342pp.	PC	NNC
1891	12mo.	165pp.		NNC
1891	12mo.	116pp.	NNC	CtMK
1893	12mo.	454pp.	PC ICN	NNC
1895	12mo.	454pp.	PC	NNC

1858-87 Philadelphia   Locations
COLLINS & McLEESTER.   as follows
Formerly E. Starr & Sons. Type specimens:

1858	4to.	1" thick		ICN

c.1870		specimen book.		CSmH
1871	4to.	500pp.		NN
c.1879	lg.8vo.	24 lvs.		NNC
c.1880	lg.8vo.	500pp.		NNC
c.1880	lg.8vo.	504pp.		NNC
1883	8vo.	504pp.		NNC
1885		504pp.	PC ICN	NNC
1887		504pp.		NNC

1836 New York   MWA
CONNER & COOKE. Specimen of printing
types and ornaments. 2nd ed.

c.1896-8 New York   NNC
CONNER, FENDLER & CO.   PC
(Bentley, Conner & Co.) Listed from RG
check list. Specimen book. Sm. 8vo., 212pp.

1829-91 New York   Locations
CONNOR, JAMES FOUNDRY &   as follows
CONNOR'S UNITED STATES TYPE FOUND-
RY. Type specimen books:

1829		Broadside list of type. Bullen 1933 catalog.		
1834	8vo.	63 lvs.	ICN	NNC
1836	8vo.	155 lvs.	RP MWA	NNC
1837	8vo.	13 lvs.		NNC
1841	8vo.	185 lvs.		NNC
1850	8vo.	218 lvs.		NNC
1852	4to.	139 lvs.	ICN	NNC
1854	4to.	188 plus 5 lvs.	NNC	MWA
1855	4to.	195 lvs.		NNC
1859	fol.	232 lvs.		NNC
c.1860	fol.	328 lvs.	RP	NNC
1865	fol.			RP
1866	lg.4to.	Supplement specimen book.		CtY
c.1868	4to.	specimen book.		ViU
c.1870	fol.	426 lvs.		NNC
c.1876	fol.	328pp.		NNC
c.1879	fol.	130 lvs.	PC	ICN
1885	4to.	62 lvs.		NNC

1885	4to.	80 lvs.	NNC	CSmH
1886	fol.	Bullen catalog for 1933.		
1888	8vo.	125 lvs. PC	NNC	CtMK
1889	4to.	200pp.	MWA	NNMM
1891	8vo.	663pp. PC NN		NNC

v.d. Several locations for this Foundry
were reported by ICJ. Eleventh hour
discovery of error. Apologies to ICJ
and the reader.

c.1882 Rochester, N.Y.   NNMM
CONOLLY, C.J. & CO. Ill. catalog, reference book and complete price list of stamps,
stencils - over 2500 styles in borders, ornaments, cuts, etc. Sq.8vo.,224pp.,pict.wrap.

c.1850 New York   ICN
COOLEY, J.G. & CO. Catalog of wood type
specimens.

1850-57 New York   Locations
CORTELYOU'S TYPE FOUND-   as follows
RY. Successors to Lothian Type Foundry.
Type specimen books:

1850	8vo.	82 lvs.	MH	NNC
1856	Cortelyou & Giffing 8vo. 182 lvs.			NNC
1856	8vo.	55 lvs.		NNC
1857	8vo.	286 lvs.		NNC

1899 Chicago   ICN
CRESCENT TYPE FOUNDRY. Specimens
for 1899.

1878 Chicago   ICHi
CRESWELL, WANNER & CO. Specimens of
borders, type, rules, cuts, etc. 4to., wrap.

c.1866 Boston   CSmH
CURTIS & MITCHELL. Successors to
Holmes & Curtis, 1847-1852 and E.A.Curtis,
1852-c.1863. Specimens of types, borders,
rules, cuts, etc. Young America, Prouty,
Excelsior, Star and Ruby presses, etc.
12mo., 60pp., pict. wrap.

1875 Boston   CSmH
------ Reduced price list of type, borders,
cuts, presses, etc. 12mo.,80pp.,ills.,wrap.

1886 Boston   MWA
------ Revised ill. price list of   MiD
borders, cuts, etc., printing machinery.
12mo., 216pp., wrap.

1890 Boston   ICN
------ Ill. price list. 12mo.,   MWA
205 and 56 lvs.

1874 Philadelphia   PKsL
DAUGHADAY, J.W. & CO. (W. C. Evans,
agent.) How to print and ill. catalog of type,
ornaments and presses. 30pp., wrap.

1875 Philadelphia   CSmH
------ How to print ill. catalog of type and
presses. 26pp., wrap.

1877 Philadelphia   CSmH
------ Revised ed., added ills. of type,
presses, supplies, etc. 100pp., wrap.

1877 Philadelphia   PKsL
------ Printers' model guide - short
history and ill. price list. 4to., 12pp., wrap.

DAVIDS, THADEUS & CO. See Stationery.

1883-97 New York   Locations
DeVINNE, THEODORE L. & CO. as follows
Specimens of black-letter, Roman, Italic and
other quaint types - as follows:

    1883 New and quaint type. 62pp. CSmH
                                   MWA

    c.1885 Louis Quatorze period type.
            7 lvs.   CSmH

    1887 Black-letter. 24pp. ICN   CSmH

    1891 Roman and Italic type.   CSmH
             ICJ   ICN   MWA
    (Best in America at this time.)

1897 Boston   CSmH
------ Old faces of Roman ICN   MWA
and medieval type.

1887-97 Boston   ICN

c.1890 Chicago   PKsL
DICK, A.B. CO. Edison mimeograph, in-
vented by Thomas A. Edison, mfg. by A. B.
Dick. Sq. 8vo., 12pp., fine ills., pict. wrap.
Ptd. by the Lakeside Press.

1841-95 Boston   Locations
DICKINSON TYPE FOUNDRY.   as follows
Samuel N. Dickinson, d.1848, succeeded by
Phelps & Dalton, later Phelps, Dalton & Co.
Merged with American Typefounders.
General specimen books:

    1841 Type specimen.   MWA

    1842 8vo.   24 lvs.   NNMM

    1842 8vo.   35 lvs.   ICN   NNC

    1846 Broadside list. 4pp. Bullen 1933
            catalog.

    1847 12mo. 189 lvs.   NNC
           PC   RP   ICJ   MH   MWA

1855	4to.	1/4" thick Bullen 1933 catalog.		
1856	4to.	211 lvs.		CSmH
		NNC	ICN	MWA
1859	4to.	45 lvs.		NNC
1867	4to.	149 lvs.		NNC
1868	4to.	101 lvs.	MiD	NNC
1870	4to.	127 lvs.		ICN
1872	12mo.	68 lvs.		NNC
1876	4to.	362 lvs.		NNC
		PC	ICN	MWA
1878		Bullen 1933 catalog.		
1879	4to.	363 lvs.	PC NhD	NNC
1883	4to.	251pp.	ICN	NNC
1885		Specimen pages-date in ink.		CSmH
1888	4to.	248pp.	NhD	NNC
1890	4to.	248pp.	NhD	NNC
c.1891	12mo.	41 lvs.	ICN	CtMK
1892		Bullen 1933 catalog.		
1893	4to.	438pp.		NN
1894	4to.	439pp. PC MH ICN		NNC
1895	4to.	439pp.		RP

1882 Boston   CSmH
DODD'S NEWSPAPER ADVERTISING
AGENCY. Ill. price list of printing mate-
rials and ink specimens. 59pp., col. ills.

1876 Orange, N. J.   NjOE
EDISON, THOMAS A. LABORATORY. Ill.
brochure - the Edison electrical pen and
duplicating machines. 16mo., 24pp., pict.
wrap. 2 samples of electric penmanship.

1889 New York   ICN
EMPIRE STATE TYPE FOUNDRY.   NNC
Successor to Farmer, Little & Co. Specimens of printers' type, cuts and ornaments.
4to., 62 lvs.

c.1877 Philadelphia   PKsL
EVANS, W.C. Inventor & Mfg. New self-
inking printing presses - cheapest in the
world - $7. to $10. for complete printing
office - specimens of type, ornaments and
presses. 8vo., 8pp., pict. wrap.

1871 Philadelphia   PHi
FAGAN, J. & SON. Specimens of book ornaments. 4to., 15 lvs.

1892-1900 New York   Locations
FARMER, A.D. & SON.   as follows
Successors to Farmer, Little & Co. Merged
with American Typefounders. Type specimens:

1892 lg. 4to.	CCXIV and 185pp.	NNC		
	MH	ICN	ICJ	
1895 8vo.	344pp.	ICJ	NNC	
1897 8vo.	371pp.		NNC	
		ICJ	ICN	MH
1899 8vo.	400pp.		NNC	
		PC	ICJ	ICN
1900 8vo.	400pp.	MWA		

1862-93 New York   Locations
FARMER, LITTLE & CO.   as follows
Successors to C.T. White & Co. Later
merged with American Typefounders. Type
specimen books:

1862	4to.	129 lvs.	RP	NNC	
1862	4to.	124pp. (also 259 lvs.)NNC			
1865	4to.	331 lvs. RP	NN	NNC	
1867	4to.	240 lvs.		NNC	
1868	fol.	74 lvs.	RP	NNC	
1873	fol.	107 lvs.		NNC	
1874	4to.	228 lvs.		CSmH	
		ViU	NNGr	NNC	ICN
1877	4to.	236 lvs.		NNC	
1878	4to.	112 and 16 lvs.		NNC	
1879	4to.	Latest styles. CtMK	CSmH		
1879	4to.	45 lvs.	ICN	CtMK	
1880	4to.	233 lvs.	ICN	NNC	
c.1881	4to.	9/16" thick. ICN	NNC		
1882	4to.	192pp.		CSmH	
	NNC	MH	PC	ICN	CtMK
1884	8vo.	192 and 12 lvs.		NNC	
1885 lg.8vo.		192 and 16 lvs.		CSmH	
			ICN	NNC	
1886				MH	

1887	4to.	XXXII and 48 lvs.	NNC	
		PC	ICN	MH

1889 lg.12mo. Bullen 1933 catalog.

1892	8vo.	304pp. RP	ICN	MWA
1893	8vo.	315pp.		NNC

FAULKNER, WILLIAM & SON. See
California Type Foundry.

c.1900 St. Louis   DTobI
FLORODORA TAG CO. Ill. catalog of
presents given for Tobacco - Tags, Coupons,
Cigar Bands - list of tags and bands - large
8vo., 80pp., col. pict. wrap. of labels, tags
and bands, with a double spread of bands
acceptable - in a way a col. specimen of
their work - plus ills. of presents, etc.

1871-92 Cincinnati   Locations
FRANKLIN TYPE FOUNDRY.   as follows
Allison & Smith. Originally a branch of L.
Johnson & Co. Type specimen books, large
and small:

1871	4to.	343 lvs. PC	NN	NNC
c.1876		212pp.		MiD
		Pocket book of specimens.		
1878	12mo.	246pp.		NNC
c.1880	8vo.	268pp.	NN	NNC
1883	8vo.	336pp.		NNC
1885	8vo.	336pp. PC	ICN	NNC
1888	8vo.	422pp.		NNC
1890	8vo.	422pp.		NNC
1892	8vo.	422pp. PC	ICN	NNC

c.1880 Central Falls, R. I.   ViU
FREEMAN, E.L. & CO. Ill. catalog of type,
borders, cuts and ornaments for printers.

c.1875 Columbus, Ga.   ICN
GILBERT, THOMAS. Catalog of   MH
type (no details reported.)

1874 Boston   ICN
GOLDING & CO. Ill. catalog of type, ornaments, Pearl printing presses and supplies.
8vo., 22pp., pict. wrap.

1880 Boston   NNMM
------ Ill. catalog of specimens   ICN
of cuts and ornaments. 4to., fine pls.

1882 Boston   MiDbF
------ Ill. catalog of type, presses and
supplies. 8vo., 112pp., pict. wrap.

c.1885 Boston   CSmH
------ Ill. catalog of printers' supplies,
col. plate. 8vo., 34pp., pict. wrap.

1888 Boston   MdTanSW
------ Ill. catalog   ICN   NNMM
of printers' supplies. 4to., 108pp.

1875 Boston   ViWC
GORHAM & CO. Specimen book of presses,
type, cuts, borders and ornaments. 8vo.,
60pp., dec. wrap.

1878 Boston   MWA
------ Handbook of presses and printing
materials.

1870 New Orleans   ViU
GRAHAM, L. & CO. Book of specimens of
type.

GREAT WESTERN TYPE FOUNDRY. See
Barnhart Brothers & Spindler.

1820 Boston   ICJ
GREELE & WILLIS. Specimen book for
1829.

c.1850 New York & New Orleans   NNC
GREEN, H.H. 13-5/8 x 19 broadside list of
type.

1852 New York & New Orleans   ICN
------ Specimen book of type.   NNC
8vo., 165 lvs.

1826-86 New York   Locations
HAGAR TYPE FOUNDRY.   as follows
Specimens of type:

1826	8vo.	90 lvs.		NNC
1831	8vo.	136 lvs.		NNC
1832	8vo.	337 lvs.		PPAmP
1833 sm.8vo.				ICN
1841	8vo.	288 lvs.	RP	NNC
1850	fol.	155 lvs.		NNC
1854	4to.	145 lvs.	ICN	NNC
1858	4to.	132 lvs.	MH MWA	NNC
1860	4to.	238 lvs.		NNC
1860	4to.	34 lvs.		NNC
1866	4to.	78 lvs.	NNC	CtMK

1873 and 1886 Bullen 1933 catalog, but
no longer at NNC.

1858 New York   CSmH
HAGAR, WILLIAM JR. CO. Hand-   MWA
book for printers and publishers with ills.
of specimens of plain and fancy type, ornaments, etc.

1884 Poughkeepsie   CSmH
HAIGHT, A.V. Specimens of printing types,
some in col. 39pp.

nd. Rochester, N. Y.   NR
HAMILTON & McNEAL. Ill. price list of
the Universal printing machines.

1884 Two Rivers, Wis.   ICN
HAMILTON MFG. CO. Holly wood specimens for 1884.

1891 Two Rivers, Wis.   MWA
------ Specimens of wooden type and
borders, etc.

c.1892-99 Boston   Locations
HANSEN, H.C. TYPE FOUNDRY. as follows
Type specimen books:

c.1892	12mo.	16 lvs.	NNC
1894	12mo.	94pp.	NNC
1897	12mo.	120pp.	NNC
1899	12mo.	136pp.	NNC

c.1870 Cincinnati   ICN
HARPEL, OSCAR HENRY. Typo-   MWA
graph or book of specimens with useful information by O.H.H.

1862-1880 New York   Locations
HART, FRANCIS & CO.   as follows
Specimens of black letter, pointed texts, old
type styles and ornaments.

1862	Specimens of stock cuts and ornaments.	ICN
1877	Old style types. 63pp.	CSmH
1878	Black letter, etc. 8vo., 2 lvs. and 158pp.	CSmH
1880	Script and italics. Pt. III.	CSmH

1896 New York   MWA
HEARST, WILLIAM RANDOLPH. The
Journal book of types - A Catalog.

1859-86 New York   Locations
HEINRICH, PH. Type speci-   as follows
mens:

1859		Bullen catalog for 1933.		
1878	4to.	141 lvs.		NNC
1886	4to.	146 lvs.	ICN	NNC

c.1890 New York   DSi
HEPPENKEIMER'S, F. SONS. Est. 1849.
Lithographers, Engravers & Printers.
Samples of Labels. 8vo., 4 col. lithos.,
samples for cigar boxes, pict. wrap.

1851 Boston   ViU
HOBART & ROBINS. Specimens of printing
types and ornaments for printers.

1855 Boston   ICN
------ Specimens for 1855.

1846-90 New York   Locations
HOE, R. & CO. Ill. catalogs of as follows
printing presses, special presses, shop
equipment and tools.

1846	Fol.circular 4pp.			CSmH
1852	sq.8vo.	16pp., pict. wrap. DSi		
1866				ICJ
1867	lg.8vo.	138pp., col.pls.,cl. CtY		
		ICN	RG	NNC
1870	8vo.	152pp., col.pls.,cl. CSmH		
				ICJ
1873	sm.fol.	84pp.		RG
1881	4to.	76pp.		CSmH
1881	4to.	172pp.	RG	CSmH
1890	4to.	44pp.		MH-BA

Further collections located without details.

| 1851-67 | Various sizes | DLC |
| 1854-81 | Various sizes | ICN |

1860-67 and also p.1900-1902-1897 NNC

1830 Philadelphia   NNC
HOWE, J. & CO. Specimen of   MWA
printing type and ornaments. 8vo., 41 lvs.

1867 Hartford, Conn.   CSmH
HUTCHINGS, WILLIAM C. Specimens of
new printing types. 23 lvs., title page in col.

1873-86 Chicago   Locations
ILLINOIS TYPE FOUNDING CO. as follows
Branch of Bruce Type Foundry. Specimens:

1873	8vo.	168pp.	PC ICN	NNC
1883	4to.	183pp.	PC	NNC
1886	4to.			ICJ
1887	12mo.	464pp.		NNC

INGALLS, J.F.   See Clothing.
N.B. Stamping outfits for making impres-
sions on paper or cloth are printing as one
very cooperative librarian pointed out.
Ingalls' patterns were once famous, and they
manufactured a form of type for transferring
patterns.

1895-99 Chicago   Locations
INLAND TYPE FOUNDRY.   as follows
Specimen books of type and ornaments:

1895	12mo.	95pp.		NNC
1895	12mo.	142pp.		NNC
1897	12mo.	351pp.		NNC
		RP	NN	ICN
1897	12mo.	448pp.	ICN	NNC
1898	8vo.	212pp.		NNC
1899	8vo.	355pp.	PC ICN	NNC
1899	8vo.	431pp.	PC ICJ	NNC

1834 Philadelphia   NNC
JOHNSON & SMITH. Successors   MH
to Richard Rolandson. Specimens of type
and borders. 8vo., 348 lvs.

1841 Philadelphia   PPAmP
------ 8vo., 350 lvs.   NNC

c.1877 Philadelphia & New York   PKsL
JOHNSON, CHARLES ENEU & CO.
Est. 1804. Oldest printing ink works in
America. Specimen book of standard, col.
poster, bag, label, litho. and other special
inks. 16mo., col. pls. - the best record we
have recorded in this field. Pict. cl.

1843-65 Philadelphia   Locations
JOHNSON, L. TYPE FOUNDRY. as follows
Also printed L. Johnson & Co. Type Foundry. Est. 1796. Specimens of type and
ornaments:

1843	sm.fol.	80 lvs.		NNC
1844	8vo.	386 lvs.	ICN	NNC
c.1845	fol.	120 lvs.		NNC
c.1847	fol.	162 lvs.		NNC
c.1849	fol.	89 lvs.		NNC
c.1850	fol.	92 lvs.		NNC
1853	fol.	78 lvs.	RP	NNC
1853	fol.	149 lvs.		NNC
1853	4to.	267 lvs.		NNC

1855-6	4to.	165 lvs.	MH	NNC
1856	4to.	178 lvs.		NNC
1857	fol.	195 lvs.		NNC
	OrU	OHi	MH	ICN
1859	fol.	265pp.	MH	NNC
c.1863	lg.4to.	603pp.		MH
1865	lg.4to.	584pp.		NNC
	PC	ViU	MWA	ICN

1879-89 Kansas City, Mo.   NNC
KANSAS CITY TYPE FOUNDRY. Est. 1872.
Four specimen books as follows:

1879	8vo.	232pp.
1887		288pp. Bullen 1933 catalog.
1889	sm.8vo.	288pp.
1889	12mo.	73pp.

1883 Meriden, Conn.   CtHi
KELSEY PRESS CO. (CtMK Company library locations listed elsewhere.) Oldest
press in U. S. still operating. Do Your Own
Printing. Ill. catalog of type, borders, cuts,
ornaments and presses. 4to.

nd. Meriden, Conn.   CSmH
------ Print Your Own Cards -   CtHi
as above.

1886 Meriden, Conn.   CSmH
------ Complete outfits for printers. Sq.
8vo., 32pp., pict. wrap.

1896 Meriden, Conn.   CSmH
------ Excelsior portable and O.K. Ct
presses, ornaments, cuts, etc. 4to., 24pp.,
wrap.

1898 Meriden, Conn.   RG
------ Ill. catalog of type, cuts, etc.

c.1900 Meriden, Conn.   NNU
------ Type specimen and presses for
printers.

1890-99 Philadelphia   Locations
KEYSTONE TYPE FOUNDRY.   as follows
Specimens of type, cuts and ornaments:

1800	12mo.	02 lvs.	NNC	COmII
1891	12mo.	86 lvs.		NNC
1892	23mo.	56 lvs.		NNC
1892	12mo.	208pp. PC	ICN	NNC
1899	12mo.	405pp. PC	ICN	NNC

1829 Albany, N. Y.   NNC
KINSLEY, A.W. & CO. Specimens of type
for printers. 8vo., 147 lvs.

1857 Albany, N. Y.   NNC
KNICKERBOCKER TYPE FOUNDRY. A. S.
Gilchrest. Lg. 4to., 14 lvs.

1858 Fredericksburg, O.   ICN
KNOX, D. & CO. Specimens of wood type.

c.1867-91 New York   Locations
LINDSAY TYPE FOUNDRY.   as follows
Est. by three brothers R. & A. & A.W. 1852.
Specimens of type and borders, cuts and
ornaments for printers:

c.1867	4to.	34 lvs.		ICN
1870	8vo.	65 lvs.		NNC
1870	4to.	38 lvs.		NNC
1888				MWA
1891	4to.	100 lvs.	NNC	CtMK

1806 New York   MH
LOTHIAN, ROBERT. Father of George D.
Specimen book. 8vo., 15 lvs.

1841 New York   NNC
LOTHIAN TYPE FOUNDRY. George B.
Lothian. Succeeded by T. F. Cortelyou.
Type specimens for printers. 8vo., 84 lvs.
N.B. Bullen 1933 catalog notes an 1832.

LUCAS, F. JR. & LUCAS BROTHERS. See
Baltimore Type Foundry.

1835 Albany, N. Y.   Sabin 89122
LYMAN, NATHAN. See also Buffalo Type
Foundry. Specimen of printing types. 8vo.
Title from Munsell 1872 catalog.

1053 Buffalo, N. Y.   MiD
------ Specimen book of ornamental types,
cuts, borders, etc. 4to., 200pp., pp. bear
running head Lyman, Buffalo, N. Y.

nd. Brooklyn, N. Y.   NNQ
McADAMS, JOHN. Ill. catalog of ruling
machinery, disks, pagers, strikers for bookbinders and printers. 8vo., 24pp., wrap.

1868-97 Philadelphia   Locations
MacKELLAR, SMITHS &   as follows
JORDAN. Took over Johnson Type Foundry.
Type specimen books:

1868	lg.4to.	600pp.			CSmH
			PC	NNC	ICJ
1869	lg.4to.	601 and 603pp. resp.			
				OrU	NNC
1870	7th specimen book.				ICJ

1871	4to.	431pp.	CtMK
	PC	NNC MWA	MH
1871	lg.4to.	601pp.	NNC
1871	Printers' handbook of types.		MWA
1873	4to.	433 and 601pp. resp.	ICN
			PC
1875-6	4to.	1 1/2" thick.	MH
1876-7	4to.	433pp. NN NNC	ICN
1878	lg.4to.	943pp. 11th book.	CSmH
		RP	NNC
c.1879	sm.8vo.	208pp.	NNC
1880	8vo.	248pp. 13th book.	CtMK
		NNC	ICN
1881-2	8vo.	300pp. 14th book.	ICN
			PC
1882	Reissue of 11th book.		CSmH
	943pp.	NNC	MWA
1883	4to.	10 lvs.	NNMM
1883-4	8vo.	304pp.	NNC
1884	Reissue of 11th book. ViU		NNC
1885	8vo.	416pp. 16th book.	NNC
		PC RP	ICN
1886	Reissue of 11th book.		NNC
1887	4to.	525pp. 17th book.	NNC
1887	8vo.	464pp. 18th book.	NNC
		PC	ICN
1888	Reissue of 11th book.		CSmH
			NNC
1889	Reissue of 17th book.		CSmH
		NNC	NhD
1889	4to.	467pp. NNMM	CSmH
	Reissue of 18th book.		
1890	Reissue of 11th book.		NNC
1890	Reissue of 17th book. ICN		NNC
1890	8vo.	510 and 525pp. 19th book.	
		ICN	NNC
1891			MWA
1892	Reissue of 17th book.		NNC
1892	Specimens mfg. for Tatum &		
	Bowen, San Francisco and		
	Portland, Ore.		CSmH

1892	8vo.	536pp. 20th book.	NNC
		PC	NN
1893-4	8vo.	556pp. 21st book.	NNC
		PC NN	MH
1894	Specimen sheets - Columbus #2.		CSmH
1895	Reissue of 11th book.		NNC
1896	One Hundred Years 1796-1896.		
	To Our Friends & Patrons. Fol.,		
	96pp., pict. im. vel.		NSbSM
		ICJ	PKsL
1897	8vo.	350pp.	NNC
1897	8vo.	522pp.	NNC

1878 Santa Fe   CSmH
MANDERFIELD & TUCKER. New Mex(ican)
specimens for printers from 1862. 26pp.
A rare record, probably unique, even though
New Mexican rodents did their level best to
destroy it.

1887 New York   NNC
MANHATTAN TYPE FOUNDRY. Purchased
by Union Type Foundry of Chicago 1888.
Specimens for printers. Sq. 8vo., 44pp.

1859-95 Chicago   Locations
MARDER, LUSE & CO.   as follows
Chicago Type Foundry. Branch of T. C.
White & Co. until 1863. Specimens of type,
cuts and ornaments for printers.

1859	4to.	118pp.		ICHi
1862	4to.	250 lvs.		NNC
c.1870	4to.	223 lvs.	PC	NNC
1874	4to.	223 lvs.		MH
1875	16mo.	192pp.		PC
1875	4to.	91 lvs.		NNC
1876	4to.	105 lvs.		NNC
1878	4to.	Reported 3/4" thick.		MH
1879	4to.	216pp.	PC	NNC
1881	16mo.	271pp.	PC	NNC
1883	4to.	91 lvs. PC	ICN	NNC
1883	16mo.	320pp. 6th ed.		CSmH
		PC		NNC
1883	4to.	114 lvs.		NNC
1885	16mo.	384pp.		NNC

1886	4to.	136 lvs.	PC	NNC

1889	4to.	88 lvs.	CSmH
		NN NNC	CtMK

Huntington copy reads Abridged Specimen Book.

1890	16mo.	544pp.	PC	NNC	CSmH

1893	16mo.	641pp.	ICN	NNC	CSmH

1895	12mo.	727pp.	NNC

1885 Rochester, N.Y.   CSmH
MAXSON, F.W. Catalog and specimen book of stamps of business cuts, ornaments, type, etc. 8vo., 40pp., pict. wrap.

c.1888 Rochester, N.Y.   NNMM
------ Catalog and reference book for dealers, agents and printers. Ills. of printing wheels, type, stamps, presses, cuts, etc. 8vo., 128pp., pict. wrap.

1880 Chicago   NNC
MECHANICS TYPE FOUNDRY.   ICN
Later became Union Type Foundry - Creswell, Wanner & Co. and later Wanner, Weber & Co. Specimens of type for printers. Creswell, Wanner & Co. 4to., 114 lvs.

1882 Chicago   NNC
------ Specimens of type by Wanner, Weber & Co. 4to., 155 lvs.

1891-2 Baltimore   NNC
MENGEL, J.G. & CO. Type specimens. 2 specimen books:

c.1891	4to	158 lvs.

c.1892	4to.	155 lvs.

1894-99 New York   Locations
MERGENTHALER LINOTYPE   as follows
CO. Specimens of linotype faces, etc.

1894	Specimens		MWA
1895	Specimens		MWA
1896	Specimens		ICN
1899	Specimens	MWA	ICJ

c.1894 Brooklyn, N.Y.   NNQ
MILLER, WILLIAM P. Ill. catalog of Ingersol improved presses.

c.1881 St. Paul, Minn.   NNC
MINNESOTA TYPE FOUNDRY. Formerly a branch of Barnhart Brothers & Spindler. Type specimens 4to., 219pp.

c.1880 Philadelphia   OHi
MODEL PRESS CO. Formerly J.W. Daughaday & Co. Specimen book of job type and printing materials. 83pp., ills.

nd. Middletown, N.Y.   ICN
MORGANS & WILCOX MFG. CO. Specimens of wood type.

c.1900 New York   CSmH
MUNSON, V.B. Successor to George Bruce's Sons. Specimens of types, borders, cuts for printers, etc.

c.1880 New York   NNMM
NATHAN, ALBERT. (Agent for Beit & Co.) Specimens of German printing inks. 12mo., 100 lvs. of col. pls. with col. designed title page. Most outstanding ink catalog of all time.

1887 New York   ICN
NATIONAL PRINTERS' MATERIALS CO. Enameled wood type specimens.

NEW ENGLAND ENGRAVING CO. See Undertakers' Equipment. N.B. Although these Yankee gentlemen advise us that they specialize in engraving on wood and print grandiose catalogs for manufacturers, the only example is for tombstone designs.

c.1827-82 Boston   Locations
NEW ENGLAND TYPE FOUND-   as follows
RY. Various proprietors and agents. Type specimen books:

c.1827	Baker & Greele			
	8vo.			PC

1829	Greele & Willis			
	8vo.	130 lvs.		PC

1834	Henry Willis, agent			
	8vo.	175 lvs.		NNC
		RP	MII	NhD

1838	Geo. A. & J. Curtis		
	8vo.	216 lvs.	NNC

1841	8vo.	230 lvs.	ICN	NNC

1842	Geo. A. Curtis		
-50	8vo.	45 lvs.	NNC

1851	Hobart & Robbins successors to Geo. A. Curtis				
	4to.	162 lvs.	MH	MWA	NNC

1855	4to.	192 lvs.	NNC

1855	4to.	41 lvs.	ICN	NNC

1859	4to.	MH

c.1860		MH

1868   Chandler, Cousens & Co.
       4to.   92 lvs.   NNC

1882   A. B. Packard
                 137 lvs.   NNC   CtMK

1851   Cincinnati   NNC
OHIO TYPE FOUNDRY. Specimens of type.
8vo., 80 lvs.

1885   Oakland, Calif.   CSmH
PACIFIC PRESS PUBLISHING HOUSE.
Specimen book of electrotypes of Pacific
Coast scenery, etc. for Pacific Coast
printers. 278pp.

1889-99 San Francisco   Locations
PACIFIC STATES TYPE   as follows
FOUNDRY. Type specimens:

    1889   Hawks & Shattuck
           8vo.   38 and 94 lvs.   NNC

    1893   Specimen book.   CSmH

    1899   A. E. & W. F. Shattuck
           8vo.   XLVIII and 200 lvs. NNC

1872-87 Greenville, Conn.   Locations
PAGE, WILLIAM H. & CO.   as follows
Specimen books and albums of chromatic
wood type, cuts and ornaments.

    1872   CSmH

    c.1875 Specimen book with fine col. pls.
                                     NNMM

    1876   MWA

    1878   CSmH

    1879   Page's wood type album. CSmH

    1879   Wood type albums #3 and 4. CSmH

    1860-7 Five specimen books of wood type.
                                      ICN

1884-96 San Francisco   Locations
PALMER & REY. Originally   as follows
branch of Marder, Luse & Co. Type specimens:

    1884 lg.8vo.   70 lvs.   NNC

    1886   Libro de muestros de tipos.
                                     CSmH

    1887 sm.4to.   240, 24 and 48 lvs. NNC

    1889 7x10   120pp.   NNC

    1889 7x10   362 and 62pp.
                  4th book.   ICN   NNC

1892 7x10   450 and 64pp.
              5th book.   NNC   CSmH

1896 12mo.   625pp.   NNC

1840 New York (formerly Boston)   ICN
PELOUZE, EDWARD. Specimen book. 8vo.
2'' thick. np.

1888 Richmond, Va.   ViU
PELOUZE, H. L. & SON. Specimens ICN
from foundry of . . . See also Baltimore
Type Foundry.

1849-92 Philadelphia   Locations
PELOUZE, LEWIS. Philadel-   as follows
phia Type Foundry. Type specimen books:

    1849 sm.8vo.   177 lvs.   ICN   NNC

    1856 4to.   146 lvs.   MH   NNC

    1892 16mo.   49 lvs.   NNC   CtMK

1897 Boston   NNMM
PETERS, C.J. & SON. Specimens of electrotypes, ill. and priced. 96pp.

1884 St. Paul, Minn.   PPL
PIONEER PRESS CO. Price list of papers,
boards, inks and printers' supplies. 60pp.

c.1886 Boston   ICJ
POINT SPECIMEN BOOK CO. Cover title
Dickinson type, etc.

1894 New York   ICN
POLHEMUS, JOHN. Book of specimens.

c.1895 New York   ViU
------ Specimens of type - faces, stock
cuts, initials, logotypes, etc.

1877 Plainfield, N. J. & New York   OrU
POTTER, C. JR. & CO. Ill. catalog of
power printing presses and steam engines.
16pp., col. litho., pict. wrap.

1889 Plainfield, N. J.   PKsL
------ New catalog to printers - power
presses, latest models. 16mo., 16pp. of
ills., pict. wrap.

1857 Boston   MWA
PRENTISS & SAWYER. Specimens of type,
borders and ornaments.

1871-78 Boston   Locations
RAND, GEORGE C. & AVERY,   as follows
Rand, Avery & Co. Specimens, stereotype
engraving, binding and printing catalogs.

    1871   Specimens for 1871.   ICN

    1874   Ill. catalog of . . .   MWA

| 1875 | Specimens for 1875. | | MWA |
| 1878 | Specimens . . . | MiD | MWA |

1818 Philadelphia   NNC
REICH, STARR & CO. Specimen book of
type. 12mo., 11 lvs.

1873 Richmond, Va.   Locations
RICHMOND TYPE FOUNDRY.   as follows
H.L. Pelouze. See also H. L. Pelouze.
Type specimens for printers:

1873	4to.	57 lvs.			NNC
1888	8vo.	185pp. ViU	ICN		NNC
1888	16mo.	190pp.			NNC

1883 New York   CSmH
RINGLER, F.A. & CO. Specimens of electrotype calendars, presses and printers'
supplies.

1844-c.1847 Philadelphia   Locations
ROBB, ALEXANDER.   as follows
Specimens of type and ornaments:

1844	8vo.	367 lvs.	NNC
1846	8vo.	1 3/4'' thick	MH
c.1847	broadside 12x19 specimens.		NNC

1836 Philadelphia   NNC
ROBB & ECHLIN. Specimens of   MWA
printing types and ornaments. 8vo., 294 lvs.

1871 Boston   MWA
ROCKWELL & CHURCHILL. Specimens of
type used in office of . . .

1816-22 Philadelphia   Locations
RONALDSON, JAMES.   as follows
Successor to Binny & Ronaldson. Est. 1768.

1816	sm.8vo.	90 lvs.	NNC	MWA	NNGr
1816	12mo.	45 lvs.	MH	NNC	MWA
1822	sm.8vo.	48 lvs.		NNC	CSmH
1822	8vo.	384pp.			NNC
1822	4to.	54 lvs.			PPAmP

c.1823 Philadelphia   ICN
RONALDSON, RICHARD. Successor to
James Ronaldson. Broadside specimen
sheet of type.

c.1855-77 Chicago   ICHi
ROUNDS, S. P., Publisher.   PC   ICN
Rounds' Printers' Cabinet. Quarterly.
Many trade periodicals in this period, though
not actual catalogs, are today fully as valuable for research. Each issue contains an
average catalog's ills. and prices in any
special field - some of Mr. Rounds' issues
are as good as a type specimen including
presses, tools, shop furniture and samples
of work.

1806 Boston   CSmH
RUSSELL & CUTLER. A specimen of
printing types and ornaments. Photostat of
title page only. Only located copy - PC.

1881-94 Baltimore   Locations
RYAN, JOHN TYPE FOUNDRY.   as follows
Est. 1854. Specimens of type and ornaments:

1881	lg.8vo.	184 lvs.			NNC
1887	7x10	290pp. NN	NhD		NNC
1889	7x10	336pp.			NNC
1891	7x10	394pp.			NNC
1893	7x10	435pp.		ICN	NNC
1894	7x10	547pp.			NNC

c.1000 St. Louis   MoSHi
ST. LOUIS PRINTERS' SUPPLY CO. Ill.
catalog of superior copper mixed types and
ornaments.

1854-93 St. Louis   NNC
ST. LOUIS TYPE FOUNDRY. Est. 1840.
First foundry west of Miss. Re-est. 1861.
Type specimen books:

1854	4to.	231 lvs.
1882	12mo.	144pp.
1886	5x8	205pp.
c.1886	4to.	97pp.
1887	8vo.	205pp.
c.1890	lg.4to.	145 lvs.
1893	8vo.	300pp.

1887 Plainfield, N. J.   PKsL
SCOTT, WALTER & CO. Ill. catalog of
Scott roll feed printing machines, lithographic presses, paper folders, etc. 4to.,
64pp., pict. wrap.

1888-89 Plainfield, N. J.   PKsL
------ Folder of loose pls. of machines.

c.1900 Plainfield, N. J.   ICJ
------ 5 catalogs of type reported c.1900
with no further details.

1879 Chicago   MWA
SHNIEDEWEND & LEE CO. Specimens of
electrotype cuts, borders and ornaments.

1888 Chicago   ICN
------ Specimens of MacKellar, Smiths &
Jordan type and ornaments.

c.1900 Boston   CSmH
SKINNER BARTLETT & CO. Specimens of
book and job types. Updike copy.

1842 Philadelphia   PC
SMITH & JOHNSON. Series of designs of
borders, type ornaments and cuts. 12 lvs.

1869 n.p.   CSmH
SPECIMENS - January 1. Title as above,
nd., np., 41 lvs. N.B. How do things like
this happen?

1874 Boston   NNMM
SPENCER, S.M. Ill. catalog of stencil dies,
ills. of designs for many uses. 8vo., 24pp.,
wrap.

1895 Chicago   NNC
STANDARD TYPE FOUNDRY. Specimens.
12mo., 192 lvs.

1828 Albany, N.Y.   NNC
STARR, LITTLE & CO. Albany Type
Foundry, 1826-1833. Specimen of type.
8vo., 75 lvs.

1826 Albany, N.Y.   CSmH
STARR, R. & CO. Letter-founder. Specimen of printing type. Sabin 90560. Hoe
sale.

c.1820 New York   NNC
STARR'S NEW YORK TYPE FOUNDRY.
Type specimen. 16mo., 2 lvs.

nd. Boston   ICN
STEVENS TYPE & PRESS CO. Steel type
specimens.

c.1895 Columbus, O.   CSmH
SURGUY & CO. Specimens of electrotype
ornaments and cuts and stereotype matrices,
etc. 4to., 190pp. of business cuts, trade
ornaments, etc. A fine pict. record.

c.1900 Columbus, O.   IU
SURGUY, HANLAN & CO. Ill. catalog of
stereotyping outfits and special machinery
for printers. 16mo., fld. circular.

nd. Chicago   ICHi
SWISHER, R.D. MFG. CO. Est. 1888.
Special catalog #47 - stamps, type, brands,
stencils for general use - machinery for
printing. 8vo., 48pp., ill. throughout, pict.
wrap.

1878 Cleveland   NNMM
TAYLOR BROTHERS & CO. Specimen book
of rubber and steel type, rubber stamping
outfits for all businesses. 50 lvs., ill.

1853 New York   NHi
TROW, JOHN F. Type Founder. Specimen
book for 1853.

1858 New York   ICN
------ Specimens for 1858.

c.1886 South Windham, Conn.   CtHi
TUBBS & CO. To the printing fraternity -
specimens of Tubbs' wood type borders and
ornaments. 4to., 20pp. of borders plus
152pp. of type. Pict. wrap.

nd. South Windham, Conn.   CtHi
------ Catalog and price list of wood type.
Fol., XIX, 151 and 2pp.

c.1895 New York   CSmH
ULLMAN, SIGMUND CO. Specimens of 292
printing inks, many ills. in col. 73pp.

1884-91 Chicago   Locations
UNION TYPE FOUNDRY. Suc- as follows
cessors to Mechanics Type Foundry.
Specimens of type and ornaments:

1884	sm.12mo.	336pp. PC ICN NNC
c.1889	16mo.	69 lvs.	NNC
1889	4to.	116pp.	PC NNC
1891	4to.	116pp.	NNC

UNITED STATES TYPE FOUNDRY. See
James Connor.

c.1900 New York   NNMM
UNIVERSAL ENGRAVING CO. Catalog #23.
Another load of new stock cuts - photo.
engravings and electrotypes for all - phone
us if you don't see what you want - we'll
make it. 4to., 144pp. of pls. of specimens,
col. pict. wrap, a fine pict. ref.

1885 New York   OrU
VANDERBURG, WELLS & CO. Ill. catalog
of wood type and borders, etc. 180pp.

1889 New York   ICN
------ Wood type specimens.

c.1863 New York   MWA
WADE, H.D. & CO. Specimens of black and
colored printing inks.

WALKER & BRESNAN. See Bresnan Type
Foundry.

WALKER & PELOUZE. See Bresnan Type
Foundry.

1882 New York   CSmH
WALKER, TUTHILL & BRESNAN. Specimen book of brass rule. 37 lvs.

1880 Boston   CSmH
WATSON, D.W. Ill. price list of complete
rotary and national printing presses with
specimens, business and social cuts and
ornaments. 8vo., 32pp.

c.1876 New York   ViU
WATSON, JOSEPH. Est. 1860. Ill. price
list of Young America and centennial printing presses, types, borders, cuts and ornaments. 4to., 32pp.

1881 New York   CHi
------ Ill. price list of Young America
presses, type, ornaments, etc. 16mo., 32pp.
Pict. wrap.

1854 New York   ICN
WELLS & WEBB. Specimens of wood type.

1891 New York   ICN
WELLS, HEBER & CO. Woodtype specimen
book.

1829 Cincinnati   DLC
WELLS, OLIVER & CO. A speci-   OHi
men of printing types and ornaments cast
by . . . 138 lvs., 4 fld.

c.1880 Seneca Falls, N.Y.   N
WESCOTT BROTHERS. Ill. price list of
printers' supplies - cutters, galleys, wood
rule, furniture and tools. 8vo., 6pp.

c.1895 St. Louis   MoSHi
WESTERN BRASS TYPE FOUNDRY CO. To
the trade - specimens of brass type. Sq.
16mo., 24pp., ill. throughout.

1804-62 New York   Locations
WHITE'S TYPE FOUNDRY.   as follows
Succeeded by Farmer, Little & Co. 1862.
Type specimens as follows, listed under the
various Whites as they took over:

Elihu White.

1812	lg.12mo.	14 lvs.		NNC
nd.	16mo.	16 lvs.		NNC
1817	sm.8vo.	52 lvs.	MWA	NNC
1818	12mo.	30pp.	NN	MWA
1821	12mo.	78 lvs.		NNC
1826	12mo.	92 lvs.		NNC
1829	8vo.	130 lvs.		NNC
1831		Sabin - not located.		

White, Hagar & Co.

1833	8vo.	151 lvs.		NNC
			ICN	DLC
1835	8vo.	240 lvs.		NNC

J. T. White

1839	Specimens of . . .		NHi	CSmH
1843	lg. 8vo.	324 lvs.	NNC	NNMM
1843	lg.8vo.	121 lvs.		NNC
1845	8vo.	337 lvs.		NNC
1849	4to.	194 lvs.	NHi	NNC
1851	4to.	71 lvs.		NNC

C. T. White & Co.

1854	4to.	258 lvs.	NNC
1855	4to.	21 lvs.	NNC
1858	4to.	186 lvs.	NNC
1860	4to.	36 lvs.	NNC
1860	4to.	248 lvs.	NNC

1871 Boston   MH-BA
WOODS, BENJAMIN O. Ill. catalog of
novelty job printing presses. Lowe's pat.
portable printing press, printers' supplies,
etc. 7x10, 20pp.

1874 Boston   MiDbF
------ Ill. catalog of type, cuts,   CSmH
ornaments and presses. 8vo., 32pp.

1881 Boston   NNMM
------ Ill. catalog of printers' supplies,
types, cuts, ornaments, presses, cutters,
etc. 4to., 40pp., pict. wrap.

1834 New York   CSmH
WRIGHT, DURAND & CO. Specimens of
xylographic engraving and printing in col.,
executed by . . . C.P. Wright, Durand & Co.
N. Smith Prentiss, perfumer, being a partner in this establishment. Fol., 16 and 2
col. pls., cover title.

1879-91 Chicago   Locations
ZEESE, A. & CO. Specimens   as follows
of electrotypes, cuts, borders and ornaments
for all trades, etc.

1879	4to.	158pp.	OrU CSmH
1885	4to.	Specimens of electrotypes.	
			MWA

| 1887 | 4to. | Special cuts for businesses. | | 1889 | 4to. | Specimens. | ICN |
| | | MWA | | 1891 | 4to. | Specimens. | MWA |

The separation of specimens and presses from samples printed purely for the purpose of soliciting business has been made at the request of several enthusiastic librarians. It has been a difficult task, and prompts me to be honest and admit that some of these black horses have slipped into the white horses' corral. Many printers founded their own type and offered it for sale; others bought type for their own use and only issued catalogs of samples of their work to get new business. Don't forget the next chapter if you want to cover this subject thoroughly.

Chapter 43

Printers' Samples of Work Catalogs

The most outstanding example is, of course, Isaiah Thomas' Specimen of printing types offered in 1785. Obviously Mr. Thomas was not offering type for sale. He boasts that his work will be done with as large and complete an assortment of type as is to be met with in any one printing office in America; he also calls the attention of his prospective client to the fact that this type has been chiefly manufactured by that great artist William Caslon, Esq. of London. From Isaiah Thomas to Currier & Ives and Louis Prang, is a long and colorful road paved with examples of American imagination, inventive genius and craftsmanship. They may not seem as important as the men who designed and manufactured the type and cuts, but without them the 19th century could not have left us the pictorial panorama of American industrial growth this guide records.

When you search the thousands of catalogs of goods and products, don't forget that most of the illustrations were produced by the type founders, lithographers and printers. Without them we would only have long, dull printed lists -- page after page of them -- the dullest reading imaginable. Although many of them specialized in producing cuts and ornaments for one field, others, in one holiday collection, spread before you the illustrations of hundreds of catalogs for every trade.

1884 Ivoryton & Clintonville, Conn.   CtHi
ACME CARD CO. - KHAM & CO. Pocket sample book of new designs for social and business cards. 7x50, folder, with dozens of color cards.

1885 Ivoryton, Conn.   PShipL
------ Album of chips - original CtHi nuggets for cards, greetings, etc. 16mo., 96pp.

1885 Ivoryton, Conn.   CtHi
------ New designs for 1885.

c.1890 Philadelphia   PKsL
ALDEN, JOHN B. Publisher. Specimens of ills. and type.

nd. Philadelphia   NNMM
ALEXANDER, J.H. Manager. Specimens of show printing being facsimiles in miniature of poster cuts and ornaments. 4 lvs. and 519pp.

1886 Durham, Conn.   CtHi
ALLING BROTHERS. Ill. catalog of sample sheets of hidden name cards for the season. 4to., bds.

nd. Durham, Conn.   CtHi
------ Ill. catalog of visiting and business cards, plain and fancy. 8pp.

1869 New York   MH-BA
AMERICAN BANK NOTE CO. Est. 1858. Ill. brochure - workmanship - samples. 8vo., 25pp.

1882 New York   PC
AMERICAN DUPLEX TICKET CO. Ill. catalog of sample tickets for railroads, stage, steamboats, parlor car, baggage, ferry, etc. Col. ills., prices.

1887 New York   MH-BA
------ Ill. catalog of railroad, coach, theatre, freight, etc. tickets. 4to., 126pp., fine ills. of samples.

c.1890 New York   NN
AMERICAN LABEL CO. Litho. and Color Printers. Ill. catalog of New York stock edgings, cigar labels - brands of the past. Tall 8vo., samples #200 to 719.

1886 Buffalo, N. Y.   MWA
AMERICAN PRINTERS' SPECIMEN EXCHANGE. Ed. H. McClure, editor. Specimens of fine printing.

1887 Buffalo, N. Y.   MWA
------ Vol. 2. Specimens of handiwork by printers in all parts of U. S.

1840 Hartford, Conn.   CtHi
ANDRUS, JUDD & FRANKLIN. Catalog of valuable stereotype copper and steel pls. - maps, views, etc. Fol., 4pp.

1898 New York   NNMM
ART LITHOGRAPH PUBLISHING CO. Formerly Obpacher Brothers. Ill. catalog of calendars, booklets, etc. 83pp., pict. wrap.

c.1890 Central Falls, R. I.   CSmH
ARTOGRAVURE CO. Ill. catalog of samples of artogravure. 25pp., fine pls.

1895 Chicago   ICHi
BINNER ENGRAVING CO. Stock catalog of half-tones for calendars, programmes, souvenirs, circulars - most modern processes on wood photos. Fol., 50pp. of pls., pict. wrap.

c.1895 Chicago   CSmH
------ Ill. catalog of stock cuts and tinted pls. N.B. After August 15 price of this catalog $1.50. Fol. wrap.

BLANC, A. & CO. See Seedsmen and Nurserymens' Products.

1883 Chicago   ICHi
BLOMGREN BROTHERS & CO. Specimens of electrotype cuts and ornaments - clothing, boots, barnyard fowl, livestock, humor, landscapes, genre. Fol., 308pp. Exhaustive ref.

c.1893 San Francisco   CHi
BOLTON & STRONG. Ill. catalog of printing plates, half-tones, engravings, col. pls. 4to., fine pls., pict. wrap.

1871 Providence, R. I.   OCP&G
BOYCE, H.P. Publisher. The Shakespearian Advertiser. Between the American slang adapted Shakespearian quotes, this little booklet serves as a sample book for mfg. of beer and billiards, safes or sewing machines. 16mo., pict. wrap.

1897 Kansas City, Mo.   MoSHi
BROWN & COOK STATIONERY CO. Ill. catalog of valentines for the season.

1888 Beverly, Mass.   MdTanSW
BROWN, GEORGE P. Catalog and price list of school reward cards, oil chromos, embossed prints, art novelties. Fol., lists.

c.1890 Beverly, Mass.   NNMM
------ Catalog and price list of school reward cards, merit cards, chromos, etc. Fol., 4pp.

c.1890 New York   DSi
BRUNS, HERMAN & SON. Ill. catalog and sample book of cigar box labels. 8vo., 10 col. pls. Bruns lithos.

c.1890 New York   NNMM
BUTT, CHARLES. Ill. catalog of engravings on wood. 20pp., wrap.

1864 New York   NHi
CALDWELL & CO. Trade catalog for dealers, agents and canvassers. Ills. of valentines, playing cards, maps, charts, Civil War uniform title pages, book ills., etc. Large 4to., 12pp.

1886 Boston   NNMM
CHANDLER, VICTOR L. Ill. catalog of wood engravings. 11 lvs.

1890 Boston   MBSPNEA
CONANT, JAMES S. Ill. catalog of shoe cuts and ornaments, electro half-tones, designs for show advts. Fol., 18pp. of cuts, pict. wrap.

1860 New York   NNMM
CORLIES, MACY & CO. Ill. sample book and catalog of bank checks, bill and letterheads, drafts, samples for 20 state banks, etc. 3-1/2 x 9, 20 lvs. of sample work.

1876 New York   MH-BA
------ Ill. catalog of engravings and samples, blank books, stationery, etc. 7 x 10, 56pp. See also Stationery.

1884 New York   NNMM
CURRIER & IVES. Publishers.   PBS
Ill. and desc. list of celebrated fire pictures - series of 6 pls. and 4 pls. 8vo., 8pp., 4pls. N.B. There must be other examples of Currier & Ives' catalogs in museums and libraries -- won't you help report them?

1894 Norwood, Mass. & Boston   NNC
CUSHING, J.S. & CO. Norwood Press. Publishers. Specimens of border types, cuts and ornaments, book faces, etc. 4to., fine pls., dec. cl.

c.1890 Glen Allen, Va.   V
CUSSONS, MAY & CO. Reference and memorandum book with compliments of . . . Specimens of cuts for calendars and advt. specialties - locomotives, signals, weather flags, presidents, mottoes, etc. 64mo., dec. wrap.

nd. West Chester, Pa.   PHi
DAVIS PRINTING OFFICE. Samples of work. 12mo., 4pp., ills.

1883 New York   NNMM
DEMPSEY & CARROLL. Ill. catalog of art stationery, engravings, sentiments, samples - 70 lvs, glt. stamped cl.

1885 New York   CFs
------ Annual souvenir for 1885 - Wedding Bells. Pls. of sample work, music, verse, engravings. 4to.

1897 Baltimore   MdHi
DORMAN, J.F.W. CO. Ill. catalog #8 - samples of wholesale stock of stamps, tags, stencils, badges, etc. 12mo., 64pp., pict. wrap.

nd. New York   NNMM
FELLOWS, J.B. & CO. Ill. catalog and price list of samples of druggists' labels. 8vo., 48pp., pls., wrap.

c.1886 Durham, Conn.   CtHi
FOOTE, S.M. Seven lists of premiums for
agents - reduced price list of visiting cards,
rewards of merit, etc. Ill. collection.

1898 Warren, Pa.   NNMM
FOUCH, A.J. & CO. Catalog of chromo
cards, books, school supplies and art novelties. 40 lvs., wrap.

1885 New York   NNMM
FOULDS, ROBERT. Ill. catalog of valentines for 1885 - comic, love, bijou, cupids,
in satin, etc. 12mo., 16pp., col. pict. wrap.
See also Toys, Games and Entertainment.

1896 New Haven   CtHi
FRANKLIN PRINTING CO. Two 8vo., 4
page ill. price lists of stamps, samples of
work, monograms and novelties. Also
agents' sample book of col. cards - business
and greeting.

1880 San Francisco   CHi
GIBBONS, ELEANOR. Samples of engraving and ills. 4to., pict. wrap.

c.1876 Wallingford, Conn.   CtHi
GLOBE CARD CO. List #27 - concealed
name cards and new list of novelty cards.
4to., 4pp.

c.1876 Boston   NNMM
GOULD, J. JAY. Ill. catalog of chromos for
advertisers and printers. 60pp.

c.1900 Grand Rapids, Mich.   MiU-H
GRAND RAPIDS ENGRAVING CO. Est.1880.
The Cargill Press. To our many friends in
the carriage industry this work is dedicated,
etc. - samples of catalog work for mfg. in a
dozen states. Tall 4to., pls., 3 in col., 16
views of plant, col. pict. wrap.

c.1895 Philadelphia   PKsL
HARRIS, GEORGE S. & SONS. Color litho.
samples of holiday labels for all occasions.
8vo., 18 col. pls., wrap.

c.1880 Boston   NNMM
HASKELL & ALLEN. Catalog and price
list of chromos - ill. mats, .24¢ to $50. per
1000 - Yosemite views, winter sports, etc.
12mo., 4pp.

c.1882 Boston   NNMM
------ Ill. catalog of fine colored and
plain prints - fast horses and sporting
scenes - 5 ills. of prints - Almont at stud,
etc. 4to., 4pp.

c.1885 Boston
------ 14 x 18 broadside - cheap prints.
Lists.

c.1890 Boston   NRGE
HELIOTYPE PRINTING CO. Ill. catalog of
reproduced ills. with samples and specimens of designs and work. Large 8vo., 24
and 8pp., pict. wrap.

nd. Cincinnati   NNMM
HENNEGAN & CO. Condensed catalog and
price list of posters for all occasions.
8 lvs., wrap.

c.1890 New York   NNMM
HEPPENKEIMER'S SONS. Est. 1849.
Lithographers & Printers. Samples of
cigar box labels. 8vo., 4 col. lithos., pict.
wrap.

c.1890 New York   NNMM
HEYWOOD-STRASSER & VOIGT LITHO CO.
Ill. catalog of imported cigar bands made by
Gebruder Weigang, Bautzen, Germany.
9 lvs. of examples.

1884 New Bedford   ICHi
HOWLAND, PAUL JR. Specimen book of
printing types, borders, cuts and ornaments.
Large 4to., 85pp., 23 pls., stiff wrap.

nd. Clintonville, Conn.   CtHi
IVY CARD CO. Agent's sample book of
greeting cards. 32 col. cards in booklet.

KELLOGG, E.B. & E.C. Lithographers.
See Seedsmen and Nurserymens' Products.

c.1865-70 Boston   NNMM
          MWA NhD IaU ICHi
KILBURN, S.S. Specimen of designs and
engravings on wood, fine pls. 4to., 45 pls.,
col. title and 8pp., cl.

1885 Chicago   CSmH
LAWRENCE, J.F. PRINTING CO. Samples
of printed and litho. labels, some in col.,
for various purposes. 16 lvs., wrap.

1883 New York   NNMM
LEVEY, FRED'K. H. & CO. Holiday catalog
of the American Pictorial Co. 12 lvs., ills.,
wrap.

c.1890 New Britain, Conn.   Ct
LEWIS & ATWELL. Lewis & Atwell specimen of photo. engravings. 4to., 16pp. plus
16 pls., wrap.

1877 Allentown, Pa.   DNLM
LOCHMAN, C.L. Catalog of dose and price
labels of principal articles of materia
medica used in U. S., active and poisonous
articles, etc. 8vo.

1882-90 New York   MiDbF
McLOUGHLIN BROTHERS. Valentines for
1882. Ill. catalog of valentines for the season. 8vo., fine ills., pict. wrap. Also ill.
catalogs of valentines for 1883 and 1890.

c.1875 Philadelphia   NNMM
MANN, WILLIAM. Lithographer. Color
tinted poster 17 x 22 offering ornamental
printing, engraved pict. checks, blank books,
etc. N.B. New store - tack this up and
oblige.

1877 Philadelphia   PHi
MARKS BROTHERS. Album of engraving
samples. 8vo., 10pp.

nd. New York   NNMM
MATHEWS & CO. Monograms - 423 numbered examples. 48 and 4 lvs., cl.

1893 Chicago   NNMM
MERCHANTS PUBLISHING CO. Ill. catalog
of druggists' labels, boxes and other printed
supplies. 192 lvs., a fine ref.

1887 White House, N. J.   PKsL
MORGAN, WILLIAM. Our 4th year - Ill.
catalog of school reward cards, Christmas,
Easter, birthday cards, chromos and novelties. Sm. fol., 8pp.

nd. New York   PHi
MOSS ENGRAVING CO. Moss type specimens. 8vo., 32pp.

c.1890 New York   DSi
NEUMAN, LOUIS E. & CO. Lithographer &
Printer. Cigar Box Labels, prices net.
5-1/2 x 8, 7 fine col. samples, pict. wrap.

1876 Chicago   NNMM
NORRIS, B.F. & CO. Ill. catalog of letter
designs for jewelers and engravers - plain
and fancy. 38pp., cl.

nd. Southbury, Conn.   CtHi
NUTTINGHAME CO. Ill. catalog of half-
tones and other samples of specimens used.

1834-76 New York   NNMM
ORR, JNO. W. Collection of 5 scrapbooks
of office proofs of work.

c.1900 Newark, N. J.   NNMM
OSBORNE, THE CO. Ill. catalog of
Osborne's fine art calendars. Fol., col.pls.

1880-84 Bloomington, Ill.   IHi
PANTAGRAPH PRINTING CO. Ill. catalog
of half-tones, cuts and ornaments of famous
horses, racing cuts, livestock, wagons,
sulkies, locomotives, comics, etc. 8vo.
Three ill. catalogs for 1880, 1883 and 1884.

1874 New York   MoSHi
PATTEN, J.L. & CO. Ill. catalog and price
list of dec. - new designs and styles.

1897 Boston & New York   NNMM
PETTINGILL & CO. Ill. catalog of type,
cuts and ornaments for an advt. agency.
68 lvs., fine ills., cl.

c.1870 Warren, Pa.   NNMM
PHOENIX STEAM PRINTING CO. Ill. price
list of merit cards, stock and visiting cards,
Merry Xmas, etc., fine paper and stationery.
4to., 4pp.

1887 New York   NNMM
THE PHOTO-ENGRAVING CO. Autumn
1887. Specimen book of pls. 4to., 16pp. of
pls., pict. wrap.

1860-92 Boston   Locations
PRANG, L. & CO. Albums of   as follows
color designs for social and business occupations, cards, chromos, book ills., greetings, alphabets, art work and even undertaking - all fine ill. catalogs of the first water.

1860   NNMM
Designs for monuments and headstones.
58 pls.

1863   NNMM
Slate pictures #2. Booklet of designs.
16mo., wrap.

1864   NNMM
Album of 162 color cards of butterflies, moths,
wild flowers, leaves and mosses.

1864   NNMM
The American Album - sample chromos
seaweeds, ferns, wildlife, etc. 4to., 41 pls.

1868   NNMM
Prang's Chromo - Popular art journal and
ill. catalog Vol. 1, #1 - 4.

1873   NNMM
Ill. catalog of publications. 8pp.

1876   PC   NhD   MBAt CSmH NNMM
Litho. specimen of state arms of the Union,
45 col. pls., col. pict. title, 4to., cl. Fine
ref.

1876   ICHi
Ill. catalog of art publications. 8vo., 39pp.,
fine ills., pict. wrap.

1878   CSmH
Prang's standard alphabets. 32 col. pls.

1880   MeBa
Alphabets plain, ornamental and illuminated.
A selection. Tall 8vo., 4 ill. in col.

1883-84   NNMM
Ill. catalog of prints. 30pp., wrap.

1884-85   NNMM
Ill. catalog of Christmas and New Years
cards, desc. and priced. 24pp.

1885   NNU
Ill. catalog of cards and novelties, fine ills.
of many familiar ones. 4to., 48pp.

1885-86   NNMM
Ill. catalog of cards for the season. 48pp.

1886   CSmH
Prang's standard alphabets - revised ed.
Tall 4to., 36 pls., many in col.

1886-87   NNMM
Ill. catalog of seasons cards. 48pp.

1887   CSmH NNMM
Ill. catalog of cards and novelties. 46 pp.

1887-88   NNMM
Catalog of seasons cards, fine ills. 45pp.

1888-89   NNMM
Ill. catalog of fine art studies, water colors,
pictures and prints. 30pp.

1890   NNMM
Ill. catalog with 36 fine pls., wrap.

1891-92   NNMM
Ill. catalog of fine art studies, etc. 48pp.

nd. Philadelphia   PHi
QUINT, S.H. & SONS. Quint's stencil,
stamp and letter works. Ill. catalog of supplies. 8vo., 69pp.

nd. North Haven, Conn.   CtHi
RAY CARD CO. Folder #1 - new pocket
sample book of social, greeting and business
cards. Folded to 16mo., 5 in col.

c.1900 Hamilton, O.   OHi
REPUBLICAN PUBLISHING CO. The building of high grade vehicles catalogs - plates
of Ohio's carriage builders, plants, models,
styles and parts. Possibly done for a
client, but more likely for more carriage
catalog work. Tall 4to., Gibson Girl driving
tandem. Pict. wrap. A great job.

1893 Providence, R. I.   RHi
RHODE ISLAND PRINTING CO. A book of
specimens. 4to., 100 pls., some in col.,
col. pict. title.

c.1881 Boston   NNMM
ROBINSON ENGRAVING CO. Fol.   PC
book of examples of work - 277 pls. of hotel
and summer resort cards, letterheads,
menus, billheads and sample brochures.

c.1880 Rochester, N. Y.   NR
ROCHESTER LITHO CO. Catalog of col.
samples - plants, shrubs, trees, etc. -
probably for nurserymen. 12mo., col. pls.

c.1900 New York   NNMM
ROTOGRAPH CO. Catalog F - #1 samples
of actual photo. postal cards. 16 lvs., wrap.

ROUSS. See Department Stores and
General Merchandise.

1879 Philadelphia   NNMM
ROWLEY & CHEW PRINTING HOUSE. Jno.
A. Haddock. Ill. catalog and price list of
printers' printed stock, etc. - cards, circulars, borders and tinted borders, letterheads.

1888 Rochester, N. Y.   NNC
STECHER LITHOGRAPH CO. Salesman's
fld. sample case of 50 fine col. examples
from fine nurserymens' catalogs of flowers,
fruits, shrubs, etc. A swell ref.

c.1890 St. Louis   MoSHi
STANNARD ENGRAVING CO. Ill. catalog
of designs and engravings for printers and
publishers, etc.

1884 Clintonville, Conn.   CtHi
STAR CARD CO. C.W. Talmadge, Prop.
Revised price list of fashionable visiting
and business cards. 4to., ills., bds.

1785 Worcester, Mass.   RPJCB
THOMAS, ISAIAH.   MWA CSmH
A specimen of Isaiah Thomas's printing
types being as large and complete an assortment as is to be met with in any one printing
office in America. See The Colonial Scene.
MWA 1950.

c.1895 New York   NNMM
THOMPSON, J. WALTER. Ill., desc. and
priced catalog of examples and designs for
an advertising company. 120pp., wrap.

nd. Clintonville, Conn.   NNMM
TODD CARD CO. Pocket sample book of
visiting cards, ill. and priced. 16 lvs.,
wrap.

1876 Philadelphia   PKsL
TOUDY, H.J. & CO. Color lithograph circular showing R. Hoe building at Centennial.
All orders for lithography, engraving and
printing promptly executed. A clever way
to advertise Hoe's presses and Toudy's
work on them.

1864-76 Rutland, Vt.   NNMM
TUTTLE & CO. Scrapbook of 208 examples
of printers' samples of work from 1864-76,
executed by the Tuttle firm.

1880 North Haven, Conn.   CtHi
TUTTLE BROTHERS. Agents' sample book
of designs for cards, visiting, social and
business. 15pp., each with 2 new col. samples.

c.1840 Philadelphia   PC
UNDERWOOD, BALD, SPENCER & HUFTY,
and DANFORTH, UNDERWOOD & CO., N.Y.
An unusual specimen book of samples of fine
engravings of eagles, locomotives, ships,
seals, many trades, etc. 4to., 22 pls., wrap.

c.1880 Columbus, O. OHi
UNION CARD CO. Agents' sample OC
book - fancy greeting cards, calling cards,
business cards, many in col. 16mo., 14
samples, bds.

1870 Bristol, Pa. NNMM
UNITED STATES LABEL PRINTING ESTAB-
LISHMENT. The Druggists' Printer. Vol.
2, #3. 22pp., fine ills. - fully as good as
most drug label catalogs.

1891 Cincinnati NNMM
UNITED STATES PRINTING CO. The card
players' Companion - ill. and priced catalog
of cards and popular games. 40pp., wrap.

1890 New York NHi
WAGNER, LOUIS C. Ill. catalog of fine
cigar labels and bands. 4to., 138 colorful
designs for box top and cigars. Fine ref.,cl.

c.1885 Philadelphia MdTanSW
WANAMAKER & BROWN. Oak Hall advertising sketches - appendix advertising cuts
with prices for business advertising. 12mo.
36pp.

c.1894 Akron, O. NNMM
WERNER, THE L. PRINTING & OHi
LITHO. CO. Type specimens of lithography,
an ill. catalog of samples - ills. of departments, plant, etc. as well, with history.
8vo., floral pict. wrap., 42 pls.

c.1878 New York & Chicago NNMM
WITSCH & SCHMITT. ICN DSi
Lithographers. Specimen book of front
brands and morticed borders, cigar bands
and box cover designs - ills. of colorful
lithos. of bathing beauties, butterflies, eagles,
fire engines, locomotives, steamboats,
chorus gals, great lovers with guitars - take
your pick - any way you look at it these col.
pls. are an important record. Sq. 8vo., 100
to 183 col. pls., cl. cvs.

c.1900 New York & Chicago DSi
------ Sample book of cigar box labels.
8vo., looseleaf, about 100 specimens in full
col. depicting commerce, trade, love and
the Spanish American War.

1884 Woodstock, Vt. VtHi
WOODBURY & CO. Ill. catalog of druggists'
labels, some in full col. - bay rum, castor
oil, gingerale, beer, whiskey and wine as
well as drugs - a swell litho. record. Sm.
4to., 84pp. of specimens.

1888 Yalesville, Conn. NNMM
YALESVILLE CARD CO. Agents' sample
book of cards, circular and printed samples
of work. 14 lvs. of col. samples.

If your interest is in the early type founders specimens, don't forget that these gentlemen could not
have stayed in business and continued designing and manufacturing without the printers who purchased
their wares and sold their pictorial harvest to the American public. Also, please bear with me;
I have not been able to examine many of these listings - they are offered to you through the cooperation of three dozen librarians and curators - some of the black horses may have been painted white.

Chapter 44

Pumps & Water Wheels

I heard you distinctly. Why don't these pumps and water wheels belong in the chapter on Plumbing? Why don't you include Windmills in this one? Why didn't you list pumps in the section covering Hardware - Miscellaneous Machinery? My answer is as arbitrary as my classifications. Through a good many years American libraries have purchased catalogs as classified in this guide. It seems to me these are the groupings in which they will be most easily found.

Although the first patent for a water wheel was granted in 1806, and in spite of the fact that Washington issued over three hundred patents from this date to 1857, the earliest printed and illustrated record with prices we can locate is about 1850. According to Mr. Bishop, the first force pumps were built for fire engines and ships before the Revolution. The first illustrated record might be the S. V. Merrick & Co. improved fire engines and other hydraulic machines c.1815 -- see Fire Engines. As a trade catalog this 8 page brochure might be debatable. It would be safer to check the illustrations in such catalogs as George C. Barrett in the Seedsmen and Nurserymens' catalogs from about 1830. Briefly, by 1869, the 20 in. turbines were doing many times the work once produced by the 25 ft. wheels. This is industrial history for which we have no room in a volume intended only to guide the reader to catalog records.

I feel sure that with a little work you can find illustrations and prices of the best pumps and water wheels of the 19th century -- the water wheels that built the industry and the pumps to serve them.

1878 Mt. Holly, N. J.   PKsL
ALCOTT, T.C. & SON. Ill. catalog of late improved turbine water wheels and mill machinery. 8vo., 68pp., pict. wrap.

c.1887 Mt. Holly, N. J.   PKsL
------ Ill. catalog of water wheels. 64pp.

1890 Mt. Holly, N. J.   PKsL
------ Ill. catalog of high duty turbine water and mill specialties. 112pp., pls.

1893 Mt. Holly, N. J.   DSi
------ Ill. catalog, 8vo., 64pp., pict. wrap.

See also Risdon, Theodore H. & Co.

1862 Milwaukee   WHi
ALLIS, EDWARD P. Reliance Works. Ill. catalog of patterns in French burr mill stones and water wheels, etc. 16mo., 52pp. Pict. wrap.

1897 New York   PP
AMERICAN IMPULSE WHEEL CO. Ill. catalog of the perfect American hurdy-gurdy Gazin power wheels. Large 8vo., diagrams and plans, cl.

c.1900 San Francisco   CHi
AMERICAN STEAM PUMP CO. Inc. 1873. Catalog #14. Ill. catalog of Marsh steam pumps for water power, boats, etc. Sq. 8vo., 136pp., pict. wrap.

1870 Boston   DeWe
AMERICAN WATER WHEEL CO. Ill. catalog of Warren's new patented graduating turbine water wheels, shaftings and castings for mills, etc. 12mo., 24pp., wrap.

c.1869 New York   MH-BA
ANDREWS, WILLIAM D. & BROTHER. Ill. catalog of patented (1846) improved anti-friction centrifugal pumps. 8vo., 8pp.

1870 Providence, R. I.   RHi
ANGELL, OTIS N. & SONS, MFG. Ill. circular and price list of Angell's Rhode Island water wheels. 16mo., 30pp., pict. wrap.

1877 Athens, O.   InHi
ATHENS WATER WHEEL & MACHINERY CO. Ill., desc. catalog of Case improved turbine water wheels and mill machinery. 8vo., 56pp., pict. wrap.

c.1872 Philadelphia   DSi
ATLANTIC MFG. CO. Ill. catalog of aquo-meter pistonless steam pumps for all purposes. 4to.

1881 Newark, N. J.   MH-BA
BACKUS WATER MOTOR CO. Ill. catalog
#7 of motors with instructions and tests.
8vo., 20pp., wrap.

c.1895 Newark, N. J.   DSi
------ Ill. catalog of water motors and
appliances. 38pp.

c.1886 Minneapolis   MnHi
BALL & NAYLOR. Ill. catalog of wood and
iron pumps for farm and town. Wrap.
Three catalogs noted, all c.188?. No other
data.

1892 Philadelphia   PP
BARR PUMPING ENGINE CO. Ill. catalog
of duplex steam pumps.

c.1900 Lancaster, Pa.   PKsL
BARRY & ZECHER CO. Ill. catalog of light
lift pumps, force and lift, hand or power.
8vo., 28pp., frs. of plant with pict. wrap. of
Penn RR., etc.

1896 Battle Creek   PP
BATTLE CREEK STEAM PUMP CO. Ill.
catalog of Marsh steam pumps.

c.1850 East Pepperell, Mass.   MBSPNEA
BLAKE BROTHERS. Ill. circular of Blake's
pat. improved water wheels with prices,
sizes, power velocity, etc. 4to., 4pp.

1889 New York, Philadelphia and San
        Francisco.   DSi
BLAKE, GEORGE F. MFG. CO. Ill. catalog
of Blake's improved steam pumps and pumping engines. 80pp.

1890 New York, Philadelphia and San
        Francisco.   CSmH
------ Ill. catalog. 78pp.

1900 New York, Philadelphia and San
        Francisco.   PP
------ Ill. catalog for 1900.

c.1874 Philadelphia   DSi
BLATCHLEY, CHARLES G. Ill. catalog of
cucumber wood pumps, wooden aqueduct
pipes, ice cream freezers, etc. 12pp., pict.
wrap.

c.1876 Philadelphia   PHi
------ Ill. circular of cucumber wood
pumps. 4pp.

1868 Mt. Morris, N. Y. & Westfield, Mass.
BODINE & CO. MFG. Ill. catalog of Jonval
turbine water wheels, mill gearings, shaftings, pulleys, etc. 16mo., 38pp., 2 pls.,
wrap.

c.1875 New Haven   Ct
BRADLEY, R.B. & CO. New Haven Agricultural Warehouse. Ill. 8 page folder of

premium cucumber wood pumps, for well
and cisterns in farm yard and back yard.

1868 Bridgeport, Conn.   MH-BA
BRIDGEPORT MFG. CO. Ill. catalog of
American submerged pumps, pat. 1864.
8vo., 4pp.

1890 Bridgton, Me.   DSi
BRIDGTON MACHINE CO. Catalog of the
Perry hydraulic turbines. 8vo., 42pp., ills.

1889 Buffalo, N. Y.   DSi
BUFFALO STEAM PUMP CO. Ill. catalog
of steam pumping machinery. 41pp., wrap.

1872 Philadelphia   PHi
BURR, DAVID A. Ill. catalog of Prall con-
densing steam pumps. 8vo., 12pp.

1874 St. Johnsbury, Vt.   VtHi
BUZZELL, LUKE. Mfg. Ill. price list of
the Giant Water Wheel - 20 to 50 in., 4to.,
4pp.

1877 New York   DSi
CAMERON, A.S. Ill. catalog of steam
pumps. 26pp.

c.1872 New York   DSi
CARR, A. & CO. Ill. price list of Selden
steam pumps. 16pp.

1894 Orange, Mass.   DSi
CHASE TURBINE MFG. CO. Ill. catalog of
turbine water wheels. 68pp.

1895 Christiana, Pa.   PP
CHRISTIANA MACHINE CO. Ill. catalog of
turbine water wheels.

c.1875 Philadelphia   PKsL
CONDE, C.A. & CO. Ill. price list of
Conde's pat. - 1872 - Challenge steam
pumps. 8vo., 8pp.

c.1885 Toledo, O.   OHi
CONSOLIDATED PUMP CO. Ill. catalog
#28 - wood pumps. 8vo., 16pp., 2 col. pls.,
pict. wrap.

1875 Chicago   DSi
CRANE BROTHERS MFG. CO. Ill. catalog
of steam pumps. 12pp.

1881 Ogdensburg, N. Y.   N
CURTIS IRON WORKS. Est. 1848. Ill. catalog of Curtis' improved turbine water
wheels mfg. by Gates Curtis. 12mo., 73pp.,
pict. wrap. of works.

1893 New York   PP
DAVIDSON, M.T. & CO. Ill. catalog of
Davidson's improved steam pumps, pumping
engines and mill machinery.

1892 Dayton, O.   DSi
DAYTON GLOBE IRON WORKS. Ill. catalog
of new American hydraulic turbines. 8vo.,
150pp.

1895 Dayton, O.   DSi
------ Ill. catalog. 8vo., 115pp.

1891 Indianapolis   PP
DEAN BROTHERS' STEAM PUMP WORKS.
Ill. catalog of steam pumping machinery.

1878-90 New York   PP
DEANE STEAM PUMP WORKS. Ill. catalog
of steam pumps and machinery. Also ill.
catalog for 1890.

1897 Holyoke, Mass.   PP
DEANE STEAM PUMP CO. Ill. catalog of
steam and power pumps, and pumping
machinery.

c.1884 New York   MH-BA
DELAMETER, C.H. & CO. IRON   DSi
WORKS. Ill. catalog of Ericsson's new hot
air pumping engines and Selden's steam
pumps. 8vo., 8pp.

1893 Salem, O.   OHi
DEMING, THE CO. Ill. catalog of   PP
iron and brass pumps, portable force pumps
for spraying fruit orchards, etc. 12mo.,
16pp., pict. wrap.

1854 Middletown, Conn.   CtHi
DOUGLAS, W. & B. Ill. and desc. catalog
of patent metallic pumps, hydraulic rams,
chain pumps, garden engines, etc. 12mo.,
28pp., pict. wrap.

1895 San Francisco   CHi
DOW STEAM PUMP WORKS. Ill. catalog of
pumping and hydraulic machinery. 8vo.,
86pp., bds.

1889 Philadelphia   PKsL
FRANCIS BROTHERS - Kensington Engine
Works, Ltd. Ill. catalog of Dow positive
piston pumps. 8vo., 12pp., fine pls.

1897 Chicago   PP
FRASER & CHALMERS. Ill. catalog of
Riedler pumps, compressors and blowing
engines. See also Hardware - Miscellaneous Machinery - Mining.

1893 Quincy, Ill.   PP
GARDNER GOVERNOR CO. Ill. catalog of
duplex steam pumps.

1883-87 San Francisco   CHi
GARRATT, W.T. & CO. Ill. catalog of brass
and iron goods, bells, pumps and pumping
machinery. 4to., fine ills., bds. Same for
1887. Ill. catalog.

1895 San Francisco   CHi
GIRARD WATER WHEEL CO. Ill. catalog
of water wheels. 8vo., fine ills.

1888 Hamilton, O.   PP
GORDON STEAM PUMP CO. Ill. catalog of
steam pumps and machinery.

1877 Goshen, Ind.   In
GOSHEN, THE PUMP CO. Ill. catalog and
price list of pumps for all purposes. 8vo.,
16pp.

1877-95 Seneca Falls, N. Y.   Locations
GOULD MFG. CO. Est. 1848.   as follows
Ill. catalog of pumps, hydraulic machinery,
rams, fire engines, garden engines, bells
and heavy hardware.

1877	8vo.	206pp.	dec. cl.	DSi
1880	8vo.	232pp.	dec. cl.	DSi
1881-2	8vo.	240pp.	dec. cl.	PKsL
1892	8vo.	282pp.	dec. cl.	PKsL
1895	8vo.	356pp.	dec. cl.	DSi PC

See also Fire Engines.

c.1865 Cincinnati   OC
GREENWOOD, MILES MFG. Ill. circular
of Leffel's American double turbine water
wheels. Great economy in water power, etc.
4to., 4pp. N.B. From OC - Greenwood was
the first paid fire chief in the world, and a
well known western builder of engines.

1883 Brooklyn, N. Y.   DSi
GUILD & GARRISON. Ill. catalog of steam
pumping machinery. 48pp.

c.1874 Hartford, Conn.   DSi
HARTFORD PUMP CO. Ill. catalog of compressed air pumps. 18pp.

1894-5 Anderson, Ind.   PP
HILL MACHINE CO. Ill. catalog of steam
artesian and deep well pumping machinery.

1887 San Francisco   CHi
HOLBROOK, MERRILL & STETSON. Ill.
catalog #35 - pumps and pumping machinery
and accessories.

1883 Lockport, N. Y.   PPL
HOLLY MFG. CO. Ill. catalog of rotary,
turbine and pressure pumps of various
types and designs. 24pp.

1884 Lockport, N. Y.   PP
------ Ill. catalog of Gaskill's steam
pumps for 1884.

1891 Lockport, N. Y.   PP
------ Ill. catalog of high duty pumps, etc.

1885 Worcester, Mass.   DSi
HOLYOKE MACHINE CO. Ill. catalog of
Hercules hydraulic turbines. 8vo., 90pp.

1895 Worcester, Mass.   DSi
------ Ill. catalog. 8vo., 88pp., ills.

c.1895 Keene, N. H.   DSi
HUMPHREY MACHINE CO. Ill. catalog of
the I.X.L. and X-L C-R hydraulic turbines.
8vo., 24pp.

1885 Orange, Mass.   DSi
HUNT, RODNEY MACHINE CO. Ill. catalog
of hydraulic turbines and woolen mill machinery. 8vo., 106pp.

1897 Orange, Mass.   DSi
------ Ill. catalog. 188pp.

1882 Goshen, Ind.   In
THE I X L PUMP CO. Ill. price list of
IXL cucumber pumps and improved porce-
lain lined pumps, etc. 8vo., 4pp.

1883 Goshen, Ind.   In
------ 4 page ill. circular of pumps.

1884 Goshen, Ind.   In
------ Ill. catalog. 12mo., 24pp., pict.
wrap. Ptd. South Bend.

1892 Chicago   DSi
JEWELL, O.H. FILTER CO. Ill. circular
of Jewell improved water purifiers - for
all pumps. 39pp.

1868 Warren, Mass.   MH-BA
KNOWLES & SIBLEY. Ill. circular of
Knowles' pat. steam pumps. 8vo., 8pp.

1874 Warren, Mass.   MH-BA
------ Ill. price list. 8vo., 8pp.

1890 Boston   DSi
KNOWLES STEAM PUMP WORKS. Ill.
circular of water supply and pumping machinery. 65pp., 35 pls.

1881 Logansport, Ind.   InHi
KNOWLTON & DOLAN. Obenshain's improved Little Giant turbine water wheels.
8vo., 36pp., fine ills., pict. wrap.

1899 San Francisco   CHi
KROGH MFG. CO. Ill. catalog #20 - pumping machinery for irrigation and reclaiming
lands. 8vo., fine photo. ills. Also a brochure for 1900.

1896 Cincinnati   PP
LAIDLAW-DUNN-GORDON CO. Ill. catalog
of pumping machinery.

1867 Portland, Ore.   CU
LEFFEL & MYERS. Ill. catalog of James
Leffel's double turbine water wheels. 56pp.,
tables, diagrams, wrap.

1868-97 Springfield, O.   Locations
LEFFEL, JAMES & CO.   as follows
Est. c.1860. Ill. catalogs of Leffel's American double turbine water wheels, booklets on
mill dams, Bookwalter's Millwright, etc.:

1868   In   OHi
Ill. catalog of Leffel's American double turbine water wheels. Pat. 1862, list of users
from Maine to California. 8vo., 80pp.

1869   OHi In   CtHi
Ill. catalog with diagrams of mills in operation, etc. 8vo., 104pp., pict. wrap.

1874   NStIHi OHi In   InHi
Construction of Mill Dams, with ill. catalog
of water wheels, etc. 12mo., 228pp., pls.
and diagrams - a fine ref.

1879   OHi   MH-BA
Ill. catalog. 8000 in use in U.S.A. Large
8vo., 96pp.

1881   InHi In   MeBa
Ill. catalog including Bookwalter's Millwright and Mechanic. Fine job.

1881-2   PKsL
Ill. handbook and catalog. 12mo., 160pp.

1882   DSi   MnHi
Catalog of Bookwalter engines. 12mo.,
30pp., fine ills.

1883   DSi   DeWe
Handbook and catalog of water wheels in
operation from Maine to Texas. 12mo.,
160pp., pls., dec. cl.

1887   MnHi
New ed. of handbook and catalog.

1888   DSi   ICHi
Handbook and ill. catalog for 1888-9. 12mo.,
128pp., pls., pict. wrap.

1890   OHi
Ill. catalog and handbook. 12mo., 108pp.

1891   OHi
Ill. catalog of hydraulic turbines. 8vo.,
104pp.

1893   OHi   InHi
Ill. circular of the Sampson water wheels.
16mo., pict. wrap.

1894   OHi   DSi
Ill. catalog of steam engines and boilers and
pumping machinery. 94pp.

1896   OHi   DSi
Ill. catalog of Cascade impulse hydraulic
turbines. 8vo., 44pp., pict. wrap.

1897   OHi
Booklet #73. Ill. catalog of Leffel's engines
and boilers and pumps. 24pp.

See also Hardware - Miscellaneous Machinery.

MARSH STEAM PUMPS. See American
Steam Pump Co.

c.1900 Oakland, Calif.   DSi
OAKLAND IRON WORKS. Ill. catalog of
Tutthill's pat. water wheels. 146pp.

1891 San Francisco   CHi
PACIFIC IRON WORKS. Ill. catalog of
Dodd's sigmoidal water wheels. 8vo.,49pp.,
wrap.

1858 Cincinnati   OC
PALMER & CO. Palmer's rotary, hydraulic lifting and forcing pumps for fire
purposes, hotels and factories and for water
supply to mills, breweries, distilleries,
railroad stations and bilge and fire pumps
for ocean, lake and river steamers and
ships. 8vo., 40pp., fine ills., wrap.

1889-92 San Francisco   CHi
PELTON WATER WHEEL CO. Two ill.
catalogs of details and price of the Pelton
water wheels.

    1889   2nd ed.   8vo.   30pp.   wrap.

    1892   5th ed.   8vo.   98pp.   wrap.

1883 Baltimore   PP
POOLE & HUNT. Engineers & Machinists.
Ill. catalog of Poole & Hunt Leffel turbine
water wheels and engines.

c.1880 Baltimore   PKsL
POOLE, ROBERT & SON. Ill. catalog of
Poole-Leffel turbine water wheels. 12mo.,
81pp., pls., wrap.

1896 Baltimore   DSi
------ Ill. catalog of turbines and power
transmission machinery. 236pp.

1880 Coatesville, Pa.   PWcHi
RIDGWAY, CRAIG & SON. Ill. catalog of
William H. Ridgway's perfection water
wheels for paper, cotton, flour and sawmills.
8vo., 48pp., pict. wrap.

1882 Coatesville, Pa.   PKsL
------ Ill. circular of Ridgway's perfection water wheels. 8vo., 89pp., fine pls.

c.1880 Mt. Holly, N. J.   DSi
RISDON, THEODORE H. & CO. Ill. catalog
of Risdon's cylinder gate hydraulic turbine
water wheels. 8vo., 74pp.

c.1900 Mt. Holly, N. J.   DSi
RISDON-ALCOTT TURBINE CO. Ill. catalog of hydraulic turbines. 8vo., 120pp.

1877 Barnard, Vt.   VtHi
SAFFORD, JOSEPH E. Ill. and desc. circular price list of Safford's pat. improved turbine water wheels. Pat. 1874. 10pp.

nd. Norwich, Conn.   CtHi
SCHOLFIELD, NATHAN. Ill. circular of
water wheels.

c.1885 York, Pa.   DSi
SMITH, S. MORGAN. Ill. catalog of Smith's
improved Success hydraulic turbines. 8vo.,
84pp.

c.1890 York, Pa.   DSi
------ Ill. catalog of gearings, pulleys and
mill machinery. 92pp., 8vo.

c.1874 Dayton, O.   DSi
SMITH, VAILE & CO. Ill. catalog of steam
pumps. 6pp.

1899 Philadelphia   PP
SNIDER-HUGHES CO. Ill. catalog of pumping machinery.

1897 Buffalo, N. Y.   PP
SNOW STEAM PUMP WORKS. Ill. catalog
of Snow steam pumps.

1869 New York   DSi
STEVENSON, J.E. Ill. catalog of Stevenson's duplex turbine water wheels. 8vo.,
44pp.

1872-99 Dayton, O.   Locations
STILWELL & BIERCE MFG. CO. as follows
Ill. catalogs of the Victor turbines and
double Eclipse turbine water wheels.

    1872   CSmH
    Ill. catalog of Eclipse double turbine water
    wheels. 44pp.

    1876   MH-BA
    Ill. catalog of Eclipse wheels and parts.
    12mo., 28pp.

    1883   InHi
    The Victor Turbines. 12mo., 80pp., plans,
    diagrams, pls., pict. wrap.

    1891   PP
    Ill. catalog of Victor turbines.

    1898   DSi
    Ill. catalog of turbines. 8vo., 180pp.

1899   PP
Ill. catalog of pumping machinery.

1869 Dayton, O.   DSi
STOUT, MILLS & TEMPLE. Globe Iron
Works. Ill. catalog of American hydraulic
turbine water wheels. 8vo., 104pp., wrap.

1872 North Chelmsford, Mass.   DeWe
SWAIN TURBINE CO., THE. Ill. and desc.
catalog of Swain turbine water wheels, accessories, etc. with tests of apparatus - to
mill owners. 8vo., 52pp., pict. wrap. and
fld. plate.

1897 Lowell, Mass. (Moved)   DSi
SWAIN TURBINE & MFG. CO. Ill. catalog
of Swain hydraulic turbines. 8vo., 29pp.

c.1895 Springfield, O.   DSi
TRUMP MFG. CO. Ill. catalog of the Trump
hydraulic turbines. 8vo., 84pp., ills.

1869 West Lebanon, N. H.   InHi NhD
TYLER, JOHN. Ill. catalog of Tyler's improved turbine water wheels. 24mo., 40pp.,
pict. wrap.

1874 West Lebanon, N. H.   NhHi
------ Ill. catalog of new improved water
wheels and parts. Pat. 1848. 16mo., 48pp.,
wrap.

1879 New Britain, Conn.   CtHi
UNION MFG. CO. Ill. catalog and price
list of hydraulic rams, garden engines, iron,
brass and copper pumps for all purposes.
8vo., 142pp., fine ills., pict. wrap.

1891 New Britain, Conn.   CtHi
------ Ill. catalog of pumps. 8vo., 190pp.,
fine ills., cl.

c.1900 Battle Creek   PP
UNION STEAM PUMP CO. Ill. catalog of
Union steam pumps.

1875 Sandy Hill, N. Y.   DeWe
WASHINGTON MACHINE CO. Ill. catalog of
Wait's Hudson River Champion water wheels.
12mo., 44pp., pict. wrap.

c.1886 Fultonville, N. Y.   DSi
WEMPLE'S, WILLIAM B. SONS. The Lesner
hydraulic turbines. 8vo., 58pp., ills.

1882 Providence, R. I.   RHi
WHITMAN, JOSIAH W. Interesting ill. and
desc. circular of Whitman's fountain pumps.
The new portable pump and sprinkler for all
occasions. 8vo., 16pp., pict. wrap.

1881-2 St. Paul, Minn.   MnHi
WILSON & ROGERS. Ill. and desc. catalog
of lift and force pumps of various designs.
8vo., ill. throughout for 1881 and 1882.

1886 Philadelphia   TxU
WOOD, R.D. & CO. Desc. and ill. price
lists of pumps, turbines, pipes, hydrants for
gas and water.

1887-93 New York   Locations
WORTHINGTON, HENRY R.   as follows
Est. 1840. Ill. catalogs of Worthington
steam pumps, pumping engines, condensers
and water meters, etc.

1887   Ill. catalog.   152pp.   DSi

1892   Ill. catalog.   PP

1893   Ill. catalog.   PP

(Now the well known Worthington Corp.)

Naturally there are hundreds of catalogs listed under Agricultural Implements, Fire Engines, Hardware, and, as pointed out, Seedsmen and Nurserymens' Products, that record and illustrate both
water wheels and pumps. Don't forget that bars and soda fountains also use pumps for instance.
See also Plumbing. This would be a very sad world without water, and don't for one minute let it
out of your mind.

Chapter 45

Railroad Equipment—Locomotives, Rolling Stock & Supplies

Although there are several outstanding library collections in this field, I must point out again that the catalogs listed represent only a small percentage of those available for research. The DeGolyer Foundation probably has in the neighborhood of a thousand locomotive catalogs; catalogs of equipment and supplies would number a great many more. The outstanding examples are located thanks to Mr. DeGolyer's enthusiastic support.

A report has just come in from the National Museum of Transport, St. Louis, Missouri. The entire library is in the process of moving to new quarters, but the librarian states that the collections contain a great many trade catalogs in the field of American transportation which will soon be cataloged. There are undoubtedly other collections I have not been able to contact, and still others without staff and time to lend a hand. I feel satisfied that the material to which we guide you, and the institutions whose symbols appear, will be able to supply the most exacting student and historian.

c.1911 Chicago   TxDaDeG
ADAMS & WESTLAKE CO. Est. 1857.
Special ill. catalog of Adlake railroad car
lighting fixtures - by acetylene, candles,
electricity, gas and oil. Lamps and lanterns for locomotives, stations, etc. 4to.,
175pp., a fine ref. <u>See</u> also Lighting for
earlier examples.

1885 St. Louis   MoSHi
AMERICAN BRAKE CO. 4to. catalog with
23 pls. of brakes and locomotives, scale
drawing, fld., wrap.

1898 St. Louis   MH-BA
------ Westinghouse Air Brake Co., lessee.
Ill. catalog of locomotive brakes, 4to., 70pp.,
cl.

v.d. New York   TxDaDeG
AMERICAN LOCOMOTIVE CO. Est. 1837.
Now Alco Products, Inc. TxDaDeG reports
a complete set of ill. bulletins.

1887 New York   MiDbF
AMERICAN MFG. & SUPPLY CO. Ill. catalog of railroad and steamship supplies - ills.
of cars, lamps, signals, track, work cars,
tools, accessories. 8vo., 450pp. of ills.,
dec. cl.

1874 Chicago   MH-BA
ANGLE-IRON RAILWAY CONSTRUCTION &
EQUIPMENT CO. Ill. catalog of track and
heavy hardware for construction. 8vo., 24pp.

1866 New York   DSi
ASHCROFT, JOHN. Ill. catalog of railway,
steamship and engineers' supplies, railway
car findings, boilers, locomotives, lanterns,
tools and machinery. 4to., 120pp.

nd. Cleveland   TxDaDeG
ATLAS CAR & MFG. CO. Ill.   OHi
catalog of railroad cars, trucks and supplies.

c.1871-1900 Philadelphia   Locations
BALDWIN LOCOMOTIVE   as follows
WORKS. W. Baird & Co. and Burnham,
Parry, Williams & Co.

Ill. catalogs of Baldwin locomotives with as
fine pls. as any brochures and pamphlets in
this period; various sizes, wraps. and cl.
A fine record.

Both PHi and TxDaDeG have complete files
as far as it is possible to know.

c.1871-2   TxDaDeG
     MiU-T PHi   PKsL CSmH MH-BA
Ill. catalog of locomotives. 4to., 134pp.,
varying number of litho. and photo. pls., cl.
Dated 1872 and nd

c.1873   MiU-T
Ill. catalog with weights and traction power
of narrow-gauge locomotives. 46pp.

1876   PHi   PKsL
Exhibit at Centennial, 4to., frs. and 5 pls.
of locomotives. 29pp.

1878   PHi   PKsL   TxDaDeG
Ill. catalog similar to 1872. Fine pls., cl.

1879   PHi   TxDaDeG
Ill. catalog of locomotives - in Portuguese -
4to., 47pp., wrap.

1881   Three variants listed, as follows:
                                  TxDaDeG
        4to., 101pp., photos. and diags., cl.
                                  MH-BA
        4to., 148pp., photos., drawings, cl.
              PHi   PKsL   TxDaDeG
        4to., 2nd ed., 164pp., 18 photos.
        with drawings and diags., cl.

1885   PHi   TxDaDeG
Ill. catalog of mine locomotives. 36pp.

1885   PHi   TxDaDeG
Ill. catalog of locomotives. 4to., 100pp.,
fine pls., details, cl.

1887   PHi   TxDaDeG
Ill. catalog - in Portuguese. 4to., 104pp.,
fine pls.

1890   PHi   TxDaDeG
Ill. catalog of noiseless motors and steam
street cars for city and suburban railroads.
4to., 24pp., 3rd ed., pict. wrap.

1896   PHi   TxDaDeG
Electric locomotives - David L. Barnes.
8vo., 123pp., fine ills., pict. wrap.

N.B. From TxDaDeG - noteworthy as the
first catalog of electric locomotives (as
opposed to street cars) issued - to my knowledge. Electric equipment supplied by
Westinghouse.

1897   PHi   TxDaDeG
Ill. catalog - Japanese ed. issued by Frazar
& Co. Ptd. Lippincott.

c.1899   MiU-T
Ill. catalog of compound passenger locomotives, American type. Circular #3.

1900   MiU-T
Ill. catalog of narrow gauge locomotives.
542pp., cl.

1875-1915   TxDaDeG
Collection of catalogs from exhibitions, fine
ills., wrap. and cl. I am sure most of these
may also be found at PHi though I do not
have a list to report.

1890-1902   PHi   PKsL   TxDaDeG
Records of Recent Construction. A series
of excellent brochures with the finest pls.
of models. # 1-100, with pict. wrap., one of
the best locomotive records.

1840   Philadelphia   MiU-T
BALDWIN, VAIL & HUFTY. Firm formed
in 1839 by Matthew W. Baldwin, founder of
the Baldwin Locomotive Works. Built locomotives for export in this year. Ill. catalog
of locomotives. 10pp. Earliest catalog
record.

c.1914 Yonkers, N. Y.   TxDaDeG
BELL LOCOMOTIVE WORKS. Record #7.
Ill. catalog of industrial steam locomotives
burning liquid fuel. 8vo., 23pp.

1883   New Britain, Conn.   TxDaDeG
BERNEY & CO. Ill. circular of CtHi
Berney's straight stack spark consumer and
double grate smoke preventer. 4to., 4pp.

nd. Boston   MH-BA
BICKFORD RAILWAY STATION INDICATOR
CO. Ill. catalog of Bickford electric train
signals. 8vo., 10pp.

1856   New York   PKsL
BOARDMAN COAL BURNING LOCOMOTIVE
BOILER CO. Desc. circular of 16pp.

1872   San Francisco   TxDaDeG
BOOTH, H.J. & CO. Union Iron Works. Ill.
circular and pattern list of locomotives,
marine engines, mining machinery, mills,
car wheels, etc. 8vo., XVI and 274pp.,
complete ref.

1896   San Francisco   CHi
------ Ill. catalogs - #1, 2 and 3.

1891   New York   TxDaDeG
BOYNTON BICYCLE RAILWAY   PC
SYSTEM. Ill. brochure showing track,
locomotives, parlor, coach and dining double
decker cars, details of construction, costs,
etc. 8vo., 48pp., pict. wrap. A fantastic
single track dream of the Gay Nineties.

1892   Philadelphia   MiU-T
BRILL, J.G. & CO. Ill. catalog of   PHi
street railways - everything for construction, operation and maintenance. 425pp.,
fine ills.

nd. Philadelphia   MiU-T
------ Ill. catalog of Brill motor   PHi
cars. 23pp.

1899   Philadelphia   MiU-T
------ Ill. catalog of standard   PHi
American electric cars, 3rd ed. 48pp.

N.B. PHi reports a collection of almost
every catalog, pamphlet or brochure published, as well as photographs.

c.1876 New York   MH-BA
BROOKS, E.J. & CO. Ill. catalog of railroad
supplies - a Hamilton bolt to a conductor's
punch. 8vo., 10pp.

1893 Dunkirk, N. Y.   TxDaDeG
BROOKS LOCOMOTIVE WORKS. Ill. bro-
chure of Brooks Locomotives at the World's
Fair. 4to., fine pict. record.

1894 Dunkirk, N. Y.   TxDaDeG
------ Ill. catalog of locomotives and railway equipment. 237pp.

1895 Dunkirk, N. Y.   TxDaDeG
------ Ill. catalog of locomotives, parts
and accessories. 4to., 160pp., diags., etc.

1899 Dunkirk, N. Y.   TxDaDeG
------ & AMERICAN LOCOMO-   PKsL
TIVE CO. Ill. catalog with history of plant,
list of clients, pls. of models, etc. - annual
capacity 400. Sq. 8vo., 336pp., pict. wrap.

1887 St. Louis   MoSHi
BROWNELL CAR CO., Mfg. Electric Cars.
Ill. catalog of street and trolley cars.

c.1895 St. Louis   TxDaDeG
------ How a Good Car Differs MoSHi
from a Poor One, and How to Get it. Combination guide and catalog - 55 ills. of twin
door and accelerator designs, wheels to roof
history of street cars. 176pp. of pure
Americana.

1877 St. Louis   MoSHi
BUCK, M.M. & CO. Ill. catalog of materials for construction and operation of railroads. Ill. of cars, cab and parlor, locomotives, lamps, seats, stoves and trimmings.
4to., 202pp., dec. cl.

1900 St. Louis   TxDaDeG
------ Railway, Machinists' and Miners'
Supplies - everything for the railroads -
ills. of cars, lamps, lanterns, locomotives,
ditchers, rolling stock. 12mo., 596pp.

1883 Boston   MH-BA
BURTON STOCK CAR CO. Est. 1882. Ill.
catalog with tests. 8vo., 32pp.

1883 Boston   MH-BA
------ Tests. for private distribution.
24mo., 20pp. Not a catalog but full of details of cars and service.

1887 Boston   MH-BA
------ Ill. catalog. 8vo., 36pp.

c.1890 Philadelphia   PKsL
BUSH INTERLOCKING BOLT CO. Ill. brochure of tracks, couplings, bolts and tools
in use on 30 railroads. 4to., 6pp.

c.1900 Corry, Pa.   TxDaDeG
CLIMAX MFG. CO. 4 ill. catalogs, undated.
Ill. catalog of Climax Patented Tramway
Locomotives. 8vo., 51pp., fine ills. 4 ex-
amples about the same size and content.

1855 Buffalo, N. Y.   TxDaDeG
COLE, GEORGE. Contractor's book of
working drawings of tools and machinery for
railroads, canals, etc. - costs of timbers,
steel, etc. Oblong fol., 15 pls., 2 in col. A
stunning depiction of - railway - construction technology.

1895 Paterson, N. J.   TxDaDeG
COOKE LOCOMOTIVE & MACHINE CO.
Ill. catalog of locomotives. 8vo., 71pp.,
Albertype Co. pls.

nd. Corry, Pa.   TxDaDeG
CORRY LOCOMOTIVE WORKS. 4 ill. catalogs of . . . no data.

nd. Chicago   MiU-T
CRERAR, ADAMS & CO. Price list of railway supplies. 47pp.

1889 Chicago   ICHi
------ Ill. catalog of railway supplies -
locomotives, cars, parlor cars, lights, signals, lamps, velocipede, inspection and
telegraph cars, work cars, furnishings.
12mo., VII, index and 445pp. of ills.

nd. Cleveland   TxDaDeG
CUYAHOGA STEAM FURNACE CO. Ill.
catalog of bolts and screws for railway construction. Built locomotives in 1850 - 1860
period but no catalogs known.

nd. Davenport, Ia.   TxDaDeG
DAVENPORT LOCOMOTIVE WORKS. Re-
ports 11 ill. catalogs, undated. No details,
but for a guide, this will do.

1886 Scranton, Pa.   TxDaDeG
DICKSON LOCOMOTIVE WORKS. Ill. catalog of locomotives. 8vo., 76pp., plans and
drawings, tables. 1/2 lea.

1898 Scranton, Pa.   TxDaDeG
------ Ill. catalog of locomo-   MH-BA
tives. 8vo., 72pp.

1900 Scranton   TxDaDeG
------ & AMERICAN LOCOMO-   PC
TIVE CO. Ill. catalog - Spanish and Eng-
lish ed. - large 8vo., 78pp., pls. of models.

DODGE, HALEY & CO. See Hardware -
Miscellaneous Machinery.

c.1886 St. Louis   MoSHi
DODSON NUT LOCK & RAILWAY SUPPLY
MFG. CO. Ill. catalog of railway supplies.

1850 New York   TxDaDeG
DUGGAN, GEORGE. Not a trade catalog
but a fine record. Specimens of stone, iron
and wood bridges, viaducts, tunnels, culverts,
etc. of the railroads of the U.S. - plans, elevations, etc. Tall fol., 60 pls., cl.

c.1890 Boston & Watertown, Mass. TxDaDeG
EAMES VACUUM BRAKE CO.   MiU-T
Ill. brochure of driver brakes. 4to., text
and 13 fine pls.

nd. Beloit, Wis.   TxDaDeG
FAIRBANKS-MORSE CO. Reported as mfg.
of locomotives. See also Hardware - Miscellaneous Machinery, Scales and Windmills.

FAY, J.A. & CO. See Hardware - Miscellaneous Machinery.

1881 Riverside, R. I.   RHi
FLAGG, LYSANDER. Flagg's railway safety gates. 12mo., 24pp., ills., pict. wrap.

FOCHT, GEORGE IRON WORKS. See
Hardware - Miscellaneous Machinery.

1845 Philadelphia   TxDaDeG
FRENCH, BAIRD & CAMPBELL. Ill. catalog of F.D. & C. pat. smoke-pipe and spark
arrester for locomotives. 8vo., 8pp., wrap.

1899 New York   MH-BA
GOLD CAR HEATING & LIGHTING CO.
Est. 1884. Ill. catalog of railway car heating and lighting apparatus and equipment.
4to., 80pp. of fine ills., cl.

c.1900 New York   TxDaDeG
------ Ill. catalog of Gold systems of
railroad car lighting and heating - plans and
pls. - the last word in light and comfort for
over 40,000 locomotives and cars, cl.

c.1882 Paterson, N. J.   TxDaDeG
GRANT LOCOMOTIVE WORKS. Later
moved to Chicago. Desc. catalog of locomotives with 11 photos. of models. Fol.,
bds. - one of the rarest in the field.

1855 St. Johnsbury, Vt.   MH-BA
HALE, R., MAGOON & CO. Formerly
Magoon & Price. Ill. brochure of pat. feed
water heaters for locomotives. 8vo., 18pp.

1890 New York & Chicago   TxDaDeG
HALL SIGNAL CO. Ill. catalog of block signals. Tall fol. with 15p. text and 53 pls.,
tinted in red, diags., etc. Pict. wrap.

nd. Erie, Pa.   TxDaDeG
HEISLER LOCOMOTIVE WORKS. Later
Stearns Mfg. Co. Ill. catalog of locomo-
tives and railway supplies.

1875 Philadelphia   MH-BA
HENDERSON HYDRAULIC CAR BRAKE CO.
Ill. catalog of hydraulic brakes for railroad
cars. 8vo., 12pp.

c.1900 West New Brighton, S. I., N. Y.
              NStIHi   TxDaDeG
HUNT, C.W. CO. Ill. catalog of Hunt indus-

trial railways - special dump, flat, shop,
oven, mining, trolley cars and electric locomotives, elevators, etc. 24mo., 44pp.

1889 Rahway, N. J.   TxDaDeG
JOHNSON RAILROAD SIGNAL CO.   NjR
Ill. catalog of Johnson signals, lanterns,
signal towers, switches, etc. 4to., 140pp.,
glt. pict. cl.

nd. Anniston, Ala.   TxDaDeG
KILBY LOCOMOTIVE & MACHINE WORKS.
Later Kilby Car & Foundry Co. Ill. cata-
logs #4, 5 and 6, undated but well after 1900.
Ills. of flat cars, loggers, etc. and later
standard freight.

1857 Buffalo, N. Y.   NNMM
KITTLE, S.P. Ill. flyer for railroad rests.

1891 St. Louis   MH-BA
LANSBERG BRAKE CO. Ill. catalog of air
brakes for passenger and freight cars.
4to., 24pp.

1890-1900 Dunkirk, N. Y.   TxDaDeG
LIMA LOCOMOTIVE WORKS & LIMA
LOCOMOTIVE & MACHINE CO. Collection
of 11 ill. catalogs from c.1890-1900 -
example. Circular #1. Ills. of locomotives
and railway supplies. 4to., 32pp. for 1893.

nd. Dunkirk, N. Y.   MiU-T
------ & AMERICAN LOCOMOTIVE CO.
Ill. catalogs of Shay locomotives. Well
after 1900.

LOVELL, F.H. CO. See Lighting for railroad lamps, etc.

MANCHESTER LOCOMOTIVE WORKS.
See Fire Engines.

MANNING, MAXWELL & MOORE. Locomotive headlights, car furnishings, station
equipment, etc. See Hardware - Miscellaneous Machinery.

1879 Taunton, Mass.   TxDaDeG
MASON MACHINE WORKS.   MTaOC
Mason Mfg. Co. Est. 1842. Inc. 1873. Ill.
catalog of Narrow Gauge Bogie locomotives.
8vo., 30pp., fine photos. of engines, glt.
pict. cl.

MIDDLETON, C.W. & H.W. See Hardware -
Miscellaneous Machinery.

nd. Milwaukee, Wis.   TxDaDeG
MILWAUKEE LOCOMOTIVE WORKS. Ill.
catalog of small gas and diesel engines.

1891 Hamilton, O.   OHi
NILES TOOL WORKS. Ill. catalog of railway cars, machines, tools and railway
equipment. Large 8vo., fine ills., cl.

1893 Boston   TxDaDeG
PALMER VENTILATOR CAR CO. Ill. circular #3 of a new system of ventilating
railroad cars, diags., 16mo., 8pp., pict.wrap.

1879 Baldwin Station & Philadelphia, Pa.
PENNSYLVANIA STEEL CO. Ill.   PHi
catalog of steel rails, billets, blooms, forgings, frogs, safety switches, crossings,
car replacers, etc. 4to., 106pp.

1896 Steelton, Pa.   PKsL
PENNSYLVANIA STEEL CO. Est. 1865.
1865-1896 ill. catalog of rails for cable,
electric and street railways - photos. of
track, stations and crossings. 4to., cl.

1893 Pittsburgh, Pa.   TxDaDeG
PITTSBURGH LOCOMOTIVE &   MiU-T
CAR CO. Ill. catalog of exhibit at World's
Exposition. 41pp. and fine pls.

v.d. Pittsburgh, Pa.   TxDaDeG
------ Several ill. catalogs reported without details.

1882-1900 Pittsburgh, Pa.   TxDaDeG
PORTER, H.K. & CO. Ill. cata-   PC
logs of locomotives. 1882 is the earliest
located, being the 2nd ed.

1872 Cincinnati   MH-BA
POST & CO. Catalog #3. Ill. catalog of
railway car trimmings and furnishings,
steam gauges, locomotive headlights and
railway supplies.

1871 New York   NjOE
POST & GODDARD. Ill. catalog of railroad
supplies, machinists' equipment, tools, etc.
87pp. with a majority of ills. for railroads.

1852 New York   MH-BA
RAILROAD CAR VENTILATING CO. Ill.
catalog of H.M. Paine's pat. apparatus for
ventilating cars, etc. 8vo., 12pp.

1889 Hillburn & Ramapo, N. Y.   TxDaDeG
RAMAPO IRON WORKS and RAMAPO
WHEEL & FOUNDRY CO. Ill. catalog of
track, wheels, brake shoes, rings, boxes,
etc. for railroad locomotives and rolling
stock. 4to., 114pp., fld. pls.

c.1890 Ramapo, N. Y.   TxDaDeG
------ Ill. catalog of track and truck
equipment. Oblong 4to., fine ills., mostly
car wheels. DeVinne Press.

1884 Providence, R. I.   TxDaDeG
RHODE ISLAND LOCOMOTIVE WORKS.
Ill. catalog of standard gauge locomotive
weights, dimensions, scale drawings and
tables. 124pp.

nd. Providence, R. I.   TxDaDeG
------ Ill. catalog. 4to., 54pp.

1900 Boston   MiU-T
RIDLON, FRANK CO. Ill. catalog of street
railway supplies.

c.1870 Paterson, N. J.   TxDaDeG
ROGERS LOCOMOTIVE & MACHINE CO.
Est. 1831. Ill. catalog of Rogers locomotives. 18 fine photos. of models, 2 to the
page, fol., bds. One of the earliest and
scarcest.

1876 Paterson, N. J.   TxDaDeG
------ Ill. catalog with history from 1831 -
1876. 2nd catalog issued. 4to., 149pp.

1886 Paterson, N. J.   TxDaDeG
------ Ill. catalog, including historical
sketch. 4to., 200pp. fine pls.

1893 Paterson, N. J.   TxDaDeG
------ Ill. catalog. 117pp.

1897 Paterson, N. J.   TxDaDeG
------ Ill. catalog with plans, diags. and
pls. 121pp. Historical sketch.

1882 St. Paul, Minn.   MnHi
RUGG, H.P. & CO. Ill. catalog and price
list of railway supplies, mill equipment,
pumps, brass fittings, belting, machinery
and tools. 4to., 541pp. of ills.

nd. Detroit, Mich.   TxDaDeG
RUSSELL WHEEL & FOUNDRY CO. Ill.
catalog of Russell cars, heavy duty and dump
cars, etc. Complimentary note - My First
Catalog. 4to., tinted ills.

1895 St. Charles, Mo.   TxDaDeG
ST. CHARLES CAR CO. Ill. catalog of railroad cars. 4to., 125pp.

1888 Schenectady   TxDaDeG
SCHENECTADY LOCOMOTIVE WORKS.
Est. 1848. Ill. catalog of locomotives from
1848-1888. Fine ills. and pls. 8vo., np.

1893 Schenectady   TxDaDeG
------ Ill. catalog covering models from
1848-1893. 8vo., 115pp., 53 pls. of models.

1897 Schenectady   TxDaDeG
------ Ill. catalog of simple   MH-BA
and compound locomotives - annual capacity
450 engines. 4to., 224pp.

1001 Schenectady   TxDaDeG
------ Ill. catalog of locomotives recently
constructed. 4to., 138pp., fine pls.

c.1890 Three Rivers, Mich.   TxDaDeG
SHEFFIELD CAR CO. Est. 1879. Ill. catalog of light cars. Ills. of plant, canopy top
cars, workmens' cars with sails, Ortley
Beach, N. J. trolley with a fine surrey fringe

on top, velocipede cars, logging cars, coke buggies. 8vo., 96pp. This one will take you back a ways.

1912 Pittsburgh, Pa.   TxDaDeG
STANDARD MOTOR TRUCK CO. Catalog #4. Standard electric railway trucks for all classes of service - city, suburban, interurban. Without any question the finest ill. record of American trolley cars issued.

8-3/4 x 11-3/4, 94pp., mostly models, engines, equipment, with 12 EXCELLENT COLOR PLATES, each with blue print line drawing on back. Dec. wrap. Though 1912, these col. pls. must be located.

1912 Pittsburgh, Pa.   NNMM
------ 8 of above col. pls. issued on heavy stock - I believe - for mailing to towns and cities.

1900 New York   MiD
STAR BRASS MFG. CO. Ill. catalog of railroad car furnishings - lamps, gongs, seats, plaques, valves, stoves, curtains, window catches, toilet accessories, etc. 8vo., 168pp., cl.

1858 Cincinnati & Covington, Ky.   OC
STEPHENS & JENKINS. Ill. catalog of rails for the iron horse. Tubular rails, switches, etc. 8vo., 22pp., pict. wrap.

1899 Troy, N.Y.   TxDaDeG
TAYLOR ELECTRIC TRUCK CO. Ill. catalog of highest grade trucks for electric service. Oblong 4to., 39pp., fine pls. One of the earliest street car catalogs.

1870 Cleveland, O.   MH-BA
THILMANY, W. U.S. Agent. Ill. brochure - method of preserving wood for railroad ties, telegraph poles, etc. Pat. 1869. 8vo., 17pp.

1890 Boston   RPB
THOMPSON-HOUSTON ELECTRIC CO. Ill. catalog of electric railway apparatus, arc lights, lamps for trolley cars, street lighting, etc. 4to., 167pp., fine ills., cl.

nd. San Francisco   TxDaDeG
UNION IRON WORKS. Ill. catalog of rolling stock, appliances for railroads, etc.

1883 Pittsburgh, Pa.   MH-BA
UNION SWITCH & SIGNAL CO. Ill. catalog of railroad signal appliances. 4to., 90pp., fine pls.

VALENTINE. See Paint - for railroad cars and coaches.

c.1900 Wilkes-Barre   TxDaDeG
VULCAN IRON WORKS. Collection of 12 ill. catalogs of locomotives and rolling stock.

1892 Cincinnati   OC
WEIR FROG CO. Ill. catalog #2 - frogs, switches, track, crossings, signals, etc. 8vo., 190pp. of ills., cl.

1894 Pittsburgh, Pa.   MH-BA
WESTINGHOUSE AIR BRAKE CO. Ill. catalog of Westinghouse automatic air brakes for rolling stock. 4to., 78pp., cl.

1890 Pittsburgh, Pa.   MH-BA
WESTINGHOUSE MACHINE CO. Ill. catalog of standard automatic locomotive engines. 12mo., 62pp.

Once again the same old warning. In the chapter Hardware - Miscellaneous Machinery, you will find many outstanding catalogs with details and fine illustrations of materials and supplies for railroads, well mixed with machinery for mills, mines, steamships, docks and other construction. Locomotive bells may be found in the Bell Chapter, in many Agricultural catalogs, and even under Hardware - Machine Tools, for the Miller, Miner and Textile manufacturer. When you stop to think of the tools used in building a railroad as well as operating one, you know you have to start with picks and shovels. Before you finish the picture you may well have used catalogs covering fifty other industries and trades. Here they are - you take over.

Chapter 46

Refrigerators

The English language does not lend itself easily to compiling, classifying and indexing such a motley crew of printed works. Properly, this heading should read: Ice and Refrigeration, Natural and Artificial Supplies, Apparatus for Procuring and Manufacturing, as well as Manufactures for Containing and Retaining. With this to start with there would be no need for an introduction. Properly also, every other chapter in this book could stand more complete and Johnsonian reconstruction. However, the clearer the chapter headings, the more utterly impossible the index becomes. So be it.

This group of catalogs includes the printed and illustrated records of American refrigeration, from cutting the ice on the ponds to manufacturing its equivalent. It naturally covers all of the many contrivances from c.1800 for preserving this natural and artificial food preserver. Transportation of ice is a fascinating history all the way from Thomas Moore's little boxes for farm wagons to the famous Knickerbocker scenic hand painted wagons and finally the railroad's refrigerator cars. Through the index, I think the catalogs listed in several chapters will guide you to a complete picture of refrigeration in the 19th century.

1872 Bridgeport, Conn. & Indianapolis
ALLEGRETTI REFRIGERATOR CO. CtHi
Ill. catalog of refrigerators and ice boxes,
special wine and beer models, oysters and
ice cream styles. 24mo., 32pp., pict. wrap.

1890 Baltimore   PKsL
ARMIGER, R. & SON. Mfg. Ill. catalog of
Armiger refrigerators. Fine ills. of Ster-
lings, Climax models, buffet, Daisy, Beauty,
Charm and Regal. The Princess combination buffet is swell. 8vo., 32pp. of ills., glt.
ptd. wrap.

1887 Belding, Mich.   MnHi
BELDING MFG. CO. Ill. catalog of Belding
refrigerators.

c.1877 Sanbornton, N. H.   NhHi
BLAISDELL & BURLEY. Ill. circular of
the Household Favorite - pat. elevator
refrigerator - delightful ills. of the calm
housewife and the astonished guests at dinner. 8vo., 8pp.

1877 Boston   MH-BA
BOSTON SCIENTIFIC REFRIGERATOR CO.
Est. 1865. Ill. catalog of refrigerators -
drying and ventilating schemes. 8vo., 18pp.

1877 Mishawaka, Ind.   MnHi
BOSTWICK REFRIGERATING CO. Ill. catalog of models for 1877.

1881-82 Buffalo, N. Y.   MnHi
BUFFALO REFRIGERATOR MFG. CO. Ill.
catalog of models for 1881 and 1882.

1870 Philadelphia   PHi
BUJAC, M.J. Ill. catalog of Carre,   NHi
Mignon & Rouart's continuous freezing apparatus. Ice by direct heat. 8vo. ill. catalog with fld. plate, wrap.

1889 Cleveland, O.   MnHi
CHADWICK, L.D. Ill. catalog of Monroe
Brothers' Patent refrigerators.

1891 Grand Haven, Conn.   MiU-H
CHALLENGE ICEBERG REFRIGERATOR
CO. Ill. catalog #6 of ice boxes and refrigerators, special sideboard models and special styles.

1882 North Cambridge, Mass.   DSi
CUTTER, J. HARRIS & CO. Est. 1850.
(Agent, Joseph Breck & Sons.) Ill. catalog
of Cutter's ice tools and ice boxes. 8vo.,
26pp., pict. wrap.

See Breck under Agricultural Implements,
Tools and Machinery for earlier refrigerators.

1887 New York   DSi
De La VERGNE REFRIGERATION MACHINE
CO. Ill. catalog of ammonia refrigeration
compressors and apparatus. 113pp.

1890 New York   NNNAM
------ Ill. catalog of mechanical refrigeration, processes and apparatus. 90pp. and
3 lvs.

1897 New York   N
------ Refrigeration for home, brewery,
saloon, hotel and skating rink apparatus.
8vo., 128pp., tinted ills., cl.

1894 Boston   N
EDDY, D. & SONS. Est. 1847. Ill. catalog
of Eddy's refrigerators. 8vo., 36pp., pict.
wrap.

c.1900 Boston   MBSPNEA
------ New ill. catalog of . . . 50 years
without an equal - new models. Sq. 12mo.,
44pp., wrap.

1890 Waynesboro, Pa.   PHi
FRICK CO. Ill. and desc. catalog   DSi
of ammonia refrigeration compressors and
apparatus. 268pp.

1887 Hudson, N. Y.   DSi
GIFFORD BROTHERS. Desc. price list of
ice elevating machinery, tools, wagons and
apparatus. 8vo., 28pp., pict. wrap.

See also Hardware - Tools and Machine
Tools for the Iceman.   p.1900 catalogs
available at N.

1900 New York   NNC
HAMMACHER, SCHLEMMER & CO. Ill.
catalog #90. Refrigerator and bar trimmings, apparatus and equipment, ice box
hardware, etc. Sq. 12mo., 46pp., wrap.

1891 Chicago   DSi
HERCULES IRON WORKS. Ill. catalog of
ice making and refrigerating machinery,
ammonia compressors and apparatus. 71pp.

1878 Philadelphia   NjOE
HOLDEN, D.L. & BROTHERS. Penn Iron
Works. Ill. catalog of ice machines and
fine refrigerators, etc. 24pp., pict. wrap.

1886 Buffalo, N. Y.   NBuHi
JEWETT, JOHN C. MFG. CO. 1886 ill.
price list and catalog of Jewett pat. refrigerators - styles Queen, Crown, Nonpareil,
Labrador, Victor, New Palace, etc. fancy
ice chests. 24mo., 48pp., pict. wrap.

1874 New York   NHi
MACE, L.H. & CO. Ill. catalog of beer and
meat safes - no more leaks - models with
iron bottoms, etc. Special chests for lager
beer. 8vo., 20pp., pict. wrap.

1877 New York   ICHi
------ Ill. catalog of ice chest models, etc.
including some woodenware, etc. 8vo., 32pp.
Pict. wrap.

1888 St. Paul, Minn.   MnHi
MINNESOTA REFRIGERATOR CO. Ill.
catalog of Simmon's world-renowned patent

refrigerators, ice chests and cold storage
rooms, etc. 12mo., 32pp.

1803 Baltimore   PC
MOORE, THOMAS. Inventor. An Essay on
the Most Eligible Construction of Ice Houses,
also a desc. of a Newly Invented Machine
Called the Refrigerator. 8vo., 28pp.

N.B. Like Benjamin Franklin's Essay on
Stoves, this is a printed record of the first
American ice box. The principle of air space,
rabbit's fur, and double wood boxes is ahead
of the times. Models for farm wagons and
homes - plans for nationwide distribution
make it a trade catalog in essence.

1893 Oakland, Calif.   CHi
OAKLAND IRON WORKS. Desc. and ill.
catalog of refrigerating and ice machinery.
8vo., 111pp., pict. wrap.

c.1885 Buffalo, N. Y.   NBuHi
PIERCE, GEORGE N. & CO. Ill. catalog of
Pierce's dry air polar refrigerators - charcoal filled for double circulation - models
for homes, hotels, grocers, beer parlors -
sideboard styles, in oak, pine and walnut.
16mo., 48pp., col. pict. wrap. Gies Litho. Co.

1800 London, England   DSi
PONTIFEX & WOOD. Desc. pamphlet on
absorption refrigeration equipment. 14pp.

N.B. This is listed only as a companion
piece to the Thomas Moore 1803. It makes
you wonder who was really first. It also
assures us it wasn't Russia.

1886 Conneaut, O.   OHi
RECORD MFG. CO. Ill. catalog of George
J. Record's tight packages for preserving
butter, lard, oysters - wood shipping cans,
etc. Probably constructed with Thomas
Moore's air space scheme. 8vo., 16pp.,
pict. wrap.

1888 St. Louis   MnHi
ST. LOUIS REFRIGERATOR & WOOD GUT-
TER CO. Ill. catalog showing various
styles of ice boxes and refrigerators.

c.1900 Chicago   ICHi
SEARS ROEBUCK & CO. Special   & V.L.
ill. catalog of refrigerators and ice chests
for home, grocer, hotel, beer parlor and
butcher. Chests of Michigan ash with flow-
ered panels, etc. Sq. 12mo., 32pp., pict.
wrap. of plant.

See also Department Stores for other locations.

1882 Michigan City, Ind.   MnHi
SMITH REFRIGERATOR & MFG. CO. Ill.
catalog of models and styles.

c.1900 Chicago   ICHi
SMYTH, JOHN M. Special ill. catalog of
refrigerators. Buy the Purity Cleanable!
Get your money's worth. Ills. of models -
Purity Cleanable, Snow Flake, Champion -
for family, grocer or hotel. Sq. 8vo., 32pp.,
pict. wrap.

1884 Buffalo, N. Y.   NBuHi
VOGT, PETER A. Ill. catalog of pat. refrigerators for beer - for home or hotel. 8vo.,
16pp., pict. wrap.

1886 Buffalo, N. Y.   MnHi
------ Ill. catalog of ice chests, etc. Same
for 1887.

c.1860 New Haven   CtHi
WINSHIP & CO. Ill. catalog of Winship's

pat. self-ventilating refrigerators for meats,
game, fish and fowl. 12mo., 12pp., pict. wrap.

1881-90 Boston & Arlington, Mass. MH-BA
WOOD, WILLIAM T. & CO.   DSi
Ill. catalogs of ice making machinery, ice
tools, hardware and woodenware, etc. 15
catalogs. 8vo., ill., pict. wrap., totaling
about 300pp. A fine ref.

See also Hardware - Tools and Machine Tools
for the Iceman.

1892 York, Pa.   PKsL
YORK MFG. CO., LTD. Ill. catalog of York
and St. Clair compound ice and refrigerating
machines. 8vo., 126pp., pls., cl.

Under Alcohol and Tobacco there are records of bar refrigerating equipment. House Furnishings
also offers some of the finest oak ice chests, and Carriages and Wagons point out some of the
finest ice wagons ever built.

Chapter 47

Road Building Machinery & Equipment

Roads and highways are certainly close to food, clothing and shelter at the top of the ladder that leads to human survival. From 1806, when the Cumberland or National Road became one of the nation's greatest undertakings, we have struggled with forests, mountains and swamps to build passable paths throughout the country. A glance at the photographs in such periodicals as The Bulletin and Good Roads, Official Organ of the League of American Wheelmen, during the Gay Nineties will make you realize how far we were even then from what we call highways today. It has been a long, interesting and colorful battle.

There is far more popular appeal in the development of a great network of iron track from coast to coast on which to run the powerful "puffinbellies" of railroad history. There are countless histories of the American iron horse, and we now have many museums where one can see these first steam monsters in all their historical glory. I cannot state that there are no surviving models of Samuel Pennock's road machines of 1873, but I doubt it.

This group of catalogs has been segregated from general machinery because it records and illustrates American ingenuity and progress in road building, and even street cleaning, from about 1857 on. There are, of course, many tools such as picks, shovels and scoops illustrated in earlier catalogs for the farmer, for who but the farmer, many of whom were the pioneers, built the first country roads that led to the western settlements? From street sweeping machines to scrapers and levelers and finally to the mighty steam rollers, this chapter attempts to cover the picture with available located materials.

1876 Akron, O.   OHi
AKRON SEWER PIPE ASSOCIATION. Ill.
catalog of Akron sewer pipe, its importance
to proper road construction, etc. 16mo.,
28pp., lithos. by Morgan Litho. of Cleveland.

nd. Zanesville   NNMM
AMERICAN ENCAUSTIC TILING CO. Ill.
catalog of designs for tile pavements. 16 lvs.

See also Architectural Building Materials.

1890 Kennett Square, Pa.   PWcHi
AMERICAN ROAD MACHINE CO.   PKsL
Formerly S. Pennock & Sons. Est. 1873.
Ill. catalog of improved road graders.
16mo., 24pp., delightful ills., pict. wrap.

1898 Kennett Square, Pa.   PWcHi
------ Ill. catalog   N   PHi   PKsL
of Champion street and road machinery.
4to., 36pp.
See S. Pennock & Sons.

AMERICAN STEEL SCRAPER CO. See
Sidney Steel Scraper Co.

1879 North Easton, Mass.   DSi
AMES, OLIVER & SONS CO. Ill.   PC
price list of shovels, spades, scoops and

drainage tools and equipment - for farm or
highway. 8vo., 50pp., pict. wrap.

1889 Chicago   ICHi
AUSTIN, F.C. MFG. CO. Ill.   MnHi
catalog of crushers, ditchers, graders,
scrapers and sprinklers.

1890 Chicago   DSi
------ Contractors' catalog of new era
wagons and improved road building tools and
equipment. Ill. of Mars searching the earth
for dirt moving machinery and discovering
Austin. 4to., 48pp., pict. wrap.

1892 San Francisco   CHi
BOWERS RUBBER CO. Ill. price list of
hose, belting, sprinklers, etc. 12mo., 32pp.,
wrap.

nd. Bryan, O.   MnHi
BRYAN MFG. CO. Ill. catalog of road levelers, rollers, scrapers and equipment.

1892 Cincinnati   OC
BURKE, M.D. Ill. brochure-brick for street
pavements - accounts of experiments. Fine
ills. of various city streets, etc. 8vo., 86pp.
cl. Possibly not a trade catalog, but a good
sales job of which any advt. agency might be
proud.

1899 Philadelphia   PHi
CHAMPION ROAD MACHINERY CO. Ill.
catalog of sprinklers, steam rollers, water
wagons and scrapers. 4to., 36pp., swell
pict. wrap.

1871 Chicago   MH-BA
CHICAGO SCRAPER & DITCHER CO. Price
list with list of users and test. letters.
8vo., 16pp., pict. wrap.

1893 Marathon, N. Y.   N
CLIMAX ROAD MACHINE CO. Ill. catalog
of crushers, scrapers, steam rollers and
machinery. 8vo., 44pp., pict. wrap.

1895 Marathon, N. Y.   MiU-T
------ Ill. catalog with opinions of users.
16mo., 48pp., pict. wrap.

1899 Paterson, N. J.   CU-A
COOKE LOCOMOTIVE CO. Ill. catalog of
Oastler steam road rollers. 4to., 24pp.,
fine pls. See also Railroads.

1886 Chicago   MnHi
GOULDS & AUSTIN. Ill. catalog of shovels,
spades, picks, scoops and equipment.

1890 Harrisburg, Pa.   PShipL
HARRISBURG CAR MFG. CO. Ill. catalog
of Paxton's portable single and double engine steam rollers. 4to., 40pp., pict. wrap.

1893 Harrisburg, Pa.   PKsL
------ Ill. catalog of Harrisburg steam
rollers with fine pls. of picking, plowing,
building, rolling, etc. - showing models for
1880, 1884, 1887 and 1893. Fol.

1888 Racine, Wis.   MnHi
HURLBUT MFG. CO. Ill. catalog of road
building machinery.

nd. Cincinnati   OHi
INDIAN REFINING CO. Price list and catalog of liquid asphalt for road builders.

c.1898 Fort Wayne   In
INDIANA ROAD MACHINE CO. Ill. catalog
with just a few hints to road builders. 24mo.,
55pp., fine ills.

c.1899 Fort Wayne   In
------ What They Say of the Indiana Stone
Crusher. Ill. folder of machinery.

c.1899 Fort Wayne   In
------ Ill. catalog of Indiana reversible
road graders, stone crushers and rollers.
24mo., 24pp., pict. wrap.

1898 Kansas City, Mo.   MiU-T
KANSAS CITY WHEEL SCRAPER CO. Ill.
catalog of wheel dirt scrapers, grading
plows, carts and wagons for road builders.
12mo., 32pp., pict. wrap.

c.1893 Springfield, O.   OHi
KELLY, THE O.S. CO. Ill. catalog of steam
road rollers, with fld. plate - a great pict.
record. Tall fol., 12pp. of pls., pict. wrap.

1883 Columbus, O.   MnHi
KILBOURNE & JACOBS MFG. CO. Ill. catalog of road building machinery.

1881 Littleton, Mass.   ICHi
KIMBALL BROTHERS. Ill. circular of the
Eureka road machine, pat. 1880 with fine pls.
12mo., 16pp. with delightful pict. wrap.

N.B. Similar to the Pennock model for
1873 - Price $175.00.

1883 Media, Pa.   PKsL
LAMBORN ROAD MACHINES CO.,   PHi
LTD.   4 page ill. circular of the Lamborn
machine, pat. 1883, tests. and directions -
delightful woodcut. $150.00.

N.B. People will no longer tolerate poor
roads . . . If your machine had to be ordered from the Ft. Wayne, Ind. plant, it was
$155.00.

1885-1887 Lansing, Mich.   MnHi
LANSING WHEELBARROW CO. Two ill.
catalogs of barrows, picks, shovels, etc.
For 1885 and 1887.

1892 Monticello, Ia.   IaHi
MILNE, JAMES & SON. Annual ill. catalog
of Hawkeye grub and stump machines, the
I.X.L. grubber and Milne's wire rope
couplers, etc. 8vo., 60pp., ills. of machines
at work, pict. wrap. that sold the goods.

1878 Providence, R. I.   MH-BA
NEW ENGLAND COMPOUND ASPHALT
BLOCK CO. Desc. circular of asphalt
blocks for street paving. 8vo., 16pp.

c.1890 Boston   MH-BA
NEW ENGLAND PAVING CO. Est. 1889.
Price list of machinery and supplies for
road makers, pavers, etc. 8vo., 20pp.

1865 New York   MH-BA
NEW YORK SANITARY & CHEMICAL COM-
POST MFG. CO. Ill. catalog of street cleaning machines, sanitary carts, garbage
wagons, pavement building equipment - machinery for docks, piers, and sewers. 8vo.,
32pp.

1885 Oshkosh, Wis.   MnHi
NORTHWESTERN SEWER PIPE CO. Ill.
catalog of pipes, brick, cement, lime and
road building supplies.

1881 New York & Paterson, N. J.   CtY
OASTLER, W.C. Cooke Locomotive Works.
Hints about roadways and steam road-roll-

ing with plans and specs. Aveling & Porter steam rollers. 7 x 10, fine pls., one fld., pict. wrap.

1885 Kennett Square, Pa.   PKsL
PENNOCK, S. & SONS CO. Est. 1881. Ill. catalog of the new Victor reversible road machines, Pennock road workers, etc. Tall 16mo., 24pp., pict. wrap.

Samuel Pennock invented the first road machine 1873, founded the business in 1881, organized the American Road Machine in 1886, inc. 1913. Moved west in 1948. Samuel Pennock was known as the patriarch of Kennett Square.

1896 Buffalo, N. Y.   NBuHi
PITTS AGRICULTURAL WORKS. Est.1837. Ill. catalog of steam rollers and road building machinery. 4to., 20pp., pict. wrap.

1898 Buffalo, N. Y.   N
        Ill. catalog of steam road rollers. 4to., 8pp., fine photos.

1899 Buffalo, N. Y.   MiU-T
------ Ill. catalog of Buffalo Pitts steam rollers and tractors. 4to., 24pp., col. pict. wrap.

1901 Buffalo, N. Y.   N
------ Ill. catalog of steam rollers.

See Agricultural Implements, Tools and Machinery for further listings.

1892 Chicago   ICHi
POPE, R.C. Pope's scientific and mechanical improvement in street rollers. 8vo., 30pp., fine ills. with pict. wrap.

1884 Massilon, O.   MnHi
RUSSELL & CO. Ill. catalog of improved farm and road machinery - improved tractors, threshers, scrapers and rollers. 16mo., 32pp.

1885 Massilon, O.   MiU-T
------ 44th annual ill. catalog -   OHi
farm and road building machines - the Russell steam roller, etc. 4to., 29pp., pict. wrap.

See Agricultural Implements, Tools and Machinery for complete list.

1886 St. Louis   MnHi
ST. LOUIS SHOVEL CO. Price list of picks, scoops, drainage tools, spades, shovels, etc.

1884-85 Sidney, O.   MnHi
SIDNEY STEEL SCRAPER CO. Ill. catalogs of scrapers, levelers, gutter cleaners, rollers and sweepers for 1884 and 1885.

1857 Philadelphia   MH
SMITH, ROBERT A. Ill. desc. of   NN
Smith's pat. street sweeping machines, sanitary or scavenger carts, etc. 8vo., 35pp., pat. 1855.

1868 Philadelphia   MH
------ American plan of street cleaning. Ill. brochure on new machinery for road work. 16pp., ills., bds.

1857 Philadelphia   Sabin #62298
STREET SWEEPING & FERTILIZING CO. OF PHILADELPHIA. Its objects, facilities and prospects of operation in Philadelphia and other cities and towns in the U. S. 8vo., 24pp. Possibly Robert A. Smith's machines were involved but Sabin gives no further data.

c.1885 Aurora, Ill.   CtY
WESTERN WHEELED SCRAPER CO. Ill. catalog of earth moving machinery and road building equipment. 16mo., 24pp., pict. wrap.

1893 Aurora, Ill.   ICHi
------ Col. ill. catalog of Western N
reversible road machines at World's Fair. Goes Lithos. 12mo., 16pp., pict. wrap.

c.1900 Aurora, Ill.   IHi
------ Ill. catalog of ditchers, graders, plows, etc. 8vo., 96pp., photos., pict. wrap.

1858 Philadelphia   PKsL
WILLIS, W.W. Ill. and desc. circular of Willis' pat. stump extractor, pat. 1855. For farmer, contractor, mechanic, road builder and speculator - imaginative ills. of trees, stumps, boulders, etc. being whisked out of the way of progress and civilization. 12mo., 16pp.

Please use the Hardware - Miscellaneous Machinery section as well. As pointed out several times, American manufacturers farmed out their production to jobbers. Agricultural Implements also lists catalogs offering road machinery.

Chapter 48

Scales & Weighing Devices

Almost before we are able to give that first baby yell we are thrown on the scales and weighed. When we have managed to survive the first forty years we are told to watch the scales and cut down. Most of the stuff we buy to eat and live is calculated at so much an ounce or pound. No matter what you do to make a living, balances and scales weigh you in and out of this small world.

Although there are thousands of price lists and illustrations of scales in hundreds of general catalogs throughout the guide, those of the manufacturers who made weighing their business will be found in this chapter. From Benjamin Dearborn's proportional balances of 1804 to Fairbanks' finest in 1895 we offer a good selective list of illustrated reference catalogs. Baby scales, druggists' balances, scales for the home and hotel kitchen, and the general store, are all represented. There are more rugged scales for the mill, farm wagon, factory, warehouse and railroad car.

Just where the 18th century whittled maple balances fit, I am not sure, but I am fairly certain that the country cabinetmakers and carpenters who made them didn't issue catalogs. If you are hunting a manufacturer whose name is not listed here I suggest you cover the Hardware chapters, the House Furnishings chapter, and the Miscellaneous Store catalogs. Many a small business sold its entire output to a jobber or retailer backalong, and unless the jobber or retailer issued catalogs, there is no printed or illustrated record of the name or product. Hundreds are hidden away and many never come to light unless you -- and you -- dig them out.

1878 Chicago   ICHi
BORDEN, SELLECK & CO. Ill. catalog of improved Howe scales. 36pp. with a fine pict. wrap.

1874 Buffalo, N. Y.   MBSPNEA
BUFFALO SCALE CO. Ill. price list of scales for druggist and general store and home kitchen. 16mo., 28pp., fine ills.

1880-97 Chicago   Locations
CHICAGO SCALE CO.   as follows
Ill. catalogs, various sizes, pict. wrap.

1880   ICHi
Ill. catalog of Union Family Scales. 16pp.

1882   ICHi
Ill. catalog of the Little Detective scale, weighs up to 251 lbs. 4to.

1883   ICHi
Ill. catalog of U. S. Standard scales.

1883   MnHi
Reduced price list of all scales for family, farm, mill, railroad, factory, store and warehouse - coffee mills, etc. 24mo., 64pp. Fine ills., pict. wrap.

c.1890   ICHi
Ill.catalog of scales for all purposes and trades.

1897   OrU
Ill. catalog of standard scales of all sizes and varieties.

1804 Boston
DEARBORN, BENJAMIN. Ill. price list of proportional balances, weights, beams, gold standard scales for banks, hydraulic balances, etc. Fol. broadside.

Dearborn's system of weighing with ease, dispatch and precision purchased for half the cost of scales and weights, and used with half the labor.

DURYEA, FORSYTH & CO. See Rochester Scale Works.

1847 St. Johnsbury, Vt.   VtHi
FAIRBANKS, E. & T. CO. Est. 1830. Later Fairbanks, Morse & Co. Catalog of Fairbanks Platform and Counter Scales. 16mo., 20pp., woodcuts, list of agents, pict. wrap.

1851 St. Johnsbury, Vt.   NNU-W
------ Fairbanks Platform Scales. 16mo., 54pp., woodcuts, wrap.

1859 St. Johnsbury, Vt.   VtHi
------ Fairbanks Pocket Atlas of U.S. and Miniature Railway Guide - with ills. and desc. of Fairbanks Standard and Counter

Scales. 16mo., advt., V and 61pp., col. tinted maps - Maine to California with woodcuts and data on scales quaintly slipped in with guide. Pict. wrap. A very unusual catalog.

1861 St. Johnsbury, Vt.   VtHi
------ Catalog of scales for every business. 16mo., 36pp. List of American Railroads using Fairbanks. Ills., pict. wrap.

c.1867 St. Johnsbury, Vt.   VtHi
------ Fairbanks Standard Scales. 32pp., ills., wrap.

1874 St. Johnsbury, Vt.   ICHi
FAIRBANKS, MORSE & CO. v.p. Ill. catalog of Scales. 24pp., wrap.

1875 St. Johnsbury, Vt.   VtHi
------ Catalog of iron frame track scales for Railroads, foundries, mills and stores. 8vo., 48pp., ills., glt. pict. wrap.

1876 St. Johnsbury, Vt.   NNMM
------ Price list of Spring Balances, Counter and Union Scales - steelyards with stencil desc. 8vo., 69pp., cl.

1878 St. Johnsbury, Vt.   VtHi
------ Standard Weighing Machines - latest improvements - important facts. 16mo., 32pp., fine ills., wrap.

1884 St. Johnsbury, Vt.   MnHi
------ v.p. Ill. price list of standard scales.

1885 St. Johnsbury, Vt.   MnHi
------ Jan. 1st catalog of scales, barrows, cars, mills, cannisters, etc. 8vo., 76pp., ills., wrap.

1889 St. Johnsbury, Vt.   MnHi
------ Ill. catalog of Fairbanks Scales. 16mo., ill., wrap.

1891 St. Johnsbury, Vt.   VtHi
------ Ill. price list of Standard Scales. 8vo., 118pp., col. plate, cl.

1893 St. Johnsbury, Vt.   VtHi
------ Ill. price list for Druggists, Confectioners, Jewelers, etc. 16mo., 58pp., pict. wrap.

1893 St. Johnsbury, Vt.   VtHi
------ Souvenir - World's Columbian Exposition.

1895 St. Johnsbury, Vt.   NNNAM
------ Ill. price list - April 1st. Fairbanks Standard Scales. 122pp., cl.

c.1900 New York   PKsL
FORSCHNER, CHARLES & SON. Ill. catalog and price list of beams, scales and spring balances.

1874 Chicago   ICHi
GILBERT, A.M. & CO. Branches in St. Louis and Cincinnati. Ill. catalog of scales, spring balances, money drawers, etc. 56pp.

1876 Chicago   MH-BA
------ Ill. circular of Howe railroad track scales, list of users, etc. 8vo., 16pp.

1878 Chicago   ICHi
------ Ill. catalog of railroad track scales, truck and barrow scales, etc. 16pp.

1879-1909 Rutland, Vt.   VtHi
HOWE SCALE CO. Ill. catalogs as follows:

   1879 Ill. price list of Howe scales for home, store and manufacturers.

   1880 Ill. catalog of Howe scales.

   1885 Ill. catalog. 16mo., 56pp.

   1909 Ill. price list. 176pp. of ills. with view of plant. Wrap.

1898 Binghamton, N.Y.   N
JONES OF BINGHAMTON. Ill. catalog F of U.S. Standard Jones Scales with rather nice col. pls. 16mo., pict. wrap.

c.1900 Jersey City & New York   NjR
KOHLBUSCH, HERMAN MFG. CO. Est. 1859. Ill. catalog of balances and weights, scales of precision for druggist, chemist and laboratories. 8vo., 40pp.

nd. Philadelphia   PHi
PHILADELPHIA SCOOP & SCALE MFG. CO. New ill. catalog.

PITTSBURGH NOVELTY WORKS. See Hardware - General Hardware Goods.

1851 Rochester, N.Y.   ICHi
ROCHESTER SCALE WORKS.   NNU
Duryea, Forsyth & Co. Ill. catalog of scales for various purposes including sugar mills, stores, etc. Also letter presses, etc. 16mo., 40pp., pict. wrap. of scales.

1889 Philadelphia   DSi
TROEMNER, HENRY. Price list of fine scales and weights. 68pp. April 1889. See also Drugs and Pharmaceuticals.

Chapter 49

Seedsmen & Nurserymen's Products

The classification of arts, crafts, occupations and trades is probably another of those arenas that sensible angels avoid. What would history be without a few fools?

The Dictionary of American Biography names Grant Thorburn America's first seedsman. Even a hasty study of the trade catalogs of American seedsmen that have survived disproves this statement, unless it can be proven that seedsmen did not grow and sell bulbs, plants, shrubs and trees, and that nurserymen never produced and sold seeds. The very catalogs listed in this chapter will make it quite plain that, being progressive Americans, both professions raised and sold everything pertaining to and included under agriculture and horticulture; many of them even wrote and sold books as well as compiling descriptive catalogs for the benefit of their customers.

This chapter will serve as a guide to examples from 1771 to 1900, and locates both large and small collections from Maine to Florida, across to Texas, up the coast to Oregon and back through Chicago to Albany and Boston. It includes the earliest and best from such great collections as DA, NIC-B, NNQ and OCL but does not pretend complete coverage of the thousands still uncataloged. We offer thorough details of the compilations of such outstanding seedsmen and nurserymen as William Prince, Bernard M'Mahon, W. Atlee Burpee, D. M. Ferry, Peter Henderson and Grant Thorburn, but we do not neglect some of the little fellows like Isaac Thompson of New London, Conn., whose 1806 list of seeds has been forgotten and unknown for generations.

1879 West Chester, Pa.   PKsL
ACHELIS, GEORGE. Prop. of the Morris Nurseries. Ill. trade list of seeds. 8vo., 10pp.

1871 Rahway, N. J.   NjOE
ACKERS, HENRY E. Annual desc. catalog of choice vegetable and flower seeds. 25pp.

ALBANY NURSERIES. See S. Moulton & Co.

ALBANY NURSERY. See Jesse Buel & Co.

ALLEN, A.B. See Agricultural Implements, Tools and Machinery.

c.1860 Richmond, Va.   Vi
ALLEN & JOHNSON. Prop. of Hermitage Nurseries. Ill. catalog of fruit trees, plants and shrubs - plants for the Virginia Wine Co., etc. 8vo., 48pp., 2 col. pls., pict. wrap.

1879 Brattleboro   VtHi
ALLEN, C.E. Seedsman. Spring   NIC-B
catalog. 8vo., XII and 96pp. with fine ills. of seeds, flowers, shrubs, etc. Dec. wrap.

1869-1880 Brooklyn & Garden City, N. Y.
ALLEN, C.L. & CO. Annual   Locations
spring and fall ill. catalogs: as follows

1869   NNQ
Ill. catalog of seeds, bulbs, plants, etc.

1871   NNQ
Autumn catalog of hyacinths, lilies, tulips, etc. 8vo., 24pp., fine ills.

1872   NNQ
6th annual ill. catalog for spring 1872 - seeds, flowers, baskets, stands, sprays, arrangements, aquariums and supplies. 8vo., 144pp.

1872   NIC-B
Flower Garden Advertiser. XVIII and 38pp.

1879-80   NNQ
Annual catalog. 12mo., 20pp., ills.

1890 Ithaca   NIC-B
ALLEN, F.R. & CO. Circular - fruit trees our specialty.

1870-79 New York   NIC-B
ALLEN, R.H. & CO. Ill. catalogs of flower, fruit, herb, field and vegetable seeds, agricultural implements and supplies, as follows:

1870 Ill. catalog   32pp.

1871 Ill. catalog   48pp.

1872 Ill. catalog   64pp.

1879 Ill. catalog   80pp.

1875   Chicago   ICHi
ALLEN, W.D. Ill. catalog of greenhouse
plants, pots, hanging baskets, wire plant
stands, etc.

1892-99 Salisbury, Md.   NIC-B
ALLEN, W.F. JR. Allen's desc. and ill.
catalogs of choice strawberry plants. 16 to
32pp., pict. wrap., 1899 in col. For 1892,
1893, 1895, 1896, 1897, 1898 and 1899.

1894   Rochester, N.Y.   NIC-B
ALLIANCE NURSERY CO. Ill. catalog of
fruit trees, small fruits and ornamentals.
40pp.

1884-93 Rockford, Ill.   NIC-B
ALNEER BROTHERS. Ill. garden directory
and seed catalogs, including everything for
the flower and vegetable garden: ill., ptd.
and pict. wrap., 40 to 56pp. each. For 1884,
1885, 1886, 1889, 1890, 1891, 1892 and 1893.

1877-79 West Chester, Pa.   NIC-B
ALTOFER, G. Wholesale price lists for
1877 and 1878-9. Each 4pp.

1892   Seven Oaks, Fla.   F
AMERICAN EXOTIC NURSERIES. Ill. catalog of tropical plants. 8vo., 89pp. of fine
ills., wrap.

AMERICAN SEED GARDENS. See Johnson,
Robbins & Co. and B.N. Strong & Co.

1880-96 Union Springs, N.Y.   NIC-B
ANDERSON, H.S. Cayuga Lake Nurseries.
Successor to Farley & Anderson.
Ill. catalogs as follows:

   1880   Desc. catalog #3 - roses. 16pp.

   1886   Catalog of flowers. 22pp.

   1889   Catalog of foreign fruit trees, orna-
          mental seedlings, shrubs, roses,
          etc. 8pp.

   1892   Autumn trade list with ills. 8pp.

   c.1896 Catalog of ornamental fruit trees,
          grapevines, shrubs, roses, etc.
          64pp.

1887-99 Chestnut Hill, Pa.   NIC-B
ANDORRA NURSERIES. Ill. catalogs of
choice hardy trees, shrubs, plants, roses
and fruits, v.p., some pls. and mostly pict.
wrap., 16 to 72pp. For 1887, 1892, 1893,
1894, 1895, 1896, 1898 and 1899.

1899   Boulder, Colo.   NIC-B
ANDREWS, D.M. Ill. catalog of hardy per-
ennials, cacti, Colorado wild flowers and
novelties. 28pp.

1899   Boulder, Colo.   NIC-B
------ Ill. catalog of rare conifers and
novelties in Rocky Mountain plants. 12pp.

1892   Oshkosh, Wis.   NIC-B
ANGELL, C.E. & CO. Badger State Seed
Farms. Ill. catalog of vegetable seeds. 32pp.

1875   San Francisco   CHi
APPLEBY, WILLIAM. Ill. nursery catalog
of seeds and plants. 8vo., pict. wrap.

1899   Carthage, Mo.   NIC-B
ARCHIAS, L.E. SEED CO. Ill. catalog. 36pp.

ARKANSAS NURSERY. See W.K. Tipton.

AROOSTOOK NURSERY. See E.W. Merritt.

ASHLAND NURSERY. See Tolman & Blake.

1891   Astoria, N.Y.   NIC-B
ASTORIA NURSERIES. Formerly Wm. C.
Wilson. Est. 1848. Ill. catalog of bulbs,
plants and seeds. 18pp., wrap. See also
Wm. C. Wilson.

1898   Orange, N.J.   NIC-B
ATKINSON, GEORGE. Successor to T.H.
Spaulding. Ill. catalog of chrysanthemums,
cannas, begonias, etc. 32pp., wrap.

1895   Normal, Ill.   NIC-B
AUGUSTINE & CO. Semi-annual wholesale
price list. 8pp.

1892-94 Downer's Grove, Ill.   NIC-B
AUSTIN, A.B. Two catalogs of fruit and
ornamental trees, plants and shrubs. 36pp.
1892-3 and 1893-4.

1896-98 Bridgman, Mich.   NIC-B
BABCOCK, WILLIAM C. Hillside Nursery
& Fruit Farm. Four ill. and desc. catalogs
of high grade fruits and plants. 1896, 1897,
1898 and spring 1898.

1890   Leavenworth   NIC-B
BAIN, VARNEY & CO. Annual seed catalog.
56pp., ills., wrap.

1896   Springfield, O.   NIC-B
BAINES, MISS ELLA V. Ill. catalog of bulbs,
roses and plants - the best and choicest. 32pp.

1891-99 Fort Worth   NIC-B
BAKER BROTHERS. Twelve ill. and desc.
catalogs of plants, seeds, shrubs, trees,
roses, grapevines, bulbs and specialties,
with 20 years of experience behind them,
etc. Annual, spring and fall, 32 to 56pp.,
fine ills. and dec. with pict. wrap. 1891,
1892, 1892, 1893, 1893, 1894, 1894, 1895,
1896, 1897, 1898 and 1899.

1897-99 Bridgman, Mich.   NIC-B
BALDWIN, O.A.E. Railroad View Fruit
Plant Farms. Price lists of blackberry,
raspberry and strawberry plants, currants,
grapevines and gooseberry bushes, etc. 16
to 26pp., with hist. details from 1889. For
1897, 1897, 1898 and 1899. First catalog
issued 1889, first ill. catalog 1900.

1898 Seneca, Kan.   NIC-B
BALDWIN, S.J. The Seneca Nursery.
Annual price list. 16pp.

1894-99 Cedar Falls, Ia.   NIC-B
BANCROFT, JOSEPH. Ill. catalogs. Good
things for farm and garden, pretty things
for all places - cut flower prices, 10 to
40pp., pict. wrap. For spring 1894, spring
and fall 1898 and spring 1899.

1890-99 Chicago   NIC-B
BARNARD, W.W. & CO. Formerly Hiram
Sibley & Co. of Rochester, N. Y. Ill. catalogs of Barnard's tested seeds for all crops,
all climates, all soils and garden implements. Five catalogs as follows:

1890	128pp.	1891	84pp.
1892	88pp.	1893	96pp.
	1899	104pp.	

1897 Denton, Md.   NIC-B
BARNHART, JOHNS. 32nd semi-annual
trade list of peach trees and grapevines. 4pp.

1898 Middle Hope, N. Y.   NIC-B
BARNS, W.D. & SON. Desc. circular and
price list of Hunn strawberries. 4pp.

1833 Boston   MStOSV
BARRETT, GEORGE C. Ill. catalog of
kitchen, garden, herb, flower, grass, shrub
seeds, bulbous roots, farm and garden implements and books. 4th ed. 64pp., fine
woodcuts, dec. wrap.

1835 Boston   MStOSV
------ Ill. catalog of seeds, mills, yokes,
garden fire engines, cornshellers, churns,
pumps, winnowers, etc. 16mo., 80pp.,wrap.

1836 Boston   NIC-B
------ Annual catalog of seeds, etc. with
ills. of implements for sale by Joseph R.
Newell. 6th ed., 16mo., 72pp., pict. wrap.

1868 Providence, R. I.   RHi
BARRETT, W.E. & CO. Ill. catalog of
seeds and farm tools. 12mo., 28pp., woodcuts, pict. wrap.

1882 Providence, R. I.   RHi
------ Ill. catalog.

1888-99 Lawrence, Kan.   NIC-B
BARTELDES, F. & CO. Kansas   KU
Seed House. Ill. catalogs of bird, flower,
field, grass, herb and vegetable seeds, nursery stock, fertilizers and implements, v.p.,
wraps.

1888, 1891, 1892, 1893, 1894
                                NIC-B
1895, 1896, 1897, 1898, 1899

1896 - as above   KU

1807 Philadelphia   PPL
BARTRAM, JOHN. A catalog of   DA
trees, shrubs and herbaceous plants indig-
enous to the U. S., cultivated and disposed
of by John Bartram & Son at their Botanical
Gardens. PPL lists as 33pp. DA copy adds
a catalog of foreign plants, etc.

1814 Philadelphia   PKsL
------ Same as above but for   DA
slight change in wording of title page.

1891-98 Hammonton, N. J.   NIC-B
BASSETT, WM. F. & SON. Bellevue Nursery. Ill. catalogs of fruit and ornamental
trees, plants and vines native to America -
We specialize in large orders for public and
private parks, etc. From 4 to 28pp., ptd.
and pict. wrap., as follows:
1891, 1895, 1896, 1897-8 and 1898.

1892 South St. Louis   NIC-B
BAYLES, S.M. Annual catalog and price
list of fruit trees, berry bushes and shrubs.
32pp.

1877 New York   NIC-B
BEACH, SON & CO. Ill. catalog of bulbs,
plants and seeds, vegetable and flower, etc.
32pp., wrap.

1879 New York   NIC-B
------ Ill. catalog. 36pp., wrap.

1895-6 Atlanta   NIC-B
BEATTIE, W.D. Atlanta Nurseries. Desc.
and ill. catalogs of fruit and ornamental
trees, plants and roses. 32pp. Two catalogs - 1895 and 1896.

1895-98 Neville Island, Pa.   NIC-B
BECKERT BROTHERS. Wholesale Growers.
Three ill. catalogs of carnations, violets,
chrysanthemums, Bougainvilleas, etc. 8pp.
each for 1895, 1897 and 1898.

1889-99 Allegheny   NIC-B
BECKERT, WILLIAM C. Seedsman. 19
ill. and desc. catalogs of bulbs, flower seeds
and implements, 16 to 72pp. with ptd. and
pict. wrap. A fine ref. collection.

1898   Fremont, N. H.   NIC-B
BEEDE, GEORGE F. Catalog and price list
of strawberry plants. 12pp.

BELLE COTTAGE NURSERIES. See George
J. Kellogg & Sons.

BELLEVUE NURSERY. See William F.
Bassett & Son.

BELMONT HILL NURSERIES. See C. O.
Saunders.

1871   Flatbush, L.I., N. Y.   NNQ
BENNETT & DAVIDSON. Spring catalog of
new plants - roses, pelargoniums, verbenas,
fuchsias, dahlias and other choice plants.
8vo., 32pp., ills.

1880   Philadelphia   NIC-B
BENSON, MAULE & CO. Ill. and desc. catalog of reliable seeds - small fruits, bulbs,
plants and implements. 48pp., pict. wrap.

1887-90   Douglaston, N. Y.   NIC-B
BENZ, ALBERT. Two ill. catalogs - annual
price lists of German fancy pansies, Viola
tricolor maxima. 6th and 8th., 4pp. each.
1887-8 and 1889-90.

1888-1900   San Francisco   NIC-B
BERGER, H.H. & CO. Ten ill. trade lists
and catalogs of oriental plants, bulbs, fruit
trees and flowers - from China, Australia
and Japan. 8 to 42pp., pict. wrap.

1888	1889-90	1889-90
1891-92	1892-93	1893-94
1894-95	1895-96	1898

and 1899-1900.

1899   Canal Dover, O.   NIC-B
BETSCHER BROTHERS. A select list of
bulbs, seeds and plants. 28pp., ill.

1887   NIC-B
BEYER, H. Annual ill. catalog of garden
and flower seeds by Hugo Beyer. 32pp.

c.1897   Chadd's Ford, Pa.   NIC-B
BIDDLE, FRANCIS C. Price list of small
fruit plants, evergreens, shrubbery and
hedges. 8pp.

1896-98   Hopewell, N. Y.   NIC-B
BIRDSEY & SON. Two price lists of nursery stock. 1896 - 6pp. and 1898 - broadside.

1897   Kittrell, N. C.   NIC-B
BLACKNALL, O.W. Ill. catalog of strawberry plants for spring of . . . 32pp.

1888-98   Philadelphia   NIC-B
BLANC, A. & CO. Seedsmen,   PKsL
nurserymen, engravers, electrotypers and
largest growers of cacti in America. See
also Printers.

Twenty odd ill. catalogs, pict. wrap., 16 to
200pp. as follows:

1888   NIC-B
Hints on cacti, priced catalog, 68pp.

1889   NIC-B
Ill. catalog of rare cacti. 24pp.

1890   NIC-B
Ill. catalog of electros of fruits, trees -
thousands of specimens. 200pp.

1890   NIC-B
Ill. catalog of cacti. 24pp.

1891   PKsL NIC-B
Ill. price list of cacti. 112pp.

1892   NIC-B
Ill. catalog of bulbs. 16pp.

1893   PKsL NIC-B
Ill. catalog of rare cacti. 32pp.

1894   NIC-B
Ill. catalog of electrotypes of flowers, plants
and shrubs for nurserymen. Pict. wrap.
36pp.

1894   PKsL NIC-B
Ill. catalog of rare cacti. 32pp.

1894   NIC-B
Ill. catalog of novelties.

1895   NIC-B
Ill. catalog of specialties. 24pp.

1896   NIC-B
Specimens of electrotypes of fruits, vegetables, etc. 1st supplement. 24pp.

1896   NIC-B
Specimens for nurserymen. 76pp.

1896   NIC-B
Ill. catalog of plants and bulbs. 32pp.

1898   NIC-B
Ill. catalog of rare plants. 32pp.

1899   NIC-B
Wholesale price list of new American and
foreign cannas. 4pp. and 32pp.

N.B. The only printer-nurseryman so far
       located. Ralph Green locates two
specimen books for 1884 and 1886. The catalogs listed here would seem to be samples

of their engravings, rather than electros and cuts offered for sale.

1860-89 Springfield, Mass. & New York
BLISS, BENJAMIN K. and from   NIC-B
1869 - B.K. & SON.

One of the finest collections of one American seedsman located. Ill. catalogs from 20 to 212pp. with fine ills., col. pls., pict. wrap., including the Bliss Floral Guide and Gardeners' Almanacs. First catalog was issued c.1852, the 1860 being their 8th annual. From herbs to flowers, shrubs to trees, for parlor and kitchen and market gardens. We offer nearly three dozen - all at NIC-B.

1819-20 Flushing, L.I., N.Y.   NIC-B
BLOODGOOD, JAMES & CO.   NNQ
Bloodgood Nursery. A catalog of fruit and forest trees, flowering plants and shrubs - at their nurseries near New York, etc. Sq. 12mo., 12pp., ptd. J. Gray & Co.

c.1820 Flushing, L.I., N.Y.   NIC-B
------ Catalog. 24mo., 39pp., stitched, ptd. Gray & Bunce, Franklin Square. Comment on Capt. Selby's $320. crop from 34 peach trees. Deplores practice by his fellow seedsmen of making a catalog into an essay, pointing out that THIS is a catalog.

1831 Flushing, L.I., N.Y.   NNQ
------ Catalog of fruit and ornamental trees, evergreens, flowering shrubs and plants. 24mo., 40pp., ptd. Wm.A.Mercein.

BLOOMINGTON NURSERIES. See F.K. Phoenix.

1884 Bloomington, Ill.   ICHi
BLOOMINGTON NURSERY CO.   IHi
Ill. catalog of bulbs, flowers, plants, trees and shrubs for the Prairies.

1896 Westfield, N.J.   NIC-B
BLOWERS, H.W. Wholesale price list of grapevines with map of Chatauqua grape belt.

1889-93 Auburn, Calif.   NIC-B
BOARDMAN, A.F. & CO. Ill. and desc. catalogs of fruits, plants and trees, pict. wrap., as follows:

1889	28pp.	wrap.
1892	74pp.	pict. wrap.
1893-4	42pp.	wrap.

1866 Rochester, N.Y.   NIC-B
BOARDMAN, S. & CO. Est. 1828. Ill. and desc. catalog of roses, vines, shrubs and ornamental fruit trees. 72pp.

1896 Hamilton, O.   NIC-B
BOCK, THEODORE. Price list of choice chrysanthemums. 4pp.

1898 Cheswold, Del.   NIC-B
BOGGS, CALEB. Ill. summer and fall catalog of pot-grown strawberry, celery, tomato, pepper and egg plants. 12pp.

1890 Marysville, Calif.   NIC-B
BOGUE, JAMES T. Price list of fruit trees. 4pp.

1899 Batavia, N.Y.   NIC-B
BOGUE, NELSON. Batavia Nurseries. Supplementary catalog of fruits - fine col. pls. 32pp.

1889 Waterloo, N.Y.   NIC-B
BONNELL, GEORGE H. Ill. and desc. catalog of garden seeds and potato plants. 16pp.

1810 Baltimore - Frederick-Town Road,
      half a mile from Baltimore.   DA
BOOTH, WILLIAM. A catalog of kitchen garden seeds and plants, physical seeds and plants, seeds to improve lands, fruit trees, annual and biennial and perennial flowers, herbaceous plants, bulbous roots, forest trees, flowering shrubs and evergreens, greenhouse and stove plants. Ptd. Baltimore by G. Dobbin & Murphy.

1854 Boston   NIC-B
BOWDITCH, AZELL. Desc. catalog of flower seeds at Mass. Horticultural Seed and Fruit Store. 12pp.

c.1890 Boston   NIC-B
BOWDITCH, WILLIAM C. Ill. and desc. catalog of flower and vegetable seeds, bulbs, plants, etc. 68pp., pict. wrap.

1883 San Francisco   CHi
BOWEN, E.J. Nurseryman. Ill. catalog of seeds, plants and garden implements. 8vo., 128pp., pict. wrap.

1899 San Francisco, Portland, Ore. and Seattle.
------ Ill. and desc. catalog. 120pp., wrap.

N.B. American growth and expansion; 1883 one nursery, 1899 three.

1897 Newport, Ark.   NIC-B
BOWEN, W.M. Ill. catalog of greenhouse and bedding plants, grapevines, fruit trees and ornamental shrubbery. 16pp., wrap.

1899 Rochester, N.Y.   NIC-B
BOWMAN, THOMAS W. & SON. Rochester Star Nurseries. Price list #4 - surplus stock. 4pp.

1890 Schiocton, Wis.   NIC-B
BOYNTON, W.D. Priced catalog of evergreens for hedges, wind breaks and nursery
planting fruit stock, Christmas trees, etc.
8pp.

1872 Denmark, Ia.   IaHi
BRACKETT, G.B. Ill. catalog of fruit and
ornamental trees.

1889-92 Bremen, O.   NIC-B
BRANDT, D. Brandt's Nursery. Four ill.
catalogs of strawberry and raspberry plants,
roses, grapevines and fruit trees, 20 to 56pp.
Fine ills., pict. wraps. For 1889, 1890,
1891 and 1892.

1838-1900 Boston   NIC-B
BRECK, JOSEPH & SONS. See Agricultural
Implements, Tools and Machinery for details
of 1838, 1880, 1897 and 1900 issues.

1885 to 1899 as follows: Ill. and desc. catalogs of garden, field and flower seeds, bulbs,
agricultural implements and machines, novelties, etc. 44 to 164pp., col. pls. and pict.
col. wrap. For 1885 to 1899, with two or
more in some years, annuals and specials.

1886-7 Fayetteville, N. C.   NIC-B
BREECE, J.A. Catalog of fruit trees -
pears, apples, peaches, plums, apricots,
pecans, cherries, Japan persimmons, grapes,
etc. 8pp.

1892 Clinton, Mass.   NIC-B
BREED, E.W. Florist. Ill. catalog - Gems
of Nature - bulbs, roses, shrubs, fruit trees,
ferns, etc. 52pp. with ill. advts. of merchants.

1897 Detroit, Mich.   NIC-B
BREITMEYER, JOHN & SONS. Price list of
carnations and chrysanthemums. 4pp.

1862-99 New York   NIC-B
BRIDGEMAN, ALFRED & ANDREW. Est.
1824. Another fine ref. collection of about
forty ill. and desc. catalogs, with col. pls.
and pict. wrap. for a period of nearly 40
years, running from 12 to 64pp., offering
everything from flower seeds to garden and
farm implements, tools and horticultural
books. These comprise 1862, 1869, 1876
and 1881; the rest are all dated from 1891-
1899! Trade catalogs paid obviously.

1871-86 Rochester, N. Y.   Locations
BRIGGS & BROTHERS.   as follows
Est. 1845. A fine collection of ill. catalogs
with some col. pls., col. pict. wrap. of flower, garden and vegetable seeds, as follows:

1870   NR
Ill. catalog of bulbs and seeds.

1871   NR   NIC-B
Ill. catalog, fine pls. 112pp.

1872   NR
Ill. catalog. 64pp. Fine ills.

1873   NR   NIC-B
Ill. catalog and floral work. 16pp.

1874   NR   ICHi   NIC-B
Ill. catalog of bulbs and plants, flower and
vegetable seeds, advance list 32pp.

1875   NR   MdTanSW
Price list of seeds, etc. 32pp., wrap.

1876   NR   NIC-B
Quarterly ill. catalog and floral work. Col.
pls., col. pict. wrap., 32pp.

1877-85   NR
Ill. catalogs as desc., v.p., wrap.

1886   NIC-B
Desc. catalog of garden seeds. 32pp.

1833 Brighton, Mass.   NIC-B
BRIGHTON NURSERIES. Annual catalog #1
of fruit and ornamental trees and plants.
40pp., ills.

1841 Brighton, Mass.   NIC-B
------ Ill. catalog of ornamental trees,
roses, vines, creepers, medicinal and culinary plants and esculent roots. 48pp.

1897-8 Brighton, N. Y.   NIC-B
BRIGHTON CENTRAL NURSERIES.
J. Frank Norris, Prop. Est. 1842. Two
semi-annual trade lists of fruit and ornamental trees, roses, etc.

1891 Rochester, Mich.   NIC-B
BROTHERTON, WILFRED A. Catalog of
Michigan wild flowers. 20pp.

1898-9 Fairpoint, O.   NIC-B
BROWN & HERSHEY. Florists & Seedsmen.
Three ill. catalogs, wrap., of bulbs, plants,
seeds and vines, etc.

1898   32pp.   1899   32pp.

Autumn 1899   8pp.

1895-6 Wyoming, Del.   NIC-B
BROWN, A.N. Brown Seed Co. Two circular price lists - 1895. The three greatest
things in agriculture - crimson clover, cow
peas and winter oats. 10pp. Desc. catalog
of high grade farm seeds. 8pp.

c.1890 Rochester, N. Y.   NR
BROWN BROTHERS CONTINENTAL NURS-
ERIES. Ill. catalog of fruit and ornamental
trees, plants, shrubs, roses, etc. with landscape plans, 100 col. pls., pict. wrap.

c.1892 Rochester, N. Y.   NR
------ Ill. catalog with 96 col. pls.

1898 Rochester, N. Y. & Ontario, Canada
------ Canadian Branch. Ill. and   NIC-B
desc. catalog with pls., 80pp., pict. wrap.

1899 Rochester, N. Y.   NIC-B
------ Ill. catalog with col. pls. and pict.
wrap. 166pp.

1897 Oxford, O.   NIC-B
BROWN, WALDO F. Price list of sugar
cane, sweet potatoes and fruit trees.

1889-98 Rockford, Ill.   NIC-B
BUCKBEE, H.W. Three ill. catalogs and
plant guides with litho. col. pls.

        1889   48pp.   1894   80pp.

                1898   126pp.

1895-6 Greenville, O.   NIC-B
BUECHLY, E.M. Two ill. catalogs of fruit
and ornamental trees, vines, roses and novelties. Wrap.

        1895   16pp.   1896   16pp.

BUEL & WILSON. See Moulton & Co.

1839-40 Albany, N. Y.   NIC-B
BUEL, JESSE & CO. Albany Nursery. Catalog of fruit and ornamental trees, shrubs,
greenhouse plants, etc. 32pp.

1842 Albany, N. Y.   NIC-B
------ Catalog of fruit and ornamental
trees, etc. 24pp.

1853-99 Philadelphia   Locations
BUIST, ROBERT. Later   as follows
Robert Jr. Rosedale Nursery. Ill. catalogs
with garden guides and almanacs of prize
medal seeds, plants, etc. as follows.

        1853   PPL
Ill. catalog of rare and popular flowering
greenhouse, hothouse and hardy plants. 56pp.

        1869   PHi
Ill. catalog with pict. wrap. of nursery.

        1880   PPL
Ill. price list of bulbous plants, etc. 14pp.

        1890-99   NIC-B
Ill. catalogs and price lists, from 16 to
160pp. Pict. wrap.

1880-99 Santa Rosa, Calif.   NIC-B
BURBANK, LUTHER. Santa Rosa Nursery.
Catalogs and price lists with fine ills., pict.
wrap. and some col. pls. of fruit, nut and
ornamental trees, shrubs, bulbs, walnut

trees, new creations in fruit and flowers,
etc. For 1880, 1883-4, 1885, 1885-6, 1888,
1890, 1892, 1893, 1894, 1895, 1898 and 1899.

1857 Providence, R. I.   RHi
BURDICK & BARRETT. Ill. catalog of field
and garden seeds and garden implements.
8vo., 12pp.

1879-1914 Philadelphia   Locations
BURPEE, W. ATLEE & CO.   as follows
Ill. farm annuals, seed and plant catalogs,
implements and blooded stock - everything
for the farm and garden. Fine col. pls. and
litho. pict. wrap.

        1879   PKsL MoSHi
Burpee's ill. annual seed catalog.

        1880   PKsL
Burpee's ill. farm annual and catalog.

        1882   NIC-B
Farm annual - seeds to swine. 48pp.

        1884-5   PHi   NIC-B
Farm annual, col. pls., 120pp.

        1892-9   PHi   NIC-B
Farm annuals, ill. catalogs, col. pls., pict.
wrap., 32 to 56pp. from 1892-99.

        1886-1914   PKsL
A fine ref. collection, col. pls., etc. as above.

1883 St. Louis   MoSHi
BUSH & SON, & MEISSNER. Bushberg
Vineyards & Grape Nurseries. Ill. catalog
of American grapevines.

1884-99 St. Louis   NIC-B
------ Semi-annual price lists of grapevines, v.p. with ill. flyers on individual
varieties. Nice collection.

1898-99 Cromwell, Conn.   NIC-B
BUTLER & JEWELL CO. The Cromwell
Nursery. Two ill. catalogs of plants, vines
and fruit and ornamental trees, each 24pp.

BUTTERFIELD, M. See Lee's Summit Star
Nurseries.

1896 Chambersburg, Pa.   NIC-B
BYERS BROTHERS. Byers' Friend - catalog of flower, vegetable and ornamental plant
seeds. 16pp.

1890-93 Niles, Calif.   CHi
CALIFORNIA NURSERY CO. Three ill. catalogs of flowers, plants, shrubs, trees and
seeds.
        1890   8vo.   50pp.   wrap.

        1891   8vo.   48pp.   pict. wrap.

        1893   8vo.   55pp.   pict. wrap.

CALLA GREEN HOUSES. See L. Templin
& Sons.

1870 Chicago   ICHi
CARPENTER, JOHNSON & COLES. Ill. catalog of Landreth's seeds.

CASCADE NURSERIES CO. See E. Y. Teas
& Co.

CAYUGA LAKE NURSERIES. See H. S.
Anderson.

CHAMPION CITY GREENHOUSES. See
Good & Reese Co.

1875 Geneva, N. Y.   MH-BA
CHASE, R.G. & CO. Nurseryman. Price
list of fruit trees, vines, roses and shrubs.
8vo., 48pp.

1756 Philadelphia   Evans 7631
CHATTIN, JAMES. Printer. A catalog of
a very curious collection of prints, consisting of several hundred representations of
trees, shrubs, plants, herbs, fruits, flowers,
etc. To be sold cheap, the lowest price
being marked in the catalog.

1856 West Chester, Pa.   PHi
CHERRY HILL NURSERIES. Ill. catalog of
seeds, plants, shrubs and ornamental trees.
24pp.

1859 Philadelphia   PHi
------ Ill. catalog. 35pp.

1871 West Chester, Pa.   PPL
------ Ill. catalog of flowers, shrubs, trees
and vines. 92pp.

1881 West Chester, Pa.   PHi
------ Ill. catalog #5 for spring. 8vo.,
18pp., pict. wrap. Semi-annual trade list.

1886 Chicago   ICHi
CHICAGO FLORAL CO. Ill. catalog of bulbs,
plants and seeds.

1872-3 Los Angeles   CHi
CHILDS & CO. Price list of seeds and
plants. 8vo., 8pp., wrap.

1879-1901 Floral Park, N. Y.   MoSHi
CHILDS, JOHN LEWIS.   NNQ   NIC-B
A fine ref. collection located in three repositories. Ill. catalogs of bulbs, flowers,
fruits and vegetables, seeds, trees and garden implements. 12mo., 8vo. and 4to., with
fine ills., col. pls. and col. pict. wrap.

        1879-1901   NNQ

        1879-1897   NIC-B

        1892-1897   MoSHi

CLAIRMONT NURSERIES, near Baltimore.
See Sinclair & Moore.

1874 Claremont, N. H.   NhD
CLOSSON, H.P. Ill. and desc. catalog of
greenhouse and bedding plants, bulbs, seeds,
trees, etc.

c.1850 Philadelphia   PKsL
COATES, JOSEPH H.P. Est. c.1810. PHi
A catalog of garden seeds. 16mo., 16pp.

1819 New York & Philadelphia   MWA
COBBETT, WILLIAM. A list of field and
garden seeds contained in one of the boxes
to be sold for five dollars . . . , also hints
respecting the sowing and cultivation, etc.
Sold at William Cobbett's Seed and Book
Store, no. 63 Fulton Street and by Mr. John
Morgan in Philadelphia. 16mo., 30pp.

1793 Richmond, Va.   Original at DA
                        Photostat copy at MBH
COLLINS, MINTON. A list of garden and
grass seeds with a choice collection of
flower roots and seeds just imported.
Broadside. January 24.

1870-73 Columbus, O.   OHi
COLUMBUS NURSERY. Est. 1855. R. G.
Hanford, Prop. Four ill. catalogs of seeds,
new plants, flowers, shrubs, etc., wrap.

    1870 8vo. 32pp.   1871 8vo. 48pp.

    1872 8vo. 48pp.   1873 8vo. 60pp.

c.1849 Wethersfield, Conn.   CtHi
COMSTOCK, FERRE & CO. The gardener's
calendar with a desc. catalog of garden seeds,
with directions for planting , cultivating, etc.
16mo., XII and 48pp., title vignette, wrap.

1850 Wethersfield, Conn.   CtHi
------ Desc. and ill. catalog of seeds,
herbs, implements, etc. 16mo., 48pp., pict.
wrap.

1853 Wethersfield, Conn.   NIC-B
------ Gardener's Almanac. 4pp., ill.

1855 Wethersfield, Conn.   NIC-B
------ Gardener's Almanac. Ill.
                                        ~
1894-1908 West Grove, Pa.   NIC-B
CONARD, ALFRED A. Fine runs   PKsL
of this well known seedsman's ill. and desc.
catalogs of seeds, plants, trees, bulbs and
garden implements, etc. 8vo. with col. pls.,
and col. pict. wrap.

CORSE, WILLIAM. See Sinclair & Moore.

1893 San Francisco   CHi
COX SEED CO. Ill. catalog of fine nursery
stock for home and farm.

1884 San Francisco   CHi
COX, THOMAS A. & CO. Ill. nursery catalog. 4to., pict. wrap.

1848 New Bedford   Sabin 17421
CRAPO, H. H. Desc. catalog of trees. 8vo.,
28pp.

1871 Boston   PPL
CURTIS & COBB. Ill. and desc. catalog of
flower and vegetable seeds, garden implements, etc. 140pp.

1877 Boston   PPL
------ Ill. catalog. 34pp.

1859 West Chester, Pa.   PHi
DARLINGTON, J.L. & CO. Ill. catalog of
fruit and ornamental trees. 8vo., 37pp.

1897 Purcellville, Va.   Vi
DAVIS, A.B. & SON. Ill. catalog. Everything for the Garden and Greenhouse. 8vo.,
40pp., dec. wrap.

DEWEY, D.M. Nurseryman. See E.B. &
E.C. Kellogg.

c.1875 Philadelphia   PPL
DICK, JOHN. Brief desc. price list of
flowers, plants and seeds. 14pp.

1874-1900 West Grove, Pa.   Locations
DINGEE & CONARD CO. Est. as follows
1850. Ill. and desc. catalog of new and
beautiful roses, basket plants, flowering
shrubs, Yucca, vines, vegetables, etc. 8vo.,
fine illo., pict. wrap. As follows:

    Twelve issues 1874-1900   NIC-B

    8vo., 36pp., pict. wrap., 1875   PKsL

    Roses by mail-8vo., 56pp., 1879
                               MdTanSW

    New Guide to Rose Culture.   PHi
    8vo., 77pp. 1886.

1873 Albany, N. Y.   MH-BA
DOUW, V.P. & CO. Est. 1831. Ill. catalog
of garden and flower seeds, agricultural
implements and supplies. 8vo., 48pp.

1839 Newburgh, N. Y.   NNMM
DOWNING, A.J. & CO. Architect, horticul-
turist and landscape gardener. See D.A.B.
Annual desc. and priced catalog of fruit
trees and shrubs. 32pp., wrap.

1863-83 Philadelphia   Locations
DREER, HENRY A.   as follows
Ill. catalogs, Garden Calendars and wholesale price lists with fine ills. and pict. wrap.
of seeds, bulbs, roses, shrubs, etc. and gardening tools. Col. pls.

1863   NIC-B
Spring catalog. 24pp.

1870   NIC-B
Desc. catalog, etc. 32pp.

1872   NIC-B
Dreer's Garden Calendar. 156pp.

1873-4   NIC-B
Ill. catalog. 40pp.

1874   NIC-B
Garden Calendar. 168pp.

1877   PHi   NIC-B
Ill. catalog. 58pp.

1878   NIC-B
Dreer's Garden Calendar. 192pp.

1879   NIC-B
Dutch bulbs and tubers. 4pp.

1880   NIC-B
Wholesale price list. 16pp.

1881   PPL   NIC-B
Desc. catalog of bulbs, etc. 32pp.

1882   PPL   NIC-B
Ill. catalog. 32pp.

1883   PPL   NIC-B
Garden Calendar - tools, implements, etc.
128pp., col. pls.

1885   PPL   NIC-B
Ill. and desc. catalog.

1883 - date - Complete file.   NIC-B

Issues not reported also at DA   PKsL

1874-76 Nashua, N. H.   NhHi
DUNLAP, A.H. & SON. Three ill. catalogs
of choice flower seeds with desc. and instructions, etc. 8vo., v.p. with pict. wrap.

1853-76 Naperville, Ill.   ICHi
DuPAGE COUNTY NURSERIES. Three ill.
catalogs of seeds, plants, shrubs, trees, etc.
for 1853, 1875 and 1876.

1890   NIC-B
ELLETSON, J. Auburn Grape Nurseries.
Trade price list of grapevines. 4pp.

1876 Chicago   ICHi
ELLINWOOD, W.J. Ill. catalog of seeds for
farm and garden.

ELLIOT, WYMAN. See Shuman & Co.

1839 Boston   MStOSV
ELLIS & BOSSON. Annual catalog of flower,
tree, garden and vegetable seeds, bulbous

roots, garden and agricultural implements
and horticultural books. Fine woodcuts of
mills, presses and tools. Yankee Farmer
Office. 16mo., 74pp., dec. wrap.

1883 Keene, N. H.   NhD
ELLIS BROTHERS. Ill. catalog of fruit
trees, plants, seeds and vines. 8vo., 44pp.

1892-93 Keene, N. H.   NhHi
------ Two ill. catalogs, 8vo. with Brett
litho. ills. 1892 and 1893.

1848-90 Rochester, N. Y.   Locations
ELLWANGER & BARRY.   as follows
Mt. Hope Garden and Nurseries. Est. 1840.

Desc. price lists and periodical catalogs of
roses, ornamental trees, shrubs and flowers,
strawberries and small fruits, mostly 8vo.,
v.p., mostly pict. wrap.

1848-1800   NIC-B
Fifteen ill. catalogs: 1848-9, 1858, 1860,
1869, 1872, 1876, 1880, 1881, 1882, 1886,
1888, Fall 1888, 1889 and 1891. Also complete run from 1891-1917.

1858-1888   NR
Collection of twenty-four catalogs.

1852-1883   PPL
Lot of five catalogs.

1875   MH-BA
Catalog #3. 29th ed. 56pp.

1888 Philadelphia   PHi
ELY, Z. DeFOREST & CO. Trade price list.
8vo., pict. wrap., ills.

Marietta, Pa.
ENGLE & BRO. See Marietta Nurseries.

1875 Clinton, Ia.   IaHi
ENNIS & PATTON'S WESTERN NURSERIES.
Ill. catalog of shrubs, trees, etc.

1883-1930 Boston   NIC-B
FARQUHAR, ROBERT & JAMES. Seedsmen.
Ill. catalog of reliable seeds. 54pp., wrap.
Sample entry. Complete file to 1930.

1875-1959 Detroit, Mich.   NIC-B
FERRY, D.M. & CO.   CHi   MiU-H

Ill. seed annuals and catalogs, mostly 8vo.
from 98 to 168pp. loaded with ills. and col.
pls. and wrap. in fine col. pict. lithos. by
the Calvert Litho. Co. Excellent ref.

1884   CHi
Ill. catalog, col. pls., 164pp.

1880-1900   MiU-H
Fine collection.

1875-1959   NIC-B
One of the best. Twelve catalogs 1875-1891;
complete file from 1892-1959.

1871 New York   NIC-B
FLEMING, JAMES. Successor to Henderson & Fleming. Annual desc. catalog of
flowering roots, etc. 16pp.

1872 New York   NIC-B
------ Ill. annual of choice seeds, including garden implements. 84pp., col. pls.

1823 New York   NIC-B
FLOY, MICHAEL. Nurseryman. A catalog
of ornamental trees, flowering shrubs,
herbaceous plants, bulbous roots, fruit trees
and flower seeds. 16mo., 40pp., title
vignette. One of the first and best - a competitor of the cantankerous William Cobbett.

1895 Santa Barbara, Calif.   NIC-B
FRANCHESCI, F. Handbook of Santa Barbara exotic flora imported and grown here.
The doctor introduced hundreds of species.
88pp.

1897 Santa Barbara, Calif.   NIC-B
------ General catalog #5. 1500 sorts of
plants with desc. and guide. 94pp.

1875-81 Rochester, N. Y.   NR
FROST, EDWARD A. Genessee Valley Nurseries. Eight ill. catalogs starting with #2
for 1875, 8vo., v.p., ills., pict. wrap.

1869 Fruitport, Mich.   MiU-H
FRUITPORT ORCHARD & VINEYARD. Ill.
catalog of trees and vines.

1893-94 Floral Park, N. Y.   NNQ
FULLER, J. ROSCOE & CO. Three ill.
catalogs of bulbs, plants, shrubs, implements and adornments, 4to., pict. wrap.:

1893 Select catalog of home adornments.

1893 New fall list of bulbs.

1894 Complete catalog for spring.

1895-96 Denver   CoD
GALLUP'S. Ill. catalogs of florist's and
gardener's implements, insecticides, fertilizers, supplies as well as seeds, plants and
trees. Ill. catalogs for 1895 and 1896.

1836 Jamaica, N. Y.   NNQ
GARRETSON, G.R. Annual catalog of seeds,
plants, roots, etc., implements, supplies and
books for horticulturists.

GENESSEE SEED STORE. See Rapelje &
Briggs.

GENESSEE VALLEY NURSERIES. See
Frost.

1886 Georgetown, Fla.   F
GEORGETOWN NURSERIES. Aaron Warr,
Prop. Desc. catalog of shrubs, trees and
fruits. 12mo., 18pp., dec. wrap.

1892 Springfield, O.   OHi
GOOD & REESE CO. Champion City Greenhouses. Ill. 8vo. catalog of bulbs, roses,
etc. for fall and winter.

1878-81 Rochester, N. Y.   NR
GOULD BROTHERS. Monroe County Nurseries. Six ill. catalogs, mostly 8vo., 16pp.,
pict. wrap, spring and fall, etc.

1853-54 Brooklyn, N. Y.   NNQ
GRAEF, H.A. Horticultural Establishment.
Preliminary catalog of seeds and plants.

1895 Colma, Calif.   CHi
GRALLERT & CO. Ill. catalog of nursery
stock, 4to., wrap.

1870 Princeton, Mo.   MoSHi
GRAND RIVER NURSERY. Ill. spring catalog of plants, shrubs, trees, etc.

c.1870 Rochester, N. Y.   NR
GRAVES, SELOVER, WILLARD & CO.
Washington Street Nurseries. Desc. and
ill. catalog #2 - ornamental dept. - flower
seeds and plants, etc. 8vo., 64pp., col. pls.

1879 Rochester, N. Y.   NR
GREEN'S NURSERY CO. Ill. catalog of Red
Cross currants, fruit bushes and trees, etc.
8vo., 42pp.

1862-99 Marblehead, Mass.   NIC-B
GREGORY, JAMES T.H. A fine ref. collection of ill. lists and catalogs, various sizes,
pict. wrap., 2 to 56pp., as follows:
1862 through 1899, lacking only 1871 and
1879. Also complete file from 1900-1936.

1886 Marblehead, Mass.   MnHi
------ Ill. catalog as above. 56pp.

1883 South Glastonbury, Conn.   CtHi
HALE BROTHERS. Elm Fruit Farm. Ill.
catalog of small fruits - new varieties
grown for market - pedigree stock, etc.
8vo., 27pp., wrap.

1889-99 South Glastonbury, Conn. NIC-B
HALE BROTHERS, G.H. & J.H. Elm Fruit
Farm. Eleven ill. catalogs of fruit plants,
file lacking only 1892. 16-32pp., wrap.

1880-89 Queens Village or East Hinsdale,
         N. Y.   NNQ
HALLOCK, V.H. & SON, & THORPE. Seven
8vo. and 4to. ill. catalogs of the best - only
premium plants, fruits and Dutch bulbs -
Floral annuals, 40 to 80pp., fine ills., pls.,
pict. wrap. 1880, 1881, 1882, 1884, 1885,
1886 and 1889.

N.B. The Century Atlas for 1902 does not
     list either village. Had our new look
progress started to wipe out Long Island
villages even then?

1900 Fifield, Mich.   MiU-H
HAMMOND, HARRY N. Seedsman. Annual
ill. catalog of seeds for garden and field.
8vo., pict. wrap.

N.B. The only Fifields in the Century Atlas
     for 1902 are in Wisconsin and England.

1870-72 Columbus, O.   OHi
HANFORD, R.G. Three ill. catalogs of new
plants and seeds, flowers and shrubs for
spring and fall. 8vo., 32, 47 and 47pp., resp.

c.1878 Chicago   ICHi
HANNA, W.J. & CO. Ill. catalog of seeds,
plants and farm implements. In German
and English. Pict. wrap.

nd. Iowa City, Ia.   IaHi
HARKETT'S FLORAL NURSERIES. Ill.
catalog.

1879 Rochester, N. Y.   NR
HARRIS, JOSEPH. Moreton Farm. Ill. and
desc. catalog of farm, field and flower garden seeds. 8vo., 48pp., pict. wrap.

1881 Rochester, N. Y.   MH-BA
------ Ill. catalog of seeds. 42pp.

1880-99 Rochester, N. Y.   NIC-B
------ Collection of fifteen ill. catalogs,
32 to 76pp., including Harris Rural Annual.
Lacking only 1888, 1890, 1891 and 1892.

1883 Hartford, Conn.   CtHi
HAWLEY, R.D. Ill. catalog of seeds, plants
and agricultural implements. 8vo., 47pp.

1869-99 New York   NIC-B
HENDERSON, P. and FLEMING, J. Seedsmen. In 1871 the firm split, Peter Henderson going on and on for himself.

Collection of forty-seven ill. catalogs, 8vo.
to 4to. with fine col. pls. and col. pict. wrap.
of everything to plant and with which to
plant, cultivate, water, pick and harvest
at the proper times.

N.B. Though not reported, I am sure there
     are other copies in other repositories.
Complete 1900-1949 in NIC-B.

1859-60 Hermann, Mo.   MoSHi
HERMANN NURSERY. Ill. catalog of fruit
and ornamental trees, shrubs, roses and
plants.

HERMITAGE NURSERIES. See Allan &
Johnson.

1870-1900 Westbury, N. Y.   NNQ
HICKS NURSERIES. Est. 1853. Four ill.
catalogs of ornamental trees, etc. for home
landscapes, etc. 1870, 1889, fall 1889 and
1900. Also examples on to 1919.

1887 Richmond, Ind.   MH-BA
HILL & CO. Ill. catalog of roses and other
plants for garden and field. Large 8vo.,
60pp.

1886 Holden, Mo.   MoSHi
HOLDEN NURSERIES. J. F. Liddle, Prop.
Ill. price list. 12mo., 4pp.

1856-80 Rochester, N. Y.   NR
HOOKER, H.E. & CO. Rochester Commercial Nurseries. Ill. catalogs of stock and
seeds, 8vo., 8 to 52pp. for 1856, 1879 and
1880.

HOOPES BROTHERS & THOMAS. See
Cherry Hill Nurseries.

1892 Menlo Park, Calif.   CHi
HOPKINS, TIMOTHY. Prop. of Sherwood
Hall Nurseries. Ill. catalog, 8vo., 30pp.

1834-1900 Boston   ICHi
HOVEY & CO. P.B. JR. & C.M. Collection
of ninety odd, 16mo. to 4to., 12 to 200pp.,
ills., col. pls., col. pict. wrap. Sample
title:

1834-5 Catalog of vegetable, herb, tree,
    flower and grass seeds, bulbs,
tuberous flower roots; ornamental greenhouse shrubs and perennial flowering plants,
agricultural, horticultural and botanical
books, etc. 32pp., dec. wrap. Everything to
plant and everything with which to harvest it.

1871-75 Chicago   ICHi
HOVEY & CO. There is no indication that
this was a branch of the Boston Hoveys.
Three ill. catalogs of seeds, plants, trees,
etc. with fine ills. of garden vases, furniture
and ornaments as well as tools and implements. 1871, 1872 and 1875.

1869-70 Chicago   NIC-B
HOVEY & HEFFRON. Desc. catalog of
flowering bulbs, imported seeds, etc. 32pp.

nd. New Canaan, Conn.   CtHi
HOYT'S, STEPHEN SONS. Successors to
Stephen Hoyt & Sons. Ill and desc. catalog
of fruit and ornamental trees, grapevines,
small fruits, shrubs, plants, roses, etc.
New ed., 8vo., 64pp., wrap.

1892 Springfield, O.   OHi
INNISFALLEN GREEN HOUSES. Charles A.
Ressor, Prop. Ill. catalog of plants, etc.
4to., 112pp., col. pls., pict. col. wrap.

1842 Cincinnati   OC
JACKSON, S.S. Nurseryman. A catalog of
plants, etc. 12mo., 26pp.

1855 Wethersfield, Conn.   CtHi
JOHNSON, ROBBINS & CO. Est. 1838.
Desc. catalog of seeds, plants, tools and
garden implements. 12mo., 48pp.

1863 Wethersfield, Conn.   CtHi
------ Ill. catalog of seeds, plants and
garden implements. 16mo., 48pp.

1882 Fredonia, N. Y.   MH-BA
JOSSELYN, GEORGE S. Fall catalog of
nursery stock, American grapevines, small
fruits, plants and trees. 8vo., 14pp., wrap.

c.1865 Hartford, Conn. & Rochester, N. Y.
KELLOGG, E.B. & E.C.   CSmH
Lithographers for D.M.Dewey, Nurseryman.

The nurseryman's specimen book of American Floriculture and Horticulture, with 66
col. pls. of flowers, fruits, roses, shrubs,
ornamental trees, etc. 4th ed. 4to., col.
litho. title.

1872 Hartford & Rochester   CSmH
------ Nurseryman's specimen book -
pocket ed. for salesman - calf, 8vo., 92 col.
lithos., pict. title showing farm before and
after. (Jobber, F. W. Hinman & Co.)

1889 Janesville, Wis.   NIC-B
KELLOGG, Geo. J. & SONS. Later the
Belle Cottage Nurseries. Price list of
fruits and nursery stock - apples, grapes,
plums, etc. 6pp.

1872 West Chester, Pa.   PHi
KIFT, JOSEPH. Annual catalog of roses
and bedding out plants. 8vo., 20pp.

KISSENA NURSERIES. See Parsons & Co.

1868 Vincennes, Ind.   In
KNOX NURSERIES. Est. 1852. Ill. catalog
of fruit and ornamental trees, roses, grapevines, shrubs, etc.

1811 Philadelphia   DA
LANDRETH, DAVID & CUTHBERT. A catalog of greenhouse plants, hardy trees, evergreen shrubs, flowering shrubs, bulbous
rooted and herbaceous plants arranged by
their botanic and English names - with a
collection of the most esteemed varieties of
fruit trees.

1826 Philadelphia   PPL
------ Price list of flowers, shrubs, trees
and vines, etc. 56pp.

nd. Philadelphia   PHi
------ A catalog of agricultural and horticultural implements and machinery. 8vo.,
37pp.

1832 Philadelphia   PHi
------ Landreth's periodical catalog of
fruit and ornamental trees, etc. 12mo.,
112pp.

1845-46 Philadelphia   NIC-B
------ Landreth, David and Fulton - late
D. & C. Landreth. Catalogs continue, however, as David Landreth and Sons at a later
date. Abridged annual catalog of hothouse
and greenhouse plants, etc. 24pp.

1868 Philadelphia   Sabin 38846-7
------ Landreth, David. Rural Register
and Almanac for 1868. 64pp.

N.B. Sabin also reports with no date the
     Floral Magazine issued by David and
Cuthbert Landreth #38847. It seems too bad
that he recorded only these two relatively
late catalogs of one of our earliest and most
outstanding horticulturists - the creator of
Philadelphia's famous 1783 gardens, and
surely one of our foremost catalogers.

1879 Philadelphia   PHi
------ Wholesale prices of seeds. 8vo.,
8pp.

1883 Philadelphia   NNMM
------ Rural Register   PPL   MnHi
and Almanac - desc., ill. and priced. 82pp.

1885 Philadelphia   MnHi
------ Rural Register and   PPL
Almanac. Ill. and priced as above.

1886-1889 Philadelphia   MnHi
------ Rural Register and Almanacs.
Various issues, various months, ill. and
priced, with col. pict. wrap.

1897 Philadelphia   PHi
------ Ill. seed catalog.

N.B. As stated before, this is a sampling of
     the ill. catalogs of an American pio-
neer seedsman. Undoubtedly there are other
issues at DA, PKsL, OCL, NIC-B, etc.

1798 New York   Sabin #33978
LANGDON, JOHN. A catalog of English
kitchen, garden and fancy flower seeds, imported in the snow - sic. - probably ship
Hazard from London, and for sale at the
store of John Langdon, No. 6. Fletcher St.
near the Fly Market, wholesale and retail.
Broadside. Not located.

1886-87 Plattsburgh, N. Y.   MH-BA
LAPHAM, JOSEPH K. Price list of greenhouse and nursery seeds and plants. 8vo.,
30pp.

1823 Flushing, N. Y.   NNQ
LAWRENCE & MILLS. Nurserymen. A
treatise and catalog of fruit and ornamental
trees, shrubs, etc. from the Prince Nursery.

Apparently a branch nursery - see Prince.

c.1878 Lebanon, Mo.   MoSHi
LEBANON NURSERY. W. S. Stebbins, Prop.
Ill. and desc. catalog of nursery stock,
wholesale and retail.

1898 Lee's Summit, Mo.   NIC-B
LEE'S SUMMIT STAR NURSERIES. Est.
1869. M. Butterfield, Prop. Ill. and desc.
catalog. 48pp., wrap.

1880 Richmond, Ind.   Ind.
LEEDS & CO. Ill. catalog for spring, 8vo.,
56pp., col. plate, pict. wrap.

1881 Richmond, Ind.   CHi
------ Ill. catalog. 8vo., 80pp.

1882 Richmond, Ind.   In
------ General ill. catalog of seeds, roses
and garden implements. 8vo., 48pp., col.
pls., pict. wrap.

1884 Rochester, N. Y.   NR
LITTLE, WILLIAM S. Rochester Commercial Nurseries. Ill. catalog of nursery
stock. 12mo., wrap.

1870 Milwaukee & Portland, Ore.   OrHi
LUELLING, SETH. Seth Luelling's catalog
of fruit trees, shrubbery, etc. 16mo., 16pp.

nd. Boston   MdTanSW
McCARTHY, N.F. & CO. Est. 1885. First
general catalog of florists' supplies - pails,
baskets, tubs, special designed sprinklers,
vases, urns, umbrella stands, etc. 12mo.,
80pp., ill., index, cl.

1864 Springfield, Mass.   MH-BA
McELWAIN BROTHERS. Ill. catalog of supplies for seedsmen and florists. 7th ed.,
8vo., 68pp.

1804 Philadelphia   PHi
M'MAHON, BERNARD. D.A.B.   DA
spells this McMahon, the catalogs spell it
M'Mahon. A close friend of David Landreth.
In 1806 he gave to America its first notable
horticultural book the American Gardener's
Calendar. See D.A.B.

A catalog of American seeds. 8vo., 30pp.

1806 Philadelphia   PPL
------ A list of vegetable, herb, flower,
tree and shrub seeds, also garden tools and
books, etc. 36pp.

1888-1897 Olney, Va.   NIC-B
McMATH BROTHERS. Accomak Nurseries.
Ill. catalog of fruit and ornamental trees,
small fruits; roses, shrubs, etc.

Collection not listed separately.

1885 Crescent City, Fla.   F
MANVILLE NURSERY CO. Desc. catalog
and price list for season 1885-6. 8vo., dec.
wrap., 28pp.

1867 Astoria, N. Y.   NNQ
MARC & WHITMAN. Desc. and ill. catalog
of bedding plants, roses, petunias, etc. 8vo.,
32pp., pict. wrap.

1872 Astoria & Woodside, N. Y.   NNQ
MARC, GABRIEL. Ill. and desc. catalog of
azaleas, roses, dwarfs, greenhouse and
hardy plants and ornamental trees. 12mo.,
34pp., dec. wrap.

1871 Marietta, Pa.   OHi
MARIETTA NURSERIES. Engle & Brother,
successor to Daniel Engle. Desc. catalog
#1 - fruit trees, vines and plants, etc. 8vo.,
20pp., pict. wrap.

1896 Floral Park, N. Y.   NNQ
MARTIN, MARY E. Ill. seed catalog.

1885 Philadelphia   PPL
MAULE, WILLIAM HENRY. Ill. and desc.
price list of seeds, flowers and plants. 56pp.

1892 Philadelphia   PHi
------ Maule's seed catalog. 8vo., ills.,
Phil. views, pict. wrap.

nd. Philadelphia   PHi
------ How I Conduct the Seed and Plant
Business. Forty photos.

c.1881 St. Paul, Minn.   MnHi
MAY, L.L. & CO. Ill. and desc. catalog of
fruit and ornamental trees, vines, small
fruits, shrubs, roses, etc. 8vo., 72pp., dec.
wrap.

1886 San Francisco   CHi
MEHERIN, THOMAS. Nurseryman. Ill.
price list. 8vo., 27pp., wrap.

1890 Houlton, Me.   NIC-B
MERRITT, E.W. Guide to fruit culture with
desc. catalog and price list of Aroostook
Nursery. 13th ed., 28pp., wrap.

1888 Maspeth, N. Y.   NNQ
MEYER, C. Desc. catalog of Acme fertilizer.

1882-83 St. Louis   MoSHi
MICHEL PLANT & SEED CO. Two ill. catalogs. Spring 1882 and complete nursery
catalog for 1883.

1875 Philadelphia   PPL
MILLER & HAYES. Mt. Airy Nurseries.
Price list of roses. 21pp.

1880-85 Wading River, N. Y.   NNQ
MILLER, E.S. Five desc. catalogs of bulbs,
orchids, aquatics, ferns, bedding plants,
trees, etc. 12mo., various pp., wrap.

1879 San Francisco   CHi
MILLER, F.A. & CO. Ill. catalog of nursery
stock, fine seeds, etc. 4to., 24pp., wrap.

1876 San Francisco   CHi
MILLER, SIEVERS & CO. Ill. catalog of
exotic garden and conservatory plants, rare
species, trees and shrubs. 8vo., 32pp.

1891 Islip, N. Y.   NNQ
MILNE BROTHERS. Ill. catalog for florists
and growers.

1849 West Chester, Pa.   PHi
MORRIS & STOKES. Nurserymen. Ill. catalog of evergreens, plants, shrubs and trees.
16mo., 24pp.

MORRIS NURSERIES. See Geo. Achelis.

1827 Albany, N. Y.   N
MOULTON, S. & CO. A catalog of fruit and
ornamental trees, herbs, shrubs and greenhouse plants. 12mo., 24pp., wrap. Raised
by S. Moulton, and for sale at Albany Nursery
by Buel & Wilson.

MT. AIRY NURSERIES. See Miller & Hayes.

MT. HOPE NURSERIES. See Ellwanger &
Barry.

1870 Cincinnati   OC
MT. WASHINGTON NURSERIES. Circular
and retail price list. 4pp.

1900 Washington, D. C.   Vi
MUNSON, D.O. Ill. catalog of ornamental
fruit trees.

1894 Cincinnati   OC
MUTH, CHARLES F. & SON. Ill. catalog of
honey, beeswax and garden seeds. 8vo.,
24pp., pict. wrap.

1897 Bridgeville, Del.   NIC-B
MYER & SON. Ill. catalog of fruit and nut
trees. 50pp., pict. wrap.

1857 Dixon, Ill.   ICHi
NACHUSA NURSERY. Ill. catalog of fruit
and ornamental trees, shrubs, etc.

1885-88 Canajoharie, N. Y.   MnHi
NELLIS, A.C. & CO. Four ill. catalogs of
nursery stock. 1885, 1886, 1887 and 1888.

NEWELL, JOSEPH R. See John B. Russell.

1865 New York   MH
NEW YORK SANITARY AND CHEMICAL
COMPOST MFG. CO. 8vo., 32pp.

NONANTUM VALE GARDENS. See J.L.L.F.
Warren.

1885 St. Paul, Minn.   MnHi
NORTH STAR SEED FARMS. Ninth annual
ill. catalog of field, garden and flower seeds,
tree pruners, potato diggers and agricultural
implements. 8vo., 24pp., pict. wrap.

Rochester, N. Y.
NOTT & ELLIOT. See Agricultural Implements, Tools and Machinery.

1868 Rochester, N. Y.   NR
O'KEEFE, M. SON & CO. FLORAL HALL.
Ill. catalog of flowers, herbs, plants, shrubs,
etc. 8vo., 52pp., pict. wrap.

1841-85 Flushing, N. Y.   NNQ
PARSONS & CO. Est. 1840. Subsequently
R. B. Parsons & Co. and R. B. Parsons &
Sons. Kissena Nurseries.

A fine collection of ill., desc. and priced catalogs and price lists of seeds and plants,
shrubs and vines, fruit and ornamental trees,
azaleas, roses, etc. 16mo. to 4to., mostly
pict. wrap. as follows: 1841, 1842, 1843,
1845, 1858, 1861, 1863, 1866, 1870, 1876-7,
1877-8, 1878-9, 1879, 1880, 1881, 1883 and
1885. Unusually fine file.

1818 Cambridge, Mass.   MBAt
PECK, W.D. A catalog of American and
foreign plants cultivated in Botanic Garden
at . . . 8vo., 1 leaf and 60pp.

1875 Chicago   IChi
PETERSON, P.S. Rose Hill Nurseries. Ill.
and desc. catalog of bulbs, shrubs, trees,
etc. Pict. map wrap.

c.1900 Toledo, O.   OT
PHILIPPS, THE HENRY SEED & IMPLE-
MENT CO. Ill. catalog of the pioneer seed
house of Toledo. 8vo., 88pp., pict. wrap.

1875 Oxford, Pa.   PHi
PHILLIPS, JOSEPH T. Sunnyside Farm.
Spring catalog of plants from Sunnyside
greenhouses. 8vo., 32pp.

1876 Oxford, Pa.   PHi
------ Spring catalog. 8vo., 32pp.

c.1865 Bloomington, Ill.   IHi
PHOENIX, F.K. Bloomington Nurseries.
Est. 1852. The Prairies for Trees - Trees
for the Prairies -- Ill. catalog of bulbs,
plants and ornamental fruit trees. 8vo.,
100pp., dec. wrap.

1868 Bloomington, Ill.   NIC-B
------ Ill. and desc. catalog #3 - new
plants - carnations to verbenas, vegetables,
vases and baskets, etc. 28pp., 2 ills.

1870 Bloomington, Ill.   NIC-B
------ Ill. catalog #3. 32pp.

1871 Bloomington, Ill.   NIC-B
------ Wholesale price list. 24pp.

1871 Bloomington, Ill.   IChi
------ Ill. catalog #5. Flower and vegetable seeds, plants, summer flowering bulbs,
etc. 8vo., 72pp., fld. plate.

1871-72 Bloomington, Ill.   NIC-B
------ Ill. and desc. catalog #4. Basket
plants to tulips. 42pp.

1873 Bloomington, Ill.   NIC-B
------ Phoenix plant and seed catalog,
novelties, etc. 64pp.

1883 Bloomington, Ill.   NIC-B
------ Abridged catalog, priced and ill.,
fruit and ornamental trees, etc. 100pp.

N.B. For later catalogs of the Bloomington
nurseries, see Tuttle, Sidney & Co.

1893 Jessamine, Fla.   NIC-B
PIKE & ELLSWORTH. Catalog of   F
rare Florida flowers and seeds. 4to., 76pp.,
col. plate, ill., pict. wrap.

1894 Jessamine, Fla.   F
------ Catalog for 1894. 4to., 64pp., ill.,
col. plate, wrap.

1853-1900 St. Louis   MoSHi
PLANT, WILLIAM M. & CO. St. Louis
Agricultural Warehouse and Seed Store.

A fine ref. collection of thirteen ill. catalogs,
priced gardener's almanacs, etc. of grass,
garden and field seeds, novelties, horticultural implements and machines, etc. 16mo.
to 4to., 32 to 73pp., dec. and pict. wrap. for:
1853, 1855, 1857, 1860, 1867, 1880, 1890,
1893, 1894, 1896, 1898, 1899 and 1900.

nd. Cheshire, Conn.   CtHi
PLATT & BARNES. Successors to F. S.
Platt. Ill. catalog of the Cheshire Nursery.
8vo., 16 (2) pp.

1891 New Haven   CtHi
PLATT, FRANK S. Desc. and ill. catalog of
vegetable, field and flower seeds and sundry
articles for the garden. 8vo., 108pp., wrap.

1839 Cranston, R. I.   RHi
POTTER, FERDINAND & CO. Annual cata-
log of fruit and ornamental trees for sale at
Botanic Garden. Sq. 16mo., 22pp., dec.wrap.

1875 Providence, R. I.   RHi
PRAY, THOMAS JR. Pray's ill. catalog #1
of bulbs, plants and floral requisites - urns,
vases, garden furniture, shrubs, etc. 8vo.,
48pp., dec. wrap.

1887 Greenpoint, N. Y.   NNQ
PRESTON FERTILIZER CO. Catalog of
fertilizer products, etc.

1771-1866 Flushing, N. Y.   Locations
PRINCE, WILLIAM. Est. c.1750. as follows
William Prince Nurseries survived three
generations and was finally sold in 1866.
See D.A.B., Evans #12206, 22816, 35955 and
Sabin #65619, 65620 and 65621.

NNQ has rescued and preserved an outstanding collection of the catalog records of this
nursery. Until proven wrong I shall name
William Prince the first American seedsman
who took advantage of the mail order business.

To make the following tabulation more his-
torically interesting, read the entries for
William Prince, William and Benjamin
Prince, William R. Prince and LeBaron
Bradford Prince. To really appreciate the
choice of words and catalog technique of the
Prince family you'll have to check in at one
of the many repositories and read for yourself; there isn't room in this guide for the
ten pages necessary for proper cataloging.

From folio broadside to pict. wrap., 16mo.,
1771 to 1866, as follows:

1771   Evans 12206
Broadside. List of fruit trees.

1771   DLC   PPL
Broadside. To be sosd (sic) a large collection of fruit trees.

1790   DLC   PPL
Broadside. A catalog of . . . adding shrubs
to list. Evans 22816. Hugh Gaine.

1790   Photostat only MBH
Broadside - variant - William and Benjamin
Prince - 6 columns - orders left at Hull and
Brown, Pearl St., New York or forwarded by
post, etc. Ptd. T. & J. Swords.

1799   MH
Broadside - A catalog - includes flowering
shrubs and plants - at Flushing Landing.

1808   PPL
Broadside - Fruit and forest trees.

1818   DA
Broadside - List of trees and shrubs.

1819   DA
Broadside - List of ornamental trees, etc.

1820   NNQ
Treatise on nursery stock at Linnaean
Botanic Garden of . . . with a catalog.
16mo., 82pp., dec. wrap.

1820   NNQ
Catalog of bulbous and fibrous rooted plants.

1822   NIC-B
Catalog - 21st ed. - adds greenhouse plants.
Orders may be left at Adams Foster, agent,
Providence, R. I. 140pp.

1823   NNQ   MStOSV
Treatise and catalog - 22nd ed.

1825   PPL
Price list, etc. 120pp.

1825   NNQ
Annual catalog and treatise. 148pp.

1827   NNQ   PKsL
Annual catalog and treatise. 24th ed.148pp.

1828   NNQ   PKsL
Treatise and wholesale catalog. 196pp.

1829-1844   NNQ
Combination treatises and catalogs, special
selected catalogs of small fruits and vines,
flowers, etc., annual catalogs, various sizes
and pp. with dec. wrap.

1844-1845   NNQ
Annual catalog in which Mr. Prince denounces
Winter & Co. - see Winter & Co. - as an
imposter and thief, warning his customers
to have no part of him. Also two special
catalogs - 1844-5.

1846   NNQ
Esculent vegetables and seeds.

1846   NIC-B
Bulbous rooted flowers. 24pp.

1846-1847   NIC-B
Supplementary catalog of new and rare
fruits in addition to 34th ed. 12pp.

1848-1866   NNQ
Twenty odd issues of annual and special catalogs, 16mo., 12mo. and 8vo., dec.and pict.
wrap., mostly ill., even to Chinese potatoes,
from 16 to 64pp.

N.B. Although the Prince Nurseries survived the Revolution, when the British
took over and destroyed countless cherry
trees to be used for barrel hoops, it seems
as though the Civil War ended this colorful
history.

1844 Boston   MH-BA
PROUTY, DAVID & CO. Ill. catalog of the
Farmers' Warehouse and Seed Store. 12mo.,
24pp.

1898 Ukiah, Calif.   NIC-B
PURDY, CARL. Retail price list of California
bulbs. 28pp., wrap.

1883 New London, Conn.   NNQ
QUINNIPIAC FERTILIZER CO. Price list
of Quinnipiac fertilizers. (Elisha King,
agent, Sag Harbor.)

1850 Rochester, N.Y.   NHi
RAPELJE & BRIGGS. Genesee   N
Seed Store. Ill. catalog of seeds, fanning
mills, bill hooks, yokes, pumps and other
agricultural implements and machines. 8vo.,
48pp., dec. wrap.

1852 Brooklyn, N.Y.   NNQ
RAUCH, J.E. Florist. Ill. and desc. catalog of stove, greenhouse and herbaceous
plants for 1852-53.

N.B. Greenwood stages pass our gate every
5 minutes - orders left at Tryon's
agricultural warehouse will be promptly delivered. 12mo., 24pp., pict. wrap.

1852 Schenectady   Sabin 68219
REAGLES, C. & SON. Union Nurseries. A
catalog of fruit and ornamental trees cultivated at the Union Nurseries. 12mo., 12pp.

1887 n.p.   F
REASONER BROTHERS. Royal Palm Nurseries. Ill. catalog.

REESOR, CHARLES A. See Innisfallen
Green Houses.

1852 Elizabeth, N.J.   PPL
REID, WILLIAM. Reid's Nurseries. Price
list of fruit and ornamental trees, flowering
shrubs, etc. 18pp.

1855 Elizabeth, N.J.   PPL
------ Price list of fruit trees. 2pp.

1867 Elizabeth, N.J.   NjR
------ Ill. catalog of fruit trees, shrubs,
etc. 8vo., 32pp., pict. wrap.

ROCHESTER COMMERCIAL NURSERIES.
See H. E. Hooker & Co. and Wm. S. Little.

1882 Newburgh, N.Y.   MWA
ROE, EDWARD PAYSON. Est. 1838. E.P.
Roe's ill. catalog of small fruits and grape-
vines, etc., title vignette, 20pp.

1878-79 New York   NNMM
ROELKER, AUGUST & SONS. Ill. and desc.
priced wholesale catalog of bulbs, seeds and
florists' supplies - fancy baskets, etc. 64pp.

ROSE HILL NURSERIES. See P.S. Peterson.

1836 Greece, Monroe Co., N.Y.   NIC-B
ROWE, ASA. Seedsman. Annual catalog of
fruit and ornamental trees, shrubs, roots,
herbaceous plants, greenhouse stock, etc.
16mo., 46pp., ptd. at Rochester by Luther
Tucker. N.B. Postage under 100 miles
3¢, over 100 miles 4¢.

1841-42 Greece, Monroe Co., N.Y. NIC-B
------ Ill. catalogs for 1841 and 1842.
16mo., 60 and 64pp., wrap.

ROYAL PALM NURSERIES. See Reasoner
Brothers.

1894-95 Highlands, N.C.   NIC-B
RUSSELL BROTHERS. Altifirm Nursery.
Wholesale ill. catalog of native American
plants, rare trees, shrubs from Allegheny
Mts. 8pp.

1829 Boston
RUSSELL, JOHN B. Issued with Joseph R.
Newell. A catalog of kitchen garden, herb,
field, flower seeds, bulbs, roots, shrubs and
fruit trees - with a list of garden and farm
implements, tools, beehives, horse powers,
threshing machines, lamps, lightning rods,
pumps, etc. 16mo., 94pp. Also agricultural
and horticultural books.

ST. LOUIS AGRICULTURAL WAREHOUSE
& SEED STORE. See Wm. M. Platt & Co.

1877 Chicago   ICHi
SANDERS, EDGAR. Price list of plants,
etc. 4pp.

1877 Washington, D.C. & Baltimore, Md.
SAUL, JOHN. Est. 1852.   F   NIC-B
Ill. catalog #6 - new, rare and beautiful
plants for spring of . . . 8vo., 96pp., wrap.

1878 Washington & Baltimore   PKsL
------ Ill. catalog #3. 8vo., 32pp.

1880 Washington & Baltimore   PKsL
------ Catalog #6. 8vo., 120pp., ills.

1889-90 Washington & Baltimore   PKsL
------ Wholesale catalog for autumn and
spring. 8vo., 20pp.

1883 Everett, Mass.   NIC-B
SAUNDERS, C.O. Belmont Hill Nurseries.
Desc. catalog of shrubs, roses, climbing
vines, trees and desirable novelties. 32pp.

1888 St. Louis   MoSHi
SCHAPER, E. Ill. catalog of seeds for farm
and garden.

1871 La Porte, Ind.   In
SCOTT, ROBERT. Price list of ornamental
nursery stock and fruit trees. 4to circular.

1881 Mt. Lebanon, N. Y.   N
SHAKERS. Shakers' desc. and ill. catalog
of flower, herb and kitchen garden seeds,
with a guide to gardening, compiled by
William Anderson. 12mo. with fine ills.

N.B. Though not reported as yet, it is
     reasonable to suggest that Shaker
seed catalogs may be preserved in any or
all of the extensive collections at Williams,
Yale, Dartmouth, Ohio Historical, Newberry,
Western Reserve, Wayside Museums, Inc.,
Berkshire Museum and the Shaker Museum
at Old Chatham, N. Y.

1873 Plantsville, Conn.   CtHi   MH-BA
SHEPARD, S.R. Spring catalog of new, rare
and beautiful plants. 8vo., 26pp.

SHERWOOD HALL NURSERIES. See
Timothy Hopkins.

1885 Minneapolis   MnHi
SHUMAN & CO. Successor to Wyman
Elliot. Ill. and desc. annual catalog of farm,
garden and flower seeds, early vegetable
plants, drills and garden tools, etc. 8vo.
Also ill. catalogs for 1886 and 1887.

1879-84 Rochester, N. Y.   NR   ICHi
SIBLEY, HIRAM & CO. Ill. catalogs of
garden, field and flower seeds, bulbs and
plants, and nursery stock. 8vo., fine ills.,
40 to 156pp. resp., pict. wrap. for: 1879,
1880, 1881, 1882, 1883 and 1884.

1834 Near Baltimore
SINCLAIR & MOORE, Prop. Clairmont
Nurseries. A catalog of gruit and ornamental trees, shrubs, plants and garden seeds -
with cursory remarks - well worth reading,
ed's. note. Ptd. J. D. Toy, Baltimore.
16mo., 34pp., marbled wrap.

1848 Near Baltimore
----- William Corse, successor to Sinclair
& Corse, successors to Sinclair & Moore.
A catalog of . . . 16mo., 45pp. Same cur-
sory remarks continued.

1867 Cincinnati   OC
SMITH, AMOR. Improved super-phosphate
of lime - Important to Farmers! Price list

with tests. that would surprise Rube Gold-
berg. 24mo., 34pp., ptd. wrap.

1896 Geneva, N. Y.   NNMM
SMITH, W. & T. Nurseryman. Ill. catalog
#277 - fruits and flowers. 196 ill. lvs., lea.
cvs.

1885 Philadelphia   PPL
SMITH, W.H. Desc. price list of flower and
vegetable seeds with ills. and wrap. 96pp.

1874 Boston   MH-BA
SPOONER, W.H. Late W.C. Strong & Co.
Ill. gardening guide and seed catalog. 8vo.,
88pp.

1897 Louisiana, Mo.   NIC-B
STARK BROTHERS NURSERIES. Stark's
fruit book - 64pp., 48 col. pls., a fine col.
pict. record.

STEBBINS, W.S. See Lebanon Nursery.

1876-81 Painesville, O. & Rochester, N. Y.
STORRS & HARRISON CO.   NR
Eight ill. catalogs of nursery stock - floral,
kitchen, herbal and field. 8vo., 16 to 48pp.

1892 Painesville & Rochester   OHi
------ Ill. catalog #2 - spring 1892. 4to.,
164pp., col. pls., col. pict. wrap. N.B.
American business seldom remains one
plant in one place long - it had to expand
even back in 1890.

1852 Wethersfield, Conn.   CtHi
STRONG, B.N. & CO. American Seed Garden. Est. 1838. Desc. catalog of seeds for
garden and field. 12mo., 50pp., dec. wrap.

1871 Boston   MH-BA
STRONG, W.C. & CO. Est. 1837. Catalog
of Dutch bulbs and flower roots. 12mo., 12pp.

1894-97 San Francisco   CHi
SUNSET SEED & PLANT CO. Ill. catalogs
of plants, seeds, shrubs, etc. 4to., 64 and
29pp. resp. for 1894 and 1897.

TALCOTT MOUNTAIN NURSERIES. See
E. A. Whiting & Co.

1873-78 Richmond, Ind.   In
TEAS, E.Y. & CO. Cascade Nursery Co.
Twenty-ninth annual price list with ills.,
8vo., 8pp. for 1873. Ill. catalog for spring
1878, 4pp.

1896 Calla, O.   OHi
TEMPLIN, L. & SONS. Calla Green Houses.
Special bargain catalog of seeds, plants and
nursery stock. 4to., fine ills.

1806 New London, Conn.   MWA
THOMPSON, ISAAC. Broadside - Important
to Gardeners - the great importance of
changing seeds - with a two column price
list of flower seeds.

1821 New York   NHi
THORBURN, GRANT & SON.   NN
Later George C. Thorburn.

See D.A.B. First American Seedsman and
compiler of first seed catalog - 1812. Entirely
false as this chapter proves. However,
he was one of our first and best, and he put
William Cobbett out of the seed business.

The Gentleman and Gardeners' Kalendar -
with ample directions, etc. - price lists of
seeds, horticultural books, almanacs, etc.
16mo., 132pp., 3rd ed., pict. title.

1821 New York   ICHi
------ A catalog of kitchen garden, field
and flower seeds, bulbs, etc. 8vo., 34pp.,
pict. title.

1828 New York   NjR
------ Catalog of herb, flower, tree and
grass seeds, flower tools, greenhouse plants,
gardening books, tools and implements and a
short treatise on cultivation, etc. 16mo.,
IV, 5-100 and errata., dec. wrap.

1836 New York   NjR
THORBURN, GEORGE C. Catalog of seeds,
bulbs, plants, shrubs, trees, etc. and garden
tools and books. 16mo., 124pp., ptd. wrap.

N.B. Mr. Thorburn took pains with his cat-
      alogs and even planned one acre
gardens with the best seeds and estimated
costs with probable harvest.

1880 Brooklyn, Conn.   CtHi
THURBER, WILLIAM R. A catalog of seeds
and plants. 8vo., 40pp., wrap.

1892 Little Rock   NIC-B
TIPTON, W.K. Arkansas Nursery. Desc.
catalog of fruit, shade and ornamental trees,
evergreens, flowering shrubs, roses, vines,
berry plants, etc. 32pp., wrap.

.1858 Ashland, Jackson Co., O.T.   OrHi
       (Oregon Territory)
TOLMAN & BLAKE'S ASHLAND NURSERY.
Broadside catalog of fruit trees.

.1800 Northampton, Mass. & v.p.   DA
         Photostat copies only MBH
TRACY, DAVID. A catalog of fruit trees,
etc. for sale at the nurseries of the sub-
scriber in the following towns Viz: T. M.
Pomroy, Northampton, Norwich, Leverett,
Pittsfield, Suffield and West Hartford, but

the stone fruit only at the nurseries in
Brimfield, Williamstown and Groton (Conn.)
Broadside. Date written in pencil.

1879-86 San Francisco   CHi
TRUMBULL, R.J. & CO. Four ill. catalogs
of seeds, plants and trees. 8vo., 48 to 60pp.
Pict. wrap.

1887-92 Bloomington, Ill.   NIC-B
TUTTLE, SIDNEY & CO. Successor to F.K.
Phoenix. Est. 1852. General desc. catalog
of fruit, ornamental and evergreen trees,
hardy shrubs, roses, etc. Western trees
for western planters. From 10 to 20 page
wholesale catalogs, fine ills., pict. wrap.
For: 1887, 1889, 1890, 1891 and 1892.

UNION NURSERIES. See C. Reagles & Son.

1891-93 Chicago   ICHi
VAUGHAN'S SEED STORE. Ill. catalogs for
1891, 1892 and 1893.

1868-90 Rochester, N. Y.   Locations
VICK, JAMES.   as follows
Vick's Nurseries. Vick's ill. catalog and
floral guide of seeds, plants, shrubs, flowers,
florists' supplies - hyacinth bulb vases,
hanging baskets, brackets, tools, implements,
bowls, aquariums, etc. As follows:

    1868-90   NR
    Collection of 41 issues. 16- 32 pp.

    1870   MH-BA
    9th annual ill. catalog. 8vo., 84pp.

    1872   NNMM
    Desc. and ill. catalog. 120pp.

    1888   MoSHi
    Ill. catalog and floral guide.

1884 San Francisco   CHi
VINCENT, SEVIN & CO. Ill. nursery catalog. 8vo., 80pp., pict. wrap.

1853 New Bedford   Sabin 52481
WACHUSETT NURSERIES. Desc. catalog
of fruit and ornamental trees. 8vo., 32pp.

1880 St. Mary's, Vigo Co., Ind.   In
WARD, THOMAS J. Prop. Semi-annual
price list of fruits, etc. 8vo., 8pp., crude
woodcuts, pict. wrap.

WARR, AARON. See Georgetown Nurseries.

1853-54 Sacramento   CHi
WARREN & SON'S GARDEN & NURSERIES.
Desc. catalog of flowers, plants, etc. 8vo.,
62pp., wrap.

1844 Boston   NIC-B
WARREN, J.L.L.F. Warren's Floral
Saloon. Warren's desc. catalog of trees,
plants and seeds cultivated at Nonantum
Vale Gardens, Brighton. 10pp., wrap.

1870 Boston   PPL
WASHBURN & CO. Ill. and desc. price list
and guide to flower and vegetable seeds.
128pp.

1893 Rochester, N.Y.   ICHi
WEAVER, PALMER & RICHMOND. Ill.
catalog of tools, implements and supplies
for nurserymen. 8vo., 56pp., pict. wrap.

1879 San Francisco   CSmH
WELLINGTON, B.F. Ill. catalog of flower,
shrub, tree, vegetable seeds, bulbs, shrubs,
etc. 12mo., 32pp., pict. wrap.

1870 Houston, Tex.   TxLT
WHITAKER, A. A catalog of choice fruit
trees, etc.

c.1885 Rochester, N.H.   MH-BA
WHITE BROTHERS. The Floral Messenger.
A catalog of flowering plants. 8vo., 54pp.,
pict. wrap.

1849 Avon, Conn.   CtHi
WHITING, E.A. & CO. Talcott Mountain
Nurseries. A catalog of fruit and ornamental trees, shrubs, vines and plants cultivated
at . . . near Hartford. 8vo., 28pp.

1861 Franklin Grove, Ill.   ICHi
WHITNEY, A.R. Ill. catalog of shrubs,
trees, vines, etc.

1869-80 Astoria, N.Y.   NNQ
WILSON, W.C. Nurseryman. Est. 1848.
Desc. and ill. catalogs of annuals, bedding
plants, roses, dahlias, fuschias, etc. 8vo.,
v.p., pict. wrap. For 1869, 1871 and 1880.

1862 Detroit, Mich.   MiU-H
WINDSOR NURSERIES. J.J. Rennie. Catalog of fruit and ornamental trees, shrubs,
roses, plants, etc. to be sold at auction.
8vo., 16pp.

c.1800 Brighton, Mass.
WINSHIP, FRANCIS. (Catalog) Trees,
shrubs, etc. Acacia roses to walnut trees,
also varieties of bulbous roots and flower
seeds, etc. On the Mill Dam Road from
Boston to Watertown. Broadside, 4to., with
2 column list.

1844-45 Flushing, N.Y.   NNQ
WINTER & CO. See William Prince catalog
1844-45. Desc. catalog of fruit and orna-
mental trees, plants, shrubs, vines, etc.
Late Prince's Linnaean Botanic Garden
Nursery.

1884 Flushing, N.Y.   PPL
------ Desc. catalog and price list. 92pp.,
dec. wrap.

Don't forget that the most enterprising seedsmen and nurserymen manufactured and sold agricultural implements with which to raise their bread and butter. No craftsman or inventor knew better
what shaped hoe, plow or fork best cultivated the seed and the plant. Few of the best illustrated
catalogs of agricultural warehouses neglected anything ranging from the smallest seed to the latest thing
in horse powers and threshers. Please remember that Chapter One is loaded with seeds, plants,
shrubs and trees of the highest order, even though implements, machinery and tools predominate.

If you are further interested in running down firms for whose catalogs we have no locations, I
recommend The Directory of Florists, Nurserymen and Seedsmen of the United States and Canada
and Reference Book. The first issue was published by the American Florist Co. of Chicago in 1887.
It is to the best of my knowledge the only 19th century directory in this field that includes lists of
Firms That Issue Catalogs. These rosters run from 250 to 300 names. I am proud to say that
thanks to cooperative librarians we have located a good majority. NIC-B boasts the 1890, 1892,
1896 and 1899 issues. DAIA locates one copy for 1891.

Chapter 50

Sewing Machines & Accessories

The Globe Needle Co. in its c.1876 catalog offers attachments and needles for twenty-four American sewing machines. Although we cannot locate catalogs for all of these manufacturers, this chapter covers the pictorial records in this field thoroughly. The following were the outstanding machines at the time of the Philadelphia Centennial:

Singer	Howe	Davis (Old Style)
Home	Wilson	Common Sense
Blees	American	Victor
Domestic	Manning	W. & W.
G. & B.	Dauntless	Elliptic
Weed	St. John	Secor
Remington	White	Finkle & Lyon
Aetna Improved	Manhattan	Florence

Probably many of them never issued catalogs, preferring to sell direct to a jobber and leave the expenses of distribution to him. By 1890 many of them had failed or sold out to the larger companies, and according to Seeger & Guernsey, the number of outstanding manufacturers stood at twenty-one.

Most of the catalogs listed are illustrated with pictures of the latest models, and some like the Grover & Baker make interesting and amusing reading. They have the true Barnum touch. They sold machines, and now that the machines have gone for scrap metal in two world wars, they remain in many libraries to tell the story for the historian.

c.1890 Chicago   ICHi
AMERICAN MACHINE CO. Ill. circular of the New Princess, style C sewing machines, new cabinet models - 6 ills. of styles 1-6, 16mo., 16pp.

ARLINGTON & KENWOOD. See Cash Buyers' Union.

c.1900 Chicago   ICHi
CASH BUYERS' UNION. Est. 1885. Ill. catalog of sewing machines, the celebrated Arlington & Kenwood models. 4to., 32pp., pict. wrap.

1873 New York   PPL
DOMESTIC SEWING MACHINE CO. Ill. brochure of Domestic styles. Pict. wrap.

1876 New York   MnHi
------ Trade catalog of Domestic machines, parts, attachments, etc. 4to., 26pp., pict. wrap.

1876 New York   MH-BA
------ How to Choose a Sewing Machine - desc. of with 3 ills. 12mo., 12pp.

c.1880 New York   NHi
------ Ill. catalog, 10pp., col. pict. wrap.

1883 New York   NNMM
------ Domestic fashions - Summer patterns, etc. Ill. and priced. 20pp., wrap.

c.1870 Rhinebeck, N. Y.   NHi
DuLANEY, G.L. & CO. Ill. price list and desc. of styles - a revolution in sewing machines - the Little Monitor sewing machine, Tucker binder and gauge, etc. View of plant. 16mo., 12pp.

1891 Belvidere, Ill.   OrU
ELDREDGE MFG. CO. Ill. and desc. circular of the Eldredge B sewing machine. 4to., 4pp.

c.1876 Middleborough, Mass.   MMidHi
GLOBE NEEDLE CO. Est. 1858. Offices
in New York. Trade price list of sewing
machine needles, attachments, supplies,
Griest's new improved ruffler, Wm. F. Nye
pure sperm oil - for 26 American sewing
machines. 16mo., 8pp.

1882 Chicago   MnHi
GOODRICH, H.B. Trade price list for Fall,
attachments and parts for sewing machines
with ills. of parts and machines. 8vo., 28pp.

c.1860 New York   MWelHi
GROVER & BAKER SEWING   ICHi
MACHINE CO. A Home Scene: Mr.Ashton's
first evening with a Grover & Baker. Amusing ills. 16mo., 32pp., pict. wrap.

1861 New York   MWelHi
------ Directions for using   NHi
family shuttle machine, with designs and
models. 16mo., 18pp.

c.1868 New York & Bridgeport, Conn. NHi
HOWE SEWING MACHINE CO.   OHi
23 principal offices.

A History of Sewing Machines by James
Parton - from Atlantic Monthly 1867 - with
a 10 page ill. catalog - Models: family,
panel, gothic, cabinet - pearled and silver
mounted, etc. A, B, C, D, E. 8vo., 32 and
10pp., pict. wrap.

c.1876 New York & Bridgeport, Conn. CtHi
------ Howe exhibition catalog of   NNMM
cases and machines with brief history of
Elias Howe, Jr. 8vo., 32pp., port., ills.

1882 New York & Bridgeport, Conn. NNMM
------ Ill. and priced catalog of sewing
machines. 10 lvs.

NATIONAL SEWING MACHINE CO. See
Bicycles. Although this is entirely a bicycle
catalog it boasts the production of 500 sewing
machines a day as well as 200 bicycles.

1878 Philadelphia   PKsL
NEW AMERICAN SEWING MACHINE CO.
Ill. catalog of models and styles with some
pls., views of offices, etc. 12mo., 32pp.,
pict. wrap.

nd. Orange, Mass.   MdTanSW
NEW HOME SEWING MACHINE CO. Ill.
catalog of sewing machines with prices of
styles. 24mo., 16pp.

nd. Providence, R.I.   NNMM
PROVIDENCE TOOL CO. Ill., desc. and
priced catalog of sewing machines for family
use and mfg. purposes. 6 lvs., pict. wrap.

1875 Ilion, N.Y.   N
REMINGTON SEWING MACHINE CO. Ill.
catalog and price of the Remington Family
models, attachments, parts, etc. 12mo.,
42pp., fine ills., pict. wrap.

1884 Ilion, N.Y.   MdTanSW
------ Instruction book for Remington hand
sewing machines - no. 4 machines, parts,
etc. with prices and ills. 26pp.

1894 Ilion, N.Y.
------ See Sporting Goods.

nd. Springfield, O.   MdTanSW
ST. JOHN SEWING MACHINE CO. Ill. and
priced circular of six royal St. John's sewing machines. 16mo., 12pp.

1880 Elizabeth, N.J. & New York   MnHi
SINGER SEWING MACHINE   MB NNU
CO. Genius Rewarded, or the Story of the
Singer Sewing Machine. Ills. of plants,
models and attachments. Sq. 12mo., 64pp.,
col. pict. wrap.

c.1882 Elizabeth, N.J. & New York MdTanSW
------ Price list of family and mfg.
machines, button hole machines and parts.
24mo., 16pp. with ills.

1893 Elizabeth, N.J. & New York   CSmH
------ Ill. catalog for 1893.   MB NHi
16mo., 32pp., col. pict. wrap.

1897 Elizabeth, N.J. & New York   MnU
------ The Story of the Sewing Machine -
with prices and ills. of machines and parts.
12mo., 38pp., pict. wrap.

1871 Baltimore   NcGW
WEED SEWING MACHINE CO. History of
Weed machines, J.P. Stambaugh. The
Great Trial at 22nd exhibition at Maryland
Institute - models of Weeds and other
machines. Fine Ills. 8vo., 56pp., wrap.

1858 Bridgeport, Conn.   MoSHi
WHEELER & WILSON MFG. CO.   PHi
Desc. booklet and ill. catalog of sewing
machines - history - directions. Large
8vo., 32pp., wrap.

1859 Bridgeport, Conn.   Ct
------ Ill. catalog of machines and parts,
instructions, etc. 8vo., 44pp., wrap.

1860 Bridgeport, Conn.   OHi
------ Improved sewing machines, OC
tests., ills., details. 8vo., 40pp., wrap.

1863 Bridgeport, Conn.   CtHi
------ Ill. catalog of models and styles
with history of invention, progress, etc.
16mo., 24pp., pict. wrap.

1868 Bridgeport, Conn.   ICHi
------   The Golden Calendar. Ill. catalog
of styles and models. 16mo., 48pp., pict.
wrap.

1877 Bridgeport, Conn.   OHi
------   The Royal Calendar of sewing
machines, models, parts, etc.

1875 New York   ICHi
WILLCOX & GIBBS SEWING MACHINE CO.
New Silent Sewing Machine with automatic
tension. 24mo. folder, unfolded to 16pp.
with 9 ills. of models, cabinets, etc. Pict.
wrap. of plant.

Naturally you will find illustrations of models and styles in Miscellaneous Department Stores, Hardware and House Furnishings Chapters. Remington, for instance, in the Sporting Goods section,
throws a few sewing machines in with his revolvers, rifles and shotguns in case Mother reads the
catalog.

Chapter 51

Silverware

Studied through illustrated catalogs, there is about as much difference between jewelers and silver-smiths as there is between the Two Black Crows' white horses and black horses; the silversmiths use more metal, as a rule, for larger pieces. They also fashioned their contributions to human appreciation of the finer arts in pewter, Britannia, plate and gold, as well as silver.

This chapter is an attempt to segregate flatware, tableware, hollow ware, etc. from the general run of badges, brooches, pins and rings that seem to constitute jewelry. From the earliest located price list of the founders of Reed & Barton in 1837 to their folio, gilt edged, gold pictorial covered catalog of 1884, containing over 4000 engravings and reputed to have cost $100,000., we offer a small but carefully selected group of examples. The results of the perfection of electrotypography catalog-wise are more easily explained in this field than any other. Although the outstanding silversmiths in New England tried woodcut illustrated price lists as an improvement over sending complete tea sets out on approval, the process was pretty expensive before the Civil War. (See The Whitesmiths of Taunton - A History of Reed & Barton 1824-1943 by George S. Gibb. Harvard University Press, pp. 200-205.)

Perhaps one of these days some book scout will turn up a small folio price list of Paul Revere's bowls and tankards -- but I doubt it. Even a one leaf circular of Nathaniel Hurd's silverware printed by Paul Revere would be useful. However, for 18th century price lists we must admit that trade catalogs are licked, and must give ground to the time honored manuscript records; at least for the present.

1897 Philadelphia   NNMM
BAILEY, BANKS & BIDDLE CO. Ill., desc. and priced catalog of sterling silver cutlery, toilet ware, coffee and tea sets, etc. 80pp. with 38 pls., bds.

nd. Philadelphia   PKsL
------ Ill. handbook of silverware. p.1900.

1870 East Haddam, Conn.   CtHi
BOARDMAN, LUTHER & SONS'   DLC
WORKS. Est. 1840. Ill. catalog of silver-ware, Britannia ware, flatware, new designs, etc. 8vo., 54pp., frs. of plant and fine pls. throughout, dec. cl.

1875 East Haddam, Conn.   PShipL
------ Special catalog D   Ct   NNMM
and net price list of flat tableware. 8vo., 36pp., pls., wrap.

1773 Philadelphia   Sabin 61927
BOGLE, SAMUEL & MR. COX. By the me-dium of the curious numerical machine in-vented by the ingenious Mr. Cox are to be disposed of the following lots of rich orna-mented plated goods just imported by Samuel Bogle. Fol. broadside.

c.1896 Taunton, Mass.   MdTanSW
COHANNET SILVER CO. Unbound collec-tion of 28 litho. pls. of candlesticks, fern dishes, shaving mugs, tea sets, pickle casters with glass inserts, etc.

1874 Derby, Conn.   CtHi
DERBY SILVER CO. Standard 1874 price list of the finest grades of designs of orna-mented silver goods. Fol., 4pp., fine ills. of plant and many designs.

c.1870 New York   NNMM
FRADLEY, J.F. & CO. Ill. and desc. cata-log of fine gold and silver headed walking canes. 13 lvs., cl.

1875-1900 Providence & New York   RHi
GORHAM MFG. CO. Est. 1831. Factory - Providence. Showrooms - New York. Large collection of catalogs, circulars and book-lets, ills., litho. pls., col. work. 16mo. to 4to., wrap. and cl. The best in designs for ref., as dated.

1889 Providence & New York   DLC
------ Ill. catalog, 4to., fine pls.

nd. Providence & New York   NNMM
------ Ill. catalog, 34 lvs., cl.

1893 Providence & New York   NNMM
------ Desc. and ill. catalog of exhibition
of silversmiths at Columbian Exposition.
72pp., pict. wrap.

1876 Bridgeport, Conn.   MnHi
HOLMES & EDWARDS. Ill. catalog of silverware, flatware and fancy hollow ware.

1875 Waterbury, Conn.   NjOE
HOLMES, BOOTH & HAYDENS. Ill. catalog
of sheet brass, copper, wires and silver-
plated ware. 70pp., wrap.

See also Hardware - Miscellaneous Supplies.

LANDERS, FRARY & CLARK. See House
Furnishings.

LEONARD, H. & SONS. See House Furnishings.

1893 Salem, Mass.   NNMM
LOW, DANIEL & CO. Catalog D. Ills. of
sterling silver novelties, etc. 40pp., wrap.

1897 Salem, Mass.   NNMM
------ Supplement to catalog J. Ills. of
sterling silver novelties, etc. wrap.

c.1860 West Meriden, Conn.   CtHi
MERIDEN BRITANNIA CO. Ill. price list
of silverware.

c.1862 West Meriden, Conn.   NNMM
------ Scrapbook of half-tone proofs and
wood engravings for a silverware catalog,
ill., desc. and priced. 120 lvs.

1867 West Meriden, Conn.   DLC
------ Ill. price list of silverware - tea
sets, wine sets, whale oil lamps, novelties.
Large 4to., 192pp. of pls., col. frs., dec. cl.

1867 West Meriden, Conn.   CtHi
------ Ill. price list for August 1867 and
appendix for June 1868. Caster sets, toothpick holders, napkin rings, etc. Fol., 34pp.

1871 West Meriden, Conn.   NNMM
------ Ill. catalog and price list of heavily
plated goods, including old price list of 1867,
patterns of porcelain-lined ice pitchers, ice
urns, etc. for 1874. Cl.

1873 West Meriden, Conn.   NNMM
------ Appendix to price list of   MH-BA
July 1, 1871 of heavily plated goods. Ill.,
desc. and priced. Title, pp. 3-79. Pls., cl.

c.1876 West Meriden, Conn.   NNMM
------ Ill. catalog and price list of patent
perfection granite ironware, nickel plated,
Britannia and planished goods. Fine pls., cl.

1876 West Meriden, Conn.   CtHi
------ Catalog of Britannia metal spoons.
Fol., 12pp., pls.

1877 West Meriden, Conn.   NNMM
------ Ill. price list of electro silver plate.
231pp. of pls.

1878 West Meriden, Conn.   NNMM
------ Ill. catalog and price list of electro
silver plate goods. Trademarks for spoons,
etc. 1847 Rogers Bros. A1. Fol., 123pp.
of pls., cl.

c.1881 West Meriden, Conn.   NNMM
------ Catalog #36 of 1847 Roger Bros.
plate. Ill., desc. and priced. 163pp., cl.

1882 West Meriden, Conn.   NNMM
------ Ill. catalog and price list of fine
electro gold and silver plate. 4to., 358pp.,
fine pls., cl.

1886-7 West Meriden, Conn.   MH-BA
------ Ill. catalog of silverware. 450pp.
of fine pls., dec. cl.

1893 West Meriden, Conn.   CtHi
------ World's Fair exhibition catalog -
Rogers 1847 plate, the finest and best.
16mo., 8pp., pict. wrap.

c.1900 West Meriden, Conn.   MdTanSW
New York Salesrooms. (C.F.Monroe, agent.)
------ Photo. ill. and priced catalog of
prize cups and trophies in sterling silver
and other metals, also cut glass trophies.
24pp.

1869 West Meriden, Conn.   NNMM
PARKER & CASPER CO. Ill. and desc.
price list of silver plated ware. 41pp., cl.

c.1875 Waterbury, Conn.   NjOE
PLUME & ATWOOD MFG. CO. Price list
of sheet brass, copper and German silver
wire, buttons and novelties. 12mo., 57pp.

c.1875 Taunton, Mass. & New York   NNMM
REED & BARTON. Formerly Leonard,
Reed & Barton. Est. 1824.

See introduction, and read George S. Gibb's
The Whitesmiths of Taunton - Reed & Bar-
ton. Harvard University Press, 1943.
Earliest price list recorded: Prices of
Ware Manufactured by Leonard, Reed &
Barton. Fancy Tea Ware, Fancy Urns,
Lamps and Caster Frames. 1 leaf, 1837.
Catalog of electro plate. 2 lvs. with 2 ills.

1877 Taunton, Mass.   MTaR&B
------ Ill. catalog of electro   MH-BA
silver plate, heavy white metal ware, nickel
and plated. Fine pls., many in col., caster
and wine sets, tea and coffee sets, trays,

flatware, prize trophies, etc. Fol. 224pp., fine pict. cl.

c.1880   MH-BA
------ Revised price list of jewelry, watches, silverware and fancy goods.

N.B. MH-BA has an excellent collection of company records in manuscript including many price lists and catalogs not listed.

1884 Taunton, Mass.   MH-BA
------ Ill. catalog of silver and   DLC
gold plate, sterling and nickel for every purpose. The best pls. ever issued in black and white, and full col., fol., glt. and col. pict. cl. with the American eagle greeting the morning sun - a masterpiece. 372pp. of the best in American silverware.

c.1900. Rochester, N.Y.   NR
ROCHESTER STAMPING CO. Household Helps - a Month's Menus for the Epicurean, being a dissertation on appropriate tableware. 12mo., 16pp., ills., pict. wrap.

1881 Greenfield, Mass.
ROGERS & SPURR MFG. CO. Ill. price list of electro silver plated ware, with steel engraver's note: This is our first catalog.

1860-1887 Wallingford, Meriden, West Meriden & Hartford, Conn.   Locations
                                 as follows
ROGERS, WILLIAM A., ROGERS & BROS., WILLIAM ROGERS MFG. CO. & ROGERS, SMITH & CO.

This group of manufacturers became the Meriden Britannia Co., which in turn, in 1898 became the International Silver Co.

See The Whitesmiths of Taunton. 1943.

1860 ROGERS, SMITH & CO. Ill. catalog of plated goods - unsurpassed, etc. - fine pls., 8vo., fine pls. with manuscript notes on blank sheets throughout. Salesman's copy.

v.d.   NNMM
Rogers, Smith and others. Five scrapbooks of silverware and plate designs. Excellent ref. nd.

1871   CtHi
Rogers, Smith & Co. Price list.

1872   CtHi
Rogers, Smith & Co. Genuine Rogers goods - facts about trademarks, with ills. and prices. 4to., pict. wrap.

1873
Rogers, Smith & Co. Ill. catalog of heavily plated silverware with fine pls. Fol., 79 pls.

1874 Waterbury, Conn.   CtHi
ROGERS & BROTHERS. Revised price list of electro plate spoons, forks, knives, ladles and flatware. 16mo., 34pp., 15 ills., designs, col. pict. wrap.

1877   TxDa
ROGERS, WILLIAM A. CO. Ill. catalog of plated silver hollow ware, tea sets, casters, etc. 148pp., fine pls., wrap.

1878   CtHi
------ I offer to the trade - superior patterns in flatware, etc. 12mo., 16pp. of designs with prices. Order from Wm. Rogers or Simpson, Hall & Miller, Wallingford, Conn.

1878 West Meriden, Conn.   CtHi
ROGERS, SMITH & CO. Revised price list of electro plated silver spoons. 12mo., 46pp., fine ills.

1881   TxDa
ROGERS, WILLIAM A. Ill. catalog of Rogers A1 knives, forks, spoons, etc. 106pp.

1882 Hartford, Conn.   CtHi
ROGERS, WM. MFG. CO. Ill.   DLC
catalog and price list of electro silver plated table ware. Fol., 112pp. of fine pls., cl.

1883   TxDa
ROGERS, WM. A. Ill. catalog of   CtHi
Oxford silver plate, flatware and table ware. 80pp. of pls.

c.1885   MdTanSW
------ Price list of Rogers & Bros. A1. Issued by Horace Partridge & Co. 8vo., 16pp., ill. patterns and prices.

1887   TxDa
------ Ill. catalog of carving sets, CtHi
berry dishes, cigar jars, shaving mugs, candlesticks, etc. 116pp. fine pls.

1892   NNMM
------ Ill. price list. 114pp., cl.

1895 Rochester, N.Y.   NR
SANITARY COMMUNION OUTFIT CO. Ill. catalog of individual communion cups and sets for as many as needed. 12mo., 16pp. of ills., pict. wrap.

1878 Wallingford, Conn.   DLC
SIMPSON, HALL, MILLER & CO. Ill. catalog and price list of fine electro silver plated ware, heavy plate on white metal and nickel, etc. Fine pls. - butter dishes to caster sets, fire chiefs' horns, novelties and napkin rings, etc. Fol., 186pp., dec. cl.

nd. Wallingford, Conn.   NNMM
------ Price list #46 of Wm. Rogers silver plated wares. Ill. and desc., 88pp., wrap.

1856 Albany, N. Y.   NNMM
SMITH & CO. Ill., desc. and priced catalog
of Britannia and silver plated ware. 13pp.

nd. Boston   NNMM
STANDARD SILVER-WARE CO. Ill., desc.
and priced catalog of silver plated ware.
16pp., wrap.

1893 Derby, Conn.   CtHi
STERLING CO. Est. 1866. Ill. catalog of
fine silverware. 8vo., 32pp., pict. wrap.

1898 Derby, Conn.   CtHi
------ Ill. catalog of artistic silver. 32pp.,
test. letters, pict. wrap.

c.1900 Newburyport, Mass.   MdTanSW
TOWLE MFG. CO. Ill. brochure MSaE
price lists of patterns: Colonial, Franklin,
Georgian, Lafayette, Revere, Newbury, etc.
Large 8vo., one complete catalog for each
pattern, with fine pls. and pict. wrap. One
of the best pict. records at the turn of the
century.

c.1890 Boston   NNMM
TUFTS, JAMES W. Ill. and priced catalog
of Tuft's quadruple silver plated ware. 4to.,
128pp., fine pls., dec. bds.

nd. Boston   NNMM
------ Ill. catalog of fine plated ware.
68pp., cl.

See also Food and Drink for other locations.
Tufts also made soda waters, beverages and
the wherewithal to serve and drink them.

1890 Wallingford, Conn.   NNMM
WALLACE, R. & SONS MFG. CO. Ill., desc.
and priced catalog of sterling silverware,
silver plate and fine cutlery. 151pp., fine
pls., cl.

1868 West Meriden, Conn.   NNMM
WILCOX SILVER PLATE CO. Ill., desc.
and priced catalog of electro plated ware.
56pp., cl.

c.1877 West Meriden, Conn.   MdTanSW
------ Ill. catalog and price list of Perfection granite ironware, Britannia, copper and
planished goods, nickel and silver plated
ware - tea sets, coffee knobs, caster frames,
stopples, bells, flatware, etc. 4to., 117pp.,
fine pls., index, cl.

c.1890 West Meriden, Conn.   CtHi
------ Afternoon Tea. Sq. 8vo., pict. wrap.

It seems almost needless to add warnings about the contents of Jewelry catalogs. When you find
Bailey, Banks & Biddle Co. heading this chapter, but fail to find Tiffany & Co. bringing up the rear
of the alphabet, you may well be puzzled. Please use both chapters, and, if any arbitrary classification still troubles you, roll up your sleeves and compile another edition for your own use.

Chapter 52

Sporting Goods

All firearms are not sporting goods, nor are all sporting goods firearms; some of us can enjoy exercise and keen competition without destroying life. Consequently, if this apparent duplication of Chapter 21 baffles you, consider the baseball, basketball, football and hockey games you have played in or watched. Think of the angler, archer, badminton player, bowler, boxer, croquet expert, fencer, golfer, polo player, swimmer, skater, tennis enthusiast and trackman -- and a hundred other sportsmen. Firearms is but a small facet of American sport.

This chapter will provide you with references that should uncover practically everything from a Gay Ninety bathing suit to a tent. Remember that when you were about ten years old it was pretty good sport to sleep out in the back yard, or go on a camping trip. Even the poker chips in the billiard and pool room are sporting equipment -- and why not the cards, cues and beer mugs that thrived in the same smoky dens of iniquity? As we have found throughout this guide, the overlap between classifications is unavoidable. You will find pistols, rifles and shotguns too, but in most cases offerings for other sports predominate. A complete and proper introduction to Spalding's 1888 Gymnasium catalog would take two pages.

1884 New York   OC
  ABBEY & IMBRIE. Ill. catalog and price list of fine fishing tackle. Sm. 4to., 24 and 2pp., 91 pls. One of the best pict. records.

1889 New York
  ------ Ill. catalog of fine fishing tackle. 4to., 136pp. of fine ills., pict. wrap. Price of this catalog 25¢.

1890 San Francisco   CHi
  ALLEN, E.T. Catalog #38 - firearms, baseball togs, athletic goods, police goods, fishing tackle. 4to., ills., wrap.

c.1880 St. Paul, Minn.   PPL
  AUERBACH, FINCH & VAN SLYCK. Ill. price list of tents, awnings, tarpaulins and other camping equipment, etc. 24pp.

c.1900 Kansas City, Mo.   MoSHi
  BAKER & LOCKWOOD MFG. CO. Successor to Caleb J. Baker. Ill. catalog of show tents, awnings, blankets, flags, horse covers, circus tents, camping tents, wagon covers, merry go-round tents and all manner of camping equipment. 8vo., 128pp., fine ills., pict. wrap. of merry-go-round.

1883 Springfield, Mass.   MiEM
  BARNEY & BERRY. Barney & Berry skates are known in every land where water freezes, etc. Ice and roller skates. Ills. of models and styles. 18mo., 16pp., fine ills., pict. wrap.

1884 Springfield, Mass.   MiEM
  ------ Ill. catalog of ice and roller skates. 20pp. with a fine litho. of the plant - Joy.

1888 Springfield, Mass.   MnHi
  ------ Ill. catalog of skates. 40pp., wrap.

1892 Providence, R. I.   RHi
  BLISS, R. MFG. CO. Ill. catalog of lawn tennis sets, rackets, complete outfits - racket models: Harvard, Oxford, Newport, Talisman, Alexandria, etc. 16mo., 48pp., fine ills., col. pict. wrap.

1808 Bridgeport, Conn.   Ct
  BRIDGEPORT GUN IMPLEMENT CO. (Hartley & Graham, agents, New York.) Golf catalog - ills. of clubs, balls, bags, markers, supplies with prices, instructions, photos. of players and clubhouses. 12mo., 102pp., pict. wrap.

1891 Boston   ICHi
  BRIGGS, OLIVER L. & SONS. Ill. catalog of billiard and pool tables, cues, balls, racks, cushions, furnishings for clubs and saloons, etc. 8vo., 28pp., pict. wrap.

c.1892 Boston   ICHi
  ------ Ill. catalog of tables and furnishings with rules and instructions, etc. 8vo., 32pp. Pict. wrap.

1888 Cambridge, Mass. &   ICHi
       New Haven, Conn.
BRINE, JAMES W. College Outfitter.
Annual ill. catalog - prices and desc. of
baseball, football, lacrosse, polo, bicycling
and gym uniforms and sporting goods. 8vo.,
52pp., a fine pict. record, wrap.

c.1875 Philadelphia   PHi
BUEHLER, BONBRIGHT & CO. Ill. catalog
of ice and roller skates - The Paragon for
men, The Alaska for the ladies. 8vo., 16pp.

1887 St. Paul, Minn.   MnHi
BURKHARD, WILLIAM R. Ill. catalog of
firearms, ammunition, fishing tackle and
sporting goods. 4to., fine ills.

1888 St. Paul, Minn.   MnHi
------ Ill. catalog of sporting goods.

c.1883 Santa Cruz, Calif.   PKsL
CALIFORNIA POWDER WORKS.   CHi
Mills and offices - San Francisco. Price
list of Santa Cruz gunpowder, ills. of labels
a fine pict. record: Eureka, Cabinet, Duck
powder, California sporting, Pacific rifle,
Quail powder, Sea & River, Valley Mills -
in col., pistol, shot and ammunition - also
blasting powder, etc. 8vo., cl., an outstanding catalog.

N.B. See History of Explosives in America
      by Van Gelder & Schlatter. Eventually
bought out by duPont after the war.

1880 New York   OAKf
CAMMEYER, ALFRED J. Ill. price list of
sporting goods.

1895 Chicago   ICHi
CARPENTER, GEORGE B. & CO. Est. 1840.
Ill. catalog of awnings, flags, sails and tents.

1899 Chicago   ICHi
------ Ill. catalog of tents, camping outfits, etc. 4to., 88pp., wrap.

1889 Post Mills, Vt.   NhD
CHUBB, THOMAS H. Est. 1869. Ill. catalog of fishing rods and anglers' supplies.
8vo., 72pp., fine ills., wrap.

1890 Post Mills, Vt.   VtHi
------ Retail catalog of fishing rods and
anglers' supplies. 4to., 80pp. with excellent
ills., pict. wrap.

Also, acquired with circulars and papers, a
47 page ill. catalog inscribed with the compliments of Thomas H. Chubb. This one is
unfortunately undated.

1897 Post Mills, Vt.   VtHi
------ Ill. catalog of anglers' supplies.
8vo., 116pp., fine ills., col. pict. wrap.

p.1900 Post Mills, Vt.   VtHi
------ Later catalog available.

1884 New York   NSbSM
CROOK, J. B. & CO. Est. 1837. Ill. catalog
of fishing tackle, guns, pistols, games, cricket,
archery, etc. 8vo., 158pp., ill. throughout.

1885 Decatur, Ill.   ICHi
CROWN ROLLER SKATE CO. Ill. catalog
of skates and sporting goods.

1883 Cazenovia, N. Y.   NSbSM
CRUTTENDEN & CARD. Ill. catalog of
rifles and sportsmens' goods. Ills. of rods,
reels, flies, glass ball traps, etc. 8vo., 28pp.,
pict. wrap.

1880 Boston
DAME, STODDARD & KENDALL. Est. 1800.
Successors to Bradford & Anthony. Ill.
catalog of angling implements, flies, hooks,
tackle, reels, rods, stenciled bait boxes,
flasks, etc. 8vo., 56pp., pict. wrap.

c.1882 New York   MH-BA
DANIELL & SONS. Ill. catalog of mens'
furnishings and athletic equipment. Some
col. pls., 8vo., 40pp.

c.1900 Wilmington, Del.   OAKf
DELAWARE RUBBER CO. Mail order
catalog - everything in rubber - bicycles,
sundries, accessories, rubber goods, etc.
16mo., 72pp., ills., pict. wrap.

c.1884 New Haven   MH-BA
DOLE, LESTER C. & CO. Ill. catalog of
sporting equipment. 8vo., 40pp.

1888 St. Louis   MnHi
DOUGHERTY BROTHERS. Ill. catalog of
awnings, tents and camping goods.

DuPONT of Delaware. See Firearms.

1876 Chicago   ICHi
EATON, E. E. Ill. price list of guns, powder,
fishing tackle, flies, baits and sporting goods.
4to., 8pp., fine ills.

1856 Boston   MiDbF
FARRAR, A. F. Successor to Geo. N. Davis.
Ill. and desc. catalog of India rubber and
gutta percha goods - camping equipment,
gun cases, flasks, boats, diving armor,
powder flasks, etc. The whiskey flasks and
powder flasks are great - I wonder how long
it took for the whiskey to eat through the
rubber; must have tasted swell about the
fourth day out. 8vo., 96pp., a fine pict. record,
dec. cl. Even a plate of painted dolls and
toys!

c.1886 St. Paul, Minn.   MnHi
FARWELL, OZMAN & JACKSON. Ill. circular of ice skates, hand painted stenciled
sleds and sleigh bells. 4to., 16pp.

c.1875 Rochester, N. Y.   NR
FIELD, JAMES. Est. 1843. Catalog of
U.S. awnings, flags, ship chandlery, tents
and camping equipment. 8vo., 32pp., ills.
of all manner of tents, pict. wrap.

c.1880 New York   NNMM
FISH & SIMPSON. Ill. catalog of skates,
guns, tricks, novelties, sporting goods and
toys. Fol., 4pp.

c.1882 New York   NNMM
------ List of sporting goods, baseball
uniforms, also firemens', yachtsmens' and
hunters' - flies, flasks, rods, guns, etc.
Fol., a fine pict. record.

1885 New York   MH-BA
GRANBERY, D. W. & CO. Formerly Hall,
Nicoll & Granbery. Wholesale catalog of
lawn tennis supplies with directions for playing, etc. 8vo., 20pp., ills., wrap.

1899 New York   NHi
HEMMENWAY, S. & SON. Sail Makers.
Ill. catalog of flags, tents, wagon, horse and
truck covers, tarpaulins for circus, park
and camping purposes. 56pp., fine ills.,
flags in col., pict. wrap. Also sails and
covers for boats.

1893 New Haven   CtHi
HENDRIX, ANDREW B. CO. Ill. catalog of
fishing reels by Hendrix for the trade. 8vo.,
84pp., pict. wrap.

1883 Pittsburgh, Pa.   PKsL
JOHNSTON, J. H. Great Western Gun Works.
Ill. catalog of baits, flies, equipment, hooks,
line, reels, rods for the angler. Large 8vo.,
24pp., fine ills., pict. wrap. See also Firearms.

nd. Philadelphia   PKsL
KIRK, W. STOKES. Catalog #19. Rifles,
guns, ammunition also sporting and army
uniforms and clothing. 12mo., 48pp., 48
ills., pict. wrap.

v.d. Boston
LOVELL, JOHN P. CO. See Bicycles and
Firearms.

1891 Chicago   ICHi
McCLURG, A. C. & CO. Ill. catalog of
sporting goods - hammocks, tents, awnings,
etc.

1890 Brooklyn, N. Y.
MARSTERS, JAMES F. Mfg. of Fine Fishing Tackle. Est. 1860. Ill. catalog of fine

fishing tackle with fine ills. of flies, hooks,
line, reels, rods - everything for the American angler. 4to., 60pp., pict. wrap.

1887 Kansas City, Mo.   MoSHi
MENGES, E. E. & CO. General catalog of
sporting goods, baseball and all sports,
fishing tackle, etc.

1891-2 New York   NNNAM
MERWIN, HULBERT & CO. Ill. catalog of
pulley weights, rowing machines and all
gymnasium apparatus and fixtures. 40pp.

c.1890 New York   ICHi
MILBURY ATLANTIC SUPPLY CO. Ill.
catalog of bathing suits and other sports-
wear.

1884-87 St. Louis   MnHi
MISSOURI TENT & AWNING CO. Ill. catalogs of tents and awnings for all purposes,
camping, etc. 1884, 1885 and 1887.

1884 Chicago   NNMM
MURRAY & BAKER. Ill. catalog of tents
and camp furniture and equipment. 48pp.

1891 Providence, R. I.   RHi
NARRAGANSETT MACHINE CO. Ill. catalog of gymnasium apparatus, machines and
fixtures, showing 400 gymns. from Ala. to
Texas equipped by N.M. Co. 4to., pict.
wrap. Swell photo. ills.

1892 Providence, R. I.   RHi
------ Catalog D. 16mo., 48pp., ill., wrap.

1892 Providence, R. I.   RHi
------ Catalog C. Standard gymnasium
equipment. 178pp., fine ills.

c.1900 Providence, R. I.   RHi
------ Ill. catalog H. Playground apparatus. 32pp.

1893 Cincinnati   OC
NATIONAL BILLIARD MFG. CO. Est. 1880.
To our patrons - A catalog of billiard and
pool tables, mfg. with 30 years experience -
ills. of tables, balls, cues, bottles, racks,
lamps, bar checks, cards, poker chips, dice,
alleys: Model tables - Competitor, Pride
of the West, Phoenix, Brilliant, Exposition,
Manhattan, Crescent, Climax, Columbia,
etc. 4to., 16pp., excellent ills., pict. col.
wrap.

1896 Cincinnati   OC
------ Ill. catalog of tables, new models,
apparatus, equipment, etc. 8vo., 32pp., col.
pict. wrap.

1875 New York   MdTanSW
NEWHOUSE TRAPS. Hunters' and Trap-
pers' complete guide. 12mo., 92pp. with

11 page price list of traps, etc. at end. A guide issued for the purpose of selling traps.

Listed because to some morons this is a sport. There was a period when trapping was justified for food, clothing and shelter. Today it should be condemned as a human crime against nature.

1888   Manchester, Vt.   VtHi
ORVIS, CHARLES F. Est. 1856. Catalog #7. The finest flies, reels and fishing rods for all anglers, etc. with a fine editorial - Fishin' Jimmy, from New Princeton Review for May 1888. Sq. 8vo., 64pp. with fine ills.

N.B. Orvis was the first to create new light rods to replace the cane poles.

p.1900   Manchester, Vt.   VtHi
------ Later fine ill. catalogs available.

1873   New York   ICHi
PECK & SNYDER. Trade price list of baseball supplies and sporting goods, skates - American Club, Ladies' rink, etc. 12mo., 16pp., fine ills., pict. wrap.

1877   New York   NSbSM
------ Guide to shooting with bow and arrow with 20 page ill. catalog of fishing tackle and sporting goods. 12mo., 72pp.

1878   New York   ICHi
------ Ill. price list and guide to sports and pastimes, with fine ills. of angling and baseball outfits, sporting equipment and even toys and tricks. 12mo., 192pp., pict. wrap.

1878   New York   ICHi
------ Archers' complete guide. Use of long bow - with ills. and prices. 12mo., 32pp., fine ills., pict. wrap.

1882   New York   NNU
------ Ill. price list - baseball to foils - to gunning. 12mo., fine ills., wrap.

1891   New York   ICHi
------ Catalog for the trade only - ills. of genuine American Club skates, bellywhoppers with fine stencils, bob-sleds, firearms, etc. 8vo., 16pp., wrap.

v.d.   Cincinnati   OCl
POWELL, P. & SON and POWELL   OC
& CLEMENT. See Firearms.

c.1880   Detroit, Mich.   MiD
RAYL, T. B. & CO. Detroit recreation depot. Ill. catalog of bicycles - high wheelers and tricycles, supplies for baseball, skating, lacrosse, all sports - toys and novelties.

c.1882   Philadelphia   PHi
REACH, A. K. & CO. Ill. catalog of general sporting goods. 8vo., 72pp., fine ills.

c.1888   Philadelphia   ICHi
------ Ill. catalog of baseball supplies, boxing, fencing, etc. equipment.

c.1892   Philadelphia   ICHi
------ Ill. catalog of sporting goods.

1894   Ilion, N. Y.   N
REMINGTON ARMS CO. Ill. catalog of firearms, bicycles, sewing machines and sporting apparatus. See also Firearms.

c.1898   Philadelphia, Pa.   NNMM
ROSENBLATT, H. M. & CO. Leather and canvas goods and holiday specialties. Ill., desc. and priced. 70pp., glt. dec. wrap.

1894   Akron, O.   OHi
SCHUMACHER GYMNASIUM CO. Ill. catalog #12. Universal gymn. goods and apparatus. 8vo., 128pp., pict. wrap.

1899   Chicago   MH-BA
SEARS ROEBUCK & CO. Ill. catalog #110- Sporting Goods. 4to., 60pp., fine ill. record.

p.1900   Chicago   ICHi
------ Play Ball! Sample book of Sears Roebuck baseball uniforms and supplies. 12mo., 7pp. of col. samples - swatches - and 4 col. pls. of uniforms, 44pp. in all. Uniforms $1.65 to $7.90, col. pict. wrap.

1888   Chicago   MnHi
SEEBERGER, A. F. & CO. Ill. catalog of guns, camping outfits, fishing tackle, ammunition, cutlery, optical goods and sporting supplies. Large 8vo., fine ill. record.

1889   Chicago   MnHi
------ Ill. catalog of sporting supplies.

1900   Kalamazoo   MiK
SHAKESPEARE, WILLIAM JR. Ill. catalog of William Shakespeare's fine fishing tackle. 16mo., 58pp. of swell ills., pict. wrap.

c.1900   Kalamazoo   MiK
------ Ill. catalog of fine reels and baits that really catch fish. 16mo., 52pp., wrap.

N.B. Shades of Lady MacBeth! Aye, Sire, with these fine lines I'll tie thy throat and tie it well. ed's note.

c.1900   Chicago   ICHi
SMYTH, JOHN M. CO. Ill. catalog of bicycles, cameras, and all manner of sporting supplies.

1886   New York & Chicago   ICHi
SPALDING, A. G. & BROTHERS. Complete ill. catalog #22 - bicycles, guns, sporting goods and velocipedes.

1887 New York & Chicago   NNU
------ Ill. catalog #25 for fall and winter.
4to., 88pp., fine ills.

1887-8 New York & Chicago   ICHi
------ Ill. catalog of sporting goods.

1888 New York & Chicago   NNU
------ Gymnasium catalog #8. Ills. of
YMCA machines and apparatus, uniforms
such as The Perisalt - nature's own remedy-
push yourself against it and eliminate the
pendulous abdomen and constipation, etc.
4to., 32pp., all sports equipment, pict. wrap.

1892 New York & Chicago   ICHi
------ Ill. catalog of athletic uniforms.
44pp.

1892 Toledo, O.   NNMM
STEVENS, B. A. Catalog B. Only the best.
Ills. of billiard room and bar supplies,
saloon fittings and fixtures, furniture -
mahogany bars, spittoons, cards, dice, novelties. Sm. 4to., 209pp. of ills. with a col.
pict. wrap. Compiled by Geo. H. Stevens.
One of the best records.

1892 Toledo, O.   OHi
------ Condensed ed. May. 4to.,   OT
58pp., fine ills.

1895 Toledo, O.   OHI
------ Ill. catalog, 12mo., 128pp., wrap.

1891 Syracuse, N. Y.   NSyHi
SYRACUSE BAMBOO FURNITURE CO. Ill.
price list of fine split bamboo fishing rods,
gang spoons, American spinners, trolling
baits, rod cases, etc. Tall 8vo., 24pp.

1867 Philadelphia   PHi
TRYON, EDWARD K. Ill. catalog of rifles,
pistols and shotguns.

1872 Philadelphia   PHi
------ Ill. catalog of the new protector
revolvers.

1886 Philadelphia   PHi
------ For the trade only. Ill. catalog of
guns, rifles and sporting goods.

1895 Philadelphia   PKsL
------ Ill. catalog and price list of firearms, bicycles, uniforms and general sporting goods - with rules for shooting - a

dictionary of guns and revolvers, police
goods, decoys, etc. Gun models 1886-95.
4to., 80pp., pict. wrap. A swell job.

c.1893 Philadelphia   ICHi
------ Ill. catalog - athletic department -
gymnasium outfits, sports equipment, league
balls -- supplies for all sports.

1899 Philadelphia   PKsL
------ Ill. catalog. 4to., 40pp., ills.

1873-4 Boston   VtSM
UNION HARDWARE CO. (N. B. Stevens,
agent.) Ill. catalog of skates, straps -
Ladies' and Gentlemens' American parlor
or floor, New York Club or rink - also dog
collars, tools and novelties. 16mo., 48pp.,
pict. wrap.

1881 Chicago   ICHi
WILKINSON, JOHN CO. Ill. catalog of gymnasium and sporting goods, high wheel bicycles, baseball, fishing and archery supplies.
4to., 16pp., fine ills.

1882 Chicago   ICHi
------ Ill. catalog of sporting goods, also
boating and gymn. goods.

1886 Chicago   ICHi
------ Ill. catalog of sporting goods, gymnasium equipment, theatrical supplies and
home entertainment.

1888 Worcester, Mass.   MWA
WINSLOW, SAMUEL SKATE CO. 1888-89
ill. price list of skates. 16mo., 32pp. of
ills. of models and styles. Pict. wrap.

1893 Boston
WOOD, JOHN JR. Ill. catalog of sporting
goods - fine ills. of bicycles, firearms, fish-
ing tackle, cutlery, etc. Ills. of models of
guns by Baker, Colt, Greener, Lefever,
Ithaca, Marlin, Parker, Scott, Remington,
L. C. Smith, Smith & Wesson and Winchester.
A fine pict. record.

1889 Boston   ICHi
WRIGHT, GEORGE & DITSON, HENRY A.
Catalog #21. Ill. catalog of lawn tennis,
baseball, cricket, lacrosse, croquet supplies,
bathing and boating outfits, gymn. apparatus,
etc. 8vo., 80pp., fine pict. record, wrap.

The word sport is almost as inclusive as hardware: there just isn't any end to it. If your sport is
bicycling, riding, driving or hunting, you have chapters covering the equipment and supplies for each.
Toys include, as far as possible, games for young and old in case your sporting list runs to parcheesi
and tiddlywinks. Naturally Automobiles will have to do for racing records and special cars. Many

of the Hardware catalogs offer ice and roller skates, gymnasium equipment, bicycle parts and fishing rods. Under Clothing it has been impossible to segregate all sporting uniforms, of course, so don't give up.

The New York Public Library's Spalding Collection is probably the best all inclusive location in this field. Although hidden under such titles as Spalding's Athletic Library, with authoritative directions, instructions and rules compiled by top sportsmen of the day, almost every one of them is a literary vehicle carrying a fine illustrated catalog of American sporting goods. Don't overlook this great reference library whether you are hunting angling, baseball, fencing, football, hockey, lacrosse or skating - the name is confusing - it isn't all baseball at all. It contains the guide books and illustrated catalogs of Peck & Snyder, Reach, Spalding, Wright & Ditson and others, and it covers just about every American sport covered in this chapter. Keep NN in mind.

There -- now roll up your sleeves, turn to the index, and go to work.

Chapter 53

Stationery

This heading should read Account Books, Blackboards, Charts, Globes, Cutters for Counting Houses, Ledgers, Office Equipment and Furnishings, Furniture, School Apparatus, Library Furnishings, Papers for all Purposes, Quills, Pens, Parchment . . . or . . . Stationery. However, time is money and most of us won't take the time to read such a heading or title. I hide it here just in case there are a few who really want to know what this chapter contains. Ink wells, spikes and paper weights are also included in some catalogs.

Available business histories offer every last detail in each field listed in our Contents; the difficult job is to remember that this guide is only for the selection of the catalog and it's location for research. Quill pens, for example, could write a chapter all by themselves -- but, this guide is concerned only with the catalogs that actually list them for sale. Further suggestions at the end of this group may include a few comments you hadn't thought about.

c.1820 Boston   MWA
ALLEN, ANDREW J. A catalog of pat. account books, stationery plain and fancy, ledgers, memo-books, pencils, wallets and navigation books, etc.

c.1875 New York   NHi
BAKER, PRATT & CO. Mfg. Ill. catalog of finest library and school globes. 4to., 4pp., 32 ills. of styles.

c.1876 New York
------ Partial list of school apparatus and furnishings, globes, blackboards, etc. 4to., 8pp., fine ills.

1880 New York   NNMM
------ Ill., desc. and priced catalog of foreign and domestic stationery - for dealers only. 140pp., wrap.

nd. New York   NNMM
------ Ill. and priced flyer of globes. 1 leaf.

c.1870 Indianapolis   In
BOWEN, STUART & CO. Emporium for Books, Paper and Stationery. Ill. catalog of school books, pads, pencils, etc. 16mo., 48pp., wrap.

1875 Indianapolis   In
------ Ill. catalog of supplies - file spikes, paper weights, wall hangers, cutters for counting houses, clips, pen racks, match safes, files and ink stands.

BROWN & COOK STATIONERY CO. See Printers' Samples - Valentines.

1887 Adams, Mass.   MH-BA
BROWN, L. L. PAPER CO. Est. 1850. Greylock Mills. Brochure and ill. catalog with history of mill - standard linen ledgers, record paper, samples, sizes and weights, etc. 7x10, 74pp., fine job.

c.1886 Chicago   DSi
BRYANT & STRATTON SHORTHAND MACHINE CO. Popular treatise - phonography modernized with price list of new machines, office equipment, etc. 4to., 52pp., pict. wrap.

c.1874 New York   NNMM
BURT & PRENTICE. Ill., desc. and priced catalog of books, stationery and merchandise. 10 lvs.

c.1874 Cincinnati   OC
BUTLER, J. J. Price list of combined writing and copying blue and La Belle violet excelsior writing fluid. 16mo., 4pp.

1897 Chicago   MnHi
CAMERON, AMBERG & CO. Catalog of office supplies and specialties.

c.1887 Boston   MH-BA
CLARK, CARROLL W. Headquarters for Useful Labor Saving Devices. Ill. price list of home, office, library and school supplies. 12mo., 48pp., wrap.

1879 Chicago   MH-BA
CLARK, FRIEND, FOX & CO. Catalog of paper for dealers, publishers, printers, lithographers, stationers, bookbinders, inks, twines, etc. 8vo., 68pp.

c.1845 Philadelphia   PHi
CLOTHIER, JOHN W. Ill. catalog of fancy
and staple stationery - bargains always on
hand from auctions - please preserve this
catalog for reference. 32mo., 16pp., wrap.

c.1850 Philadelphia   PKsL
CLOTHIER, JOHN W. & CO. Ill. catalog of
fancy and staple stationery bargains from
auction always available - superior quills,
inkstands, slates, Japan ware, chessmen and
boards, etc. 32mo., 16pp., dec. wrap.

1893 Chicago   NHi
COMPTOMETER CO. Mechanical arithme-
tic - the comptometer does the work - for
offices, etc., tests. Sq. 16mo., ills., wrap.

1874 New York   NNMM
CORLIES, MACY & CO. Ill. catalog of
stationery, glass inkwells, paper weights,
presses, stamps, furnishings and supplies.
4to., 56pp. See also Printers' Samples.

1845 Rochester, N. Y.   NIC
CORNELL, SILAS. Desc. of Silas   N
Cornell's improved terrestrial globes. 2nd
ed. 16mo., X, (11) - 36pp., frs.

c.1830 New York   MWA
COTTONS & BARNARD. A catalog of drawing and letter paper, artificial flower paper,
cards, brushes, candle ornaments, pens and
pencils, inkstands and paint boxes, slates,
games, etc. Fol. broadside with 3 columns
of goods.

1892 San Francisco   CHi
CROCKER, H. S. CO. Ill. catalog of legal
blanks, letter files, stamps, typewriters,
etc. 8vo., 62pp., wrap.

1860 New York   NHi
DAVIDS, THADEUS & CO. Est. 1824. History of Ink, plus price list and 24 fine col.
pls. and col. frs. by Snyder, Black & Sturn,
and notices of the press. 12mo., 72pp., cl.
The best ill. catalog of inks located.

DEMPSEY & CARROLL. See Printers'
Samples.

c.1886 Boston, New York & Philadelphia
DENNISON MFG. CO.   NNMM
Est. Framingham, Mass., 1844. Ill. catalog
of samples, some in col., gummed paper and
labels. 16mo., stiff wrap.

nd. Philadelphia   PHi
------ Dennison's Bogie Book. 12mo.,
32pp., ptd. Philadelphia.

c.1900 Philadelphia   PHi
------ Stationers' ill. catalog of tags,
labels and specialties. 4to., 158pp.

1873 Jersey City   PPL
DIXON, JOSEPH CRUCIBLE CO. Ill. brochure - uses of plumbago and graphite -
lead pencils, lubrications, stove polish and
Dixon pencils.

1894 Jersey City   PKsL
------ History of a Lead Pencil by Walton
Day. 12mo., 16pp., pict. wrap.

1898 Jersey City   PKsL
------ Pencillings - col. lithos. by Bien,
16pp., col. pict. wrap.

1855 Boston   MH-BA
DUTTON, E. P. & CO. Formerly Ide and
Dutton. Ill. catalog of maps, books, school
apparatus and stationery. 12mo., 72pp.

1872 Philadelphia   PHi
ELDER, DAVID D. & CO. New ready reference list of books and stationery. 12mo.

1876 Camden, N. J.   PKsL
ESTERBROOK STEEL PEN CO. Ill. price
list of steel pens and holders. 12pp.

1875 New York   NNMM
FOLEY, JOHN. Est. 1848. MH-BA PKsL
Invention of John Foley's diamond pointed
pens - history - with ill. catalog of pens,
fancy and plain, magic pencils, machines
for making, machines in action - even making toothpicks. 8vo. with 80 fine litho. pls.,
glt. dec. cl. Best pen catalog located.

c.1800 Trenton, N. J.   NjR
GORDON, PETER. A catalog of books,
stationery, quills, ink powders, inkstands,
mathematical instruments, parchment, writing papers - at Peter Gordon's Store near
the Market House. Fol. broadside, 3 columns
of goods.

c.1870 Boston   MH-BA
HAMMETT, J. L. Ill. catalog of school supplies. 8vo., 60pp.

1872 Boston   MH-BA
------ Desc. and ill. catalog of school
furniture - blackboards, charts, maps, bells,
seats, globes, scientific apparatus, etc.
8vo., 116pp.

c.1883 Boston   MH-BA
------ Ill. catalog of school supplies, stationery, etc. 8vo., 56pp.

1885 Chicago   MnHi
HANSON, C. H. Ill. catalog of engraving
stencils, stamps, brass and rubber date
stamps, seals and office equipment.

c.1841 Philadelphia   MH-BA
HART, S. & SON. Est. 1828. Catalog of
portable writing desks, all manner of sta-

tionery, games, fancy goods and novelties. 16mo., 32pp.

1869 Hartford, Conn.   OC
HIRST PATENT GOLD PEN CO. Price list of Hirst's Patent Pens. 32mo., 20pp.

c.1874 Cincinnati   OC
HOLLAND, JOHN. Ill. price list of Holland's gold pens, the best and cheapest, etc. 12mo., 4pp.

1860 New York   NSbSM
HOSFORD & CO. Ill. catalog #14 of blank books, litho. and letter press stationery, stamps, presses, fountain pens, inkstands, paper weights, etc. Tall 16mo., 36pp.

c.1860 Boston   MiDbF
JOSLIN, GILMAN &   NHi   NhD   ICRMc
SONS. Joslin's terrestrial and celestial globes - How to Use - etc. with 8 pls. An ill. catalog. 12mo., 44pp., pict. cl.

1790 New York   Evans #22594
JOYCE & SNOWDEN. Joyce & Snowden's American ink powders for records, equal to any imported or offered for sale in the Thirteen United States - sold by most stationers and ironmongers in principal towns and cities. 4to. Listed as a label engraved in English and Dutch with directions.

If it's good enough for Evans, it's a good early record of American ink for sale - and that constitutes a catalog for me.

1890 San Francisco   CHi
KLINKNER, C. A. & Co. Ill. catalog of rubber stamps, brass plates, burning stamps and brands, office furnishings, etc. 8vo.

1885 Boston   MH-BA
LIBRARY BUREAU. Est. 1876.   NNMM
Classified ill. catalog of supplies, standard fittings, holiday selections, furnishings, etc. 8vo., 100pp.

1888 Boston   MH-BA
------ Special holiday selections. 8vo., 16pp.

1891 Boston   NNNAM
------ Classified ill. catalog of library and office supplies. 172pp.

1895 Boston   NNNAM
------ Ill. catalog of card index outfits. 48pp.

1900 Boston   NNNAM
------ Ill. catalog of 161pp.

nd. Philadelphia   PHi
MAURICE, WILLIAM H. Ill. catalog of blank books and plain and fancy stationery. 12mo., 22pp.

1894 San Francisco   CHi
MOISE, L. H. Ill. catalog of rubber stamps, stencils, badges, metal signs, office equipment, etc. 16mo., 192pp., wrap.

c.1890 Philadelphia   PKsL
NOLL, E. P. & CO. New desc. and ill. catalog of wall and pocket maps, guides, globes, atlases, rollers, etc. for offices, etc.

c.1886 St. Paul, Minn.   MnHi
NORTHWESTERN STAMP WORKS. Ill. catalog and price list of rubber date stamps, seals, dies, office supplies, etc. 8vo., 32pp.

1889 Rochester, N. Y.   MH-BA
OFFICE SPECIALTY MFG. CO. Ill. catalog of document files, shelves, indexes, cabinets, rapid roller copiers, office equipment, etc. 4to., 40pp.

1892 San Francisco   CHi
PAYOT, UPHAM & CO. Ill. catalog of stationery, globes, pens and pencils, writing and record paper, everything for school, office, etc. 4to., 320pp., wrap.

PHOENIX STEAM PRINTING CO. See Printers' Samples.

1887 Chicago   MnHi
RIDER, M. D. Ill. catalog of blank books, stationery, office equipment, etc.

1876 Boston   NjOE
RITCHIE'S. Ritchie's ill. catalog of school apparatus. 40pp., wrap.

1900 Denver   CoD
SACHS-LAWLER MACHINE MFG. CO. Ill. catalog of numbering machines, seals, pads, stamps, daters, punchers and office supplies.

1874 New York   MH-BA
SCHERMERHORN, J. W. & CO. Ill. catalog of school materials. 90th ed. 8vo., 224pp., fine pict. ref.

nd. Chester, Conn.   NNMM
SILLIMAN, S. & CO. Ill. and desc. price list of inkstands. 1 leaf.

1874 Philadelphia   PHi
SMITH, JOHN L. Successor to R.L. Barnes. Ill. catalog and price list of maps and globes, drawing and tracing paper, tracing linen, wall maps, spring rollers, office equipment, etc. 8vo., (2), VII, 36pp., wrap.

c.1890 Philadelphia   PHi
------ Ill. catalog of maps, globes, etc. and stationery furnishings. 16mo., 108pp.

1900 Chicago   ICHi
STAFFORD, E. H. MFG. CO. Ill. catalog #31 - office and bank furnishings, desks,

iron hat trees, spittoons, etc. 4to., 56pp., pict. wrap.

c.1880 New York
STEIGER, E. & CO. Ill. catalog #30B - Kindergarten supplies, globes, maps, occupational furnishings, etc. 8vo., 32pp., dec. wrap.

c.1875 New York   NNMM
TIFFANY & CO. Est. 1837. Ill. catalog of French and English stationery, reception and visiting cards, arms, crests, monograms, etc. 18 lvs., wrap.

1883 Albany, N.Y.   MH-BA
UNION SCHOOL FURNITURE CO. Ill. catalog of school furnishings and supplies, automatic school seats, etc. 8vo., 18pp.

1885 Albany, N.Y.   MH-BA
------ Ill. catalog of stationery and school supplies. 8vo., 34pp.

nd. Philadelphia   PHi
WHITE RUBBER STAMP CO. Several ill. catalogs of rubber daters, seals, stamps and office supplies.

1887 Chicago   ICHi
WORLD RUBBER STAMP CO. Specimen book of rubber and steel stamps, stencils, seals, checks, blanks and office equipment. Tall 24mo., 108pp. of ills., ptd. wrap.

Glass ink wells will also be found under Glass, Hardware and House Furnishings. Paper of many manufacturers and hues will be found under Printers' Specimens and Printers' Samples, and wallpapers in a very small group under Miscellany. Stationers have sold books for generations but just when they got into the department store division of merchandising it is as hard to say as just when The A & P became a pseudo Sears Roebuck & Co. Like Topsy, many of these changes have just plumb growed up around us, making classification even more impossible than ever. Optical and Scientific Apparatus offers many catalogs of school equipment. Although against the advice of some librarians, Printers' Specimens and Presses contain catalogs of date stamps and other office equipment. Try your luck and if you get lost, run for the index.

Chapter 54

Stoves & Heating Equipment

To leave those four words at the head of a chapter to do the work of fifty is unfair to both the English language and the reader. Fishing hastily in but a few of the located catalogs, one comes up with cooking utensils, broilers, ovens, sad irons, fire bricks, stove lining, tiles, gas logs, fireplaces, fancy grates and fire frames, ventilators and registers, special stoves and heaters for various trades, furnaces, patent smoke blowers and even toy stoves as well as ornamental ironwork cast in many stove foundries.

Although I have tried not to use private collection locations, I feel they are important as a record of existence even though at the moment they may not be available for research. Mrs. Josephine Pierce is one of the few historians who has not only used illustrations from American trade catalogs (Fire on the Hearth - 1951) but also cataloged them properly. Most of the PC listings in this chapter are from her own library.

Starting chronologically with Benjamin Franklin's Essay in 1744, checking M. N. Stanley's Stoves for 1836 and J. L. Parker's in 1839, the reader can trace American cooking and heating right through to the Superior steel furnaces for banks, churches and hotels manufactured at Little Falls, N. Y. in 1893.

1881 Chicago   ICHi
ADAMS & WESTLAKE. Ill. price list of improved oil stoves. 16mo., pict. wrap.

1882 Chicago   ICHI
------ Ill. catalog of stoves.

1883 Chicago   MnHi
------ Ill. catalog of stove boards and heating accessories for stoves.

1880-80 Chicago   MnHi
------ Three ill. catalogs of vapor and oil stoves, boards and equipment.

See Lighting for other locations.

1879 Concord, N. H.   MH-BA
ALLEN, D. N. Ill. catalog of pat. steam heating apparatus. 8vo., 16pp.

1859 New Bedford   PC
ALMY & SWAIN. Stove annual for 1859-60. Fine ills.

1855 New Haven   OC
AMERICAN AUTOMATIC STEAM CO. (Thomas B. Wing, agent, Cincinnati.) Ill. and desc. price list of Stephen J. Gold's steam heating apparatus of Newark, N. J. 20pp. Subscriber holds pat. right for Ohio and Indiana.

1888 Gardner, Mass.   PC
AMERICAN OIL STOVE CO. (Thomas Kirk, agent, Atlanta, Ga.) Condensed ed. of 1888 ill. catalog of models: Young America, Susan R. Knox, stoves and sad iron heaters. 6x6, 36pp.

1894 Chicago, New York & v.p.   ICHi
AMERICAN RADIATOR CO. Factories in Buffalo & Detroit. Ill. catalog of radiators, special designs for corners, stairways, windows, cabinet styles for dining rooms, etc. 16mo., 90pp., wrap.

1873 Philadelphia   PKsL
AMERICAN STOVE & HOLLOW WARE CO. Price list of models: Best, Cottage, Prince Royal, Star, Oriental, Waverly, Wellington, Red Jacket, Diadem, Grey Jacket, Keystone, Amazon, Naomi, American, Bantam, Paul Revere, Hecla, etc. Pats. 1862-1870. Fine list. 16mo., 32pp.

See also Baltimore Stove Works.

1837 Northampton, Mass.   PC
ARNOLD'S PATENT YANKEE COOKING STOVES. No details.

1885 Boston   MnHi
ASBESTOS PACKING CO. Catalog of asbestos cement felting for covering steam pipes and boilers.

1889 Boston   MnHi
------ Covers for steam heating apparatus.

1887-89 Cleveland, O.   MnHi
AURORA VAPOR STOVE CO. Three ill.
catalogs for 1887, 1888 and 1889.

nd. Taunton, Mass.   MTaOC
BABBITT, JEROME. Ill. catalog   PC
of stove pipes and parts, iron, tin and japanned ware, toys, etc.

c.1892 Williamsport, Pa.   PKsL
BACKUS MFG. CO. Ill. catalog of Backus'
pat. portable steam radiators, radiating
mantels, tiles, open fireplace, gas logs, etc.
8vo., 44pp., pict. wrap. of plant.

1881 Baltimore   PKsL
BALTIMORE STOVE WORKS. John Kern,
Jr. successor to American Stove & Hollow
Ware Co. of Philadelphia. Ill. catalog with
fine pls. of iron founders' goods, stoves,
ranges, furnaces, hollow ware, parlor mantels. 4to., 110pp., some col. pls., stiff pict.
wrap.

1886 Pottsville, Pa.   MH-BA
BANNAN, F. B. STEAM HEATING &
MACHINE WORKS. Ill. catalog of steam
and hot water radiators. 4to., 20pp.

1886 Boston   PC
BANNISTER ROCKING GRATE CO. Ill.
catalog of Bannister grates for all stoves
and heating plants.

1875-6 Philadelphia   MH-BA
BARBER, HENRY A. Ill. catalog of self-
regulating, improved low pressure heating
and ventilating apparatus. 8vo., 20pp.

BARROWS, SAVERY & CO. See Agricultural Implements, Tools and Machinery.

1852-96 Providence, R. I.   RHi
BARSTOW, A. C. STOVE MFG. CO. A fine
collection of ill. catalogs, 16mo. to 4to., with
pls. and pict. wrap. Stoves for the home,
office and factory, as well as special stoves
and heaters for various trades. Twenty
odd: 1852, 1867 and nearly a complete run
from 1870 to 1896.

1880 Providence, R. I.   NNMM
------ Ill. catalog of stoves. 72pp.

c.1880 Providence, R. I.   NNMM
------ Ill. broadside of models.

1878-87 Neenah, Wis.   MnHi
BERGSTROM BROTHERS & CO. Ill. catalogs of stoves for 1878, 1879 and 1887.

c.1850 Troy, N. Y.   PC
BILLINGS & STOW. Ill. broadside price
list of heaters, ranges and hollow ware.

c.1886 Pittsburgh, Pa.   PKsL
BISSELL & CO. Ill. catalog of Peerless
shaking and dumping grates - ills. of mantels, iron fire frames, fire backs and grates.
Sq. 16mo., 56pp., fine ills., wrap.

1885 Erie, Pa.   PKsL
BLACK & GERMER. Mfg. The Radiant
Home Base Burner. 16mo., 4 page folder
with col. ills. of three styles.

c.1885 Springfield, O.   MnHi
BLAKENEY FOUNDRY CO. Catalog of the
cupola furnace.

c.1874 Burlington, Vt.   PPL
BLODGETT & SWEET. Desc. and ill. catalog of models and styles of ovens - 9 ills.

1880 Boston   PC
BOSTON SOAPSTONE FURNACE CO. Ill.
desc. of soapstone heaters - advantages and
economy - with a condemnation of iron furnaces. 8vo., 22pp.

1888 Salem, O.   MnHi
BOYLE & CAREY. Keystone Stove Works.
Ill. catalog of styles, etc.

1873-88 Milwaukee   MnHi
BRAND & CO. Empire Stove Works. A
fine ref. collection of seven ill. and desc.
catalogs of models and styles, improvements,
etc. 1873, 1876, 1878, 1879, 1886-7 and 1888.

1863-98 St. Louis   NNMM
BRIDGE & BEACH MFG. CO. Empire Stove
Works. A fine collection of price lists, ill.
catalogs and circulars of models and styles,
improved stoves and ranges, hollow ware,
Superior models, etc., various sizes, ptd.
and pict. wrap. Thirty odd catalogs for ref.

1899 St. Louis   MoSHi
------ Ill. catalog of Superior Stoves and
ranges.

1890 Cleveland, O.   OHi
BRIGHTMAN STOKER CO. Mechanical
stoker and smoke preventing furnaces, pat.
1885, styles and models. 8vo., 26pp., with
4to. pict. circular, col. pict. wrap. by the
Werner Litho. Co.

1868 Troy, N. Y.   MH-BA
BUSSEY, McLEOD & CO. Oakwood Stove &
Hollow Ware Works. Ill. price list of Oakwood stoves and hollow ware, cooking stoves,
etc. 8vo., 16pp.

1871 Troy, N. Y.   MnHi
------ Ill. catalog of stoves and hollow ware.

1880 Troy, N. Y.   NNMM
------ Ill. catalog of stoves for wood and
coal. 40pp., wrap.

1897 St. Louis   MoSHi
CHARTER OAK STOVE & RANGE WORKS.
Ill. catalog of styles.

1862 Philadelphia   PC
CHASE, SHARPE & THOMPSON. Ill. catalog of cooking, parlor and hall stoves.

1872-86 Chicago   MnHi
CHICAGO STOVE WORKS. Three ill. catalogs of styles and models of stoves for all
purposes and fine hollow ware. 1872, 1880
and 1886.

1844 Boston   MWA
CHILSON, GARDNER. Fol. broadside with
woodcuts of the Trojan, Pioneer, Utter's pat.
airtight for parlors and offices, Espey's pat.
smoke blower for chimneys, airtight cooking
stoves, etc. Price list.

1851 Boston   PPL
CHILSON, RICHARDSON & CO.   PHi
Ill. catalog of pat. air warming and ventilating furnaces, improved grates, etc. 8vo.,
32pp. List of purchasers.

1881-85 Chicago   MnHi
CLARK, CHARLES E. Three ill. catalogs
of stoves and fine hollow ware for 1881, 1882
and 1885.

1891 Chicago & New York   PC
CLARK, GEORGE M. & CO. The key to
economy - a catalog of stoves.

c.1881 Cleveland, O.   MnHi
CLEVELAND COOPERATIVE STOVE CO.
St. Paul, Minn. branch. Ill. catalog of cooking and heating stoves, the best ranges and
fine hollow ware. 4to., 48pp. with circular
insert.

1894 Cleveland, O.   PC
CLEVELAND FOUNDRY CO. Ill. catalog of
stoves and hollow ware. 64pp., pict. wrap.

1887 Quincy, Ill.   MnHi
COMSTOCK-CASTLE STOVE CO. Ill. catalog of styles and models.

1855 New Haven   CtHi
CONNECTICUT STEAM HEATING CO.
Desc. notice of apparatus pat. by Stephen J.
Gold, mfg. by . . . 8vo., 22pp., diags.

1901   NNQ
CONTINENTAL IRON WORKS. Ill. catalog
of furnaces, boilers and apparatus.

1873 Cincinnati   OC
CONTINENTAL STOVE WORKS. Ill. price
list of 34 models and types of stoves for all
purposes. Ills. in green and black, broadside.

nd. Cincinnati   PHi
------ Catalog of varnishes and blackings
for preserving stoves, etc.

nd. Rochester, N. Y.   NR
CO-OPERATIVE FOUNDRY CO. Hail to the
Chief! The Crown Jewel - most powerful
heater and most perfect baker. Col. ill.
circular.

1884 Philadelphia & Lansdale, Pa.   MnHi
COX, ABRAM STOVE CO. Ill. catalog of
styles and models.

1888 Philadelphia   PKsL
------ Ill. catalog of styles and models,
fancy cast fireplace linings, hollow ware.
16mo., 124pp., fine pict. ref., pict. wrap.

1871 Philadelphia   PC
COX, WHITEMAN & COX. Ill. catalog of
stoves.

1878 New York   OC
CRARY CLAY HEATER CO. The Crary
clay heater produces pure heated atmos-
phere, etc. 16pp., pict. wrap. of heater.

1879 New York   NHi
CREAMER, W.G. & CO. Ill. catalog of hot
air registers, etc.

1885 Cleveland, O.   MnHi
DANGLER STOVE & MFG. CO. and
DANGLER VAPOR & REFINING CO. Ill.
catalog of vapor and oil stoves.

c.1886 Cleveland, O.   NNMM
------ Ill. and desc. priced catalog of the
Gem blue and white flame cook stoves. 8 lvs.

1888 Cleveland, O.   MnHi
------ Ill. catalog of stoves, etc.

1882-84 Cincinnati   MnHi
DAVIS, W. C. & CO. Favorite Stove Works.
Four ill. catalogs of models and styles.

1873-99 Detroit, Mich.   MnHi
DETROIT STOVE WORKS. Six ill. catalogs
from 8pp. to 300pp., 8vo. to 4to. with fine
ills. and pls. of pot-bellies, Shaker type,
wood and coal for home, farm, hotel, store
and factory. A fine ref. including catalogs
for 1873, 1876, 1879, 1886, 1888 and 1899.

1901 Detroit, Mich.   NNMM
------ Ill. catalog and price list #71 of
Jewell stoves and ranges. Fine pls., 300pp.

c.1880 Philadelphia   PKsL
DICK, JOHN. Ill. price list of John Dick's
pat. boiler for heating hothouses, greenhouses and dwellings. 8vo., 8pp.

1882 New York   NHi
DIETZ, R. E. Est. 1840. Ill. price list of
Dietz tubular oil stoves, models, styles, etc.
See Dietz - Lighting Chapter.

c.1890 Dighton, Mass.   MTsOC
DIGHTON STOVE LINING CO. Fire brick
for cupolas, stoves, ranges, etc. 16mo.,
12pp., ills. and diags., pict. wrap.

nd. Cleveland, Tenn.   PC
DIXIE FOUNDRY CO. General ill. catalog
of heaters, stoves and ranges for all purposes and places.

c.1868 Albany, N. Y.   MH-BA
DOYLE, WILLIAM. Ill. catalog of cooking
stoves and 2 single pls. of styles. 12mo.,
12pp.

c.1887 Norwood, N. Y.   MH-BA
DUCOLIN, S. Price list of hot water heating furnaces, pat. 1882, with tests.

1853 Boston   MH-BA
DUNKLEE, B. W. & CO. Ill. price list of
warming and ventilating apparatus. 8vo.,
56pp. See Pond & Dunklee.

1885 Geneva, N. Y.   MnHi
DUNNING, W. B. Ill. catalog of Dunning pat.
boilers and apparatus for steam heating.

c.1870 New York   NHi
DUPARQUET & HUOT. Ill. broadside of
models and styles of stoves for all purposes.

1877 Milwaukee   MnHi
DUTCHER, VOSE & ADAMS. Ill. catalog of
stoves and hollow ware.

1882 Milwaukee   MnHi
DUTCHER, VOSE & CO. Ill. catalog of
stoves.

1860 Troy, N. Y.   NNMM
EDDY, CHARLES & CO. Victor   OHi
Foundry. Ill. and desc. catalog of stoves,
patterns and designs, styles and models.
8vo., 42pp., pict. wrap.

EMPIRE STOVE WORKS. See Brand & Co.,
Bridge & Beach Mfg. Co. and Swett, Quimby
& Perry.

N.B. Three empires in three different
American cities.

1884-87 St. Louis   MnHi
EXCELSIOR MFG. CO. Four ill. catalogs
of stoves for home, workshop, factory, farm

and hotel - all places and purposes. 1884,
1885, 1886 and 1887. See House Furnishings.

EXCELSIOR STOVE WORKS. See Giles F.
Filley.

FAVORITE STOVE WORKS. See W. C.
Davis & Co.

1881 Boston   MH-BA
FELTON, B. W. Ill. and desc. catalog of
furnaces and ventilators - heating apparatus.
Large 8vo., 16pp.

1860 St. Louis   MoSHi
FILLEY, GILES F. Excelsior   IHi
Stove Works. Wholesale price list of un-
trimmed stoves for family, hotel, boarding
houses - also toy stoves. Parlor, box and
cooking. 4to., 4pp., ill. of foundry and hotel
model.

FIRE BRICK WORKS. See Architectural
Building Materials.

1744 Philadelphia   Evans 5395
        PHi   DLC   MWA   RPJCB
FRANKLIN, BENJAMIN. An account of the
new invented Pennsylvanian fireplaces;
wherein their construction and manner of
operation is particularly explained, their advantages above every other method of warming rooms demonstrated; and all objections
that have been raised against the use of them
answered and obviated. Directions for putting them up and for using them to the best
advantage. With a copper plate, in which
several parts of the machine are exactly
laid. 8vo., pp. (2), 37 (1), plate.

On the verso of the title page: Advertisement The Fire-Places are made in the best
manner, and are sold by R. Grace in Philadelphia. They are also sold by J. Parker in
New York, and J. Franklin in Boston. The
within described is of the middle and most
common size. There are others to be had
both larger and smaller.

See The Colonial Scene. (1602-1800) A
Catalog of Books exhibited at the John Carter
Brown Library in the Spring of 1949, augmented by related titles from the Library of
the American Antiquarian Society.
                            Worcester 1950.
Lawrence Wroth notes that this brochure
was printed in 1744 at the expense of Robert
Grace who mfg. the stoves. He does not
agree with me that it IS a trade catalog.
However, it is my contention that though Dr.
Franklin believed that inventions were for
the benefit of mankind, Mr. Grace distrib-
uted it to SELL STOVES.
                            Evans 5395
            MWA   RPJCB

John Carter Brown Library also has a sixth
ed. printed in French and English c.1782.

1888 Chicago   MnHi
FULLER & WARNER CO. Ill. catalog of
stoves and heaters.

1883 Cleveland, O.   OHi
FULLER & WARREN. Mfg. Ill. catalog of
hot air stoves and furnaces. 60pp., wrap.

c.1850 Troy, N. Y.   MH-BA
FULLER, WARREN & MORRISON. Ill. catalog of cooking stoves. 12mo., 14pp.

1860 Troy, N. Y.   MH-BA
------ Ill. price list of P. P. Stewart's
improved cooking stoves. Pat. 1859. 12mo.,
24pp., pict. wrap.

1875 Troy, N. Y.   PKsL
FULLER, WARREN & CO. for J.A. Lawson
of Philadelphia. Ill. catalog of Columbia,
Ruby and Pearl styles and models.

1876 Troy, N. Y.   NNMM
------ Ill. and desc. price list of Spirit of
'76, with photo top or cast iron caged reservoir. 1 leaf.

1877 Troy, N. Y. & Chicago   MnHi
------ Ill. catalog of stoves.

1885 Troy, N. Y. & Chicago   MnHi
------ Ill. catalog of stoves.

nd. Detroit, Mich.   PC
GANSON & CO. Ill. circular of the
Defiance #9.

c.1875 Cincinnati   OC
GAUSSEN'S GAS STOVE STORE. Atmos-
pheric gas the fuel of the future - gas cooking and heating stoves of every variety.
12mo., 25pp., wrap.

c.1876 Cincinnati   OC
------ A new departure in domestic
economy - scientific principles - make family cooking at more nominal cost - $75. for
the best, operates at 10¢ an hour - oven or
roaster on the ground floor - to keep the
cook's figure. 8vo., 46pp., wrap.

1868 New York   PC
GIBBS, S. W. Founder. Ill. catalog of
stoves and hollow ware.

nd. Chelsea, Mich.   PC
GLAZIER STOVE CO. Ill. catalog of styles
and models.

1868 Central Falls, R. I.   RHi
GREAT AMERICAN STEAM RANGE CO.
Ill. price list of J.W. Patterson's pat. wrought
iron portable steam ranges, steam coffee

urns, mocha coffee pots, etc. for hotels,
steamships, etc. 24mo., 8pp., fld. plate.

1882-89 Chicago   MnHi
GRIBBEN, SEXTON & CO. Three ill. catalogs of stoves and hollow ware. 1882, 1888
and 1889.

1885 Jersey City   MnHi
GRIFFING, A. A. IRON CO. Ill. catalog and
price list of Bundy pat. direct and indirect
radiators. 8vo., 46pp.

1876 Cincinnati   OC
GROSSIUS, JOHN. Ill. catalog of schoolhouse ventilating stoves and warm air furnaces, registers, etc. 4to., 46pp., frs.

1879 Cincinnati   OC
------ Ill. circular of new improved pat.
schoolhouse ventilating stoves. 4to., 4pp.

1896 Boston   MH-BA
GURNEY HEATER MFG. CO. Ill. price
list of hot water heaters and steam boilers.
4to., 8pp.

1886 Chicago   MnHi
HAY & PRENTICE CO. Ill. price list of
class 2 boilers, radiators, valves and steam
heating specialties to the trade.

1899 St. Louis   MoSHi
HEINE SAFETY BOILER CO. Ill. catalog of
Helios boilers for furnaces and heating plants.

nd. Lancaster, Pa.   PC
HERR & CO. Ill. catalog of heating appliances
and accessories.

1852 Philadelphia   PC
HILL & SCHOOCH. Successors to Frederick
Leibrandt - Union Factory. Ill. catalog of
heaters, ranges and stoves for all purposes.

1881 Buffalo, N. Y.   MnHi
HUBBELL STOVE CO. Ill. catalog of stoves
and hollow ware.

1887 Cleveland, O.   MnHi
HULL VAPOR STOVE CO. Catalog and price
list of vapor stoves, gas and vapors.

nd. Philadelphia   PHi
HYATT & CO., INC. Ill. catalog and price
list of L-Bow heater, stove and furnace pipes
and fittings.

1900 New York   NNMM
JACKSON, EDWIN A. & BROS. Ill., desc.
and priced catalog of ventilating grates, etc.
32pp., wrap. See Architectural Building
Materials and House Furnishings.

c.1884   MBSPNEA
JARVIS FURNACE CO. Ill. circular of
Jarvis pat. furnaces for burning all kinds of
waste, etc. 16mo., 32pp., pict. wrap.

1877 Buffalo, N. Y.   MnHi
JEWETT & ROOT. Ill. catalog of stove
models and styles.

1890 Buffalo, N. Y.   PC
JEWETT, SHERMAN S. & CO. Ill. price
list of stoves for all purposes.

c.1900 Kalamazoo   NNMM
KALAMAZOO STOVE CO. Ill., desc. and
priced catalog of stoves and ranges for all
purposes. 112pp., wrap.

KERN, JOHN JR. & CO. See Baltimore
Stove Works.

1869 New York   NhDY
KEYSER, J. H. & CO. Ill. and desc. list of
furnaces, ranges and stoves. 12mo., 58pp.,
pict. wrap.

KEYSTONE STOVE WORKS. See Boyle &
Carey.

1887 St. Louis   MoSHi
KRAATZ & BROTHER. Ill. catalog of Jumbo
Golden Anvil ranges.

1860 Philadelphia   PC
LEIBRANDT & McDOWELL. Philadelphia
Stove Works & Hollow Ware Foundries. Ill.
catalog of models and styles for all purposes,
hollow ware, etc.

1861 Philadelphia   PHI
------ Ill. catalog of 6 plate models, fancy
styles, irons, kettles, spiders, etc. 8vo.,
88pp. and 3, wrap.

1887 Philadelphia   PHi
------ Ill. catalog of famous oil ranges,
hollow ware, etc. 12mo., 12pp.

1866 Albany, N. Y.   KU
LITTLEFIELD STOVE CO. Origin of the
base-burning stove and mode of operation,
by one who has made a study for thirteen
years. Ill. catalog of the parlor furnace,
Morning Glory model pat. 1860 and 1863.
32mo., 40pp.

nd. Albany, N. Y.   NNMM
------ Ill., desc. and priced catalog of the
West Shore Range and other models. 48pp.

c.1874 Albany, N. Y.   MSwanHi
------ Ill. circular of the Morning Glory
hot-blast cooking stoves and other models
for various places.

c.1895 Waynesboro, Va.   Vi
LOTH'S HEATING CO. Ill. supplement to
#4 catalog - Loth's air-tight heaters for
coal, coke and wood. High grade - low price!

1856 Cincinnati   OC
LOTZE, ADOLPHUS. Remarks upon warming and ventilating public and private buildings and ill. price list of Lotze's pat. furnace. 4to., 24pp.

nd. Albany, N. Y.   NNMM
McCOY & CLARK. Stove Mfg. Ill. catalog
of stoves for all purposes. 28pp.

1856 Albany, N. Y.   NNMM
------ Ill. and desc. circular of stoves.
39pp.

1857 Albany, N. Y.   NNMM
------ Ill. circular. 41pp.

1872 Chelsea, Mass.   PC
MAGEE FURNACE CO. Ill. catalog of furnaces, ranges, cooking and parlor stoves.

1885 Troy, N. Y.   MnHi
MAHONEY, M. Ill. catalog of hot air furnaces.

1899 St. Louis   MoSHi
MAJESTIC MFG. CO. Ill. catalog of stoves
for all purposes.

1874-75 Philadelphia (Limerick Station)
MARCH, SISLER & CO. Ill. cata-   PHi
log of heaters, ranges and stoves - models
and styles. 4to., 40pp., wrap.

c.1858 Westfield, Mass.   MH-BA
MASSACHUSETTS STEAM & WATER HEAT-
ING CO. H. B. Smith Co. Gold's pat. sectional low pressure steam and water heating
apparatus, tests., list of users. 8vo., 24pp.

c.1875 Cincinnati   OC
MEARS, OLHABER & CO. Grand Western!
New coal cook stoves. 4to. broadside.

nd. Cincinnati   OHi
------ Wettengel's continental stove varnish for all heating apparatus. 4to. broadside.

1879-82 Detroit, Mich.   MnHi
MICHIGAN STOVE CO. Est. 1871. Branches
at Buffalo and Chicago. Unusually fine ill.
and desc. catalogs for 1879, 1881 and 1882.
Fine litho. ills. by Cosack & Co. - stoves for
wood and coal, pot belly to Shaker styles -
for farm, church, home, factory, hotel and
store. Pict. wrap.

1900 Philadelphia   PKsL
MODEL HEATING CO. Ill. catalog #5 with
desc. and photos. of models. 8vo., 32pp.

1888   Cleveland, O. & Boston   PC
MONITOR OIL STOVE CO. Ill. catalog -
The Monitor is the only safe oil stove in the
world. Something familiar about that statement.

1880   Danbury, Conn.   CtHi
MORRIS, E. S. & CO. Ill. price list of
Baxter furnaces.

nd.   Middleboro, Mass.   NNMM
MURDOCK PARLOR GRATE CO. Sales
offices in Boston. Ill., desc. and priced circular. 2 lvs.

1886   Middleboro, Mass.   MMidHi
------ Ill. catalog of brass goods,   PC
open fireplaces, fire frames, grates, andirons, Franklin type stoves, parlor stoves,
etc. Tall 8vo., 80pp. of fine ills., wrap.

c.1889 Middleboro, Mass.   NNMM
------ Series 10. Ill. catalog. 200pp. of
ills., dec. wrap.

1853   Philadelphia   PHi
NORTH, CHASE & NORTH. Iron Foundry.
Ill. catalog of cooking, parlor and hall
stoves for every home and shop, hollow ware,
etc. 8vo., 26pp., pict. wrap.

1858   Philadelphia   PHi
------ Price list of hollow ware and hardware goods, etc.

1860   Philadelphia   NNMM
------ Ill. catalog of stoves for   PHi
all purposes. 8vo., 84pp., pict. wrap.

See Sharpe & Thompson, successors 1867.

nd.   North Manchester, Ind.   In
NORTH MANCHESTER FOUNDRY. Price
list of laundry and heating stoves.

1889   Chicago   MnHi
NORTHWESTERN STOVE REPAIR CO. Ill.
catalog of stoves for every trade.

1881   Minneapolis   MnHi
NORTHWESTERN STOVE WORKS. Ill. catalog and price list of superior stoves and
hollow ware. 8vo., 30pp., wrap.

OAKWOOD STOVE & HOLLOW WARE
WORKS. See Bussey, McLeod & Co.

ORIENTAL & AMERICAN STOVE WORKS.
See Perry & Co.

c.1874 Reading, Pa.   PKsL
ORR, PAINTER & CO. Ill. catalog of stoves,
models Anchor, LaBelle, etc.

1886   New York   NHi
PALMER MFG. CO. Price list of stove
boards, stove pipe, collars, stove legs, etc.

c.1871 Troy, N. Y.   NNMM
PARIS, DANIEL E. & CO. Ill. and desc.
catalog of the Mansard cook and Dome Reservoir stoves. 22pp., wrap.

1839   Troy, N. Y.   N
PARKER, S. Pocasset Iron Co. Price list
of parlor wood stoves, Nine-Plate, Guard-
Plate, Flat, Franklin Six-Plate and box
stoves. Mss. note. 1 leaf with 2 engravings. Hollow ware offered from the Pocasset
Iron Co.

1886   New Haven   CtHi
PECK BROTHERS & CO. Ill. catalog of
brass work, pipes, steam fittings, boilers,
radiators, etc. for heating and comfortable
bathing. 8vo., 1070pp. of ills., cl. See
Plumbing.   N.B. When is a plumber not
a plumber -- when he's a steam fitter.

1876   Utica, N. Y.   N
PECKHAM, J. S. & M. Stove Works. Ill.
catalog of stoves and hollow ware - pot
bellies, the Home Radiant, double base burning double duty models, ranges, kettles, pans
and pots. 4to., 12pp., pict. wrap.

1881-82 Utica, N. Y.   MnHi
------ Ill. catalog.

1887-88 Utica, N. Y.   MnHi
------ Ill. catalog.

1882-83 Detroit, Mich.   MnHi
PENINSULAR STOVE CO. Ill. catalog of
stoves, heaters, etc. for kitchen and parlor.

1888   Detroit, Mich.   MnHi
------ Ill. catalog of furnaces and stoves.

1868   Albany, N. Y.   NNMM
PERRY & CO. Oriental & American Stove
Works. Ill. catalog of stoves and furnaces.
48pp., wrap.

1870   Albany, N. Y.   MH-BA
------ Ill. catalog of Oriental base burning
warm air furnaces - St. Albans model, improved hot blast cooking stoves, etc. 8vo.,
36pp.

1875   Albany, N. Y.   NNMM
------ Ill. catalog. 44pp., wrap.

1880   Albany, N. Y.   NNMM
------ Annual catalog with fine pls. and
ills. with details of models. 112pp., cl.

1881   Albany, N. Y.   NNMM
------ Supplementary catalog of new models with fine ills. 48pp., wrap.

1868-95 Albany, N. Y.   PC
------ Ill. catalogs and circulars for 1868,
c.1870, 1878, 1881 and 1895.

1891 Geneva, N. Y.   PC
PHILLIPS & CLARK STOVE CO. Ill. catalog and price list, fine pls. of models and
styles. 12mo., 128pp., pict. stiff wrap. of
works.

1874 Plymouth, Mass.   PC
PLYMOUTH FOUNDRY CO. Ill. catalog of
stoves for ships, cabooses and other specialties.

POCASSET IRON CO. See S. Parker.

1855 Boston   NNMM
POND & DUNKLEE. Ill. catalog of ventilating heaters, Boylton's pat., portable furnaces,
the Coronet, wood stoves for railway cars,
etc. See Architectural Building Materials.

1861 Troy, N. Y.   MH-BA
PORTER & CO. Ill. catalog of stoves -
annotated. Large 8vo., 40pp.

c.1867 Boston   NNMM
PRATT & WENTWORTH. Peerless stoves
for coal or wood. 1 leaf, 1 ill.

nd. Boston   NNMM
------ Retail price list of stoves and
hollow ware. 2 lvs.

1885 St. Paul, Minn.   MnHi
PRUDEN STOVE CO. Ill. catalog and price
list of heaters, ranges and stoves, especially
adapted to wants of the Northwest. 4to., 24pp.

QUAKERTOWN STOVE WORKS. See
Thomas, Roberts & Stevenson.

1872-74 Albany, N. Y.   PC
RANSOM STOVE WORKS. Ill. catalog of
stoves and hollow ware.

1882 Albany, N. Y.   MnHi
------ Ill. catalog.

1887 Albany, N. Y.   NNMM
------ Ill. catalog of stoves and all manner
of hollow ware. 108pp., wrap.

1853 Albany, N. Y.   NNMM
RATHBONE & CO. Ill. and desc. catalog of
stoves, styles and models. 36pp.

1854 Albany, N. Y.   MH-BA
------ Rathbone & Kennedy -   NNMM
formerly Rathbone & Co. Ill. catalog of
stoves and hollow ware. Large 8vo., 56pp.

1855 Albany, N. Y.   NNMM
------ Ill. circular. 50pp.

1856 Albany, N. Y.   NNMM
------ Ill. catalog. 16 lvs.

1857 Albany, N. Y.   NNMM
------ Ill. catalog of stoves and hollow
ware. 41 lvs.

1859 Albany, N. Y.   NNMM
------ Ill. catalog of new models. 56pp.

1859 Albany, N. Y.   ICHi
------ Ill. circular of the Good Samaritan
cooking stove. 16mo., 31pp., pict. wrap.

c.1859 Albany, N. Y.   NNMM
------ Catalog of the original smoke and
gas burner - The Albanian model. 30pp.

1861 Albany, N. Y.   MH-BA
------ John F. Rathbone - formerly Rathbone & Kennedy. Ill. circular of the Good
Samaritan Cooking Stove. Pat. 1859. 16mo.,
32pp., wrap.

1861 Albany, N. Y.   MH-BA
------ Ill. catalog of new model stoves and
hollow ware. 7x10, 58pp., wrap.

1889 Albany, N. Y.   N
Branches in Detroit & Chicago.
RATHBONE, SARD & CO. Ill. catalog of
Acorn stoves and ranges, pls. of foundries
and works, models and styles from Shaker
designs to vapor varieties for parlor, bedroom and bath. 16mo., 125pp., glt. pict. wrap.

c.1889 Middletown, Pa.   MdTanSW
RAYMOND & CAMPBELL. Ill. catalog in
guise of a cook book: Good Old Pennsylvania
Cooking Recipes. Ills. of models; Grand
Perfect, Capital, New Pullman, Anna, Grand
Climax, Pride, Susquehanna and Hustler
heaters. 32pp.

1876 Reading, Pa.   PHi
READING HARDWARE CO. Ill. catalog of
warm air registers, etc. 12mo., 26pp., fine
ills. - for September.

1874 Reading, Pa.   PKsL
READING STOVE & HOLLOW   PHi
WARE WORKS. Orr, Painter & Co. Ill.
catalog and price list of stoves, kettles,
caldrons, grates, castings, index, fine pls.
4to., 92pp.

1876 Reading, Pa.   PHi
------ Ill. catalog of warm air registers.
12mo., 26pp., pict. wrap.

1878 Reading, Pa.   PHi
------ Ill. catalog and several circulars
and supplements.

1883-84 Cincinnati   MnHi
REDWAY & BURTON. Ill. catalog of Fault-
less stoves in various sizes and styles.

1887 Chicago   MnHi
RENDTORFF, H. & CO. Ill. catalog of stove
boards.

1852 Cincinnati   OC
RESOR, W. & R. P. & CO. Ill. catalog of
Chilson's pat. air warming and ventilating
furnaces for public and private buildings.
8vo., 48pp.

N.B. Both the Plymouth Church, Brooklyn,
     N. Y. and the Reverend Henry Ward
Beecher were warmed by this furnace.
Probably that scandal would hever have happened if the lady had not stopped by to warm
up beside Chilson's patent air warming furnace. I strongly suspect that the real story
is that the furnace was out of order, and the
good pastor being a gentleman offered to
keep her warm -- and, well, one thing led to
another -- and the story got out.

1878 Cincinnati   OC
RESOR, WILLIAM & CO. Wholesale ill.
price list of stoves and hollow ware for all.
12mo., 76pp.

1884 Cincinnati   MnHi
------ Ill. catalog of improved stove models and hollow ware.

1885 Cincinnati   MnHi
------ Ill. catalog.

1879 Providence, R. I.   RHi
RETORT GAS STOVE CO. Ill. catalog of
new designs for parlor and kitchen. 14pp.,
glt. pict. wrap.

1882 Providence, R. I.   RHi
------ Ill. catalog of stoves and cooking
utensils, pots and pans, etc. 12mo., 20pp.,
glt. pict. wrap.

c.1873 Philadelphia   DSI
REYNOLDS, J. & SON. Ill. and desc. catalog of heating furnaces. 62pp.

1885 New York & Chicago   MnHi
RICHARDSON & BOYNTON. Ill. trade price
list of hot air heaters, furnaces, fireplaces,
etc.

1886 New York & Chicago   MnHi
------ The new Perfect warm air and
steam heating stoves and furnaces.

1891 New York & Chicago   ICU
------ Ill. catalog of Perfect heaters, furnaces and ranges. 8vo., 72pp., pict. wrap.

nd. New York   NNMM
RICHARDSON & MORGAN CO. Pilgrim
combination heating and cooking ranges and
stoves. 1 leaf.

1885 Norwich, Conn.   CtHi
RICHMOND STOVE CO. Ill. circular of the
Fern-Base oil burners, pict. wrap.

1886 Norwich, Conn.   MnHi
------ Ill. catalog of Richmond warm air
ranges, stoves and furnaces.

1882 Evansville   MnHi
ROELKER, JOHN H. & CO. Ill. catalog of
Fame cookery stoves.

1888 Utica, N. Y.   MnHi
SAYRE, OWENS & CO. Ill. catalog of Union,
Oneida and Tubular hot air furnaces.

1892 Cleveland, O.   OHi
SCHNEIDER & TRENKAMP CO. Ill. catalog
of Reliable gas stoves.

c.1875 Providence, R. I.   MH-BA
SELF-ACTING HEAT GOVERNOR CO. Ill.
circular of Tingley's automatic heat governor for hot air furnaces. 8vo., 36pp.

1870 Royer's Ford, Pa.   PC
SHANTZ & KEELEY. Springville Stove &
Hollow Ware Works. Ill. catalog of models
of improved stoves.

1867 Philadelphia   PHi
SHARPE & THOMPSON. Successors to
North, Chase & North. Ill. catalog of ranges,
heaters, stoves, plain, turned and tinned
hollow ware, fire frames, vases, castings
and urns. 8vo., 56pp., wrap.

1868-69 Philadelphia   PHi
------ Ill. catalog with fld. pls. 8vo., 64pp.

1863 Albany, N. Y.   MH-BA
SHEAR, PACKARD & CO. Ill.   PC
catalog of American hot air gas burning cooking stoves for coal or wood. 12mo., 24pp.

SHEELER & BUCKWALTER. See Hardware
- General Goods.

1892 Philadelphia & Baltimore   MH-BA
SHEPPARD, ISAAC & CO. Hints about Heating - ill. catalog of Paragon steel plate furnaces. Pat. 1890. 12mo., 64pp., pict. wrap.

c.1900 Brooklyn, N. Y.   NNQ
SILVER & CO. Ill. catalog of oil heaters
and stoves.

1889 Toledo, O.   DAIA
                        IU   IHi   DSi
SMEAD, ISAAC D. & CO. Warming and
Ventilation of Buildings. Sm. 4to., 154pp.,
col. pls. as well as fine black and white of
models of Smead Stoves and Furnaces -
under 13 pat. - and pls. of school and public
buildings all over the country, costs, etc.

Everything but a price list. Cl. N.B. Last minute decision - locations not complete.

1885 Boston   PC
SMITH & ANTHONY STOVE CO. Some Artistic Fireplaces. Ills. of models - Hub Franklin, Canopy Franklin, Rideau, Lion Backs, andirons, firebacks, etc. Sq.12mo., 40pp., pict. wrap.

1886 Boston   DSi
------ Our Homes - How to Heat   ICU
and Ventilate Them. Ills. of stoves, etc. Hubs, ranges, furnaces. 8vo., 96pp., wrap.

1887 Boston   NNMM
------ Ill. catalog of some artistic fireplaces and heating stoves. 48pp.

1887 Boston   MH-BA
------ Ill. catalog of Anthony steel plate furnaces - Homes and how to heat them - 12mo., 112pp., pict. wrap.

c.1875 Westfield, Mass.   MH-BA
SMITH, H. B. & CO. Est. 1853. Ill. catalog of Gold's steam and water warming and ventilating apparatus. List of users. 8vo., 42pp.

1892 Providence, R. I.   RHi
SPICER STOVE CO. Ill. catalog of Model and Grand Model ranges, stoves and furnaces - open model Franklin stoves, charcoal furnaces, field stoves - often mislabeled Civil War and Revolutionary by the uninformed - hollow ware. Fol., 80pp. of pls.

1892 New York & v.p.   PC
STANDARD OIL CO. Two col. ill. circulars with styles and prices; Summer Comfort, and Here's What the Newspapers Say.

N.B. Have we already thrown out all of the early Standard Oil catalogs?

1835 New York   PC
STANLEY, M. N. & CO. Ill. catalog of Stanley's pat. rotary cooking stoves - remarks and directions - woodcut on title page. 32mo., 12pp., ptd. G. F. Bunce.

1836 New York   NHi
------ Catalog for 1836. 32mo., 12pp.

c.1886 Boston   MH-BA
STEVENS, LEVI. Ill. circular of Stevens' regenerative boiler furnaces. 8vo., 5pp.

1844 Chicago   PC
STEWART, P. P. Stewart's pat. Summer and Winter air tight cooking stoves.

c.1860 Chicago   PC
------ Ill. circular of Stewart's pat. Greenman & Northrup air tight stoves for all. 12mo., wrap.

1865 Chicago   ICHi
------ Ill. catalog of Stewart's large oven air tight cooking stoves. 12mo., 24pp., pict. wrap.

1896 Boston   DSi
STURTEVANT, B. F. & CO. A treatise on heating and ventilation. 169pp. I suspect a good sales talk in this with ills., though I have to confess I am relying on the librarian.

1893 Little Falls, N. Y.   PC
SUPERIOR FURNACE CO. Ill. catalog. Some fine col. lithos. Steel furnaces, combination steam and hot water heaters for churches, homes, hotels, banks, schools, stores, etc. Lithos. by J. Ottmann Litho. Co. 8vo., 48pp.

1893 Philadelphia   PKsL
SWEENY, GEORGE & CO. Mfg. Ill. catalog of stove linings, fire bricks, cylinders, bakers' ovens, heater and range linings, etc.

1869 Troy, N. Y.   PC
SWETT, QUIMBY & PERRY. Empire Stove Works. Ill. circular of the New Empire - Hot air, gas and base burning stoves for coal and wood.

c.1890 Taunton, Mass.   MTaHi
TAUNTON IRON WORKS. Ill.   PC
catalog of the Quaker Price stoves.

1868 Quakertown & Philadelphia, Pa. PHi
THOMAS, ROBERTS, STEVENSON & CO. FOUNDRY. Ill. catalog of fine stoves and hollow ware, fancy gates, fences and ornamental ironwork. 4to., 24pp., fine pls.

1869 Quakertown & Philadelphia, Pa. NNMM
------ Ill. catalog and price list PHi
of fine stoves and hollow ware, iron railings, gate posts, etc. Fine pls., wrap.

1874 Quakertown & Philadelphia, Pa. PHi
------ Ill. catalog of new styles and models. 4to., 22pp., pict. wrap.

1860 Troy, N. Y.   MH-BA
TIBBITS & McCOUN. Mfg. Ill. circular of the new Steward - a new tight large oven cooking stove. Pat. 1860. 8vo., 8pp.

1860 Albany, N. Y.   N
TREADWELL, W. & J. Perry & Norton, Eagle Foundry. Ill. catalog of The Economist, Star of the North - models for wood or coal, with or without the new Sand ovens. Pat. J. Easterly 1858. 16mo., 24pp., pict. wrap.

1886 New York & St. Louis   MoSHi
TUTTLE & BAILEY MFG. CO.   NNMM
Pullis Brothers, Mississippi Iron Works. Ill. and desc. catalog of warm air registers, ventilators with iron and soapstone borders,

ornamental screens, etc. 12mo., 32pp., wrap. Also 1879 and 1882 records privately owned.

1876-78 Peekskill, N. Y.   MnHi
UNION STOVE WORKS. Two ill. catalogs of models and styles.

1865 Boston   MH-BA
UNION WARMING & VENTILATING CO. Ill. catalog of steam and water warming and ventilating apparatus mfg. under Gold's pat. with Campbell's improvements. List of users. 12mo., 20pp.

1889 Elizabeth, N. J.   PC
UNITED STATES FUEL CO. Sestalit, the marvelous fuel - with ill. and desc. catalog of stoves and heaters for using this new fuel.

1889 St. Paul, Minn.   MnHi
UNITED STATES STOVE CO. Ill. catalog of straw and hay furnaces, also coal and wood stoves for cooking, and cooking utensils and specialties. 8vo., 16pp. with broadside tipped in.

1850 Troy, N. Y.   NNMM
VIALL, HOUSE & MANN. Ill. and desc. price list of stoves for parlor and kitchen. 15pp., wrap.

VICTOR FOUNDRY, THE. See Charles Eddy & Co.

1853 Albany, N. Y.   NNMM
VOSE & CO. Ill. Book of Stoves - models and styles. 87 lvs. with pls. 1 to XXVII.

1870 Troy, N. Y.   MnHi
WAGER, FALES & CO. Ill. catalog of stoves and hollow ware.

1883 Boston   MnHi
WAINWRIGHT MFG. CO. Ill. catalog of Wainwright heaters, condensers and filters.

1869 Boston   NNMM
WALKER, GEORGE W. & CO. Ill., desc. and priced circular for Walker's tubular dome furnace. 2 lvs.

c.1873 Lebanon, Pa.   PKsL
WEIMER MACHINE WORKS. Est. 1856. Ill. price list of Weimer's shell coil tuyeres. Pat. 1871.

1887 Philadelphia   PKsL
WEIR & NIXON. Ill. catalog of Weir & Nixon's steam and hot air heating apparatus. 8vo., 24pp., pict. wrap.

1879 Taunton, Mass.   MTaHi
WEIR STOVE CO. Ill., desc. and   NNMM
priced trade list of models and styles of improved stoves. 16pp., wrap.

nd. Taunton, Mass.   NNMM
------ Ill. catalog of Glenwood stoves and ranges. 6 lvs., wrap.

1879 Utica, N. Y.   MnHi
WHEELER, RUSSELL, SON & CO. Ill. catalog of stoves and hollow ware.

c.1883 Utica, N. Y.   MnHi
------ Ill. catalog of ranges, stoves and hot air furnaces - models Shaker type, pot belly, cylinder, etc. Hollow ware of all kinds, etc. Large 4to., 74pp., fine pls., pict. wrap.

1862 Taunton, Mass.   MTaOC
WHITTENTON STOVE FOUNDRY. L. M. Leonard, Prop. List of stoves and hollow ware and circular of prices. Ills. of Orion, Spartan, Monteveu, Corinthian, Gazelle, Boston Belle, Enterprise, Arctic, Tropic. Dish kettles, scotch bowls, one armed griddles, etc. 8vo., 20pp., fine ills., glt. dec. wrap.

nd. Philadelphia   PHi
WILLIAM, CHARLES. Price list of heating and ventilating apparatus. 8vo., 25pp.

1895 Chicago   MH-BA
WIRETON HEATING CO. Ill. circular D - celebrated lowdown double burner magazine and Panama furnaces. 8x8, 34pp.

c.1886 St. Paul, Minn.   MnHi
WOLTERSTORFF & MORITZ. St. Paul Tin & Sheet Iron Works. Ill. catalog of the Commander wrought iron ranges, steam tables, carving tables, broilers, bar, coffee and tea urns and new Commander and Harris furnaces. 4to., 8pp.

1896 St. Louis   MoSHi
WROUGHT RANGE STOVE CO. Est. 1864. Ill. catalog of home comfort steel ranges for private families, hotels, restaurants, army posts, dining cars, steamboats - also cooking utensils, etc. with col. pict. wrap., plate of plant, list of steamboats and railroads, showing distribution throughout the country. 4to., 126pp., pls. and pict. wrap.

STOVES

As long ago as 1844, when James J. Walworth and Joseph Nason installed a system for heating the lobby and halls of the famous old Astor House on Broadway, the plumber and steam fitter was the mechanic who not only drew your bath but heated it for you. This may be a slight exaggeration, but when you examine the James J. Walworth illustrated catalogs of goods and equipment for plumbers and steam fitters in 1870 you will agree that, give or take a few years, his connection with heating and cooking is almost as important as his indispensability as Master of the Bath. When this chapter has you all warmed up and snug as a bug, and you need a shower, remember to follow through. Check Plumbing, and of course Hardware - Miscellaneous Supplies for the bathing facilities c.1860.

Chapter 55

Telephones

There are two ways of looking at telephones. If you are just out of college and just starting in business, they are a plastic convenience that by pressing buttons and dialing numbers put you in instant touch with any prospect in the country. If you are the blushing bride housewife species, they are little delicately fashioned gadgets, colored to match your eyes or the sofa, that bring you the local and national gossip. On the other hand, if you have survived for say sixty or seventy years and watched them change, they are a more personal part of your life. They always remind me of Fibber McGee. I still like to pick up the instrument and chat with the operators. It was more fun to drop in at the corner store, twirl the old bell and have a little trouble getting your girl on the other end, than to dial a cold impersonal automatic machine that only buzzes at you in answer.

Throughout this chapter you will find illustrated records of those early personal telephones. You will also find telegraphic apparatus and other electrical instruments that have been swallowed up and forgotten in our mad rush into this great atomic world of conveniences that will eventually make us a race of money making machines. Since machines have no appreciation of conveniences, and less of history, what price progress.

1887 Portland, Me.   MBT&T
AMERICAN ACOUSTIC CO. Ill. circular of mechanical, or acoustic telephones and signals. 16mo., 20pp., pict. wrap.

1882 Boston   MBT&T
AMERICAN BELL TELEPHONE   PC
CO. A Description of the Telephone and of the Apparatus Used in Connection Therewith, with ills. 8vo., 29pp., 14 detailed sketches of apparatus and a complete price list, wrap.

1869 New York   MH-BA
AMERICAN COMPOUND TELEGRAPH WIRE CO. Desc. circular of wires and instruments. 18mo., 30pp.

1870 Charlotte, Mich.   MiU-T
CHARLOTTE TELEPHONE CO. Ill. circular of the new Charlotte telephones and vocal phonometer - most wonderful invention of the age - complete $10. with a half mile of wire.

1861 New York   Sabin #12515
CHESTER, C.T. & J.N.   MH   NHi
Ill. catalog of telegraphic materials. 8vo., 42pp., appendix, wrap.

1868 New York   PC
------ Ill. catalog. 8vo., 48pp., glt. dec. wrap.

c.1882 Boston   MBT&T
DOLBEAR TELEPHONE CO. Owners of the Dolbear System. Desc. of Dolbear tele-

phones. 8vo., 24pp. with ills., wrap.

N.B. Not a catalog exactly but an ill. record. Issued because of a suit, with a history from 1837 to 1882.

c.1885 Boston   MH-BA
ELECTRIC PROTECTOR CO. OF NEW ENGLAND. Desc. circular of automatic safety devices for use with telephones and other electric instruments. 8vo., 46pp.

1889 Mooresville, Ind.   In
(Moved to Martinsville, Ind.)
ELLIOT TELEPHONE CO. (sic) Spelled Elliott in catalog. Ill. catalog of Elliott non electric telephones, unequaled for low prices, works to perfection two miles or less. Have you a wife? Ask her to read this! 16mo., 32pp., pict. wrap.

nd. New York   PKsL
GREELEY, E. S. & CO. Special ill. catalog of telegraph and telephone supplies, wire, batteries, tools, etc. See also Homacoustic Apparatus Co.

1878 Mallet Creek, O.   ICTPA
HOLCOMB'S ACOUSTIC TELE-   OHi
PHONE CO. Ill. circular for Holcomb's acoustic speaking telephones, pat. Only telephone having a clear title - compound diaphram with nickel mountings - guaranteed for one mile. 16mo., 4pp.

1893 Chicago (?)   PC
HOMACOUSTIC APPARATUS CO. Ill. catalog of Cutmore's pat. at the World's Fair, Space 13, Group J. (E.S. Greeley, agent.) 16mo., 24pp., delightful cuts, pict. wrap.

1888 Portland, Me. & Boston   MH-BA
LORD ACOUSTIC TELEPHONE MFG. CO. Portland headquarters - leased to Mass.

Sketch of advantages and business with 6 pls. showing telephones in operation in home, factory and warehouse. 12mo., 20pp., glt. pict. wrap.

1896 New York   MH-BA
MANHATTAN ELECTRIC SUPPLY CO. Ill. catalog of electric telephones and electrical supplies. 12mo., 64pp.

1888 New York   N
MANHATTAN TELEPHONE CO. Manhattan telephones, guaranteed to work - sold outright at moderate prices. Ill. circular, 12mo., 24pp., pict. wrap.

c.1875 Philadelphia   PKsL
PATRICK & CARTER. Ill. catalog of telephones and electric instruments and supplies. 8vo., 48pp., pict. wrap.

c.1884 Providence, R. I.   MH-BA
RHODE ISLAND TELEPHONE & ELECTRIC CO. Ill. catalog of telephones and electric supplies. Large 8vo., 14pp.

1887 Rochester, N. Y.   NR
ROCHESTER TELEPHONE CO. Ill. circular of telephone instruments, batteries, bells, etc.

1890 New York
SHAVER CORP. Molecular telephones and central office apparatus - private lines, etc. 8vo., 20pp., ills. of styles A, B, C, D, E, F, G, H and J boards, etc., pict. wrap.

1893 New York   N
STANLEY & PATTERSON. Ill. catalog of telephones, bells, batteries, parts - not to mention toy telephones, boats, trains, etc. - fans, lights, cigar lighters, etc. Sq. 12mo., 432pp., dec. wrap.

c.1870 New York   NjOE
TILLOTSON, L. G. & CO. Ill. price list of telegraphic machines and instruments, parts and supplies. 116pp., pict. wrap.

c.1872 New York   NHi
------ Ill. catalog. 8vo., 248pp., 18th ed., wrap.

c.1880 Brooklyn, N. Y.   NNQ
TUCKER, CHARLES A. Ill. price list of electric goods - telephone supplies, bells, alarms, batteries and instruments. 16mo., 12pp., dec. wrap.

c.1898 Peoria, Ill.   N
U. S. ELECTRIC SUPPLY CO. Ill. catalog #20 - telephones and electrical apparatus, batteries, bells, battery jobs in oak cases with ringers. Swell record. 4to., 96pp.

1876 Chicago   NjOE
WESTERN ELECTRIC MFG. CO. Ill. catalog of telegraph instruments and supplies, electro-medical batteries, telegraph printing instruments, etc. 88pp., pict. wrap.

1878 Chicago   NjOE
------ Ill. catalog for 1878.

1898 Boston   MBT&T
WHITMAN & COUCH. Ill. catalog C - Telephones, complete equipment, exchanges, private lines, Bi-Polar receivers and attachments, etc.

There are business repositories that have not been checked. If you want to search further, I suggest such libraries as American Tel. and Tel., New England Tel. and Tel., and the Telephone Pioneers of America. I am sure there are other telephone catalogs in our state historical society libraries and state libraries. I am quite sure the Smithsonian Institution must have unreported issues. I have done a good deal of work in many fields; if you find more, let me know - there can always be a second, revised edition.

Chapter 56

Toys, Games & Entertainment

From the maternity ward to the cemetery the human animal never tires of toys. Rattles and rag dolls may change to miniature railroads and baseball bats but the fundamental passion for being entertained never blacks out entirely. Even when the undertaker has his eye on great grandfather, the old chap is often found waving a rattle or watching the latest Ives creation in Sonny's playroom. This is only a guide to source material. If you want reading matter about this colorful thing we call life, take a look at the Freeman's Cavalcade of Toys, published by Century House in 1942, or Riding the Tinplate Rails by Louis H. Hertz, Model Craftsman Publishing Corp., 1944. Both books will not only trace the history of toys and toy making, but prove the importance and value of trade catalogs.

Toys were probably created in the Stone Age. When Father made a huge killer-diller out of a small tree trunk split at one end to hold a boulder, he may have handed little Jimmy a twig and explained how to swat a bug with it. Just when toy making became an industry is hard to say. Charles Morrow Wilson believes that the Yankee craftsmen of Vermont were the first to make toys as toys and not merely as miniature copies of grownup gadgets. This American development had its start in Vermont about 1810, and even before the Civil War, was flooding the markets at home and abroad.

From the catalog standpoint, although blacksmiths, carpenters and tinsmiths made toys for their little ones as a sideline from the earliest times, there are very few listings before 1850. Collectors, historians and students will find in this chapter a selective sampling well placed in many of our best reference libraries.

nd. New Haven   CtHi
ART FABRIC MILLS. Price list of cloth toys, rag dolls and art pillows - ptd. in oil colors on durable cloth. Large 8vo., 4pp.

1860 Cincinnati   OC
BART & HICKCOX. Ill. and desc. catalog of India rubber and gutta percha goods - fancy goods and childrens' toys - firemens' coats, opera hats, diving suits, flasks, etc., rubber animals and novelties. 8vo., 96pp., dec. cl.

BATES, G.H.W. & CO. See Musical Instruments.

c.1872 Paterson   NjR
BEGGS, EUGENE. One of the first - if not the first - American mfg. of toy steam engines, locomotives, steamboats, etc. Beggs' miniature steam locomotive and rail-way. Price list with engraving. 1 leaf, Pat. Sept. 19, 1871.

1879-80 Springfield, Mass.   N
BRADLEY, MILTON & CO. Est. 1860. Still in business and going strong. Ill. cat-alog of Bradley's home amusements, toys and novelties - the Centennalia, panoramas, tableaux, steam fire engines, Hippodrome, Texas ranch, railroads, etc. 8vo., 32pp. and 4pp., pict. wrap.

1884 Springfield, Mass.   ICHi
------ Ill. catalog with fine col. pls. of American menagerie, Aquarium, Zeotrope, historiscope, American fire dept., etc. 8vo., 56pp., col. pict. wrap.

1873 New York   NNMM
BUCKMAN MFG. CO. Ill. catalog of novel-ties - steam toys a specialty - steamboats, steam fire engines and locomotives. 4to., 12pp.

Beggs and Buckman were the pioneers in this field. See Drepperd and Freeman - suggested homework and bedtime reading.

1871 Upper Falls, Vt.   NNMM
BURKE, COOK & TAYLOR. Ill.   VtHi
catalog of dolls' beds, tops, toy towel racks, etc. - also turned wood handles for brushes, shovels, pails, forks, rakes and other tools. 12mo., 8pp., wrap.

Recently, a soft pink plastic handle on a dish mop came off in my hands - why wouldn't it? The atomic machine that made the gadget only allowed the wire a 1/2 in. purchase - I found an old c.1870 wooden one in the barn. I'm still using it and am sure it will outlast the mop.

1871 New York   NNMM
BURKE, GEORGE H. Agent.   VtHi
Combination catalog of toys mfg. by Burke,
Cook & Taylor, R. Cobleigh, Smith, Burr &
Co. and Springfield Toy Co. See each for
details of this catalog.

BUTLER BROTHERS. See Department and
Miscellaneous Stores.

1899 Cincinnati   OC
CARLISLE & FINCH CO. (Agent for Ohio
Electric Works.) Ill. catalog B, #4. Electric novelties, experimental apparatus,
dynamos and motors, gas engines - toy
trains, etc. 12mo., 40pp., wrap.

c.1900 Cincinnati   OC
------ Ill. catalog of miniature electric
railways, locomotives, passenger and freight
cars, switches, tracks, stations, etc. 12mo.,
78pp., pict. wrap.

c.1900 Ludington, Mich.   NNMM
CARROM-ARCHARENA CO. Ill., desc. and
priced catalog of games, game boards and
toys. 32pp., pict. wrap.

c.1878 Albany, N. Y. & Philadelphia
CLARK, IRVING D. & CO. Please preserve
this circular - Pat. Leaping Horses for boys
and girls, swings, velocipedes, etc. 64mo.,
4pp., 4 ills.

1871 Chester, Vt.   NNMM
COBLEIGH, R. Ill. catalog of   VtHi
childrens' and dolls' stenciled carriages,
sleds, wagons, etc. Gipsy Gig, chaise,
perambulators, sleds, sleighs, etc. 12mo.,
20pp., pict. wrap.

1866 Waterbury, Vt.   MH-BA
COLBY BROTHERS & CO. Ill. catalog of
childrens' carriages, willow ware, baskets,
etc. 24mo., 24pp.

1890 Columbia, Pa.   PKsL
COLUMBIA GREY IRON CO. Ill. catalog of
novelties and toys - iron pull toys, penny
banks - and also match safes, boot jacks,
pot rests, etc. 12mo., 112pp., pict. wrap.

c.1885 Hartford, Conn.   CtHi
CONNECTICUT MFG. CO. Ill. monthly catalog of books, novelties, toys, games, etc.
8vo., pict. wrap.

nd. Noank, Conn.   CtHi
CONNECTICUT TOY & NOVELTY MFG.
CO. American made toys - toy soldiers
specialties. 4to., 1 leaf, ill.

c.1870 Boston   NHi
CUTTER, HYDE & CO. Est. 1861. Twenty
third annual catalog of staple and fancy
goods, toys, etc. - ills. of penny banks - Race

Course Bank! - dolls, hot air toys, tea sets,
doll houses, tops, cap pistols, pull toys,
trains, etc. 12mo., 48pp., pict. wrap. Since
1861 - the best stock in America!

1878 New York   MH-BA
DARE, C. W. F. Ill. and desc.   NNMM
catalog of perambulators, bicycles, rocking
horses, wagons, etc. 12mo., 8pp., pict. wrap.

1862 Springfield, Vt.   VtHi
ELLIS, BRITTON & EATON NOVELTY
WORKS. Desc. and ill. catalog of childrens'
toys, doll carriages, carts, wagons, stilts,
cannon, building toys, doll houses, etc.
12mo., 22pp., pict. wrap.

1866 Springfield, Vt.   VtHi
------ Ill. supplement to price list - new
toys, sleds, dolls' rocking chairs, beds, play
houses - so constructed as to be taken all to
pieces and rebuilt - a fine record. 12mo.,
12pp., wrap.

1869 Springfield, Vt.   PC
------ Ill. catalog of hobby horses, dolls,
doll furniture, iron toys, pull toys, sleds,
wagons and a complete line of wooden ware.

ENTERPRISE MFG. CO. See House
Furnishings.

1856 Boston   MiDbF
FARRAR, A. F. Successor to George N.
Davis. Ill. and desc. catalog of India rubber
and gutta percha goods. Painted toys, dolls,
animals firemen and other human figures
for the kids, as well as camp equipment,
flasks, diving armor, boats and clothing.
8vo., 96pp., cl.

c.1890 New York   NSbSM
FARRELL, CHARLES. Ill. catalog of the
latest, best and fastest selling novelties,
games, tricks and toys. 8vo., 32pp.

1880 Providence, R. I.   RHi
FERRIN, FRANK C. Catalog of toys, fancy
goods, novelties, ornaments, air pistols,
valentines, etc. 12mo., 60pp., wrap.

1880 New York   NNMM
FISH & SIMPSON. Ill. catalog of skates,
guns, novelties, tricks and toys. Fol., 4pp.

c.1880 New York   NNMM
------ List of sporting goods - flies, flasks,
uniforms for all sports, games and toys.
Fol.

c.1885 New York   NhHi
FOULDS, ROBERT. (Foulds was agent for
several small toy manufacturers.) Ill. catalog and price list of domestic and imported
toys, dolls, dolls' clothes, penny banks, pull
and mechanical iron toys, tin toys, music

boxes, cap pistols, rattles, magic lanterns
and slides, etc. 8vo., 72pp., pict. wrap.

c.1886 New York   MdTanSW
------ Ill. catalog of dolls, fireworks, toys,
etc. 8vo., 68pp., pict. wrap.

GOULD, W. R. See West & Lee.

1895 Lockport, N. Y.   N
GRAND CENTRAL NOVELTY CO. Ill. catalog of novelties - penny banks, games,
emblems, watches, toys and tricks. 4to.,
32pp., pict. wrap.

HASLET, FLANAGEN & CO. (Toy banks
and tin toys) See House Furnishings.

1870 Philadelphia   PKsL
HINRICH'S. Formerly Werckmeister's.
70th annual display - Santa Claus is coming -
tinted ills. - lists of toys and novelties with
Clement Moore's Night Before Christmas
thrown in for good measure. 8vo., 8pp.,
pict. wrap.

nd. New Haven   CtHi
HULL'S HOBBIES. Fun for every member
of the family - 50 exciting hobby and craft
items selected by a panel of merchandisers.
8vo., 15pp., ills., ptd. in red and black.

nd. Port Huron, Mich.   ICHi
INTERSTATE MFG. CO. Introductory ill.
catalog of rocking horses, goats and swans
for little ones. 16mo., 12pp. of delightful
creations.

1878 Chicago   ICHi
INVENTORS' AGENCY. Our Monthly pamphlet of newly pat. articles for agents - ills.
of magic lanterns, coin box machines, novelties, tricks, etc. Sq. 16mo., 16pp., ills.,
wrap. A useful catalog in a way since it
ills. contemporary inventions and creations.

nd. Bridgeport, Conn.   CtHi
IVES MFG. CORP. Ill. catalog of Ives toys -
electrical and mechanical miniature railways, etc. 8vo., 24pp., pict. wrap.

N.B. CtHi also has later Ives catalogs.

c.1866 n.p.   NNMM
JUVENILE CARRIAGE WORKS. Ill. catalog
of doll perambulators, velocipedes, shoo-
fly horses, round-back shoo-fly and rattan
gig rockers, goat wagons and chariots, new
style sleds and spring style rocking horses,
etc. 8vo., 20pp. Incomplete, but a fine ill.
record of a whale of a lot of toys our youngsters will never even know about unless we
take care of the catalogs. You can count on
NNMM's print department to preserve what
others discard through lack of imagination
and historical appreciation.

1882 New York   NHi
LAUER, C. F. Desc. catalog of notions,
fancy goods, toys, penny banks, pull and
mechanical toys. 8vo., 52pp., wrap.

LEWIS, G. W. See Art Fabric Mills.

1874 Ludlow, Vt.   VtHi
LUDLOW TOY MFG. CO. Ill. catalog of
doll perambulators, carts, wagons, sleighs
and sleds, wheelbarrows, etc. - and other
toys. 16mo., 18pp., pict. wrap.

1886 Ludlow, Vt.   VtHi
------ Fall catalog. 14th ill. price list of
dolls and toys, etc. 16mo., 28pp., pict.wrap.

c.1890 New York   NSbSM
LYON, AMOS M. Ill. catalog of dolls, tin
and iron toys, games, penny banks, drums,
etc. 4to., 24pp., pict. wrap.

1890 New York   NNMM
MACE, J.H. & CO. Ill., desc. and priced
catalog of domestic and imported toys - tin,
wood, iron - pull and mechanical. 80pp.

1898 New York   NHi
MARTINKA & CO. Ill. and desc. catalog of
conjuring wonders, sets and cabinets of
tricks. 8vo., pict. wrap.

1856 Durham, Conn.   CtHi
MERRIAM MFG. CO. Price list of Japanned
and stamped tinware, tin toys, etc. and Britannia ware. 16mo., 19pp.

c.1866 New York   PC
NEW BRUNSWICK RUBBER CO. Prices
current of balls, dolls and toys - footballs,
lions, monkeys, dogs, cats, eagles, soldiers,
roly-polys and even elephants. 4to., 4pp.

1876 Worcester, Mass.   MWA
NOYES, SNOW & CO. Ill. catalog of games
and home amusements. 12mo., 32pp., wrap.

OHIO ELECTRIC WORKS. See Carlisle &
Finch Co.

1885 Salem, Mass.   PC
PARKER BROTHERS. Mfg. of Toys and
Games. Est. 1883. Company has complete
collection of all catalogs issued from first
in 1885. Notably 1885, 1890, 1895 and 1900,
being resp. 4pp., 44pp., 32pp. and 48pp. Ill.
with pict. wrap.

POMMEROY, A. H. See Hardware -
Carpenters' Tools.

1881 New York   NSbSM
RIDEOUT, E. G. & CO. Semi-   NHi
annual ill. catalog of novelties, notions,
jokes, tricks, games and toys. Sm. 4to.,
32pp., pict. wrap. N.B. Several others
from 1879-1884 located in private collections.

1887 Chicago   NNMM
ST. NICHOLAS TOY CO. Ill. fall and winter
catalog of chairs, desks and bureaus for
youngsters, stenciled sleds, express wagons,
rocking horses, bicycles, tricycles, etc. Sq.
8vo., 48pp., pict. wrap.

1898 New York   MiD
SCHWARZ, F. O. A. Schwarz Christmas
Review & Exhibition of dolls, boats, animals,
costumes, iron pull and mechanical toys,
trains, doll houses - everything. Fol., 12pp.
with fine ills.

c.1900 New York   PC
------ Broadside ill. price list of mechanical railroads - complete trains, stations,
track, signals, bridges, etc. Large 4to.,
76 ills.

c.1890 New York   NHi
SELCHOW & RIGHTER. Est. 1867. Ill.
catalog of childrens' carriages, guns and
games - Dickens on the Turf - bow guns and
sparrow guns, etc. 32mo., 32pp., pict. wrap.

SHEPARD, SIDNEY & CO. See House Furnishings.

c.1885 South Orange, N. J.   NNMM
SHEPARDSON, E. B. New   NjR
catalog of fancy goods, jokes, music boxes,
penny banks, toys, tricks. 4to., 16pp.,
amusing ills.

SPELMAN BROTHERS. See House Furnishings.

1871 Springfield, Vt.   NNMM
SPRINGFIELD TOY CO. Ill.   VtHi
catalog of dolls' carriages, carts, perambulators, revolving Easter eggs, sleds, etc.
12mo., 16pp., glt. pict. wrap.

STANLEY & PATTERSON. See Telephones.

1859-61 Cromwell, Conn.   CtHi
STEVENS, J. & E. Co. Est. 1843. Ill. catalogs #1, 2 and 3. Iron toys. 8vo. with fine
ills. and wrap.

Dated through the cooperation of a private
collector who also reports ill. catalogs for
1867, 1880 and several others to 1924. 1859
was the first catalog issued. CtHi also reports later issues.

nd. New York   NNMM
STIRN & LYON. Desc. and ill. price list of
toys. 132pp., pict. wrap.

STRATTON, JOHN F. & CO. See Musical
Instruments.

1880 New York   DLC
TRAVERS, GEORGE W. Ill. catalog of baby
and doll carriages, express wagons, dog
carts, fancy carts and wagons with lace parasol tops, etc. Sm. 4to., 58pp., pict. wrap.

1887 St. Louis   MnHi
UDELL & CRUNDEN. Spring catalog - ill.
price list of childrens' carriages, boys'
wagons, velocipedes, baseball goods, equipment for lawn tennis, croquet, etc. Tall
8vo., 80pp.

1882 New York & East New York   NHi
UNEXCELLED FIREWORKS CO. Inc. 1874.
Western depot St. Louis, Mo. Ill. price
list - ills. of the Monkey pistol, Chinese
Must Go., Alert, Buster, Peerless and
Mamoth - as well as bombs, lanterns, etc.
24mo., 40pp., fine ills., pict. wrap.

1885 New York   NStIHi
------ Nct ill. price list. 24mo., 72pp.,
ills. of Running Horse with Jockey, Giant
Bank, Walking Boy, Butting Match Pistol,
etc. Pict. wrap. of warehouse.

See Celebration & Decoration Chapter.

1891 Cincinnati   NNMM
UNITED STATES PLAYING CARD CO.
Card players' companion. 16mo., 40pp.,
with fine col. pls. of decks, and a pict. wrap.
A fine selling job.

This company is listed as Est. in 1894.
Obviously this is an error - also quite as
obviously this must be their first issue.
Perhaps I should add, toys for young and old.

UNITED STATES PRINTING CO. See
Printers' Samples.

1888 Portland, Conn. & New York   MiDbF
UNITED STATES STAMPING CO. Ill. catalog of toys, penny banks, Japanned tin toys
with fine stencils, iron pull and mechanical
toys -- and a hundred others. Large 8vo.,
151pp., ill. throughout, pict. wrap.

1885 Springfield, Vt.   VtSM
VERMONT CHILDRENS' CARRIAGE MFG.
CO. 22nd annual ill. and desc. catalog of
toy carts, express wagons, toy surreys with
fringed tops, mats and parasols. 8vo., 24pp.

c.1880 Springfield, Vt.   VtHi
VERMONT NOVELTY WORKS CO. Est.
1859. Annual ill. catalog of childrens' toys,
carriages, wagons, sleds, dolls, etc. Organized 1859, washed away 1864, washed away
again 1869, burned out June 1878 - and -
We're Still Alive! 16mo., 64pp., fine ills.,
pict. wrap.

1887 Augusta, Me.   PC
VICKERY, P. O. Ill. catalog of novelties and games - also firearms and jewelry. 4to., 16pp., wrap.

1874 Worcester, Mass.   MSC
WEST & LEE GAME CO. Ill. catalog of games and home amusements. 8vo., 20pp., pict. wrap.

1875 Worcester, Mass.   MSC
------ Ill. catalog of games, etc.

1876 Worcester, Mass.   NSbSM
------ W. R. Gould, successor. Ill. catalog of games, etc.

1892 WHITNEY, F. A. See Carriages for Children.

WILL & FINCK CO'S. BAZAAR. See House Furnishings.

1880 New York   PC
YOUNG, M. Young's monthly publication - being an ill. catalog of toys, tricks, games, penny banks, cigar lighters, juvenile printing presses, cap pistols, etc. Fol.

c.1870 New York   MdTanSW
ZINN, CHARLES & CO. Ill. catalog of fancy stands, toy baskets, doll furniture and wagons, willow ware tea sets, childrens' furniture, etc., 4to., 32pp., pict.wrap. of interior.

Although we have not been able to locate catalogs of Kenton Hardware Co., Hubley Mfg. Co., Gong Bell Mfg. Co., Pratt & Letchworth, Ives-Blakeslee & Co., N. N. Hill Brass Co. and Watrous Mfg. Co., I list them because I know they exist in at least one private collection. Quite naturally, the owners do not choose to be pestered with requests to use their collections; this is the province of the library and museum.

I have cross-indexed as many more general catalogs as seemed necessary, but if you are still at a loss to find some record of a trademark or manufacturer's name, be sure to check Hardware, Ornamental Iron and Sporting Goods. Also don't forget that Stove founders cast many miniatures for the kids, and that the manufacturers of fireworks (under Celebration, Decoration and Theatrical Goods) also made the best cap pistols. I hardly think it necessary to mention Best & Co., Marshall Field & Co., Butler Brothers, Montgomery Ward & Co., Sears Roebuck and a dozen other Miscellaneous Department and General Stores, but I will anyway.

Chapter 57

Typewriters

If you will read The Story of the Typewriter 1873-1923, compiled and published by the Herkimer County Historical Society, you will more clearly understand why I have segregated this group of catalogs instead of burying them under Hardware, House Furnishings and Department Stores. Today millions think no more of them than they do the telephones, automobiles and planes. The luxuries of yesterday have become our necessities.

On January 7th, 1714 the British patent office recorded an attempt to invent a typewriter. In 1829 the first American patent on a typewriter was granted to William Austin Burt of Detroit. The next effort was recorded in France in 1833. Burt's was advertised as "a simple, cheap and pretty machine for printing letters." The French machine was described as a Ktypographic machine or pen that would print almost as fast as one could write. From 1840 to 1866 over a dozen patents were issued and recorded but none of these machines were really practical enough to warrant manufacture. It remained for E. Remington & Sons to actually manufacture the Sholes and Glidden patent. The contract was signed March 1, 1873. Model #1 Remington, Shop #1, is now in the Remington collection. It is mounted on a sewing machine base and the foot treadle operates the carriage return.

I include this very short sketch in case your library does not have a copy of the history. The important part for this guide is the complete details of the first catalog which is also in the Remington archives. The compiler unfortunately does not give the familiar size, pagination, illustration, printer and wrapper data. It tells the prospective purchaser that the machine resembles the family sewing machine. It is graceful and ornamental -- a beautiful piece of furniture for office, study or parlor. It claims that people travelling by sea can write with it when pen writing is impossible. Legibility, rapidity, ease, convenience and economy are the main selling points. It was especially recommended to reporters, lawyers, authors and clergymen -- the mere businessmen and manufacturers were not at the time even considered good prospects. Merchants and bankers and all men of business were added as an afterthought. The illustrations of the machine itself, and of Dad and Sister "settin' up to their machines" in the typical chairs of the period are as delightful (if, of course, you like this kind of history) as the gentleman in the brown derby tipping his hat to the young lady as he whirls by on his high wheeler bike.

The testimonials include a letter from Mark Twain. Apparently back in 1874, Mr. Clemens and his sidekick D. R. Locke, better known as Petroleum V. Nasby, passed the Remington store window. They entered to inspect the strange looking contraption. Mark Twain at once purchased a machine. In 1875 he wrote the manufacturers a note as only he could have written it. The gist of the message was that he had stopped using their type-writer because he couldn't write a single letter without someone asking him to tell all about the durned thing. He closes with - "I don't like to write letters, and so I don't want people to know I own this curiosity breeding little joker." There are many others. One man was worried for fear his insurance broker thought he couldn't read his writing, and begged him not to go to the expense of having the letters printed. Again I am slipping into the pages of history you can find for yourselves. As to the present location of this catalog, all I am sure of is that in 1923 it was in the Remington historical library.

As will appear obvious in the following locations, the Smithsonian Institution has the outstanding collection for research. In the American Writing Machine Company catalogs, the models have already lost their sewing machine stands - but, as records of what used to be, they are really quite "sum punkins."

1883 Hartford, Conn.   DSi
AMERICAN WRITING MACHINE CO. The
Caligraph. Some would call this a house
organ, but in this case it is an ill. catalog.
Vol. 1, #4. December. 8vo., pict. wrap.

1885 Hartford, Conn.   PC
------ It Stands at the Head - The Caligraph Writing Machine. 12mo., 104pp., ills.
of models #1 and 2, sample work, tests.,
pict. wrap.

1887 Hartford, Conn.   CtHi
------ The Caligraph. 16mo., 36pp., ills.
of models, cases, desks and tables. Pict.
wrap.

c.1888 Hartford, Conn.   DSi
------ Catalog. Models # 1, 2 and 3, ill.,
pict. wrap.

c.1895 Hartford, Conn.   DSi
------ The Caligraph. 8vo., 36pp., ill.,
pict. wrap.

1890 Boston   DSi
ANDERSON'S SHORTHAND TYPEWRITER
CO. Model for 1890. 4pp., ills.

nd. Harrisburg, Pa.   DSi
BENNETT TYPEWRITER, THE. Ill. catalog.

1897 Stamford, Conn.   DSi
BLICKENSDERFER MFG. CO. Ill. catalog
of models #5 and #7 with instructions.
12mo., 12pp., wrap.

nd. Stamford, Conn.   CtHi
------ New improved Blick aluminum
typewriter. Featherweight secretary of the
traveler and for the home. Mfg. by . . .
12mo., ill.

nd. Stamford, Conn.   CtHi
------ Ill. catalog of Blickensderfer typewriters #2. 8vo., 31pp.

nd. Stamford, Conn.   CtHi
------ Ill. catalog. 12mo., 21 (1)pp.

1899 Stamford, Conn.   DSi
------ The Blick. Ills. of models, desks,
tables, etc. Sq. 16mo., 24pp., wrap.

BROOKS. See Union Writing Machine Co.

c.1900 Washington, D.C.   DSi
CAHILL ELECTRIC CO., THE. The Cahill
Electrical Typewriter. 12pp., ills., wrap.

nd. Chicago   DSi
CHICAGO WRITING MACHINE CO. Circular of Model - $35.00.

c.1885 New York   DSi
COLUMBIA TYPE WRITING MACHINE CO.
The Columbia Type Writer. A perfect
writing machine. Tall. 12mo., 12pp., with
fine ills. and sample of work.

c.1894 New York   DSi
------ The Bar Lock Modern Writing
Machine #6. Ill. circular.

1885 New York   PC
CRANDALL TYPE WRITER CO. (John A.
Caldwell, agent.) 4 page ill. circular -
machine and type roller, etc. Tests.

c.1888 New York   DSi
------ The New Model Crandall. Ill. catalog of 24pp., pict. wrap. Tests.

1886 New York   NNC
MINER, E. N. & L. A. Miner's specialties
for shorthand writers and type writer operators. Ills. of the Ingersol, Prouty, Horton,
Hammond and Hall models. 8vo., 32pp.,
pict. wrap.

c.1883 Ilion, N. Y. & New York   PPL
REMINGTON, E. & SONS. Ill. catalog of
Remington sewing machines, tables, stands,
accessories, etc.

c.1884 Ilion, N. Y. & New York   DSi
------ Directions for using models #1
through #4. 15pp., ill.

c.1885 Ilion, N. Y.   PPL
------ (Wyckoff, Seamans &   DSi
Benedict, agents.) Ill. catalog of models,
stands, desks, copy holders, covers and supplies, with a short history from 1714. Mentions pat. issued to Charles Thurber of
Worcester and to Fairbanks in 1848 that
proved good for nothing. Sq. 16mo., 64pp.,
fine ills., pict. wrap.

c.1886-7 Ilion, N. Y.   DSi
------ Ill. catalog of Remington Standard
Typewriters. 48pp., wrap.

c.1894 Ilion, N. Y.   DSi
------ Instructions for using model #6.
20pp., ills., pict. wrap. See Western
Electric.

1874-75 Herkimer, N. Y.   DSi
SHOLES & GLIDDEN. Ill. leaflet. Dated
between spring 1874 and #1 1875 when the
machines were marked Remington. See
Introduction, Remington and Western Electric.

c.1900 Syracuse, N. Y.   CtHi
SMITH PREMIUM TYPEWRITER   DSi
CO. Smith Premier Typewriter. Method
of operation and instructions, etc. 8vo.,
12pp., ills., col. pict. wrap.

c.1890 Boston   DSi
TOWER CO., THE. (Agents.) The New
Franklin Cutter Typewriter. 4 page ill.
circular.

c.1900 Boston   ICHi
TYPEWRITER EXCHANGE, THE. Catalog
of makes bought and sold, new and old,
rented or exchanged. Fine ills. of models -
fine ref. list:-

Brooks   Franklin

Crandall   Blickensderfer

Chicago or   Densmore
   Munson
                    New Century
Fay Sho
                    National
Fox
                    Bar Lock
Caligraph
                    Hammond
Hartford
                    Pittsburg
Jewett   Visible

Oliver   Underwood

Remington   Wellington

Keystone   Williams

Manhattan A   Yost

          Peerless

Tall 24mo., 24pp., wrap.

c.1890 New York   DSi
   UNION WRITING MACHINE CO. The Brooks
   Typewriter. Ill. catalog of models and sup-
   plies. 16pp., wrap.

nd. Various   DSi
   VARIOUS. Ill. catalogs of the following
   makes, undated and probably all after 1900:-

   The Emerson Wonder - $60.00.

   Fox Mfg. Co. "It's a Fox."
      Col. pict. wrap.

   Lambert Typewriters for Almost
      Everybody.

   New Hammond Multiplex

   The Noiseless

   The Oliver #3 model.

   Sterling Typewriters

   The Victor

   The Woodstock Typewriter.

c.1885 Chicago   DSi
   WESTERN ELECTRIC MFG. CO. Ill. circular of the Sholes & Glidden typewriter --
   $125.00.

Chapter 58

Undertakers' Equipment & Paraphernalia

An excellent chapter to peruse with a frightful hangover. It will cheer you up no end to see the lovely caskets one used to be able to crawl into with an undertaker on each side, with all the trimmings, for about $19.00. Of course the family could spend $50. to $1000. if you left them the wherewithal, but the nice part of it was you didn't have to lie there during the show knowing that the funeral would leave them busted.

NNMM has the best collection in the field but don't let this cast a shadow; the Print Department of the Metropolitan boasts the most delightfully, enthusiastically, completely and dynamically alive staff in the entire country. I do not belittle other locations, but if you really want a magnificent red velvet lined model with silver and gold angels, mounted on a bronze stand with griffon legs and feet, and a beveled French window through which to watch the performance, try NNMM.

Checking Seeger & Guernsey's Cyclopaedia for the undertakers' supplies for 1890, this seemingly short chapter covers the outstanding manufacturers pretty thoroughly.

1889 Bristol, Vt.   MH-BA
BRISTOL MFG. CO. Ill. catalog of fine burial caskets. Large 8vo., 84pp., fine engravings, cl.

1889 Buffalo, N. Y.   N
CENTRAL MFG. CO. Ill. catalog of fine burial caskets, stands, angel pedestals, robes, covers, etc. with 112 pls. Tall 8vo., limp mor. in salesman's case. 40pp. of desc. and text, price list, etc.

1897 Boston   NNMM
COOK & WATKINS. #4 design book of granite and marble monuments and memorials, ill. and numbered. 61pls., glt. dec. cl.

1877 Baltimore   NNMM
DUER, JOHN & SONS. Ill. catalog of coffin trimmings, hardware and ornaments. 67pp.

1850 Newtown, L. I., N. Y.   PC
FISK & RAYMOND. Ill. catalog of Fisk's pat. metallic burial cases - airtight and indestructible, for protecting and preserving the dead - ordinary interment for vaults, for transportation or any other desirable purpose. Won 4 medals in 1849. Tests. include a graphic detailed desc. of Mrs. Madison's funeral by Mr. Ritchie of The Union - this was the first Fisk casket used. No copy man before or since did a better job - it is truly great. 16mo., 16pp., pict. wrap.

c.1870 Newtown, L. I., N. Y.   PC
FISK METALLIC BURIAL CASE CO. W. M. Raymond & Co. Ill. catalog of coffins, cases, ornaments and trimmings with a back wrap showing a swell hearse. 8vo., 18pp., pict. wrap.

1892 Brooklyn, N. Y.   NNQ
GRANITE CUTTERS' NATIONAL UNION. Kings County Branch. Bill of prices current for monumental and cemetery work.

1886 New York   NNMM
HORNTHAL, NOBLE & CO. Ill. catalog of casket and coffin ornaments and trimmings. 265pp., glt. lettered cl., a great ref.

1865 East Hampton, Conn.   CtHi
MARKHAM & STRONG. Revised price list with ills. of coffin ornaments and trimmings, hardware, handles, etc. 8vo., 48pp., wrap.

1884 New York   NNMM
METALLIC BURIAL CASE CO. Ill. catalog with 21 fine col. pls. of gold and silver ornaments, full satin linings, full glass, lightest ever mfg. - each page with details, sizes, etc. Prices - models D, K, L, M and N. 4to., 43 lvs., glt dec. wrap.

1882 Bridgeport, Conn.   NNMM
MONUMENTAL BRONZE CO. Ill. catalog of white bronze monuments, statuary, portrait medallions, busts, statues and ornamental art work for cemeteries, private and public parks. 4to., 127pp., pict. bds.

c.1896 New York   N
NATIONAL CASKET CO. Ill. Casket Catalog #F with fine pls. of caskets - $45. to
$1000. - 21 distributors, desc., details, col.
pict. wrap.

c.1900 New York   MMidHi
------ Ne Plus Ultra catalog of Candelabra,
funeral clothing, fancy and plain caskets,
stands, trimming tables, tool chests, hardware. Fol., 200pp. of ills.

1896 New Britain   CtHi
NEW BRITAIN HARDWARE MFG. CO. Ill.
catalog of casket hardware, handles, plates,
decorations, trimmings, etc. Fol., 84 pls.

1879 Middletown, Conn.   CtHi
NEW ENGLAND ENGRAVING CO. For Asa
B. and J. B. Stowe. Album of granite and
marble designs for cemetery monuments.
8vo., 30 photos., cl.

1877 Philadelphia   PHi
PAXSON, COMFORT & CO. Reduced wholesale price list of undertakers' supplies -
hardware, ornaments and trimmings. 16mo.,
32pp., pict. wrap.

1878 Philadelphia   PC
------ 4to. ill. catalog of fine plates - a
great book to look over some morning with
a good hangover.

c.1894 Philadelphia   NNMM
PHILADELPHIA WHITE BRONZE MONU-
MENT CO. Ill., desc. and priced catalog of
monuments, tombs, statues, busts and ornaments. 108pp., wrap.

PRANG, L. & CO. Designs for monuments.
See Printers' Samples.

1893 St. Louis   MoSHi
RIDDLE, F.C. & BRO. CASKET CO. Ill.
catalog of supplies, gowns and robes for
funeral directors, pall bearers and corpses,
pat. embalming tables, showcases and caskets, hearses, plumes, hardware, trimmings,
urns, fancy stands - even screw drivers for
special spots with instructions for ordering
by wire! Pat. dates run from 1883 to 1893.
A great ref. if you are in the mood. Fol.,
127pp. of ills., wrap.

1888 Meriden, Conn.   CtHi
ROGERS, C. & BROTHERS. Ill. catalog of
coffin and casket hardware - silver plaques,
handles, buttons, trimmings - from angels
to doves, society emblems, etc. View of
plant - mfg. plant, of course. Fol., 194pp.
of pls., dec. bds.

1846 New York   NNMM
SMITH, J. JAY. Designs for monuments
and mural tablets adapted to rural cemeter-

ies, church yards, churches and chapels.
30pp. of desc. and text with 30 fine pls.

c.1870 New York (in the Bowery)   PC
SMITH, WINSTON & CO. Ill. catalog of
caskets and coffins. Tall 8vo., 24pp. and
20 pls. of new models and styles for the
most pernickety corpses.

N.B. Had previously depended on photos.
for customers, but could now issue
ill. catalogs. See Silver Chapter. Undoubtedly their first ill. catalog.

STOWE. See New England Engraving Co.

1870 Winsted, Conn.   CtHi
STRONG, D. & CO. Mfg. Ill. catalog of
Undertakers' Goods. Coffins, clothes, ice
coolers, trimmings, etc. 7x10-1/2, title
and 62 pls. plus appendix of 16 pls., mor.
Probably salesman's copy.

1879 New York   NNMM
TAYLOR, H.E. & CO. Ill. catalog of undertakers' sundries. 225pp. of fine ills., wrap.

1885 New York   NNMM
------ Ill. catalog of caskets and coffins -
latest models and styles, ill. and desc.,
100 pls., cl.

1885 New York   NNMM
THORN, LANGDON & ARROWSMITH. Ill.
catalog of caskets and coffins. 84pp. of pls.
and ills., cl.

1897 Proctor, Vt.   NNMM
VERMONT MARBLE CO. Ill. price list of
Rutland, Sutherland Falls, Blue and Mountain Dark Marbles for Tombstones. 574pp.
of fine pls., cl.

See Architectural Building Materials.

1875 Watertown, Conn.   CtHi
WARREN, C.A. Patentee. Ill. catalog of
Warren's pat. festoons, emblems, banners,
floral and evergreen decorations - horn of
plenty baskets for church funerals, etc.
8vo., 20pp., pict. wrap.

1877 Watertown, Conn.   NNMM
------ Catalog and price list of pat. emblems, floral decorations, etc. 7 lvs.

c.1899   NNMM
WENDELL, H.F. & CO. Ill., desc. and
priced catalog of fine memorial goods. 16pp.
including pict. wrap, fine ills.

1894 Bridgeport, Conn.   CtHi
  WHITE MFG. CO. Ill. catalog and price
  list of finely finished hearse mountings,
  trappings, ornaments and lamps. 4to., 62pp.
  of ills., pict. wrap.

1897 Bridgeport, Conn.   CtHi
  ------ Ill. catalog of fine hearse   NNMM
  mountings, lamps, etc. 4to., 70pp. of pls.,
  wrap.

  See Carriages, Wagons, etc.

For other illustrations of silver mountings, plates and ornaments, be sure to check the chapter on
Silverware. The Statuary section under Miscellany also lists several monument makers who supplied cemetery markers and fancy tombs. The Hardware chapter also offers handles for coffins and
tools for undertakers, and, of course, the Carriage, Wagon and Accessories section lists some of
the best hearses built in the 19th century.

Chapter 59

Washing Machines

This must be another very short and incomplete looking chapter. Half a catalog is better than none, especially when the half you own has the best illustrations, prices and details. Even half of one percent of the possible locations is better than no guide at all. The collector who wants only the earliest known copy of a catalog or a book is not a historian.

This section offers a selective few with illustrations that probably were used in most catalogs and brochures issued. As you know from studying the printers' specimen books of the 19th century, the same cuts were repeated by many manufacturers. Although several are located in a private collection, and are not available for research, they are records of what is undoubtedly available in libraries that have not as yet reported their holdings. Publishers and opportunities will not wait forever. This guide is the first step. Don't be too critical and be thankful for a start in the right direction.

Thanks to a private collector and personal friend, I am able to at least add the following illustrated circulars as being extant records that will some day be available to the public:

Campbell's Patent - showing one model.

Eagle Washers - one model.

Eureka Washing Machines - one model.

Gaskill Washers - one model.

Keystone Washers - two models at $6.00 and $8.00.

Nonpareil - three models at $13.50, $22.50 and $27.00.

Rice's patent - one model.

Sea Foam - one model.

Snowflake Washers - one model.

Wood's Washing Machines - one model.

c.1900 Cincinnati   OC
    BOSS WASHING MACHINE CO. Boss Wash-
    ing Machines - by hand, water and electric
    power. Fine ills. of plant and models:

Banner	Springless
Champion	Uneeda
Cincinnati	Veribest

    4to., 20pp., folded to 40, wrap.

1890 Sidney, O.   OHi
    BUCKEYE CHURN CO. Special catalog of
    churns, washing machines, etc. 2 ills.

1890 North East, Pa.   PC
    BUTT & SICKLEY. Ill. circular of the
    Atlantic Washing Machine. 16mo., 8pp.,
    one model.

c.1875 Chicago   PC
    CALKINS CHAMPION WASHER CO. Ill.
    catalog of Calkins Champion Washers and
    Wringers. 16mo., 16pp., pict. wrap.

c.1899 Syracuse, N.Y.   PC
    DODGE & QUILL MFG. CO. Ill. catalog of
    Easy Washing Machines. 16mo., 6pp., wrap.

    DOTY'S CLOTHES WASHER. See Metro-
    politan Washing Machine Co.

    ERKENBRECHER. See Food and Drink.

c.1845 Baltimore & New York   PC
    GASKILL, C.T. & CO. Mfg. Baltimore,
    (A. H. Mallory, agent, New York.) Luken's
    pat. washing machine - simple as truth, with
    comment from Baltimore Sun. 4to. circu-
    lar, woodcut of machine.

c.1870 New York   PC
    HALEY, MORSE & CO. Mfg. Ill. circular
    of celebrated pat. Union Washing Machine
    and clothes wringer combination, American
    mangle or ironing machine, and the Reliance
    Wringer - prizes won 1863 and 1867 - also
    the Welcome Carpet Sweeper - $3.50. 8pp.

1852 Baltimore   NNU-W
KING, T. J. Ill. catalog of King's Washing
Apparatus, pat. 1851 - A child can handle it -
50 pieces of clothing in 5 minutes! 12mo.,
24pp., pict. wrap. Dealers listed by states.

1866 New York   PC   PKsL
METROPOLITAN WASHING MACHINE CO.
Ill. circular of Doty's Clothes Washer.
24mo., 16pp., pict. wrap.

c.1867 Newark, N. J. & New York   NjR
------ (C.G. Crane & Co., Newark, agents.)
Ill. catalog of Universal Clothes Wringers
with cog wheels and pat. stop gears - mfg.
by Metropolitan. 300,000 in use! 24mo.,
16pp., pict. wrap.

c.1870 New York   PC
------ Ill. catalog of Doty's Improved
Washer with Metropolitan Balances. 16mo.,
24pp., pict. wrap.

1873 New York   MH-BA
------ Doty's washing machines and Universal clothes wringers - revised price list,
large 8vo., 2pp., ills.

1877 New York   MH-BA
------ Wholesale ill. price list of Universal, National and Reliance clothes wringers.
16mo., 8pp.

1900 Binghamton   PC   ICHI
NINETEEN HUNDRED WASHER CO., THE.
Ill. catalog and price list of 1900 washers -
ill. of the baby running the washer with a
big smile. 16mo., 16pp., pict. wrap.

c.1900 Binghamton   ICHi
------ Booklet of reprinted   PC
tests. 16mo., 32pp., wrap.

c.1900 Binghamton   N
------ Electric Wash Day - Keep your serv-
ants contented - let them darn and mend
while the old electric washes! 16mo., 16pp.
Swell pict. wrap.

SHAKER WASHING MACHINES. See Furniture.

c.1896 Chicago   ICHi
STEEL ROLL MANGLE & MACHINE CO.
Ill. catalog of heated steel roll ironing machines, shirt ironers, starchers and washers.
Gas and gasoline - models and styles - even
including wooden shoes for wash rooms.
8vo., 160pp., fine ills., pict. wrap.

WALWORTH, JAMES J. & CO. See Hardware - Miscellaneous Machinery.

1891 Fort Wayne   In
WAYNE, ANTHONY MFG. CO. Ill. catalog
of Anthony Wayne Washers. 16mo., 24pp.,
pict. wrap. showing the old way on front
cover - sweating away over the wooden tub,
and the back cover with the smiling lady
twirling the washer handle like an organ
grinder. Can you imagine a high school
girl having to turn the handle today? Why
she'd be worn out doing one blouse.

Perhaps you have an idea that whereas distribution of American goods and manufactures today is so complicated and vast that the layman cannot possibly understand it, during the 19th century it was all relatively simple. This was not the case at all. Although drummers, manufacturers' catalogs and the stores carried the brunt of selling goods to the public, the general catalogs offered everything from a pin to a silo.

If you merely want to see what a washing machine looked like from 1845 to 1900, or if you are hunting a firm whose washer has come down in the family, this chapter may make a direct hit. On the other hand, if it doesn't, be sure to search such catalogs as Joseph Breck & Son under Agricultural Implements, House Furnishings and Hardware. In 1899 Breck carried the Horton Stave Leg Rotary Washer manufactured in Fort Wayne, Indiana. At the turn of the century, for instance, Sears Roebuck & Co. offered illustrations of Fulton's American Washing Machine, The Chicago American, The Desplaines, The Curtis, The Acme, Continental, Genuine Improved Scott's Western Washer, Quick & Easy Washer, Seroco, Richmond Rotary and The Electric! We offer here individual washing machine manufacturers' creations and inventions, but you must use other obvious chapters to complete the story.

Chapter 60

Weathervanes

Although students of American design may not agree, wrought iron has produced the most fascinating workmanship of all the examples that have been preserved for us through the ages. Others prefer brass, bronze, glass and pottery. To me wrought iron has a substance that lends itself to both delicate and rugged individual creation. From the crudest curling irons, butterfly hinges, pot hooks, trammels and turnkeys to the most magnificent peacock weathervanes, wrought iron artifacts offer an outstanding record.

The catalogs offered and located are the best that have been preserved, at least as far as it has been possible to ascertain from library catalogs. Cross indexing is not as thorough as I would like to make it but indicates the necessity of using the Ornamental Ironwork Chapter carefully for stray illustrations not duplicated here. This group of catalogs has been segregated because of its importance as a top facet in the index of American design.

In a guide of this nature there is little room for chit-chat. Personal experiences and side lights must bow to research. However, let me, like the Ancient Mariner hold you for a moment. On an old barn in Bridgewater, Mass. a magnificent peacock vane still swings to the New England weather. The last time I approached the owner he told me that if I would pay him a thousand dollars, climb the building and take it out without breaking my neck, I might have it. This is a clever offer. If I broke my neck obviously I didn't take title to the vane. I wonder if this peacock will ever find its way to one of our national museums.

As pointed out in connection with bells, andirons and other fine examples of the blacksmith's work, there probably were no catalogs in the 17th and 18th centuries. The best reference is, of course, Albert H. Sonn's monumental work "Early American Wrought Iron." Mere trade catalogs must admit defeat as pictorial records during this early period of American development. Many of them do however recreate fine examples of the earliest cocks, arrows, Indians, sheep, ships, plows and motifs of these pioneer craftsmen. Let me add here that many of the finest examples were carved and whittled out of pine, maple and oak.

BARBEE, W. T. IRON & WIRE WORKS.
See Ornamental Ironwork.

BARNUM, E. T. See Ornamental Ironwork.

c.1875 Portchester, N. Y.   NNMM
BENT, SAMUEL S. & SON. Est. 1843. Ill. catalog of cast iron chairs, settees, vases, crestings, tree guards, summer houses, hitching posts, croquet stands with pitcher and water glass holders built in - and fine weathervanes. Large 4to., 34pp. of pls., pict. wrap.

BERGER, L. D. BROTHERS. See Hardware.

BRECK, JOSEPH & SONS. See Agricultural Implements and House Furnishings.

1883 Waltham   NNMM
CUSHING, L.W. & SONS. Est.1852. TxDa
Ill. catalog #9 - Weathervanes - ill. designs of cow, deer, dog, fox, eagle, grasshopper,

butterfly, fish, full rigged ship, peacocks, horse - with and without rider and sulky, rooster, sheep, squirrel, key, etc. Sheet and full bodied copper. 4to., 20pp. of pls., pict. wrap.

c.1885 New York   MH-BA
FISKE, J.W. Ill. catalog of copper weathervanes, finials and crestings. 4to., 100pp., pict. wrap. One of the best.

See Ornamental Ironwork and Architectural Building Materials.

c.1865 Boston   NNMM
HARRIS & CO. Ill. circu-   TxLT   MiDbF
lar of Boston Copper Weathervanes, iron crestings, etc.

c.1870 Boston   VtSM
------ Ill. price list with 45   N
designs. 16mo.

c.1870 Boston   TxDa
------ Ill. folder of copper weathervanes,
lightning rods, garden furniture, crestings,
etc. 8pp.

1866 New York   NNMM
JEWELL, A.L. & CO. Ill. catalog of copper
weathervanes for May 1st. Complete list
with 4 ills. Brigs, schooners, steamers,
ships, military figures, birds and animals.

1871 Providence, R. I.   RHi
MILLER IRON CO. Founders. Ill. catalog
of ornamental ironwork for lawns, gardens,
homes, etc. Bird houses, furniture, ornaments and weathervanes. 12mo., 22pp.,
wrap.

c.1883 Providence, R. I.   RHi
------ Ill. catalog and price list of hollow
ware, stable fittings and weathervanes.
4to., 126pp., pict. wrap. A fine ref.

MOTT, J.L. IRON WORKS. See Architectural Building Materials and Ornamental
Ironwork.

MULLINS, W.H. & CO. See Architectural
Building Materials and Statuary.

1884 Detroit, Mich.   MiU-H
NATIONAL IRON & WIRE CO. Ill. catalog
of fancy plant stands, hitching posts, elegant
railings, crestings, hat and cane stands,
fire screens and weathervanes - not to mention the best mouse traps. 4to., 72pp., fine
pls., pict. wrap.

c.1850 Philadelphia   PHi
SAVORY & CO. Founders. (Curtis & Hand,
agents.) Ill. catalog of fine iron castings,
hollow ware, crestings, furniture and
weathervanes. 8vo., 56pp. of fine pls., pict.
wrap.

c.1883 Boston   NNMM
SNOW, W.A. & CO. Catalog B, ill., desc.
and priced of chairs, settees, vases, crestings and weathervanes. 16pp.

1889 Boston   CCuMGM
------ Ill. catalog of stable   NhDY
fixtures, garden furniture and ornaments,
crestings and weathervanes. 4to., 92pp.,
pict. wrap.

1894 Boston   NNMM
------ Ill. catalog of wrought   CBaK
and cast iron work, stable fixtures and fine
weathervanes. Fine pls. and ref. Large
8vo., 148pp., pict. wrap.

SPOKANE ORNAMENTAL IRON & WIRE
WORKS. See Ornamental Ironwork.

1880 Moline, Ill.   IHi
UNION MALLEABLE IRON CO. Ill. catalog
of malleable iron castings for plow, carriage,
pump and designs for weathervanes, etc.
Pict. litho. wrap in col. by Shober & Carqueville.

c.1895 Buffalo, N. Y.   NNMM
WALBRIDGE & CO. Ill. catalog of iron
reservoir vases, garden ornaments, crestings and weathervanes. 4to., 58pp., wrap.

nd. Chicago   NNMM
WESTERN GRILLE MFG. CO. Ill. catalog
of fancy iron and wire work designs. 60
engravings, fol.

1883 New York   NNMM
WESTERVELT, A.B. & W.T. CO. Catalog
#6. Ill. catalog of copper weathervanes,
bannerets, crestings and finials. The best
catalog in the field. 100pp. of vanes for
architects, brewers, fire stations, railroads,
steamship companies, etc. - dragons, pens,
fire engines, horse cars, locomotives, ships,
animals - and even the Angel Gabriel blowing his horn. Large sq. 8vo., 100pp., wrap.

1884 New York   MnHi
------ Catalog #7. Ill. catalog of   MiD
weathervanes, crestings, stable ornaments,
architectural finials, etc. Another masterpiece of 100pp. of pls. of the finest American
designs.

c.1890 New York   NNMM
------ Ill. catalog of bannerets, crosses,
finials, crestings and weathervanes - adding
such vanes as Sun Flower, Hook & Ladder,
etc. Large 4to., 16pp., fine pls., wrap.
Little, but OH My!

PLEASE consult Architectural Building Materials, Hardware and Ornamental Ironwork before you
conclude that this section is sadly incomplete. I chose to make a separate chapter with this heading
to honor the artists in wrought iron, yet even as I write it, I have to admit that many illustrated in
the catalogs are manufactured of copper! They are weathervanes nevertheless. The dissertation
on wrought iron is only for those who feel about it as I do.

Chapter 61

Windmills

Why, you may wonder, are windmills ferreted out of this maze of American manufactures for special treatment. In the first place they just do not fit any other classification. They served the Pilgrim, pioneer, farmer, manufacturer, miner, railroad builder and cattleman -- they produced water for drinking and power for work -- they served mankind. It would be ridiculous to bury them in the Hardware - Miscellaneous Machinery Chapter unless one chose to have in the index a full page of references for this one all important American machine.

Many would prefer to go to Holland and see the dummies set up in the glorious gardens for the tourists, but for my money, as the fella says, I'd prefer a contemporary lithograph of an American Champion at work in America. Our museums have rescued and restored some of the finest examples, but the authentication, dating and explanation of the parts and accessories is the province of the lowly trade catalog. I well remember one at Narragansett Pier that actually pumped water to wash the old Pierce Arrow as well as water the horses c.1910. I wonder if it is still there?

nd. Waupun, Wis.   MnHi
ALTHOUSE, WHEELER & CO. Ill. catalog of pumps, windmills and well equipment.

1881-82 Aurora, Ill.   MnHi
AMERICAN WELL WORKS. Ill. catalogs of pumps and windmills for 1881 and 1882.

BANKS, W.H. & CO. See Agricultural Implements.

1888 Beloit, Wis.   TxDaDeG
BELOIT STEEL MILL CO. (E.H. Wheeler, Boston agent.) Ill. circular of windmills and tanks. 8vo., 4pp.

c.1900 Louisville, Ky.   KyU
CALDWELL, W.E. & CO. Ill. catalogs of high grade tanks, towers and tubs, complete water systems, bell towers, sprinkler systems. 4to, 36pp., pict. wrap. Also later issues after 1900, 8vo., to 44pp. with pict. wrap.

1880 Batavia, Ill.   MnHi
CHALLENGE WIND MILL & FEED MILL CO. Ill. catalog of Challenge windmills.

1887 Batavia, Ill.   MnHi
------ Ill. catalog of windmills,   IHi large 8vo., 44pp., pict. wrap. showing windmill at work supplying farmhouse, barns, grounds with fountain playing, workshop with men at machines - one of the best located.

c.1883 New York   MnHi
DELAMETER IRON WORKS. Ill. catalog of pumps and windmills.

1883 Beloit, Wis.   MH-BA
ECLIPSE WIND ENGINE CO.   WHi
Ill. catalog of Eclipse pumping and geared windmills, tests. 19th ed. Large 8vo., 32pp., wrap.

1892 Beloit, Wis.   ICJ
------ Ill. catalog. 4to., 54pp.,   WHi pict. wrap. Unusually fine ills. of farms, dairies, residences, grinding mills in operation with wind power - fountains to saw mills.

c.1884 Chicago & St. Paul, Minn.   MnHi
FAIRBANKS, MORSE & CO. Ill. catalog of the original solid steel wheel Eclipse windmill, self-regulating for all mills and machines. Large 8vo., 32pp.

c.1890 Chicago & St. Paul, Minn.   TxDaDeG
------ Ill. price list of Eclipse windmills, pumps, tanks, etc. 16mo., 16pp., pict. wrap.

1879 Chicago   MnHi
FIELDHOUSE, DUTCHER & BELDER. Ill. catalog of pumps, windmills and wind power equipment.

1891 Kendallville, Ind.   In
FLINT & WALLING MFG. CO. Ill. catalog of Star wind engines, windmills, Hoosier automatic tubs, tanks and well machines. Post 1900 issues at TxDaDeG.

1885 Springfield, O.   MnHi
FOOS MFG. CO. Ill. catalog of windmills, wind power engines, scientific mills, portable forges, etc. 16mo., 32pp., pict. wrap.

1888 Springfield, O.   OHi
------ Ill. catalog - To our friends and
patrons, etc. 12mo., 48pp., col.pict.wrap.

1889 Springfield, O.   MnHi
------ Ill. catalog. 12mo., 48pp., wrap.

1884 Chicago   MnHi
GOULDS & AUSTIN. Ill. catalog of pumps,
well digging equipment and windmills.

1882 Saline, Mich.   MiU-H
GROSS, J.G. & BROTHER.   CU-A
Ill. catalog of improved Saline standard windmills, Champion anti-freezing force pumps,
etc. 12mo., 8pp., swell pict. wrap.

1883 Chicago   MnHi
HAY & PRENTICE. Ill. catalog of pumps
and windmills.

1885 Mansfield, O.   MnHi
HUMPHREYS MFG. CO. Ill. catalog of
pumps, well equipment, windmills and tanks.

1884 Dubuque, Ia.   MnHi
McDONALD, A.Y. Ill. catalog of pumps and
windmills. Also have 1886 issue.

1874 Chicago   MnHi
McDONALD BROTHERS. Ill. catalog of
pumps, well digging equipment, tanks, tubs
and windmills.

1884 Springfield, O.   MnHi
MAST, FOOS & CO. Ill. catalog of pumps,
water systems, windmills and equipment.

c.1890 Springfield, O.   OHi
------ Ill. catalog #10. Buckeye force
pumps, iron turbine wind engines, Columbia
steel windmills, derricks, fencing, crestings
and ironwork. 8vo., 144pp., cl.

1887 Ashland, O.   MnHi
MYERS, F.E. & BROTHER.   OHi
Ill. catalog of pumps, spray pumps, windmills, tubs, tanks, equipment and farm
accessories.

nd. Chicago   MnHi
NEEDHAM, RUPP & CO. Ill. catalog of
pumps and windmills.

PAGE, GEORGE. See Hardware - Tools
and Machines by Trades - Millers' Machinery.

1859 Salem, O.   KU
PEABODY, FRANCIS. Ill. catalog of wind
turbines, new engines for grist mills, flouring mills and machinery and equipment for
farmer and mechanic. 12mo., 30pp., pict.
wrap.

1888 Mishawaka, Ind.   In
PERKINS WIND MILL & AXE CO. Ill. catalog of Perkins' windmills and accessories.

1900 Mishawaka, Ind.   In
------ Ill. catalog #28. Perkins' Mills,
towers, tools and machinery for wind engines,
mills, light, power and water. 8vo., 218pp.,
pict. wrap.

1891 Kalamazoo   TxDaDeG
PHELPS & BIGELOW WIND MILL CO. Ill.
catalog of I X L windmills and power wind
engines - action shots of wind power in work-
shops and mills. 8vo., 32pp., pict. wrap.

1897 Kalamazoo   MiU-H
------ Ill. catalog #20. Tall 8vo.,   MiD
20pp., fine pict. wrap.

1882 Waukegan   MStOSV
POWELL & DOUGLAS.   IHi
Ill. catalog and price list of Star wood pumps,
Champion wind power mills and equipment.
12mo., 32pp., pict. wrap.

1883 Waukegan   MnHi
------ Ill. catalog of Champion   ICHi
wind engines, pumps and tanks.

1886 Waukegan   MnHi
------ R.J. Douglas & Co. Ill. catalog of
windmills, pumps, etc.

c.1890 Sandwich, Ill.   ICHi
SANDWICH ENTERPRISE CO. Ill. catalog
of windmills, pumps and agricultural machinery.

1891 Kalamazoo   PC
SMITH & POMEROY. Ill. catalog of Eureka
self-regulating windmills. 8vo., 12pp., pict.
wrap.

1894 Freeport, Ill.   IHi
STOVER MFG. CO.   PC
Ill. catalog of Ideal windmills, pumps, tanks,
tubs, accessories and farm hardware - cuts
and photos., wrap.

1886 New Carlisle, O.   MnHi
SUPERIOR MACHINE CO. Ill. catalog of
pumps, windmills and accessories.

1895 Boston   MBSPNEA
TYLER, GEORGE. Agent. Ill. catalog of
wind engines and water supply goods. 8vo.,
62pp., wrap.

1873 Batavia, Ill.   CU-A
U.S. WIND ENGINE & PUMP CO. Ill. catalog of Halliday's Wind Engines, pumps, tanks,
etc. with fine engravings of its power uses.
8vo., 52pp., pict. wrap.

1879 Batavia, Ill.   MnHi
------ Ill. catalog. 23rd ed.

1880 Batavia, Ill.   ICHi
------ Ill. catalog of Victorious Halliday
Standard Wind Mills. 96pp.

1882 Batavia, Ill.   IHi
------ Ill. price list for March - windmills, pumps, tanks, etc.

1886 Batavia, Ill.   MnHi
------ Ill. catalog. Jan. 1.   IHi
Windmills, including haying tools and farm
equipment. 8vo., 24pp.

c.1886 Batavia, Ill.   ICHi
------ Ill. catalog. Halliday Standard,
U.S. Solid Wheel and vaneless windmills.

Engravings of windmills in use on Ohio,
Illinois and Michigan farms, and even pumping brine from the salt wells in Texas. One
of the best. Sq. 8vo., 112pp. of ills; with
col. pict. wrap.

1886 Rockford, Ill.   MnHi
WARD, FRANK. Ill. catalog of pumps, well
digging equipment and standard windmills.

1883 Racine, Wis.   MnHi
WINSHIP BROTHERS MFG. CO. Ill. catalog of pumps, well digging equipment and
mills.

Under Hardware - Miscellaneous Machinery there may be a few strays in these more general catalogs.
Throughout this guide it should be evident that few American products were sold and cataloged only
by the manufacturers. If you have the name, the index should direct you to the right spot. The best
book for serious study of the American windmill is unquestionably Alfred R. Wolff's "The Windmill
as a Prime Mover," John Wiley & Sons, New York, 1885. (Second edition 1888)

Chapter 62

Miscellany

A Grouping Of Six Classifications
With Too Few Locations To Warrant Separate
Chapters, But Too Important To Bury In Any One General Heading.

LIGHTNING RODS	SAFES & VAULTS
POST OFFICE EQUIPMENT	STATUARY
REAL ESTATE	WALLPAPER

To delve into the histories of these six facets of Americana is not within the province of a guide. My stated purpose is to locate the reference material for the student and historian, and to point out the importance of available untapped sources. I am convinced that each one of these groups deserves attention and have therefore kept them in semi-private rooms.

The lightning rod seems to have come and gone. I do not mean to say that they are no longer manufactured and used, but as the catalogs indicate, there was a day when the whole country was flooded not only with newly invented and impractical rods but with crooked get rich quick salesmen shoving them down peoples' throats. Without these illustrated catalogs and circulars the active, turbulent, useful life of the American lightning rod can never be written.

1853 Philadelphia   PHi
ARMITAGE, THOMAS. Armitage's Patent Electro-Magnet Lightning Rods - best insurance against lightning. 12mo., 12pp.

c.1866 Chicago   ICHi
BRITTAN, NATHAN & CO. Ill. catalog of building materials including lightning conductors, etc.

1879 Cincinnati   OC
CHAMBER'S NATIONAL LIGHTNING PROTECTION CO. An exposition of the laws and modes of action of electricity applicable to means of protection, etc. 8vo., 32pp. P.S. They sold lightning rods.

c.1866 Chicago   ICHi
KISSELL & BLICKENSDERFER. Ill. catalog of Brittan's system of protection from thunder storms. 8vo., 32pp., pict. wrap. See #2. Did Brittan go broke, or were these gentlemen his agents?

1854 New York   NHi
LYON MFG. CO. Ill. catalog of Otis' patent lightning rods - for absolute protection. 12mo., 28pp., pict. wrap.

1858 Indianapolis   MH-BA
MUNSON, DAVID. Ill. (one only) catalog of copper tubular lightning rods - with a story on thunder and lightning, cause and effect. 12mo., 20pp.

PRATT, JAMES. See L. Wilcox.

QUIMBY. See Edward N. Williams.

1854 New York   N
SPRATT, J. Ill. catalog of Spratt's patent lightning rods and conductors - the only sure one manufactured. 8vo., 12pp., pict. title and wrap.

c.1851 Hartford, Conn. & Cincinnati   CtHi
WILCOX, L. Assignee. Ill. circular of James Pratt's patent lightning rods - details of protection, etc. 8vo., 4pp.

1879 New York   NHi
WILLIAMS, EDWARD H. Ill. circular of Quimby's improved lightning rods for homes and vessels - list of rods in use all over the country. Sq. 16mo., 20pp., dec. wrap.

Although our museums have rescued many old post office cabinets, boxes and windows, and set them up for the curious tourist, it is fitting and proper that our libraries have the printed pictorial records filed for future research and restoration.

c.1900 Buffalo, N. Y.   N
AUTOMATIC TRANSPORTATION CO. A
New Era in Transportation - postal service
in rural areas, photo. ills. of post and merchandise deliveries being made by complete
automatic system while the crowds cheer,
maps of tracks, tubes, vehicles, etc. 2 circulars, 4to., 12pp., and sq. 8vo., 20pp.

1874 Milford, N. H.   NhHi
McLANE, JOHN. Ill. catalog of patent wire
post office boxes, cabinets, fronts, equipment, etc. What an up to date Post Office
should have. 8vo., 34pp., wrap.

1887 Milford, N. H.   NhD
------ Catalog #10. Patent #4 wire bot-
tomed boxes, windows, tables, pict. - with
eagles - or plain. 8vo., 60pp., pict. wrap.

1895 Baltimore   PKsL
SADLER CO. Everything for Postmasters.
Being an ill. catalog of windows, cabinets,

counters, fronts, safes, stamps, etc. Tall
4to., 60pp., with tinted pict. wrap. of the
modern Post Office lobby.

1873 Wheeling, W. Va.   NHi
U.S. POST OFFICE BULLETIN. Vol. 2, #4.
Actually an ill. catalog of badges, hand
stamps, stencils, cancellations and supplies.
Fol., 4pp.

See John H. Zevely.

1886 Stamford, Conn.   CtHi
YALE & TOWNE MFG. CO. Ill. catalog of
Yale standard new style post office cabinets
and outfits. Tall 8vo., 96pp., pict. wrap.
An exhaustive ref.

1877 Charleston, W. Va.   Wv-Ar
ZEVELY, JOHN H. U.S. Post Office Bulletin. Vol. X, #2. See U.S. Post Office Bulletin also Vol. 2, #4.

The real estate catalogs hardly belong in this guide, and yet though they do not offer merchandise for sale, they do record the prices and values that will never return. The fact that so few are located does not mean they are rare. They are only included to show that catalogs cover the entire field of Americana, and if they are ever needed, will be on hand.

1884 Orlando, Fla.   F
LIVINGSTON & WALLACE. Desc. list of
properties for 1884. 12mo., 24pp., 40
acres for $450.00!

1869 Baltimore   MdTanSW
NEWTON, WILLIAM H. & CO. Desc. catalog of southern farms, mills, plantations,
etc. 8vo., 56pp.

c.1863 Baltimore   MH-BA
TEMPLEMAN, R.W. & CO. Land agents,
surveyors and brokers.

Desc. catalog of Maryland lands, lists by
parcels, many with log dwellings. 8vo.,
50pp., wrap.

Tales and stories of fires and crooks are written and rewritten every other week, and when enough of them are put between two covers and published, they constitute history. The American safes, vaults and locks illustrated in these catalogs from c.1835, are the source material that can and will authenticate the truth of these histories. Small and weak though they look today compared with modern fireproofing and burglar alarms, they are the kids in the family album most of us like to remember.

1841 New York   MH-BA
AMERICAN BANK LOCK CO. Est. 1835.
2nd annual catalog of locks, with list of
banks now using patent combination models.
8vo., 16pp.

1854 New Haven   CtHi
BACON, WILLIAM W. Ill. catalog. Protection against burglars! Cheapest and only
reliable security extant! Impregnable as
the Rock of Gibralta! Bankers . . . will at

once supply themselves with this Yale patent improved duplex lock! Large 8vo., 64pp.

1859 New Haven   CtHi
------ Ill. catalog of Bacon's burglar-proof safes - a circular for bankers. 4to., 8pp., tests.

1858 Boston   MH-BA
BIGELOW, M.B. & HARDY, ANSON. Ill. catalog of Maryland's patent fire-proof safes. 16mo., 24pp., wrap.

1885 Canton, O.   DSi
DIEBOLD SAFE & LOCK CO. Ill. catalog of patent round-cornered fire and burglar-proof safes - fine pls. showing glt. and col. stenciled scenic dec., interior cabinets, gates, etc. 4to., 124pp., pict. wrap.

c.1877 Boston   MH-BA
EQUITABLE SAFE DEPOSIT CO. Ill. circular showing safe storage for valuable property. 16mo., 16pp. This isn't a trade catalog of safes, but it is an ill. record.

1859 Philadelphia   PKsL
EVANS, G.G. & WATSON. Ill. catalog of Evans & Watson's Premier Salamander Philadelphia Safes. Safe against the world - fine pict. record with dozens of tales of fires and robberies thwarted. 12mo. with a fine pict. wrap.

1860 Philadelphia   PKsL
------ Special catalog of safes with ills. of the best.

1864 Chicago, New York & Philadelphia
HERRING & CO. Est. c.1840.   MH-BA
Ill. catalog of iron safes, bank vaults and impregnable combination locks. 4to., 28pp.

1874 New York   TxDaDeG
HERRING & FARRELL. Actual experiences of Herring's celebrated safes, fighting fire

for thirty-three years, one thousand trials - records of famous fires - fine ills. of stencil dec. safes with prices and details. 8vo., 144pp., pict. wrap.

nd. Boston   NNMM
MORRIS, E.C. & CO. Ill. and desc. catalog of fire or burglar-proof vault doors. 16pp., wrap.

1872 Cincinnati   OC
MOSLER, BAHMANN & CO. Ill. catalog of Mosler, Bahmann fire and burglar-proof safes, vaults, locks. Stories and tests. by clients. 8vo., 59pp., wrap.

1889 Cleveland, O.   OHi
NATIONAL SAFE & LOCK CO. Ill. catalog of fire and burglar-proof safes. 8vo., 16pp., wrap.

1889 Pittsburgh   MnHi
NATIONAL SAFE DEPOSIT & VAULT MFG. CO. Ill. catalog of Hough & Harper burglar and mob proof vaults. 4to., 30pp., fine pict. ref.

1800 New York   NHi
VALENTINE & BUTLER. Ill. catalog of Valentine & Butler's Aluminum patent fire and burglar-proof safes and locks - tales and records of robberies - ills. of handsome stencil dec. models with fancy cabinets, etc. 8vo., 38pp., wrap.

1857 Boston   PC
WILDER, JOHN E. MFG. CO. Ill. catalog of Wilder's new style fire-proof safes - 12 sizes ill., desc. and priced. 16mo., 48pp., pict. wrap.

nd. York, Pa.   PHi
YORK SAFE & LOCK CO. Ill. catalog of fire and burglar-proof safes and vault doors. 4to., 69pp., one of the best ill. records.

The statuary catalogs tell their own story. To hide John Rogers with only one index reference would be unkind to the millions who collect his famous groups. To neglect that period in our history when every city, town and hamlet decided to order a monument to some distinguished citizen for the park or square would be criminal. It is a small group but it does offer many of the best catalogs issued.

---

c.1900 Chicopee, Mass.   NNMM
AMES MFG. CO., LTD. Ill. catalog and price list of bronze statuary - unpaged with mounted photos. throughout, lea. cvs.

c.1868 New York & York, Pa.   MiDbF
FISKE, J.W. IRON WORKS. Works   NNMM
in York, Pa. Ill. catalog of iron vases, lawn

animals, fountains and statues for estates and parks. 4to., 18pp.

1874 York, Pa. & New York   DLC
------ Ill. catalog of iron and zinc fountains, aquariums, group statues, lawn and park ornaments - cranes, dolphins, park lights, etc. Fol., 48pls., cl.

c.1876 York, Pa. & New York   ICHi
------ Ill. catalog of zinc statuary for hall
lights, indoors and out, cigar store Indians,
Squaws, Jockey and Chinese figures, hitching posts, vases, lawn animals, etc. Fol.,
68 pls., cl.

See Architectural Building Material and
Ornamental Ironwork.

1875 Milwaukee   MnHi
HENNECKE, C. & CO. Ill. catalog of ornamental statuary for house, garden, park and
cemetery.

1886 Milwaukee   NNMM
------ Ill., desc. and priced catalog #3.
Florentine statuary for home and park -
lawn figures, etc. 64pp.

1887 Milwaukee   NHi
------ Ill. catalog #5 of   WM
Hennecke's Florentine statuary - vases,
lawn figures, busts, plaques, monuments,
etc. 4to., 12pp., pict. wrap.

METAL STAMPING & SPINNING CO. See
Ornamental Ironwork.

MONUMENTAL BRONZE CO. See Undertakers' Equipment.

1890 New York   NNMM
MOTT, J.L. IRON WORKS. Ill. catalog M.
Statuary and ornamental animal lawn fig-
ures, garden vases, etc. 4to., 64pp., wrap.

See Ornamental Ironwork and Architectural
Building Materials.

1896 Salem, O.   OHi
MULLINS, W.H. CO. Ill. catalog   DeU
of architectural sheet metal work and statuary. Pls. of 72 huge statues designed and

built for the Cotton States and International
Exposition. Tall 4to., 172pp., pict. wrap.

See Architectural Building Materials.

c.1894 Philadelphia   PHi
PHILADELPHIA WHITE BRONZE MONU-
MENT CO. Ill. catalog of statuary.

c.1870 New York   IHi
ROGERS, JOHN. Rogers' Groups of Sculp-
ture, an ill. catalog of 16pp. and 16 pls.,
16mo., wrap.

1876 New York   NCooHi
------ Ill. catalog of statuary. Fol., wrap.

c.1877 New York   NHi
------ Groups of statuary by John Rogers.
4to., 6pp., ills., pict. wrap.

1882 New York   NCooHi
------ Ill. catalog of statuary. Fol.

1892 New York   NCooHi
------ Ill. catalog of statuary. Fol.

1895 New York   CaNBSM
ROGERS' STATUARY CO. Ill. and desc.
catalog of group statuettes from the studio
of John Rogers - revised prices. Sq. 12mo.,
88pp. with 87 pls. Feb. 1st.

c.1875 Philadelphia   PKsL
STEAVENSON & CASSEL. Successors to
C. Friese. Fairhill Terra Cotta & Lava
Works. Broadside price list of plain and
fancy terra cotta and lava statuary. Ornaments for aquariums, rustic logs, hanging
baskets, etc.

WERNER, GEORGE F. ART METAL WORKS.
See Ornamental Ironwork.

Wallpaper design is not only important but popular and I am sorry not to be able to locate hundreds.
It would seem that, like the brass and wire manufacturers of Connecticut, many of our paper makers
banded together and issued pool price lists. I merely suggest this as a possibility. Perhaps study
of the Janeway and Carpender 1884 catalog will inspire someone to dig out the facts and account for
the apparent scarcity of American wallpaper catalogs before 1900. After 1900, of course, Sears
Roebuck, Montgomery Ward and others printed many colorful records, which have already been
recognized and preserved for future use. I hope someone will locate them for future historians who
may want to write about our 20th century.

1795 Boston   Evans 28428
CLOUGH, EBENEZER.   RPJCB
Boston Paper Staining Manufactory.

Ebenezer Clough, paper stainer, manufactures and keeps constantly for sale a great
variety of paper hangings.

A billhead engraved by Samuel Hill - not a
catalog, but a pict. record that shows American paper making and staining from start
to finish under the American Eagle and the
motto Protection. Why didn't he list his
designs and prices?

c.1827 Portsmouth, N. H.   MWA
FOSTER, JOHN W. Room papers of the newest patterns at lowest factory prices -- as well as spectacles to suit any age, musical instruments, etc. 25 cents to $10.00. Broadside, 2 engravings, and a fine Bible and spectacle border.

c.1890 Brooklyn, N. Y.   NNMM
HALBERT, GEORGE. Painter, Decorator & Designer of Paper Hangings. Catalog of designs of wallpapers, also 7 pls. of parquet floors and stained glass windows. 4to., 12pp. Unfortunately, the wallpapers are not ill.

1884 New Brunswick, N. J.   NNMM
JANEWAY & CARPENDER. To the Trade - Wallpapers of all grades - independent of all pools and paper mfg. combinations - with caustic comment on price fixing in the jobbers' pool. Small 4to., 5 fine col. pls. of designs. 6pp., dec. wrap.

1883 Chicago   NNMM
McGRATH, JOHN J. To the Trade with compliments of . . . Practical suggestions for ceiling docorations and paper hangings of every variety. 10x14, 6 litho. pls. by Schober & Carqueville and full col. design

wallpaper wrap. Makes quite a point about competitors who claim best papers and designs. Prefers to let the customer judge for himself.

c.1840 Boston   MWA
MARSH, JOHN. Paper & Stationery Warehouse. Broadside with 3 columns of paper and stationery for sale.

c.1835 Boston   MWA
MERIAM & BROTHERS. Paper hangings manufactured, band, cap, hat and muff boxes with new designs to order, pict. window shades, French and Philadelphia papers with rich gilt frescoes, etc. Broadside with fine contemporary border.

1899 New Brighton, Pa.   PHi
PITTSBURG WALL PAPER CO. Ill. catalog of wallpapers with fine col. pls. 8vo., fine ref.

c.1800 Portsmouth, N. H.   MWA
SHORES, JAMES F. & CO. Room papers of every design and price in the newest patterns, spectacles for all ages, stationery, etc. Broadside with 3 columns of goods.

C H E E R I O   A N D   G O O D   L U C K !

When people visit with people, whether family, friends or business associates, for dinner or for a long vacation, they usually part company with sincere farewells, thank the Good Lord it's over goodbyes, or some sort of until we meet again sentiments. After all, no matter how it may read to you, this has been a long, long, long visit! Much as I deplore the necessity of haranguing you further on the importance of trade catalogs to the unwritten history of American business, I can't just jump in the car and ride off without a friendly smile and a simple so long. Besides, according to the mysteries of pagination, we need a few lines to make things come out right.

I hope my arbitrary selection of these sixty two chapters has been helpful. My purpose is to pinpoint those goods, products and manufactures time has proven the leaders in the development of the United States economically, politically and socially. Dr. Franklin's stove, John Tweedy's turnkey, William Prince's nursery, Thomas Moore's refrigerator, the first Baldwin locomotive, the first automatic cow milker and a hundred other printed and pictorial records have paved the way to our present luxurious 20th century way of life and world industrial supremacy. Manuscript material and printed reports are indispensable, but the catalogs that actually sold the nation the inventions and improvements are the backbone of business history.

From the simple solid statements of Benjamin Franklin to the wild exaggerations of the Gay Nineties, American enthusiasm for living coupled with Yankee imagination have left us an enviable heritage. Don't take this catalog panorama for granted. Don't rely on Evans and Sabin for a complete education in O. P. Americana. Revere them for what they are as far as they go, but remember that America has done a heap o' livin' since 1876. Consider the number of library locations used in these monumental bibliographies, and then check Bowker's American Library Directory for 1960 with over fifteen thousand entries. Think of the number of museum libraries and business libraries that have grown like Topsies during the past fifty years. Use your imagination -- it's an Americanism that belongs to you. Don't forget what has happened in your home, your office, your factory and on your familiar highways since you were a kid. Bear in mind that history is being made every day, that you are part of it, and that some of the best of it has been and is being recorded in American Trade Catalogs.

MISCELLANY

And now Gentle Reader, as many of the works listed in the Book Chapter delighted in saying, I will let you get back to your own lives. I have provided you with locations of the best examples to be found in over one hundred and sixty repositories that have recognized these catalogs as worthy Americana. The book is yours.

BIBLIOGRAPHICAL SUGGESTIONS

GEORGE H. ADAMS & SON'S NEW CO-
LUMBIAN RAIL ROAD ATLAS, AND
PICTORIAL ALBUM OF AMERICAN
INDUSTRY. Many of the full page
illustrated advertisements are catalogs
in themselves. New York and London,
1879. (Several later editions).

THE AMERICAN ADVERTISING DIREC-
TORY FOR MANUFACTURERS AND
DEALERS IN AMERICAN GOODS FOR
1831. The first attempt to the best of
my knowledge. Compiled and published
by Jocelyn, Darling & Co., New York,
1831. Also another edition for 1832.

AMERICAN BIBLIOGRAPHY by Charles
Evans. A Chronological Dictionary of
Books, Pamphlets and Periodical Publi-
cations printed in the United States of
America from 1639 to 1820. New York,
1903.

AMERICAN BOOK AUCTION CATALOGUES
by George L. McKay with an introduction
by Clarence S. Brigham. 1713-1934.
New York Public Library, 1937.

AMERICAN CLOCKS AND CLOCKMAKERS
by Carl W. Drepperd. Fine illustrations
and plates, many were taken directly
from catalogues located in this Guide.
Doubleday & Co., Inc., Garden City, N. Y.

AMERICAN FIREARMS MAKERS by A.
Merwyn Carey. A cyclopedia of the
makers of American firearms fully
described and arranged in more than
2100 entries. When, Where, and What
they Made. From the Colonial Period
to the End of the Nineteenth Century.
Published by Thomas Y. Crowell Co.,
New York, 1953.

THE ARTS AND CRAFTS IN NEW YORK,
1726-1776. Advertisements and News
items from New York City Newspapers.
The New York Historical Society, 1938.

ASSOCIATION OF CENTENARY FIRMS
AND CORPORATIONS OF THE UNITED
STATES. Published by Christopher
Sower Co., Philadelphia, 1892.

THE BOOK IN AMERICA by Hellmut
Lehmann-Haupt in collaboration with

Lawrence C. Wroth and Rollo G. Silver.
No one who speaks Americana should be
without a copy. Published by R. R.
Bowker Co., New York, 1951.

THE BUCKEYE BOOK OF DIRECT ADVER-
TISING by Carl Richard Greer. Fine
illustrations of 20th century trade catalogs. The Beckett Paper Co., Hamilton,
Ohio, 1926.

THE BUSINESS FOUNDING DATE DIREC-
TORY by Etna M. Kelley. Listing over
9000 business firms founding dates from
1687-1915. Over 200 years of business
growth. Published by Morgan & Morgan,
Scarsdale, N. Y., 1954.

CATALOGUES AND COUNTERS. A history
of Sears, Roebuck and Company by Boris
Emmett and John E. Jeuck. Published
by The University of Chicago Press, 1950.

CAVALCADE OF THE RAILS by Frank P.
Morse. Published by E. P. Dutton & Co.,
Inc., New York, 1940.

CAVALCADE OF TOYS by Ruth and Larry
Freeman. A good reference well illustrated from many of the catalogs located
in the Guide. Century House, New York,
1942.

A CENTURY OF DEPENDABILITY. A Story
of One Hundred Years of Hardware Mfg.
Published by Wilcox, Crittenden & Co.,
Inc., Middletown, Conn., 1947.

A CENTURY OF SERVICE TO DENTISTRY.
1844-1944. Published by the S. S. White
Dental Mfg. Co., Philadelphia, Pa., in
commemoration of its one hundredth
anniversary.

THE COLONIAL SCENE. 1602-1800. A
Catalogue of Books exhibited at the John
Carter Brown Library in the Spring of
1949, augmented by related titles from
the Library of the American Antiquarian
Society. Published in Worcester, Mass.,
1950.

CYLINDER RECORDS. A description of the
numbering systems, physical appearance
and other aspects of cylinder records
made by the major American companies.

Written and published by Duane D. Deakins, M. D., Stockton, Calif. 1st edition 1856, 2nd edition 1958.

A DICTIONARY OF BOOKS RELATING TO AMERICA FROM ITS DISCOVERY TO THE PRESENT TIME by Joseph Sabin. New York, 1868.

THE EARLY FULLING MILLS OF NEW JERSEY by Harry B. Weiss. Illustrations from trade catalogs. New Jersey Agricultural Society, Trenton, N. J., 1957.

THE EARLY GRIST MILLS OF NEW JERSEY by Harry B. Weiss. Illustrations from trade catalogs. New Jersey Agricultural Society, Trenton, N. J., 1956.

"ENJINE! - ENJINE!" A STORY OF FIRE PROTECTION by Kenneth Holcomb Dunshee. Published by Harold Vincent Smith for the Home Insurance Company, New York, 1939.

ESSAYS HONORING LAWRENCE C. WROTH. Chapter - American Booksellers' Catalogues. 1734-1800. By C. S. Brigham. Portland, 1951.

FIRE ON THE HEARTH - THE EVOLUTION AND ROMANCE OF THE HEATINGSTOVE by Josephine H. Peirce. Illustrations from trade catalogs used to good advantage. Published by the Pond-Ekberg Company, Springfield, Mass., 1951.

THE GREAT INDUSTRIES OF THE UNITED STATES by Horace Greeley and others. An Historical Summary of the origin, growth and perfection of the Chief Industrial Arts of this Country, with over 450 illustrations. Published by J. B. Burr & Hyde, Hartford, 1872.

GREEN MOUNTAIN TOYS by Charles Morrow Wilson. Illustrations from the best of American toy catalogs, appearing in "Vermont Life", Vol. XII, No. 2, Winter, 1958-59.

GUIDE TO BUSINESS HISTORY by Henrietta M. Larson. Materials for the study of American business history and suggestions for their use. Published by Harvard University Press, Cambridge, Mass., 1950.

GUNS AND SHOOTING. A Bibliography by Ray Riling. Published by Greenbery, 1951.

HIGHLIGHTS IN THE HISTORY OF AMERICAN MASS PRODUCTION by Roy T. Bramson. Published by The Bramson Publishing Co., Detroit, Mich., 1945.

Illustrations from the Carl W. Drepperd Collection.

A HISTORY OF AMERICAN MANUFACTURES from 1606-1860 by J. Oleander Bishop, M. D. In two volumes. Published by Young & Co., Philadelphia, 1861.

HISTORY OF THE AMERICAN STEAM FIRE ENGINE by William T. King. The Pinkham Press, 1896.

THE HISTORY & DEVELOPMENT OF ADVERTISING by Frank Presbrey. Published by Doubleday & Co., Inc., Garden City, N. Y.

HOROLOGICAL BOOKS AND PAMPHLETS IN THE LIBRARY OF THE FRANKLIN INSTITUTE. Compiled by Walter A. R. Pertuch, Librarian. April, 1956.

THE HORSE & BUGGY AGE IN NEW ENGLAND by Edwin Valentine Mitchell. A fine picture of 19th century carriage making. Published by Coward, McCann, Inc., New York, 1937.

KNIGHT'S NEW MECHANICAL DICTIONARY by Edward H. Knight, A.M., LL.D. A description of tools, instruments, machines, processes and engineering. Published by Houghton, Mifflin & Co., Boston, 1882-1883.

LIGHT ON OLD LAMPS by Larry Freeman. Published by Century House, Watkins Glen, N. Y., 1944.

THE MEN AND TIMES OF PEPPERELL. An account of the first one hundred years of the Pepperell Mfg. Co. Inc. February 16, 1844. Published by Pepperell Mfg. Co., Boston, 1945.

NEWARK INDUSTRIAL EXHIBITION. Report and Catalogue of the First Exhibition of Newark Industries, exclusively. 1872, 1873, 1874 and 1875. Reprinted by special request by the Holbrooks' Steam Printery, 11 Mechanic Street, Newark, N. J., 1882.

THE OLD COUNTRY STORE by Gerald Carson. Trade catalog references, and well worth the time if you haven't yet read it. Published by Oxford University Press, New York, 1954.

PILLS, PETTICOATS & PLOWS - THE SOUTHERN COUNTRY STORE by Thomas D. Clark. Published by The Bobbs-Merrill Company, New York, 1944.

THE POWDER FLASK BOOK by Ray Riling. Treating of the history and use of the flask as a principal accessory to the firearm, from its inception, through the ages. Introductory chapter by Harold D. Peterson, Chief, Historical Investigations Branch, National Park Service. Fine illustrations from catalogs. Published by Robert Halter, The River House, New Hope, Pa., 1953.

THE PRIMER OF AMERICAN ANTIQUES by Carl W. Drepperd. Published by Doubleday, Doran & Co., Inc., Garden City, N. Y., 1944.

PRINTING IN THE AMERICAS by John Clyde Oswald. An excellent background for anything both American and bibliographical. The Gregg Publishing Co., 1937.

RECLAIMED RUBBER by J. M. Ball. The Story of an American Raw Material. Rubber Reclaimers Association, Inc., New York, 1947.

RIDING THE TINPLATE RAILS by Louis H. Hertz. Toy and Model Railroads. Published by Model Craftsman Publishing Corporation, Ramsey, N. J., 1944.

SEEGER AND GUERNSEY'S CYCLOPAEDIA OF THE MANUFACTURES AND PRODUCTS OF THE UNITED STATES. The most exhaustive reference compiled in the 19th century. New York, 1890.

SHAKER FURNITURE, THE CRAFTSMANSHIP OF AN AMERICAN COMMUNAL SECT by Edward Deming and Faith Andrews. Dover Publications, 1950.

THE STORY OF THE TYPEWRITER, 1873-1923. Published in commemoration of the Fiftieth Anniversary of the Writing Machine by the Herkimer County Historical Society. Herkimer, N. Y., 1923. Illustrations from catalogs with amusing details.

SUBJECT COLLECTIONS compiled by Lee Ash. Published by R. R. Bowker Co., New York, 1958.

SUN ON THE RIVER by Margaret S. Rice. 100th Anniversary Book of the Bailey Co., Inc. A fine pictorial record of 19th century carriage making. Privately printed at the Rumford Press, Concord, N. H., 1955.

TEN OLD GUN CATALOGS compiled by L. D. Satterlee. Ten reprints of the best 1864 to 1880 with notes. The Gun Digest Co., Chicago, 1957.

TREASURES IN TRUCK AND TRASH by Carl W. Drepperd. A fine chapter on trade catalogs in which he gives a list of the American manufactures he considers most important to collectors and to history. Published by Doubleday & Co., Inc., Garden City, N. Y., 1949.

WALTHAM INDUSTRIES by Edmund L. Sanderson. A Collection of Sketches of Early Firms and Founders. Published by Waltham Historical Society, Inc. in cooperation with The Waltham Chamber of Commerce, 1957.

WEBB'S NEW ENGLAND RAILWAY AND MANUFACTURERS' STATISTICAL GAZETEER. Short sketches loaded with manufacturing details. Webb Brothers, Providence, R. I., 1869.

THE WHITESMITHS OF TAUNTON by George Sweet Gibb. A History of Reed & Barton, 1824-1943 with facsimiles of price lists and illustrations from catalogs. Published by Harvard University Press, 1943.

THE WINDMILL AS A PRIME MOVER by Alfred R. Wolff. Exhaustive, excellent plates, diagrams and details. Published by John Wiley & Sons, New York, 1885. Second edition, 1888.

INDEX

405

407

411

413

414

416

417

422